GUI
SOCCER
WHO'S WHO

Jack Rollin

Cover design: David Roberts

First published in 1984
Second edition 1986
Third edition 1989
Fourth edition 1990

Published in Great Britain by Guinness Publishing Ltd,
33 London Road, Enfield, Middlesex

Typeset in Linotron 202 Times Roman
Typeset, printed and bound in Great Britain by
BPCC Hazell Books Ltd
Member of BPCC Ltd
Aylesbury, Bucks, England

British Library Cataloguing in Publication Data

Rollin, Jack, 1932–
Guinness soccer who's who. – 4th ed.
1. Great Britain. Association football – biographies.
Collections
I. Guinness Who's Who in Soccer
796.3340922

ISBN 0-85112-930-7

THE AUTHOR

Jack Rollin was born in London in 1932 and educated at King's, Harrow. There he played soccer, while later at Westcliff-on-Sea High School it was rugby. Within ten days of joining the Royal Air Force he was playing in a Welsh Cup tie for RAF Bridgnorth and in the services he learned shorthand and typing, resuming his career in journalism and covering the 1954 World Cup in Switzerland in a freelance capacity.

In 1958 an ankle injury ended his own career during which, at the age of 14, he had been offered a trial with the United States club Chicago Maroons. He wisely declined a one-off re-appearance in 1971 against the European Cup finalists Panathinaikos of Greece.

For ten years Jack Rollin was Editor of the weekly magazine *Soccer Star* and its companion monthly *World Soccer* before becoming a freelance again in 1970. Since then he has researched football for BBC Television, acted as an assistant to commentators on 'Match of the Day', spoken on radio and appeared on television programmes. He has contributed to *What's on in London* and *Radio Times* and in 1975 he won the Designers and Art Directors Association Silver Award for *Radio Times World Cup Special* for the most outstanding specialist feature of the year.

In 1972 he became one of the compilers of the *Rothmans Football Yearbook* and later became its Editor. He has provided advice on the football sections of the *Encyclopaedia Britannica* and *Guinness Book of Records*. He is a football columnist for the *Sunday Telegraph*.

Jack Rollin contributed to three part-works: *The Game* (8 vols. 1970); *Book of Football* (6 vols. 1972) and *Football Handbook* (1979–80). His articles have appeared in programmes for matches at Wembley Stadium since 1963. He has produced handbooks which include *World Soccer Digest* 1961, 1962 and 1963 and *World Cup Digest* 1966.

In 1978 he carried out the international research for the BBC Television series 'The Game of the Century' and produced the first edition of *The Guinness Book of Soccer Facts and Feats*.

Other books he has written: *England's World Cup Triumph* (1966), *A Source Book of Football* (1971), *The History of Aldershot Football Club* (1975), *World Cup Guide* (1982), *Who's Who in Soccer* (1984, 1986, 1989), *Soccer at War 1939–45* (1985), *Soccer: The Records* (1985), *Soccer: Records, Facts and Champions* (1988), *Soccer Shorts* (1988), *The World Cup 1930—1990* (1990), and *The Football Fact Book* (1990). In 1974 he contributed the South American section for John Moynihan's *Football Fever*.

The author is married to June and has a daughter Glenda.

FOREWORD

I am delighted to welcome the fourth edition of the *Guinness Soccer Who's Who* by Jack Rollin. It is certainly on a par with all the quality reference books in the Guinness library and will prove an invaluable help to all administrators, managers, soccer writers and supporters of football throughout the United Kingdom.

It is a difficult task to keep abreast of the changing face of personnel at clubs and Jack Rollin is to be congratulated on achieving this task successfully. There are precise details of professional players in England, Wales and Scotland which can be found by quick and easy alphabetical reference and it provides all the information necessary for a football fact-finder.

The book will occupy a prominent place on my desk and I do not hesitate to recommend it.

Gordon Taylor

Gordon Taylor,
Chief Executive, The Professional Footballers' Association

Front cover, clockwise from top left:
Tommy Tynan (Plymouth Argyle), Rodney Wallace (Southampton), Mixu Paatelainen (Dundee United), Paul Longden (Scunthorpe United), Steve Nicol (Liverpool) and Mark Bowen (Norwich City).

INTRODUCTION

This book features the statistical League careers of all players who made Barclays League appearances during the 1989–90 season as well as those in the Scottish Premier Division. It also includes others who were contracted professionally with Football League clubs at the start of the 1989–90 season and who remained there during the season and others recently playing on the continent.

Club names in italics indicate temporary transfers where they have not become permanent moves in the same season. Italic figures refer to Lincoln City in the GM Vauxhall Conference. All appearances include those as substitute.

The Editor would like to thank Alan Elliott for providing details of Scottish League players and also acknowledge the co-operation and assistance of the Football League in the compilation of this book and in particular Mike Foster, Sheila Murphy and Debbie Birch. Thanks also to Mavis Suckling.

Bibliography: *Rothmans Football Yearbook*

Also published by Guinness:
Soccer Shorts
The Football Fact Book
The World Cup 1930–1990
Guinness Book of Records

Season	Club	League Appearances/Goals	

ABBOTT, Greg

Born Coventry 14.12.63. Ht 5 9
Wt 10 07
Midfield. From Apprentice.

1981–82	Coventry C	—	—
1982–83	Bradford C	11	—
1983–84		35	3
1984–85		42	6
1985–86		39	10
1986–87		33	7
1987–88		32	5
1988–89		28	4
1989–90		35	3

ABEL, Graham

Born Runcorn 17.9.60. Ht 6 2 Wt 13 00
Defender. From Northwich V and Runcorn.

1985–86	Chester C	23	2
1986–87		41	1
1987–88		45	2
1988–89		40	3
1989–90		41	7

ABERCROMBY, Billy

Born Paisley 14.9.58 Ht 5 9 Wt 10 13
Midfield. From St Mirren BC

1975–76	St Mirren	—	—
1976–77		3	—
1977–78		30	3
1978–79		31	2
1979–80		15	—
1980–81		29	1
1981–82		30	—
1982–83		25	1
1983–84		34	4
1984–85		31	2
1985–86		23	2
1986–87		28	—
1987–88		9	—
1988–89	Partick T	10	—
1989–90	Dunfermline Ath	9	—

ABLETT, Gary

Born Liverpool 19.11.65 Ht 6 0
Wt 11 04
Defender. From Apprentice. England Under-21.

1983–84	Liverpool	—	—
1984–85		—	—
1984–85	*Derby Co*	6	—
1985–86	Liverpool	—	—
1986–87	*Hull C*	5	—
1986–87	Liverpool	5	1
1987–88		17	—
1988–89		35	—
1989–90		15	—

ABRAHAMS, Tony

Born Liverpool 8.12.69.

Midfield. From Trainee.

1987–88	Nottingham F	—	—
1988–89		—	—
1989–90	Blackpool	—	—

ABRAHAM, Gareth

Born Merthyr Tydfil 13.2.69. Ht 6 4
Wt 12 11
Defender. From Trainee.

1987–88	Cardiff C	2	1
1988–89		31	2
1989–90		37	1

ACHAMPONG, Kenny

Born London 26.6.66. Ht 5 9 Wt 11 01
Forward. From Apprentice.

1984–85	Fulham	10	3
1985–86		35	3
1986–87		21	6
1987–88		15	3
1988–89		—	—

Season	Club	League Appearances/Goals	
1988–89	*West Ham U*	—	—
1989–90	Charlton Ath	10	—

ADAMS, Mick

Born Sheffield 8.11.61. Ht 5 6 Wt 10 04
Defender. From Apprentice. England Youth.

Season	Club	Apps	Goals
1979–80	Gillingham	4	—
1980–81		13	—
1981–82		31	2
1982–83		44	3
1983–84	Coventry C	17	1
1984–85		31	3
1985–86		31	3
1986–87		11	2
1986–87	Leeds U	17	1
1987–88		40	—
1988–89		16	1
1988–89	Southampton	8	—
1989–90		15	—

ADAMS, Neil

Born Stoke 23.11.65. Ht 5 7 Wt 10 06
Forward. From Local. England Under-21.

Season	Club	Apps	Goals
1985–86	Stoke C	32	4
1986–87	Everton	12	—
1987–88		8	—
1988–89		—	—
1988–89	*Oldham Ath*	9	—
1989–90	Oldham Ath	27	4

ADAMS, Steve

Born Sheffield 7.5.59. Ht 5 8 Wt 10 12
Forward. From Manawatu U, Rotherham U, Blackpool, Worksop T.

Season	Club	Apps	Goals
1987–88	Scarborough	28	2
1988–89		20	3
1989–90		—	—
1989–90	Doncaster R	30	1

ADAMS, Tony

Born London 10.10.66. Ht 6 1 Wt 13 3
Defender. From Apprentice. England Youth, B, Under-21, 17 full caps.

Season	Club	Apps	Goals
1983–84	Arsenal	3	—
1984–85		16	—
1985–86		10	—
1986–87		42	6
1987–88		39	2
1988–89		36	4
1989–90		38	5

ADCOCK, Tony

Born Bethnal Green 27.2.63 Ht 5 11 Wt 11 09
Forward. From Apprentice.

Season	Club	Apps	Goals
1980–81	Colchester U	1	—
1981–82		40	5
1982–83		30	17
1983–84		43	26
1984–85		28	24
1985–86		33	15
1986–87		35	11
1987–88	Manchester C	15	5
1987–88	Northampton T	18	10
1988–89		46	17
1989–90		8	3
1989–90	Bradford C	28	5

ADKINS, Nigel

Born Birkenhead 11.3.65. Ht 5 11 Wt 13 04
Goalkeeper. From Apprentice. England Schools.

Season	Club	Apps	Goals
1982–83	Tranmere R	10	—
1983–84		4	—
1984–85		38	—
1985–86		34	—
1986–87	Wigan Ath	8	—
1987–88		2	—
1988–89		30	—
1989–90		13	—

AGANA, Tony

Born London 2.10.63. Ht 5 11 Wt 12 02
Forward. From Weymouth.

Season	Club	Apps	Goals
1987–88	Watford	15	1
1987–88	Sheffield U	12	2

Season	Club	League Appearances	Goals
1988–89		46	24
1989–90		31	10

AGBOOLA, Reuben

Born London 30.5.62. Ht 5 10 Wt 11 09
Defender. From Apprentice.

Season	Club	League Appearances	Goals
1979–80	Southampton	—	—
1980–81		6	—
1981–82		5	—
1982–83		37	—
1983–84		33	—
1984–85		9	—
1984–85	Sunderland	8	—
1985–86		12	—
1986–87	*Charlton Ath*	1	—
1986–87	Sunderland	11	—
1987–88		38	—
1988–89		29	—
1989–90		36	—

AGNEW, Gary

Born Dumfries 27.1.71. Ht 5 11
Wt 12 03
Midfield. From Trainee.

Season	Club	League Appearances	Goals
1988–89	Middlesbrough	—	—
1989–90		—	—

AGNEW, Paul

Born Lisburn 15.8.65. Ht 5 9 Wt 10 07
Defender. From Cliftonville. Northern Ireland Schools, Youth, Under-23.

Season	Club	League Appearances	Goals
1983–84	Grimsby T	1	—
1984–85		12	—
1985–86		16	—
1986–87		29	—
1987–88		38	1
1988–89		34	—
1989–90		24	2

AGNEW, Steve

Born Shipley 9.11.65. Ht 5 9 Wt 10 06
Midfield. From Apprentice.

Season	Club	League Appearances	Goals
1983–84	Barnsley	1	—
1984–85		10	1
1985–86		2	—
1986–87		33	—
1987–88		25	6
1988–89		39	6
1989–90		46	8

AINSCOW, Alan

Born Bolton 15.7.53. Ht 5 8 Wt 11 00
Midfield. From Apprentice. England Youth.

Season	Club	League Appearances	Goals
1971–72	Blackpool	18	3
1972–73		37	10
1973–74		19	3
1974–75		31	4
1975–76		35	2
1976–77		17	2
1977–78		35	4
1978–79	Birmingham C	31	2
1979–80		37	6
1980–81		40	8
1981–82	Everton	17	2
1982–83		11	1
1982–83	*Barnsley*	2	—
From Eastern			
1984–85	Wolverhampton W	42	5
1985–86		16	—
1985–86	Blackburn R	5	2
1986–87		17	2
1987–88		28	1
1988–89		15	—
1989–90	Rochdale	20	—

AINSCOW, Andy

Born Orrell 1.10.68. Ht 5 10 Wt 10 11
Forward. From Trainee.

Season	Club	League Appearances	Goals
1986–87	Wigan Ath	—	—
1987–88		15	4
1988–89		7	—
1989–90	Rotherham U	1	—

AIREY, Carl

Born Wakefield 6.2.65. Ht 6 0 Wt 12 05
Forward. From Apprentice.

Season	Club	League Appearances	Goals
1982–83	Barnsley	11	2
1983–84		27	3
1984–85	*Bradford C*	5	—
1985–86	Darlington	41	16

Season	Club	League Appearances/Goals	
1986–87		34	12
From Charleroi			
1986–87	Chesterfield	26	4
1987–88	Rotherham U	32	11
From Charleroi			
1988–89	Torquay U	17	3
1989–90		12	8
1989–90	*Shamrock R*	—	—

AITKEN, Roy

Born Irvine 24.11.58 Ht 6 0 Wt 13 00
Midfield. From Celtic BC. Scotland Schools, Under-21, 56 full caps.

Season	Club	League Appearances/Goals	
1975–76	Celtic	12	—
1976–77		33	5
1977–78		33	2
1978–79		36	5
1979–80		35	3
1980–81		33	4
1981–82		33	3
1982–83		33	6
1983–84		31	5
1984–85		33	3
1985–86		36	—
1986–87		42	1
1987–88		43	1
1988–89		32	—
1989–90		18	2
1989–90	Newcastle U	22	1

AIZLEWOOD, Mark

Born Newport 1.10.59. Ht 6 0 Wt 13 03
Midfield. From Apprentice. Wales Under-21, 17 full caps.

Season	Club	League Appearances/Goals	
1975–76	Newport Co	6	—
1976–77		5	—
1977–78		27	1
1977–78	Luton T	—	—
1978–79		39	—
1979–80		10	—
1980–81		23	—
1981–82		26	3
1982–83		—	—
1982–83	Charlton Ath	22	1
1983–84		31	1
1984–85		38	3
1985–86		35	3
1986–87		26	1
1986–87	Leeds U	15	—
1987–88		17	—
1988–89		38	3
1989–90	Bradford C	39	1

ALBISTON, Arthur

Born Edinburgh 14.7.57. Ht 5 7
Wt 11 03
Defender. From Apprentice. Scotland Schoolboy, Under-21, 14 full caps.

Season	Club	League Appearances/Goals	
1974–75	Manchester U	2	—
1975–76		3	—
1976–77		17	—
1977–78		28	—
1978–79		33	—
1979–80		25	—
1980–81		42	1
1981–82		42	1
1982–83		38	1
1983–84		40	2
1984–85		39	—
1985–86		37	1
1986–87		22	—
1987–88		11	—
1988–89	WBA	43	2
1989–90	Dundee	10	—

ALDRIDGE, John

Born Liverpool 18.9.58 Ht 5 11
Wt 11 10
Forward. From South Liverpool. Eire. 35 caps.

Season	Club	League Appearances/Goals	
1978–79	Newport Co	—	—
1979–80		38	14
1980–81		27	7
1981–82		36	11
1982–83		41	17
1983–84		28	20
1983–84	Oxford U	8	4
1984–85		42	30
1985–86		39	23
1986–87		25	15
1986–87	Liverpool	10	2
1987–88		36	26

Season	Club	League Appearances/Goals	
1988–89		35	21
1989–90		2	1

To Real Sociedad

ALEXANDER, Graham

Born Coventry 10.10.71. Ht 5 10
Wt 11 00
Defender. From Trainee.

1989–90	Scunthorpe U	—	—

ALEXANDER, Ian

Born Glasgow 26.1.63. Ht 5 8 Wt 10 07
Defender. From Leicester J.

1981–82	Rotherham U	8	—
1982–83		3	—
1983–84	Motherwell	16	1
1984–85		8	1
1984–85	Morton	7	1
From Pezoporikos			
1986–87	Bristol R	22	1
1987–88		45	1
1988–89		42	—
1989–90		43	1

ALEXANDER, Keith

Born Nottingham 14.11.58. Ht 6 4
Wt 13 06
Forward. From Barnet.

1988–89	Grimsby T	44	14
1989–90		38	12

ALLARDYCE, Sam

Born Dudley 19.10.54 Ht 6 2 Wt 14 00
Defender. From Apprentice.

1971–72	Bolton W	—	—
1972–73		—	—
1973–74		7	—
1974–75		18	3
1975–76		40	5
1976–77		41	6
1977–78		41	4
1978–79		20	1
1979–80		17	2
1980–81	Sunderland	25	2
1981–82		—	—
1981–82	Millwall	36	1
1982–83		27	1
1983–84	Coventry C	28	1
1984–85	Huddersfield T	37	—
1985–86	Bolton W	14	—
1986–87	Preston NE	37	2
1987–88		39	—
1988–89		14	—
1989–90	WBA	1	—

ALLEN, Bradley

Born Harold Wood 13.9.71. Ht 5 7
Wt 10 00
Forward. From schoolboys.

1988–89	QPR	1	—
1989–90		—	—

ALLEN, Clive

Born London 20.5.61. Ht 5 10 Wt 12 03
Forward. From Apprentice. England Schools, Youth, Under-21, 3 full caps. Football League.

1978–79	QPR	10	4
1979–80		39	28
1980–81	Arsenal	—	—
1980–81	Crystal Palace	25	9
1981–82	QPR	37	13
1982–83		25	13
1983–84		25	14
1984–85	Tottenham H	13	7
1985–86		19	9
1986–87		39	33
1987–88		34	11
From Bordeaux			
1989–90	Manchester C	30	10

ALLEN, Jason

Born Belfast 8.6.70. Ht 6 0 Wt 11 02
Defender. From Trainee.

1989–90	Oldham Ath	—	—

ALLEN, Malcolm

Born Dioniolen 21.3.67. Ht 5 8
Wt 11 02

Forward. From Apprentice. Wales Youth, 9 full caps.

1984–85	Watford	—	—
1985–86		13	2
1986–87		4	—
1987–88		22	3
1987–88	*Aston Villa*	4	—
1988–89	Norwich C	23	5
1989–90		12	3
1989–90	Millwall	8	2

ALLEN, Martin

Born Reading 14.8.65 Ht 5 10 Wt 11 00
Midfield. From school. England Youth, Under-21.

1983–84	QPR	—	—
1984–85		5	—
1985–86		31	3
1986–87		32	5
1987–88		38	4
1988–89		28	4
1989–90		2	—
1989–90	West Ham U	39	9

ALLEN, Paul

Born Aveley 28.8.62. Ht 5 7 Wt 10 10
Midfield. From Apprentice. England Youth, Under-21.

1979–80	West Ham U	31	2
1980–81		3	1
1981–82		28	—
1982–83		33	—
1983–84		19	—
1984–85		38	3
1985–86	Tottenham H	33	1
1986–87		37	3
1987–88		39	3
1988–89		37	1
1989–90		32	6

ALLINSON, Ian

Born Hitchin 1.10.57. Ht 5 9 Wt 12 09
Forward. From Apprentice.

1974–75	Colchester U	1	—
1975–76		5	—
1976–77		39	7
1977–78		45	6
1978–79		46	5
1979–80		38	2
1980–81		46	6
1981–82		42	21
1982–83		46	22
1983–84	Arsenal	9	—
1984–85		27	10
1985–86		33	6
1986–87		14	—
1987–88	Stoke C	9	—
1987–88	Luton T	27	3
1988–89		5	—
1988–89	Colchester U	25	7
1989–90		13	3

ALLISON, Michael

Born Elderslie 17.3.66. Ht 5 11
Wt 11 08
Goalkeeper. From Horwich RMI

1989–90	Chesterfield	—	—

ALLISON, Wayne

Born Huddersfield 16.10.68. Ht 6 1
Wt 12 06
Forward.

1986–87	Halifax T	8	4
1987–88		35	4
1988–89		41	15
1989–90	Watford	7	—

ALLPRESS, Tim

Born Hitchin 27.1.71. Ht 6 0 Wt 12 00
Defender. From Trainee.

1989–90	Luton T	1	—

ALLON, Joe

Born Gateshead 12.11.66. Ht 5 10
Wt 11 12
Forward. From Trainee England Youth.

1984–85	Newcastle U	1	—
1985–86		3	1
1986–87		5	1
1987–88	Swansea C	32	11
1988–89		2	—

Season	Club	League Appearances/Goals	
1988–89	Hartlepool U	21	4
1989–90		45	18

AMPADU, Kwame

Born Bradford 20.12.70. Ht 5 10
Wt 10 13
Forward. From Trainee. Eire Youth.

Season	Club	League Appearances/Goals	
1988–89	Arsenal	—	—
1989–90		2	—

ANDERSEN, Vetle

Born Kristiansand 20.4.64.
Forward.

Season	Club	League Appearances/Goals	
1989–90	WBA	1	—

ANDERSON, Colin

Born Newcastle 26.4.62. Ht 5 8
Wt 10 08
Midfield. From Apprentice.

Season	Club	League Appearances/Goals	
1979–80	Burnley	—	—
1980–81		2	—
1981–82		4	—
1982–83	Torquay U	42	5
1983–84		39	4
1984–85		28	2
1984–85	*QPR*	—	—
1984–85	WBA	—	—
1985–86		11	—
1986–87		28	1
1987–88		23	1
1988–89		42	6
1989–90		13	—

ANDERSON, Darren

Born Merton 6.9.66. Ht 6 1 Wt 13 5
Defender. From QPR Schoolboy and Coventry C Apprentice. England Youth.

Season	Club	League Appearances/Goals	
1983–84	Charlton Ath	1	—
1984–85		9	1
1985–86		—	—
1985–86	*Crewe Alex*	5	—
1986–87	Aldershot	24	—
1987–88		25	1

Season Club League Appearances/Goals

Season	Club	League Appearances/Goals	
1988–89		33	2
1989–90		16	1

ANDERSON, John

Born Dublin 7.11.59. Ht 5 11 Wt 11 06
Defender. From Apprentice. Eire, Youth Under-21. 16 full caps.

Season	Club	League Appearances/Goals	
1977–78	WBA	—	—
1978–79		—	—
1979–80	Preston	5	—
1980–81		8	—
1981–82		38	—
1982–83	Newcastle U	33	1
1983–84		41	1
1984–85		35	1
1985–86		38	3
1986–87		32	1
1987–88		35	1
1988–89		21	1
1989–90		37	4

ANDERSON, Nicky

Born Lincoln 29.3.69 Ht 5 10 Wt 10 10
Midfield. From Trainee.

Season	Club	League Appearances/Goals	
1986–87	Mansfield T	7	—
1987–88		12	—
1988–89		1	—
1989–90	Lincoln C	1	—

ANDERSON, Viv

Born Nottingham 29.8.56. Ht 6 0
Wt 11 08
Defender. From Apprentice. England Under-21 B, 30 full caps, Football League.

Season	Club	League Appearances/Goals	
1974–75	Nottingham F	16	—
1975–76		21	—
1976–77		38	1
1977–78		37	3
1978–79		40	1
1979–80		41	3
1980–81		31	—
1981–82		39	—
1982–83		25	1
1983–84		40	6
1984–85	Arsenal	41	3
1985–86		39	2

Season	Club	Apps	Goals
1986–87		40	4
1987–88	Manchester U	31	2
1988–89		6	—
1989–90		16	—

ANDERTON, Steven

Born Lancaster 2.10.69
Midfield. From Trainee.

Season	Club	Apps	Goals
1989–90	Preston NE	1	—

ANDREWS, Gary

Born Nottingham 12.5.68. Ht 5 11
Wt 12 01
Defender. From Apprentice.

Season	Club	Apps	Goals
1985–86	Nottingham F	—	—
1986–87		—	—
1987–88		—	—
1988–89	Peterborough U	33	—
1989–90		10	—

ANDREWS, Ian

Born Nottingham 1.12.64. Ht 6 2
Wt 12 02
Goalkeeper. From Apprentice. England Youth.

Season	Club	Apps	Goals
1982–83	Leicester C	—	—
1983–84		2	—
1983–84	*Swindon T*	1	—
1984–85	Leicester C	31	—
1985–86		39	—
1986–87		42	—
1987–88		12	—
1988–89	Celtic	5	—
1988–89	*Leeds U*	1	—
1989–90	Celtic	—	—
1989–90	Southampton	3	—

ANDREWS, Simon

Born Macclesfield 26.9.70. Ht 5 9
Wt 10 11
Forward. From Trainee.

Season	Club	Apps	Goals
1988–89	Manchester U	—	—
1989–90	Wigan Ath	—	—

ANGELL, Brett

Born Marlborough 20.8.68 Ht 6 1
Wt 12 03
Forward. From Portsmouth and Cheltenham T.

Season	Club	Apps	Goals
1987–88	Derby Co	—	—
1988–89	Stockport Co	26	5
1989–90		44	23

ANGUS, Ian

Born Glasgow 19.11.61. Ht 5 10
Wt 10 03
Midfield. From Eastercraigs.

Season	Club	Apps	Goals
1979–80	Aberdeen	—	—
1980–81		19	1
1981–82		1	1
1982–83		5	3
1983–84		12	—
1984–85		28	2
1985–86		17	2
1986–87		2	1
1986–87	Dundee	29	4
1987–88		40	6
1988–89		15	—
1989–90		4	—
1989–90	*Plymouth Arg*	—	—

ANSAH, Andy

Born Lewisham 19.3.69. Ht 5 10
Wt 11 01
Forward. From Crystal Palace.

Season	Club	Apps	Goals
1988–89	Brentford	7	2
1989–90		1	—
1989–90	Southend U	7	1

ANTHROBUS, Steve

Born Lewisham 10.11.68. Ht 6 2
Wt 12 13
Forward.

Season	Club	Apps	Goals
1986–87	Millwall	—	—
1987–88		3	—

Season Club League Appearances/Goals

Season	Club	Apps	Goals
1988–89	....	3	—
1989–90	....	15	4
1989–90	*Southend U*	—	—
1989–90	Wimbledon	10	—

ARCHDEACON, Owen

Born Greenock 4.3.66. Ht 5 9 Wt 10 08
Forward. From Gourock United. Scotland Youth, Under-21.

Season	Club	Apps	Goals
1982–83	Celtic	—	—
1983–84	....	1	—
1984–85	....	3	1
1985–86	....	23	3
1986–87	....	29	2
1987–88	....	10	1
1988–89	....	10	—
1989–90	Barnsley	21	3

ARCHIBALD, Steve

Born Glasgow 27.9.56. Ht 5 10
Wt 11 02
Forward. From Fernhill Ath. Scotland Under-21, 27 full caps.

Season	Club	Apps	Goals
1974–75	Clyde	4	—
1975–76	....	16	2
1976–77	....	31	3
1977–78	....	14	2
1977–78	Aberdeen	10	4
1978–79	....	32	13
1979–80	....	34	12
1980–81	Tottenham H...........	41	20
1981–82	....	27	6
1982–83	....	31	11
1983–84	....	32	21
From Barcelona			
1987–88	Blackburn R............	20	6
1988–89	Hibernian	31	13
1989–90	....	13	2

ARDILES, Ossie

Born Cordoba, Argentina 3.8.52. Ht 5 6
Wt 9 10
Midfield. From Huracan. Argentina 42 full caps.

Season	Club	Apps	Goals
1978–79	Tottenham H...........	38	3
1979–80	....	40	3
1980–81	....	36	5
1981–82	....	26	2
1982–83	Paris St. Germain	14	1
1982–83	Tottenham H...........	2	—
1983–84	....	9	—
1984–85	....	11	2
1985–86	....	23	1
1986–87	....	25	—
1987–88	....	28	—
1987–88	*Blackburn R*	5	—
1988–89	QPR	8	—
1989–90	Swindon T	2	—

ARMSTRONG, Chris

Born Newcastle 19.6.71. Ht 6 0
Wt 11 00
Forward.

Season	Club	Apps	Goals
1988–89	Wrexham	—	—
1989–90	....	22	3

ARMSTRONG, Gordon

Born Newcastle 15.7.67. Ht 6 0
Wt 11 10
Midfield. From Apprentice.

Season	Club	Apps	Goals
1984–85	Sunderland.............	4	—
1985–86	....	14	2
1986–87	....	41	5
1987–88	....	37	5
1988–89	....	45	8
1989–90	....	46	8

ARNOTT, Doug

Born Lanark 5.8.64. Ht 5 7 Wt 10 07
Forward. From Pollok Juniors.

Season	Club	Apps	Goals
1986–87	Motherwell..............	1	—
1987–88	....	2	—
1988–89	....	14	1
1989–90	....	30	5

ARNOTT, Kevin

Born Bensham 28.9.58. Ht 5 10
Wt 11 12
Midfield. From Apprentice.

Season	Club	Apps	Goals
1976–77	Sunderland..............	20	3
1977–78	....	21	3

Season	Club	League Appearances/Goals	
1978–79		15	—
1979–80		37	8
1980–81		34	2
1981–82		6	—
1981–82	*Blackburn R*	17	2
1982–83	Sheffield U	7	1
1982–83	*Blackburn R*	12	1
1982–83	*Rotherham U*	9	2
1983–84	Sheffield U	46	6
1984–85		27	3
1985–86		18	1
1986–87		23	—
From Vasalund			
1987–88	Chesterfield	19	1
1988–89		36	—
1989–90		16	3

ASH, Mark

Born Sheffield 22.1.68. Ht 5 9 Wt 11 04
Defender. From Apprentice.

Season	Club	League Appearances/Goals	
1985–86	Rotherham U	—	—
1986–87		17	—
1987–88		2	—
1988–89		1	—
1989–90	Scarborough	11	—

ASHBY, Barry

Born London 21.11.70. Ht 6 2 Wt 12 03
Defender. From Trainee.

Season	Club	League Appearances/Goals	
1988–89	Watford	—	—
1989–90		18	1

ASHLEY, Kevin

Born Birmingham 31.12.68. Ht 5 7
Wt 10 04
Defender. From Apprentice.

Season	Club	League Appearances/Goals	
1986–87	Birmingham C	7	—
1987–88		1	—
1988–89		15	—
1989–90		31	1

ASHURST, Jack

Born Coatbridge 12.10.54 Ht 6 0
Wt 12 04
Defender. From Apprentice.

Season	Club	League Appearances/Goals	
1971–72	Sunderland	—	—
1972–73		11	—
1973–74		19	1
1974–75		6	—
1975–76		21	—
1976–77		31	—
1977–78		38	2
1978–79		11	1
1979–80		3	—
1979–80	Blackpool	25	—
1980–81		28	3
1981–82	Carlisle U	46	1
1982–83		30	—
1983–84		41	1
1984–85		42	—
1985–86		35	—
1986–87	Leeds U	41	1
1987–88		41	—
1988–89		7	—
1988–89	Doncaster R	30	1
1989–90		43	—

ASKEW, Billy

Born Lumley 2.10.59. Ht 5 5 Wt 10 07
Midfield. From Apprentice.

Season	Club	League Appearances/Goals	
1977–78	Middlesbrough	—	—
1978–79		—	—
1979–80		1	—
1980–81		5	—
1981–82		6	—
1981–82	*Blackburn R*	—	—
1982–83	Hull C	36	6
1983–84		33	1
1984–85		46	6
1985–86		33	2
1986–87		27	—
1987–88		30	3
1988–89		16	—
1989–90		32	1
1989–90	Newcastle U	4	—

ASPIN, Neil

Born Gateshead 12.4.65. Ht 6 0 Wt 12 3
Defender. From Apprentice.

Season	Club	League Appearances/Goals	
1981–82	Leeds U	1	—
1982–83		15	—
1983–84		21	1

Season	Club	League Appearances/Goals	
1984–85		32	1
1985–86		38	2
1986–87		41	1
1987–88		26	—
1988–89		33	—
1989–90	Port Vale	42	—

ASPINALL, Warren

Born Wigan 13.9.67. Ht 5 8 Wt 10 6
Forward. From Apprentice. England Youth.

Season	Club	League Appearances/Goals	
1984–85	Wigan Ath	10	1
1985–86		—	—
1985–86	Everton	1	—
1985–86	*Wigan Ath*	41	21
1986–87	Everton	6	—
1986–87	Aston Villa	12	3
1987–88		32	11
1988–89	Portsmouth	40	11
1989–90		3	—

ATHERTON, Peter

Born Orrell 6.4.70. Ht 5 11 Wt 12 03
Defender. From Trainee.

Season	Club	League Appearances/Goals	
1987–88	Wigan Ath	16	—
1988–89		40	1
1989–90		46	—

ATKIN, Paul

Born Nottingham 3.9.69. Ht 6 0
Wt 12 04
Defender. From Trainee. England Youth.

Season	Club	League Appearances/Goals	
1987–88	Notts Co	—	—
1988–89		—	—
1988–89	Bury	1	—
1989–90		9	1

ATKINS, Bob

Born Leicester 16.10.62. Ht 6 0
Wt 12 02
Defender. Local.

Season	Club	League Appearances/Goals	
1982–83	Sheffield U	8	—
1983–84		16	3
1984–85		16	—
1984–85	Preston NE	13	—
1985–86		34	2
1986–87		41	1
1987–88		45	1
1988–89		39	—
1989–90		28	1

ATKINS, Ian

Born Birmingham 16.1.57. Ht 6 0
Wt 12 03
Midfield. From Apprentice.

Season	Club	League Appearances/Goals	
1974–75	Shrewsbury T	—	—
1975–76		32	4
1976–77		43	7
1977–78		41	10
1978–79		44	11
1979–80		39	3
1980–81		39	6
1981–82		40	17
1982–83	Sunderland	37	4
1983–84		40	2
1984–85		—	—
1984–85	Everton	6	1
1985–86		1	—
1985–86	Ipswich T	21	2
1986–87		40	1
1987–88		16	1
1987–88	Birmingham C	8	1
1988–89		40	3
1989–90		45	2

ATKINS, Mark

Born Doncaster 14.8.68. Ht 6 1
Wt 12 00
Defender.

Season	Club	League Appearances/Goals	
1986–87	Scunthorpe U	26	—
1987–88		22	2
1988–89	Blackburn R	46	6
1989–90		41	7

ATKINSON , Brian

Born Darlington 19.1.71. Ht 5 10
Wt 12 00
Midfield. From Trainee.

Season	Club	Apps	Goals
1988–89	Sunderland	3	—
1989–90		13	—

ATKINSON, Dalian

Born Shrewsbury 21.3.68. Ht 6 1
Wt 12 10
Forward. England B.

Season	Club	Apps	Goals
1985–86	Ipswich T	1	—
1986–87		8	—
1987–88		17	8
1988–89		34	10
1989–90	Sheffield W	38	10

ATKINSON, Graeme

Born Hull 11.11.71.
Midfield. From Trainee.

Season	Club	Apps	Goals
1989–90	Hull C	13	1

ATKINSON, Pat

Born Singapore 22.5.70. Ht 5 8
Wt 10 11
Forward. From Sheffield U Trainee.

Season	Club	Apps	Goals
1988–89	Hartlepool U	13	3
1989–90		8	—

ATKINSON, Paul

Born Chester-le-Street 19.1.66 Ht 5 9
Wt 10 02
Midfield. From Apprentice. England Youth.

Season	Club	Apps	Goals
1983–84	Sunderland	8	1
1984–85		9	1
1985–86		13	—
1986–87		8	—
1987–88		22	3
1988–89	Port Vale	4	3
1989–90		—	—
1989–90	*Hartlepool U*	11	1

ATKINSON, Paul

Born Otley 14.8.61. Ht 5 10 Wt 11 05
Forward. From Apprentice.

Season	Club	Apps	Goals
1979–80	Oldham Ath	38	6
1980–81		30	2
1981–82		33	—
1982–83		42	3
1983–84	Watford	11	—
1984–85		—	—
1985–86	Oldham Ath	26	1
1986–87	*Swansea C*	18	3
1986–87	*Bolton W*	3	—
1987–88	Oldham Ath	7	—
1988–89	Burnley	14	1
1989–90		8	—

ATTEVELD, Ray

Born Amsterdam 8.9.66. Ht 5 10
Wt 12 00
Midfield. From Haarlem.

Season	Club	Apps	Goals
1989–90	Everton	18	1

AUSTIN, Dean

Born Hemel Hempstead 26.4.70.
Defender. From St. Albans C.

Season	Club	Apps	Goals
1989–90	Southend U	7	—

AWFORD, Andy

Born Worcester 14.7.72.
Defender. From Worcester C, Portsmouth Trainee.

Season	Club	Apps	Goals
1988–89	Portsmouth	4	—
1989–90		—	—

AYLOTT, Trevor

Born London 26.11.57. Ht 6 1 Wt 14 00
Forward. From Apprentice.

Season	Club	Apps	Goals
1976–77	Chelsea	—	—
1976–77	*QPR*	—	—
1977–78	Chelsea	11	2
1978–79		15	—
1979–80		3	—
1979–80	Barnsley	18	4
1980–81		37	11
1981–82		41	11
1982–83	Millwall	32	5
1982–83	Luton T	12	2
1983–84		20	8
1984–85	Crystal Palace	35	8

Season	Club	League Appearances/Goals	
1985–86	....	18	4
1985–86	*Barnsley*	9	—
1986–87	Bournemouth	37	10
1987–88	....	43	9
1988–89	....	40	6
1989–90	....	18	2

BABB, Phil

Born Lambeth 30.11.70. Ht 6 0
Wt 12 03
Defender.

Season	Club	League Appearances/Goals	
1988–89	Millwall	—	—
1989–90	....	—	—

BACON, Paul

Born London 20.12.70. Ht 5 9 Wt 10 04
Defender. From Trainee.

Season	Club	League Appearances/Goals	
1988–89	Charlton Ath	—	—
1989–90	....	—	—

BAILEY, Danny

Born Leyton 21.5.64. Ht 5 7 Wt 12 07
Midfield. From Wealdstone.

Season	Club	League Appearances/Goals	
1989–90	Exeter C	46	1

BAILEY, Dennis

Born Lambeth 13.11.65. Ht 5 10
Wt 11 06
Forward. From Fulham, Farnborough T.

Season	Club	League Appearances/Goals	
1987–88	Crystal Palace	5	1
1988–89	....	—	—
1988–89	*Bristol R*	17	9
1989–90	Birmingham C	43	18

BAILEY, John

Born Liverpool 1.4.57. Ht 5 8 Wt 11 03
Defender. From Apprentice.

Season	Club	League Appearances/Goals	
1975–76	Blackburn R	6	—
1976–77	....	34	—
1977–78	....	41	1
1978–79	....	39	—
1979–80	Everton	42	2
1980–81	....	31	—
1981–82	....	12	—
1982–83	....	37	1
1983–84	....	33	—
1984–85	....	15	—
1985–86	....	1	—
1985–86	Newcastle U	28	—
1986–87	....	8	—
1987–88	....	4	—

Season	Club	Apps	Goals
1988–89	Bristol C	35	—
1989–90		38	1

BAILIE, Colin

Born Belfast 31.3.64. Ht 5 11 Wt 10 11
Defender. From Apprentice.

Season	Club	Apps	Goals
1981–82	Swindon T	1	—
1982–83		26	1
1983–84		38	3
1984–85		42	—
1985–86	Reading	26	—
1986–87		37	1
1987–88		21	—
1988–89	Cambridge U	23	1
1989–90		36	—

BAIN, Kevin

Born Kirkcaldy 19.9.72. Ht 6 0
Wt 11 09
Defender. From Abbey Star. Scotland U-16.

Season	Club	Apps	Goals
1989–90	Dundee	1	—

BAIRD, Ian

Born Rotherham 1.4.64. Ht 6 0
Wt 12 10
Forward. From Apprentice.
England Schools.

Season	Club	Apps	Goals
1981–82	Southampton	—	—
1982–83		11	2
1983–84		6	1
1983–84	*Cardiff C*	12	6
1984–85	Southampton	5	2
1984–85	*Newcastle U*	5	1
1984–85	Leeds U	10	6
1985–86		35	12
1986–87		40	15
1987–88	Portsmouth	20	1
1987–88	Leeds U	10	3
1988–89		43	10
1989–90		24	4
1989–90	Middlesbrough	19	5

BAKER, Clive

Born N. Walsham 14.3.59. Ht 5 9
Wt 11 00
Goalkeeper. From Amateur.

Season	Club	Apps	Goals
1977–78	Norwich C	2	—
1978–79		2	—
1979–80		—	—
1980–81		10	—
1981–82		—	—
1982–83		—	—
1983–84		—	—
1984–85	Barnsley	37	—
1985–86		42	—
1986–87		39	—
1987–88		44	—
1988–89		46	—
1989–90		37	—

BAKER, Graham

Born Southampton 3.12.58. Ht 5 9
Wt 10 08
Midfield. From Apprentice. England Under-21.

Season	Club	Apps	Goals
1977–78	Southampton	3	1
1978–79		22	5
1979–80		23	4
1980–81		39	8
1981–82		26	4
1982–83	Manchester C	27	4
1983–84		36	8
1984–85		29	4
1985–86		10	—
1986–87		15	3
1987–88	Southampton	36	5
1988–89		21	4
1989–90		3	—
1989–90	*Aldershot*	7	2

BAKER, Paul

Born Newcastle 5.1.63. Ht 6 1 Wt 12 10
Midfield. From Bishop Auckland.

Season	Club	Apps	Goals
1984–85	Southampton	—	—
1985–86	Carlisle U	35	2
1986–87		36	9
1987–88	Hartlepool U	39	19

Season	Club	League Appearances/Goals	
1988–89		40	7
1989–90		43	16

BAKER, Steve

Born Newcastle 2.12.61. Ht 5 5 Wt 10 08
Midfield. From Apprentice.

Season	Club	League Appearances/Goals	
1979–80	Southampton	—	—
1980–81		1	—
1981–82		5	—
1982–83		7	—
1983–84		8	—
1983–84	*Burnley*	10	—
1984–85	Southampton	9	—
1985–86		13	—
1986–87		26	—
1987–88		4	—
1987–88	Leyton Orient	9	3
1988–89		46	3
1989–90		32	—

BALAVAGE, John

Born Bellshill 15.10.60. Ht 6 2 Wt 12 00
Goalkeeper. From Albion Rovers BC.

Season	Club	League Appearances/Goals	
1978–79	Albion R	27	—
1979–80		33	—
1980–81		33	—
1981–82		31	—
1982–83		22	—
1983–84		20	—
1984–85	St Johnstone	5	—
1985–86		38	—
1986–87		26	—
1987–88		37	—
1988–89		39	—
1989–90		38	—

BALL, Kevin

Born Hastings 12.11.64. Ht 5 9 Wt 12 00
Defender. From Apprentice.

Season	Club	League Appearances/Goals	
1983–84	Portsmouth	1	—
1984–85		—	—
1985–86		9	—
1986–87		16	—
1987–88		29	1

Season	Club	League Appearances/Goals	
1988–89		14	1
1989–90		36	2

BALL, Steve

Born Colchester 2.9.69 Ht 6 0 Wt 12 01
Midfield. From Trainee.

Season	Club	League Appearances/Goals	
1987–88	Arsenal	—	—
1988–89		—	—
1989–90	Colchester U	4	—

BALTACHA, Sergei

Born Ukraine 17.2.58 Ht 6 0 Wt 12 00
Midfield. From Dynamo Kiev. USSR full caps.

Season	Club	League Appearances/Goals	
1988–89	Ipswich T	20	1
1989–90		8	—

BAMBER, Dave

Born St. Helens 1.2.59 Ht 6 3 Wt 13 10
Forward. From Manchester Univ.

Season	Club	League Appearances/Goals	
1979–80	Blackpool	7	1
1980–81		15	3
1981–82		38	15
1982–83		26	10
1983–84	Coventry C	19	3
1983–84	Walsall	10	3
1984–85		10	4
1984–85	Portsmouth	4	1
1985–86		—	—
1985–86	Swindon T	23	9
1986–87		42	9
1987–88		41	13
1988–89	Watford	18	3
1988–89	Stoke C	23	6
1989–90		20	2
1989–90	Hull C	19	3

BANGER, Nicky

Born Southampton 25.2.71. Ht 5 8 Wt 10 06
Forward. From Trainee.

Season	Club	League Appearances/Goals	
1988–89	Southampton	—	—
1989–90		—	—

BANKS, Ian

Born Mexborough 9.1.61. Ht 5 9
Wt 13 00
Midfield. From Apprentice.

Season	Club	League Appearances/Goals	
1978–79	Barnsley	2	—
1979–80		38	3
1980–81		45	14
1981–82		42	15
1982–83		37	5
1983–84	Leicester C	26	3
1984–85		33	9
1985–86		31	2
1986–87		3	—
1986–87	Huddersfield T	37	8
1987–88		41	9
1988–89	Bradford C	30	3
1988–89	WBA	4	—
1989–90	Barnsley	37	3

BANNISTER, Gary

Born Warrington 22.7.60. Ht 5 8
Wt 11 05
Forward. From Apprentice.
England Under-21.

Season	Club	League Appearances/Goals	
1978–79	Coventry C	4	1
1979–80		7	—
1980–81		11	2
1981–82	Sheffield W	42	21
1982–83		39	20
1983–84		37	14
1984–85	QPR	42	17
1985–86		36	16
1986–87		34	15
1987–88		24	8
1987–88	Coventry C	8	1
1988–89		24	8
1989–90		11	2
1989–90	WBA	13	2

BANNON, Eamonn

Born Edinburgh 18.4.58. Ht 5 9
Wt 11 11
Midfield. From Links BC.
Scotland Schools, Under-21, 9 full caps.

Season	Club	League Appearances/Goals	
1976–77	Hearts	13	1
1977–78		39	12
1978–79		19	5
1978–79	Chelsea	19	1
1979–80		6	—
1979–80	Dundee U	24	4
1980–81		34	8
1981–82		36	12
1982–83		32	10
1983–84		33	7
1984–85		35	10
1985–86		31	11
1986–87		39	9
1987–88		26	1
1988–89	Hearts	30	2
1989–90		33	2

BANTON, Dale

Born Kensington 15.5.61. Ht 5 10
Wt 11 05
Forward. From Apprentice.

Season	Club	League Appearances/Goals	
1979–80	West Ham U	4	—
1980–81		—	—
1981–82		1	—
1982–83	Aldershot	45	24
1983–84		46	19
1984–85		15	4
1984–85	York C	30	12
1985–86		35	10
1986–87		29	6
1987–88		33	16
1988–89		11	4
1988–89	Walsall	10	—
1988–89	*Grimsby T*	8	1
1989–90	Aldershot	23	1

BARACLOUGH, Ian

Born Leicester 4.12.70.
Forward. From Trainee.

Season	Club	League Appearances/Goals	
1988–89	Leicester C	—	—
1989–90		—	—
1989–90	*Wigan Ath*	9	2

BARBER, Fred

Born Ferryhill 26.8.63. Ht 5 10 Wt 12 00
Goalkeeper. From Apprentice.

Season	Club	League Appearances/Goals	
1981–82	Darlington	—	—
1982–83		12	—
1983–84		46	—
1984–85		45	—
1985–86		32	—
1985–86	Everton	—	—
1986–87		—	—
1986–87	Walsall	36	—
1987–88		46	—
1988–89		44	—
1989–90		25	—
1989–90	*Peterborough U*	6	—

BARBER, Philip

Born Tring 10.6.65. Ht 5 11 Wt 12 05
Forward. From Aylesbury.

Season	Club	Apps	Goals
1983–84	Crystal Palace	9	2
1984–85		23	4
1985–86		39	9
1986–87		31	5
1987–88		37	7
1988–89		46	6
1989–90		30	1

BARDSLEY, David

Born Manchester 11.9.64. Ht 5 10
Wt 11 00
Defender. From Apprentice. England Youth.

Season	Club	Apps	Goals
1981–82	Blackpool	1	—
1982–83		28	—
1983–84		16	—
1983–84	Watford	25	—
1984–85		17	—
1985–86		13	2
1986–87		41	5
1987–88		4	—
1987–88	Oxford U	34	1
1988–89		37	6
1989–90		3	—
1989–90	QPR	31	1

BARHAM, Mark

Born Folkestone 12.7.62. Ht 5 7
Wt 11 00
Midfield. From Apprentice. England Youth, 2 full caps.

Season	Club	Apps	Goals
1979–80	Norwich C	4	—
1980–81		35	1
1981–82		27	4
1982–83		38	4
1983–84		11	2
1984–85		14	1
1985–86		35	9
1986–87		13	2
1987–88	Huddersfield T	26	1
1988–89		1	—
1988–89	Middlesbrough	4	—
1989–90	WBA	4	—
1989–90	Brighton	17	2

BARKER, Simon

Born Farnworth 4.11.64. Ht 5 9
Wt 11 00
Midfield. From Apprentice.
England Under-21.

Season	Club	Apps	Goals
1982–83	Blackburn R	—	—
1983–84		28	3
1984–85		38	2
1985–86		41	10
1986–87		42	11
1987–88		33	9
1988–89	QPR	25	1
1989–90		28	3

BARLOW, Andy

Born Oldham 24.11.65. Ht 5 9 Wt 11 01
Defender.

Season	Club	Apps	Goals
1984–85	Oldham Ath	33	—
1985–86		26	—
1986–87		29	2
1987–88		26	—
1988–89		15	—
1989–90		44	1

BARLOW, Martin

Born Barnstable 25.6.71
Midfield. From Trainee.

Season	Club	League Appearances/Goals	
1988–89	Plymouth Arg	1	—
1989–90		1	—

BARNARD, Leigh

Born Worsley 29.10.58. Ht 5 8 Wt 11 07
Midfield. From Apprentice.

Season	Club	Apps	Goals
1977–78	Portsmouth	11	—
1978–79		28	7
1979–80		5	—
1980–81		18	1
1981–82		17	—
1981–82	*Peterborough U*	4	—
1982–83	Swindon T	46	4
1983–84		36	7
1984–85		32	2
1984–85	*Exeter C*	6	2
1985–86	Swindon T	38	3
1986–87		41	3
1987–88		17	2
1988–89		2	—
1989–90		5	—
1989–90	Cardiff C	35	8

BARNES, Bobby

Born Kingston 17.12.62. Ht 5 7
Wt 10 09
Forward. From Apprentice.

Season	Club	Apps	Goals
1980–81	West Ham	6	1
1981–82		3	—
1982–83		—	—
1983–84		13	2
1984–85		20	2
1985–86		1	—
1985–86	*Scunthorpe U*	6	—
1985–86	Aldershot	14	8
1986–87		25	11
1987–88		10	7
1987–88	Swindon T	28	10
1988–89		17	3
1988–89	Bournemouth	10	—
1989–90		4	—
1989–90	Northampton T	37	18

BARNES, David

Born London 16.11.61. Ht 5 10
Wt 11 01
Defender. From Apprentice.
England Youth.

Season	Club	Apps	Goals
1979–80	Coventry C	3	—
1980–81		—	—
1981–82		6	—
1981–82	Ipswich T	—	—
1982–83		6	—
1983–84		11	—
1984–85		—	—
1984–85	Wolves	23	1
1985–86		38	1
1986–87		26	2
1987–88		1	—
1987–88	Aldershot	30	—
1988–89		39	1
1989–90	Sheffield U	24	—

BARNES, John

Born Jamaica 7.11.63 Ht 5 11 Wt 12 00
Forward. From Sudbury Court.
England Under-21, 58 full caps.

Season	Club	Apps	Goals
1981–82	Watford	36	13
1982–83		42	10
1983–84		39	11
1984–85		40	12
1985–86		39	9
1986–87		37	10
1987–88	Liverpool	38	15
1988–89		33	8
1989–90		34	22

BARNES, Paul

Born Leicester 16.11.67. Ht 5 10
Wt 10 06
Forward. From Apprentice.

Season	Club	Apps	Goals
1985–86	Notts Co	14	4
1986–87		—	—
1987–88		11	2
1988–89		15	7
1989–90		13	1
1989–90	Stoke C	5	—

BARNES, Robert

Born Stoke 26.11.69 Ht 5 8 Wt 10 08
Defender. From Trainee.

Season	Club	League Appearances/Goals	
1988–89	Manchester C	—	—
1989–90	Wrexham	8	—

BARNETT, David

Born Swindon 20.11.69 Ht 5 6 Wt 9 13
Defender. From Trainee.

Season	Club	Apps	Goals
1988–89	Swindon T	—	—
1989–90		—	—

BARNETT, Gary

Born Stratford 11.3.63. Ht 5 6 Wt 9 13
Forward. From Apprentice.

Season	Club	Apps	Goals
1980–81	Coventry C	—	—
1981–82		—	—
1982–83	Oxford U	22	2
1982–83	*Wimbledon*	5	1
1983–84	Oxford U	19	7
1984–85		2	—
1984–85	*Fulham*	2	1
1985–86	Oxford U	2	—
1985–86	Fulham	36	6
1986–87		42	9
1987–88		42	9
1988–89		28	5
1989–90		32	1

BARNSLEY, Andy

Born Sheffield 9.6.62. Ht 6 0 Wt 11 07
Defender. From Denaby U.

Season	Club	Apps	Goals
1984–85	Rotherham U	—	—
1985–86		28	—
1986–87	Sheffield U	42	1
1987–88		32	—
1988–89		3	—
1988–89	Rotherham U	27	—
1989–90		37	3

BARR, Billy

Born Halifax 21.1.69. Ht 5 11 Wt 11 07
Defender. From Trainee.

Season	Club	Apps	Goals
1987–88	Halifax T	30	—
1988–89		43	4
1989–90		23	2

BARRASS, Tony

Born Teeside 29.3.71
Forward. From Trainee.

Season	Club	Apps	Goals
1988–89	Hartlepool U	3	—
1989–90		9	—

BARRATT, Tony

Born Salford 18.10.65. Ht 5 7 Wt 10 03
Defender. From Billingham T.

Season	Club	Apps	Goals
1985–86	Grimsby T	22	—
From Billingham T			
1986–87	Hartlepool U	23	—
1987–88		43	3
1988–89		32	1
1988–89	York C	12	—
1989–90		46	4

BARRETT, Earl

Born Rochdale 28.4.67 Ht 5 10 Wt 11 00
Defender. From Apprentice. England Under-21.

Season	Club	Apps	Goals
1984–85	Manchester C	—	—
1985–86		1	—
1985–86	*Chester C*	12	—
1986–87	Manchester C	2	—
1987–88		—	—
1987–88	Oldham Ath	18	—
1988–89		44	—
1989–90		46	2

BARRETT, Scott

Born Derby 2.4.63. Ht 5 10 Wt 13 04
Goalkeeper. From Ilkeston T.

Season	Club	Apps	Goals
1984–85	Wolverhampton W	4	—
1985–86		21	—
1986–87		5	—
1987–88	Stoke C	27	—
1988–89		17	—
1989–90		7	—

Season	Club	League Appearances/Goals	
1989–90	*Colchester U*	13	—
1989–90	*Stockport Co*	10	—

BARRICK, Dean

Born Hemsworth 30.9.69. Ht 5 9
Wt 11 04
Midfield. From Trainee.

Season	Club	Apps	Goals
1987–88	Sheffield W	—	—
1988–89		8	2
1989–90		3	—

BARRON, Dougie

Born Edinburgh 25.10.61 Ht 5 11
Wt 11 00
Defender. From Bainsford F.

Season	Club	Apps	Goals
1980–81	St Johnstone	1	—
1981–82		17	—
1982–83		5	1
1983–84		20	2
1984–85		37	1
1985–86		37	2
1986–87		35	—
1987–88		38	1
1988–89		38	—
1989–90		17	—

BARROW, Graham

Born Chorley 13.6.54. Ht 6 2 Wt 13 07
Midfield. From Altrincham.

Season	Club	Apps	Goals
1981–82	Wigan Ath	41	12
1982–83		28	3
1983–84		42	5
1984–85		38	9
1985–86		30	7
1986–87	Chester C	41	5
1987–88		38	4
1988–89		35	3
1989–90		28	1

BARTLETT, Kevin

Born Portsmouth 12.10.62. Ht 5 9
Wt 10 12
Forward. From Apprentice.

Season	Club	Apps	Goals
1980–81	Portsmouth	2	—
1981–82		1	1
From Fareham			
1986–87	Cardiff C	23	4
1987–88		37	12
1988–89		22	9
1988–89	WBA	17	3
1989–90		20	7
1989–90	Notts Co	14	8

BARTON, Warren

Born London 19.3.69. Ht 6 0 Wt 11 00
Defender. From Leytonstone/Ilford.

Season	Club	Apps	Goals
1989–90	Maidstone U	42	—

BARTRAM, Vince

Born Birmingham 7.8.68. Ht 6 2
Wt 13 04
Goalkeeper. From Local.

Season	Club	Apps	Goals
1985–86	Wolverhampton W	—	—
1986–87		1	—
1987–88		—	—
1988–89		—	—
1989–90		—	—
1989–90	*Blackpool*	9	—

BASHIR, Naseem

Born Amersham 12.9.69 Ht 5 6
Wt 10 06
Midfield.

Season	Club	Apps	Goals
1988–89	Reading	—	—
1989–90		3	1

BASTOCK, Paul

Born Leamingtom 19.5.70. Ht 5 8
Wt 10 00
Goalkeeper. From Coventry C Trainee.

Season	Club	Apps	Goals
1987–88	Cambridge U	10	—
1988–89		2	—
1989–90		—	—

BASTOW, Ian

Born Torquay 12.8.71 Ht 5 8 Wt 9 02
Midfield. From Trainee.

Season	Club	League Appearances/Goals	
1988–89	Torquay U	2	—
1989–90		9	—

BATES, Jamie

Born London 24.2.68. Ht 6 1 Wt 12 12
Defender. From Trainee.

Season	Club	Apps	Goals
1986–87	Brentford	24	1
1987–88		23	1
1988–89		36	1
1989–90		15	—

BATTY, David

Born Leeds 2.12.68. Ht 5 7 Wt 10 07
Midfield. From Trainee. England B, Under-21.

Season	Club	Apps	Goals
1987–88	Leeds U	23	1
1988–89		30	—
1989–90		42	—

BATTY, Lawrence

Born London 15.2.64 Ht 6 0 Wt 13 07
Goalkeeper. From Farense.

Season	Club	Apps	Goals
1984–85	Fulham	—	—
1985–86		2	—
1986–87		2	—
1987–88		—	—
1987–88	*Crystal Palace*	—	—
1988–89	Fulham	1	—
1989–90		2	—

BATTY, Paul

Born Edington 9.1.64. Ht 5 7 Wt 10 07
Midfield. From Apprentice.

Season	Club	Apps	Goals
1981–82	Swindon T	—	—
1982–83		39	1
1983–84		41	4
1984–85		28	2
1985–86	Chesterfield	26	—
1986–87	Exeter C	33	2
1987–88		32	6
1988–89		15	1
1989–90		20	2
1989–90	*Cambridge U*	—	—

BAURESS, Gary

Born Liverpool 19.1.71. Ht 6 0
Wt 12 00
Defender. From Trainee.

Season	Club	Apps	Goals
1989–90	Tranmere R	1	—

BAYES, Ashley

Born Lincoln 19.4.72.
Goalkeeper. From Trainee.

Season	Club	Apps	Goals
1989–90	Brentford	1	—

BAZELEY, Darren

Born Northampton 5.10.72.
Forward. From Trainee.

Season	Club	Apps	Goals
1989–90	Watford	1	—

BEADLE, Peter

Born London 13.5.72
Midfield. From Trainee.

Season	Club	Apps	Goals
1988–89	Gillingham	2	—
1989–90		10	2

BEAGRIE, Peter

Born Middlesbrough 28.11.65. Ht 5 9
Wt 10 08
Midfield. From Local. England B, Under-21.

Season	Club	Apps	Goals
1983–84	Middlesbrough	—	—
1984–85		7	1
1985–86		26	1
1986–87	Sheffield U	41	9
1987–88		43	2
1988–89	Stoke C	41	7
1989–90		13	—
1989–90	Everton	19	—

BEARDSLEY, Peter

Born Newcastle 18.1.61. Ht 5 8
Wt 12 00
Forward. From Wallsend BC. England 45 full caps. Football League.

Season	Club	League Appearances/Goals	
1979–80	Carlisle U	37	8
1980–81		43	10
1981–82		22	4
From Vancouver Whitecaps			
1982–83	Manchester U	—	—
From Vancouver Whitecaps			
1983–84	Newcastle U	35	20
1984–85		38	17
1985–86		42	19
1986–87		32	5
1987–88	Liverpool	38	15
1988–89		37	10
1989–90		29	10

BEARDSMORE, Russell

Born Wigan 28.9.68. Ht 5 6 Wt 8 10
Midfield. From Apprentice. England Under-21.

Season	Club	League Appearances/Goals	
1986–87	Manchester U	—	—
1987–88		—	—
1988–89		23	2
1989–90		21	2

BEASANT, Dave

Born Willesden 20.3.59. Ht 6 4 Wt 13 00
Goalkeeper. From Edgware T. England B, 2 full caps.

Season	Club	League Appearances/Goals	
1979–80	Wimbledon	2	—
1980–81		34	—
1981–82		46	—
1982–83		46	—
1983–84		46	—
1984–85		42	—
1985–86		42	—
1986–87		42	—
1987–88		40	—
1988–89	Newcastle U	20	—
1988–89	Chelsea	22	—
1989–90		38	—

BEASLEY, Andy

Born Sedgley 5.2.64. Ht 6 1 Wt 12 02
Goalkeeper. From Apprentice.

Season	Club	League Appearances/Goals	
1981–82	Luton T.	—	—
1982–83		—	—
1983–84		—	—
1983–84	*Mansfield T*	—	—
1983–84	*Gillingham*	—	—
1984–85	Mansfield T	3	—
1985–86		—	—
1986–87		—	—
1986–87	*Peterborough U*	7	—
1987–88	Mansfield T	8	—
1987–88	*Scarborough*	4	—
1988–89	Mansfield T	6	—
1989–90		26	—

BEATTY, Steve

Born Larne 1.9.69 Ht 6 0 Wt 12 10
Defender. From Trainee.

Season	Club	League Appearances/Goals	
1988–89	Chelsea	—	—
1989–90		—	—

BEAUCHAMP, Joe

Born Oxford 13.3.71 Ht 5 11 Wt 11 10
Forward. From Trainee.

Season	Club	League Appearances/Goals	
1988–89	Oxford U	1	—
1989–90		3	—

BEAUMONT, Chris

Born Sheffield 5.12.65 Ht 5 11 Wt 11 07
Forward. From Denaby.

Season	Club	League Appearances/Goals	
1988–89	Rochdale	34	7
1989–90	Stockport Co	22	5

BEAUMONT, David

Born Edinburgh 10.12.63. Ht 5 10 Wt 11 05
Midfield. 'S' Form. Scotland Youth, Under-21.

Season	Club	League Appearances/Goals	
1980–81	Dundee U	—	—
1981–82		—	—
1982–83		—	—
1983–84		2	—
1984–85		18	1
1985–86		13	—
1986–87		28	—
1987–88		10	1
1988–89		18	1

Season	Club	League Appearances/Goals	
1988–89	Luton T	15	—
1989–90		19	—

BEAUMONT, Nigel

Born Pontefract 11.2.67. Ht 6 1
Wt 12 07
Defender

Season	Club	Apps	Goals
1984–85	Bradford C	—	—
1985–86		2	—
1986–87		—	—
1987–88		—	—
1988–89	Wrexham	21	—
1989–90		43	3

BEAVON, Stuart

Born Wolverhampton 30.11.58. Ht 5 6
Wt 10 04
Midfield. From Apprentice.

Season	Club	Apps	Goals
1976–77	Tottenham H	—	—
1977–78		—	—
1978–79		1	—
1979–80		3	—
1979–80	*Notts Co*	6	—
1980–81	Reading	37	6
1981–82		40	5
1982–83		46	4
1983–84		36	7
1984–85		46	2
1985–86		44	3
1986–87		42	3
1987–88		34	2
1988–89		39	9
1989–90		32	3

BECK, John

Born Edmonton 25.5.54. Ht 5 11
Wt 11 09
Midfield. From Apprentice.

Season	Club	Apps	Goals
1972–73	QPR	1	—
1973–74		5	—
1974–75		29	1
1975–76		5	—
1976–77	Coventry C	40	3
1977–78		23	2
1978–79		6	1
1978–79	Fulham	32	2
1979–80		40	2
1980–81		37	8
1981–82		5	1
1982–83		—	—
1982–83	*Bournemouth*	4	—
1982–83	Bournemouth	11	3
1983–84		45	3
1984–85		36	1
1985–86		41	5
1986–87	Cambridge U	35	5
1987–88		35	2
1988–89		40	4
1989–90		2	—

BECKFORD, Darren

Born Manchester 12.5.67. Ht 6 1
Wt 11 01
Forward. From Apprentice. England Youth.

Season	Club	Apps	Goals
1984–85	Manchester C	4	—
1985–86		3	—
1985–86	*Bury*	12	5
1986–87	Manchester C	4	—
1986–87	*Port Vale*	11	4
1987–88	Port Vale	40	9
1988–89		42	20
1989–90		42	17

BECKFORD, Jason

Born Manchester 14.2.70. Ht 5 9
Wt 12 04
Forward. From Trainee. England Youth.

Season	Club	Apps	Goals
1987–88	Manchester C	5	—
1988–89		8	1
1989–90		5	—

BEEDIE, Stuart

Born Aberdeen 16.8.60. Ht 5 10
Wt 11 00
Midfield. From Sunnybank A.

Season	Club	Apps	Goals
1978–79	Montrose	10	—
1979–80		34	4
1980–81		36	9
1981–82	St Johnstone	26	5
1982–83		34	2
1983–84		34	2

Season	Club	League Appearances/Goals	
1984–85	Dundee U	28	3
1985–86		18	3
1986–87	Hibernian	9	2
1986–87	Dunfermline Ath	6	—
1987–88		36	2
1988–89		23	2
1989–90	Dundee	21	3

BEEKS, Steve

Born Ashford 10.4.71. Ht 5 10 Wt 11 05
Midfield. From Trainee.

Season	Club	Apps	Goals
1989–90	Aldershot	1	—

BEENEY, Mark

Born Pembury 30.12.67. Ht 6 4
Wt 14 07
Goalkeeper.

Season	Club	Apps	Goals
1986–87	Gillingham	—	—
1987–88	Maidstone U	—	—
1988–89		—	—
1989–90		33	—
1989–90	*Aldershot*	7	—

BEESLEY, Paul

Born Wigan 21.7.65. Ht 6 1 Wt 11 11
Defender. From Marine.

Season	Club	Apps	Goals
1984–85	Wigan Ath	2	—
1985–86		17	—
1986–87		39	—
1987–88		42	1
1988–89		44	2
1989–90		11	—
1989–90	Leyton Orient	32	1

BEESTON, Carl

Born Stoke 30.6.67. Ht 5 9 Wt 11 13
Midfield. From Apprentice. England Under-21.

Season	Club	Apps	Goals
1984–85	Stoke C	1	—
1985–86		5	—
1986–87		—	—
1987–88		12	—
1988–89		23	2
1989–90		38	2

BEGLIN, Jim

Born Waterford 29.7.63. Ht 5 11
Wt 11 00
Defender. From Shamrock R. Eire B, 15 full caps.

Season	Club	Apps	Goals
1982–83	Liverpool	—	—
1983–84		—	—
1984–85		10	1
1985–86		34	1
1986–87		20	—
1987–88		—	—
1988–89		—	—
1989–90	Leeds U	19	—
1989–90	*Plymouth Arg*	5	—

BELL, Doug

Born Paisley 5.9.59. Ht 5 11 Wt 12 01
Midfield. From Cumbernauld.
Scotland Under-21.

Season	Club	Apps	Goals
1977–78	St Mirren	2	1
1978–79		—	—
1979–80	Aberdeen	9	—
1980–81		17	1
1981–82		13	1
1982–83		23	1
1983–84		24	3
1984–85		22	—
1985–86	Rangers	23	—
1986–87		12	1
1986–87	*St Mirren*	4	—
1986–87	Hibernian	16	2
1987–88		16	1
1987–88	Shrewsbury T	15	2
1988–89		26	1
1988–89	*Hull C*	4	—
1989–90	Shrewsbury T	9	3
1989–90	Birmingham C	15	—

BELL, Michael

Born Newcastle 15.11.71.
Midfield. From Trainee.

Season	Club	League Appearances/Goals	
1989–90	Northampton T	6	—

BELLAMY, Gary

Born Worksop 4.7.62. Ht 6 2 Wt 11 05
Defender. From Apprentice.

Season	Club	Apps	Goals
1980–81	Chesterfield	3	—
1981–82		25	—
1982–83		42	—
1983–84		38	1
1984–85		22	2
1985–86		12	2
1986–87		42	2
1987–88	Wolverhampton W	24	2
1988–89		43	1
1989–90		39	3

BENALI, Francis

Born Southampton 30.12.68. Ht 5 9
Wt 11 01
Forward. From Apprentice.

Season	Club	Apps	Goals
1986–87	Southampton	—	—
1987–88		—	—
1988–89		7	—
1989–90		27	—

BENBOW, Ian

Born Hereford 9.1.69. Ht 5 10 Wt 11 00
Midfield. From Trainee.

Season	Club	Apps	Goals
1987–88	Hereford U	21	2
1988–89		34	1
1989–90		27	1

BENJAMIN, Ian

Born Nottingham 11.12.61. Ht 5 11
Wt 12 00
Midfield. From Apprentice. England Youth.

Season	Club	Apps	Goals
1978–79	Sheffield U	2	2
1979–80		3	1
1979–80	WBA	—	—
1980–81		2	—
1981–82	Notts Co	—	—
1982–83	Peterborough U	46	6
1983–84		34	8
1984–85	Northampton T	44	18
1985–86		46	22
1986–87		46	18
1987–88		14	1
1987–88	Cambridge U	25	2
1988–89	Chester C	22	2
1988–89	Exeter C	20	3
1989–90		12	1
1989–90	Southend U	15	4

BENNETT, Dave

Born Manchester 11.7.59. Ht 5 9
Wt 10 07
Forward. From Amateur.

Season	Club	Apps	Goals
1978–79	Manchester C	1	—
1979–80		25	2
1980–81		26	7
1981–82		—	—
1981–82	Cardiff C	36	6
1982–83		41	12
1983–84	Coventry C	34	6
1984–85		34	2
1985–86		38	6
1986–87		31	7
1987–88		28	4
1988–89		7	—
1988–89	Sheffield W	10	—
1989–90		18	—

BENNETT, Gary

Born Liverpool 20.9.63. Ht 6 1 Wt 12 06
Forward. Local.

Season	Club	Apps	Goals
1984–85	Wigan Ath	20	3
1985–86	Chester C	43	13
1986–87		33	13
1987–88		43	10
1988–89		7	—
1988–89	Southend U	17	2
1989–90		25	4
1989–90	Chester C	8	1

BENNETT, Gary

Born Manchester 4.12.61. Ht 6 1
Wt 12 01
Defender. From Amateur.

Season	Club	Apps	Goals
1979–80	Manchester C	—	—
1980–81		—	—

Season	Club	League Appearances/Goals	
1981–82	Cardiff C	19	1
1982–83		36	8
1983–84		32	2
1984–85	Sunderland	37	3
1985–86		28	3
1986–87		41	4
1987–88		38	2
1988–89		40	3
1989–90		36	3

BENNETT, Gary

Born Enfield 13.11.70 Ht 5 7 Wt 9 13
Midfield. From Trainee.

Season	Club	League Appearances/Goals	
1988–89	Colchester U	9	1
1989–90		36	4

BENNETT, Martyn

Born Birmingham 4.8.61. Ht 6 0
Wt 13 06
Defender. From Apprentice. England Schools.

Season	Club	League Appearances/Goals	
1978–79	WBA	1	—
1979–80		4	—
1980–81		16	1
1981–82		23	2
1982–83		23	1
1983–84		29	—
1984–85		39	—
1985–86		25	2
1986–87		15	2
1987–88		6	1
1988–89		—	—
1989–90		1	—

BENNETT, Michael

Born London 27.7.69. Ht 5 10 Wt 11 11
Midfield. From Apprentice. England Youth.

Season	Club	League Appearances/Goals	
1986–87	Charlton Ath	2	—
1987–88		16	1
1988–89		11	—
1989–90		6	1
1989–90	Wimbledon	7	1

BENNETT, Mike

Born Bolton 24.12.62. Ht 5 8 Wt 10 07
Defender. From Apprentice.
England Youth.

Season	Club	League Appearances/Goals	
1979–80	Bolton W	8	—
1980–81		6	1
1981–82		35	—
1982–83		16	—
1983–84	Wolverhampton W	6	—
1983–84	Cambridge U	11	—
1984–85		34	—
1985–86		31	—
1986–87	Bradford C	—	—
1986–87	Preston NE	42	1
1987–88		34	—
1988–89		—	—
1989–90		10	—

BENNETT, Tom

Born Falkirk 12.12.69 Ht 5 11 Wt 11 08
Defender. From Trainee.

Season	Club	League Appearances/Goals	
1987–88	Aston Villa	—	—
1988–89	Woverhampton W	2	—
1989–90		30	—

BENNYWORTH, Ian

Born Hull 15.1.62. Ht 6 0 Wt 12 07
Defender. From Apprentice.

Season	Club	League Appearances/Goals	
1979–80	Hull C	1	—
From Gainsborough T, Nuneaton			
1987–88	Scarborough	39	1
1988–89		35	2
1989–90		15	—
1989–90	Hartlepool U	27	2

BENSTEAD, Graham

Born Aldershot 20.8.63. Ht 6 2
Wt 12 04
Goalkeeper. From Apprentice. England Youth.

Season	Club	League Appearances/Goals	
1981–82	QPR	—	—
1982–83		—	—

Season	Club	League Appearances/Goals	
1983–84		—	—
1984–85		—	—
1984–85	*Norwich C*	1	—
1985–86	Norwich C	—	—
1986–87		13	—
1987–88		2	—
1987–88	*Colchester U*	18	—
1987–88	*Sheffield U*	8	—
1988–89	Sheffield U	39	—
1989–90		—	—

BENT, Junior

Born Huddersfield 1.3.70. Ht 5 5
Wt 10 06
Forward. From Trainee.

Season	Club	Apps	Goals
1987–88	Huddersfield T	7	—
1988–89		22	5
1989–90		7	1
1989–90	*Burnley*	9	3
1989–90	Bristol C	1	—

BERESFORD, John

Born Sheffield 4.9.66. Ht 5 5 Wt 10 08
Midfield. From Apprentice.
England Schools, Youth.

Season	Club	Apps	Goals
1983–84	Manchester C	—	—
1984–85		—	—
1985–86		—	—
1986–87	Barnsley	27	1
1987–88		34	3
1988–89		27	1
1988–89	Portsmouth	2	—
1989–90		28	—

BERESFORD, Marlon

Born Lincoln 2.9.69. Ht 6 1 Wt 12 06
Goalkeeper. From Trainee.

Season	Club	Apps	Goals
1987–88	Sheffield W	—	—
1988–89		—	—
1989–90		—	—
1989–90	*Bury*	1	—
1989–90	*Ipswich T*	—	—

BERGSSON, Gudni

Born Iceland 21.7.65 Ht 5 10 Wt 10 07
Defender. From Valur. Iceland full caps.

Season	Club	League Appearances/Goals	
1988–89	Tottenham H	8	—
1989–90		18	—

BERNAL, Andy

Born Canberra 16.7.66. Ht 5 10
Wt 12 05
Midfield.

Season	Club	Apps	Goals
1987–88	Ipswich T	9	—
1988–89		—	—
1989–90		—	—

BERRY, George

Born West Germany 19.11.57. Ht 6 0
Wt 13 02
Defender. From Apprentice. Wales 5 full caps.

Season	Club	Apps	Goals
1975–76	Wolverhampton W	—	—
1976–77		1	—
1977–78		7	—
1978–79		30	3
1979–80		41	—
1980–81		25	1
1981–82		20	—
1982–83	Stoke C	31	5
1983–84		8	—
1984–85		32	1
1984–85	*Doncaster R*	1	—
1985–86	Stoke C	41	3
1986–87		40	8
1987–88		36	5
1988–89		33	4
1989–90		16	1

BERRY, Greg

Born Essex 5.3.71
Forward. From East Thurrock.

Season	Club	Apps	Goals
1989–90	Leyton Orient	9	1

BERRY, Les

Born Plumstead 4.5.56. Ht 6 2 Wt 11 13
Defender. From Apprentice.

Season	Club	Apps	Goals
1973–74	Charlton Ath	—	—
1974–75		—	—
1975–76		15	1
1976–77		39	2

Season	Club	League Appearances/Goals	
1977–78		41	2
1978–79		38	1
1979–80		42	2
1980–81		44	2
1981–82		25	—
1982–83		39	1
1983–84		42	—
1984–85		26	—
1985–86		7	—
1986–87	Brighton	23	—
1986–87	*Gillingham*	11	—
1987–88	Gillingham	20	—
1988–89		—	—
1989–90	Maidstone U	38	—

BERRY, Neil

Born Edinburgh 6.4.63. Ht 6 0 Wt 12 00
Defender. From Apprentice. Scotland Youth.

Season	Club	Apps	Goals
1980–81	Bolton W	—	—
1981–82		3	—
1982–83		9	—
1983–84		14	—
1984–85		6	—
1984–85	Hearts	3	—
1985–86		32	2
1986–87		30	3
1987–88		35	—
1988–89		32	1
1989–90		10	1

BERRY, Steve

Born Gosport 4.4.63. Ht 5 7 Wt 11 06
Midfield. From Apprentice.

Season	Club	Apps	Goals
1980–81	Portsmouth	—	—
1981–82		27	2
1982–83		1	—
1983–84		—	—
1983–84	*Aldershot*	7	—
1984–85	Sunderland	34	2
1985–86		1	—
1985–86	Newport Co	26	3
1986–87		34	3
1986–87	Swindon T	1	—
1987–88		3	—
1987–88	Aldershot	36	6
1988–89		12	—
1988–89	Northampton T	34	3
1989–90		41	2

BERRYMAN, Stephen

Born Blackburn 26.12.66
Goalkeeper.

Season	Club	Apps	Goals
1989–90	Hartlepool U	1	—

BERTSCHIN, Keith

Born Enfield 25.8.56. Ht 6 1 Wt 11 08
Forward. From Barnet. England Youth, Under-21.

Season	Club	Apps	Goals
1973–74	Ipswich T	—	—
1974–75		—	—
1975–76		3	2
1976–77		29	6
1977–78	Birmingham C	42	11
1978–79		9	2
1979–80		37	12
1980–81		30	4
1981–82	Norwich C	36	12
1982–83		40	8
1983–84		33	7
1984–85		5	2
1984–85	Stoke C	25	2
1985–86		42	19
1986–87		21	8
1986–87	Sunderland	11	2
1987–88		25	5
1988–89	Walsall	20	—
1989–90		35	9

BETT, Jim

Born Hamilton 25.11.59. Ht 5 11
Wt 12 03
Midfield. From school. Scotland Schools, Under-21, 25 full caps.

Season	Club	Apps	Goals
1976–77	Airdrieonians	1	—
1977–78		7	—
From Iceland and Lokeren			
1980–81	Rangers	34	4
1981–82		35	11
1982–83		35	6
From Lokeren			
1985–86	Aberdeen	24	3
1986–87		38	4

Season	Club	Apps	Goals
1987–88		38	10
1988–89		31	5
1989–90		30	3

BIGGINS, Wayne

Born Sheffield 20.11.61. Ht 5 11
Wt 11 00
Forward. From Apprentice.

Season	Club	Apps	Goals
1979–80	Lincoln C	—	—
1980–81		8	1
From Matlock Town and King's Lynn			
1983–84	Burnley	20	8
1984–85		46	18
1985–86		12	3
1985–86	Norwich C	28	7
1986–87		31	4
1987–88		20	5
1988–89	Manchester C	32	9
1989–90	Stoke C	35	10

BILLING, Peter

Born Liverpool 24.10.64. Ht 6 2
Wt 13 00
Defender. From South Liverpool.

Season	Club	Apps	Goals
1985–86	Everton	1	—
1986–87		—	—
1986–87	Crewe Alex	19	—
1987–88		32	—
1988–89		37	1
1989–90	Coventry C	18	—

BINGHAM, David

Born Dunfermline 3.9.70. Ht 5 10
Wt 10 11
Forward. From Inverkeithing U.

Season	Club	Apps	Goals
1989–90	St Johnstone	1	—

BIRCH, Paul

Born Reading 3.12.68. Ht 6 0 Wt 12 05
Forward. From Arsenal Trainee, Portsmouth.

Season	Club	Apps	Goals
1987–88	Brentford	16	2
1988–89		2	—
1989–90		—	—

BIRCH, Paul

Born West Bromwich 20.11.62 Ht 5 6
Wt 10 04
Midfield. From Apprentice.

Season	Club	Apps	Goals
1980–81	Aston Villa	—	—
1981–82		—	—
1982–83		—	—
1983–84		22	2
1984–85		25	3
1985–86		27	2
1986–87		29	3
1987–88		38	6
1988–89		12	—
1989–90		12	—

BIRD, Adrian

Born Bristol 8.7.69. Ht 6 1 Wt 11 07
Defender. From School.

Season	Club	Apps	Goals
1986–87	Birmingham C	6	—
1987–88		9	—
1988–89		12	—
1989–90		—	—

BIRTLES, Garry

Born Nottingham 27.7.56. Ht 6 0
Wt 12 03
Forward. From Long Eaton U.
England Under-21, B, 3 full caps.

Season	Club	Apps	Goals
1976–77	Nottingham F	1	—
1977–78		—	—
1978–79		35	14
1979–80		42	12
1980–81		9	6
1980–81	Manchester U	25	—
1981–82		33	11
1982–83		—	—
1982–83	Nottingham F	25	7
1983–84		34	15
1984–85		13	2
1985–86		25	—
1986–87		28	14
1987–88	Notts Co	43	7

Season	Club	Apps	Goals
1988–89		20	2
1989–90	Grimsby T	38	8

BISHOP, Charlie

Born Nottingham 16.2.68. Ht 6 0
Wt 12 01
Defender. From Stoke C Apprentice.

Season	Club	Apps	Goals
1986–87	Watford	—	—
1987–88	Bury	17	—
1988–89		38	3
1989–90		30	1

BISHOP, Eddie

Born Liverpool 28.11.62 Ht 5 8
Wt 11 07
Midfield. From Winsford U, Northwich Vic, Altrincham, Runcorn.

Season	Club	Apps	Goals
1987–88	Tranmere R	5	1
1988–89		35	8
1989–90		28	7

BISHOP, Ian

Born Liverpool 29.5.65. Ht 5 9 Wt 10 12
Midfield. From Apprentice.

Season	Club	Apps	Goals
1983–84	Everton	1	—
1983–84	*Crewe Alex*	4	—
1984–85	Everton	—	—
1984–85	Carlisle U	30	2
1985–86		36	6
1986–87		42	3
1987–88		24	3
1988–89	Bournemouth	44	2
1989–90	Manchester C	19	2
1989–90	West Ham U	17	2

BISSETT, Nicky

Born Fulham 5.4.64 Ht 6 2 Wt 12 10
Defender. From Barnet.

Season	Club	Apps	Goals
1988–89	Brighton	16	—
1989–90		29	6

BLACK, Eric

Born Bellshill 1.10.63. Ht 5 8 Wt 10 04
Forward. Unattached. Scotland Schools, Youth, B, Under-21, 2 full caps.

Season	Club	Apps	Goals
1981–82	Aberdeen	13	3
1982–83		31	12
1983–84		18	6
1984–85		27	17
1985–86		26	8

To Metz

BLACK, Kenny

Born Stenhousemuir 29.11.63. Ht 5 8
Wt 10 11
Defender. From Linlithgow Rose.
Scotland Schools, Youth.

Season	Club	Apps	Goals
1980–81	Rangers	—	—
1981–82		8	—
1982–83		14	1
1983–84	Motherwell	17	—
1984–85	Hearts	32	7
1985–86		29	2
1986–87		42	1
1987–88		42	4
1988–89		33	1
1989–90	Portsmouth	41	2

BLACK, Kingsley

Born Luton 22.6.68. Ht 5 8 Wt 10 11
Midfield. From school. Northern Ireland, 10 full caps.

Season	Club	Apps	Goals
1986–87	Luton T	—	—
1987–88		13	—
1988–89		37	8
1989–90		36	11

BLACK, Tom

Born Lanark 11.10.62. Ht 5 8 Wt 10 12
Defender. From Bellshill YM.

Season	Club	Apps	Goals
1980–81	Airdrieonians	—	—
1981–82		—	—
1982–83		5	—
1983–84		32	4
1984–85		37	1
1985–86		12	—
1986–87		24	1
1987–88		29	1

Season	Club	League Appearances/Goals	
1988–89		37	4
1989–90	St Mirren	31	1

BLACKIE, Billy

Born Edinburgh 4.10.63. Ht 5 11
Wt 11 07
Forward. From Musselburgh A Jun.

Season	Club	Apps	Goals
1985–86	Berwick R	2	3
1985–86	Cowdenbeath	1	1
1986–87		23	14
1987–88	Forfar Ath	34	8
1987–88	Dumbarton	4	—
1988–89		9	—
1988–89	Alloa	18	4
1989–90		4	—
1989–90	St Johnstone	10	—

BLACKMORE, Clayton

Born Neath 23.9.64. Ht 5 9 Wt 11 06
Midfield. From Apprentice. Wales Schools, Youth, Under-21, 25 full caps.

Season	Club	Apps	Goals
1982–83	Manchester U	—	—
1983–84		1	—
1984–85		1	—
1985–86		12	3
1986–87		12	1
1987–88		22	3
1988–89		28	3
1989–90		28	2

BLACKWELL, Dean

Born London 5.12.69 Ht 6 1 Wt 12 10
Defender. From Trainee.

Season	Club	Apps	Goals
1988–89	Wimbledon	—	—
1989–90		3	—
1989–90	*Plymouth Arg*	7	—

BLACKWELL, Kevin

Born Luton 21.12.58. Ht 5 11 Wt 12 10
Goalkeeper. From Boston U, Barnet.

Season	Club	Apps	Goals
1987–88	Scarborough	21	—
1988–89		15	—

Season	Club	League Appearances/Goals	
1989–90		8	—
1989–90	Notts C	—	—

BLADES, Paul

Born Peterborough 5.1.65. Ht 6 0
Wt 10 12
Defender. From Apprentice. England Youth.

Season	Club	Apps	Goals
1982–83	Derby Co	6	—
1983–84		4	—
1984–85		22	—
1985–86		30	—
1986–87		16	—
1987–88		31	—
1988–89		38	1
1989–90		19	—

BLAKE, Mark

Born Portsmouth 19.12.67. Ht 6 1
Wt 12 08
Defender. From Apprentice. England Youth.

Season	Club	Apps	Goals
1985–86	Southampton	1	—
1986–87		8	1
1987–88		6	1
1988–89		3	—
1989–90		—	—
1989–90	*Colchester U*	4	1
1989–90	*Shrewsbury T*	10	—

BLAKE, Mark

Born Nottingham 16.12.70 Ht 5 11
Wt 12 03
Midfield. From Trainee. England Schools, Youth, Under-21.

Season	Club	Apps	Goals
1989–90	Aston Villa	9	—

BLAKE, Nathan

Born Cardiff 27.1.72
Defender. From Chelsea Trainee and Cardiff C Trainee.

Season	Club	League Appearances/Goals	
1989–90	Cardiff	6	—

BLAKE, Noel

Born Jamaica 12.1.62. Ht 6 0 Wt 13 11
Defender. From Walsall Amateur and Sutton Coldfield T.

Season	Club	Apps	Goals
1979–80	Aston Villa	3	—
1980–81		—	—
1981–82		1	—
1981–82	*Shrewsbury T*	6	—
1982–83	Aston Villa	—	—
1982–83	Birmingham C	37	3
1983–84		39	2
1984–85	Portsmouth	42	3
1985–86		42	4
1986–87		41	3
1987–88		19	—
1988–89	Leeds U	44	4
1989–90		7	—
1989–90	Stoke C	18	—

BLISSETT, Gary

Born Manchester 29.6.64. Ht 6 1 Wt 11 13
Forward. From Manchester C, Manchester U. Amateur, and Altrincham.

Season	Club	Apps	Goals
1983–84	Crewe Alex	22	3
1984–85		29	9
1985–86		38	11
1986–87		33	16
1986–87	Brentford	10	5
1987–88		41	9
1988–89		36	6
1989–90		37	11

BLISSETT, Luther

Born W. Indies 1.2.58. Ht 5 10 Wt 12 03
Forward. From Juniors. England Under-21, B, 14 full caps.

Season	Club	Apps	Goals
1975–76	Watford	3	1
1976–77		4	—
1977–78		33	6
1978–79		41	21
1979–80		42	10
1980–81		42	11
1981–82		40	19
1982–83		41	27
1983–84	AC Milan	30	5
1984–85	Watford	41	21
1985–86		23	7
1986–87		35	11
1987–88		25	4
1988–89		3	1
1988–89	Bournemouth	30	19
1989–90		46	18

BLOOMER, Bob

Born Sheffield 21.6.66. Ht 5 10 Wt 11 06
Midfield.

Season	Club	Apps	Goals
1985–86	Chesterfield	6	—
1986–87		31	3
1987–88		38	1
1988–89		44	10
1989–90		22	1
1989–90	Bristol R	—	—

BLUNDELL, Chris

Born Billinge 7.12.69 Ht 5 10 Wt 10 09
Defender. From Trainee.

Season	Club	Apps	Goals
1987–88	Oldham Ath	1	—
1988–89		2	—
1989–90		—	—

BOARDMAN, Craig

Born Barnsley 30.11.70. Ht 6 0 Wt 11 08
Defender. From Trainee.

Season	Club	Apps	Goals
1988–89	Nottingham F	—	—
1989–90		—	—

BODIN, Paul

Born Cardiff 13.9.64. Ht 6 0 Wt 13 01
Midfield. From Chelsea Amateur. Wales Youth, Under-21, 1 full cap.

Season	Club	Apps	Goals
1981–82	Newport Co	—	—
1982–83	Cardiff C	31	—
1983–84		26	3
From Bath C			
1987–88	Newport Co	6	1
1987–88	Swindon T	5	1

Season	Club	League Appearances/Goals	
1988–89		16	1
1989–90		41	5

BODLEY, Mike

Born Hayes 14.9.67. Ht 5 9 Wt 10 06
Defender. From Apprentice.

Season	Club	Apps	Goals
1985–86	Chelsea	—	—
1986–87		—	—
1987–88		6	1
1988–89		—	—
1988–89	Northampton T	20	—
1989–90		—	—

BOGIE, Ian

Born Newcastle 6.12.67. Ht 5 7
Wt 10 02
Midfield. From Apprentice. England Schools.

Season	Club	Apps	Goals
1985–86	Newcastle U	—	—
1986–87		1	—
1987–88		7	—
1988–89		6	—
1988–89	Preston NE	13	1
1989–90		35	3

BOLDER, Bob

Born Dover 2.10.58. Ht 6 3 Wt 14 06
Goalkeeper. From Dover.

Season	Club	Apps	Goals
1976–77	Sheffield W	—	—
1977–78		23	—
1978–79		19	—
1979–80		31	—
1980–81		39	—
1981–82		42	—
1982–83		42	—
1983–84	Liverpool	—	—
1984–85		—	—
1985–86		—	—
1985–86	Sunderland	22	—
1985–86	*Luton T*	—	—
1986–87	Charlton Ath	26	—
1987–88		35	—

Season	Club	League Appearances/Goals	
1988–89		38	—
1989–90		38	—

BOND, Jonathan

Born Sheffield 5.11.69. Ht 5 10
Wt 11 00
Midfield. From Trainee.

Season	Club	Apps	Goals
1989–90	Barnsley	—	—

BOND, Kevin

Born London 22.6.57. Ht 6 2 Wt 13 10
Defender. From Bournemouth.
Apprentice. England B.

Season	Club	Apps	Goals
1974–75	Norwich C	—	—
1975–76		1	—
1976–77		3	—
1977–78		28	—
1978–79		42	2
1979–80		40	9
1980–81		28	1
From Seattle S			
1981–82	Manchester C	33	3
1982–83		40	3
1983–84		34	4
1984–85		3	1
1984–85	Southampton	33	1
1985–86		34	1
1986–87		34	1
1987–88		39	3
1988–89	Bournemouth	27	1
1989–90		31	—

BONNER, Pat

Born Donegal 25.5.60. Ht 6 2 Wt 13 01
Goalkeeper. From Keadie Rovers. Eire, 43 full caps.

Season	Club	Apps	Goals
1978–79	Celtic	2	—
1979–80		—	—
1980–81		36	—
1981–82		36	—
1982–83		36	—
1983–84		33	—
1984–85		34	—
1985–86		30	—
1986–87		43	—
1987–88		32	—

Season	Club	League Appearances/Goals	
1988–89		26	—
1989–90		36	—

BONNYMAN, Phil

Born Glasgow 6.2.54. Ht 5 11 Wt 12 04
Midfield. From Anniesland W.

Season	Club	Apps	Goals
1971–72	Rangers	—	—
1972–73		—	—
1973–74	Hamilton A	13	—
1974–75		35	5
1975–76		23	2
1975–76	Carlisle U	9	—
1976–77		37	1
1977–78		33	8
1978–79		45	7
1979–80		28	10
1979–80	Chesterfield	11	3
1980–81		42	8
1981–82		46	14
1982–83	Grimsby T	40	1
1983–84		29	3
1984–85		37	8
1985–86		29	3
1985–86	*Stoke C*	7	—
1986–87	Grimsby T	16	—
1987–88	Darlington	38	3
1988–89		12	2
1989–90	Dunfermline Ath	1	—

BOOKER, Bob

Born Watford 25.1.58. Ht 6 3 Wt 13 03
Midfield. From Bedmond Sports.

Season	Club	Apps	Goals
1978–79	Brentford	3	—
1979–80		12	6
1980–81		26	7
1981–82		38	4
1982–83		39	6
1983–84		29	4
1984–85		38	7
1985–86		44	8
1986–87		2	—
1987–88		12	—
1988–89		8	—
1988–89	Sheffield U	26	2
1989–90		42	8

BOOTH, Scott

Born Aberdeen 16.12.71 Ht 5 7
Wt 10 03
Forward. From Schools.

Season	Club	Apps	Goals
1988–89	Aberdeen	—	—
1989–90		2	—

BOOTHROYD, Adrian

Born Bradford 8.2.71. Ht 5 8 Wt 10 12
Defender. From Trainee.

Season	Club	Apps	Goals
1989–90	Huddersfield T	10	—

BOOTY, Martyn

Born Kirby Muxloe 30.5.71. Ht 5 8
Wt 12 01
Defender. From Trainee.

Season	Club	Apps	Goals
1989–90	Coventry C	—	—

BORROWS, Brian

Born Liverpool 20.12.60 Ht 5 10
Wt 10 12
Defender. From Amateur. England B.

Season	Club	Apps	Goals
1979–80	Everton	—	—
1980–81		—	—
1981–82		15	—
1982–83		12	—
1982–83	Bolton W	9	—
1983–84		44	—
1984–85		42	—
1985–86	Coventry C	41	—
1986–87		41	1
1987–88		33	—
1988–89		38	1
1989–90		37	1

BOSNICH, Mark

Born Sydney (Australia) 13.1.72.
Goalkeeper.

Season	Club	League Appearances/Goals	
1989–90	Manchester U	1	—

BOUGHEY, Darren

Born Stoke 30.11.70. Ht 5 9 Wt 10 13
Forward. From Trainee.

1989–90	Stoke C	7	—

BOULD, Stephen

Born Stoke 16.11.62. Ht 6 3 Wt 13 04
Defender. From Apprentice.

1980–81	Stoke C	—	—
1981–82		2	—
1982–83		14	—
1982–83	*Torquay U*	9	—
1983–84	Stoke C	38	2
1984–85		38	3
1985–86		33	—
1986–87		28	1
1987–88		30	—
1988–89	Arsenal	30	2
1989–90		19	—

BOWDEN, Jon

Born Stockport 21.1.63. Ht 6 1
Wt 12 07
Midfield. From Local.

1979–80	Oldham Ath	—	—
1980–81		—	—
1981–82		5	2
1982–83		31	2
1983–84		31	1
1984–85		15	—
1985–86		—	—
1985–86	Port Vale	36	3
1986–87		34	4
1987–88	Wrexham	26	1
1988–89		42	10
1989–90		33	1

BOWEN, Mark

Born Neath 7.12.63. Ht 5 8 Wt 11 13
Defender. From Apprentice. Wales Schools, Youth, Under-21, 11 full caps.

1981–82	Tottenham H	—	—
1982–83		—	—
1983–84		7	—
1984–85		6	—
1985–86		2	1
1986–87		2	1
1987–88	Norwich C	24	1
1988–89		35	2
1989–90		38	7

BOWLING, Ian

Born Sheffield 27.7.65 Ht 6 3 Wt 14 08
Goalkeeper. From Gainsborough T.

1988–89	Lincoln C	8	—
1989–90		—	—
1989–90	*Hartlepool U*	1	—

BOWMAN, David

Born Tunbridge Wells 10.3.60. Ht 5 10
Wt 11 02
Midfield. From Salvesen BC. Scotland Under-21.

1980–81	Hearts	17	1
1981–82		16	1
1982–83		39	5
1983–84		33	—
1984–85		11	1
1984–85	Coventry C	10	—
1985–86		30	2
1986–87	Dundee U	29	—
1987–88		39	1
1988–89		29	1
1989–90		24	1

BOWYER, Gary

Born Manchester 22.6.71
Defender.

1989–90	Hereford U	14	2

BOWYER, Ian

Born Ellesmere Port 6.6.51. Ht 5 10
Wt 11 11
Midfield. From Apprentice.

1968–69	Manchester C	6	1
1969–70		34	12
1970–71		10	—
1971–72	Orient	42	14

Season Club League Appearances/Goals

Season	Club	Apps	Goals
1972–73		36	4
1973–74		—	—
1973–74	Nottingham F	28	6
1974–75		32	6
1975–76		40	13
1976–77		41	12
1977–78		29	4
1978–79		29	4
1979–80		19	1
1980–81		21	3
1980–81	Sunderland	9	1
1981–82		6	—
1981–82	Nottingham F	24	1
1982–83		40	4
1983–84		42	6
1984–85		39	2
1985–86		26	3
1986–87		34	3
1987–88	Hereford U	29	1
1988–89		9	—
1989–90		2	—

BOYD, Charlie

Born Liverpool 20.9.69. Ht 5 6 Wt 9 04
Forward. From Trainee.

Season	Club	Apps	Goals
1987–88	Liverpool	—	—
1988–89		—	—
1989–90		—	—

BOYD, Tom

Born Glasgow 24.11.65. Ht 5 11
Wt 11 04
Defender. 'S' Form. Scotland Youth, B, Under-21.

Season	Club	Apps	Goals
1983–84	Motherwell	13	—
1984–85		36	—
1985–86		31	—
1986–87		31	—
1987–88		42	2
1988–89		36	1
1989–90		33	1

BOYLE, Terry

Born Ammanford 29.10.58. Ht 5 10
Wt 12 06
Defender. From Apprentice. Wales Schools, Under-21, 2 full caps.

Season	Club	Apps	Goals
1975–76	Tottenham H	—	—
1976–77		—	—
1977–78		—	—
1977–78	Crystal Palace	1	—
1978–79		—	—
1979–80		5	—
1980–81		20	1
1981–82	*Wimbledon*	5	1
1981–82	Bristol C	23	—
1982–83		14	—
1982–83	Newport Co	29	—
1983–84		45	1
1984–85		46	3
1985–86		46	7
1986–87	Cardiff C	46	1
1987–88		46	4
1988–89		36	2
1989–90	Swansea C	27	1

BRABIN, Gary

Born Liverpool 9.12.70
Midfield. From Trainee.

Season	Club	Apps	Goals
1989–90	Stockport Co	1	—

BRACEWELL, Paul

Born Stoke 19.7.62. Ht 5 8 Wt 10 09
Midfield. From Apprentice. England Under-21, 3 full caps.

Season	Club	Apps	Goals
1979–80	Stoke C	6	—
1980–81		40	2
1981–82		42	1
1982–83		41	2
1983–84	Sunderland	38	4
1984–85	Everton	37	2
1985–86		38	3
1986–87		—	—
1987–88		—	—
1988–89		20	2
1989–90		—	—
1989–90	Sunderland	37	2

BRACEY, Lee

Born Ashford 11.9.68 Ht 6 1 Wt 12 08
Goalkeeper. From Trainee.

Season	Club	League Appearances/Goals	
1987–88	West Ham U	—	—
1988–89	Swansea C	30	—
1989–90		31	—

BRACK, Mark

Born Liverpool 18.9.70. Ht 6 0
Wt 12 02
Goalkeeper. From Trainee.

Season	Club	Apps	Goals
1988–89	Liverpool	—	—
1989–90		—	—

BRADLEY, Darren

Born Birmingham 24.11.65. Ht 5 7
Wt 11 12
Defender. From Apprentice. England Youth.

Season	Club	Apps	Goals
1983–84	Aston Villa	—	—
1984–85		2	—
1985–86		18	—
1985–86	WBA	10	—
1986–87		14	1
1987–88		19	—
1988–89		26	—
1989–90		27	2

BRADLEY, Russell

Born Birmingham 28.3.66.
Midfield. From Dudley T.

Season	Club	Apps	Goals
1987–88	Nottingham F	—	—
1988–89		—	—
1988–89	*Hereford U*	12	1
1989–90	Hereford U	33	1

BRADSHAW, Carl

Born Sheffield 2.10.68. Ht 6 0 Wt 11 00
Forward. From Apprentice. England Youth.

Season	Club	Apps	Goals
1986–87	Sheffield W	9	2
1986–87	*Barnsley*	6	1
1987–88	Sheffield W	20	2
1988–89		3	—
1988–89	Manchester C	5	—
1989–90		—	—
1989–90	Sheffield U	30	3

BRADSHAW, Darren

Born Sheffield 19.3.67. Ht 5 11
Wt 11 04
Midfield. From Matlock T.

Season	Club	Apps	Goals
1987–88	Chesterfield	18	—
1987–88	York C	25	1
1988–89		34	2
1989–90		—	—
1989–90	Newcastle U	12	—

BRADSHAW, Mark

Born Ashton 7.6.69. Ht 5 10 Wt 11 05
Defender. From Trainee.

Season	Club	Apps	Goals
1986–87	Blackpool	4	—
1987–88		16	—
1988–89		—	—
1989–90		21	1

BRADSHAW, Paul

Born Altrincham 28.4.56. Ht 6 3
Wt 13 04
Goalkeeper. From Apprentice. England Youth, Under-21.

Season	Club	Apps	Goals
1973–74	Blackburn R	18	—
1974–75		—	—
1975–76		12	—
1976–77		41	—
1977–78		7	—
1977–78	Wolverhampton W	34	—
1978–79		39	—
1979–80		37	—
1980–81		38	—
1981–82		42	—
1982–83		—	—
1983–84		10	—
From Vancouver W			
1984–85	WBA	—	—
1985–86		8	—
1986–87	Bristol R	5	—
1987–88	Newport Co	23	—

Season	Club	League Appearances/Goals	
1988–89	WBA	2	—
1989–90		4	—

BRADY, Kieron

Born Glasgow 17.9.71 Ht 5 9 Wt 11 13
Midfield. From Trainee.

Season	Club	Apps	Goals
1989–90	Sunderland	11	2

BRADY, Liam

Born Dublin 13.2.56. Ht 5 7 Wt 11 01
Midfield. From Apprentice. Eire, 72 full caps. Football League.

Season	Club	Apps	Goals
1973–74	Arsenal	13	1
1974–75		32	3
1975–76		42	5
1976–77		38	5
1977–78		39	9
1978–79		37	13
1979–80		34	7
1980–81	Juventus	28	8
1981–82		29	5
1982–83	Sampdoria	29	2
1983–84		28	4
1984–85	Internazionale	29	2
1985–86		29	3
1986–87	Ascoli	17	—
1986–87	West Ham U	12	2
1987–88		22	2
1988–89		22	3
1989–90		33	2

BRAMHALL, John

Born Warrington 20.11.56. Ht 6 2
Wt 13 06
Defender. From Amateur.

Season	Club	Apps	Goals
1976–77	Tranmere R	8	—
1977–78		10	—
1978–79		35	2
1979–80		45	1
1980–81		37	1
1981–82		35	3
1981–82	Bury	9	—
1982–83		46	6
1983–84		45	6
1984–85		42	4
1985–86		25	1
1985–86	*Chester C*	4	—
1986–87	Rochdale	46	9
1987–88		40	4
1988–89	Halifax T	39	3
1989–90		23	2
1989–90	Scunthorpe U	21	—

BRAMWELL, Steve

Born Stockport 9.10.70
Defender. From Trainee.

Season	Club	Apps	Goals
1988–89	Oldham Ath	1	—
1989–90		—	—
1989–90	*Wigan Ath*	—	—

BRANAGAN, Keith

Born Fulham 10.7.66. Ht 6 1 Wt 13 00
Goalkeeper.

Season	Club	Apps	Goals
1983–84	Cambridge U	1	—
1984–85		19	—
1985–86		9	—
1986–87		46	—
1987–88		35	—
1987–88	Millwall	—	—
1988–89		—	—
1989–90		16	—
1989–90	*Brentford*	2	—

BRAY, Ian

Born Neath 6.12.62. Ht 5 8 Wt 11 06
Defender. From Apprentice.

Season	Club	Apps	Goals
1980–81	Hereford U	—	—
1981–82		16	2
1982–83		27	—
1983–84		23	1
1984–85		42	1
1985–86	Huddersfield T	32	1
1986–87		13	—
1987–88		30	—
1988–89		—	—
1989–90		14	—

BRAZIL, Derek

Born Dublin 14.12.68. Ht 5 11 Wt 10 05
Defender. From Rivermount BC. Eire Youth, B, Under-21, Under-23.

Season	Club	League Appearances/Goals	
1985–86	Manchester U	—	—
1986–87		—	—
1987–88		—	—
1988–89		—	—
1989–90		1	—

BRAZIL, Gary

Born Tunbridge Wells 19.9.62. Ht 5 11 Wt 9 13
Forward. From Crystal Palace Apprentice.

Season	Club	Apps	Goals
1980–81	Sheffield U	3	—
1981–82		1	—
1982–83		33	5
1983–84		19	2
1984–85		6	2
1984–85	*Port Vale*	6	3
1984–85	Preston NE	17	3
1985–86		43	14
1986–87		45	18
1987–88		36	14
1988–89		25	9
1988–89	Newcastle U	7	—
1989–90		16	2

BREACKER, Tim

Born Bicester 2.7.65. Ht 5 11 Wt 13 00
Defender. England Under-21.

Season	Club	Apps	Goals
1983–84	Luton T	2	—
1984–85		35	—
1985–86		36	—
1986–87		29	1
1987–88		40	1
1988–89		22	—
1989–90		38	1

BREMNER, Des

Born Aberchider 7.9.52. Ht 5 10 Wt 11 08
Midfield. From Deveronvale. Scotland Schools, Youth, Under-23, 1 full cap.

Season	Club	Apps	Goals
1972–73	Hibernian	11	—
1973–74		21	2
1974–75		30	2
1975–76		32	3
1976–77		36	4
1977–78		33	2
1978–79		31	5
1979–80		5	—
1979–80	Aston Villa	36	3
1980–81		42	2
1981–82		38	3
1982–83		37	—
1983–84		17	—
1984–85		4	1
1984–85	Birmingham C	30	—
1985–86		32	—
1986–87		40	4
1987–88		37	—
1988–89		29	1
1989–90	Fulham	16	—
1989–90	Walsall	6	—

BREMNER, Kevin

Born Banff 7.10.57. Ht 5 9 Wt 12 05
Forward. From Keith.

Season	Club	Apps	Goals
1980–81	Colchester U	34	8
1981–82		46	21
1982–83		15	2
1982–83	*Birmingham C*	4	1
1982–83	*Wrexham*	4	1
1982–83	*Plymouth Arg*	5	1
1982–83	Millwall	17	6
1983–84		42	16
1984–85		37	11
1985–86	Reading	22	7
1986–87		42	15
1987–88	Brighton	44	8
1988–89		41	15
1989–90		43	13

BRENNAN, Mark

Born Rossendale 4.10.65. Ht 5 10 Wt 10 13
Midfield. From Apprentice. England Youth, Under-21.

Season	Club	Apps	Goals
1982–83	Ipswich T	—	—
1983–84		19	1
1984–85		36	2
1985–86		40	3
1986–87		37	7
1987–88		36	6

Season	Club	League Appearances/Goals	
1988–89	Middlesbrough	25	3
1989–90		40	3

BRESSINGTON, Graham

Born Eton 8.7.66 Ht 6 0 Wt
Defender. From Wycombe W.

Season	Club	League Appearances/Goals	
1987–88	Lincoln C	*12*	—
1988–89		30	1
1989–90		43	2

BREVETT, Rufus

Born Derby 24.9.69
Defender. From Trainee.

Season	Club	League Appearances/Goals	
1987–88	Doncaster R	17	—
1988–89		23	—
1989–90		42	—

BRIEN, Tony

Born Dublin 10.2.69. Ht 5 11 Wt 11 09
Defender. From Apprentice.

Season	Club	League Appearances/Goals	
1986–87	Leicester C	—	—
1987–88		15	1
1988–89		1	—
1988–89	Chesterfield	29	1
1989–90		43	3

BRIGGS, Gary

Born Leeds 8.5.58 Ht 6 3 Wt 12 10
Defender. From Apprentice

Season	Club	League Appearances/Goals	
1977–78	Middlesbrough	—	—
1977–78	Oxford U	20	2
1978–79		39	—
1979–80		46	1
1980–81		42	1
1981–82		45	1
1982–83		37	1
1983–84		38	3
1984–85		42	4
1985–86		38	—
1986–87		40	3
1987–88		18	1

Season	Club	League Appearances/Goals	
1988–89		15	1
1989–90	Blackpool	17	2

BRIGHT, Mark

Born Stoke 6.6.62. Ht 6 0 Wt 13 00
Forward. From Leek T.

Season	Club	League Appearances/Goals	
1981–82	Port Vale	2	—
1982–83		1	1
1983–84		26	9
1984–85	Leicester C	16	—
1985–86		24	6
1986–87		2	—
1986–87	Crystal Palace	28	8
1987–88		38	25
1988–89		46	20
1989–90		36	12

BRIGHTWELL, David

Born Lutterworth 7.1.71.
Midfield. From Trainee.

Season	Club	League Appearances/Goals	
1987–88	Manchester C	—	—
1988–89		—	—
1989–90		—	—

BRIGHTWELL, Ian

Born Lutterworth 9.4.68. Ht 5 10
Wt 11 07
Midfield. From Congleton T. England Schools, Youth, Under-21.

Season	Club	League Appearances/Goals	
1986–87	Manchester C	16	1
1987–88		33	5
1988–89		26	6
1989–90		28	2

BRILEY, Les

Born Lambeth 2.10.56. Ht 5 7 Wt 11 00
Midfield. From Apprentice.

Season	Club	League Appearances/Goals	
1974–75	Chelsea	—	—
1975–76		—	—
1976–77	Hereford U	34	1
1977–78		27	1
1977–78	Wimbledon	14	1
1978–79		26	1
1979–80		21	—
1979–80	Aldershot	12	—

Season	Club	League Appearances/Goals	
1980–81		44	—
1981–82		37	2
1982–83		28	—
1983–84		36	1
1984–85	Millwall	33	—
1985–86		39	1
1986–87		33	3
1987–88		44	4
1988–89		31	2
1989–90		26	2

BRIMACOMBE, John

Born Plymouth 25.11.58. Ht 5 11
Wt 11 12
Defender. From Liskeard and Saltash.

Season	Club	League Appearances/Goals	
1985–86	Plymouth Arg	1	1
1986–87		11	—
1987–88		42	1
1988–89		24	1
1989–90		20	—

BRISCOE, Robert

Born Derby 4.9.69. Ht 5 8 Wt 10 13
Defender. From Trainee.

Season	Club	League Appearances/Goals	
1987–88	Derby Co	—	—
1988–89		—	—
1989–90		10	1

BROADBENT, Graham

Born Halifax 20.12.58
Forward. From Emley.

Season	Club	League Appearances/Goals	
1988–89	Halifax T	12	2
1989–90		13	—

BROCK, Kevin

Born Middleton Stoney 9.9.62. Ht 5 9
Wt 10 12
Midfield. From Apprentice. England Schools, Under-21.

Season	Club	League Appearances/Goals	
1979–80	Oxford U	19	2
1980–81		26	5
1981–82		28	5
1982–83		37	4
1983–84		45	3
1984–85		37	6
1985–86		23	—
1986–87		31	1
1987–88	QPR	26	2
1988–89		14	—
1988–89	Newcastle U	21	2
1989–90		44	2

BROCKIE, Vincent

Born Greenock 2.2.69. Ht 5 8 Wt 10 10
Defender. From Trainee.

Season	Club	League Appearances/Goals	
1987–88	Leeds U	2	—
1988–89		—	—
1988–89	Doncaster R	23	2
1989–90		24	3

BRODDLE, Julian

Born Laughton 1.11.64. Ht 5 9 Wt 11 07
Midfield. From Apprentice.

Season	Club	League Appearances/Goals	
1981–82	Sheffield U	1	—
1982–83		—	—
1983–84	Scunthorpe U	13	1
1984–85		45	14
1985–86		41	7
1986–87		38	10
1987–88		7	—
1987–88	Barnsley	19	1
1988–89		38	3
1989–90		20	—
1989–90	Plymouth Arg	9	—

BROMAGE, Russel

Born Stoke 9.11.59. Ht 5 11 Wt 11 05
Defender. From Apprentice.

Season	Club	League Appearances/Goals	
1977–78	Port Vale	6	—
1978–79		20	2
1979–80		29	1
1980–81		45	4
1981–82		45	—
1982–83		46	2
1983–84		38	1
1983–84	*Oldham Ath*	2	—
1984–85	Port Vale	37	1
1985–86		40	1
1986–87		41	1
1987–88	Bristol C	30	—

Season	Club	Apps	Goals
1988–89		13	1
1989–90		3	—

BROOKE, Gary

Born Bethnal Green 24.11.60. Ht 5 6
Wt 10 5
Midfield. From Apprentice.

Season	Club	Apps	Goals
1978–79	Tottenham H	—	—
1979–80		—	—
1980–81		18	3
1981–82		16	4
1982–83		23	7
1983–84		12	—
1984–85		4	1
1985–86	Norwich C	13	2
1986–87		1	—
From Gröningen			
1988–89	Wimbledon	10	—
1989–90		2	—
1989–90	*Stoke C*	8	—

BROOK, Gary

Born Dewsbury 9.5.64. Ht 5 10
Wt 12 04
Forward. From Frickley Ath.

Season	Club	Apps	Goals
1987–88	Newport Co	14	2
1987–88	Scarborough	5	—
1988–89		44	12
1989–90		15	3
1989–90	Blackpool	25	6

BROOKMAN, Nick

Born Manchester 28.10.68. Ht 5 9
Wt 10 07
Midfield. From Trainee.

Season	Club	Apps	Goals
1986–87	Bolton W	4	—
1987–88		26	6
1988–89		25	4
1989–90		2	—
1989–90	Stockport Co	6	—

BROOKS, Shaun

Born London 9.10.62. Ht 5 7 Wt 11 00
Midfield. From Apprentice. England Schools, Youth.

Season	Club	Apps	Goals
1979–80	Crystal Palace	1	—
1980–81		17	—
1981–82		25	2
1982–83		7	2
1983–84		4	—
1983–84	Orient	36	9
1984–85		29	5
1985–86		38	7
1986–87		45	5
1987–88	Bournemouth	37	6
1988–89		36	3
1989–90		35	4

BROTHERSTON, Noel

Born Belfast 18.11.56. Ht 5 8 Wt 11 05
Midfield. From Apprentice. Northern Ireland Schools, Youth, Under-21, 27 full caps.

Season	Club	Apps	Goals
1973–74	Tottenham H	—	—
1974–75		—	—
1975–76		1	—
1976–77		—	—
1977–78	Blackburn R	40	11
1978–79		35	2
1979–80		41	7
1980–81		33	3
1981–82		38	2
1982–83		39	6
1983–84		21	1
1984–85		33	7
1985–86		19	1
1986–87		18	—
1987–88	Bury	36	4
1988–89		2	—
1988–89	*Scarborough*	5	—
1989–90	Bury	—	—

BROWN, David

Born Hartlepool 28.1.57. Ht 6 1
Wt 12 08
Goalkeeper. From Horden C.W.

Season	Club	Apps	Goals
1976–77	Middlesbrough	—	—
1977–78		10	—
1978–79		—	—
1979–80		—	—
1979–80	*Plymouth Arg*	5	—
1979–80	Oxford U	18	—

Season	Club	League Appearances/Goals	
1980–81		3	—
1981–82		—	—
1981–82	Bury	27	—
1982–83		45	—
1983–84		28	—
1984–85		46	—
1985–86		—	—
1986–87	Preston NE	24	—
1987–88		27	—
1988–89		23	—
1988–89	*Scunthorpe U*	5	—
1989–90	Halifax T	27	—

BROWN, Gary

Born Beverley 3.1.69. Ht 5 10 Wt 11 02
Midfield. From Blackburn R.

Season	Club	League Appearances/Goals	
1987–88	Bolton W	—	—
1988–89		—	—
1989–90		—	—

BROWN, Grant

Born Sunderland 19.11.69. Ht 6 0 Wt 11 12
Defender. From Trainee.

Season	Club	League Appearances/Goals	
1987–88	Leicester C	2	—
1988–89		12	—
1989–90	Lincoln C	34	2

BROWN, John

Born Stirling 26.1.62. Ht 5 11 Wt 10 02
Midfield. From Blantyre Welfare.

Season	Club	League Appearances/Goals	
1979–80	Hamilton A	19	—
1980–81		38	6
1981–82		28	5
1982–83		9	—
1983–84		39	—
1984–85	Dundee	34	7
1985–86		29	11
1986–87		31	10
1987–88		20	3
1987–88	Rangers	9	2
1988–89		29	1
1989–90		27	1

BROWN, Kenny

Born Barking 11.7.67. Ht 5 8 Wt 11 06
Defender. From Apprentice.

Season	Club	League Appearances/Goals	
1984–85	Norwich C	—	—
1985–86		—	—
1986–87		18	—
1987–88		7	—
1988–89	Plymouth Arg	39	1
1989–90		44	—

BROWN, Kevan

Born Andover 2.1.66 Ht 5 9 Wt 11 08
Defender.

Season	Club	League Appearances/Goals	
1983–84	Southampton	—	—
1984–85		—	—
1985–86		—	—
1986–87		—	—
1986–87	Brighton	15	—
1987–88		35	—
1988–89		3	—
1988–89	Aldershot	28	—
1989–90		42	2

BROWN, Malcolm

Born Salford 13.12.56. Ht 6 2 Wt 13 01
Defender. From Apprentice.

Season	Club	League Appearances/Goals	
1973–74	Bury	1	—
1974–75		—	—
1975–76		5	—
1976–77		5	—
1977–78	Huddersfield T	30	1
1978–79		42	—
1979–80		46	2
1980–81		46	3
1981–82		46	1
1982–83		46	9
1983–84	Newcastle U	—	—
1984–85		39	—
1985–86	Huddersfield T	37	—
1986–87		33	1
1987–88		25	—
1988–89		1	—

1988–89 Rochdale 11 —
1989–90 Stockport Co 37 2

BROWN, Mike

Born Birmingham 8.2.68. Ht 5 9
Wt 10 12
Forward. From Apprentice.

1985–86 Shrewsbury T — —
1986–87 22 2
1987–88 41 5
1988–89 41 —
1989–90 43 1

BROWN, Nicky

Born Hull 16.10.66. Ht 6 0 Wt 12 07
Forward. From Local.

1984–85 Hull C — —
1985–86 1 —
1986–87 — —
1987–88 10 —
1988–89 13 —
1989–90 34 2

BROWN, Phil

Born Sheffield 16.1.66. Ht 5 8 Wt 9 07
Forward. From Apprentice.

1982–83 Chesterfield 1 —
1983–84 16 6
1984–85 29 9
1985–86 31 3
1986–87 10 1
1986–87 Stockport Co 23 1
1987–88 Lincoln C *40* *16*
1988–89 38 3
1989–90 5 —

BROWN, Phil

Born South Shields 30.5.59 Ht 5 11
Wt 11 06
Defender. Local.

1978–79 Hartlepool U — —
1979–80 10 —
1980–81 46 1
1981–82 44 4
1982–83 44 2
1983–84 31 —
1984–85 42 1
1985–86 Halifax T 45 2
1986–87 46 12
1987–88 44 5
1988–89 Bolton W 46 4
1989–90 46 1

BROWN, Steve

Born Northampton 6.7.66
Forward.

1985–86 Northampton T — —
From Irthlingborough D
1989–90 Northampton T 21 1

BROWN, Tony

Born Bradford 17.9.58. Ht 6 2 Wt 12 07
Defender. From Thackley.

1982–83 Leeds U 1 —
1983–84 22 1
1984–85 1 —
1984–85 *Doncaster R* 14 —
1985–86 Doncaster R 38 2
1986–87 35 —
1986–87 Scunthorpe U 22 —
1988–89 32 2
1989–90 Rochdale 43 —

BROWNING, Marcus

Born Bristol 22.4.71. Ht 5 11 Wt 12 00
Forward. From Trainee.

1989–90 Bristol R 1 —

BRUCE, Marcel

Born Detroit, USA 15.3.71 Ht 5 10
Wt 11 07
Defender. From Trainee.

1989–90 Colchester U 29 1

BRUCE, Steve

Born Newcastle 31.12.60 Ht 6 0 Wt 12 6
Defender. From Apprentice. England
Youth.

1978–79 Gillingham — —

Season	Club	League Appearances/Goals	
1979–80		40	6
1980–81		41	4
1981–82		45	6
1982–83		39	7
1983–84		40	6
1984–85	Norwich C	39	1
1985–86		42	8
1986–87		41	3
1987–88		19	2
1987–88	Manchester U	21	2
1988–89		38	2
1989–90		34	3

BRUSH, Paul

Born Plaistow 22.2.58. Ht 5 11 Wt 12 02
Defender. From Apprentice.

Season	Club	Apps	Goals
1976–77	West Ham U	—	—
1977–78		24	—
1978–79		42	—
1979–80		27	—
1980–81		11	—
1981–82		13	—
1982–83		6	—
1983–84		10	—
1984–85		18	1
1985–86		—	—
1985–86	Crystal Palace	26	2
1986–87		15	1
1987–88		9	—
1987–88	Southend U	14	1
1988–89		28	—
1989–90		31	—

BRYCE, Steven

Born Shotts 30.6.69. Ht 5 8 Wt 10 07
Forward. From Motherwell BC.

Season	Club	Apps	Goals
1987–88	Motherwell	—	—
1988–89		9	—
1989–90		3	—

BRYSON, Ian

Born Kilmarnock 26.11.62 Ht 5 11
Wt 11 11
Midfield.

Season	Club	Apps	Goals
1981–82	Kilmarnock	14	3
1982–83		28	1

Season	Club	League Appearances/Goals	
1983–84		25	4
1984–85		36	3
1985–86		38	14
1986–87		32	10
1987–88		42	5
1988–89	Sheffield U	37	8
1989–90		39	9

BUCKLE, Paul

Born Hatfield 16.12.70.
Midfield. From Trainee.

Season	Club	Apps	Goals
1987–88	Brentford	1	—
1988–89		—	—
1989–90		10	—

BUCKLEY, John

Born Glasgow 10.5.62. Ht 5 9 Wt 10 13
Forward. From Queen's Park and Celtic.

Season	Club	Apps	Goals
1982–83	Partick T	8	1
1983–84		37	4
1984–85	Doncaster R	39	6
1985–86		45	5
1986–87	Leeds U	9	1
1986–87	*Leicester C*	5	—
1987–88	Leeds U	1	—
1987–88	*Doncaster R*	6	—
1987–88	Rotherham U	26	—
1988–89		36	5
1989–90		40	7

BUCKLEY, Neil

Born Hull 25.9.68. Ht 6 2 Wt 13 06
Defender. From Trainee.

Season	Club	Apps	Goals
1986–87	Hull C	1	—
1987–88		—	—
1988–89		13	—
1989–90		10	1
1989–90	*Burnley*	5	—

BULL, Steve

Born Tipton 28.3.65. Ht 5 11 Wt 11 04
Forward. From Apprentice. England
Under-21, B, 11 full caps.

Season	Club	Apps	Goals
1985–86	WBA	1	—
1986–87		3	2

Season	Club	Apps	Goals
1986–87	Wolverhampton W	30	14
1987–88	....	44	34
1988–89	....	45	37
1989–90	....	42	24

BULLIMORE, Wayne

Born Sutton-in-Ashfield 12.9.70 Ht 5 9
Wt 10 06
Midfield. From Trainee. FA Schools.

Season	Club	Apps	Goals
1988–89	Manchester U	—	—
1989–90	....	—	—

BULLOCK, Steven

Born Stockport 5.10.66. Ht 5 9
Wt 11 08
Midfield. From school.

Season	Club	Apps	Goals
1983–84	Oldham Ath	1	—
1984–85	....	9	—
1985–86	....	8	—
1986–87	Tranmere R	30	1
1987–88	Stockport Co	41	—
1988–89	....	22	—
1989–90	....	27	—

BUMSTEAD, John

Born Rotherhithe 27.11.58. Ht 5 7
Wt 10 05
Midfield. From Apprentice.

Season	Club	Apps	Goals
1977–78	Chelsea	—	—
1978–79	....	8	1
1979–80	....	28	3
1980–81	....	41	1
1981–82	....	21	4
1982–83	....	36	4
1983–84	....	31	7
1984–85	....	25	3
1985–86	....	32	1
1986–87	....	29	8
1987–88	....	17	1
1988–89	....	29	2
1989–90	....	29	2

BUNN, Frankie

Born Birmingham 6.11.62. Ht 6 0
Wt 11 00
Forward. From Apprentice.

Season	Club	Apps	Goals
1980–81	Luton T	3	1
1981–82	....	2	—
1982–83	....	4	—
1983–84	....	30	3
1984–85	....	20	5
1985–86	Hull C	42	14
1986–87	....	35	4
1987–88	....	18	5
1987–88	Oldham Ath	21	9
1988–89	....	28	12
1989–90	....	29	5

BURGESS, Daryl

Born Birmingham 20.4.71. Ht 5 11
Wt 12 03
Defender. From Trainee.

Season	Club	Apps	Goals
1989–90	WBA	34	—

BURGESS, Dave

Born Liverpool. Ht 5 10 Wt 11 04
Defender. Local.

Season	Club	Apps	Goals
1981–82	Tranmere R	46	1
1982–83	....	46	—
1983–84	....	44	—
1984–85	....	41	—
1985–86	....	41	—
1986–87	Grimsby T	31	—
1987–88	....	38	—
1988–89	Blackpool	46	—
1989–90	....	19	1

BURKE, David

Born Liverpool 6.8.60. Ht 5 10
Wt 11 00
Defender. From Apprentice. England Youth.

Season	Club	Apps	Goals
1977–78	Bolton W	—	—
1978–79	....	20	1
1979–80	....	27	—
1980–81	....	22	—
1981–82	Huddersfield T	41	1
1982–83	....	44	1
1983–84	....	42	—
1984–85	....	31	1
1985–86	....	—	—

Season	Club	League Appearances/Goals	
1986–87		21	—
1987–88		10	—
1987–88	Crystal Palace	31	—
1988–89		39	—
1989–90		11	—

BURKE, Mark

Born Solihull 12.2.69. Ht 5 10 Wt 11 08
Forward. From Apprentice. England Youth.

Season	Club	League Appearances/Goals	
1986–87	Aston Villa	1	—
1987–88		6	—
1987–88	Middlesbrough	16	—
1988–89		29	5
1989–90		12	1

BURLEY, Craig

Born Ayr 24.9.71. Ht 6 1 Wt 11 07
Midfield. From Trainee.

Season	Club	League Appearances/Goals	
1989–90	Chelsea	—	—

BURLEY, George

Born Cumnock 3.6.56. Ht 5 9 Wt 11 02
Defender. From Apprentice. Scotland Schools, Youth, Under-21, Under-23, 11 full caps.

Season	Club	League Appearances/Goals	
1973–74	Ipswich T	20	—
1974–75		31	—
1975–76		42	—
1976–77		40	2
1977–78		31	1
1978–79		38	1
1979–80		38	—
1980–81		23	—
1981–82		29	—
1982–83		31	1
1983–84		28	—
1984–85		37	—
1985–86		6	—
1985–86	Sunderland	27	—
1986–87		27	—
1987–88		—	—

Season	Club	League Appearances/Goals	
1988–89	Gillingham	46	2
1989–90	Motherwell	34	—

BURNETT, Wayne

Born London 4.9.71
Midfield. From Trainee.

Season	Club	League Appearances/Goals	
1989–90	Leyton Orient	3	—

BURNS, Hugh

Born Lanark 13.12.65. Ht 6 0 Wt 11 07
Defender. From Cambuslang R.

Season	Club	League Appearances/Goals	
1982–83	Rangers	—	—
1983–84		4	—
1984–85		15	—
1985–86		28	3
1986–87		3	—
1986–87	*Leeds U*	—	—
1986–87	Hamilton A	5	1
1987–88	Hearts	24	—
1988–89		—	—
1988–89	Dunfermline Ath	15	—
1989–90		—	—
1989–90	*Fulham*	6	—

BURNS, Phil

Born Stockport 18.12.66
Goalkeeper. From Huddersfield T, Trainee, Army.

Season	Club	League Appearances/Goals	
1988–89	Reading	—	—
1989–90		—	—

BURNS, Steve

Born Salford 28.10.68. Ht 6 0 Wt 12 07
Defender.

Season	Club	League Appearances/Goals	
1988–89	Blackpool	—	—
1989–90		—	—

BURNS, Tommy

Born Glasgow 16.2.56. Ht 5 11
Wt 11 03
Midfield. From Maryhill Juniors. Scotland Under-21, 8 full caps.

Season	Club	League Appearances/Goals	
1974–75	Celtic	1	—
1975–76		5	—

Season	Club	League Appearances/Goals	
1976–77		22	1
1977–78		23	3
1978–79		29	3
1979–80		15	—
1980–81		33	4
1981–82		33	9
1982–83		17	7
1983–84		33	9
1984–85		27	7
1985–86		34	5
1986–87		17	—
1987–88		27	2
1988–89		32	2
1989–90		9	—
1989–90	Kilmarnock	22	3

BURNS, Willie

Born Motherwell 10.12.69. Ht 5 11
Wt 10 10
Defender. From Trainee. Scottish Youth.

Season	Club	Apps	Goals
1987–88	Manchester C	—	—
1988–89		—	—
1989–90	Rochdale	44	1

BURRIDGE, John

Born Workington 3.12.51. Ht 5 11
Wt 13 03
Goalkeeper. From Apprentice.

Season	Club	Apps	Goals
1968–69	Workington	1	—
1969–70		—	—
1970–71		26	—
1970–71	Blackpool	3	—
1971–72		34	—
1972–73		22	—
1973–74		30	—
1974–75		38	—
1975–76		7	—
1975–76	Aston Villa	30	—
1976–77		35	—
1977–78		—	—
1977–78	*Southend U*	6	—
1977–78	Crystal Palace	10	—
1978–79		42	—
1979–80		36	—
1980–81		—	—
1980–81	QPR	19	—
1981–82		20	—
1982–83	Wolverhampton W	42	—
1983–84		32	—
1984–85		—	—
1984–85	*Derby Co*	6	—
1984–85	Sheffield U	30	—
1985–86		42	—
1986–87		37	—
1987–88	Southampton	31	—
1988–89		31	—
1989–90		—	—
1989–90	Newcastle U	28	—

BURROWS, Adrian

Born Sutton 16.1.59. Ht 5 11 Wt 11 12
Defender. Local.

Season	Club	Apps	Goals
1979–80	Mansfield T	17	—
1980–81		20	3
1981–82		41	2
1982–83	Northampton T	43	4
1983–84		45	—
1984–85	Plymouth Arg	39	—
1985–86		7	2
1986–87		17	1
1987–88		23	1
1987–88	*Southend U*	6	—
1988–89	Plymouth Arg	43	1
1989–90		46	1

BURROWS, David

Born Dudley 25.10.68. Ht 5 9 Wt 11 07
Defender. From Apprentice. England B, Under-21.

Season	Club	Apps	Goals
1985–86	WBA	1	—
1986–87		15	1
1987–88		21	—
1988–89		9	—
1988–89	Liverpool	21	—
1989–90		26	—

BURTON, Mike

Born Birmingham 5.11.69 Ht 5 8
Wt 11 00
Forward. From Trainee.

Season	Club	League Appearances/Goals	
1988–89	Birmingham C	4	—
1989–90		—	—

BURTON, Paul

Born Hereford 6.8.73
Midfield.

Season	Club	Apps	Goals
1989–90	Hereford U	2	—

BURVILL, Glen

Born Canning Town 26.10.62. Ht 5 9
Wt 10 10
Midfield. From Apprentice.

Season	Club	Apps	Goals
1980–81	West Ham U	—	—
1981–82		—	—
1982–83		—	—
1983–84	Aldershot	38	12
1984–85		27	3
1984–85	Reading	14	—
1985–86		16	—
1985–86	*Fulham*	9	2
1986–87	Aldershot	36	2
1987–88		43	9
1988–89		42	7
1989–90		33	3

BUTCHER, Terry

Born Singapore 28.12.58. Ht 6 4
Wt 14 0
Defender. From Amateur. England Under-21 B, 77 full caps

Season	Club	Apps	Goals
1976–77	Ipswich T	—	—
1977–78		3	—
1978–79		21	2
1979–80		36	2
1980–81		40	4
1981–82		27	1
1982–83		42	—
1983–84		34	1
1984–85		41	2
1985–86		27	4
1986–87	Rangers	43	3
1987–88		11	1
1988–89		34	2
1989–90		34	3

BUTLER, Barry

Born Farnworth 4.6.62. Ht 6 2 Wt 13 0
Defender. From Atherton T.

Season	Club	Apps	Goals
1985–86	Chester C	14	—
1986–87		44	—
1987–88		16	—
1988–89		35	—
1989–90		44	4

BUTLER, Brian

Born Salford 4.7.66. Ht 5 7 Wt 10 05
Defender. From Apprentice.

Season	Club	Apps	Goals
1984–85	Blackpool	—	—
1985–86		19	1
1986–87		37	3
1987–88		18	1
1988–89	Stockport Co	32	2
1989–90	Halifax T	30	3

BUTLER, John

Born Liverpool 7.2.62. Ht 5 11
Wt 11 10
Defender. From Prescot Cables.

Season	Club	Apps	Goals
1981–82	Wigan Ath	1	—
1982–83		40	5
1983–84		41	3
1984–85		45	3
1985–86		36	—
1986–87		36	—
1987–88		26	1
1988–89		20	3
1988–89	Stoke C	25	1
1989–90		44	—

BUTLER, Martin

Born Hull 3.3.66. Ht 5 8 Wt 12 01
Forward. From Trainee.

Season	Club	Apps	Goals
1984–85	York C	19	3
1985–86		14	—
1985–86	*Aldershot*	2	1
1986–87	York C	15	3
1986–87	*Exeter C*	4	1

Season	Club	Apps	Goals
1987–88	York C	5	—
1988–89		12	3
1988–89	*Carlisle U*	1	—
1989–90	Scunthorpe U	2	—
1989–90	Scarborough	6	—

BUTLER, Lee

Born Sheffield 30.5.66. Ht 6 2 Wt 14 02
Goalkeeper. From Haworth Colliery.

Season	Club	Apps	Goals
1986–87	Lincoln C	30	—
1987–88	Aston Villa	—	—
1988–89		4	—
1989–90		—	—

BUTLER, Peter

Born Halifax 27.8.66. Ht 5 9 Wt 11 02
Midfield. From Apprentice.

Season	Club	Apps	Goals
1984–85	Huddersfield T	4	—
1985–86		1	—
1985–86	*Cambridge U*	14	1
1986–87	Bury	11	—
1986–87	Cambridge U	29	4
1987–88		26	5
1987–88	Southend U	15	3
1988–89		35	2
1989–90		41	2

BUTLER, Steve

Born Birmingham 27.1.62. Ht 6 2
Wt 13 00
Forward. From Windsor and Eton, Wokingham.

Season	Club	Apps	Goals
1984–85	Brentford	3	1
1985–86		18	2
To Maidstone U (1986)			
1989–90		44	21

BUTTER, Jim

Born Dundee 14.12.66. Ht 6 1 Wt 12 02
Goalkeeper. From Blairgowrie Jun.

Season	Club	Apps	Goals
1987–88	St Johnstone	2	—
1988–89		—	—
1989–90		1	—

BUTTERS, Guy

Born Hillingdon 30.10.69
Defender. From Trainee. England Under-21.

Season	Club	Apps	Goals
1988–89	Tottenham H	28	1
1989–90		7	—
1989–90	*Southend U*	16	3

BUTTERWORTH, Garry

Born Peterborough 8.9.69 Ht 5 8
Wt 10 11
Midfield. From Trainee.

Season	Club	Apps	Goals
1986–87	Peterborough U	1	—
1987–88		11	—
1988–89		8	—
1989–90		39	3

BUTTERWORTH, Ian

Born Crewe 25.1.65. Ht 6 1 Wt 12 10
Defender. From Apprentice. England Under-21.

Season	Club	Apps	Goals
1981–82	Coventry C	14	—
1982–83		30	—
1983–84		24	—
1984–85		22	—
1985–86	Nottingham F	23	—
1986–87		4	—
1986–87	Norwich C	28	—
1987–88		35	—
1988–89		37	2
1989–90		22	—

BUTTIGIEG, John

Born Sliema 5.10.63 Ht 6 0 Wt 11 13
Defender. From Sliema W. Malta full caps.

Season	Club	Apps	Goals
1988–89	Brentford	18	—
1989–90		22	—

BUXTON, Steve

Born Birmingham 13.3.60. Ht 5 5
Wt 11 02

Forward. From Amateur.

Season	Club	Apps	Goals
1977–78	Wrexham	1	—
1978–79		13	2
1979–80		13	1
1980–81		14	2
1981–82		9	3
1982–83		39	10
1983–84		20	3
1984–85	Stockport Co	18	1
1985–86	Torquay U	—	—
1985–86	Wrexham	5	3
1986–87		30	8
1987–88		35	6
1988–89		30	4
1989–90		21	4

BYRNE, David

Born London 5.3.61. Ht 5 8 Wt 10 09
Forward. From Kingstonian.

Season	Club	Apps	Goals
1985–86	Gillingham	23	3
1986–87	Millwall	40	4
1987–88		23	2
1988–89		—	—
1988–89	*Cambridge U*	4	—
1988–89	*Blackburn R*	4	—
1988–89	Plymouth Arg	13	1
1989–90		32	1
1989–90	*Bristol R*	2	—

BYRNE, John

Born Manchester 1.2.61. Ht 6 0
Wt 12 04
Forward. From Apprentice. Eire, 19 full caps.

Season	Club	Apps	Goals
1978–79	York C	—	—
1979–80		9	2
1980–81		38	6
1981–82		29	6
1982–83		43	12
1983–84		46	27
1984–85		10	2
1984–85	QPR	23	3
1985–86		36	12
1986–87		40	11
1987–88		27	4

To Le Havre

BYRNE, Mick

Born Dublin 14.1.60 Ht 5 11 Wt 12 03
Forward. From Shamrock R.

Season	Club	Apps	Goals
1988–89	Huddersfield T	37	7
1989–90		19	4
1989–90	*Shelbourne*	—	—

BYRNE, Paul

Born Dublin 30.6.72. Ht 5 9 Wt 11 6
Midfield. From Trainee.

Season	Club	Apps	Goals
1989–90	Oxford U	3	—

BYWATER, Paul

Born Bridgnorth 10.8.71. Ht 5 11
Wt 13 05
Defender. From Trainee.

Season	Club	Apps	Goals
1989–90	Shrewsbury T	—	—

Season Club League Appearances/Goals

CADETTE, Richard

Born Hammersmith 21.3.65. Ht 5 8
Wt 11 07
Forward. From Wembley.

Season	Club	Apps	Goals
1984–85	Orient	21	4
1985–86	Southend U	44	24
1986–87		46	24
1987–88	Sheffield U	28	7
1988–89	Brentford	32	12
1989–90		16	1
1989–90	*Bournemouth*	8	1

CAESAR, Gus

Born London 5.3.66. Ht 6 0 Wt 12 00
Defender. From Apprentice. England Under-21.

Season	Club	Apps	Goals
1983–84	Arsenal	—	—
1984–85		—	—
1985–86		2	—
1986–87		15	—
1987–88		22	—
1988–89		2	—
1989–90		3	—

CALDERWOOD, Colin

Born Stranraer 20.1.65. Ht 6 0 Wt 12 00
Defender. From Amateur.

Season	Club	Apps	Goals
1981–82	Mansfield T	1	—
1982–83		28	—
1983–84		30	1
1984–85		41	—
1985–86	Swindon T	46	2
1986–87		46	1
1987–88		34	1
1988–89		43	4
1989–90		46	3

CALDWELL, Dave

Born Aberdeen 31.7.60. Ht 5 10
Wt 12 02
Forward. From Inverness Caley.

Season	Club	Apps	Goals
1979–80	Mansfield T	3	—
1980–81		28	8
1981–82		33	9
1982–83		35	10
1983–84		38	21
1984–85		20	9
1984–85	*Carlisle U*	4	—
1984–85	*Swindon T*	5	—
1985–86	Chesterfield	22	3
1986–87		36	14
1987–88		10	—
1987–88	Torquay U	24	4
From KV Overpelt			
1989–90	Torquay U	17	6

CALDWELL, Tony

Born Salford 21.3.58. Ht 5 9 Wt 11 07
Forward. From Salford, Irlam, Hyde and Horwich RMI.

Season	Club	Apps	Goals
1983–84	Bolton W	33	19
1984–85		31	18
1985–86		40	10
1986–87		35	11
1987–88	Bristol C	16	3
1987–88	*Chester C*	4	—
1988–89	Bristol C	1	—
1988–89	Grimsby T	3	—
1988–89	Stockport Co	24	5
1989–90		2	—

CALLAGHAN, Aaron

Born Dublin 8.10.66. Ht 5 11 Wt 11 2
Defender. From Apprentice. Eire Youth, Under-21.

Season	Club	Apps	Goals
1984–85	Stoke C	5	—
1985–86		—	—
1985–86	*Crewe Alex*	8	—
1986–87	Stoke C	2	—
1986–87	Oldham Ath	5	—
1987–88		11	2
1988–89	Crewe Alex	41	4
1989–90		41	2

CALLAGHAN, Nigel

Born Singapore 12.9.62. Ht 5 9
Wt 10 00
Midfield. From Apprentice. England Under-21.

Season	Club	Apps	Goals
1979–80	Watford	1	—
1980–81		21	2

Season	Club	League Appearances/Goals	
1981–82		37	5
1982–83		41	9
1983–84		41	10
1984–85		38	8
1985–86		23	4
1986–87		20	3
1986–87	Derby Co	18	4
1987–88		40	4
1988–89		18	2
1988–89	Aston Villa	16	1
1989–90		8	—

CALVERT, Mark

Born Consett 11.9.70 Ht 5 9 Wt 11 05
Forward. From Trainee.

Season	Club	Apps	Goals
1988–89	Hull C	5	—
1989–90		—	—

CAM, Scott

Born Sheffield 3.5.70. Ht 5 10 Wt 10 07
Defender. From Trainee. England Youth.

Season	Club	Apps	Goals
1987–88	Sheffield W	—	—
1988–89		—	—
1989–90		—	—

CAME, Mark

Born Exeter 14.9.61. Ht 6 0 Wt 12 13
Defender. From Winsford U.

Season	Club	Apps	Goals
1983–84	Bolton W	—	—
1984–85		23	1
1985–86		35	1
1986–87		43	—
1987–88		43	5
1988–89		2	—
1989–90		19	—

CAMERON, Ian

Born Glasgow 24.8.66. Ht 5 9 Wt 10 04
Midfield. 'S' Form. Scotland Schools, Youth.

Season	Club	Apps	Goals
1983–84	St Mirren	8	—
1984–85		9	1
1985–86		12	—
1986–87		31	6
1987–88		41	8
1988–89		26	2
1989–90	Aberdeen	11	—

CAMPBELL, Alan

Born Dublin 10.8.60. Ht 5 10 Wt 11 11
Forward. From Berchem.

Season	Club	Apps	Goals
1989–90	Dundee	15	2

CAMPBELL, David

Born Eglinton 2.6.65. Ht 5 10 Wt 11 02
Midfield. From Oxford BC(NI). Northern Ireland, 10 full caps.

Season	Club	Apps	Goals
1983–84	Nottingham F	—	—
1984–85		1	—
1985–86		18	3
1986–87		14	—
1986–87	*Notts Co*	18	2
1987–88	Nottingham F	8	—
1987–88	Charlton Ath	21	1
1988–89		9	—
1988–89	*Plymouth Arg*	1	—
1988–89	Bradford C	12	1
1989–90		23	3

CAMPBELL, Duncan

Born Paisley 11.9.70 Ht 5 7 Wt 10 12
Forward. From Jerviston BC.

Season	Club	Apps	Goals
1988–89	Dundee	8	1
1989–90		15	1

CAMPBELL, Garv

Born Belfast 4.4.66
Defender.

Season	Club	Apps	Goals
1983–84	Arsenal	—	—
1984–85		—	—
From Local			
1988–89	WBA	—	—
1989–90		—	—
1989–90	Leyton Orient	8	—

CAMPBELL, Greg

Born Portsmouth 13.7.65. Ht 5 11
Wt 11 05
Forward. From Manchester U. Amateur and West Ham U. Apprentice.

1982–83	West Ham U	—	—
1983–84		—	—
1984–85		2	—
1985–86		3	—
1986–87		—	—
1986–87	*Brighton*	2	—
1987–88	West Ham U	—	—
From Sparta			
1988–89	Plymouth Arg	13	3
1989–90		22	3

CAMPBELL, Kevin

Born Lambeth 4.2.70. Ht 6 0 Wt 13 01
Forward. From Trainee.

1987–88	Arsenal	1	—
1988–89		—	—
1988–89	*Leyton Orient*	16	9
1989–90	Arsenal	15	2
1989–90	*Leicester C*	11	5

CAMPBELL, Stephen

Born Dundee 20.11.67. Ht 5 9 Wt 11 02
Midfield. From Downfield BC. Scotland Under-21.

1985–86	Dundee	5	—
1986–87		4	—
1987–88		7	1
1988–89		24	—
1989–90		2	—

CANHAM, Tony

Born Leeds 8.6.60. Ht 5 9 Wt 11 07
Midfield. From Harrogate Railway.

1984–85	York C	3	1
1985–86		41	13
1986–87		38	9
1987–88		18	2
1988–89		41	9
1989–90		34	4

CARBERRY, Jimmy

Born Liverpool 13.10.69 Ht 5 7
Wt 10 06
Midfield. From Trainee.

1988–89	Everton	—	—
1989–90	Wigan Ath	32	3

CARMICHAEL, Matt

Born Singapore 13.5.64. Ht 6 2
Wt 11 07
Forward. From Army.

1989–90	Lincoln C	26	5

CARR, Cliff

Born London 19.6.64. Ht 5 5 Wt 10 04
Midfield. From Apprentice. England Under-21.

1982–83	Fulham	6	1
1983–84		41	4
1984–85		38	4
1985–86		35	4
1986–87		25	1
1987–88	Stoke C	41	—
1988–89		41	1
1989–90		22	—

CARR, Darren

Born Birmingham 4.11.69 Ht 5 7
Wt 10 04
Midfield. From Burton Albion.

1989–90	Crystal Palace	—	—

CARR, Darren

Born Bristol 4.9.68. Ht 6 2 Wt 13 00
Defender.

1985–86	Bristol R	1	—
1986–87		20	—
1987–88		9	—
1987–88	Newport Co	9	—
1987–88	Sheffield U	3	—
1988–89		10	1
1989–90		—	—

CARR, Franz

Born Preston 24.9.66. Ht 5 7 Wt 10 12
Midfield. From Apprentice. England Schools, Youth, Under-21.

1984–85	Blackburn R	—	—

Season	Club	Apps	Goals
1985–86	Nottingham F	23	3
1986–87		36	4
1987–88		22	4
1988–89		23	3
1989–90		14	1
1989–90	*Sheffield W*	12	—

CARR, Graham

Born Darlington 8.12.70. Ht 5 11 Wt 11 04
Goalkeeper. From Trainee.

Season	Club	Apps	Goals
1989–90	Hartlepool U	1	—

CARROLL, John

Born Dublin 13.10.71. Ht 6 1 Wt 11 08
Defender. From Home Farm.

Season	Club	Apps	Goals
1988–89	Liverpool	—	—
1989–90		—	—

CARSON, Tom

Born Alexandria 26.3.59 Ht 6 0 Wt 12 00
Goalkeeper. From Vale of Leven.

Season	Club	Apps	Goals
1978–79	Dumbarton	—	—
1979–80		3	—
1980–81		33	—
1981–82		39	—
1982–83		37	—
1983–84		37	—
1984–85	Dundee	20	—
1985–86		—	—
1986–87	*Hibernian*	2	—
1987–88	*Partick T*	6	—
1987–88	*Queen of S*	7	—
1987–88	*Dunfermline Ath*	5	—
1987–88	*Ipswich T*	1	—
1987–88	Dundee	6	—
1988–89		2	—
1989–90		16	—

CARSTAIRS, Jim

Born St. Andrews 29.1.71 Ht 6 0 Wt 12 05
Defender. From Trainee.

Season	Club	Apps	Goals
1988–89	Arsenal	—	—
1989–90		—	—

CARTER, Danny

Born Hackney 29.6.69
Forward. From Billericay.

Season	Club	Apps	Goals
1988–89	Leyton Orient	1	—
1989–90		31	5

CARTER, Graeme

Born Castle Eden 18.11.69. Ht 6 0 Wt 12 00
Defender. From Trainee.

Season	Club	Apps	Goals
1988–89	Newcastle U	—	—
1989–90		—	—

CARTER, Jimmy

Born London 9.11.65. Ht 5 10 Wt 10 08
Midfield. From Apprentice.

Season	Club	Apps	Goals
1983–84	Crystal Palace	—	—
1984–85		—	—
1985–86	QPR	—	—
1986–87	Millwall	12	1
1987–88		26	—
1988–89		20	5
1989–90		28	2

CARTER, Tim

Born Bristol 5.10.67. Ht 6 2 Wt 13 11
Goalkeeper. From Apprentice. England Youth.

Season	Club	Apps	Goals
1985–86	Bristol R	2	—
1986–87		38	—
1987–88		7	—
1987–88	*Newport Co*	1	—
1987–88	Sunderland	1	—
1988–89		2	—
1988–89	*Bristol C*	3	—
1989–90	Sunderland	18	—

CARTWRIGHT, Neil

Born Stourbridge 20.2.71
Forward. From Trainee.

Season	Club	League Appearances/Goals	
1988–89	WBA	1	—
1989–90		7	—

CASCARINO, Tony

Born St Paul's Cray 1.9.62. Ht 6 2
Wt 13 12
Forward. From Crockenhill. Eire 26 full caps.

Season	Club	Apps	Goals
1981–82	Gillingham	24	5
1982–83		38	15
1983–84		37	12
1984–85		43	16
1985–86		34	14
1986–87		43	16
1987–88	Millwall	39	20
1988–89		38	13
1989–90		28	9
1989–90	Aston Villa	10	2

CASE, Jimmy

Born Liverpool 18.5.54. Ht 5 9
Wt 12 08
Midfield. From Sth Liverpool. England Under-23.

Season	Club	Apps	Goals
1973–74	Liverpool	—	—
1974–75		1	—
1975–76		27	6
1976–77		27	1
1977–78		33	5
1978–79		37	7
1979–80		37	3
1980–81		24	1
1981–82	Brighton	33	3
1982–83		35	3
1983–84		35	4
1984–85		24	—
1984–85	Southampton	10	1
1985–86		36	2
1986–87		39	3
1987–88		38	—
1988–89		34	—
1989–90		33	3

CASEY, Paul

Born Rinteln 6.10.61 Ht 5 8 Wt 10 06
Defender. From Apprentice.

Season	Club	Apps	Goals
1979–80	Sheffield U	8	1
1980–81		5	—
1981–82		12	—
From Boston			
1987–88	Lincoln	*10*	—
1988–89		8	—
1989–90		12	—

CASEY, Stuart

Born Plymouth 5.9.69 Ht 5 7 Wt 10 07
Midfield. From Trainee.

Season	Club	Apps	Goals
1988–89	Plymouth Arg	—	—
1989–90		—	—

CASH, Stuart

Born Tipton 5.9.65. Ht 5 11 Wt 11 10
Defender. From Halesowen.

Season	Club	Apps	Goals
1989–90	Nottingham F	—	—
1989–90	*Rotherham U*	8	1

CASS, David

Born Forest Gate 27.3.62.
Goalkeeper. From Billericay.

Season	Club	Apps	Goals
1986–87	Leyton Orient	7	—
1987–88		—	—
1988–89		—	—
1989–90		—	—

CASSELLS, Keith

Born London 10.7.57. Ht 5 10 Wt 11 12
Forward. From Wembley T.

Season	Club	Apps	Goals
1977–78	Watford	—	—
1978–79		3	—
1979–80		7	—
1979–80	*Peterborough U*	8	—
1980–81	Watford	2	—
1980–81	Oxford U	18	3
1981–82		27	10
1981–82	Southampton	6	2
1982–83		13	2
1982–83	Brentford	16	7
1983–84		30	9
1984–85		40	12
1985–86	Mansfield T	40	13
1986–87		46	16

Season	Club	League Appearances/Goals	
1987–88		40	9
1988–89		37	14
1989–90		—	—

CASTLE, Steve

Born Barkingside 17.5.66. Ht 5 11
Wt 12 05
Midfield. From Apprentice.

Season	Club	Apps	Goals
1984–85	Orient	21	1
1985–86		23	4
1986–87		24	5
1987–88		42	10
1988–89		24	6
1989–90		27	7

CATON, Tommy

Born Liverpool 6.10.62. Ht 6 2
Wt 13 00
Defender. From Apprentice. England Schools, Youth, Under-21.

Season	Club	Apps	Goals
1979–80	Manchester C	42	—
1980–81		30	—
1981–82		39	1
1982–83		38	5
1983–84		16	2
1983–84	Arsenal	26	—
1984–85		35	1
1985–86		20	1
1986–87		—	—
1986–87	Oxford U	17	2
1987–88		36	1
1988–89		—	—
1988–89	Charlton Ath	13	1
1989–90		24	1

CAWLEY, Peter

Born London 15.9.65. Ht 6 4 Wt 13 00
Defender. From Chertsey.

Season	Club	Apps	Goals
1986–87	Wimbledon	—	—
1986–87	*Bristol R*	10	—
1987–88	Wimbledon	—	—
1988–89		1	—
1988–89	*Fulham*	5	—
1989–90	Bristol R	3	—

CECERE, Michele

Born Chester 4.1.68. Ht 6 0 Wt 11 04
Forward. From Apprentice.

Season	Club	Apps	Goals
1985–86	Oldham Ath	—	—
1986–87		14	4
1987–88		25	2
1988–89		13	2
1988–89	Huddersfield T	31	4
1989–90		23	4
1989–90	*Stockport Co*	1	—

CHALMERS, Paul

Born Glasgow 31.10.63. Ht 5 10
Wt 10 03
Forward. From Eastercraigs. Scotland Youth.

Season	Club	Apps	Goals
1980–81	Celtic	—	—
1981–82		—	—
1982–83		—	—
1983–84		—	—
1984–85		1	1
1985–86		3	—
1985–86	*Bradford C*	2	—
1986–87	St Mirren	23	2
1987–88		36	10
1988–89		33	11
1989–90		9	—
1989–90	Swansea C	16	4

CHAMBERLAIN, Alec

Born March 20.6.64. Ht 6 2 Wt 13 00
Goalkeeper. From Ramsey T.

Season	Club	Apps	Goals
1981–82	Ipswich T	—	—
1982–83	Colchester U	—	—
1983–84		46	—
1984–85		46	—
1985–86		46	—
1986–87		46	—
1987–88	Everton	—	—
1987–88	*Tranmere R*	15	—

Season	Club		
1988–89	Luton T	6	—
1989–90		38	—

CHAMBERLAIN, Mark

Born Stoke 19.11.61. Ht 5 9 Wt 10 07
Forward. From Apprentice. England Schools, Under-21, 8 full caps.

Season	Club		
1978–79	Port Vale	8	—
1979–80		11	—
1980–81		31	9
1981–82		46	8
1982–83	Stoke C	37	6
1983–84		40	7
1984–85		28	1
1985–86		7	3
1985–86	Sheffield W	21	2
1986–87		24	5
1987–88		21	1
1988–89	Portsmouth	28	6
1989–90		38	6

CHAMBERS, Steve

Born Worksop 20.7.68 Ht 5 10 Wt 10 10
Defender. From Apprentice.

Season	Club		
1985–86	Sheffield W	—	—
1986–87	Mansfield T	5	—
1987–88		8	—
1988–89		5	—
1989–90		7	—

CHANDLER, Jeff

Born Hammersmith 19.6.59. Ht 5 7
Wt 10 01
Midfield. From Apprentice. Eire Under-21, 2 full caps.

Season	Club		
1976–77	Blackpool	—	—
1977–78		13	2
1978–79		24	5
1979–80		—	—
1979–80	Leeds U	17	2
1980–81		9	—
1981–82		—	—
1981–82	Bolton W	33	2
1982–83		37	4
1983–84		46	14
1984–85		41	16
1985–86	Derby Co	37	10
1986–87		9	—
1986–87	*Mansfield T*	6	—
1987–88	Bolton W	3	2
1988–89		20	2
1989–90		1	—
1989–90	Cardiff C	24	—

CHANNING, Justin

Born Reading 19.11.68. Ht 5 10
Wt 10 02
Defender. From Apprentice. England Youth.

Season	Club		
1986–87	QPR	2	—
1987–88		14	1
1988–89		9	1
1989–90		23	2

CHAPMAN, Craig

Born Middlesbrough 9.12.70. Ht 5 7
Wt 10 05
Defender. From Trainee.

Season	Club		
1988–89	Newcastle U	—	—
1989–90		—	—

CHAPMAN, Gary

Born Leeds 1.5.64 Ht 5 10 Wt 12 00
Forward. Local.

Season	Club		
1988–89	Bradford C	2	—
1989–90		3	—
1989–90	Notts Co	19	4

CHAPMAN, Ian

Born Brighton 31.5.70. Ht 5 8 Wt 11 05
Defender. FA Schools.

Season	Club		
1986–87	Brighton	5	—
1987–88		—	—
1988–89		19	—
1989–90		42	—

CHAPMAN, Lee

Born Lincoln 5.12.59. Ht 6 1 Wt 13 00
Forward. From Amateur. England Under-21.

Season	Club	League Appearances/Goals	
1978–79	Stoke C	—	—
1978–79	*Plymouth Arg*	4	—
1979–80	Stoke C	17	3
1980–81		41	15
1981–82		41	16
1982–83	Arsenal	19	3
1983–84		4	1
1983–84	Sunderland	15	3
1984–85	Sheffield W	40	15
1985–86		31	10
1986–87		41	19
1987–88		37	19
From Niort			
1988–89	Nottingham F	30	8
1989–90		18	7
1989–90	Leeds U	21	12

CHAPMAN, Les

Born Oldham 27.9.48. Ht 5 9 Wt 11 11
Midfield. From High Barn.

Season	Club	League Appearances/Goals	
1966–67	Oldham Ath	16	—
1967–68		10	1
1968–69		41	7
1969–70		9	1
1969–70	Huddersfield T	10	—
1970–71		14	1
1971–72		39	3
1972–73		22	2
1973–74		33	1
1974–75		15	1
1974–75	Oldham Ath	24	—
1975–76		41	2
1976–77		42	2
1977–78		38	4
1978–79		42	3
1979–80	Stockport Co	32	1
1979–80	Bradford C	14	2
1980–81		45	—
1981–82		34	1
1982–83		46	—
1983–84	Rochdale	45	—
1984–85		43	—
1985–86	Stockport Co	38	3
1986–87	Preston NE	36	1
1987–88		17	—
1988–89		—	—
1989–90		—	—

CHAPMAN, Vincent

Born Newcastle 5.12.67. Ht 5 9
Wt 11 00
Defender. From Tow Law T.

Season	Club	League Appearances/Goals	
1987–88	Huddersfield T	6	—
1988–89		—	—
1988–89	*York C*	—	—
1989–90	Rochdale	4	—

CHAPPLE, Phil

Born Norwich 26.11.66. Ht 6 2 Wt 12 07
Defender. From Apprentice.

Season	Club	League Appearances/Goals	
1984–85	Norwich C	—	—
1985–86		—	—
1986–87		—	—
1987–88		—	—
1987–88	Cambridge U	6	1
1988–89		46	3
1989–90		45	5

CHARD, Phil

Born Corby 16.10.60. Ht 5 8 Wt 11 03
Midfield. From Nottingham F. Amateur.

Season	Club	League Appearances/Goals	
1978–79	Peterborough U	6	1
1979–80		20	2
1980–81		—	—
1981–82		39	3
1982–83		44	4
1983–84		38	7
1984–85		25	1
1985–86	Northampton T	41	7
1986–87		40	12
1987–88		34	8
1987–88	Wolverhampton W	9	2
1988–89		19	3
1989–90		6	—
1989–90	Northampton T	29	2

CHARLERY, Ken

Born Stepney 28.11.64. Ht 6 1 Wt 12 07
Forward. From Fisher Ath, Basildon U, Beckton U (1989).

Season	Club	League Appearances/Goals	
1989–90	Maidstone U	30	2

CHARLES, Gary

Born London 13.4.70. Ht 5 9 Wt 10 13
Defender. England Under-21.

1987–88	Nottingham F	—	—
1988–89		1	—
1988–89	*Leicester C*	8	—
1989–90	Nottingham F	1	—

CHARLES, Steve

Born Sheffield 10.5.60. Ht 5 9 Wt 10 07
Midfield. From Sheffield University.
England Schools.

1979–80	Sheffield U	14	1
1980–81		31	6
1981–82		30	1
1982–83		35	—
1983–84		11	1
1984–85		2	1
1984–85	Wrexham	32	7
1985–86		40	20
1986–87		41	10
1987–88	Mansfield T	46	12
1988–89		46	7
1989–90		43	7

CHARLTON, Simon

Born Huddersfield 25.10.71. Ht 5 7
Wt 10 11
Defender. From Trainee.

1989–90	Huddersfield T	3	—

CHEETHAM, Michael

Born Amsterdam 30.6.67 Ht 5 11
Wt 11 05
Midfield. From Army.

1988–89	Ipswich T	3	—
1989–90		1	—
1989–90	Cambridge U	36	10

CHEREDNIK, Aleksey

Born USSR 12.12.60. Ht 5 9 Wt 11 07
Defender. From Dnepr.

Season	Club	League Appearances/Goals	
1989–90	Southampton	8	—

CHERRY, Paul

Born Derby 14.10.64. Ht 6 0 Wt 11 07
Defender. From Salvesen BC.

1984–85	Hearts	3	—
1985–86		5	—
1986–87	Cowdenbeath	35	5
1987–88		35	8
1988–89	St Johnstone	39	2
1989–90		39	4

CHERRY, Steve

Born Nottingham 5.8.60. Ht 5 11
Wt 11 00
Goalkeeper. From Apprentice. England
Youth.

1977–78	Derby Co	—	—
1978–79		—	—
1979–80		4	—
1980–81	*Port Vale*	4	—
1981–82	Derby Co	4	—
1982–83		31	—
1983–84		38	—
1984–85	Walsall	41	—
1985–86		30	—
1986–87		—	—
1986–87	Plymouth Arg	21	—
1987–88		37	—
1988–89		15	—
1988–89	*Chesterfield*	10	—
1988–89	Notts Co	18	—
1989–90		46	—

CHETTLE, Steve

Born Nottingham 27.9.68. Ht 6 1
Wt 12 00
Defender. From Apprentice. England
Under-21.

1986–87	Nottingham F	—	—
1987–88		30	—

Season	Club	League Appearances/Goals	
1988–89		28	2
1989–90		22	1

CHIEDOZIE, John

Born Nigeria 18.4.60. Ht 5 7 Wt 10 10
Forward. From Apprentice. Nigeria full caps.

Season	Club	Apps	Goals
1976–77	Orient	15	—
1977–78		21	2
1978–79		36	6
1979–80		37	3
1980–81		36	9
1981–82	Notts Co	32	1
1982–83		39	5
1983–84		40	9
1984–85	Tottenham H	34	5
1985–86		18	7
1986–87		1	—
1987–88		—	—
1988–89	Derby Co	2	—
1989–90		—	—
1989–90	Notts Co	1	—
1989–90	Chesterfield	7	—

CHILDS, Gary

Born Birmingham 19.4.64. Ht 5 7
Wt 10 08
Midfield. From Apprentice. England Youth.

Season	Club	Apps	Goals
1981–82	WBA	2	—
1982–83		—	—
1983–84		1	—
1983–84	Walsall	30	2
1984–85		40	2
1985–86		33	5
1986–87		28	8
1987–88	Birmingham C	32	1
1988–89		23	1
1989–90	Grimsby T	44	5

CHISHOLM, Gordon

Born Glasgow 8.4.60. Ht 6 0 Wt 12 00
Defender. From Apprentice.

Season	Club	Apps	Goals
1977–78	Sunderland	—	—
1978–79		27	1
1979–80		13	—
1980–81		34	3
1981–82		22	—
1982–83		32	1
1983–84		36	4
1984–85		32	1
1985–86		1	—
1985–86	Hibernian	29	2
1986–87		23	2
1987–88		7	—
1987–88	Dundee	15	—
1988–89		34	4
1989–90		34	3

CHIVERS, Gary

Born Stockwell 15.5.60. Ht 5 11
Wt 11 05
Defender. From Apprentice.

Season	Club	Apps	Goals
1978–79	Chelsea	5	—
1979–80		29	2
1980–81		40	2
1981–82		29	—
1982–83		30	—
1983–84	Swansea C	10	—
1983–84	QPR	—	—
1984–85		23	—
1985–86		14	—
1986–87		23	—
1987–88	Watford	14	—
1987–88	Brighton	10	—
1988–89		46	6
1989–90		41	3

CHRISTIE, Trevor

Born Newcastle 28.2.59. Ht 6 2
Wt 12 00
Forward. From Apprentice.

Season	Club	Apps	Goals
1976–77	Leicester C	—	—
1977–78		5	—
1978–79		26	8
1979–80	Notts Co	41	9
1980–81		39	14
1981–82		35	13
1982–83		33	9
1983–84		39	19
1984–85	Nottingham F	14	5
1984–85	Derby Co	20	7
1985–86		45	15

Season	Club	Apps	Goals
1986–87	Manchester C	9	3
1986–87	Walsall	35	13
1987–88		36	7
1988–89		28	2
1988–89	Mansfield T	12	1
1989–90		45	13

CLAESEN, Nico

Born Leut 1.10.62. Ht 5 8 Wt 10 00
Forward. From Standard Liege. Belgium full caps.

Season	Club	Apps	Goals
1986–87	Tottenham H	26	8
1987–88		24	10

To Antwerp

CLARIDGE, Steve

Born Portsmouth 10.4.66. Ht 5 11
Wt 11 08
Forward. From Fareham.

Season	Club	Apps	Goals
1984–85	Bournemouth	6	1
1985–86		1	—
From Weymouth			
1988–89	Crystal Palace	—	—
1988–89	Aldershot	37	9
1989–90		25	10
1989–90	Cambridge U	20	4

CLARK, Billy

Born Christchurch 19.5.67. Ht 6 0
Wt 12 03
Defender. From Local.

Season	Club	Apps	Goals
1984–85	Bournemouth	1	—
1985–86		1	—
1986–87		—	—
1987–88		2	—
1987–88	Bristol R	31	1
1988–89		11	—
1989–90		—	—

CLARK, Howard

Born Coventry 19.9.68. Ht 5 11
Wt 11 01
Defender. From Apprentice.

Season	Club	Apps	Goals
1986–87	Coventry C	—	—
1987–88		—	—
1988–89		9	1
1989–90		9	—

CLARK, John

Born Edinburgh 22.9.64. Ht 6 0
Wt 13 01
Defender. 'S' Form. Scotland Youth.

Season	Club	Apps	Goals
1981–82	Dundee U	—	—
1982–83		1	—
1983–84		9	1
1984–85		10	3
1985–86		11	1
1986–87		30	3
1987–88		28	3
1988–89		20	2
1989–90		29	1

CLARK, Martin

Born Uddington 13.10.68 Ht 5 9
Wt 10 11
Midfield. From Hamilton A.

Season	Club	Apps	Goals
1987–88	Clyde	26	—
1988–89		25	2
1988–89	Nottingham F	—	—
1989–90		—	—
1989–90	*Falkirk*	3	1
1989–90	*Mansfield T*	14	1

CLARK, Paul

Born Benfleet 14.9.58. Ht 5 9 Wt 13 13
Midfield. From Apprentice. England Schools, Youth.

Season	Club	Apps	Goals
1976–77	Southend U	25	—
1977–78		8	1
1977–78	Brighton	26	3
1978–79		33	4
1979–80		11	2
1980–81		9	—
1981–82	*Reading*	2	—
1982–83	Southend U	31	1
1983–84		20	—
1984–85		29	1
1985–86		39	1
1986–87		46	—
1987–88		30	—

Season	Club	League Appearances/Goals	
1988–89		16	—
1989–90		25	—

CLARK, Sandy

Born Airdrie 28.10.56 Ht 6 0 Wt 12 07
Forward. From Airdrie BC.

Season	Club	Apps	Goals
1974–75	Airdrieonians	3	—
1975–76		20	7
1976–77		32	8
1977–78		38	7
1978–79		38	23
1979–80		37	22
1980–81		36	10
1981–82		30	15
1982–83	West Ham U	26	7
1982–83	Rangers	10	4
1983–84		30	9
1984–85		1	—
1984–85	Hearts	25	8
1985–86		33	12
1986–87		41	8
1987–88		35	6
1988–89		2	1
1989–90	Dunfermline Ath	4	—

CLARKE, Brian

Born Eastbourne 10.10.68. Ht 6 3
Wt 13 08
Defender.

Season	Club	Apps	Goals
1987–88	Gillingham	—	—
1988–89		10	—
1989–90		3	—

CLARKE, Colin

Born Newry 30.10.62. Ht 6 0 Wt 13 06
Forward. From Apprentice. Northern Ireland, 24 full caps.

Season	Club	Apps	Goals
1980–81	Ipswich T	—	—
1981–82	Peterborough	27	4
1982–83		37	9
1983–84		18	5
1983–84	*Gillingham*	8	1
1984–85	Tranmere R	45	22
1985–86	Bournemouth	46	26
1986–87	Southampton	33	20
1987–88		40	16
1988–89		9	—
1988–89	*Bournemouth*	4	2
1988–89	QPR	12	5
1989–90		34	6

CLARKE, David

Born Nottingham 3.12.64. Ht 5 10
Wt 11 00
Midfield. From Apprentice. England Youth.

Season	Club	Apps	Goals
1982–83	Notts Co	16	—
1983–84		20	—
1984–85		22	—
1985–86		42	1
1986–87		23	6
1987–88	Lincoln C	*30*	*5*
1988–89		36	4
1989–90		30	2

CLARKE, Mick

Born Birmingham 22.12.67. Ht 5 11
Wt 11 05
Forward. From Birmingham C Apprentice.

Season	Club	Apps	Goals
1986–87	Barnsley	23	3
1987–88		14	—
1988–89		3	—
1989–90	Scarborough	36	1

CLARKE, Nicky

Born Walsall 20.8.67. Ht 5 11 Wt 12 00
Defender. From Apprentice.

Season	Club	Apps	Goals
1984–85	Wolverhampton W	—	—
1985–86		23	1
1986–87		24	—
1987–88		8	—
1988–89		8	—
1989–90		3	—

CLARKE, Stephen

Born Saltcoats 29.8.63. Ht 5 10
Wt 10 02
Defender. From Beith Juniors. Scotland Youth, Under-21, B. Football League.

Season	Club	Apps	Goals
1981–82	St Mirren	—	—

Season	Club	League Appearances/Goals	
1982–83		31	—
1983–84		33	2
1984–85		33	—
1985–86		31	3
1986–87		23	1
1986–87	Chelsea	16	—
1987–88		38	1
1988–89		36	—
1989–90		24	3

CLARKE, Wayne

Born Wolverhampton 28.2.61. Ht 6 0
Wt 11 08
Forward. From Apprentice. England Schools, Youth.

Season	Club	Apps	Goals
1977–78	Wolverhampton W	1	—
1978–79		8	1
1979–80		16	2
1980–81		24	3
1981–82		29	6
1982–83		39	12
1983–84		31	6
1984–85	Birmingham C	40	17
1985–86		28	5
1986–87		24	16
1986–87	Everton	10	5
1987–88		27	10
1988–89		20	3
1989–90	Leicester C	11	1
1989–90	Manchester C	9	—

CLARKSON, Ian

Born Birmingham 4.12.70 Ht 5 11
Wt 11 08
Defender. From Trainee.

Season	Club	Apps	Goals
1988–89	Birmingham C	9	—
1989–90		20	—

CLAYTON, Gary

Born Sheffield 2.2.63. Ht 5 11 Wt 12 08
Midfield. From Rotherham U Apprentice, Burton Alb.

Season	Club	Apps	Goals
1986–87	Doncaster R	35	5
1987–88	Cambridge U	45	5
1988–89		46	1
1989–90		10	1

CLAYTON, John

Born Elgin 20.8.61. Ht 5 11 Wt 11 07
Forward. From Apprentice.

Season	Club	Apps	Goals
1978–79	Derby C	1	—
1979–80		—	—
1980–81		9	1
1981–82		14	3
From Bulova, Hong Kong			
1983–84	Chesterfield	33	5
1984–85	Tranmere R	44	31
1985–86		3	4
1985–86	Plymouth Arg	36	12
1986–87		21	3
1987–88		20	7

To Fortuna Sittard

CLAYTON, Paul

Born Dunstable 4.1.65. Ht 5 11
Wt 11 03
Forward. From Apprentice.

Season	Club	Apps	Goals
1982–83	Norwich C	—	—
1983–84		7	—
1984–85		5	—
1985–86		1	—
1986–87		—	—
1987–88		—	—
1987–88	Darlington	12	3
1988–89		10	—
1988–89	Crewe Alex	20	6
1989–90		18	4

CLELAND, Alec

Born Glasgow 10.12.70. Ht 5 8
Wt 10 00
Defender. From S Form. Scotland Under-21.

Season	Club	Apps	Goals
1987–88	Dundee U	1	—

Season	Club	League Appearances/Goals	
1988–89	....	9	—
1989–90	....	15	—

CLEMENT, Andy

Born Cardiff 12.11.67. Ht 5 8 Wt 11 00
Defender. From Apprentice. Wales Youth.

Season	Club		
1985–86	Wimbledon	—	—
1986–87	....	4	—
1986–87	*Bristol R*	6	—
1987–88	Wimbledon	11	—
1987–88	*Newport Co*	5	1
1988–89	Wimbledon	11	—
1989–90	....	—	—

CLEMENTS, Kenny

Born Manchester 9.4.55 Ht 6 1 Wt 12 06
Defender. From Amateur.

Season	Club		
1975–76	Manchester C	27	—
1976–77	....	35	—
1977–78	....	42	—
1978–79	....	15	—
1979–80	....	—	—
1979–80	Oldham Ath	36	1
1980–81	....	40	—
1981–82	....	27	1
1982–83	....	38	—
1983–84	....	41	—
1984–85	....	24	—
1984–85	*Manchester C*	12	1
1985–86	Manchester C	30	—
1986–87	....	39	—
1987–88	....	25	—
1987–88	Bury	9	1
1988–89	....	44	—
1989–90	....	28	—

CLEMINSHAW, David

Born South Cave 1.11.70. Ht 6 1
Wt 12 09
Goalkeeper. From Trainee.

Season	Club		
1989–90	Hull C	—	—

CLOSE, Shaun

Born Islington 8.9.66. Ht 5 8 Wt 10 01
Forward. From Trainee.

Season	Club	League Appearances/Goals	
1984–85	Tottenham H	—	—
1985–86	....	—	—
1986–87	....	2	—
1987–88	....	7	—
1987–88	Bournemouth	16	6
1988–89	....	23	2
1989–90	....	—	—
1989–90	Swindon T	11	—

CLOUGH, Nigel

Born Sunderland 19.3.66. Ht 5 9
Wt 11 05
Forward. From AC Hunters, England Under-21, 1 full cap.

Season	Club		
1984–85	Nottingham F	9	1
1985–86	....	39	15
1986–87	....	42	14
1987–88	....	34	19
1988–89	....	36	14
1989–90	....	38	9

COBB, Gary

Born Luton 6.8.68. Ht 5 8 Wt 11 05
Midfield. From Apprentice.

Season	Club		
1986–87	Luton T	2	—
1987–88	....	7	—
1988–89	....	—	—
1988–89	*Northampton T*	1	—
1989–90	Luton T	—	—
1989–90	*Swansea C*	5	—

COCKERILL, Glenn

Born Grimsby 25.8.59. Ht 6 0 Wt 12 06
Midfield. From Louth U.

Season	Club		
1976–77	Lincoln C	4	—
1977–78	....	13	1
1978–79	....	35	6
1979–80	....	19	3
1979–80	Swindon T	10	1
1980–81	....	16	—
1981–82	Lincoln C	44	11
1982–83	....	38	8
1983–84	....	33	6
1983–84	Sheffield U	10	1
1984–85	....	40	7
1985–86	....	12	2

Season	Club	League Appearances/Goals	
1985–86	Southampton	30	7
1986–87		42	7
1987–88		39	2
1988–89		34	6
1989–90		36	4

COCKERILL, John

Born Cleethorpes 12.7.61 Ht 6 0
Wt 12 07
Midfield. From Stafford R.

Season	Club	League Appearances/Goals	
1988–89	Grimsby T	29	6
1989–90		33	5

COCKRAM, Allan

Born Kensington 8.10.63. Ht 5 8
Wt 10 08
Midfield. Local.

Season	Club	League Appearances/Goals	
1980–81	Tottenham H	—	—
1981–82		—	—
1982–83		—	—
1983–84		2	—
1984–85		—	—
1985–86	Bristol R	1	—
From St Albans			
1987–88	Brentford	7	2
1988–89		37	7
1989–90		26	2

CODDINGTON, Matt

Born Lytham St Annes 17.9.69 Ht 6 0
Wt 11 10
Goalkeeper. From Trainee.

Season	Club	League Appearances/Goals	
1988–89	Middlesbrough	—	—
1989–90		—	—
1989–90	*Bury*	—	—
1989–90	*Halifax T*	—	—

CODNER, Robert

Born Walthamstow 23.1.65 Ht 5 11
Wt 11 05
Midfield. From Leicester C, Barnet.

Season	Club	League Appearances/Goals	
1988–89	Brighton	28	1
1989–90		45	9

COLE, Andrew

Born Nottingham 15.10.71. Ht 5 11
Wt 11 02
Forward. From Trainee.

Season	Club	League Appearances/Goals	
1989–90	Arsenal	—	—

COLE, David

Born Barnsley 28.9.62. Ht 6 0 Wt 11 10
Defender. From Sunderland.

Season	Club	League Appearances/Goals	
1984–85	Swansea C	8	—
1984–85	Swindon T	20	—
1985–86		44	3
1986–87		5	—
1986–87	Torquay U	29	—
1987–88		46	5
1988–89		35	1
1989–90	Rochdale	43	5

COLE, Michael

Born Stepney 3.9.66. Ht 6 0 Wt 12 05
Forward. From Amateur.

Season	Club	League Appearances/Goals	
1983–84	Ipswich T	—	—
1984–85		2	—
1985–86		18	1
1986–87		16	2
1987–88		2	—
1987–88	*Port Vale*	4	1
1987–88	Fulham	9	1
1988–89		36	3
1989–90		1	—

COLEMAN, Chris

Born Swansea 10.6.70. Ht 6 2 Wt 12 10
Defender. From Apprentice. Wales
Under-21.

Season	Club	League Appearances/Goals	
1987–88	Swansea C	30	—
1988–89		43	—
1989–90		46	2

COLEMAN, David

Born Salisbury 8.4.67. Ht 5 7 Wt 10 08
Defender.

Season	Club		
1985–86	Bournemouth	1	—
1986–87		1	—
1987–88		5	—
1987–88	*Colchester U*	6	1
1988–89	Bournemouth	9	1
1989–90		27	1

COLEMAN, Nicky

Born Crayford 6.5.66. Ht 5 10 Wt 11 12
Defender. From Apprentice.

Season	Club		
1983–84	Millwall	—	—
1984–85		1	—
1985–86		6	—
1985–86	*Swindon T*	13	4
1986–87	Millwall	42	—
1987–88		36	—
1988–89		—	—
1989–90		3	—

COLEMAN, Simon

Born Worksop 13.3.68. Ht 6 0 Wt 10 08
Midfield.

Season	Club		
1985–86	Mansfield T	—	—
1986–87		2	—
1987–88		44	2
1988–89		45	5
1989–90		5	—
1989–90	Middlesbrough	36	1

COLES, David

Born Wandsworth 15.6.64 Ht 6 0
Wt 11 00
Goalkeeper. From Apprentice.

Season	Club		
1981–82	Birmingham C	—	—
1982–83		—	—
1982–83	Mansfield T	3	—
1983–84	Aldershot	45	—
1984–85		34	—
1985–86		29	—
1986–87		1	—
1987–88		11	—
1987–88	*Newport Co*	14	—
From HJK Helsinki			
1988–89	Colchester U	—	—
1988–89	Crystal Palace	—	—
1988–89	Brighton	1	—
1989–90	Aldershot	28	—

COLLIER, Darren

Born Stockton 1.12.67 Ht 5 11 Wt 11 09
Goalkeeper. From Middlesbrough.

Season	Club		
1988–89	Blackburn R	1	—
1989–90		16	—

COLLINGS, Paul

Born Liverpool 30.9.68 Ht 6 2 Wt 12 00
Goalkeeper.

Season	Club		
1988–89	Tranmere R	1	—
1989–90		—	—

COLLINS, Darren

Born Winchester 24.5.67
Forward. From Liphook, Petersfield U.

Season	Club		
1988–89	Northampton T	8	—
1989–90		35	8

COLLINS, David

Born Dublin 30.10.71. Ht 6 1 Wt 12 10
Defender. From Trainee.

Season	Club		
1988–89	Liverpool	—	—
1989–90		—	—

COLLINS, Eamonn

Born Dublin 22.10.65. Ht 5 6 Wt 9 07
Midfield. From Blackpool and Southampton Apprentice. Eire Youth, Under-21.

Season	Club		
1982–83	Southampton	—	—
1983–84		—	—
1984–85		3	—
1985–86		—	—
1986–87	Portsmouth	5	—
1987–88		—	—
1987–88	*Exeter C*	9	—

Season	Club	League Appearances/Goals	
1988–89	Portsmouth	—	—
1989–90	Colchester U	39	2

COLLINS, John

Born Galashiels 31.1.68. Ht 5 7 Wt 9 10
Midfield. From Hutchison Vale BC.
Scotland Youth, Under-21, 4 full caps.

Season	Club	Apps	Goals
1984–85	Hibernian	—	—
1985–86		19	1
1986–87		30	1
1987–88		44	6
1988–89		35	2
1989–90		35	6

COLQUHOUN, John

Born Stirling 14.7.63. Ht 5 7 Wt 10 0
Forward. From Grangemouth Inter.

Season	Club	Apps	Goals
1980–81	Stirling Albion	13	—
1981–82		37	13
1982–83		39	21
1983–84		15	11
1983–84	Celtic	12	2
1984–85		20	2
1985–86	Hearts	36	8
1986–87		43	13
1987–88		44	15
1988–89		36	5
1989–90		36	6

COLVILLE, Bob

Born Nuneaton 27.4.63. Ht 5 10
Wt 11 11
Forward. From Rhos.

Season	Club	Apps	Goals
1983–84	Oldham Ath	4	1
1984–85		7	1
1985–86		17	2
1986–87		4	—
1986–87	Bury	8	1
1987–88		3	—
1987–88	Stockport Co	40	14
1988–89		31	6
1989–90	York C	24	—

COMFORT, Alan

Born Aldershot 8.12.64. Ht 5 7
Wt 11 02
Midfield. From Apprentice. England
Youth.

Season	Club	Apps	Goals
1982–83	QPR	—	—
1983–84		—	—
1984–85		—	—
1984–85	Cambridge U	33	2
1985–86		30	3
1985–86	Orient	15	5
1986–87		45	11
1987–88		46	12
1988–89		44	19
1989–90	Middlesbrough	15	2

COMSTIVE, Paul

Born Southport 25.11.61. Ht 6 1
Wt 12 07
Midfield. From Amateur.

Season	Club	Apps	Goals
1979–80	Blackburn R	—	—
1980–81		3	—
1981–82		2	—
1982–83		1	—
1982–83	*Rochdale*	9	2
1983–84	Wigan Ath	29	2
1984–85		6	—
1984–85	Wrexham	28	3
1985–86		35	3
1986–87		36	2
1987–88	Burnley	44	8
1988–89		38	9
1989–90		—	—
1989–90	Bolton W	31	1

COMYN, Andy

Born Manchester 2.6.68. Ht 6 1
Wt 12 00
Defender. From Alvechurch.

Season	Club	Apps	Goals
1989–90	Aston Villa	4	—

CONEY, Dean

Born Dagenham 18.9.63. Ht 6 0
Wt 12 06
Forward. From Apprentice. England
Under-21.

Season	Club	Apps	Goals
1980–81	Fulham	7	3
1981–82		42	13
1982–83		37	4

Season	Club	League Appearances/Goals	
1983–84		27	7
1984–85		24	7
1985–86		37	12
1986–87		37	10
1987–88	QPR	32	7
1988–89		16	—
1988–89	Norwich C	8	1
1989–90		9	—

CONNELLY, Dino

Born Glasgow 6.1.70. Ht 5 9 Wt 10 08
Midfield. From Celtic BC, Arsenal Trainee. Scotland Schools, Youth.

Season	Club	Apps	Goals
1987–88	Arsenal	—	—
1988–89		—	—
1989–90		—	—

CONNOLLY, Patrick

Born Glasgow 25.6.70. Ht 5 8 Wt 9 04
Midfield. From S Form.

Season	Club	Apps	Goals
1986–87	Dundee U	—	—
1987–88		—	—
1988–89		2	—
1989–90		15	5

CONNOR, Robert

Born Kilmarnock 4.8.60. Ht 5 11 Wt 11 04
Midfield. From Ayr U BC. Scotland Youth, B, Under-21, 3 full caps.

Season	Club	Apps	Goals
1977–78	Ayr U	9	—
1978–79		29	—
1979–80		38	9
1980–81		39	8
1981–82		30	—
1982–83		39	4
1983–84		39	7
1984–85	Dundee	34	7
1985–86		35	2
1986–87		2	—
1986–87	Aberdeen	32	4
1987–88		34	1
1988–89		36	4
1989–90		34	1

CONNOR, Terry

Born Leeds 9.11.62. Ht 5 9 Wt 11 08
Forward. From Apprentice. England Youth, Under-21.

Season	Club	Apps	Goals
1979–80	Leeds U	23	6
1980–81		27	4
1981–82		27	4
1982–83		19	5
1982–83	Brighton	7	1
1983–84		40	13
1984–85		38	14
1985–86		33	14
1986–87		38	9
1987–88	Portsmouth	19	4
1988–89		14	5
1989–90		15	3

CONROY, Mike

Born Glasgow 31.12.65. Ht 6 0 Wt 11 00
Forward. From Apprentice.

Season	Club	Apps	Goals
1983–84	Coventry C	—	—
1983–84	Clydebank	2	—
1984–85		26	11
1985–86		28	7
1986–87		36	9
1987–88		22	11
1987–88	St Mirren	10	1
1988–89	Reading	13	4
1989–90		34	2

COOK, Andy

Born Romsey 10.8.69. Ht 5 9 Wt 10 12
Defender. From Apprentice.

Season	Club	Apps	Goals
1987–88	Southampton	2	—
1988–89		3	—
1989–90		4	1

COOK, Jason

Born Edmonton 29.12.69 Ht 5 7 Wt 10 06
Midfield. From Trainee.

Season	Club	League Appearances/Goals	
1988–89	Tottenham H	—	—
1989–90	Southend U	29	1

COOK, Mark

Born Boston 7.8.70 Ht 6 0 Wt 11 11
Midfield. From Trainee.

Season	Club	Apps	Goals
1988–89	Lincoln C	1	—
1989–90		6	—

COOK, Mike

Born Coventry Ht 5 9 Wt 10 12
Midfield. From Trainee.

Season	Club	Apps	Goals
1986–87	Coventry C	—	—
1987–88		—	—
1987–88	*York C*	6	1
1988–89	Coventry C	—	—
1989–90	Cambridge U	15	1

COOK, Mitch

Born Scarborough 15.10.61. Ht 6 0
Wt 12 0
Midfield. From Scarborough.

Season	Club	Apps	Goals
1984–85	Darlington	31	3
1985–86		3	1
1985–86	Middlesbrough	6	—
1986–87	Scarborough	—	—
1987–88		38	5
1988–89		43	5
1989–90	Halifax T	37	2

COOK, Paul

Born Liverpool 22.2.67. Ht 5 11
Wt 10 10
Midfield.

Season	Club	Apps	Goals
1984–85	Wigan Ath	2	—
1985–86		13	2
1986–87		27	4
1987–88		41	8
1988–89	Norwich C	4	—
1989–90		2	—
1989–90	Wolverhampton W	28	2

COOKE, John

Born Salford 25.4.62. Ht 5 8 Wt 11 00
Forward. From Apprentice. England Youth.

Season	Club	Apps	Goals
1979–80	Sunderland	4	1
1980–81		17	1
1981–82		10	1
1982–83		14	1
1983–84		4	—
1984–85		6	—
1984–85	*Carlisle U*	6	2
1985–86	Sheffield W	—	—
1985–86	Carlisle U	33	4
1986–87		36	2
1987–88		37	5
1988–89	Stockport Co	34	6
1989–90		24	1

COOKE, Richard

Born Islington 4.9.65. Ht 5 6 Wt 9 00
Forward. From Apprentice. England Youth, Under-21.

Season	Club	Apps	Goals
1982–83	Tottenham H	—	—
1983–84		9	1
1984–85		—	—
1985–86		2	1
1986–87		—	—
1986–87	*Birmingham C*	5	—
1986–87	Bournemouth	23	8
1987–88		34	5
1988–89		15	3
1988–89	Luton T	6	—
1989–90		11	1

COOKSON, Steve

Born Wolverhampton 19.2.72. Ht 6 1
Wt 10 10
Forward. From Trainee.

Season	Club	Apps	Goals
1989–90	Torquay U	10	1

COOMBE, Mark

Born Torquay 17.9.68 Ht 6 1 Wt 12 00
Goalkeeper. From Bournemouth Trainee.

1987–88	Bristol C	—	—
1987–88	*Carlisle U*	—	—
1988–89	Colchester U	3	—
1988–89	Torquay U	8	—
1989–90		—	—

COOMBS, Paul

Born Bristol 4.9.70 Ht 5 11 Wt 12 05
Forward. From QPR schoolboy, Aldershot trainee.

1988–89	Aldershot	1	—
1989–90		12	1

COOPER, Colin

Born Durham 28.2.67. Ht 5 10 Wt 11 01
Defender. England Under-21.

1984–85	Middlesbrough	—	—
1985–86		11	—
1986–87		46	—
1987–88		43	2
1988–89		35	2
1989–90		21	2

COOPER, David

Born London 23.6.71. Ht 5 10 Wt 11 10
Forward. From Trainee.

1989–90	Wimbledon	—	—

COOPER, Davie

Born Hamilton 25.2.56. Ht 5 8 Wt 12 05
Forward. From Hamilton Avondale. Scotland Under-21. 22 full caps.

1974–75	Clydebank	26	4
1975–76		26	13
1976–77		38	11
1977–78	Rangers	35	6
1978–79		30	5
1979–80		30	2
1980–81		25	3
1981–82		30	3
1982–83		31	5
1983–84		34	6
1984–85		32	5
1985–86		32	4
1986–87		42	8
1987–88		33	1
1988–89		23	1
1989–90	Motherwell	31	6

COOPER, Gary

Born Edgware 20.11.65. Ht 5 8 Wt 11 03
Defender. From Brentford, QPR and Fisher Ath (1989)

1989–90	Maidstone U	33	4

COOPER, Graham

Born Bolton 18.11.65. Ht 5 10 Wt 10 11
Midfield. From Amateur.

1983–84	Huddersfield T	3	1
1984–85		34	5
1985–86		—	—
1986–87		12	2
1987–88		25	5
1988–89	Wrexham	36	11
1989–90		18	3

COOPER, Leigh

Born Reading 7.5.61. Ht 5 8 Wt 10 09
Defender. From Apprentice.

1979–80	Plymouth Arg	14	—
1980–81		28	3
1981–82		43	5
1982–83		45	4
1983–84		43	2
1984–85		21	—
1985–86		40	1
1986–87		35	—
1987–88		37	—
1988–89		15	—
1989–90		2	—

COOPER, Mark

Born Cambridge 5.4.67. Ht 6 2 Wt 13 04
Forward. From Apprentice.

1983–84	Cambridge U	2	—
1984–85		18	3
1985–86		19	1
1986–87		32	13

Season	Club	Apps	Goals
1986–87	Tottenham H	—	—
1987–88		—	—
1987–88	Shrewsbury T	6	2
1987–88	Gillingham	31	8
1988–89		18	3
1988–89	Leyton Orient	14	4
1989–90		39	11

COOPER, Mark

Born Wakefield 18.12.68. Ht 5 8
Wt 11 04
Midfield. From Trainee.

Season	Club	Apps	Goals
1987–88	Bristol C	—	—
1988–89		—	—
1989–90	Exeter C	5	—
1989–90	*Southend U*	5	—

COOPER, Neale

Born India 24.11.63. Ht 6 1 Wt 12 07
Defender. From King St. Scotland Schools, Youth, Under-21.

Season	Club	Apps	Goals
1979–80	Aberdeen	—	—
1980–81		5	—
1981–82		27	3
1982–83		31	2
1983–84		26	—
1984–85		20	1
1985–86		23	—
1986–87	Aston Villa	13	—
1987–88		7	—
1988–89		—	—
1988–89	Rangers	14	1
1989–90		3	—

COOPER, Neil

Born Aberdeen 12.8.59. Ht 5 11
Wt 12 07
Defender. From Hilton Academy. Scotland Schools, Youth.

Season	Club	Apps	Goals
1974–75	Aberdeen	1	—
1975–76		2	—
1976–77		—	—
1977–78		1	—
1978–79		7	1
1979–80		1	—
1979–80	Barnsley	20	3
1980–81		30	2
1981–82		10	1
1981–82	Grimsby T	16	1
1982–83		24	1
1983–84		7	—
1983–84	St Mirren	25	—
1984–85		10	—
1985–86		30	—
1986–87		39	1
1987–88		27	1
1988–89		30	—
1989–90	Hibernian	27	—

COOPER, Paul

Born Brierley Hill 21.12.53. Ht 5 10
Wt 12 12
Goalkeeper. From Apprentice.

Season	Club	Apps	Goals
1971–72	Birmingham C	12	—
1972–73		3	—
1973–74		2	—
1973–74	Ipswich T	1	—
1974–75		2	—
1975–76		40	—
1976–77		34	—
1977–78		40	—
1978–79		41	—
1979–80		40	—
1980–81		38	—
1981–82		32	—
1982–83		35	—
1983–84		36	—
1984–85		36	—
1985–86		36	—
1986–87		36	—
1987–88	Leicester C	32	—
1988–89		24	—
1988–89	Manchester C	8	—
1989–90		7	—

COOPER, Steve

Born Birmingham 22.6.64. Ht 5 11
Wt 10 12
Forward.

Season	Club	Apps	Goals
1983–84	Birmingham C	—	—
1983–84	*Halifax T*	7	1
1984–85	*Mansfield T*	—	—
1984–85	Newport Co	38	11

Season	Club	Apps	Goals
1985–86	Plymouth Arg	38	8
1986–87		12	4
1987–88		23	3
1988–89	Barnsley	35	6
1989–90		30	5

CORK, Alan

Born Derby 4.3.59. Ht 6 0 Wt 12 00
Forward. From Amateur.

Season	Club	Apps	Goals
1977–78	Derby C	—	—
1977–78	*Lincoln C*	5	—
1977–78	Wimbledon	17	4
1978–79		45	22
1979–80		42	12
1980–81		41	23
1981–82		6	—
1982–83		7	5
1983–84		42	29
1984–85		28	11
1985–86		38	11
1986–87		30	5
1987–88		34	9
1988–89		25	2
1989–90		31	5

CORNFORTH, John

Born Whitley Bay 7.10.67. Ht 6 1
Wt 12 08
Defender. From Apprentice.

Season	Club	Apps	Goals
1984–85	Sunderland	1	—
1985–86		—	—
1986–87		—	—
1986–87	*Doncaster R*	7	3
1987–88	Sunderland	12	2
1988–89		15	—
1989–90		2	—
1989–90	*Shrewsbury T*	3	—
1989–90	*Lincoln C*	9	1

CORNWELL, John

Born Bethnal Green 13.10.64. Ht 6 0
Wt 12 00
Defender. From Apprentice.

Season	Club	Apps	Goals
1981–82	Orient	3	—
1982–83		31	3
1983–84		42	7
1984–85		36	10
1985–86		44	8
1986–87		46	7
1987–88	Newcastle U	24	1
1988–89		9	—
1988–89	Swindon T	6	—
1989–90		19	—

COSTELLO, Greg

Born Dublin 5.4.70.
Midfield.

Season	Club	Apps	Goals
1987–88	QPR	—	—
1988–89		—	—
1989–90		—	—

COSTELLO, Peter

Born Halifax 31.10.69 Ht 6 0 Wt 11 07
Forward. From Trainee.

Season	Club	Apps	Goals
1988–89	Bradford C	8	2
1989–90		12	—

COTON, Tony

Born Tamworth 19.5.61. Ht 6 2
Wt 13 07
Goalkeeper. From Mile Oak.

Season	Club	Apps	Goals
1978–79	Birmingham C	—	—
1979–80		—	—
1979–80	*Hereford U*	—	—
1980–81	Birmingham C	3	—
1981–82		15	—
1982–83		28	—
1983–84		41	—
1984–85		7	—
1984–85	Watford	33	—
1985–86		40	—
1986–87		31	—
1987–88		37	—
1988–89		46	—
1989–90		46	—

COTTEE, Tony

Born West Ham 11.7.65. Ht 5 8
Wt 11 11
Forward. From Apprentice. England
Youth, Under-21, 7 full caps.

Season	Club	League Appearances/Goals	
1982–83	West Ham U	8	5
1983–84		39	15
1984–85		41	17
1985–86		42	20
1986–87		42	22
1987–88		40	13
1988–89	Everton	36	13
1989–90		27	13

COTTERILL, Steve

Born Cheltenham 20.7.64 Ht 6 1
Wt 12 05
Forward. From Burton A.

Season	Club	Apps	Goals
1988–89	Wimbledon	4	1
1989–90		2	1

COTTON, Perry

Born Chislehurst 11.11.65
Midfield.

Season	Club	Apps	Goals
1988–89	Scunthorpe U	1	—
1989–90		17	1

COUGHLIN, Russell

Born Swansea 15.2.60. Ht 5 8 Wt 11 12
Midfield. From Apprentice.

Season	Club	Apps	Goals
1977–78	Manchester C	—	—
1978–79		—	—
1978–79	Blackburn R	11	—
1979–80		10	—
1980–81		3	—
1980–81	Carlisle U	25	3
1981–82		37	5
1982–83		38	2
1983–84		30	3
1984–85	Plymouth Arg	38	3
1985–86		45	10
1986–87		40	5
1987–88		8	—
1987–88	Blackpool	24	2
1988–89		43	5
1989–90		35	1

COUSINS, Jason

Born Hayes 14.10.70. Ht 6 0 Wt 12 07
Defender. From Trainee.

Season	Club	League Appearances/Goals	
1989–90	Brentford	13	—

COWAN, Tom

Born Bellshill 28.8.69. Ht 5 8 Wt 10 08
Defender. From Netherdale BC.

Season	Club	Apps	Goals
1988–89	Clyde	16	2
1988–89	Rangers	4	—
1989–90		3	—

COWANS, Gordon

Born Durham 27.10.58. Ht 5 7 Wt 9 8
Midfield. From Apprentice.
England Youth, Under-21, B, 9 full caps.

Season	Club	Apps	Goals
1975–76	Aston Villa	1	—
1976–77		18	3
1977–78		35	7
1978–79		34	4
1979–80		42	6
1980–81		42	5
1981–82		42	6
1982–83		42	10
1983–84		—	—
1984–85		30	1
1985–86	Bari	20	—
1986–87		38	3
1987–88		36	—
1988–89	Aston Villa	33	2
1989–90		34	4

COWDRILL, Barry

Born Birmingham 3.1.57. Ht 5 11
Wt 11 04
Defender. From Sutton Coldfield T.

Season	Club	Apps	Goals
1979–80	WBA	9	—
1980–81		10	—
1981–82		8	—
1982–83		2	—
1983–84		22	—
1984–85		9	—
1985–86		10	-
1985–86	*Rotherham U*	2	—
1986–87	WBA	29	—
1987–88		32	—

1988–89	Bolton W	38	—
1989–90		44	3

COWLING, David

Born Doncaster 27.11.58. Ht 5 7
Wt 11 04
Forward. From Mansfield T. Apprentice.

1977–78	Huddersfield T	—	—
1978–79		26	1
1979–80		40	10
1980–81		43	4
1981–82		38	8
1982–83		41	7
1983–84		41	3
1984–85		32	4
1985–86		39	6
1986–87		34	—
1987–88		6	—
1987–88	*Scunthorpe U*	1	—
1987–88	Reading	10	1
1988–89	Scunthorpe U	39	2
1989–90		32	—

COX, Brian

Born Sheffield 7.5.61. Ht 6 0 Wt 13 05
Goalkeeper. From Apprentice.

1978–79	Sheffield Wed	4	—
1979–80		15	—
1980–81		3	—
1981–82	Huddersfield T	14	—
1982–83		45	—
1983–84		23	—
1984–85		37	—
1985–86		37	—
1986–87		37	—
1987–88		20	—
1988–89	Mansfield T	39	—
1989–90		15	—

COX, Neil

Born Scunthorpe 8.10.71. Ht 5 11
Wt 12 10
Midfield. From Trainee.

1989–90	Scunthorpe U	—	—

COYLE, Tony

Born Glasgow 17.1.60. Ht 5 10 Wt 11 12
Forward. From Avoco Amats.

1977–78	Albion R	1	—
1978–79		30	1
1979–80		15	4
1979–80	Stockport Co	14	—
1980–81		34	1
1981–82		36	7
1982–83		34	5
1983–84		38	5
1984–85		38	6
1985–86		25	4
1986–87	Chesterfield	38	2
1987–88		38	2
1988–89	Stockport Co	23	3
1989–90	Exeter C	1	—

COYNE, Peter

Born Hartlepool 13.11.58. Ht 5 9
Wt 10 07
Forward. From Apprentice. England Schools.

1975–76	Manchester U	2	1
1976–77		—	—
From Ashton U			
1977–78	Crewe Alex	41	16
1978–79		36	16
1979–80		25	2
1980–81		32	13
From Hyde U			
1984–85	Swindon T	45	15
1985–86		31	10
1986–87		28	5
1987–88		5	—
1988–89		1	—
1989–90		—	—
1989–90	Aldershot	3	—

COYNE, Tommy

Born Glasgow 14.11.62. Ht 6 0 Wt 10 07
Forward. From Hillwood BC.

1981–82	Clydebank	31	9
1982–83		38	18

Season	Club	League Appearances/Goals	
1983–84		11	10
1983–84	Dundee U	18	3
1984–85		21	3
1985–86		13	2
1986–87	Dundee	20	9
1987–88		43	33
1988–89		26	9
1988–89	Celtic	7	—
1989–90		23	7

CRABBE, Scott

Born Edinburgh 12.8.68. Ht 5 7
Wt 10 00
Midfield. From Tynecastle BC. Scotland Under-21.

Season	Club	League Appearances/Goals	
1986–87	Hearts	5	—
1987–88		5	—
1988–89		1	—
1989–90		35	12

CRAIB, Mark

Born St Andrews 8.2.70. Ht 5 10
Wt 11 02
Defender. From Celtic BC.

Season	Club	League Appearances/Goals	
1987–88	Dundee	—	—
1988–89		4	—
1989–90		22	1

CRAIG, Albert

Born Glasgow 3.1.62. Ht 5 8 Wt 11 03
Midfield. From Yoker Ath.

Season	Club	League Appearances/Goals	
1981–82	Dumbarton	13	2
1982–83		32	7
1983–84		26	4
1984–85		35	4
1985–86		32	6
1986–87	Hamilton A	16	5
1986–87	Newcastle U	6	—
1987–88		3	—
1987–88	*Hamilton A*	6	1
1988–89	Newcastle U	1	—
1988–89	Northampton T	2	1
1988–89	Dundee	6	2
1989–90		20	2

CRANSON, Ian

Born Easington 2.7.64. Ht 5 11
Wt 11 07
Defender. From Apprentice. England Under-21.

Season	Club	League Appearances/Goals	
1982–83	Ipswich T	—	—
1983–84		8	—
1984–85		20	1
1985–86		42	1
1986–87		32	2
1987–88		29	1
1987–88	Sheffield W	4	—
1988–89		26	—
1989–90	Stoke C	17	2

CRAWSHAW, Gary

Born Reading 4.2.71. Ht 5 8 Wt 10 08
Forward. From Trainee.

Season	Club	League Appearances/Goals	
1989–90	Luton T	—	—

CREANEY, Gerard

Born Coatbridge 13.4.70. Ht 5 10
Wt 10 07
Forward. From Celtic BC.

Season	Club	League Appearances/Goals	
1987–88	Celtic	—	—
1988–89		—	—
1989–90		6	1

CRICHTON, Paul

Born Pontefract 3.10.68. Ht 6 1
Wt 12 05
Goalkeeper. From Apprentice.

Season	Club	League Appearances/Goals	
1986–87	Nottingham F	—	—
1986–87	*Notts Co*	5	—
1986–87	*Darlington*	5	—
1986–87	*Peterborough U*	4	—
1987–88	Nottingham F	—	—
1987–88	*Darlington*	3	—
1987–88	*Swindon T*	4	—
1987–88	*Rotherham U*	6	—
1988–89	Nottingham F	—	—
1988–89	*Torquay U*	13	—

Season	Club	League Appearances/Goals	
1988–89	Peterborough U	31	—
1989–90	....	16	—

CROFT, Brian

Born Chester 27.9.67. Ht 5 9 Wt 11 06
Midfield.

Season	Club	League Appearances/Goals	
1984–85	Chester C................	—	—
1985–86	....	1	—
1986–87	....	21	1
1987–88	....	37	2
1988–89	Cambridge U............	17	2
1989–90	Chester C................	44	3

CROMBIE, Dean

Born Lincoln 9.8.57. Ht 6 0 Wt 11 12
Defender. From Ruston Sports.

Season	Club	League Appearances/Goals	
1976–77	Lincoln C................	13	—
1977–78	....	20	—
1978–79	Grimsby T	46	1
1979–80	....	39	—
1980–81	....	33	—
1981–82	....	38	—
1982–83	....	32	1
1983–84	....	40	—
1984–85	....	39	—
1985–86	....	34	1
1986–87	....	19	—
1986–87	*Reading*....................	4	—
1987–88	Bolton W................	24	—
1988–89	....	31	—
1989–90	....	38	1

CROMPTON, Jonathan

Born Orrell 25.1.70. Ht 5 9 Wt 10 07
Forward.

Season	Club	League Appearances/Goals	
1988–89	Crewe Alex	—	—
1989–90	....	1	—

CROOK, Ian

Born Romford 18.1.63. Ht 5 8 Wt 10 06
Midfield. From Apprentice.

Season	Club	League Appearances/Goals	
1980–81	Tottenham H...........	—	—
1981–82	....	4	—
1982–83	....	4	—
1983–84	....	3	—
1984–85	....	5	1
1985–86	....	4	—
1986–87	Norwich C	33	5
1987–88	....	23	1
1988–89	....	26	1
1989–90	....	35	—

CROOKS, Garth

Born Stoke 10.3.58. Ht 5 8 Wt 12 01
Forward. From Apprentice. England
Under-21.

Season	Club	League Appearances/Goals	
1975–76	Stoke C	2	—
1976–77	....	23	6
1977–78	....	42	18
1978–79	....	40	12
1979–80	....	40	12
1980–81	Tottenham H...........	40	16
1981–82	....	27	13
1982–83	....	26	8
1983–84	....	10	1
1983–84	*Manchester U*...........	7	2
1984–85	Tottenham H...........	22	10
1985–86	WBA	19	5
1986–87	....	21	11
1986–87	Charlton Ath	7	2
1987–88	....	28	10
1988–89	....	14	2
1989–90	....	—	—

CROSBY, Gary

Born Sleaford 8.5.64. Ht 5 7 Wt 9 11
Midfield. From Lincoln U.

Season	Club	League Appearances/Goals	
1986–87	Lincoln C................	7	—
From Grantham			
1987–88	Nottingham F	14	1
1988–89	....	13	—
1989–90	....	34	5

CROSBY, Phil

Born Leeds 9.11.62. Ht 5 9 Wt 11 04
Defender. From Apprentice. England
Youth.

Season	Club	League Appearances/Goals	
1979–80	Grimsby T	4	—
1980–81		10	—
1981–82		15	1
1982–83		10	—
1983–84	Rotherham U	39	—
1984–85		33	—
1985–86		12	—
1986–87		34	—
1987–88		28	—
1988–89		37	2
1989–90	Peterborough U	42	—

CROSS, Nicky

Born Birmingham 7.2.61. Ht 5 9
Wt 11 12
Forward. From Apprentice.

Season	Club	Apps	Goals
1978–79	WBA	—	—
1979–80		—	—
1980–81		2	1
1981–82		22	2
1982–83		32	4
1983–84		25	3
1984–85		24	5
1985–86	Walsall	44	21
1986–87		39	16
1987–88		26	8
1987–88	Leicester C	17	6
1988–89		41	9
1989–90	Port Vale	42	13

CROSS, Paul

Born Barnsley 31.10.65. Ht 5 7 Wt 9 06
Midfield. From Apprentice.

Season	Club	Apps	Goals
1983–84	Barnsley	—	—
1984–85		1	—
1985–86		20	—
1986–87		18	—
1987–88		38	—
1988–89		—	—
1989–90		36	—

CROSS, Steve

Born Wolverhampton 22.12.59. Ht 5 10
Wt 11 05
Defender. From Apprentice.

Season	Club	Apps	Goals
1976–77	Shrewsbury T	5	—
1977–78		1	—
1978–79		19	2
1979–80		19	—
1980–81		35	2
1981–82		34	3
1982–83		33	5
1983–84		41	9
1984–85		40	5
1985–86		35	8
1986–87	Derby Co	6	—
1987–88		15	3
1988–89		19	—
1989–90		8	—

CROSSLEY, Mark

Born Barnsley 16.6.69. Ht 6 0 Wt 13 09
Goalkeeper. England Under-21.

Season	Club	Apps	Goals
1987–88	Nottingham F	—	—
1988–89		2	—
1989–90		8	—
1989–90	*Manchester U*	—	—

CROSSLEY, Richard

Born Huddersfield 5.9.70
Defender. From Huddersfield T Trainee.

Season	Club	Apps	Goals
1989–90	York C	1	—

CROWN, David

Born Enfield 16.2.58. Ht 5 10 Wt 12 01
Forward. From Walthamstow Ave.

Season	Club	Apps	Goals
1980–81	Brentford	38	6
1981–82		8	2
1981–82	Portsmouth	27	2
1982–83		1	—
1982–83	*Exeter C*	7	3
1983–84	Reading	45	7
1984–85		43	8
1985–86	Cambridge U	43	24
1986–87		46	12
1987–88		17	9
1987–88	Southend U	28	17

Season	Club	League Appearances/Goals	
1988–89		44	25
1989–90		41	19

CRUMPLIN, John

Born Bath 26.5.67. Ht 5 8 Wt 11 10
Midfield. From Bognor Regis.

1986–87	Brighton	5	—
1987–88		26	2
1988–89		12	—
1989–90		25	2

CULLEN, Tony

Born Newcastle 30.9.69 Ht 5 6 Wt 11 07
Forward. Local.

1988–89	Sunderland	7	—
1989–90		16	—
1989–90	*Carlisle U*	2	1

CULPIN, Paul

Born Kirby Muxloe 8.2.62. Ht 5 10
Wt 10 08
Forward.

1981–82	Leicester C	—	—
From Nuneaton			
1985–86	Coventry C	7	1
1986–87		2	1
1987–88		—	—
1987–88	Northampton T	20	10
1988–89		39	13
1989–90		4	—
1989–90	Peterborough U	12	2

CULVERHOUSE, Ian

Born Bishop's Stortford 22.9.64. Ht 5 10
Wt 11 02
Defender. From Apprentice. England Youth.

1982–83	Tottenham H	—	—
1983–84		2	—
1984–85		—	—
1985–86		—	—
1985–86	Norwich C	30	—
1986–87		25	—
1987–88		33	—
1988–89		38	—
1989–90		32	—

CUMMING, Bob

Born Airdrie 7.12.55. Ht 5 10 Wt 10 05
Midfield. From Baillieston Jnrs.

1973–74	Grimsby T	—	—
1974–75		5	—
1975–76		32	2
1976–77		41	—
1977–78		27	3
1978–79		34	9
1979–80		40	14
1980–81		32	11
1981–82		24	2
1982–83		33	7
1983–84		30	1
1984–85		20	5
1985–86		24	2
1986–87		23	1
1987–88	Lincoln C	33	7
1988–89		29	5
1989–90		12	—

CUNDY, Jason

Born Wimbledon 12.11.69 Ht 6 1
Wt 13 07
Defender. From Trainee.

1988–89	Chelsea	—	—
1989–90		—	—

CUNNINGHAM, Ken

Born Dublin 28.6.71
Defender.

1989–90	Millwall	5	—

CUNNINGHAM, Tony

Born Jamaica 12.11.57. Ht 6 1 Wt 13 02
Forward. From Stourbridge.

1979–80	Lincoln C	38	12
1980–81		34	6
1981–82		46	11
1982–83		5	3
1982–83	Barnsley	29	7
1983–84		13	4

Season	Club	League Appearances/Goals	
1983–84	Sheffield W	28	5
1984–85	Manchester C	18	1
1984–85	Newcastle U	13	1
1985–86		17	1
1986–87		17	2
1987–88	Blackpool	40	10
1988–89		31	7
1989–90	Bury	25	8

CUNNINGTON, Shaun

Born Bourne 4.1.66. Ht 5 9 Wt 11 00
Defender. From Bourne T.

Season	Club	League Appearances/Goals	
1982–83	Wrexham	4	—
1983–84		42	—
1984–85		41	6
1985–86		42	2
1986–87		46	1
1987–88		24	3
1987–88	Grimsby T	15	2
1988–89		44	1
1989–90		44	3

CURBISHLEY, Alan

Born Forest Gate 8.11.57. Ht 5 10
Wt 11 07
Midfield. From Apprentice.
England Schools, Youth, Under-21.

Season	Club	League Appearances/Goals	
1974–75	West Ham U	2	—
1975–76		14	2
1976–77		10	1
1977–78		32	1
1978–79		27	1
1979–80	Birmingham C	42	3
1980–81		29	6
1981–82		29	1
1982–83		30	1
1982–83	Aston Villa	7	—
1983–84		26	1
1984–85		3	—
1984–85	Charlton Ath	23	2
1985–86		30	4
1986–87		10	—
1987–88	Brighton	34	6
1988–89		37	6
1989–90		45	1

CURLE, Keith

Born Bristol 14.11.63. Ht 6 0 Wt 12 07
Defender. From Apprentice.

Season	Club	League Appearances/Goals	
1981–82	Bristol R	20	2
1982–83		12	2
1983–84	Bristol R	—	—
1983–84	Torquay U	16	5
1983–84	Bristol C	6	—
1984–85		40	—
1985–86		44	1
1986–87		28	—
1987–88		3	—
1987–88	Reading	30	—
1988–89		10	—
1988–89	Wimbledon	18	—
1989–90		38	2

CURRAN, Chris

Born Birmingham 17.9.71
Defender. From Trainee.

Season	Club	League Appearances/Goals	
1989–90	Torquay U	1	—

CURRAN, Chris

Born Manchester 6.1.71
Defender. From Trainee.

Season	Club	League Appearances/Goals	
1989–90	Crewe Alex	1	—

CURRAN, Henry

Born Glasgow 9.10.66. Ht 5 8 Wt 11 04
Midfield. From Eastercraigs.

Season	Club	League Appearances/Goals	
1984–85	Dumbarton	2	—
1985–86		6	—
1986–87		8	—
1986–87	Dundee U	3	—
1987–88		6	—
1988–89		6	—
1989–90	St Johnstone	31	3

CURRIE, David

Born Stockton 27.11.62. Ht 5 11
Wt 12 09
Forward. Local.

Season	Club	League Appearances/Goals	
1981–82	Middlesbrough	1	—
1982–83		8	—
1983–84		39	15
1984–85		39	12
1985–86		26	4
1986–87	Darlington	45	12
1987–88		31	21
1987–88	Barnsley	15	7
1988–89		41	16
1989–90		24	7
1989–90	Nottingham F	8	1

CURRY, Sean

Born Liverpool 13.11.66. Ht 5 8
Wt 10 10
Forward. From Apprentice.

Season	Club	League Appearances/Goals	
1984–85	Liverpool	—	—
1985–86		—	—
1986–87		—	—
1986–87	Blackburn R	11	2
1987–88		20	4
1988–89		7	—
1989–90	Hartlepool U	1	—
1989–90	Preston NE	—	—

CURTIS, Alan

Born Rhondda 16.4.54. Ht 5 10
Wt 12 04
Forward. From Amateur. Wales Under-21, Under-23, 35 full caps.

Season	Club	League Appearances/Goals	
1972–73	Swansea C	13	—
1973–74		38	4
1974–75		37	—
1975–76		41	9
1976–77		46	14
1977–78		39	32
1978–79		34	13
1979–80	Leeds U	22	4
1980–81		6	1
1980–81	Swansea C	20	6
1981–82		40	10
1982–83		21	4
1983–84		9	1
1983–84	Southampton	9	—
1984–85		30	4
1985–86		11	1
1985–86	*Stoke C*	3	—
1986–87	Cardiff C	42	4
1987–88		40	2
1988–89		35	4
1989–90		8	—
1989–90	Swansea C	26	3

CUSACK, Dave

Born Thurscroft 6.6.56. Ht 6 1 Wt 13 11
Defender. From Apprentice.

Season	Club	League Appearances/Goals	
1975–76	Sheffield W	37	—
1976–77		27	—
1977–78		31	1
1978–79		—	—
1978–79	Southend U	37	1
1979–80		36	1
1980–81		42	6
1981–82		43	5
1982–83		28	4
1982–83	Millwall	14	1
1983–84		39	—
1984–85		45	8
1985–86	Doncaster R	43	2
1986–87		40	1
1987–88		17	1
1987–88	Rotherham U	18	—
From Boston U			
1989–90	Doncaster R	1	—

CUSACK, Nicky

Born Rotherham 24.12.65. Ht 6 0
Wt 11 13
Forward. From Alvechurch.

Season	Club	League Appearances/Goals	
1987–88	Leicester C	16	1
1988–89	Peterborough U	44	10
1989–90	Motherwell	31	11

CUTLER, Chris

Born Manchester 7.4.64. Ht 5 11
Wt 11 09
Forward. From Amateur.

Season	Club	League Appearances/Goals	
1981–82	Bury	2	—
1982–83		5	—
1983–84		12	2
1984–85		4	1
1985–86	Crewe Alex	28	6
1986–87		35	5

Season	Club	Apps	Goals
1987–88	....	36	6
1988–89	....	3	2
1989–90	....	38	5

CYGAN, Paul

Born Doncaster 4.3.72
Midfield. From Trainee.

Season	Club	Apps	Goals
1989–90	Doncaster R............	1	—

DAISH, Liam

Born Portsmouth 23.9.68 Ht 6 2
Wt 13 05
Defender. From Apprentice. Eire Under-21.

Season	Club	Apps	Goals
1986–87	Portsmouth	1	—
1987–88	....	—	—
1988–89	Cambridge U...........	28	—
1989–90	....	42	1

DALE, Carl

Born Colwyn Bay 29.4.66. Ht 6 0
Wt 12 00
Forward. From Bangor C.

Season	Club	Apps	Goals
1987–88	Chester C................	—	—
1988–89	....	41	22
1989–90	....	31	9

DALEY, Peter

Born Liverpool 14.2.70
Midfield. From Liverpool Trainee.

Season	Club	Apps	Goals
1989–90	Southend U.............	5	1

DALEY, Philip

Born Walton 12.4.67
Forward. From Newton.

Season	Club	Apps	Goals
1989–90	Wigan Ath	33	6

DALEY, Tony

Born Birmingham 18.10.67. Ht 5 7
Wt 10 11
Forward. From Apprentice. England Youth.

Season	Club	Apps	Goals
1984–85	Aston Villa..............	5	—
1985–86	....	23	2
1986–87	....	33	3
1987–88	....	14	3
1988–89	....	29	5
1989–90	....	32	6

DALGLISH, Kenny

Born Glasgow 4.3.51. Ht 5 8 Wt 11 13
Forward. From Cumbernauld U. Scotland Youth, Under-23, 102 full caps.

Season	Club	League Appearances/Goals	
1969–70	Celtic	2	—
1970–71		3	—
1971–72		31	17
1972–73		32	23
1973–74		33	18
1974–75		33	16
1975–76		35	24
1976–77		35	14
1977–78	Liverpool	42	20
1978–79		42	21
1979–80		42	16
1980–81		34	8
1981–82		42	13
1982–83		42	18
1983–84		33	7
1984–85		36	6
1985–86		21	3
1986–87		18	6
1987–88		2	—
1988–89		—	—
1989–90		1	—

DALTON, Paul

Born Middlesbrough 25.4.67 Ht 5 11
Wt 12 00
Midfield. From Brandon.

Season	Club	Apps	Goals
1987–88	Manchester U	—	—
1988–89		—	—
1988–89	Hartlepool U	17	2
1989–90		45	11

DALY, Gerry

Born Dublin 30.4.54. Ht 5 9 Wt 11 02
Midfield. From Bohemians. Eire Under-21, 46 full caps.

Season	Club	Apps	Goals
1972–73	Manchester U	—	—
1973–74		16	1
1974–75		37	11
1975–76		41	7
1976–77		17	4
1976–77	Derby C	17	7
1977–78		37	10
1978–79		37	13
1979–80		21	1
1980–81	Coventry C	35	8
1981–82		19	4
1982–83		2	—
1982–83	*Leicester C*	17	1
1983–84	Coventry C	28	7
1984–85	Birmingham C	30	1
1985–86		2	—
1985–86	Shrewsbury T	27	4
1986–87		28	4
1986–87	Stoke C	1	—
1987–88		21	1
1988–89	Doncaster R	39	4
1989–90		—	—

DALZIEL, Ian

Born South Shields 24.10.62. Ht 5 8
Wt 11 10
Defender. From Apprentice.

Season	Club	Apps	Goals
1979–80	Derby Co	—	—
1980–81		—	—
1981–82		4	—
1982–83		18	4
1983–84	Hereford U	30	4
1984–85		26	—
1985–86		41	3
1986–87		28	—
1987–88		25	1
1988–89	Carlisle U	42	1
1989–90		24	1

DAMERELL, Mark

Born Plymouth 31.7.65. Ht 5 9 Wt 11 00
Forward. From St. Blazey.

Season	Club	Apps	Goals
1989–90	Plymouth Arg	1	—

DANIEL, Ray

Born Luton 10.12.64. Ht 5 8 Wt 11 09
Midfield. From Apprentice.

Season	Club	Apps	Goals
1982–83	Luton T	3	—
1983–84		7	2
1983–84	*Gillingham*	5	—
1984–85	Luton T	7	1
1985–86		5	1
1986–87	Hull C	9	—
1987–88		26	2

Season	Club	League Appearances/Goals	
1988–89		23	1
1989–90	Cardiff C	43	1

DANIELS, Scott

Born Benfleet 22.11.69 Ht 6 1 Wt 11 09
Midfield. From Trainee.

Season	Club		
1987–88	Colchester U	1	—
1988–89		26	—
1989–90		46	—

DANZEY, Michael

Born Widnes 8.2.71. Ht 6 1 Wt 12 12
Forward. From Trainee

Season	Club		
1988–89	Nottingham F	—	—
1989–90		—	—
1989–90	*Chester C*	2	—

DARBY, Lee

Born Salford 20.9.69. Ht 6 0 Wt 11 06
Midfield.

Season	Club		
1986–87	Portsmouth	—	—
1987–88		1	—
1988–89		—	—
1989–90		—	—

DARBY, Julian

Born Bolton 3.10.67. Ht 6 0 Wt 11 04
Defender. England Schools.

Season	Club		
1984–85	Bolton W	—	—
1985–86		2	—
1986–87		28	—
1987–88		35	2
1988–89		44	5
1989–90		46	10

D'AURIA, David

Born Swansea 26.3.70 Ht 5 8 Wt 11 00
Midfield. From Trainee.

Season	Club		
1987–88	Swansea C	4	—
1988–89		14	2
1989–90		7	—

DAVENPORT, Peter

Born Birkenhead 24.3.61. Ht 5 10
Wt 11 06
Forward. From Everton Amateur, Cammell Laird. England B, 1 full cap.

Season	Club		
1981–82	Nottingham F	5	4
1982–83		18	6
1983–84		33	15
1984–85		35	16
1985–86		27	13
1985–86	Manchester U	11	1
1986–87		39	14
1987–88		34	5
1988–89		8	2
1988–89	Middlesbrough	24	4
1989–90		35	3

DAVEY, Simon

Born Swansea 1.10.70
Forward. From Trainee.

Season	Club		
1986–87	Swansea C	1	—
1987–88		4	—
1988–89		3	—
1989–90		18	2

DAVIDSON, Jonathan

Born Cheadle 1.3.70 Ht 5 8 Wt 11 11
Defender. From Trainee.

Season	Club		
1988–89	Derby Co	—	—
1989–90		6	—

DAVIES, Alan

Born Manchester 5.12.61. Ht 5 8
Wt 11 4
Midfield. From Apprentice. Wales Under-21, 11 full caps.

Season	Club		
1981–82	Manchester U	1	—
1982–83		3	—
1983–84		3	—
1984–85		—	—
1985–86	Newcastle U	14	1
1985–86	*Charlton Ath*	1	—

Season	Club	League Appearances/Goals	
1986–87	Newcastle U	7	—
1986–87	*Carlisle U*	4	1
1987–88	Swansea C	42	3
1988–89		42	5
1989–90	Bradford C	26	1

DAVIES, Andy

Born Wolverhampton 6.6.72
Defender. From Trainee.

Season	Club	Apps	Goals
1988–89	Torquay U	3	—
1989–90		10	—

DAVIES, Billy

Born Glasgow 31.5.64. Ht 5 5 Wt 9 08
Midfield. From Pollok U BC.

Season	Club	Apps	Goals
1980–81	Rangers	—	—
1981–82		4	—
1982–83		4	—
1983–84		3	1
1984–85		—	—
1985–86		—	—
From Elfsborg			
1987–88	St Mirren	18	—
1988–89		27	4
1989–90		29	1

DAVIES, Gordon

Born Merthyr 3.8.55. Ht 5 9 Wt 11 05
Forward. From Merthyr T. Wales 18 full caps.

Season	Club	Apps	Goals
1977–78	Fulham	5	1
1978–79		32	9
1979–80		39	15
1980–81		45	18
1981–82		41	24
1982–83		38	19
1983–84		36	22
1984–85		11	5
1984–85	Chelsea	12	6
1985–86		1	—
1985–86	Manchester C	26	9
1986–87		5	—
1986–87	Fulham	21	6
1987–88		39	13
1988–89		34	14
1989–90		23	6

DAVIES, Kenneth

Born Stockton 22.12.70. Ht 6 0
Wt 11 00
Midfield. From Trainee.

Season	Club	Apps	Goals
1989–90	Hartlepool U	3	—

DAVIES, Michael

Born Stretford 19.1.66. Ht 5 8 Wt 10 07
Midfield. From Apprentice.

Season	Club	Apps	Goals
1983–84	Blackpool	3	—
1984–85		17	—
1985–86		36	5
1986–87		42	6
1987–88		38	—
1988–89		30	2
1989–90		23	—

DAVIES, Roy

Born Cardiff 19.8.71. Ht 5 6 Wt 9 06
Defender. From Trainee.

Season	Club	Apps	Goals
1989–90	Chelsea	—	—

DAVIS, Darren

Born Sutton-in-Ashfield 5.2.67. Ht 6 0
Wt 11 00
Defender. From Apprentice. England Youth.

Season	Club	Apps	Goals
1983–84	Notts Co	1	—
1984–85		4	—
1985–86		22	1
1986–87		45	—
1987–88		20	—
1988–89	Lincoln C	38	2
1989–90		34	—

DAVIS, Paul

Born London 9.12.61. Ht 5 10 Wt 10 10
Midfield. From Apprentice. England Under-21.

Season	Club	Apps	Goals
1979–80	Arsenal	2	—
1980–81		10	1

Season	Club	Apps	Goals
1981–82		38	4
1982–83		41	4
1983–84		35	1
1984–85		24	1
1985–86		29	4
1986–87		39	4
1987–88		29	5
1988–89		12	1
1989–90		11	1

DAVIS, Steve

Born Birmingham 26.7.65. Ht 6 0
Wt 12 07
Defender. From Stoke C. Apprentice.
England Youth.

Season	Club	Apps	Goals
1983–84	Crewe Alex	24	—
1984–85		40	—
1985–86		45	1
1986–87		33	—
1987–88		3	—
1987–88	Burnley	33	5
1988–89		37	—
1989–90		31	1

DAVIS, Steve

Born Hexham 30.10.68. Ht 6 2 Wt 12 08
Defender. From Trainee.

Season	Club	Apps	Goals
1987–88	Southampton	—	—
1988–89		—	—
1989–90		4	—
1989–90	*Burnley*	9	—

DAVISON, Aidan

Born Sedgefield 11.5.68. Ht 6 1
Wt 13 02
Goalkeeper. From Billingham Syn.

Season	Club	Apps	Goals
1987–88	Notts Co	—	—
1988–89		1	—
1989–90		—	—
1989–90	*Leyton Orient*	—	—
1989–90	Bury	—	—
1989–90	*Chester C*	—	—

DAVISON, Bobby

Born S. Shields 17.7.59. Ht 5 8 Wt 11 08
Forward. From Seaham C.W.

Season Club League Appearances/Goals

Season	Club	Apps	Goals
1980–81	Huddersfield T	2	—
1981–82	Halifax T	46	20
1982–83		17	9
1982–83	Derby Co	26	8
1983–84		40	14
1984–85		46	24
1985–86		41	17
1986–87		40	19
1987–88		13	1
1987–88	Leeds U	16	5
1988–89		39	14
1989–90		29	11

D'AVRAY, Mich

Born Johannesburg 19.2.62. Ht 6 2
Wt 12 11
Forward. From Apprentice. England
Under-21.

Season	Club	Apps	Goals
1979–80	Ipswich T	2	—
1980–81		5	1
1981–82		13	2
1982–83		17	2
1983–84		23	6
1984–85		33	6
1985–86		26	5
1986–87		19	4
1986–87	*Leicester C*	3	—
1987–88	Ipswich T	29	7
1988–89		32	3
1989–90		12	1

DAWES, Ian

Born Croydon 22.2.63. Ht 5 8 Wt 10 02
Defender. From Apprentice.
England Schools.

Season	Club	Apps	Goals
1980–81	QPR	—	—
1981–82		5	—
1982–83		42	—
1983–84		42	2
1984–85		42	—
1985–86		42	1
1986–87		23	—
1987–88		33	—

Season	Club	League Appearances/Goals	
1988–89	Millwall	30	1
1989–90		38	4

DAWS, Tony

Born Sheffield 10.9.66. Ht 5 9 Wt 10 12
Forward. From Apprentice. England Youth.

Season	Club	Apps	Goals
1984–85	Notts Co	7	1
1985–86		1	—
1986–87	Sheffield U	11	3
1987–88	Scunthorpe U	10	3
1988–89		46	24
1989–90		33	11

DAWSON, Ally

Born Glasgow 25.2.58. Ht 5 10 Wt 12 00
Defender. From school. Scotland Youth, Under-21, 5 full caps.

Season	Club	Apps	Goals
1975–76	Rangers	3	—
1976–77		1	—
1977–78		2	—
1978–79		23	1
1979–80		32	—
1980–81		22	2
1981–82		25	1
1982–83		25	—
1983–84		28	—
1984–85		26	1
1985–86		24	1
1986–87		7	—
1987–88	Blackburn R	22	—
1988–89		6	—
1989–90		12	—

DAWSON, Jason

Born Burslem 9.2.71
Forward. From Stoke C Schoolboy, Port Vale Trainee.

Season	Club	Apps	Goals
1989–90	Port Vale	—	—
1989–90	Rochdale	27	2

DAWSON, Robert

Born Stirling 1.8.63 Ht 5 9 Wt 10 10
Defender. From Fallin Violet.

Season	Club	Apps	Goals
1981–82	Stirling A	18	—
1982–83		36	—
1983–84		33	2
1984–85		34	—
1985–86		39	—
1986–87		39	—
1987–88	St Mirren	24	—
1988–89		9	—
1989–90		1	—

DAY, Keith

Born Grays 29.11.62. Ht 6 1 Wt 11 00
Defender. From Aveley.

Season	Club	Apps	Goals
1984–85	Colchester U	45	4
1985–86		30	5
1986–87		38	3
1987–88	Orient	41	3
1988–89		45	2
1989–90		39	1

DAY, Mervyn

Born Chelmsford 26.6.55. Ht 6 2
Wt 15 01
Goalkeeper. From Apprentice.
England Youth, Under-23.

Season	Club	Apps	Goals
1972–73	West Ham U	—	—
1973–74		33	—
1974–75		42	—
1975–76		41	—
1976–77		42	—
1977–78		23	—
1978–79		13	—
1979–80	Orient	42	—
1980–81		40	—
1981–82		42	—
1982–83		46	—
1983–84	Aston Villa	14	—
1984–85		16	—
1984–85	Leeds U	18	—
1985–86		40	—
1986–87		34	—
1987–88		44	—
1988–89		45	—
1989–90		44	—

DEAKIN, John

Born Wortley 29.9.66
Midfield. From Barnsley Apprentice.

Season	Club	League Appearances/Goals	
1985–86	Doncaster R	14	—
1986–87		9	—
1987–88	Grimsby T	—	—
From Shepshed C			
1989–90	Birmingham C	7	—

DEAKIN, Ray

Born Liverpool 19.6.59. Ht 5 8 Wt 12 04
Defender. From Apprentice.

Season	Club	League Appearances/Goals	
1977–78	Everton	—	—
1978–79		—	—
1979–80		—	—
1980–81		—	—
1981–82	Port Vale	23	6
1982–83	Bolton W	30	1
1983–84		41	1
1984–85		34	—
1985–86	Burnley	46	3
1986–87		46	—
1987–88		37	3
1988–89		14	—
1989–90		33	—

DEANE, Brian

Born Leeds 7.2.68. Ht 6 3 Wt 12 07
Forward. From Apprentice.

Season	Club	League Appearances/Goals	
1985–86	Doncaster R	3	—
1986–87		20	2
1987–88		43	10
1988–89	Sheffield U	43	22
1989–90		45	21

DEARDEN, Kevin

Born Luton 8.3.70
Goalkeeper. From Trainee.

Season	Club	League Appearances/Goals	
1988–89	Tottenham H	—	—
1988–89	*Cambridge U*	15	—
1989–90	Tottenham H	—	—
1989–90	*Hartlepool U*	10	—
1989–90	*Oxford U*	—	—
1989–90	*Swindon T*	1	—

DEARY, John

Born Ormskirk 18.10.62. Ht 5 10
Wt 12 04
Midfield. From Apprentice.

Season	Club	League Appearances/Goals	
1979–80	Blackpool	—	—
1980–81		10	—
1981–82		27	—
1982–83		45	6
1983–84		31	6
1984–85		32	13
1985–86		40	7
1986–87		44	3
1987–88		37	3
1988–89		37	5
1989–90	Burnley	41	2

DEEHAN, John

Born Solihull 6.8.57. Ht 6 0 Wt 11 03
Forward. From Apprentice. England Youth, Under-21.

Season	Club	League Appearances/Goals	
1974–75	Aston Villa	—	—
1975–76		15	7
1976–77		27	13
1977–78		36	12
1978–79		26	10
1979–80		6	—
1979–80	WBA	28	3
1980–81		15	2
1981–82		4	—
1981–82	Norwich C	22	10
1982–83		40	20
1983–84		34	15
1984–85		40	13
1985–86		26	4
1986–87	Ipswich T	29	10
1987–88		20	1
1988–89	Manchester C	—	—
1989–90		—	—
1989–90	Barnsley	—	—

DE MANGE, Ken

Born Dublin 3.9.64. Ht 5 10 Wt 11 12
Midfield. From Home Farm. Eire Youth, B.

Season	Club	League Appearances/Goals	
1983–84	Liverpool	—	—
1984–85		—	—
1985–86		—	—
1986–87		—	—
1986–87	*Scunthorpe U*	3	2
1987–88	Liverpool	—	—
1987–88	Leeds U	15	1

Season	Club	League Appearances/Goals	
1987–88	Hull C	9	1
1988–89		32	1
1989–90		21	—

DEMPSEY, Mark

Born Manchester 14.1.64. Ht 5 8
Wt 9 12
Midfield. From Apprentice.

Season	Club	League Appearances/Goals	
1981–82	Manchester U	—	—
1982–83		—	—
1983–84		—	—
1984–85		—	—
1984–85	*Swindon T*	5	—
1985–86	Manchester U	1	—
1986–87	Sheffield U	30	5
1987–88		33	4
1988–89		—	—
1988–89	*Chesterfield*	3	—
1988–89	Rotherham U	27	1
1989–90		22	3

DENNIS, Mark

Born Streatham 2.5.61. Ht 5 9 Wt 11 02
Defender. From Apprentice. England Youth, Under-21.

Season	Club	League Appearances/Goals	
1978–79	Birmingham C	31	—
1979–80		40	—
1980–81		19	—
1981–82		17	—
1982–83		23	1
1983–84		—	—
1983–84	Southampton	20	—
1984–85		31	—
1985–86		24	—
1986–87		20	2
1986–87	QPR	—	—
1987–88		11	—
1988–89		17	—
1989–90	Crystal Palace	8	—

DENNIS, Tony

Born Eton 1.12.63 Ht 5 7 Wt 10 02
Midfield. From Slough.

Season	Club	League Appearances/Goals	
1988–89	Cambridge U	18	3
1989–90		17	2

DENNISON, Robert

Born Banbridge 30.4.63. Ht 5 7
Wt 11 00
Forward. From Glenavon. Northern Ireland 7 full caps.

Season	Club	League Appearances/Goals	
1985–86	WBA	12	1
1986–87		4	—
1986–87	Wolverhampton W	10	3
1987–88		43	3
1988–89		43	8
1989–90		46	8

DEVEREUX, Jim

Born Aldershot 20.2.70 Ht 6 4 Wt 13 00
Defender. From Trainee.

Season	Club	League Appearances/Goals	
1988–89	Aldershot	1	—
1989–90		1	—

DEVEREUX, Robert

Born Ipswich 13.1.71. Ht 5 8 Wt 10 09
Midfield. From Ipswich T. Trainee

Season	Club	League Appearances/Goals	
1989–90	Colchester U	2	—

DEVINE, Steve

Born Strabane 11.12.64. Ht 5 9
Wt 11 00
Midfield. From Apprentice. Northern Ireland Youth.

Season	Club	League Appearances/Goals	
1982–83	Wolverhampton W	—	—
1983–84	Derby Co	10	—
1984–85		1	—
1985–86	Stockport Co	2	—
1985–86	Hereford U	11	1
1986–87		41	1
1987–88		43	—
1988–89		41	—
1989–90		34	1

DEVONSHIRE, Alan

Born London 13.4.56. Ht 5 11 Wt 11 07
Midfield. From Southall & Ealing Bor. England B, 8 full caps.

Season	Club	League Appearances	Goals
1976–77	West Ham U	28	—
1977–78		34	3
1978–79		41	5
1979–80		34	5
1980–81		39	6
1981–82		35	1
1982–83		39	3
1983–84		22	1
1984–85		—	—
1985–86		38	3
1986–87		20	2
1987–88		1	—
1988–89		20	—
1989–90		7	—

DIAMOND, Tony

Born Rochdale 23.8.68. Ht 5 10 Wt 10 04
Forward. From Apprentice. Northern Ireland Youth.

Season	Club	League Appearances	Goals
1986–87	Blackburn R	8	2
1987–88		7	—
1988–89		11	1
1988–89	*Wigan Ath*	6	2
1989–90	Blackburn R	—	—
1989–90	Blackpool	3	1

DIBBLE, Andy

Born Cwmbran 8.5.65. Ht 6 2 Wt 13 07
Goalkeeper. From Apprentice. Wales Schools, Youth, Under-21, 3 full caps.

Season	Club	League Appearances	Goals
1981–82	Cardiff C	1	—
1982–83		20	—
1983–84		41	—
1984–85	Luton T	13	—
1985–86		7	—
1985–86	*Sunderland*	12	—
1986–87	Luton T	1	—
1986–87	*Huddersfield T*	5	—
1987–88	Luton T	9	—
1988–89	Manchester C	38	—
1989–90		31	—

DICK, Alistair

Born Stirling 25.4.65. Ht 5 9 Wt 10 07
Forward. From Apprentice. Scotland Schools, Youth.

Season	Club	League Appearances	Goals
1981–82	Tottenham H	1	—
1982–83		2	—
1983–84		11	2
1984–85		2	—
1985–86		1	—
To Ajax			
1989–90	Brighton	—	—

DICKENS, Alan

Born Plaistow 3.9.64. Ht 5 11 Wt 12 05
Midfield. From Apprentice. England Youth, Under-21.

Season	Club	League Appearances	Goals
1982–83	West Ham U	15	6
1983–84		10	—
1984–85		25	2
1985–86		41	4
1986–87		36	3
1987–88		28	3
1988–89		37	5
1989–90	Chelsea	22	1

DICKENSON, Kevin

Born London 24.11.62. Ht 5 6 Wt 10 06
Defender. From Tottenham H Apprentice.

Season	Club	League Appearances	Goals
1979–80	Charlton Ath	1	—
1980–81		—	—
1981–82		7	—
1982–83		12	—
1983–84		42	1
1984–85		13	—
1985–86	Orient	46	1
1986–87		39	—
1987–88		22	1
1988–89		39	1
1989–90		31	—

DICKINS, Matt

Born Sheffield 3.9.70. Ht 6 4 Wt 14 00
Goalkeeper. From Trainee.

Season	Club	League Appearances/Goals	
1989–90	Sheffield U	—	—
1989–90	*Leyton Orient*	—	—

DICKINSON, Martin

Born Leeds 14.3.63. Ht 5 10 Wt 11 00
Defender. From Apprentice.

Season	Club	League Appearances/Goals	
1979–80	Leeds U	6	—
1980–81		1	—
1981–82		—	—
1982–83		31	—
1983–84		34	—
1984–85		12	1
1985–86		19	1
1985–86	WBA	7	—
1986–87		27	1
1987–88		16	1
1988–89	Sheffield U	1	—
1989–90		—	—

DICKS, Julian

Born Bristol 8.8.68. Ht 5 7 Wt 11 07
Defender. From Apprentice. England Under-21.

Season	Club	League Appearances/Goals	
1985–86	Birmingham C	23	—
1986–87		34	—
1987–88		32	1
1987–88	West Ham U	8	—
1988–89		34	2
1989–90		40	9

DIGBY, Fraser

Born Sheffield 23.4.67. Ht 6 1 Wt 12 12
Goalkeeper. From Apprentice. England Youth, Under-21.

Season	Club	League Appearances/Goals	
1984–85	Manchester U	—	—
1985–86		—	—
1985–86	*Oldham Ath*	—	—
1985–86	*Swindon T*	—	—
1986–87	Manchester U	—	—
1986–87	Swindon T	39	—
1987–88		31	—
1988–89		46	—
1989–90		45	—

DIGWEED, Perry

Born London 26.10.59. Ht 6 0 Wt 11 04
Goalkeeper. From Apprentice.

Season	Club	League Appearances/Goals	
1976–77	Fulham	1	—
1977–78		—	—
1978–79		2	—
1979–80		11	—
1980–81		1	—
1980–81	Brighton	15	—
1981–82		12	—
1982–83		15	—
1983–84		4	—
1983–84	*WBA*	—	—
1984–85	Brighton	—	—
1984–85	*Charlton Ath*	—	—
1985–86	Brighton	33	—
1986–87		22	—
1987–88	*Newcastle U*	—	—
1987–88	*Chelsea*	3	—
1988–89	Brighton	1	—
1989–90		11	—

DILLON, Kevin

Born Sunderland 18.12.59. Ht 6 0
Wt 12 07
Midfield. From Apprentice. England Youth, Under-21.

Season	Club	League Appearances/Goals	
1977–78	Birmingham C	17	1
1978–79		36	2
1979–80		31	6
1980–81		39	2
1981–82		36	1
1982–83		27	3
1982–83	Portsmouth	11	5
1983–84		36	9
1984–85		37	9
1985–86		31	5
1986–87		39	8
1987–88		32	9

Season	Club	Apps	Goals
1988–89	....	29	—
1989–90	Newcastle U	43	—

DINEEN, Jack

Born Brighton 23.9.70.
Midfield.

Season	Club	Apps	Goals
1987–88	Brighton	—	—
1988–89	....	—	—
1989–90	....	—	—

DINNIE, Alan

Born Glasgow 14.5.63. Ht 5 10
Wt 11 00
Defender. From Baillieston Jun.

Season	Club	Apps	Goals
1987–88	Partick T.................	37	1
1988–89	....	31	1
1989–90	....	14	2
1989–90	Dundee	22	—

DISLEY, Martin

Born Ormskirk 24.6.71.
Midfield.

Season	Club	Apps	Goals
1989–90	Crewe Alex	1	—

DIXON, Andy

Born Louth 19.4.68. Ht 6 1 Wt 10 11
Defender. From Apprentice.

Season	Club	Apps	Goals
1986–87	Grimsby T	1	—
1987–88	....	32	—
1988–89	....	5	—
1989–90	Southend U	24	—

DIXON, Kerry

Born Luton 24.7.61. Ht 6 0 Wt 13 00
Forward. From Tottenham H Apprentice and Dunstable. England Under-21, 8 full caps.

Season	Club	Apps	Goals
1980–81	Reading..................	39	13
1981–82	....	42	12
1982–83	....	35	26
1983–84	Chelsea	42	28
1984–85	....	41	24
1985–86	....	38	14
1986–87	....	36	10

Season Club League Appearances/Goals

Season	Club	Apps	Goals
1987–88	....	33	11
1988–89	....	39	25
1989–90	....	38	20

DIXON, Kevin

Born Blackhill 27.7.60. Ht 5 10
Wt 10 06
Forward. From Annfield Plain & Tow Law T.

Season	Club	Apps	Goals
1983–84	Carlisle U	9	—
1983–84	*Hartlepool U*	6	3
1984–85	Hartlepool U	42	12
1985–86	....	22	5
1985–86	*Scunthorpe U*...........	14	2
1986–87	Hartlepool U	43	9
1987–88	Scunthorpe U	41	4
1988–89	Hartlepool U	14	4
1988–89	York C....................	19	4
1989–90	....	19	4
1989–90	*Scarborough*	3	—

DIXON, Lee

Born Manchester 17.3.64. Ht 5 9
Wt 11 03
Defender. Local. England B, 1 full cap.

Season	Club	Apps	Goals
1982–83	Burnley	3	—
1983–84	....	1	—
1983–84	Chester	16	1
1984–85	....	41	—
1985–86	Bury	45	5
1986–87	Stoke C	42	3
1987–88	....	29	2
1987–88	Arsenal	6	—
1988–89	....	33	1
1989–90	....	38	5

DOBBIN, Jim

Born Dunfermline 17.9.61. Ht 5 10
Wt 10 06
Midfield. From Whitburn BC. Scotland Youth.

Season	Club	Apps	Goals
1980–81	Celtic	—	—
1981–82	....	—	—
1982–83	....	—	—
1983–84	....	2	—
1983–84	*Motherwell*	2	—

Season	Club	League Appearances/Goals	
1983–84	Doncaster R	11	2
1984–85		17	1
1985–86		31	6
1986–87		5	4
1986–87	Barnsley	30	4
1987–88		16	2
1988–89		41	5
1989–90		28	1

DOBBINS, Wayne

Born Bromsgrove 30.8.68. Ht 5 7
Wt 10 08
Midfield. From Apprentice.

Season	Club	Apps	Goals
1986–87	WBA	6	—
1987–88		10	—
1988–89		16	—
1989–90		5	—

DOBBS, Gerald

Born London 24.1.71. Ht 5 8 Wt 11 07
Defender. From Trainee.

Season	Club	Apps	Goals
1989–90	Wimbledon	—	—

DOBSON, Paul

Born Hartlepool 17.12.62. Ht 5 11
Wt 10 02
Forward. From Newcastle U Amateur.

Season	Club	Apps	Goals
1981–82	Hartlepool U	5	—
1982–83		26	8
From Horden			
1983–84		27	12
1984–85		38	10
1985–86		15	2
1986–87	Torquay U	39	16
1987–88		38	22
1988–89	Doncaster R	24	10
1988–89	Scarborough	18	5
1989–90		37	15

DOBSON, Tony

Born Coventry 5.2.69. Ht 6 1 Wt 12 10
Defender. From Apprentice. England Under-21.

Season	Club	Apps	Goals
1986–87	Coventry C	1	—
1987–88		1	—
1988–89		16	—
1989–90		30	—

DOCKER, Ian

Born Gravesend 12.9.69. Ht 5 8
Wt 11 02
Defender. From Trainee.

Season	Club	Apps	Goals
1987–88	Gillingham	1	—
1988–89		35	—
1989–90		20	—

DODD, Jason

Born Bath 2.11.70. Ht 5 10 Wt 11 10
Defender.

Season	Club	Apps	Goals
1988–89	Southampton	—	—
1989–90		22	—

DODDS, Billy

Born New Cumnock 5.2.69 Ht 5 7
Wt 10 00
Forward. From Apprentice.

Season	Club	Apps	Goals
1986–87	Chelsea	1	—
1987–88		—	—
1987–88	*Partick Th*	30	9
1988–89	Chelsea	2	—
1989–90	Dundee	30	13

DODDS, Davie

Born Dundee 23.9.58. Ht 5 11 Wt 11 05
Forward. 'S' Form. Scotland Schools, Youth, Under-21, 2 full caps.

Season	Club	Apps	Goals
1975–76	Dundee U	—	—
1976–77		—	—
1977–78		1	—
1977–78	*Arbroath*	6	1
1977–78	Dundee U	9	1
1978–79		27	10
1979–80		21	6
1980–81		24	14
1981–82		35	14
1982–83		36	22
1983–84		33	15
1984–85		26	8
1985–86		31	12
From Neuchatel			

Season	Club	League Appearances/Goals	
1986–87	Aberdeen	26	4
1987–88		23	9
1988–89		23	4
1989–90		1	—
1989–90	Rangers	14	4

DOIG, Russell

Born Millport 17.1.64. Ht 5 8 Wt 10 09
Forward. From St Mirren. Scottish Schools.

Season	Club	League Appearances/Goals	
1983–84	E. Stirling	38	3
1984–85		35	1
1985–86		36	5
1986–87	Leeds U	4	—
1986–87	*Peterborough U*	7	—
1987–88	Leeds U	—	—
1987–88	Hartlepool U	9	—
1988–89		19	1
1989–90		5	—

DOLAN, Eamonn

Born Dagenham 20.9.67. Ht 5 10 Wt 12 01
Forward. From Apprentice. Eire Youth, Under 21.

Season	Club	League Appearances/Goals	
1984–85	West Ham U	—	—
1985–86		—	—
1986–87		1	—
1987–88		4	—
1988–89		—	—
1988–89	*Bristol C*	3	—
1989–90	West Ham U	10	3

DOLAN, Jim

Born Salsburgh 22.2.69. Ht 5 10 Wt 10 07
Forward. From Motherwell BC.

Season	Club	League Appearances/Goals	
1987–88	Motherwell	—	—
1988–89		5	—
1989–90		12	—

DOLAN, Paul

Born Ottawa 16.4.66. Ht 6 4 Wt 13 05
Goalkeeper. From Vancouver W. Canada full caps.

Season	Club	League Appearances/Goals	
1986–87	Notts Co	—	—
1987–88		—	—
1988–89		—	—
1989–90		—	—

DONACHIE, Willie

Born Glasgow 5.10.51 Ht 5 9 Wt 11 05
Defender. From Juniors.
Scotland Under-23, 35 full caps.

Season	Club	League Appearances/Goals	
1968–69	Manchester C	—	—
1969–70		3	—
1970–71		11	—
1971–72		37	—
1972–73		40	1
1973–74		42	—
1974–75		40	1
1975–76		40	—
1976–77		42	—
1977–78		39	—
1978–79		38	—
1979–80		19	—
From Portland Timbers			
1981–82	Norwich C	11	—
From Portland Timbers			
1982–83	Burnley	23	—
1983–84		37	3
1984–85	Oldham Ath	39	—
1985–86		33	—
1986–87		33	—
1987–88		31	3
1988–89		9	—
1989–90		7	—

DONAGHY, Mal

Born Belfast 13.9.57. Ht 5 11 Wt 12 02
Defender. From Larne.
Northern Ireland Under-21, 64 full caps.

Season	Club	League Appearances/Goals	
1978–79	Luton T	40	—
1979–80		42	1
1980–81		42	—
1981–82		42	9
1982–83		40	3
1983–84		40	1
1984–85		42	1
1985–86		42	—
1986–87		42	—
1987–88		32	1

Season	Club	League Appearances/Goals	
1988–89		6	—
1988–89	Manchester U	30	—
1989–90		14	—
1989–90	*Luton T*	5	—

DONALD, Stephen

Born Paisley 24.6.70 Ht 5 10 Wt 11 02
Midfield. From Trainee.

Season	Club	League Appearances/Goals	
1989–90	Huddersfield T	—	—

DONALD, Warren

Born Hillingdon 7.10.64. Ht 5 6
Wt 10 03
Midfield. From Apprentice.
England Schools.

Season	Club	League Appearances/Goals	
1982–83	West Ham U	—	—
1983–84		2	—
1984–85		—	—
1984–85	*Northampton T*	11	2
1985–86	West Ham U	—	—
1985–86	Northampton T	32	3
1986–87		41	3
1987–88		40	2
1988–89		37	1
1989–90		27	2

DONEGAL, Glenville

Born 20.6.69. Ht 6 2 Wt 12 08
Forward. From Trainee.

Season	Club	League Appearances/Goals	
1987–88	Northampton T	10	1
1988–89		9	2
1989–90		1	—

DONNELLAN, Leo

Born Brent 19.1.65. Ht 5 10 Wt 11 08
Midfield. From Apprentice.

Season	Club	League Appearances/Goals	
1982–83	Chelsea	—	—
1983–84		—	—
1984–85		—	—
1984–85	*Orient*	6	—
1985–86	Fulham	23	—
1986–87		30	4
1987–88		11	—

Season	Club	League Appearances/Goals	
1988–89		4	—
1989–90		11	—

DONNELLY, Paul

Born Liverpool 23.12.71
Defender. From Trainee.

Season	Club	League Appearances/Goals	
1988–89	Halifax T	1	—
1989–90		1	—

DONOVAN, Kevin

Born Halifax 17.12.71. Ht 5 7 Wt 10 10
Forward. From Trainee.

Season	Club	League Appearances/Goals	
1989–90	Huddersfield T	1	—

DONOWA, Lou

Born Ipswich 24.9.64 Ht 5 9 Wt 11 00
Forward. From Apprentice. England Under-21.

Season	Club	League Appearances/Goals	
1982–83	Norwich C	1	—
1983–84		25	4
1984–85		34	7
1985–86		2	—
1985–86	*Stoke C*	4	1
From Coruna, Willem II Tilburg			
1989–90	Ipswich T	23	1

DOONER, Gary

Born St Helens 14.9.70
Midfield. From Trainee.

Season	Club	League Appearances/Goals	
1988–89	Stockport Co	1	—
1989–90		—	—

DORIGO, Tony

Born Australia 31.12.65. Ht 5 10
Wt 10 09
Defender. From Apprentice. England B, Under-21, 4 full caps.

Season	Club	League Appearances/Goals	
1983–84	Aston Villa	1	—
1984–85		31	—
1985–86		38	1
1986–87		41	—
1987–88	Chelsea	40	—

Season	Club	League Appearances/Goals	
1988–89		40	6
1989–90		35	3

DORNAN, Andy

Born Aberdeen 19.8.61. Ht 5 9
Wt 11 03
Defender. From King St. Scotland Schools, Youth.

Season	Club	League Appearances/Goals	
1978–79	Aberdeen	—	—
1979–80		—	—
1980–81		2	—
1981–82		—	—
1982–83	Motherwell	19	—
1983–84		26	2
1984–85		21	1
1985–86		26	—
1986–87	Walsall	43	—
1987–88		31	—
1988–89		26	—
1989–90		18	1

DOUGLAS, Colin

Born Hurlford 9.9.62. Ht 6 1 Wt 11 07
Forward. From Celtic.

Season	Club	League Appearances/Goals	
1981–82	Doncaster R	42	3
1982–83		38	7
1983–84		44	15
1984–85		46	10
1985–86		42	13
1986–87	Rotherham U	43	3
1987–88		40	1
1988–89	Doncaster R	46	2
1989–90		45	2

DOWIE, Iain

Born Hatfield 9.1.65 Ht 6 1 Wt 12 12
Forward. From Hendon. Northern Ireland 2 full caps.

Season	Club	League Appearances/Goals	
1988–89	Luton T	8	—
1989–90		29	9
1989–90	*Fulham*	5	1

DOWNES, Chris

Born Sheffield 17.1.69. Ht 5 10 Wt 10 08
From Trainee.

Season	Club	League Appearances/Goals	
1987–88	Sheffield U	—	—
1987–88	*Scarborough*	2	—
1988–89	Sheffield U	2	—
1989–90	Stockport Co	11	1

DOWNING, Keith

Born Oldbury 23.7.65. Ht 5 8 Wt 11 00
Midfield. From Mile Oak R.

Season	Club	League Appearances/Goals	
1984–85	Notts Co	12	—
1985–86		3	—
1986–87		8	1
1987–88	Wolverhampton W	34	1
1988–89		32	1
1989–90		31	3

DOWNS, Greg

Born Carlton 13.12.58. Ht 5 9 Wt 10 07
Defender. From Apprentice.

Season	Club	League Appearances/Goals	
1976–77	Norwich C	—	—
1977–78		1	—
1977–78	*Torquay U*	1	1
1978–79	Norwich C	3	—
1979–80		18	—
1980–81		29	2
1981–82		28	1
1982–83		28	—
1983–84		42	4
1984–85		20	—
1985–86	Coventry C	41	—
1986–87		39	2
1987–88		27	2
1988–89		22	—
1989–90		17	—

DOWSON, Alan

Born Gateshead 17.6.70
Defender. From Trainee.

Season	Club	League Appearances/Goals	
1988–89	Millwall	—	—
1989–90		—	—
1989–90	*Fulham*	4	—

DOYLE, Maurice

Born Ellesmere Port 17.10.69 Ht 5 8
Wt 10 07
Forward. From Trainee.

Season	Club	Apps	Goals
1987–88	Crewe Alex	4	—
1988–89		4	2
1989–90	QPR	—	—

DOYLE, Steve

Born Neath 2.6.58. Ht 5 9 Wt 11 01
Midfield. From Apprentice.
Wales Under-21.

Season	Club	Apps	Goals
1974–75	Preston NE	13	—
1975–76		24	1
1976–77		22	—
1977–78		32	1
1978–79		29	2
1979–80		14	—
1980–81		27	1
1981–82		36	3
1982–83	Huddersfield T	42	2
1983–84		36	2
1984–85		36	2
1985–86		42	—
1986–87		5	—
1986–87	Sunderland	33	—
1987–88		32	1
1988–89		35	1
1989–90	Hull C	36	2

DOZZELL, Jason

Born Ipswich 9.12.67 Ht 6 2 Wt 12 04
Forward. From school. England Youth, Under-21.

Season	Club	Apps	Goals
1983–84	Ipswich T	5	1
1984–85		14	2
1985–86		41	3
1986–87		42	2
1987–88		39	1
1988–89		29	11
1989–90		46	8

DRAPER, Mark

Born Derby 11.11.70 Ht 5 10 Wt 11 04
Midfield. From Trainee.

Season	Club	Apps	Goals
1988–89	Notts Co	20	3
1989–90		34	3

DREYER, John

Born Alnwick 11.6.63 Ht 6 0 Wt 11 06
Defender. From Wallingford T

Season	Club	Apps	Goals
1984–85	Oxford U	—	—
1985–86		—	—
1985–86	*Torquay U*	5	—
1985–86	*Fulham*	12	2
1986–87	Oxford U	25	2
1987–88		35	—
1988–89	Luton T	18	1
1989–90		38	2

DRINKELL, Kevin

Born Grimsby 18.6.60. Ht 5 11 Wt 12 06
Forward. From Apprentice.

Season	Club	Apps	Goals
1976–77	Grimsby T	4	2
1977–78		26	5
1978–79		28	7
1979–80		33	16
1980–81		41	7
1981–82		28	6
1982–83		39	17
1983–84		36	15
1984–85		35	14
1985–86	Norwich C	41	22
1986–87		42	16
1987–88		38	12
1988–89	Rangers	32	12
1989–90		4	—
1989–90		22	5

DRISCOLL, Andy

Born Staines 21.10.71
Midfield. From West Ham schoolboy, Brentford trainee.

Season	Club	Apps	Goals
1988–89	Brentford	1	—
1989–90		12	2

DRYDEN, Richard

Born Stroud 14.6.69. Ht 6 0 Wt 11 02
Defender.

Season	Club	Apps	Goals
1986–87	Bristol R	6	—

Season	Club	League Appearances/Goals	
1987–88		6	—
1988–89		1	—
1988–89	Exeter C	21	—
1989–90		30	7

DRYSDALE, Jason

Born Bristol 17.11.70. Ht 5 10 Wt 10 07
Defender. From Trainee.

Season	Club	League Appearances/Goals	
1988–89	Watford	—	—
1989–90		20	—

DUBLIN, Dion

Born Leicester 22.4.69. Ht 6 0 Wt 12 04
Forward.

Season	Club	League Appearances/Goals	
1987–88	Norwich C	—	—
1988–89	Cambridge U	21	6
1989–90		46	15

DUBLIN, Keith

Born Wycombe 29.1.66. Ht 5 11
Wt 12 07
Defender. From Apprentice. England Youth.

Season	Club	League Appearances/Goals	
1983–84	Chelsea	1	—
1984–85		11	—
1985–86		11	—
1986–87		28	—
1987–88	Brighton	46	5
1988–89		43	—
1989–90		43	—

DUFFIELD, Peter

Born Middlesbrough 4.2.69. Ht 5 6
Wt 10 07
Forward.

Season	Club	League Appearances/Goals	
1986–87	Middlesbrough	—	—
1987–88	Sheffield U	11	1
1987–88	*Halifax T*	12	6
1988–89	Sheffield U	38	11
1989–90		5	2

DUFFY, Darrell

Born Birmingham 18.1.71 Ht 5 11
Wt 11 00
Defender. From Trainee. FA Schools, England Youth.

Season	Club	League Appearances/Goals	
1988–89	Aston Villa	1	—
1989–90		—	—

DUFFY, Jim

Born Glasgow 27.4.59 Ht 5 10 Wt 11 04
Defender. From Maryhill Jun.

Season	Club	League Appearances/Goals	
1978–79	Celtic	—	—
1979–80		—	—
1980–81		—	—
1981–82	Morton	20	—
1982–83		27	—
1983–84		38	2
1984–85		34	1
1985–86	Dundee	36	—
1986–87		42	2
1987–88		5	—
1988–89	Falkirk manager		
1989–90	Dundee	8	—

DUGGAN, Andy

Born Bradford 19.9.67. Ht 6 3 Wt 13 00
Defender.

Season	Club	League Appearances/Goals	
1984–85	Barnsley	—	—
1985–86		—	—
1986–87		2	1
1987–88		—	—
1987–88	*Rochdale*	3	—
1988–89	Barnsley	—	—
1988–89	Huddersfield T	14	2
1989–90		15	1

DUNBAR, Ian

Born Newcastle 6.6.71
Forward.

Season	Club	League Appearances/Goals	
1989–90	Hartlepool U	1	—

DUNKLEY, Malcolm

Born Wolverhampton 12.7.61 Ht 6 5
Wt 14 00
Forward. From Bromsgrove R.

Season	Club	League Appearances/Goals	
1988–89	Lincoln C	11	4
1989–90		—	—

DUNN, Iain

Born Derwent 1.4.72. Ht 5 10 Wt 11 07
Forward. From school.

Season	Club	Apps	Goals
1988–89	York C	26	6
1989–90		18	2

DUNPHY, Sean

Born Rotherham 5.11.70 Ht 6 3
Wt 13 05
Defender. From Trainee.

Season	Club	Apps	Goals
1989–90	Barnsley	6	—

DURIE, Gordon

Born Paisley 6.12.65. Ht 6 0 Wt 11 06
Forward. From Hill of Beath Hawthorn. Scotland B, Under-21, 7 full caps.

Season	Club	Apps	Goals
1981–82	East Fife	13	1
1982–83		25	2
1983–84		34	16
1984–85		9	7
1984–85	Hibernian	22	8
1985–86		25	6
1985–86	Chelsea	1	—
1986–87		25	5
1987–88		26	12
1988–89		32	17
1989–90		15	5

DURNIN, John

Born Bootle 18.8.65. Ht 5 10 Wt 11 04
Forward. From Waterloo Dock.

Season	Club	Apps	Goals
1985–86	Liverpool	—	—
1986–87		—	—
1987–88		—	—
1988–89		—	—
1988–89	*WBA*	5	2
1988–89	Oxford U	19	3
1989–90		42	13

DURRANT, Iain

Born Glasgow 29.10.66. Ht 5 8 Wt 9 07
Midfield. From Glasgow United. Scotland Youth, Under-21, 5 full caps.

Season	Club	Apps	Goals
1984–85	Rangers	5	—
1985–86		30	2
1986–87		39	4
1987–88		40	10
1988–89		8	2
1989–90		—	—

DUXBURY, Lee

Born Skipton 7.10.69 Ht 5 10 Wt 11 07
Midfield. From Trainee.

Season	Club	Apps	Goals
1988–89	Bradford C	1	—
1989–90		12	1
1989–90	*Rochdale*	10	—

DUXBURY, Mike

Born Accrington 1.9.59. Ht 5 9
Wt 11 02
Defender. From Apprentice.
England Under-21, 10 full caps.

Season	Club	Apps	Goals
1976–77	Manchester U	—	—
1977–78		—	—
1978–79		—	—
1979–80		—	—
1980–81		33	2
1981–82		24	—
1982–83		42	1
1983–84		39	—
1984–85		30	1
1985–86		23	1
1986–87		32	1
1987–88		39	—
1988–89		18	—
1989–90		19	—

DYCHE, Sean

Born Kettering 28.6.71 Ht 6 0 Wt 11 07
Midfield. From Trainee.

Season	Club	Apps	Goals
1988–89	Nottingham F	—	—

Season	Club	App	Goals
1989–90		—	—
1989–90	Chesterfield	22	2

DYER, Alex

Born West Ham 14.11.65. Ht 5 11
Wt 12 04
Midfield. From Watford Apprentice.

Season	Club	App	Goals
1983–84	Blackpool	9	—
1984–85		36	8
1985–86		39	8
1986–87		24	3
1986–87	Hull C	17	4
1987–88		28	8
1988–89		15	2
1988–89	Crystal Palace	7	2
1989–90		10	—

DYSON, Paul

Born Birmingham 27.12.59. Ht 6 2
Wt 13 07
Defender. From Apprentice.
England Under-21.

Season	Club	App	Goals
1977–78	Coventry C	—	—
1978–79		2	—
1979–80		18	2
1980–81		41	2
1981–82		40	—
1982–83		39	1
1983–84	Stoke C	38	2
1984–85		37	3
1985–86		31	—
1985–86	WBA	11	—
1986–87		42	2
1987–88		8	2
1988–89		3	1
1988–89	Darlington	12	3
1989–90	Crewe Alex	31	2

DZIEKANOWSKI, Dariusz

Born Warsaw 30.9.62 Ht 6 1 Wt 12 13
Forward. From Legia Warsaw. Poland full caps.

Season	Club	App	Goals
1989–90	Celtic	33	8

EARLE, Robbie

Born Newcastle, Staffs. 27.1.65. Ht 5 9
Wt 10 10
Forward. From Stoke C.

Season	Club	App	Goals
1981–82	Port Vale	—	—
1982–83		8	1
1983–84		12	—
1984–85		46	15
1985–86		46	15
1986–87		35	6
1987–88		25	4
1988–89		44	13
1989–90		43	12

EASTER, Graham

Born Epsom 26.9.69 Ht 5 7 Wt 10 07
Midfield. From Trainee.

Season	Club	App	Goals
1988–89	WBA	—	—
1988–89	Huddersfield T	—	—
1989–90	Crewe Alex	3	—

EATON, Jason

Born Bristol 29.1.69 Ht 5 10 Wt 11 04
Forward. From Trowbridge.

Season	Club	App	Goals
1987–88	Bristol R	3	—
1988–89	Bristol C	2	—
1989–90		11	1

EBBRELL, John

Born Bromborough 1.10.69. Ht 5 7
Wt 9 12
Midfield. FA Schools, England Youth, Under-21.

Season	Club	App	Goals
1986–87	Everton	—	—
1987–88		—	—
1988–89		4	—
1989–90		17	—

ECKHARDT, Jeff

Born Sheffield 7.10.65. Ht 6 0 Wt 11 07
Defender.

Season	Club	App	Goals
1984–85	Sheffield U	7	—
1985–86		33	2
1986–87		22	—

Season	Club	Apps	Goals
1987–88		12	—
1987–88	Fulham	29	1
1988–89		43	2
1989–90		40	2

EDINBURGH, Justin

Born Brentwood 18.12.69 Ht 5 9
Wt 11 06
Defender. From Trainee.

Season	Club	Apps	Goals
1988–89	Southend U	15	—
1989–90		22	—
1989–90	*Tottenham H*	—	—

EDMONDS, Darren

Born Watford 12.4.71. Ht 5 9 Wt 11 06
Midfield. From Trainee.

Season	Club	Apps	Goals
1989–90	Leeds U	—	—

EDMONDS, Neil

Born Accrington 18.10.68. Ht 5 8
Wt 10 08
Defender. From Trainee.

Season	Club	Apps	Goals
1986–87	Oldham Ath	1	—
1987–88		4	—
1988–89	Rochdale	39	8
1989–90		4	—

EDWARDS, Alistair

Born Whyalia 21.6.68.
Forward. From Sydney Olympic.

Season	Club	Apps	Goals
1989–90	Brighton	1	—

EDWARDS, Andy

Born Epping 17.9.71
Midfield. From Trainee.

Season	Club	Apps	Goals
1988–89	Southend U	1	—
1989–90		8	—

EDWARDS, Dean

Born Wolverhampton 25.2.62. Ht 5 10
Wt 10 07
Forward. From Apprentice.

Season	Club	Apps	Goals
1979–80	Shrewsbury	4	—
1980–81		6	1
1981–82		3	—

From Palloseura and Telford U

Season	Club	Apps	Goals
1985–86	Wolverhampton W	23	7
1986–87		8	2
1986–87	Exeter C	11	5
1987–88		43	12
1988–89	Torquay U	40	8
1989–90		30	3

EDWARDS, Keith

Born Stockton 16.7.57. Ht 5 11
Wt 11 07
Forward.

Season	Club	Apps	Goals
1975–76	Sheffield U	3	—
1976–77		31	18
1977–78		36	11
1978–79	Hull C	46	24
1979–80		41	19
1980–81		40	13
1981–82		5	1
1981–82	Sheffield U	41	35
1982–83		42	13
1983–84		44	33
1984–85		29	13
1985–86		35	20
1986–87	Leeds U	30	6
1987–88		8	—
1987–88	Aberdeen	9	2
1987–88	Hull C	9	3
1988–89		44	26
1989–90		2	—
1989–90	Stockport Co	27	10
1989–90	*Huddersfield T*	10	4

EDWARDS, Neil

Born Aberdare 5.12.70. Ht 5 8 Wt 11 02
Goalkeeper. From Trainee.

Season	Club	Apps	Goals
1988–89	Leeds U	—	—
1989–90		—	—

EDWARDS, Paul R

Born Birkenhead 25.12.63. Ht 5 11
Wt 11 00
Defender. From Altrincham.

Season	Club	Apps	Goals
1987–88	Crewe Alex	13	1
1988–89		45	4

Season Club League Appearances/Goals

Season	Club	Apps	Goals
1989–90		28	1
1989–90	Coventry C	8	—

EDWARDS, Paul

Born Liverpool 22.2.65 Ht 5 11
Wt 11 05
Goalkeeper. From St. Helens T.

Season	Club	Apps	Goals
1988–89	Crewe Alex	10	—
1989–90		8	—

EDWARDS, Robert

Born Manchester 23.2.70 Ht 5 8
Wt 11 07
Forward. From Trainee.

Season	Club	Apps	Goals
1987–88	Crewe Alex	6	1
1988–89		4	—
1989–90		4	—

EDWARDS, Robert

Born Kendal 1.7.73.
Defender.

Season	Club	Apps	Goals
1989–90	Carlisle U	12	—

EELES, Tony

Born Chatham 15.11.70 Ht 5 7 Wt 9 12
Midfield. From Trainee.

Season	Club	Apps	Goals
1988–89	Gillingham	3	—
1989–90		33	2

ELEY, Kevin

Born Mexborough 4.3.68. Ht 5 6
Wt 9 07
Midfield. From school.

Season	Club	Apps	Goals
1983–84	Rotherham U	1	—
1984–85		6	—
1985–86		5	—
1986–87		1	—
1987–88	Chesterfield	36	2
1988–89		40	—
1989–90		5	—

ELI, Roger

Born Bradford 11.9.65. Ht 5 11
Wt 11 03
Defender. From Apprentice.

Season	Club	Apps	Goals
1983–84	Leeds U	—	—
1984–85		1	—
1985–86		1	—
1985–86	Wolverhampton W	14	—
1986–87		4	—
1987–88	Cambridge U	—	—
1987–88	Crewe Alex	27	1
1988–89	York C	4	1
1988–89	Bury	2	—
1989–90	Burnley	29	—

ELKINS, Gary

Born Wallingford 4.5.66. Ht 5 09
Wt 11 12
Midfield. From Apprentice. England Youth.

Season	Club	Apps	Goals
1983–84	Fulham	—	—
1984–85		21	—
1985–86		13	—
1986–87		9	—
1987–88		29	—
1988–89		22	1
1989–90		10	1
1989–90	*Exeter C*	5	—

ELLIOTT, Matthew

Born Surrey 1.11.68 Ht 6 3 Wt 13 06
Defender. From Epsom & Ewell.

Season	Club	Apps	Goals
1988–89	Charlton Ath	—	—
1988–89	Torquay U	13	2
1989–90		33	2

ELLIOTT, Paul

Born London 18.3.64. Ht 6 2 Wt 11 11
Defender. From Apprentice. England Youth, Under-21.

Season	Club	Apps	Goals
1980–81	Charlton Ath	—	—
1981–82		38	1
1982–83		25	—
1982–83	Luton T	13	1
1983–84		38	2
1984–85		9	1
1985–86		6	—
1985–86	Aston Villa	23	2

Season	Club	Apps	Goals
1986–87		34	5

From Bari.

Season	Club	Apps	Goals
1989–90	Celtic	27	—

ELLIOTT, Shaun

Born Haltwistle 26.1.57. Ht 6 0
Wt 11 10
Defender. From Apprentice. England B.

Season	Club	Apps	Goals
1974–75	Sunderland	—	—
1975–76		—	—
1976–77		19	1
1977–78		29	3
1978–79		41	1
1979–80		41	4
1980–81		38	—
1981–82		36	1
1982–83		20	—
1983–84		33	—
1984–85		32	—
1985–86		32	2
1986–87	Norwich C	15	2
1987–88		16	—
1988–89	Blackpool	41	—
1989–90		26	—

ELLIOTT, Steve

Born Haltwistle 15.9.58. Ht 5 11
Wt 12 00
Forward. From Apprentice.

Season	Club	Apps	Goals
1977–78	Nottingham F	—	—
1978–79		4	—
1978–79	Preston NE	7	—
1979–80		42	16
1980–81		35	9
1981–82		35	10
1982–83		45	19
1983–84		44	16
1984–85	Luton T	12	3
1984–85	Walsall	28	5
1985–86		41	16
1986–87	Bolton W	38	9
1987–88		19	2
1988–89		3	—
1988–89	Bury	31	11
1989–90		—	—
1989–90	Rochdale	22	6

ELLIOTT, Tony

Born Nuneaton 30.11.69. Ht 6 0
Wt 12 12
Goalkeeper. England Youth.

Season	Club	Apps	Goals
1986–87	Birmingham C	—	—
1987–88		—	—
1988–89		—	—
1988–89	Hereford U	23	—
1989–90		29	—

ELLIS, Mark

Born Bradford 6.1.62. Ht 5 9 Wt 10 12
Forward. Local.

Season	Club	Apps	Goals
1980–81	Bradford C	4	1
1981–82		18	—
1982–83		25	3
1983–84		37	8
1984–85		45	7
1985–86		25	3
1986–87		31	5
1987–88		22	2
1988–89		5	1
1989–90		6	—

ELLIS, Tony

Born Salford 20.10.64. Ht 5 11 Wt 11 00
Forward. From Horwich RMI, Northwich Vic.

Season	Club	Apps	Goals
1986–87	Oldham Ath	5	—
1987–88		—	—
1987–88	Preston NE	24	4
1988–89		45	19
1989–90		17	3
1989–90	Stoke C	24	6

ELSEY, Karl

Born Swansea 20.11.58. Ht 5 11
Wt 12 07
Midfield. From Pembroke Boro.

Season	Club	Apps	Goals
1978–79	QPR	3	—
1979–80		4	—
1980–81	Newport C	34	2

Season	Club	Apps	Goals
1981–82		40	7
1982–83		42	5
1983–84		7	1
1983–84	Cardiff C	29	1
1984–85		30	4
1985–86	Gillingham	46	5
1986–87		43	2
1987–88		39	6
1988–89	Reading	44	3
1989–90	Maidstone U	44	4

ELSTRUP, Lars

Born Roby, Denmark 24.3.63. Ht 5 11 Wt 11 11
Forward. From OB Odense. Denmark full caps.

Season	Club	Apps	Goals
1989–90	Luton T	23	4

EMERSON, Dean

Born Salford 27.12.62. Ht 5 10 Wt 11 07
Midfield. From Local.

Season	Club	Apps	Goals
1981–82	Stockport Co	23	1
1982–83		45	3
1983–84		44	1
1984–85		44	2
1985–86	Rotherham U	45	7
1986–87		10	1
1986–87	Coventry C	19	—
1987–88		20	—
1988–89		18	—
1989–90		12	—

ENDERSBY, Scott

Born Lewisham 20.2.62. Ht 5 10 Wt 13 00
Goalkeeper. From Kettering T and Ipswich T Apprentice. England Youth.

Season	Club	Apps	Goals
1978–79	Ipswich T	—	—
1979–80		—	—
1980–81		—	—
1981–82	Tranmere R	43	—
1982–83		36	—
1983–84	Swindon T	37	—
1984–85		46	—
1985–86		2	—
1985–86	Carlisle U	27	—
1986–87		25	—
1987–88	York C	34	—
1987–88	*Cardiff C*	4	—
1988–89	York C	1	—
1989–90		—	—

ENGLISH, Tom

Born Cirencester 18.10.61. Ht 5 9 Wt 11 06
Forward. From Apprentice. England Youth.

Season	Club	Apps	Goals
1979–80	Coventry C	30	10
1980–81		28	7
1981–82		8	—
1982–83		—	—
1983–84	Leicester C	28	3
1984–85		16	—
1985–86	Rochdale	3	1
1984–85	Plymouth Arg	4	1
1984–85	Colchester U	—	—
1985–86		23	8
1986–87		24	9

From Bishop's Stortford

Season	Club	Apps	Goals
1989–90	Colchester U	13	3

ENGLISH, Tony

Born Luton 10.10.66. Ht 6 0 Wt 12 04
Midfield. From Coventry C Apprentice. England Youth.

Season	Club	Apps	Goals
1984–85	Colchester U	22	3
1985–86		45	13
1986–87		32	7
1987–88		43	2
1988–89		36	8
1989–90		44	2

ENTWISTLE, Wayne

Born Bury 6.8.58. Ht 5 11 Wt 11 08
Forward. From Apprentice. England Youth.

Season	Club	Apps	Goals
1976–77	Bury	20	5
1977–78		11	2
1977–78	Sunderland	7	1
1978–79		36	11
1979–80		2	—
1979–80	Leeds U	11	2

Season	Club	League Appearances/Goals	
1980–81		—	—
1980–81	Blackpool	20	3
1981–82		12	3
1981–82	Crewe Alex	11	—
1982–83	Wimbledon	9	3
From Grays Ath			
1983–84	Bury	38	11
1984–85		45	21
1985–86	Carlisle U	9	2
1985–86	Bolton W	8	—
1986–87		—	—
1986–87	*Burnley*	8	2
1986–87	Stockport Co	24	5
1987–88		25	3
1988–89	Bury	2	—
1988–89	Wigan Ath	29	6
1989–90	Hartlepool U	2	—

ESHELBY, Paul

Born Sheffield 29.5.70.
Midfield.

Season	Club	League Appearances/Goals	
1989–90	Exeter C	1	—

EVANS, Allan

Born Dunfermline 12.10.56. Ht 6 1
Wt 12 13
Defender. From Dunfermline U. Scotland Youth, 4 full caps.

Season	Club	League Appearances/Goals	
1973–74	Dunfermline Ath	9	—
1974–75		26	—
1975–76		26	1
1976–77		37	13
1977–78	Aston Villa	9	1
1978–79		37	6
1979–80		35	8
1980–81		39	7
1981–82		38	2
1982–83		40	4
1983–84		36	7
1984–85		38	6
1985–86		35	3
1986–87		26	6
1987–88		20	1
1988–89		27	—
1989–90	Leicester C	14	—

EVANS, Ceri

Born Christchurch 2.10.63. Ht 6 1
Wt 14 02
Defender. From Otaga Univ, Worcester Coll. (Oxford). New Zealand full caps.

Season	Club	League Appearances/Goals	
1988–89	Oxford U	4	—
1989–90		24	2

EVANS, David

Born W. Bromwich 20.5.58. Ht 5 11
Wt 12 04
Defender. From Apprentice.

Season	Club	League Appearances/Goals	
1975–76	Aston Villa	—	—
1976–77		—	—
1977–78		—	—
1978–79		2	—
1979–80	Halifax T	45	3
1980–81		39	1
1981–82		46	2
1982–83		42	1
1983–84		46	2
1984–85	Bradford C	45	1
1985–86		35	—
1986–87		42	1
1987–88		43	1
1988–89		34	—
1989–90		24	—

EVANS, Gareth

Born Coventry 14.1.67 Ht 5 8 Wt 10 06
Forward. From Apprentice.

Season	Club	League Appearances/Goals	
1984–85	Coventry C	—	—
1985–86		6	—
1986–87		1	—
1986–87	Rotherham U	34	9
1987–88		29	4
1987–88	Hibernian	12	2
1988–89		35	5
1989–90		28	3

EVANS, Mark

Born Leeds 24.8.70 Ht 6 0 Wt 11 08
Goalkeeper. From Trainee.

Season	Club	League Appearances/Goals	
1988–89	Bradford C	3	—
1989–90		5	—

EVANS, Paul

Born Shrewsbury 16.3.72. Ht 5 7
Wt 11 01
Defender. From Trainee.

Season	Club	Apps	Goals
1989–90	Oxford U	—	—

EVANS, Stewart

Born Maltby 15.11.60 Ht 6 4 Wt 11 05
Forward.From Rotherham U Apprentice.

Season	Club	Apps	Goals
1978–79	Rotherham U	—	—
1979–80		—	—
From Gainsborough T			
1980–81	SheffieldU	—	—
1981–82	Wimbledon	18	4
1982–83		42	14
1983–84		45	12
1984–85		40	14
1985–86		30	6
1986–87	WBA	14	1
1986–87	Plymouth Arg	5	—
1987–88		37	10
1988–89		3	—
1988–89	Rotherham U	25	6
1989–90		20	4

EVANS, Terry

Born London 12.4.65. Ht 6 5 Wt 15 01
Defender. From Hillingdon B.

Season	Club	Apps	Goals
1985–86	Brentford	19	1
1986–87		1	—
1987–88		29	4
1988–89		45	5
1989–90		44	3

EYRES, David

Born Liverpool 26.2.64. Ht 5 10
Wt 11 00
Forward. From Rhyl.

Season	Club	Apps	Goals
1989–90	Blackpool	35	7

FAIRCLOUGH, Chris

Born Nottingham 12.4.64. Ht 5 11
Wt 11 02
Defender. From Apprentice. England Under-21.

Season	Club	Apps	Goals
1981–82	Nottingham F	—	—
1982–83		15	—
1983–84		31	—
1984–85		35	—
1985–86		—	—
1986–87		26	1
1987–88	Tottenham H	40	4
1988–89		20	1
1988–89	Leeds U	11	—
1989–90		42	8

FAIRCLOUGH, David

Born Liverpool 5.1.57. Ht 5 10
Wt 11 00
Forward. From Apprentice. England Under-21.

Season	Club	Apps	Goals
1973–74	Liverpool	—	—
1974–75		—	—
1975–76		14	7
1976–77		20	3
1977–78		29	10
1978–79		4	2
1979–80		14	5
1980–81		9	4
1981–82		—	—
1982–83		8	3
From Lucerne			
1984–85	Norwich C	2	—
1985–86	Oldham Ath	17	1
1986–87	Rochdale	—	—
From Beveren.			
1989–90	Tranmere R	14	1

FAIRCLOUGH, Wayne

Born Nottingham 27.4.68. Ht 5 10
Wt 9 12
Defender. From Apprentice.

Season	Club	Apps	Goals
1985–86	Notts Co	5	—
1986–87		9	—
1987–88		29	—
1988–89		20	—

Season	Club	League Appearances/Goals	
1989–90		8	—
1989–90	Mansfield T	13	—

FAIRWEATHER, Carlton

Born London 22.9.61. Ht 5 11 Wt 11 00
Forward. From Tooting & Mitcham.

Season	Club	League Appearances/Goals	
1984–85	Wimbledon	13	2
1985–86		20	7
1986–87		26	8
1987–88		21	4
1988–89		26	3
1989–90		21	1

FALCO, Mark

Born Hackney 22.10.60. Ht 6 0
Wt 12 00
Forward. From Apprentice. England Youth.

Season	Club	League Appearances/Goals	
1978–79	Tottenham H	1	1
1979–80		9	2
1980–81		3	1
1981–82		21	5
1982–83		16	5
1982–83	*Chelsea*	3	—
1983–84	Tottenham H	36	13
1984–85		42	22
1985–86		40	18
1986–87		6	—
1986–87	Watford	33	14
1987–88	Rangers	14	5
1987–88	QPR	19	5
1988–89		27	12
1989–90		21	5

FALCONER, Willie

Born Aberdeen 5.4.66. Ht 6 1 Wt 11 09
Midfield. From Lewis United. Scotland Schools, Youth.

Season	Club	League Appearances/Goals	
1982–83	Aberdeen	1	—
1983–84		8	1
1984–85		16	4
1985–86		8	—
1986–87		8	—
1987–88		36	8
1988–89	Watford	33	5
1989–90		30	3

FALLON, Shaun

Born Widnes 10.9.70
Midfield. From Trainee.

Season	Club	League Appearances/Goals	
1988–89	Wigan Ath	1	—
1989–90		2	—

FARNINGHAM, Ray

Born Dundee 10.4.61. Ht 5 8 Wt 10 07
Forward. From Celtic BC.

Season	Club	League Appearances/Goals	
1978–79	Forfar Ath	1	—
1979–80		38	5
1980–81		34	4
1981–82		39	5
1982–83		21	3
1983–84		37	6
1984–85		31	4
1985–86		37	2
1986–87		2	—
1986–87	Motherwell	29	3
1987–88		29	6
1988–89		18	3
1989–90	Dunfermline Ath	17	—

FARNWORTH, Simon

Born Chorley 28.10.63. Ht 6 0 Wt 11 13
Goalkeeper. From Apprentice. England Schools.

Season	Club	League Appearances/Goals	
1981–82	Bolton W	—	—
1982–83		—	—
1983–84		36	—
1984–85		46	—
1985–86		31	—
1986–87		—	—
1986–87	*Stockport Co*	10	—
1986–87	*Tranmere R*	7	—
1986–87	Bury	14	—
1987–88		39	—
1988–89		45	—
1989–90		7	—

FARRELL, Andy

Born Colchester 7.10.65. Ht 6 0
Wt 11 00

Season	Club	League Appearances/Goals	

Defender. From school.

1983–84	Colchester U	15	—
1984–85		38	—
1985–86		24	1
1986–87		28	4
1987–88	Burnley	45	3
1988–89		36	4
1989–90		36	2

FARRELL, Sean

Born Watford 28.2.69. Ht 6 1 Wt 12 08
Midfield. From Apprentice.

1986–87	Luton T	—	—
1987–88		—	—
1987–88	*Colchester U*	9	1
1988–89	Luton T	—	—
1989–90		1	—

FARRELL, Stephen

Born Kilmarnock 8.3.73.
Forward.

1989–90	Stoke C	2	—

FASHANU, John

Born Kensington 18.9.62. Ht 6 1
Wt 11 12
Forward. From Cambridge U. Amateur. England 2 full caps.

1979–80	Norwich C	—	—
1980–81		—	—
1981–82		5	1
1982–83		2	—
1983–84		—	—
1983–84	*Crystal Palace*	1	—
1983–84	Lincoln C	26	6
1984–85		10	4
1984–85	Millwall	25	4
1985–86		25	8
1985–86	Wimbledon	9	4
1986–87		37	11
1987–88		38	14
1988–89		30	12
1989–90		24	11

FASHANU, Justin

Born Kensington 19.2.61. Ht 6 1
Wt 13 01
Forward. From Apprentice. England Youth, Under-21, B.

1978–79	Norwich C	16	5
1979–80		34	11
1980–81		40	19
1981–82	Nottingham F	32	3
1982–83	*Southampton*	9	3
1982–83	Nottingham F	—	—
1982–83	Notts Co	15	7
1983–84		17	5
1984–85		32	8
1985–86	Brighton	16	2
1986–87		—	—

From Edmonton.

1989–90	Manchester C	2	—
1989–90	West Ham U	2	—
1989–90	Leyton Orient	5	—

FEARON, Ron

Born Romford 19.11.60 Ht 6 0 Wt 11 12
Goalkeeper. From QPR Apprentice.

1979–80	Reading	—	—
1980–81		6	—
1981–82		42	—
1982–83		13	—

From Sutton

1987–88	Ipswich T	10	—
1988–89		18	—
1989–90		—	—

FEE, Greg

Born Halifax 24.6.64. Ht 6 1 Wt 12 00
Defender.

1982–83	Bradford C	3	—
1983–84		4	—

From Boston U

1987–88	Sheffield W	16	—

Season	Club	League Appearances/Goals	
1988–89		8	—
1989–90		2	—

FEELEY, Andy

Born Hereford 30.9.61. Ht 5 10
Wt 12 00
Midfield. From Apprentice.

1978–79	Hereford U	26	—
1979–80		25	3
1979–80	*Chelsea*	—	—
1980–81	Hereford	—	—
From Trowbridge T			
1983–84	Leicester C	3	—
1984–85		35	—
1985–86		26	—
1986–87		12	—
1987–88	Brentford	34	—
1988–89		33	—
1989–90	Bury	30	2

FELGATE, David

Born Blaenau Ffestiniog 4.3.60. Ht 6 2
Wt 13 06
Goalkeeper. From Blaenau Ffestiniog.
Wales Schools, Under-21, 1 full cap.

1978–79	Bolton W	—	—
1978–79	*Rochdale*	35	—
1979–80	Bolton W	—	—
1979–80	*Bradford C*	—	—
1979–80	*Crewe Alex*	14	—
1979–80	*Rochdale*	12	—
1980–81	Bolton W	—	—
1980–81	Lincoln C	42	—
1981–82		43	—
1982–83		46	—
1983–84		46	—
1984–85		21	—
1984–85	*Cardiff C*	4	—
1984–85	*Grimsby T*	12	—
1985–86	Grimsby T	12	—
1985–86	Bolton W	15	—
1986–87		20	—
1986–87	*Rotherham U*	—	—
1987–88	Bolton W	46	—
1988–89		46	—
1989–90		40	—

FELLENGER, David

Born Edinburgh 6.6.69. Ht 5 8 Wt 10 02
Midfield. From Hutchinson Vale BC.

1987–88	Hibernian	—	—
1988–89		2	—
1989–90		12	1

FENSOME, Andy

Born Northampton 18.2.69. Ht 5 8
Wt 11 02
Midfield. From Trainee.

1986–87	Norwich C	—	—
1987–88		—	—
1988–89		—	—
1988–89	*Newcastle U*	—	—
1989–90	Cambridge U	24	—

FENWICK, Terry

Born Camden, Co. Durham 17.11.59.
Ht 5 11 Wt 11 01
Defender. From Apprentice. England
Youth, Under-21, 20 full caps.

1976–77	Crystal Palace	—	—
1977–78		10	—
1978–79		24	—
1979–80		15	—
1980–81		21	—
1980–81	QPR	19	2
1981–82		36	5
1982–83		39	3
1983–84		41	10
1984–85		41	2
1985–86		37	7
1986–87		21	1
1987–88		22	3
1987–88	Tottenham H	17	—
1988–89		34	8
1989–90		10	—

FERDINAND, Les

Born London 18.12.66. Ht 5 11
Wt 13 05

Forward. From Hayes.

1986–87	QPR	2	—
1987–88		1	—
1987–88	*Brentford*	3	—
1988–89	QPR	—	—
1988–89	*Besiktas*	—	—
1989–90	QPR	9	2

FEREDAY, Wayne

Born Warley 16.6.63. Ht 5 9 Wt 11 08
Midfield. From Apprentice. England Under-21.

1980–81	QPR	6	2
1981–82		4	—
1982–83		5	—
1983–84		17	4
1984–85		26	7
1985–86		34	2
1986–87		37	2
1987–88		37	4
1988–89		31	—
1989–90	Newcastle U	25	—

FERGUSON, Derek

Born Glasgow 31.7.67. Ht 5 8 Wt 10 11
Midfield. From Gartcosh United. Scotland Schools, Youth, Under-21, 2 full caps.

1983–84	Rangers	1	—
1984–85		8	—
1985–86		19	—
1986–87		30	1
1987–88		32	4
1988–89		16	2
1989–90		5	—
1989–90	*Dundee*	4	—

FERGUSON, Iain

Born Newarthill 4.8.62. Ht 5 7 Wt 10 07
Forward. From Fir Park BC. Scotland Youth, Under-21.

1979–80	Dundee	13	5
1980–81		11	1
1981–82		34	12
1982–83		29	9
1983–84		33	12
1984–85	Rangers	28	6
1985–86		4	—
1986–87	*Dundee*	3	2
1986–87	Dundee U	36	16
1987–88		39	11
1988–89	Hearts	29	5
1989–90		11	1
1989–90	*Charlton Ath*	1	—
1989–90	*Bristol C*	11	2

FERGUSON, Ian

Born Glasgow 15.3.67. Ht 5 10
Wt 10 11
Midfield. From Clyde BC. Scotland B, Under-21, 3 full caps.

1984–85	Clyde	2	—
1985–86		19	4
1986–87		5	—
1986–87	St Mirren	35	4
1987–88		22	6
1987–88	Rangers	8	1
1988–89		30	6
1989–90		24	—

FILLERY, Mike

Born Mitcham 17.9.60. Ht 5 11
Wt 13 00
Midfield. From Apprentice. England Schools, Youth.

1978–79	Chelsea	7	—
1979–80		41	11
1980–81		36	6
1981–82		40	6
1982–83		37	9
1983–84	QPR	30	1
1984–85		32	6
1985–86		17	—
1986–87		18	2
1987–88	Portsmouth	18	—
1988–89		17	2
1989–90		29	4

FILSON, Robert

Born St Helens 25.6.68
Defender. From Everton, Preston NE.

Season	Club	App	Goals
1988–89	Wrexham	1	—
1989–90		1	—

FINDLAY, William

Born Kilmarnock 29.8.70. Ht 5 10
Wt 10 13
Midfield. From Kilmarnock BC.

Season	Club	App	Goals
1987–88	Hibernian	—	—
1988–89		3	1
1989–90		10	—

FINLEY, Alan

Born Liverpool 10.12.67 Ht 6 3
Wt 14 03
Defender. From Marine.

Season	Club	App	Goals
1988–89	Shrewsbury T	34	1
1989–90		29	1

FINNEY, Kevin

Born Newcastle-under-Lyme 19.10.69.
Ht 6 0 Wt 12 00
Midfield. From Apprentice.

Season	Club	App	Goals
1987–88	Port Vale	15	—
1988–89		14	1
1989–90		8	—

FINNIGAN, Tony

Born Wimbledon 17.10.62. Ht 5 10 Wt 11 09
Defender. Crystal Palace Apprentice.

Season	Club	App	Goals
1980–81	Fulham	—	—
1981–82		—	—
1982–83		—	—
1983–84		—	—
1984–85	Crystal Palace	11	1
1985–86		36	3
1986–87		41	6
1987–88		17	—
1988–89	Blackburn R	17	—
1989–90		19	—

FIORE, Mark

Born Southwark 18.11.69 Ht 5 10
Wt 11 10
Midfield. From Trainee.

Season	Club	App	Goals
1988–89	Wimbledon	1	—
1989–90		—	—
1989–90	Plymouth Arg	12	1

FISHENDEN, Paul

Born Hillingdon 2.8.63. Ht 6 0 Wt 10 12
Forward. Local.

Season	Club	App	Goals
1981–82	Wimbledon	5	1
1982–83		9	4
1983–84		23	8
1984–85		20	10
1985–86		18	2
1985–86	*Fulham*	3	—
1986–87		—	—
1986–87	*Millwall*	3	—
1986–87	*Orient*	4	—
1987–88	Wimbledon	—	—
1987–88	Crewe Alex	15	3
1988–89		46	16
1989–90		20	6

FITZGERALD, Scott

Born London 13.8.69. Ht 6 0 Wt 12 02
Defender. From Trainee.

Season	Club	App	Goals
1988–89	Wimbledon	—	—
1989–90		1	—

FITZPATRICK, Gary

Born Birmingham 5.8.71 Ht 5 10
Wt 10 06
Midfield. From Trainee.

Season	Club	App	Goals
1989–90	Leicester C	1	—

FITZPATRICK, Paul

Born Liverpool 5.10.65. Ht 6 4 Wt 12 00
Midfield.

Season	Club	App	Goals
1984–85	Tranmere R	—	—
1985–86	Liverpool	—	—
1984–85	Preston NE	—	—
1984–85	Bolton W	3	—
1985–86		11	—
1986–87	Bristol C	19	2
1987–88		24	5
1988–89		1	—
1988–89	Carlisle U	32	—

Season	Club	League Appearances/Goals	
1988–89	*Preston NE*	2	—
1989–90	Carlisle U	45	4

FLECK, Robert

Born Glasgow 11.8.65. Ht 5 7 Wt 10 8
Foward. From Possil YM. Scotland Youth, Under-21, 3 full caps.

Season	Club	Apps	Goals
1983–84	Partick T	2	1
1983–84	Rangers	1	—
1984–85		8	—
1985–86		15	3
1986–87		40	19
1987–88		21	7
1987–88	Norwich C	18	7
1988–89		33	10
1989–90		27	7

FLEMING, Craig

Born Calder 6.10.71
Midfield. From Trainee.

Season	Club	Apps	Goals
1988–89	Halifax T	1	—
1989–90		10	—

FLEMING, Gary

Born Londonderry 17.2.67. Ht 5 9
Wt 11 03
Defender. From Apprentice. Northern Ireland 11 full caps.

Season	Club	Apps	Goals
1984–85	Nottingham F	2	—
1985–86		16	—
1986–87		34	—
1987–88		22	—
1988–89		—	—
1989–90	Manchester C	14	—
1989–90	*Notts Co*	3	—
1989–90	Barnsley	12	—

FLEMING, Mark

Born Hammersmith 11.8.69.
Defender. From Trainee.

Season	Club	Apps	Goals
1987–88	QPR	2	—
1988–89		1	—
1989–90	Brentford	17	—

FLEMING, Paul

Born Halifax 6.9.67. Ht 5 7 Wt 10 00
Defender.

Season	Club	Apps	Goals
1985–86	Halifax T	13	—
1986–87		15	—
1987–88		9	—
1988–89		23	—
1989–90		40	1

FLETCHER, Jason

Born Nottingham 29.9.69.
Defender. From Trainee.

Season	Club	Apps	Goals
1987–88	Nottingham F	—	—
1988–89		—	—
1989–90		—	—

FLOUNDERS, Andy

Born Hull 13.12.63. Ht 5 11 Wt 11 06
Forward. From Apprentice.

Season	Club	Apps	Goals
1980–81	Hull C	5	—
1981–82		13	5
1982–83		23	13
1983–84		30	9
1984–85		39	14
1985–86		25	10
1986–87		24	3
1986–87	Scunthorpe U	15	6
1987–88		45	24
1988–89		46	16
1989–90		44	18

FLOWERS, Tim

Born Kenilworth 3.2.67. Ht 6 2
Wt 13 09
Goalkeeper. From Apprentice. England Youth, Under-21.

Season	Club	Apps	Goals
1984–85	Wolverhampton W	38	—
1985–86		25	—
1985–86	*Southampton*	—	—
1986–87	Southampton	9	—
1986–87	*Swindon T*	2	—
1987–88	Southampton	9	—

Season	Club	Apps	Goals
1987–88	*Swindon T*	5	—
1988–89	Southampton	7	—
1989–90		35	—

FLYNN, Brian

Born Port Talbot 12.10.55. Ht 5 4
Wt 10 00
Midfield. From Apprentice.
Wales Schools, Under-23, 66 full caps.

Season	Club	Apps	Goals
1972–73	Burnley	—	—
1973–74		2	—
1974–75		26	—
1975–76		39	4
1976–77		41	2
1977–78		12	2
1977–78	Leeds U	29	1
1978–79		41	3
1979–80		24	3
1980–81		41	3
1981–82		17	1
1981–82	*Burnley*	2	—
1982–83	Leeds U	2	—
1982–83	Burnley	28	1
1983–84		43	9
1984–85		9	1
1984–85	Cardiff C	22	—
1985–86		10	—
1985–86	Doncaster R	27	—
1986–87	Bury	19	—
From Limerick			
1987–88	Doncaster R	24	1
1987–88	Wrexham	17	1
1988–89		41	1
1989–90		23	2

FLYNN, Gerry

Born Belfast 28.3.72. Ht 5 10 Wt 11 01
Midfield. From Bangor.

Season	Club	Apps	Goals
1989–90	Hull C	—	—

FLYNN, Mike

Born Oldham 23.2.69. Ht 6 0 Wt 11 00
Defender. From Trainee.

Season	Club	Apps	Goals
1986–87	Oldham Ath	—	—
1987–88		31	1
1988–89		9	—

Season	Club	Apps	Goals
1988–89	Norwich C	—	—
1989–90		—	—
1989–90	Preston NE	23	1

FOLEY, Steve

Born Liverpool 4.10.62. Ht 5 8 Wt 11 09
Forward. From Apprentice.

Season	Club	Apps	Goals
1980–81	Liverpool	—	—
1981–82		—	—
1982–83		—	—
1983–84		—	—
1983–84	*Fulham*	3	—
1984–85	Grimsby T	31	2
1985–86	Sheffield U	28	5
1986–87		38	9
1987–88	Swindon T	35	4
1988–89		40	8
1989–90		23	4

FORBES, Graeme

Born Forfar 29.7.58. Ht 6 0 Wt 13 00
Defender. From Lochee United.

Season	Club	Apps	Goals
1980–81	Motherwell	28	4
1981–82		31	6
1982–83		26	1
1983–84		32	1
1984–85		36	4
1985–86		27	—
1986–87		5	—
1986–87	Walsall	40	3
1987–88		44	3
1988–89		45	1
1989–90		44	2

FORD, Gary

Born York 8.2.61. Ht 5 8 Wt 11 10
Midfield. From Apprentice.

Season	Club	Apps	Goals
1978–79	York C	33	4
1979–80		29	2
1980–81		43	4
1981–82		41	8
1982–83		45	11
1983–84		46	11
1984–85		44	5
1985–86		40	3
1986–87		45	4

Season	Club	League Appearances/Goals	
1987–88	Leicester C	16	2
1987–88	Port Vale	23	3
1988–89		22	7
1989–90		—	—
1989–90	*Walsall*	13	2

FORD, Mike

Born Bristol 9.2.66. Ht 6 0 Wt 11 02
Defender. From Apprentice.

Season	Club	League Appearances/Goals	
1983–84	Leicester C	—	—
From Devizes			
1984–85	Cardiff C	20	1
1985–86		44	4
1986–87		36	1
1987–88		45	7
1988–89	Oxford U	10	1
1989–90		31	2

FORD, Stuart

Born Sheffield 20.7.71. Ht 5 11
Wt 11 13
Goalkeeper. From Trainee.

Season	Club	League Appearances/Goals	
1989–90	Rotherham U	1	—

FORD, Tony

Born Grimsby 14.5.59. Ht 5 8 Wt 12 13
Forward. From Apprentice. England B.

Season	Club	League Appearances/Goals	
1975–76	Grimsby T	14	—
1976–77		6	—
1977–78		34	2
1978–79		45	15
1979–80		37	5
1980–81		28	4
1981–82		35	7
1982–83		37	4
1983–84		42	8
1984–85		42	6
1985–86		34	3
1985–86	*Sunderland*	9	1
1986–87	Stoke C	41	6
1987–88		44	7
1988–89		27	—
1988–89	WBA	11	1
1989–90		42	8

FOREMAN, Darren

Born Southampton 12.2.68. Ht 5 10
Wt 10 08
Forward. England Schools.

Season	Club	League Appearances/Goals	
1986–87	Barnsley	16	1
1987–88		9	4
1988–89		—	—
1989–90		17	3
1989–90	Crewe Alex	14	3

FORREST, Craig

Born Vancouver 20.9.67. Ht 6 5
Wt 14 01
Goalkeeper. From Apprentice.

Season	Club	League Appearances/Goals	
1985–86	Ipswich T	—	—
1986–87		—	—
1987–88		—	—
1987–88	*Colchester U*	11	—
1988–89	Ipswich T	28	—
1989–90		45	—

FORREST, Gerry

Born Stockton 21.1.57. Ht 5 9 Wt 10 11
Defender. From South Bank.

Season	Club	League Appearances/Goals	
1976–77	Rotherham U	—	—
1977–78		44	—
1978–79		46	—
1979–80		43	4
1980–81		44	2
1981–82		35	1
1982–83		39	—
1983–84		45	—
1984–85		44	—
1985–86		17	—
1985–86	Southampton	22	—
1986–87		38	—
1987–88		37	—
1988–89		17	—
1989–90		1	—

FORSYTH, Mike

Born Liverpool 20.3.66. Ht 5 11
Wt 12 02

Season	Club	League Appearances/Goals	

Defender. From Apprentice. England Youth, B, Under-21

1983–84	WBA	8	—
1984–85		10	—
1985–86		11	—
1985–86	*Northampton T*	—	—
1985–86	Derby Co	—	—
1986–87		41	1
1987–88		39	3
1988–89		38	—
1989–90		38	—

FORSYTH, Stewart

Born Insch 26.10.61. Ht 6 0 Wt 11 0
Defender. From Middlefield BC.

1977–78	Arbroath	—	—
1978–79		—	—
1979–80		12	—
1980–81		28	1
1981–82		27	1
1982–83		33	—
1983–84		35	4
1984–85	Dundee	13	—
1985–86		9	1
1986–87		28	—
1987–88		41	1
1988–89		33	—
1989–90		34	1

FOSTER, Adrian

Born Kidderminster 20.7.71 Ht 5 9
Wt 11 00
Forward. From Trainee.

1989–90	WBA	14	1

FOSTER, Colin

Born Chislehurst 16.7.64. Ht 6 4
Wt 14 01
Defender. From Apprentice

1981–82	Orient	23	2
1982–83		43	2
1983–84		11	1
1984–85		42	1
1985–86		36	2
1986–87		19	2
1986–87	Nottingham F	9	1

Season	Club	League Appearances/Goals	
1987–88		39	2
1988–89		18	2
1989–90		6	—
1989–90	West Ham U	22	1

FOSTER, George

Born Plymouth 26.9.56. Ht 5 10
Wt 11 02
Defender. From Apprentice.

1973–74	Plymouth Arg	5	—
1974–75		—	—
1975–76		16	1
1976–77		15	2
1976–77	*Torquay U*	6	3
1977–78	Plymouth Arg	46	3
1978–79		28	—
1979–80		46	—
1980–81		46	—
1981–82		10	—
1981–82	*Exeter C*	28	—
1982–83	Derby Co	30	—
1983–84	Mansfield T	42	—
1984–85		44	—
1985–86		46	—
1986–87		45	—
1987–88		44	—
1988–89		42	—
1989–90		42	—

FOSTER, Steve

Born Portsmouth 24.9.57. Ht 6 1
Wt 13 13
Defender. From Apprentice. England Under-21, 3 full caps.

1975–76	Portsmouth	11	—
1976–77		31	1
1977–78		31	3
1978–79		36	2
1979–80	Brighton	38	1
1980–81		42	1
1981–82		40	2
1982–83		36	1
1983–84		16	1
1983–84	Aston Villa	7	1
1984–85		8	2
1984–85	Luton T	25	1
1985–86		35	3

Season	Club	League Appearances/Goals	
1986–87		28	2
1987–88		39	2
1988–89		36	3
1989–90	Oxford U	35	4

FOSTER, Wayne

Born Leigh 11.9.63. Ht 5 8 Wt 11 00
Forward. From Apprentice. England Youth.

Season	Club	League Appearances/Goals	
1981–82	Bolton W	23	2
1982–83		24	4
1983–84		30	3
1984–85		28	4
1985–86	Preston NE	31	3
1986–87	Hearts	31	4
1987–88		39	4
1988–89		9	1
1989–90		17	1

FOWLER, Lee

Born Nottingham 26.1.69 Ht 5 8
Wt 11 07
Forward. From Trainee.

Season	Club	League Appearances/Goals	
1987–88	Stoke C	1	—
1988–89		—	—
1989–90		15	—

FOX, Matthew

Born Birmingham 13.7.71 Ht 6 0
Wt 13 00
Defender. From Trainee.

Season	Club	League Appearances/Goals	
1988–89	Birmingham C	3	—
1989–90		—	—

FOX, Peter

Born Scunthorpe 5.7.57. Ht 5 11
Wt 13 08
Goalkeeper. From Apprentice.

Season	Club	League Appearances/Goals	
1972–73	Sheffield W	1	—
1973–74		—	—
1974–75		20	—
1975–76		27	—
1976–77		1	—
1976–77	*West Ham U*	—	—
1977–78	Sheffield W	—	—
1977–78	*Barnsley*	1	—
1977–78	Stoke C	—	—
1978–79		1	—
1979–80		23	—
1980–81		42	—
1981–82		38	—
1982–83		35	—
1983–84		42	—
1984–85		14	—
1985–86		37	—
1986–87		39	—
1987–88		17	—
1988–89		29	—
1989–90		38	—

FOX, Ruel

Born Ipswich 14.1.68. Ht 5 6 Wt 10 00
Midfield. From Apprentice.

Season	Club	League Appearances/Goals	
1985–86	Norwich C	—	—
1986–87		3	—
1987–88		34	2
1988–89		4	—
1989–90		7	3

FOYLE, Martin

Born Salisbury 2.5.63. Ht 5 10 Wt 11 02
Forward. From Amateur.

Season	Club	League Appearances/Goals	
1980–81	Southampton	—	—
1981–82		—	—
1982–83		7	1
1983–84		5	—
1983–84	*Blackburn R*	—	—
1984–85	Aldershot	44	15
1985–86		20	9
1986–87		34	11
1986–87	Oxford U	4	—
1987–88		33	11
1988–89		40	14
1989–90		13	2

FRAIL, Stephen

Born Glasgow 10.8.69. Ht 5 9 Wt 10 09
Midfield. From Possilpark YM.

Season	Club	League Appearances/Goals	
1985–86	Dundee	—	—
1986–87		—	—
1987–88		4	—

Season	Club	Apps	Goals
1988–89		23	1
1989–90		6	—

FRAIN, David

Born Sheffield 11.10.62. Ht 5 8
Wt 10 05
Forward. From Rowlinson YC.

Season	Club	Apps	Goals
1985–86	Sheffield U	7	1
1986–87		19	3
1987–88		18	1
1988–89	Rochdale	42	12
1989–90	Stockport Co	29	2

FRAIN, John

Born Birmingham 8.10.68. Ht 5 7
Wt 11 10
Midfield. From Apprentice.

Season	Club	Apps	Goals
1985–86	Birmingham C	3	—
1986–87		3	1
1987–88		14	2
1988–89		28	3
1989–90		38	1

FRANCE, Paul

Born Huddersfield 10.9.68. Ht 6 1
Wt 11 08
Midfield. From Trainee.

Season	Club	Apps	Goals
1987–88	Huddersfield T	8	—
1988–89		3	—
1988–89	*Cobh Ramblers*	—	—
1989–90	Bristol C	—	—

FRANCIS, John

Born Dewsbury 21.11.63 Ht 5 8
Wt 11 02
Forward. From Emley.

Season	Club	Apps	Goals
1988–89	Sheffield U	22	1
1989–90		20	5
1989–90	Burnley	19	4

FRANCIS, Kevin

Born Moseley 6.12.67 Ht 6 7 Wt 15 08
Forward. From Mile Oak R.

Season	Club	Apps	Goals
1988–89	Derby Co	—	—
1989–90		8	—

FRANCIS, Lee

Born London 24.10.69. Ht 5 10
Wt 10 11
Defender. From Trainee.

Season	Club	Apps	Goals
1987–88	Arsenal	—	—
1988–89		—	—
1989–90		—	—
1989–90	*Chesterfield*	2	—

FRANCIS, Sean

Born Birmingham 1.8.72. Ht 5 10
Wt 11 09
Forward. From Trainee.

Season	Club	Apps	Goals
1989–90	Birmingham C	—	—

FRANCIS, Steve

Born Billericay 29.5.64. Ht 5 11
Wt 11 05
Goalkeeper. From Apprentice. England Youth.

Season	Club	Apps	Goals
1981–82	Chelsea	29	—
1982–83		37	—
1983–84		—	—
1984–85		2	—
1985–86		3	—
1986–87		—	—
1986–87	Reading	14	—
1987–88		34	—
1988–89		22	—
1989–90		46	—

FRANCIS, Trevor

Born Plymouth 19.4.54. Ht 5 10
Wt 11 07
Forward. From Apprentice. England Youth, Under-23, 52 full caps.

Season	Club	Apps	Goals
1970–71	Birmingham C	22	15
1971–72		39	12
1972–73		31	6
1973–74		37	6
1974–75		23	13
1975–76		35	17

Season	Club	League Appearances/Goals	
1976–77		42	21
1977–78		42	25
From Detroit E			
1978–79	Birmingham C	9	3
1978–79	Nottingham F	20	6
From Detroit E			
1979–80	Nottingham F	30	14
1980–81		18	6
1981–82		2	2
1981–82	Manchester C	26	12
1982–83	Sampdoria	14	7
1983–84		15	3
1984–85		24	6
1985–86		15	1
1986–87	Atalanta	21	1
1987–88	Rangers	18	—
1987–88	QPR	9	—
1988–89		19	7
1989–90		4	5
1989–90	Sheffield W	12	—

FRANKLAND, Tony

Born Greenwich 11.10.72.
Midfield. From School.

1989–90	Exeter C	4	—

FRANKLIN, Darryl

Born Caerphilly 1.3.71. Ht 5 5 Wt 10 06
Forward. From Trainee.

1989–90	Leeds U	—	—

FREESTONE, Roger

Born Newport 19.8.68. Ht 6 2 Wt 12 03
Goalkeeper. Wales Under-21.

1986–87	Newport Co	13	—
1986–87	Chelsea	6	—
1987–88		15	—
1988–89		21	—
1989–90		—	—
1989–90	*Swansea C*	14	—
1989–90	*Hereford U*	8	—

FRENCH, Hamish

Born Aberdeen 7.2.64. Ht 5 10
Wt 11 04
Midfield. From Keith.

Season	Club	League Appearances/Goals	
1987–88	Dundee U	20	2
1988–89		18	3
1989–90		12	2

FRIDGE, Les

Born Inverness 27.8.68. Ht 5 11
Wt 11 12
Goalkeeper. From Apprentice. Scotland Youth, Under-21.

1985–86	Chelsea	1	—
1986–87		—	—
1986–87	St Mirren	1	—
1987–88		3	—
1988–89		15	—
1989–90		8	—

FRIEL, George

Born Reading 11.10.70. Ht 5 8 Wt 10 11
Forward. From Trainee.

1989–90	Reading	3	—

FRY, Chris

Born Cardiff 23.10.69 Ht 5 9 Wt 9 06
Forward. From Trainee.

1988–89	Cardiff C	9	—
1989–90		23	1

FULTON, Stephen

Born Greenock 10.8.70. Ht 5 10
Wt 11 00
Midfield. From Celtic BC.

1986–87	Celtic	—	—
1987–88		—	—
1988–89		3	—
1989–90		16	—

FUTCHER, Paul

Born Chester 25.9.56. Ht 6 0 Wt 12 03
Defender. From Apprentice. England Under-21.

1972–73	Chester	2	—
1973–74		18	—
1974–75	Luton T	19	—
1975–76		41	—

Season	Club	Apps	Goals
1976–77		40	1
1977–78		31	—
1978–79	Manchester C	24	—
1979–80		13	—
1980–81	Oldham Ath	36	1
1981–82		37	—
1982–83		25	—
1982–83	Derby Co	17	—
1983–84		18	—
1983–84	Barnsley	10	—
1984–85		36	—
1985–86		37	—
1986–87		36	—
1987–88		41	—
1988–89		41	—
1989–90		29	—

FUTCHER, Ron

Born Chester 25.9.56. Ht 6 0 Wt 12 10
Forward. From Apprentice.

Season	Club	Apps	Goals
1973–74	Chester	4	—
1974–75	Luton	17	7
1975–76		31	10
1976–77		33	13
1977–78		39	10
1978–79	Manchester C	17	7
From Minnesota K, Portland T, Tulsa R and NAC Breda			
1984–85	Barnsley	19	6
1985–86		40	17
1986–87		25	13
1986–87	Bradford C	10	4
1987–88		32	14
1988–89	Port Vale	41	17
1989–90		11	3
1989–90	Burnley	23	7

FYFE, Tony

Born Carlisle 23.2.62. Ht 6 2 Wt 12 00
Forward.

Season	Club	Apps	Goals
1987–88	Carlisle U	10	4
1988–89		25	4
1989–90		13	4
1989–90	*Scarborough*	6	1
1989–90	Halifax T	12	—

GABBIADINI, Marco

Born Nottingham 20.1.68. Ht 5 10
Wt 12 04
Forward. From Apprentice. England B, Under-21.

Season	Club	Apps	Goals
1984–85	York C	1	—
1985–86		22	4
1986–87		29	9
1987–88		8	1
1988–89		36	18
1988–89	Sunderland	35	21
1989–90		46	21

GABBIADINI, Ricardo

Born Newport 11.3.70 Ht 6 0 Wt 13 00
Forward. From Trainee.

Season	Club	Apps	Goals
1987–88	York C	1	—
1988–89	Sunderland	—	—
1989–90		1	—
1989–90	*Blackpool*	5	3
1989–90	*Brighton*	1	—
1989–90	*Grimsby T*	3	1

GAGE, Kevin

Born Chiswick 21.4.64. Ht 5 10
Wt 12 11
Defender. From Apprentice. England Youth.

Season	Club	Apps	Goals
1980–81	Wimbledon	1	—
1981–82		21	1
1982–83		26	4
1983–84		24	4
1984–85		37	2
1985–86		29	1
1986–87		30	3
1987–88	Aston Villa	44	2
1988–89		28	3
1989–90		22	3

GAHAGAN, John

Born Glasgow 24.8.58. Ht 5 9 Wt 10 07
Forward. From Shettleston Juniors.

Season	Club	Apps	Goals
1977–78	Clydebank	5	—
1978–79		—	—
1979–80	Motherwell	17	3

Season	Club	League Appearances/Goals	
1980–81		34	1
1981–82		39	7
1982–83		28	4
1983–84		30	7
1984–85		31	5
1985–86		21	3
1986–87		19	—
1987–88		23	—
1988–89		14	2
1989–90		26	3

GALE, Tony

Born London 19.11.59. Ht 6 1 Wt 13 07
Defender. From Apprentice. England Youth, Under-21.

Season	Club	Apps	Goals
1977–78	Fulham	38	8
1978–79		36	2
1979–80		42	4
1980–81		40	1
1981–82		44	1
1982–83		42	2
1983–84		35	1
1984–85	West Ham U	37	—
1985–86		42	—
1986–87		32	2
1987–88		18	—
1988–89		31	—
1989–90		36	1

GALL, Mark

Born London 14.5.63. Ht 5 10 Wt 12 00
Forward. From Wandsworth and Greenwich Borough (1988).

Season	Club	Apps	Goals
1989–90	Maidstone U	41	18

GALLACHER, Bernard

Born Johnstone 22.3.67. Ht 5 9
Wt 11 00
Defender. From Apprentice.

Season	Club	Apps	Goals
1984–85	Aston Villa	—	—
1985–86		—	—
1986–87		1	—
1987–88		43	—

Season	Club	League Appearances/Goals	
1988–89		4	—
1989–90		7	—

GALLACHER, John

Born Glasgow 26.1.69. Ht 5 10
Wt 10 08
Forward.

Season	Club	Apps	Goals
1987–88	Falkirk	2	—
1988–89		16	5
1989–90	Newcastle U	28	6

GALLACHER, Kevin

Born Clydebank 23.11.66. Ht 5 6
Wt 10 00
Forward. From Duntocher BC. Scotland Youth, B, Under-21, 4 full caps.

Season	Club	Apps	Goals
1983–84	Dundee U	—	—
1984–85		—	—
1985–86		20	3
1986–87		37	10
1987–88		26	4
1988–89		31	9
1989–90		17	1
1989–90	Coventry C	15	3

GALLAGHER, Eddie

Born Glasgow 21.11.64. Ht 5 9
Wt 10 06
Forward. From Campsie BW.

Season	Club	Apps	Goals
1985–86	Partick T	23	4
1986–87		30	5
1987–88		34	13
1988–89		3	2
1988–89	Hamilton A	14	3
1988–89	Dunfermline Ath	7	1
1989–90		14	1

GALLAGHER, Nicholas

Born Boston 28.1.71.
Midfield.

Season	Club	Apps	Goals
1989–90	Doncaster R	1	—

GALLIERS, Steve

Born Fulwood 21.8.57. Ht 5 6 Wt 9 07
Midfield. From Chorley.

Season	Club	League Appearances	Goals
1977–78	Wimbledon	27	1
1978–79		44	3
1979–80		36	2
1980–81		37	4
1981–82		11	—
1981–82	Crystal Palace	13	—
1982–83	Wimbledon	34	2
1983–84		36	1
1984–85		29	1
1985–86		32	1
1986–87		14	—
1986–87	*Bristol C*	9	—
1987–88	Wimbledon	1	—
1987–88	Bristol C	35	6
1988–89		33	—
1989–90	Maidstone U	8	—

GALLIMORE, Tony

Born Crewe 21.2.72.
Midfield. From Trainee.

Season	Club	League Appearances	Goals
1989–90	Stoke C	1	—

GALLOWAY, Mick

Born Oswestry 30.5 65. Ht 5 11
Wt 11.07
Defender. From Amateur. Scotland Youth, Under-21.

Season	Club	League Appearances	Goals
1983–84	Mansfield T	17	—
1984–85		31	3
1985–86		6	—
1985–86	Halifax T	19	—
1986–87		43	3
1987–88		17	2
1987–88	Hearts	25	6
1988–89		31	2
1989–90	Celtic	33	2

GALVIN, Tony

Born Huddersfield 12.7.56. Ht 5 9
Wt 13 05
Forward. From Goole T. Eire, 29 full caps.

Season	Club	League Appearances	Goals
1977–78	Tottenham H	—	—
1978–79		1	—
1979–80		10	4
1980–81		17	1
1981–82		32	3
1982–83		26	2
1983–84		30	1
1984–85		38	4
1985–86		23	4
1986–87		24	1
1987–88		—	—
1987–88	Sheffield W	18	—
1988–89		18	1
1989–90	Swindon T	11	—

GANNON, Jim

Born London 7.9.68. Ht 6 2 Wt 13 00
Defender. From Dundalk.

Season	Club	League Appearances	Goals
1988–89	Sheffield U	—	—
1989–90		—	—
1989–90	*Halifax T*	2	—
1989–90	Stockport Co	7	1

GANNON, John

Born Wimbledon 18.12.66. Ht 5 8
Wt 10 10
Midfield. From Apprentice.

Season	Club	League Appearances	Goals
1984–85	Wimbledon	—	—
1985–86		1	1
1986–87		2	—
1986–87	*Crewe Alex*	15	—
1987–88	Wimbledon	13	1
1988–89		—	—
1988–89	*Sheffield U*	16	1
1989–90	Sheffield U	39	3

GARDINER, Mark

Born Cirencester 25.12.66. Ht 5 10
Wt 10 07
Forward. From Apprentice.

Season	Club	League Appearances	Goals
1983–84	Swindon T	1	—
1984–85		4	—
1985–86		1	—
1986–87		4	—
1986–87	Torquay U	22	3
1987–88		27	1

Season	Club	League Appearances/Goals	
1988–89	Crewe Alex	38	10
1989–90		26	6

GARDNER, James

Born Dunfermline 27.9.67. Ht 5 10
Wt 10 02
Midfield. From Ayresome North AFC

1986–87	Queen's Park	1	—
1987–88		1	—
1988–89	Motherwell	—	—
1989–90		1	—

GARDNER, Steve

Born Teeside 3.7.68. Ht 5 9 Wt 12 8
Defender. From Apprentice.

1986–87	Manchester U	—	—
1987–88	Burnley	42	—
1988–89		44	—
1989–90		9	—

GARNER, Andy

Born Chesterfield 8.3.66. Ht 6 0
Wt 12 01
Forward. From Apprentice.

1983–84	Derby Co	13	5
1984–85		16	3
1985–86		16	5
1986–87		2	—
1987–88		24	4
1988–89	Blackpool	42	11
1989–90		46	8

GARNER, Darren

Born Plymouth 10.12.71 Ht 5 6
Wt 10 01
Midfield. From Trainee.

1988–89	Plymouth Arg	1	—
1989–90		1	—

GARNER, Simon

Born Boston 23.11.59. Ht 5 9 Wt 11 12
Forward. From Apprentice.

1978–79	Blackburn R	25	8
1979–80		28	6
1980–81		33	7
1981–82		36	14
1982–83		41	22
1983–84		42	19
1984–85		37	12
1985–86		38	12
1986–87		40	10
1987–88		40	14
1988–89		44	20
1989–90		43	18

GARNETT, Shaun

Born Wallasey 22.11.69 Ht 6 2 Wt 11 00
Midfield. From Trainee.

1987–88	Tranmere R	1	—
1988–89		—	—
1989–90		4	—

GARTON, Billy

Born Salford 15.3.65. Ht 5 11 Wt 11 08
Defender. From Apprentice.

1982–83	Manchester U	—	—
1983–84		—	—
1984–85		2	—
1985–86		10	—
1985–86	*Birmingham C*	5	—
1986–87	Manchester U	9	—
1987–88		6	—
1988–89		14	—
1989–90		—	—

GASCOIGNE, Paul

Born Gateshead 27.5.67. Ht 5 10
Wt 11 07
Midfield. From Apprentice. England B, Under-21, 17 full caps.

1984–85	Newcastle U	2	—
1985–86		31	9
1986–87		24	5
1987–88		35	7

Season	Club	League Appearances/Goals	
1988–89	Tottenham H	32	6
1989–90		34	6

GATES, Eric

Born Ferryhill 28.6.55. Ht 5 6 Wt 10 06
Forward. From Apprentice. England 2 full caps.

Season	Club	Apps	Goals
1972–73	Ipswich T	—	—
1973–74		6	—
1974–75		6	—
1975–76		13	1
1976–77		12	1
1977–78		24	2
1978–79		22	7
1979–80		36	13
1980–81		37	11
1981–82		38	9
1982–83		24	3
1983–84		37	13
1984–85		41	13
1985–86	Sunderland	39	9
1986–87		27	5
1987–88		42	19
1988–89		37	4
1989–90		36	6

GATTING, Steve

Born Park Royal 29.5.59 Ht 5 11
Wt 12 08
Defender. From Apprentice.

Season	Club	Apps	Goals
1976–77	Arsenal	—	—
1977–78		—	—
1978–79		21	1
1979–80		14	1
1980–81		23	3
1981–82		—	—
1981–82	Brighton	39	3
1982–83		40	4
1983–84		35	4
1984–85		8	—
1985–86		17	—
1986–87		40	1
1987–88		46	3
1988–89		29	3
1989–90		19	—

GAUGHAN, Steve

Born Doncaster 14.4.70 Ht 5 11
Wt 11 02
Midfield.

Season	Club	Apps	Goals
1987–88	Doncaster R	4	—
1988–89		34	2
1989–90		29	1

GAVIN, Mark

Born Baillieston 10.12.63. Ht 5 8
Wt 10 07
Midfield. From Apprentice.

Season	Club	Apps	Goals
1981–82	Leeds U	—	—
1982–83		7	1
1983–84		12	1
1984–85		11	1
1984–85	*Hartlepool U*	7	—
1985–86	Carlisle U	13	1
1985–86	Bolton W	8	1
1986–87		41	2
1987–88	Rochdale	23	6
1987–88	Hearts	7	—
1988–89		2	—
1988–89	Bristol C	29	3
1989–90		40	3

GAVIN, Pat

Born Hammersmith 5.6.67 Ht 6 0
Wt 12 00
Forward. From Hanwell T.

Season	Club	Apps	Goals
1988–89	Gillingham	13	7
1989–90	Leicester C	—	—
1989–90	*Gillingham*	34	1

GAYLE, Andy

Born Manchester 17.9.70 Ht 5 8
Wt 10 06
Midfield. From Trainee.

Season	Club	Apps	Goals
1988–89	Oldham Ath	1	—

Season	Club	Apps	Goals
1989–90	....	—	—
1989–90	Crewe Alex	1	—

GAYLE, Brian

Born London 6.3.65. Ht 6 1 Wt 12 07
Defender.

Season	Club	Apps	Goals
1984–85	Wimbledon	12	1
1985–86	....	13	—
1986–87	....	32	1
1987–88	....	26	1
1988–89	Manchester C	41	3
1989–90	....	14	—
1989–90	Ipswich T	20	—

GAYLE, Howard

Born Liverpool 18.5.58. Ht 5 10
Wt 10 09
Midfield. Local. England Under-21.

Season	Club	Apps	Goals
1977–78	Liverpool	—	—
1978–79	....	—	—
1979–80	....	—	—
1979–80	*Fulham*	14	—
1980–81	Liverpool	4	1
1981–82	....	—	—
1982–83	Liverpool	—	—
1982–83	*Birmingham C*	13	1
1982–83	*Newcastle U*	8	2
1983–84	Birmingham C	33	8
1984–85	Sunderland	25	2
1985–86	....	23	2
1986–87	Stoke C	6	2
1987–88	Blackburn R	13	1
1988–89	....	45	19
1989–90	....	30	5

GAYLE, John

Born Birmingham 30.7.64 Ht 6 4
Wt 13 01
Forward. From Burton Alb.

Season	Club	Apps	Goals
1988–89	Wimbledon	2	—
1989–90	....	11	1

GAYLE, Marcus

Born Hammersmith 27.9.70
Midfield. From Trainee. England Youth.

Season	Club	Apps	Goals
1988–89	Brentford	3	—
1989–90	....	9	—

GAYLE, Mark

Born Bromsgrove 21.10.69 Ht 6 2
Wt 12 03
Goalkeeper. From Trainee.

Season	Club	Apps	Goals
1988–89	Leicester C	—	—
1989–90	Blackpool	—	—

GAYNOR, Tommy

Born Limerick 29.1.63. Ht 6 1 Wt 13 02
Forward. From Limerick.

Season	Club	Apps	Goals
1986–87	Doncaster R	23	4
1987–88	....	10	3
1987–88	Nottingham F	12	3
1988–89	....	19	4
1989–90	....	11	—

GEDDES, Bobby

Born Inverness 12.8.60. Ht 6 0 Wt 11 4
Goalkeeper. From Ross County. Scotland Under-21.

Season	Club	Apps	Goals
1977–78	Dundee	—	—
1978–79	....	—	—
1979–80	....	—	—
1980–81	....	20	—
1981–82	....	28	—
1982–83	....	1	—
1983–84	....	24	—
1984–85	....	16	—
1985–86	....	36	—
1986–87	....	44	—
1987–88	....	38	—
1988–89	....	34	—
1989–90	....	12	—

GEDDIS, David

Born Carlisle 12.3.58. Ht 6 0 Wt 11 08
Forward. From Apprentice. England Youth, B.

Season	Club	Apps	Goals
1975–76	Ipswich T	—	—
1976–77	....	2	—
1976–77	*Luton T*	13	4
1977–78	Ipswich T	26	4

Season	Club	League Appearances	Goals
1978–79		15	1
1979–80		—	—
1979–80	Aston Villa	20	2
1980–81		9	4
1981–82		14	6
1982–83		4	—
1982–83	*Luton T*	4	—
1983–84	Aston Villa	—	—
1983–84	Barnsley	31	14
1984–85		14	10
1984–85	Birmingham C	18	12
1985–86		26	6
1986–87		2	—
1986–87	*Brentford*	4	—
1986–87	Shrewsbury T	15	5
1987–88		15	5
1988–89		9	1
1988–89	Swindon T	10	3
1989–90		—	—

GEE, Phil

Born Pelsall 19.12.64. Ht 5 9 Wt 10 04
Forward. From Riley Sports and Gresley R.

Season	Club	League Appearances	Goals
1985–86	Derby Co	4	2
1986–87		41	15
1987–88		38	6
1988–89		12	1
1989–90		8	1

GEMMILL, Scot

Born Paisley 2.1.71. Ht 5 10 Wt 10 01
Midfield. From School.

Season	Club	League Appearances	Goals
1989–90	Nottingham F	—	—

GENNOE, Terry

Born Shrewsbury 16.3.53. Ht 6 2 Wt 13 00
Goalkeeper. From Bricklayers Sports.

Season	Club	League Appearances	Goals
1972–73	Bury	1	—
1973–74		2	—
1973–74	*Blackburn R*	—	—
1974–75	Bury	—	—
1974–75	*Leeds U*	—	—
1975–76	Halifax T	26	—
1976–77		26	—
1977–78		26	—
1977–78	Southampton	—	—
1978–79		23	—
1979–80		13	—
1980–81	*Everton*	—	—
1980–81	*Crystal Palace*	3	—
1981–82	Blackburn R	35	—
1982–83		33	—
1983–84		30	—
1984–85		37	—
1985–86		32	—
1986–87		11	—
1987–88		39	—
1988–89		43	—
1989–90		28	—

GERMAN, Paul

Born Chertsey 18.4.71.
Defender. From Trainee.

Season	Club	League Appearances	Goals
1989–90	Fulham	—	—

GERNON, Irvin

Born Birmingham 30.12.62. Ht 6 1 Wt 12 08
Defender. From Apprentice. England Youth, Under-21.

Season	Club	League Appearances	Goals
1979–80	Ipswich T	—	—
1980–81		—	—
1981–82		4	—
1982–83		26	—
1983–84		19	—
1984–85		13	—
1985–86		11	—
1986–87		3	—
1986–87	*Northampton T*	9	—
1986–87	Gillingham	14	—
1987–88		21	1
1988–89		—	—
1988–89	Reading	22	—
1989–90		3	—
1989–90	Northampton T	12	1

GIBBINS, Roger

Born Enfield 6.9.55 Ht 5 10 Wt 11 09
Forward. From Apprentice. England Schools.

Season	Club	League Appearances/Goals	
1972–73	Tottenham H	—	—
1973–74		—	—
1974–75		—	—
1975–76	Oxford U	19	2
1976–77	Norwich C	20	5
1977–78		28	7
From New England Tea Men			
1979–80	Cambridge U	35	4
1980–81		30	4
1981–82		35	4
1981–82	Cardiff C	46	8
1982–83		42	4
1983–84		40	5
1984–85		11	—
1985–86	Swansea C	35	6
1986–87	Newport Co	46	8
1987–88		33	1
1987–88	Torquay U	12	2
1988–89		21	3
From Newport Co.			
1988–89	Cardiff C	12	—
1989–90		38	1

GIBBS, Nigel

Born St Albans 20.11.65. Ht 5 6
Wt 10 10
Defender. From Apprentice. England Youth, Under-21.

Season	Club	League Appearances/Goals	
1983–84	Watford	3	—
1984–85		12	—
1985–86		40	1
1986–87		15	—
1987–88		30	—
1988–89		46	1
1989–90		41	—

GIBSON, Colin

Born Bridport 6.4.60 Ht 5 8 Wt 10 11
Defender. From Apprentice. England Under-21, B.

Season	Club	League Appearances/Goals	
1977–78	Aston Villa	—	—
1978–79		12	—
1979–80		31	2
1980–81		21	—
1981–82		23	—
1982–83		23	1
1983–84		28	1
1984–85		40	4
1985–86		7	2
1985–86	Manchester U	18	5
1986–87		24	1
1987–88		29	2
1988–89		2	—
1989–90		6	1

GIBSON, Terry

Born Walthamstow 23.12.62. Ht 5 5
Wt 10 00
Forward. From Apprentice. England Schools, Youth.

Season	Club	League Appearances/Goals	
1979–80	Tottenham H	1	—
1980–81		—	—
1981–82		1	—
1982–83		16	4
1983–84	Coventry C	36	17
1984–85		38	15
1985–86		24	11
1985–86	Manchester U	7	—
1986–87		16	1
1987–88		—	—
1987–88	Wimbledon	17	6
1988–89		17	5
1989–90		18	5

GILBERT, Billy

Born Lewisham 10.11.59. Ht 5 11
Wt 12 00
Defender. From Apprentice. England Schools, Youth, Under-21.

Season	Club	League Appearances/Goals	
1976–77	Crystal Palace	—	—
1977–78		18	—
1978–79		41	1
1979–80		40	1
1980–81		39	—
1981–82		31	—
1982–83		34	—
1983–84		34	1
1984–85	Portsmouth	35	—
1985–86		36	—
1986–87		36	—
1987–88		21	—

Season	Club	League Appearances/Goals	
1988–89		12	—
1989–90	Colchester U	27	—

GILBERT, David

Born Lincoln 22.6.63. Ht 5 4 Wt 10 04
Midfield. From Apprentice.

Season	Club	League Appearances/Goals	
1980–81	Lincoln C	1	—
1981–82		29	1
1982–83	Scunthorpe U	1	—
From Boston U			
1986–87	Northampton T	45	8
1987–88		41	6
1988–89		34	7
1988–89	Grimsby T	11	3
1989–90		45	10

GILKES, Michael

Born Hackney 20.7.65. Ht 5 8 Wt 10 02
Forward.

Season	Club	League Appearances/Goals	
1984–85	Reading	16	2
1985–86		9	2
1986–87		7	—
1987–88		39	4
1988–89		46	9
1989–90		42	2

GILL, Gary

Born Middlesbrough 28.11.64. Ht 5 11
Wt 12 04
Defender. From Apprentice.

Season	Club	League Appearances/Goals	
1982–83	Middlesbrough	—	—
1983–84		6	—
1983–84	*Hull C*	1	—
1984–85	Middlesbrough	14	—
1985–86		9	—
1986–87		36	2
1987–88		3	—
1988–89		8	—
1989–90		1	—

GILL, Jeremy

Born Weston-super-Mare 8.9.70
Defender. From Trowbridge.

Season	Club	League Appearances/Goals	
1988–89	Leyton Orient	—	—
1989–90		—	—

GILL, Mark

Born Dublin 6.6.66. Ht 5 9 Wt 11 01
Forward. From Home Farm.

Season	Club	League Appearances/Goals	
1987–88	Newcastle U	—	—
1988–89		—	—
1989–90		—	—

GILL, Tony

Born Bradford 6.3.68. Ht 5 10 Wt 11 00
Midfield. From Apprentice.

Season	Club	League Appearances/Goals	
1985–86	Manchester U	—	—
1986–87		1	—
1987–88		—	—
1988–89		9	1
1989–90		—	—

GILLARD, Ken

Born Dublin 30.4.72. Ht 5 9 Wt 11 08
Defender. From Trainee.

Season	Club	League Appearances/Goals	
1988–89	Luton T	—	—
1989–90		—	—

GILLESPIE, Gary

Born Stirling 5.7.60. Ht 6 2 Wt 12 07
Defender. From school. Scotland
Under-21, 12 full caps.

Season	Club	League Appearances/Goals	
1977–78	Falkirk	22	—
1978–79	Coventry C	15	—
1979–80		38	1
1980–81		37	1
1981–82		40	2
1982–83		42	2
1983–84	Liverpool	—	—
1984–85		12	1
1985–86		14	3
1986–87		37	—
1987–88		35	4

Season	Club	League Appearances/Goals	
1988–89		15	1
1989–90		13	4

GILLHAUS, Hans

Born Helmond 5.11.63.
Forward. From PSV Eindhoven. Holland full caps.

1989–90	Aberdeen	20	8

GILLIGAN, Jimmy

Born London 24.1.64. Ht 6 0 Wt 12 06
Forward. From Apprentice. England Youth.

1981–82	Watford	1	—
1982–83		4	2
1982–83	*Lincoln C*	3	—
1983–84	Watford	12	4
1984–85		10	—
1985–86	Grimsby T	25	4
1986–87	Swindon T	17	5
1986–87	*Newport Co*	5	1
1986–87	Lincoln C	11	1
1987–88	Cardiff C	46	19
1988–89		46	15
1989–90		7	1
1989–90	Portsmouth	32	5

GILZEAN, Ian

Born Enfield 10.12.69. Ht 6 1 Wt 12 08
Forward. From Trainee.

1988–89	Tottenham H	—	—
1989–90		—	—

GINZBURG, Ben

Born Tel Aviv 11.12.64 Ht 6 0 Wt 13 00
Goalkeeper. From Maccabi Tel Aviv

1989–90	Rangers	4	—

GITTENS, Jon

Born Moseley 22.1.64. Ht 6 0 Wt 12 06
Defender. From Paget R.

1985–86	Southampton	4	—
1986–87		14	—
1987–88	Swindon T	29	—
1988–89		29	1
1989–90		40	4

GLEASURE, Peter

Born Luton 8.10.60. Ht 5 11 Wt 12 13
Goalkeeper. From Apprentice.

1978–79	Millwall	—	—
1979–80		—	—
1980–81		13	—
1981–82		38	—
1982–83		4	—
1982–83	*Northampton T*	11	—
1983–84	Northampton T	46	—
1984–85		43	—
1985–86		44	—
1986–87		46	—
1987–88		46	—
1988–89		46	—
1989–90		46	—

GLEGHORN, Nigel

Born Seaham 12.8.62. Ht 6 0 Wt 12 13
Midfield. From Seaham Red Star.

1985–86	Ipswich T	21	2
1986–87		29	7
1987–88		16	2
1988–89	Manchester C	32	6
1989–90		2	1
1989–90	Birmingham C	43	9

GOATER, Shaun

Born Bermuda 25.2.70. Ht 5 11
Wt 11 04
Forward.

1988–89	Manchester U	—	—
1989–90		—	—
1989–90	Rotherham U	12	2

GLOVER, Dean

Born West Bromwich 29.12.63. Ht 5 10
Wt 11 13
Defender. From Apprentice.

1981–82	Aston Villa	—	—
1982–83		—	—
1983–84		—	—

Season	Club	League Appearances/Goals	
1984–85		5	—
1985–86		18	—
1986–87		—	—
1987–88		5	—
1986–87	*Sheffield U*	5	—
1987–88	Middlesbrough	38	4
1988–89		12	1
1988–89	Port Vale	22	—
1989–90		44	4

GLOVER, Lee

Born Kettering 24.4.70. Ht 5 10
Wt 12 01
Forward. From Trainee. Scotland Under-21.

Season	Club	Apps	Goals
1986–87	Nottingham F	—	—
1987–88		20	3
1988–89		—	—
1989–90		—	—
1989–90	*Leicester C*	5	1
1989–90	*Barnsley*	8	—

GODDARD, Karl

Born Leeds 29.12.67. Ht 5 9 Wt 10 10
Defender. From Apprentice. England Schools.

Season	Club	Apps	Goals
1985–86	Manchester U	—	—
1986–87	Bradford C	20	—
1987–88		29	—
1988–89		23	—
1989–90		1	—
1989–90	*Exeter C*	1	—
1989–90	*Colchester U*	16	1

GODDARD, Paul

Born Harlington 12.10.59. Ht 5 8
Wt 11 13
Forward. From Apprentice. England Under-21, 1 full cap.

Season	Club	Apps	Goals
1977–78	QPR	7	1
1978–79		23	6
1979–80		40	16
1980–81	West Ham U	37	17
1981–82		39	15
1982–83		39	10
1983–84		5	1

Season	Club	League Appearances/Goals	
1984–85		40	9
1985–86		6	1
1986–87		4	1
1986–87	Newcastle U	26	11
1987–88		35	8
1988–89	Derby Co	31	7
1989–90		18	8
1989–90	Millwall	14	1

GODDEN, Tony

Born Gillingham 2.8.55. Ht 6 0
Wt 13 00
Goalkeeper. From Ashford T.

Season	Club	Apps	Goals
1975–76	WBA	—	—
1976–77		6	—
1976–77	*Preston NE*	—	—
1977–78	WBA	42	—
1978–79		42	—
1979–80		42	—
1980–81		42	—
1981–82		19	—
1982–83		12	—
1982–83	*Luton T*	12	—
1983–84	WBA	—	—
1983–84	*Walsall*	19	—
1984–85	WBA	41	—
1985–86		21	—
1985–86	*Chelsea*	8	—
1986–87	Chelsea	26	—
1987–88	Birmingham C	22	—
1988–89		7	—
1988–89	*Bury*	1	—
1988–89	*Sheffield W*	—	—
1989–90	Peterborough U	24	—

GODFREY, Kevin

Born Kennington 24.2.60. Ht 5 10
Wt 10 11
Forward. From Apprentice.

Season	Club	Apps	Goals
1976–77	Orient	—	—
1977–78		11	—
1978–79		6	—
1979–80		5	1
1980–81		9	2
1981–82		42	7
1982–83		45	11
1983–84		41	10

Season	Club	Apps	Goals
1984–85	....	40	10
1985–86	....	16	4
1985–86	*Plymouth Arg*	7	1
1986–87	Orient	36	10
1987–88	....	34	7
1988–89	Brentford	29	8
1989–90	....	27	2

GODFREY, Peter

Born Falkirk 12.10.57. Ht 6 0 Wt 11 07
Defender. From Linlithgow Rose.

Season	Club	Apps	Goals
1979–80	Stenhousemuir	2	—
1980–81	Meadowbank T	2	—
1981–82	....	30	6
1982–83	....	38	3
1983–84	....	37	3
1984–85	....	19	—
1984–85	St Mirren	15	1
1985–86	....	34	3
1986–87	....	38	1
1987–88	....	24	—
1988–89	....	27	1
1989–90	....	22	2

GOLDSMITH, Craig

Born Peterborough 27.8.63 Ht 5 7
Wt 11 03
Forward. From Blackstones.

Season	Club	Apps	Goals
1988–89	Peterborough U	40	6
1989–90	....	6	—
1989–90	Carlisle U	26	1

GOLDSMITH, Martin

Born Walsall 4.11.69 Ht 6 0 Wt 11 11
Forward. From Trainee.

Season	Club	Apps	Goals
1988–89	Walsall	2	—
1989–90	....	1	—
1989–90	*Larne*	—	—

GOLLEY, Mark

Born Beckenham 28.10.62. Ht 6 1
Wt 13 00
Midfield. From Crystal Palace, Sutton U (1988)

Season	Club	Apps	Goals
1989–90	Maidstone U	45	3

GOODACRE, Sam

Born Sheffield 1.12.70 Ht 5 10 Wt 11 00
Forward. From School.

Season	Club	Apps	Goals
1989–90	Sheffield W	—	—

GOODING, Mick

Born Newcastle 12.4.59 Ht 5 7 Wt 10 13
Forward. From Bishop Auckland.

Season	Club	Apps	Goals
1979–80	Rotherham U	34	3
1980–81	....	37	4
1981–82	....	22	2
1982–83	....	9	1
1982–83	Chesterfield	12	—
1983–84	....	—	—
1983–84	Rotherham U	26	7
1984–85	....	44	10
1985–86	....	40	8
1986–87	....	46	8
1987–88	Peterborough U	44	18
1988–89	....	3	3
1988–89	Wolverhampton W	31	4
1989–90	....	13	—
1989–90	Reading	27	3

GOODISON, Wayne

Born Wakefield 23.9.64. Ht 5 8
Wt 11 07
Defender. From Apprentice.

Season	Club	Apps	Goals
1982–83	Barnsley	3	—
1983–84	....	—	—
1984–85	....	12	—
1985–86	....	21	—
1986–87	....	—	—
1986–87	Crewe Alex	35	—
1987–88	....	34	—
1988–89	....	25	1
1989–90	Rochdale	45	4

GOODMAN, Don

Born Leeds 9.5.66. Ht 5 10 Wt 11 10
Forward. From school.

Season	Club	Apps	Goals
1983–84	Bradford C	2	—
1984–85	....	25	5

Season	Club	League Appearances/Goals	
1985–86		20	4
1986–87		23	5
1986–87	WBA	10	2
1987–88		40	7
1988–89		36	15
1989–90		39	21

GOODWIN, Mark

Born Sheffield 23.2.60. Ht 5 10
Wt 10 09
Midfield. From Apprentice.

Season	Club	League Appearances/Goals	
1977–78	Leicester C	14	3
1978–79		28	1
1979–80		30	4
1980–81		19	—
1980–81	Notts Co	10	2
1981–82		38	4
1982–83		34	4
1983–84		29	—
1984–85		38	4
1985–86		43	6
1986–87		45	4
1987–88	Walsall	36	2
1988–89		32	—
1989–90		24	—

GOODWIN, Shaun

Born Rotherham 14.6.69. Ht 5 7
Wt 8 10
Midfield. From Trainee.

Season	Club	League Appearances/Goals	
1987–88	Rotherham U	3	—
1988–89		41	4
1989–90		38	6

GOODYEAR, Clive

Born Lincoln 15.1.61. Ht 6 0 Wt 11 04
Defender. Local.

Season	Club	League Appearances/Goals	
1978–79	Luton T	—	—
1979–80		1	—
1980–81		5	1
1981–82		32	1
1982–83		35	2
1983–84		17	—
1984–85	Plymouth Arg	33	2
1985–86		41	2
1986–87		32	1
1987–88	Wimbledon	22	—
1988–89		—	—
1989–90		4	—

GORAM, Andy

Born Bury 13.4.64. Ht 5 11 Wt 11 06
Goalkeeper. From West Bromwich Apprentice. Scotland Under-21, 9 full caps.

Season	Club	League Appearances/Goals	
1981–82	Oldham Ath	3	—
1982–83		38	—
1983–84		22	—
1984–85		41	—
1985–86		41	—
1986–87		41	—
1987–88		9	—
1987–88	Hibernian	33	1
1988–89		36	—
1989–90		34	—

GORDON, Colin

Born Stourbridge 17.1.63. Ht 6 1
Wt 12 12
Forward. From Oldbury U.

Season	Club	League Appearances/Goals	
1984–85	Swindon T	33	17
1985–86		39	16
1986–87	Wimbledon	3	—
1986–87	*Gillingham*	4	2
1987–88	Reading	20	8
1987–88	*Bristol C*	8	4
1988–89	Reading	4	1
1988–89	Fulham	17	2
1989–90	Birmingham C	21	3

GORDON, Dale

Born Gt Yarmouth 9.1.67. Ht 5 10
Wt 11 08
Forward. From Apprentice. England Schools, Youth.

Season	Club	League Appearances/Goals	
1983–84	Norwich C	—	—
1984–85		23	3
1985–86		6	1
1986–87		41	5
1987–88		21	3

Season Club League Appearances/Goals

Season	Club	League Appearances/Goals	
1988–89		38	5
1989–90		26	3

GORE, Ian

Born Liverpool 10.1.68. Ht 5 11
Wt 12 04
Midfield.

Season	Club	League Appearances/Goals	
1986–87	Birmingham C	—	—
From Southport			
1987–88	Blackpool	—	—
1988–89		21	—
1989–90		34	—

GORE, Shaun

Born London 21.9.68. Ht 6 3 Wt 14 05
Defender.

Season	Club	League Appearances/Goals	
1985–86	Fulham	5	—
1986–87		7	—
1987–88		8	—
1988–89		6	—
1989–90		—	—

GORMAN, Paul

Born Dublin 6.8.63 Ht 5 10 Wt 12 00
Defender. From Apprentice. Eire Youth, Under-21.

Season	Club	League Appearances/Goals	
1980–81	Arsenal	—	—
1981–82		4	—
1982–83		—	—
1983–84		2	—
1984–85	Birmingham C	6	—
1984–85	Carlisle U	7	1
1985–86		24	—
1986–87		35	—
1987–88		37	—
1988–89		43	6
1989–90		2	—
1989–90	*Shelbourne*	—	—
1989–90	Shrewsbury T	19	1

GORMLEY, Eddie

Born Dublin 23.10.68. Ht 5 7 Wt 10 07
Midfield. From Bray W. Eire U-21.

Season	Club	League Appearances/Goals	
1987–88	Tottenham H	—	—
1988–89		—	—
1988–89	*Chesterfield*	4	—
1988–89	*Motherwell*	—	—
1989–90	Tottenham H	—	—
1989–90	*Shrewsbury T*	—	—

GORTON, Andy

Born Salford 23.9.66. Ht 5 11 Wt 11 04
Goalkeeper.

Season	Club	League Appearances/Goals	
1984–85	Oldham Ath	—	—
1985–86		1	—
1986–87		1	—
1986–87	*Stockport Co*	14	—
1987–88		24	—
1987–88	*Tranmere R*	1	—
1988–89	Stockport Co	34	—
1989–90	Lincoln C	20	—

GOSLING, Lee

Born Basingstoke 5.3.70. Ht 5 10
Wt 11 07
Midfield. From Trainee.

Season	Club	League Appearances/Goals	
1988–89	Portsmouth	—	—
1989–90		—	—

GOSNEY, Andy

Born Southampton 8.11.63. Ht 6 4
Wt 13 02
Goalkeeper. From Apprentice. England Youth.

Season	Club	League Appearances/Goals	
1981–82	Portsmouth	1	—
1982–83		—	—
1983–84		—	—
1984–85		—	—
1985–86		4	—
1986–87		—	—
1987–88		4	—
1988–89		14	—
1989–90		—	—

GOSS, Jeremy

Born Cyprus 11.5.65. Ht 5 9 Wt 10 09
Midfield. Amateur.

Season	Club	League Appearances/Goals	
1982–83	Norwich C	—	—
1983–84		1	—
1984–85		5	—

Season Club League Appearances/Goals

Season	Club	Apps	Goals
1985–86		—	—
1986–87		1	—
1987–88		22	2
1988–89		—	—
1989–90		7	—

GOTSMANOV, Sergei

Born USSR 17.3.59.
Midfield. From Dynamo Minsk.

Season	Club	Apps	Goals
1989–90	Brighton	16	4

GOUCK, Andy

Born Blackpool 8.6.72.
Midfield. From Trainee.

Season	Club	Apps	Goals
1989–90		8	1

GOUGH, Richard

Born Stockholm 5.4.62. Ht 6 0 Wt 12 00
Defender. From Witz University. Scotland Under-21, 50 full caps.

Season	Club	Apps	Goals
1980–81	Dundee U	4	—
1981–82		30	1
1982–83		34	8
1983–84		33	3
1984–85		33	6
1985–86		31	5
1986–87	Tottenham H	40	2
1987–88		9	—
1987–88	Rangers	31	5
1988–89		35	4
1989–90		26	—

GOURLAY, Archie

Born Greenock 29.6.69. Ht 5 8
Wt 10 00
Midfield.

Season	Club	Apps	Goals
1987–88	Morton	2	—
1987–88	Newcastle U	—	—
1988–89		1	—
1989–90		—	—
1989–90	*Morton*	4	—

GRACE, John

Born Dublin 16.2.64. Ht 6 2 Wt 12 07
Goalkeeper. From Tolka R.

Season	Club	Apps	Goals
1989–90	Colchester U	19	—

GRAHAM, Deniol

Born Cannock 4.10.69. Ht 5 10
Wt 10 05
Forward. From Trainee.

Season	Club	Apps	Goals
1987–88	Manchester U	1	—
1988–89		—	—
1989–90		1	—

GRAHAM, Jimmy

Born Glasgow 15.11.69 Ht 5 11
Wt 11 00
Midfield. From Trainee.

Season	Club	Apps	Goals
1988–89	Bradford C	1	—
1989–90		6	—
1989–90	*Rochdale*	11	—

GRAHAM, Mike

Born Lancaster 24.2.59. Ht 5 9
Wt 11 07
Defender. From Apprentice.

Season	Club	Apps	Goals
1976–77	Bolton W	—	—
1977–78		1	—
1978–79		9	—
1979–80		9	—
1980–81		27	—
1981–82	Swindon T	30	1
1982–83		46	—
1983–84		36	—
1984–85		29	—
1985–86	Mansfield T	45	—
1986–87		41	—
1987–88		46	1
1988–89		1	—
1988–89	Carlisle U	44	2
1989–90		43	—

GRAHAM, Milton

Born Tottenham 2.11.62. Ht 5 11
Wt 12 06
Forward. Local.

Season	Club	Apps	Goals
1981–82	Bournemouth	5	3
1982–83		20	2
1983–84		30	4

Season	Club	League Appearances/Goals	
1984–85		18	3
1985–86	Chester C	38	3
1986–87		42	4
1987–88		25	3
1988–89		24	1
1989–90	Peterborough U	15	2

GRAHAM, Tommy

Born Glasgow 31.3.58. Ht 5 10
Wt 11 10
Forward. From Arthurlie.

Season	Club	Apps	Goals
1977–78	Aston Villa	—	—
1978–79		—	—
1978–79	Barnsley	27	12
1979–80		11	1
1980–81		—	—
1980–81	Halifax T	34	9
1981–82		37	8
1982–83	Doncaster R	11	2
1982–83	Scunthorpe U	13	3
1983–84		27	4
1984–85		38	9
1985–86		31	5
1986–87	Scarborough	—	—
1987–88		44	7
1988–89		43	4
1989–90		24	—
1989–90	Halifax T	21	1

GRAINGER, Martin

Born Enfield 23.8.72.
Midfield. From Trainee.

Season	Club	Apps	Goals
1989–90	Colchester U	7	2

GRANT, Brian

Born Bannockburn 19.6.64. Ht 5 9
Wt 10 07
Midfield. From Fallin Violet.

Season	Club	Apps	Goals
1981–82	Stirling Alb	1	—
1982–83		1	—
1983–84		24	3
1984–85	Aberdeen	—	—
1985–86		—	—
1986–87		15	4
1987–88		7	1
1988–89		26	1
1989–90		31	6

GRANT, Peter

Born Bellshill 30.8.65. Ht 5 9 Wt 10 03
Midfield. From Celtic BC. Scotland Schools, Youth, B, Under-21, 2 full caps.

Season	Club	Apps	Goals
1982–83	Celtic	—	—
1983–84		3	—
1984–85		20	4
1985–86		30	1
1986–87		37	1
1987–88		37	2
1988–89		21	—
1989–90		26	—

GRANT, Roddy

Born Bloucester 16.9.66. Ht 5 11
Wt 11 00
Forward. From Strathbrock Jun.

Season	Club	Apps	Goals
1986–87	Cowdenbeath	24	14
1987–88		32	11
1988–89		8	2
1988–89	St Johnstone	28	5
1989–90		37	19

GRAY, Andy

Born Lambeth 22.2.64. Ht 5 11
Wt 13 03
Midfield. From Corinthian C. and Dulwich H. England Under-21.

Season	Club	Apps	Goals
1984–85	Crystal Palace	21	5
1985–86		30	10
1986–87		30	6
1987–88		17	6
1987–88	Aston Villa	19	1
1988–89		18	3
1988–89	QPR	11	2
1989–90	Crystal Palace	35	6

GRAY, Gareth

Born Longridge 24.2.70 Ht 6 2 Wt 11 02
Goalkeeper. From Darwen.

1988–89	Bolton W	—	—
1989–90		—	—

GRAY, Kevin

Born Sheffield 7.1.72
Midfield. From Trainee.

1988–89	Mansfield T	1	—
1989–90		16	—

GRAY, Paul

Born Belfast 28.1.70. Ht 5 9 Wt 11 13
Forward. From Trainee.

1988–89	Luton T	—	—
1989–90		7	1

GRAY, Philip

Born Belfast 2.10.68. Ht 5 10 Wt 11 07
Forward. From Apprentice. Northern Ireland Under-23.

1986–87	Tottenham H	1	—
1987–88		1	—
1988–89		1	—
1989–90		—	—
1989–90	*Barnsley*	3	—

GRAY, Steven

Born Irvine 7.2.67. Ht 5 6 Wt 10 02
Midfield. From Kilmarnock BC. Scotland Youth, Under-21.

1985–86	Aberdeen	13	1
1986–87		13	1
1987–88		7	—
1988–89		4	—
1989–90		—	—

GRAY, Stuart

Born Withernsea 19.4.60. Ht 5 10
Wt 11 05
Defender. Local.

1980–81	Nottingham F	14	1
1981–82		33	2
1982–83		2	—
1982–83	*Bolton W*	10	—
1983–84	Barnsley	17	8
1984–85		7	—
1985–86		36	2
1986–87		40	11
1987–88		20	2
1987–88	Aston Villa	20	5
1988–89		35	4
1989–90		29	—

GRAYSON, Neil

Born York 1.1.64.
Defender. From Rowntree Mackintosh.

1989–90	Doncaster R	6	1

GRAYSON, Simon

Born Ripon 16.12.69 Ht 5 11 Wt 10 11
Midfield. From Trainee.

1987–88	Leeds U	2	—
1988–89		—	—
1989–90		—	—

GRAYSON, Simon

Born Sheffield 21.10.68. Ht 6 1
Wt 12 00
Forward.

1986–87	Sheffield U	—	—
1987–88		—	—
1987–88	*Chesterfield*	8	—
1987–88	Hartlepool U	1	—
1988–89		41	12
1989–90		2	—

GREALISH, Tony

Born Paddington 21.9.56. Ht 5 7
Wt 12 00
Midfield. From Apprentice. Eire Youth, 44 full caps.

1974–75	Orient	25	2
1975–76		38	1
1976–77		33	2
1977–78		36	—
1978–79		39	5
1979–80	Luton T	41	2
1980–81		37	—
1981–82	Brighton	37	1
1982–83		38	2

Season	Club	League Appearances/Goals	
1983–84		25	3
1983–84	WBA	11	—
1984–85		38	4
1985–86		16	1
1986–87		—	—
1986–87	Manchester C	11	—
1987–88	Rotherham U	38	3
1988–89		39	3
1989–90		33	—

GREAVES, Steve

Born London 17.1.70 Ht 5 9 Wt 11 03
Midfield. From Trainee.

Season	Club	League Appearances/Goals	
1987–88	Fulham	1	—
1988–89		—	—
1988–89	*Waterford*	—	—
1989–90	Fulham	—	—
1989–90	*Brighton*	—	—

GREEN, Matt

Born Dudley 6.11.70. Ht 5 11 Wt 11 07
Midfield. From Trainee.

Season	Club	League Appearances/Goals	
1989–90	Wolverhampton W	—	—

GREEN, Richard

Born Wolverhampton 22.11.67. Ht 6 0
Wt 11 08
Defender.

Season	Club	League Appearances/Goals	
1986–87	Shrewsbury T	15	—
1987–88		31	2
1988–89		39	3
1989–90		40	—

GREEN, Ron

Born Birmingham 3.10.56. Ht 6 2
Wt 14 00
Goalkeeper. From Alvechurch.

Season	Club	League Appearances/Goals	
1977–78	Walsall	1	—
1978–79		1	—
1979–80		39	—
1980–81		24	—
1981–82		46	—
1982–83		35	—
1983–84		17	—
1983–84	*WBA*	—	—
1984–85	Shrewsbury T	19	—
1984–85	*Bristol R*	18	—
1985–86	Bristol R	38	—
1986–87	Scunthorpe U	43	—
1987–88		35	—
1988–89	Wimbledon	4	—
1988–89	*Shrewsbury T*	17	—
1988–89	*Manchester C*	—	—
1988–89	Walsall	2	—
1989–90		21	—

GREEN, Scott

Born Walsall 15.1.70
Forward. From Trainee.

Season	Club	League Appearances/Goals	
1988–89	Derby Co	—	—
1989–90		—	—
1989–90	Bolton W	5	2

GREENALL, Colin

Born Billinge 30.12.63. Ht 5 10
Wt 11 06
Defender. From Apprentice.

Season	Club	League Appearances/Goals	
1980–81	Blackpool	12	—
1981–82		18	—
1982–83		24	1
1983–84		39	4
1984–85		44	3
1985–86		43	1
1986–87		3	—
1986–87	Gillingham	37	2
1987–88		25	2
1987–88	Oxford U	12	—
1988–89		40	2
1989–90		15	—
1989–90	*Bury*	3	—

GREENMAN, Chris

Born Bristol 22.12.68 Ht 5 10
Wt 11 06
Defender. From school.

Season	Club	League Appearances/Goals	
1988–89	Coventry C	—	—
1989–90		—	—

GREENOUGH, Ricky

Born Mexborough 30.5.61. Ht 6 1
Wt 13 06

Season	Club	League Appearances/Goals	

Defender. From Boston and Alfreton T.

1984–85	Chester C	24	3
1985–86		33	5
1986–87		44	7
1987–88		31	—
1988–89	Scarborough	—	—
1988–89	York C	26	1
1989–90		3	—

GREENWOOD, Nigel

Born Preston 27.11.66. Ht 5 11
Wt 12 00
Forward. From Apprentice.

1984–85	Preston NE	15	5
1985–86		30	9
1986–87	Bury	37	15
1987–88		30	4
1988–89		23	1
1989–90		20	5
1989–90	Preston NE	5	—

GREER, Ross

Born Perth (Australia) 23.9.57.
Forward.

1989–90	Chester C	2	—

GREGORY, David

Born Sudbury 23.1.70. Ht 5 11 Wt 11 06
Midfield. From Trainee.

1987–88	Ipswich	—	—
1988–89		2	—
1989–90		4	—

GREGORY, John

Born Scunthorpe 11.5.54. Ht 6 1
Wt 11 00
Midfield. From Apprentice.

1972–73	Northampton T	9	—
1973–74		46	—
1974–75		41	1
1975–76		45	3
1976–77		46	4
1977–78	Aston Villa	26	3
1978–79		39	7
1979–80	Brighton	33	—
1980–81		39	7
1981–82	QPR	34	9
1982–83		42	15
1983–84		37	7
1984–85		37	5
1985–86		11	—
1985–86	Derby Co	22	4
1986–87		42	12
1987–88		39	6
1988–89		—	—
1989–90	Portsmouth	—	—
1989–90	Plymouth Arg	3	—
1989–90	Bolton W	7	—

GREGORY, Tony

Born Doncaster 21.3.68. Ht 5 8
Wt 11 09
Midfield. From Apprentice. England
Schools, Youth.

1985–86	Sheffield W	5	—
1986–87		10	1
1987–88		—	—
1988–89		3	—
1989–90		—	—

GREW, Mark

Born Bilston 15.2.58. Ht 5 11 Wt 12 08
Goalkeeper. From Amateur.

1976–77	WBA	—	—
1977–78		—	—
1978–79		—	—
1978–79	*Wigan Ath*	4	—
1978–79	*Notts Co*	—	—
1979–80	WBA	—	—
1980–81		—	—
1981–82		23	—
1982–83		10	—
1983–84	Leicester C	5	—
1983–84	*Oldham Ath*	5	—
1983–84	Ipswich T	—	—
1984–85		6	—
1985–86		—	—
1985–86	*Fulham*	4	—
1985–86	*WBA*	1	—
1985–86	*Derby Co*	—	—
1986–87	Port Vale	3	—
1987–88		41	—

Season	Club	League Appearances/Goals	
1988–89		37	—
1989–90		43	—

GREWCOCK, Neil

Born Leicester 26.4.62. Ht 5 6 Wt 11 09
Forward. From Apprentice.

Season	Club	Apps	Goals
1979–80	Leicester C	1	1
1980–81		7	—
1981–82		—	—
1981–82	*Gillingham*	13	1
1982–83	Gillingham	21	3
From Shepshed C			
1984–85	Burnley	46	6
1985–86		38	7
1986–87		36	9
1987–88		32	—
1988–89		13	1
1989–90		7	2

GREYGOOSE, Dean

Born Thetford 18.12.64. Ht 5 11
Wt 11 05
Goalkeeper. From Apprentice. England Youth.

Season	Club	Apps	Goals
1982–83	Cambridge U	—	—
1983–84		16	—
1984–85		10	—
1984–85	*Orient*	—	—
1985–86	Cambridge U	—	—
1985–86	*Lincoln C*	6	—
1985–86	Orient	1	—
1986–87		—	—
1986–87	C. Palace	—	—
1987–88		—	—
1987–88	Crewe Alex	43	—
1988–89		36	—
1989–90		32	—

GRICE, Neil

Born Walthamstow 18.4.71. Ht 5 9
Wt 10 07
Forward. From Trainee.

Season	Club	Apps	Goals
1989–90	Ipswich T	—	—

GRIFFIN, James

Born Hamilton 1.1.67 Ht 5 8 Wt 11 04
Defender. From Fir Park BC.

Season	Club	Apps	Goals
1985–86	Motherwell	1	—
1986–87		—	—
1987–88		6	—
1987–88		4	—
1988–89		1	—
1989–90		11	—

GRIFFITH, Colen

Born Georgetown 26.12.62. Ht 5 10
Wt 11 07
Forward. From Kettering T.

Season	Club	Apps	Goals
1989–90	Cardiff C	38	9

GRIFFITHS, Brian

Born Prescot 26.1.65
Forward. From St Helens T.

Season	Club	Apps	Goals
1988–89	Wigan Ath	29	8
1989–90		45	7

GRIFFITHS, Carl

Born Coventry 15.7.71 Ht 5 9 Wt 10 06
Forward. From Trainee.

Season	Club	Apps	Goals
1988–89	Shrewsbury T	28	6
1989–90		18	4

GRITT, Steve

Born Bournemouth 31.10.57. Ht 5 10
Wt 11 04
Midfield. From Apprentice.

Season	Club	Apps	Goals
1976–77	Bournemouth	6	3
1977–78	Charlton Ath	34	3
1978–79		39	3
1979–80		31	7
1980–81		40	—
1981–82		34	3
1982–83		27	1
1983–84		33	1
1984–85		35	1
1985–86		11	2

Season	Club	League Appearances/Goals	
1986–87		14	1
1987–88		27	—
1988–89		22	2
1989–90	Walsall	20	1
1989–90	Charlton Ath	2	—

GROBBELAAR, Bruce

Born Durban 6.10.57. Ht 6 1 Wt 13 00
Goalkeeper. From Vancouver Whitecaps. Zimbabwe full caps.

Season	Club	Apps	Goals
1979–80	Crewe Alex	24	1
From Vancouver Whitecaps			
1980–81	Liverpool	—	—
1981–82		42	—
1982–83		42	—
1983–84		42	—
1984–85		42	—
1985–86		42	—
1986–87		31	—
1987–88		38	—
1988–89		21	—
1989–90		38	—

GROVES, Paul

Born Derby 28.2.66. Ht 5 11 Wt 11 05
Midfield. From Burton Alb.

Season	Club	Apps	Goals
1987–88	Leicester C	1	1
1988–89		15	—
1989–90		—	—
1989–90	*Lincoln C*	8	1
1989–90	Blackpool	19	1

GROVES, Perry

Born London 19.4.65. Ht 5 11 Wt 12 01
Forward. From Apprentice.

Season	Club	Apps	Goals
1981–82	Colchester U	9	—
1982–83		17	2
1983–84		42	2
1984–85		44	10
1985–86		43	12
1986–87		1	—
1986–87	Arsenal	25	3
1987–88		34	6
1988–89		21	4
1989–90		30	4

GUMMER, Jason

Born Tredegar 27.10.67. Ht 5 9
Wt 11 00
Forward. From Apprentice. Wales Youth.

Season	Club	Apps	Goals
1985–86	Cardiff C	5	1
1986–87		15	3
1987–88		2	—
1988–89		11	1
1988–89	*Torquay U*	7	1
1989–90	Cardiff C	1	—

GUNN, Andy

Born Barking 2.2.71. Ht 6 0 Wt 12 01
Forward. From Trainee.

Season	Club	Apps	Goals
1988–89	Watford	—	—
1989–90		—	—
1989–90	Crewe Alex	1	—

GUNN, Bryan

Born Thurso 22.12.63. Ht 6 2 Wt 13 13
Goalkeeper. From Invergordon BC. Scotland Schools, Youth, Under-21, B, 1 full cap.

Season	Club	Apps	Goals
1980–81	Aberdeen	—	—
1981–82		—	—
1982–83		1	—
1983–84		—	—
1984–85		2	—
1985–86		10	—
1986–87		2	—
1986–87	Norwich C	29	—
1987–88		38	—
1988–89		37	—
1989–90		37	—

GUNN, Bryn

Born Kettering 21.8.58. Ht 6 2 Wt 13 7
Defender. From Apprentice.

Season	Club	Apps	Goals
1975–76	Nottingham F	11	—
1976–77		—	—
1977–78		—	—
1978–79		1	—

Season	Club	League Appearances/Goals	
1979–80		2	—
1980–81		26	—
1981–82		37	—
1982–83		33	1
1983–84		4	—
1984–85		17	—
1985–86		—	—
1985–86	*Shrewsbury T*	9	—
1985–86	*Walsall*	6	—
1985–86	*Mansfield T*	5	—
1986–87	Peterborough U	39	7
1987–88		46	—
1988–89		46	7
1989–90	Chesterfield	46	8

GUSCOTT, Lindon

Born London 29.3.72
Midfield. From West Ham schoolboy, Gillingham, Trainee.

Season	Club	League Appearances/Goals	
1988–89	Gillingham	2	—
1989–90		—	—

GYNN, Mick

Born Peterborough 19.8.61. Ht 5 5
Wt 10 10
Midfield. From Apprentice.

Season	Club	League Appearances/Goals	
1978–79	Peterborough U	11	2
1979–80		27	1
1980–81		29	7
1981–82		46	6
1982–83		43	17
1983–84	Coventry C	23	2
1984–85		39	4
1985–86		12	1
1986–87		22	5
1987–88		25	3
1988–89		8	1
1989–90		34	3

HAAG, Kelly

Born Enfield 6.10.70.
Forward. From Trainee.

Season	Club	League Appearances/Goals	
1989–90	Brentford	5	—

HACKETT, Gary

Born Stourbridge 11.10.62. Ht 5 7
Wt 11 03
Forward. From Bromsgrove R.

Season	Club	League Appearances/Goals	
1983–84	Shrewsbury T	31	3
1984–85		38	5
1985–86		42	6
1986–87		39	3
1987–88	Aberdeen	15	—
1987–88	Shrewsbury T	1	—
1988–89	Stoke C	46	5
1989–90		26	2
1989–90	WBA	14	2

HADDOCK, Peter

Born Newcastle 9.12.61. Ht 5 11
Wt 11 05
Defender. From Apprentice.

Season	Club	League Appearances/Goals	
1979–80	Newcastle U	—	—
1980–81		—	—
1981–82		30	—
1982–83		17	—
1983–84		3	—
1984–85		1	—
1985–86		6	—
1985–86	*Burnley*	7	—
1986–87	Leeds U	11	—
1987–88		40	1
1988–89		12	—
1989–90		40	—

HAGAN, Jim

Born Birmingham 10.8.56. Ht 5 10
Wt 10 09
Defender. From Larne.

Season	Club	League Appearances/Goals	
1977–78	Coventry C	—	—
1978–79		13	—
1979–80		—	—
1979–80	*Torquay U*	7	—

From Detroit Express, Seiko

Season	Club	League Appearances/Goals	
1981–82	Coventry C	3	—
1982–83	Birmingham C	32	—
1983–84		33	—
1984–85		29	—
1985–86		31	—
1986–87		12	—
From Spain			
1989–90	Colchester U	2	—

HAIG, Richard

Born Pontypridd 29.12.70
Midfield. From Trainee.

Season	Club	League Appearances/Goals	
1988–89	Cardiff C	1	—
1989–90		4	—

HAIGH, Kevin

Born Sheffield 16.7.70 Ht 5 9 Wt 11 00
Forward. Local.

Season	Club	League Appearances/Goals	
1988–89	Sheffield W	—	—
1989–90		—	—

HAINES, Ivan

Born Chatham 14.9.68. Ht 5 9 Wt 10 12
Midfield.

Season	Club	League Appearances/Goals	
1987–88	Gillingham	1	—
1988–89		12	—
1989–90		26	—

HALES, Kevin

Born Dartford 13.1.61. Ht 5 7 Wt 10 04
Defender. From Apprentice.

Season	Club	League Appearances/Goals	
1978–79	Chelsea	—	—
1979–80		7	—
1980–81		—	—
1981–82		10	2
1982–83		3	—
1983–84	Orient	43	2
1984–85		33	—
1985–86		31	2
1986–87		33	1
1987–88		42	6
1988–89		35	9
1989–90		39	2

HALL, Derek

Born Manchester 5.1.65. Ht 5 8
Wt 12 03
Midfield. From Apprentice.

Season	Club	League Appearances/Goals	
1982–83	Coventry C	1	—
1983–84		—	—
1983–84	*Torquay U*	10	2
1984–85	Torquay U	45	4
1985–86	Swindon T	10	—
1986–87	Southend U	43	9
1987–88		40	3
1988–89		40	3
1989–90	Halifax T	41	4

HALL, Gareth

Born Croydon 20.3.69 Ht 5 8 Wt 10 07
Defender. Wales Under-21, 7 full caps.

Season	Club	League Appearances/Goals	
1986–87	Chelsea	1	—
1987–88		13	—
1988–89		22	—
1989–90		13	1

HALL, Mark

Born Doncaster 11.5.70
Midfield. From Trainee.

Season	Club	League Appearances/Goals	
1987–88	Doncaster R	1	—
1988–89		1	—
1989–90		—	—

HALL, Paul

Born Manchester 3.7.72. Ht 5 9
Wt 10 02
Forward. From Trainee.

Season	Club	League Appearances/Goals	
1989–90	Torquay U	10	—

HALL, Richard

Born Ipswich 14.3.72. Ht 6 1 Wt 13 00
Defender. From Trainee.

Season Club League Appearances/Goals

Season	Club	League Appearances/Goals	
1989–90	Scunthorpe U	1	—

HALL, Wayne

Born Rotherham 25.10.68 Ht 5 8
Wt 10 04
Midfield. From Darlington.

Season	Club	League Appearances/Goals	
1988–89	York C	2	—
1989–90		27	3

HALLWORTH, Jon

Born Stockport 26.10.65. Ht 6 1
Wt 14 03
Goalkeeper. From school.

Season	Club	League Appearances/Goals	
1983–84	Ipswich T	—	—
1984–85		—	—
1984–85	*Swindon T*	—	—
1984–85	*Fulham*	—	—
1984–85	*Bristol R*	2	—
1985–86	Ipswich T	6	—
1986–87		6	—
1987–88		33	—
1988–89		—	—
1988–89	Oldham Ath	16	—
1989–90		15	—

HALPIN, John

Born Broxburn 15.11.61. Ht 5 10
Wt 11 05
Midfield. From Celtic BC. Scotland Youth.

Season	Club	League Appearances/Goals	
1981–82	Celtic	3	—
1982–83		—	—
1983–84		4	—
1984–85	*Sunderland*	—	—
1984–85	Carlisle U	19	1
1985–86		33	5
1986–87		7	—
1987–88		23	3
1988–89		33	7
1989–90		17	—

HALSALL, Mick

Born Bootle 21.7.61. Ht 5 10 Wt 11 04
Midfield. From Apprentice.

Season	Club	League Appearances/Goals	
1979–80	Liverpool	—	—
1980–81		—	—
1981–82		—	—
1982–83		—	—
1982–83	Birmingham C	12	1
1983–84		21	2
1984–85		3	—
1984–85	Carlisle U	26	5
1985–86		41	4
1986–87		25	2
1986–87	Grimsby T	12	—
1987–88	Peterborough U	45	4
1988–89		42	1
1989–90		46	10

HAMILTON, Brian

Born Paisley 5.8.67. Ht 6 0 Wt 11 07
Defender. From Pollok United BC. Scotland Schools, Under-21.

Season	Club	League Appearances/Goals	
1985–86	St Mirren	8	—
1986–87		28	3
1987–88		27	—
1988–89		23	1
1989–90	Hibernian	28	1

HAMILTON, David

Born South Shields 7.11.60. Ht 5 6
Wt 10 06
Defender. From Apprentice. England Youth.

Season	Club	League Appearances/Goals	
1978–79	Sunderland	—	—
1979–80		—	—
1980–81		—	—
1980–81	Blackburn R	3	—
1981–82		17	—
1982–83		32	2
1983–84		26	2
1984–85		3	—
1984–85	*Cardiff C*	10	—
1985–86	Blackburn R	33	3
1986–87	Wigan Ath	41	3
1987–88		45	2
1988–89		17	2
1989–90	Chester C	28	—

HAMILTON, Gary

Born Glasgow 27.12.65. Ht 5 8
Wt 12 03

Midfield. From Apprentice.

Season	Club	League Appearances	Goals
1982–83	Middlesbrough	9	2
1983–84		31	3
1984–85		36	—
1985–86		33	4
1986–87		43	7
1987–88		41	6
1988–89		36	3
1989–90		—	—

HAMILTON, Ian

Born Stevenage 14.12.67. Ht 5 9
Wt 11 03
Forward. From Apprentice.

Season	Club	League Appearances	Goals
1985–86	Southampton	—	—
1986–87		—	—
1987–88		—	—
1987–88	Cambridge U	9	1
1988–89		15	—
1988–89	Scunthorpe U	27	1
1989–90		43	6

HAMILTON, Lindsay

Born Bellshill 11.8.62. Ht 6 2 Wt 13 07
Goalkeeper. From Thorniewood.

Season	Club	League Appearances	Goals
1982–83	Stenhousemuir	4	—
1983–84		38	—
1984–85		39	—
1985–86		29	—
1986–87		13	—
1986–87	Rangers	—	—
1987–88		—	—
1988–89		—	—
1988–89	*Charlton Ath*	—	—
1989–90	Rangers	—	—
1989–90	*Leeds U*	—	—
1989–90	*Clydebank*	1	—
1989–90	*Stirling Albion*	1	—

HAMMOND, Nicky

Born Hornchurch 7.9.67. Ht 6 0
Wt 11 13
Goalkeeper. From Apprentice.

Season	Club	League Appearances	Goals
1985–86	Arsenal	—	—
1986–87		—	—
1986–87	*Bristol R*	3	—
1986–87	*Peterborough U*	—	—
1986–87	*Aberdeen*	—	—
1987–88	Swindon T	4	—
1988–89		—	—
1989–90		—	—

HANCOCK, Tony

Born Manchester 31.1.67 Ht 6 1
Wt 12 12
Forward. From Stockport Georgians

Season	Club	League Appearances	Goals
1988–89	Stockport Co	22	5
1989–90	Burnley	17	—
1989–90	Preston NE	—	—

HANNIGAN, Al

Born Islington 26.1.71 Ht 6 0 Wt 12 04
Defender. From Trainee. Northern Ireland Youth.

Season	Club	League Appearances	Goals
1988–89	Arsenal	—	—
1989–90		—	—
1989–90	*Torquay U*	7	—

HANSBURY, Roger

Born Barnsley 26.1.55. Ht 5 11 Wt 12 0
Goalkeeper. From Apprentice.

Season	Club	League Appearances	Goals
1972–73	Norwich C	—	—
1973–74		—	—
1974–75		4	—
1975–76		—	—
1976–77		4	—
1976–77	*Bolton W*	—	—
1977–78	Norwich C	14	—
1977–78	*Cambridge U*	11	—
1978–79	Norwich C	18	—
1978–79	*Orient*	—	—
1979–80	Norwich C	16	—
1980–81		22	—
1981–82		—	—
From Eastern, Hong Kong.			
1983–84	Burnley	46	—
1984–85		37	—
1985–86	Cambridge U	37	—
1985–86	Birmingham C	—	—
1986–87		31	—
1987–88		22	—
1987–88	*Sheffield U*	5	—

1988–89	Birmingham C	3	—
1988–89	*Wolverhampton W*	3	—
1989–90	Birmingham C	1	—
1989–90	*Colchester U*	4	—
1989–90	Cardiff C	35	—

HANSEN, Alan

Born Alloa 13.6.55. Ht 6 1 Wt 13 00
Defender. From Sauchie BC. Scotland Under-23, 26 full caps.

1973–74	Partick T	1	—
1974–75		29	—
1975–76		21	2
1976–77		35	4
1976–77	Liverpool	—	—
1977–78		18	—
1978–79		34	1
1979–80		38	4
1980–81		36	1
1981–82		35	—
1982–83		34	—
1983–84		42	1
1984–85		41	—
1985–86		41	—
1986–87		39	—
1987–88		39	1
1988–89		6	—
1989–90		31	—

HARBEY, Graham

Born Chesterfield 29.8.64. Ht 5 8
Wt 10 8
Defender. From Apprentice.

1982–83	Derby Co	—	—
1983–84		19	—
1984–85		4	1
1985–86		3	—
1986–87		14	—
1987–88	Ipswich T	35	1
1988–89		23	—
1989–90		1	—
1989–90	WBA	30	—

HARDWICK, Steve

Born Mansfield 6.9.56. Ht 5 11
Wt 13 00
Goalkeeper. From Amateur. England Youth.

1974–75	Chesterfield	5	—
1975–76		12	—
1976–77		21	—
1976–77	Newcastle U	—	—
1977–78		9	—
1978–79		31	—
1979–80		41	—
1980–81		4	—
1981–82		—	—
1982–83		7	—
1982–83	Oxford U	18	—
1983–84		46	—
1984–85		42	—
1985–86		23	—
1985–86	*C. Palace*	3	—
1986–87	Oxford U	23	—
1987–88		4	—
1987–88	*Sunderland*	6	—
1988–89	Huddersfield T	46	—
1989–90		21	—

HARDY, Jason

Born Burnley 14.12.69 Ht 5 10
Wt 11 04
Midfield. From Trainee.

1986–87	Burnley	1	—
1987–88		—	—
1988–89		17	1
1989–90		22	—

HARDY, Phil

Born Chester 9.4.73.
Defender.

1989–90	Wrexham	1	—

HARDYMAN, Paul

Born Portsmouth 11.3.64. Ht 5 8
Wt 11 07
Defender. Local. England Under-21.

1983–84	Portsmouth	3	—
1984–85		15	—
1985–86		21	1
1986–87		33	—
1987–88		20	1

Season	Club	League Appearances/Goals	
1988–89		25	1
1989–90	Sunderland	42	7

HARFORD, Mick

Born Sunderland 12.2.59 Ht 6 2
Wt 13 09
Forward. From Lambton St BC. England B, 2 full caps.

Season	Club	League Appearances/Goals	
1977–78	Lincoln C	27	9
1978–79		31	6
1979–80		36	16
1980–81		21	10
1980–81	Newcastle U	19	4
1981–82	Bristol C	30	11
1981–82	Birmingham C	12	9
1982–83		29	6
1983–84		39	8
1984–85		12	2
1984–85	Luton T	22	15
1985–86		37	22
1986–87		18	4
1987–88		25	9
1988–89		33	7
1989–90		4	—
1989–90	Derby Co	16	4

HARGREAVES, Christian

Born Cleethorpes 12.5.72. Ht 5 10
Wt 10 13
Forward. From Trainee.

Season	Club	League Appearances/Goals	
1989–90	Grimsby T	19	2

HARKNESS, Steven

Born Carlisle 27.8.71 Ht 5 9 Wt 10 11
Midfield. From Trainee.

Season	Club	League Appearances/Goals	
1988–89	Carlisle U	13	—
1989–90	Liverpool	—	—

HARLE, David

Born Denaby 15.8.63. Ht 5 9 Wt 11 02
Midfield. From Apprentice. England Youth.

Season	Club	League Appearances/Goals	
1979–80	Doncaster R	1	—
1980–81		34	1
1981–82		26	2
1982–83	Exeter C	37	6
1983–84		6	—
1983–84	Doncaster R	29	6
1984–85		37	9
1985–86		17	2
1985–86	Leeds U	3	—
1985–86	*Bristol C*	8	—
1986–87	Bristol C	15	2
1986–87	Scunthorpe U	26	2
1987–88		45	6
1988–89		18	2
1988–89	Peterborough U	7	—
1989–90		15	2
1989–90	Doncaster R	10	—

HARPER, Alan

Born Liverpool 1.11.60. Ht 5 9
Wt 10 10
Defender. From Apprentice. England Youth.

Season	Club	League Appearances/Goals	
1977–78	Liverpool	—	—
1978–79		—	—
1979–80		—	—
1980–81		—	—
1981–82		—	—
1982–83		—	—
1983–84	Everton	29	1
1984–85		13	—
1985–86		21	—
1986–87		36	3
1987–88		28	—
1988–89	Sheffield W	24	—
1989–90		11	—
1989–90	Manchester C	21	—

HARPER, Steve

Born Stoke 3.2.69. Ht 5 10 Wt 11 05
Forward. From Trainee.

Season	Club	League Appearances/Goals	
1987–88	Port Vale	21	2
1988–89		7	—
1988–89	Preston NE	5	—
1989–90		36	10

HARRIS, Andrew

Born Birmingham 17.11.79. Ht 5 10
Wt 12 02

Season	Club	League Appearances/Goals	

Midfield. From Trainee.

1989–90	Birmingham C	1	—

HARRIS, Mark

Born Reading 15.7.63. Ht 6 1 Wt 12 05
Defender. From Wokingham.

1987–88	Crystal Palace	—	—
1988–89		2	—
1989–90		—	—
1989–90	*Burnley*	4	—
1989–90	Swansea C	41	2

HARRISON, Frankie

Born Middlesbrough 19.9.63. Ht 6 1
Wt 12 06
Defender.

1982–83	Middlesbrough	—	—
From local.			
1985–86	Lincoln C	1	—
1986–87	Halifax T	14	—
1987–88		18	—
1988–89		13	—
1989–90		9	—

HARRISON, Gerry

Born Lambeth 15.4.72.
Midfield. From Trainee.

1989–90	Watford	3	—

HARRISON, Wayne

Born Stockport 15.11.67. Ht 5 8
Wt 10 07
Forward. From Apprentice.

1984–85	Oldham Ath	5	1
1984–85	Liverpool	—	—
1984–85	*Oldham Ath*	1	—
1985–86	Liverpool	—	—
1986–87		—	—
1987–88		—	—
1988–89		—	—
1988–89	*Crewe Alex*	3	1
1989–90	Liverpool	—	—

HARROWER, Steven

Born Exeter 9.10.61. Ht 5 8 Wt 11 01
Midfield. Local.

1983–84	Exeter C	13	1
1984–85		31	1
1985–86		38	6
1986–87		34	—
1987–88		46	2
1988–89		18	—
1989–90		7	—

HART, Nigel

Born Golborne 1.10.58. Ht 6 0 Wt 12 03
Defender. Local.

1978–79	Wigan Ath	—	—
1979–80		1	—
1979–80	Leicester C	—	—
1980–81		—	—
1981–82	Blackpool	28	—
1982–83		9	—
1982–83	Crewe Alex	28	—
1983–84		37	3
1984–85		44	6
1985–86		23	—
1986–87		10	1
1986–87	Bury	11	—
1987–88		34	2
1988–89	Stockport Co	38	2
1989–90		1	—
1989–90	Chesterfield	27	2

HART, Peter

Born Mexborough 14.8.57. Ht 5 11
Wt 12 10
Defender. From Apprentice.

1973–74	Huddersfield T	1	—
1974–75		13	—
1975–76		19	1
1976–77		44	1
1977–78		41	—
1978–79		46	1
1979–80		46	4
1980–81	Walsall	45	5

Season	Club	League Appearances/Goals	
1981–82		45	1
1982–83		45	—
1983–84		45	3
1984–85		46	—
1985–86		44	2
1986–87		46	—
1987–88		37	1
1988–89		27	—
1989–90		10	—

HARTFIELD, Charlie

Born London 4.9.71. Ht 6 0 Wt 12 00
Defender. From Trainee.

Season	Club	Apps	Goals
1989–90	Arsenal	—	—

HARTFORD, Asa

Born Clydebank 24.10.50. Ht 5 7
Wt 11 04
Midfield. From Amateur. Scotland Under-21, Under-23, 50 full caps.

Season	Club	Apps	Goals
1967–68	WBA	6	1
1968–69		26	7
1969–70		34	1
1970–71		34	2
1971–72		39	1
1972–73		41	3
1973–74		33	3
1974–75	Manchester C	30	2
1975–76		39	9
1976–77		40	4
1977–78		37	4
1978–79		39	3
1979–80	Nottingham F	3	—
1979–80	Everton	35	1
1980–81		39	5
1981–82		7	—
1981–82	Manchester C	30	3
1982–83		38	3
1983–84		7	1
From Ft Lauderdale			
1984–85	Norwich C	28	2
1985–86	Bolton W	46	5
1986–87		35	3
1987–88	Stockport Co	31	—
1988–89		14	—
1988–89	Oldham Ath	7	—
1989–90	Shrewsbury T	17	—

HARTIGAN, Richard

Born Solihull 10.9.70. Ht 5 6 Wt 9 04
Forward. From Trainee.

Season	Club	Apps	Goals
1989–90	Wolverhampton W	—	—

HARVEY, Graham

Born Musselburgh 23.4.61. Ht 5 11
Wt 11 04
Forward. From Ormiston Primrose.

Season	Club	Apps	Goals
1982–83	Hibernian	14	1
1983–84		16	2
1984–85		3	—
1984–85	Dundee	7	2
1985–86		30	5
1986–87		33	12
1987–88		29	4
1988–89		20	4
1989–90		6	1

HARVEY, Jimmy

Born Lurgan 2.5.58. Ht 5 9 Wt 11 04
Midfield. From Glenavon. Northern Ireland, Under-23.

Season	Club	Apps	Goals
1977–78	Arsenal	1	—
1978–79		2	—
1979–80		—	—
1979–80	*Hereford U*	11	—
1980–81	Hereford U	30	1
1981–82		42	5
1982–83		41	5
1983–84		44	9
1984–85		34	5
1985–86		42	9
1986–87		34	5
1986–87	Bristol C	2	—
1987–88		1	—
1987–88	*Wrexham*	6	—
1987–88	Tranmere R	33	3

Season	Club	League Appearances/Goals	
1988–89		42	4
1989–90		46	7

HARVEY, Lee

Born Harlow 21.12.66. Ht 5 11
Wt 11 07
Midfield. From Local. England Youth.

Season	Club	Apps	Goals
1983–84	Orient	4	—
1984–85		4	—
1985–86		12	2
1986–87		15	1
1987–88		23	1
1988–89		29	6
1989–90		37	6

HARVEY, Richard

Born Letchworth 17.4.69. Ht 5 9
Wt 11 10
Defender. From Apprentice. England Youth.

Season	Club	Apps	Goals
1986–87	Luton T	5	—
1987–88		—	—
1988–89		12	—
1989–90		26	—

HARVIE, Scott

Born Glasgow 22.11.68 Ht 5 7 Wt 11 02
Defender. From Rothes.

Season	Club	Apps	Goals
1986–87	Aberdeen	—	—
1987–88		—	—
1988–89		—	—
1989–90		2	—

HARWOOD, Chris

Born Hendon 19.4.70 Ht 5 11 Wt 12 00
Midfield. From Trainee. England Youth.

Season	Club	Apps	Goals
1988–89	West Ham U	—	—
1989–90		—	—

HARWOOD, Tony

Born Chatham 20.12.70. Ht 5 11
Wt 13 11
Defender. From Trainee.

Season	Club	Apps	Goals
1989–90	Coventry C	—	—

HASFORD, Jason

Born Manchester 1.4.71.
Forward. From Manchester C. Trainee.

Season	Club	Apps	Goals
1989–90	Rochdale	1	—

HATELEY, Mark

Born Liverpool 7.11.61. Ht 6 1
Wt 11 07
Forward. From Apprentice. England Youth, Under-21, 31 full caps.

Season	Club	Apps	Goals
1978–79	Coventry C	1	—
1979–80		4	—
1980–81		19	3
1981–82		34	13
1982–83		35	9
1983–84	Portsmouth	38	22
1984–85	AC Milan	21	7
1985–86		22	8
1986–87		23	2

To Monaco and Rangers.

HATHAWAY, Ian

Born Worsley 22.8.68 Ht 5 8 Wt 10 06
Forward. From WBA Apprentice. Bedworth U.

Season	Club	Apps	Goals
1988–89	Mansfield T	12	1
1989–90		22	1

HAUSER, Thomas

Born West Germany 10.4.65 Ht 6 3
Wt 12 06
Forward. From Berne OB.

Season	Club	Apps	Goals
1988–89	Sunderland	13	2
1989–90		18	6

HAWKE, Warren

Born Durham 20.9.70 Ht 5 10 Wt 10 11
Midfield. From Trainee.

Season	Club	Apps	Goals
1988–89	Sunderland	4	—
1989–90		8	1

HAWKER, Phil

Born Solihull 7.12.62. Ht 6 1 Wt 11 06
Defender. From Apprentice. England Youth.

Season	Club	Apps	Goals
1980–81	Birmingham C	11	—
1981–82		20	1
1982–83		4	—
1982–83	Walsall	5	—
1983–84		11	—
1984–85		20	—
1985–86		33	4
1986–87		23	1
1987–88		29	2
1988–89		26	2
1989–90		30	1

HAWKINS, Nigel

Born Bristol 7.9.68. Ht 5 9 Wt 10 07
Forward. From Apprentice.

Season	Club	Apps	Goals
1986–87	Bristol C	—	—
1987–88		1	—
1988–89		17	2
1989–90		—	—
1989–90	Blackpool	7	—

HAY, Alan

Born Dunfermline 28.11.58 Ht 5 11
Wt 11 03
Defender. From Bolton W. Amateur.

Season	Club	Apps	Goals
1978–79	Bristol C	—	—
1979–80		4	—
1980–81		36	1
1981–82		34	—
1981–82	*St Mirren*	—	—
1982–83	York C	42	1
1983–84		42	1
1984–85		45	—
1985–86		21	1
1986–87	Tranmere R	28	—
From Scotland			
1988–89	York C	1	—

Season	Club	Apps	Goals
1988–89	Sunderland	1	—
1989–90	Torquay U	8	—

HAYCOCK, Paul

Born Sheffield 8.7.62. Ht 6 1 Wt 12 00
Forward. From Burton Alb.

Season	Club	Apps	Goals
1986–87	Rotherham U	26	6
1987–88		35	12
1988–89		33	4
1989–90		3	—

HAYDE, Michael

Born St Helens 20.6.71.
Midfield. From Liverpool Trainee.

Season	Club	Apps	Goals
1989–90	Chester C	1	—
1989–90	*Linfield*	—	—

HAYES, Martin

Born Walthamstow 21.3.66. Ht 5 10
Wt 11 12
Forward. From Apprentice. England B, Under-21.

Season	Club	Apps	Goals
1983–84	Arsenal	—	—
1984–85		—	—
1985–86		11	2
1986–87		35	19
1987–88		27	1
1988–89		17	1
1989–90		12	3

HAYLOCK, Garry

Born Bradford 31.12.70. Ht 5 11
Wt 12 00
Midfield. From Trainee.

Season	Club	Apps	Goals
1989–90	Huddersfield T	—	—
1989–90	*Shelbourne*	—	—

HAYLOCK, Paul

Born Lowestoft 24.3.63. Ht 5 9
Wt 11 10
Defender. From Apprentice.

Season	Club	Apps	Goals
1980–81	Norwich C	—	—
1981–82		21	—
1982–83		42	1

Season	Club	League Appearances/Goals	
1983–84		39	—
1984–85		41	1
1985–86		12	1
1986–87	Gillingham	45	—
1987–88		32	—
1988–89		31	—
1989–90		44	—

HAYWARD, Steve

Born Walsall 8.9.71 Ht 5 10 Wt 11 07
Midfield. From Trainee.

Season	Club	Apps	Goals
1988–89	Derby Co	—	—
1989–90		3	—

HAZARD, Mike

Born Sunderland 5.2.60 Ht 5 7 Wt 10 05
Midfield. From Apprentice.

Season	Club	Apps	Goals
1977–78	Tottenham H	—	—
1978–79		—	—
1979–80		3	—
1980–81		4	—
1981–82		28	5
1982–83		18	1
1983–84		11	2
1984–85		23	4
1985–86		4	1
1985–86	Chelsea	18	1
1986–87		18	6
1987–88		28	2
1988–89		4	—
1989–90		13	—
1989–90	Portsmouth	8	1

HAZEL, Desmond

Born Bradford 15.7.67. Ht 5 10
Wt 10 10
Forward. From Apprentice.

Season	Club	Apps	Goals
1985–86	Sheffield W	—	—
1986–87		—	—
1986–87	*Grimsby T*	9	2
1987–88	Sheffield W	6	—
1988–89	Rotherham U	42	6
1989–90		33	2

HAZEL, Ian

Born London 1.12.67. Ht 5 10 Wt 10 04
Midfield. From Apprentice.

Season	Club	Apps	Goals
1985–86	Wimbledon	—	—
1986–87		—	—
1987–88		6	—
1988–89		1	—
1988–89	*Bristol R*	3	—
1989–90	Bristol R	8	—

HEALD, Paul

Born Wath-on-Dearne 20.8.68. Ht 6 2
Wt 12 05
Goalkeeper. From Trainee.

Season	Club	Apps	Goals
1987–88	Sheffield U	—	—
1988–89		—	—
1988–89	Leyton Orient	28	—
1989–90		37	—

HEANEY, Neil

Born Middlesbrough 3.11.71. Ht 5 9
Wt 11 01
Forward. From Trainee.

Season	Club	Apps	Goals
1989–90	Arsenal	—	—

HEARD, Pat

Born 17.3.60. Ht 5 9 Wt 11 05
Defender. From Apprentice. England Youth.

Season	Club	Apps	Goals
1977–78	Everton	—	—
1978–79		10	—
1979–80		1	—
1979–80	Aston Villa	9	—
1980–81		—	—
1981–82		8	2
1982–83		7	—
1982–83	Sheffield W	19	2
1983–84		5	1
1984–85		1	—
1984–85	Newcastle U	34	2
1985–86		—	—
1985–86	Middlesbrough	25	2

Season	Club	League Appearances/Goals	
1985–86	Hull C	8	—
1986–87		37	1
1987–88		35	4
1988–89	Rotherham U	30	4
1989–90		14	3

HEATH, Adrian

Born Stoke 11.1.61. Ht 5 6 Wt 10 01
Forward. From Apprentice.
England Under-21, B.

Season	Club	Apps	Goals
1978–79	Stoke C	2	—
1979–80		38	5
1980–81		38	6
1981–82		17	5
1981–82	Everton	22	6
1982–83		38	10
1983–84		36	12
1984–85		17	11
1985–86		36	10
1986–87		41	11
1987–88		29	9
1988–89		7	2
From Espanol			
1989–90	Aston Villa	9	—
1989–90	Manchester C	12	2

HEATH, Herbert

Born Wolverhampton 29.3.70 Ht 6 0
Wt 12 08
Defender. From Walsall Wood, Darlaston.

Season	Club	Apps	Goals
1988–89	Exeter C	5	—
1989–90		—	—

HEATH, Philip

Born Stoke 24.11.64. Ht 5 10 Wt 12 01
Forward. From Apprentice.

Season	Club	Apps	Goals
1982–83		1	—
1983–84		4	1
1984–85		36	2
1985–86		38	5
1986–87		38	1
1987–88		39	8
1988–89	Oxford U	16	1
1989–90		21	—

HEATHCOTE, Mike

Born Durham 10.9.65. Ht 6 2 Wt 12 05
Defender. From Middlesbrough, Spennymoor U.

Season	Club	Apps	Goals
1987–88	Sunderland	1	—
1987–88	*Halifax T*	7	1
1988–89	Sunderland	—	—
1989–90		8	—
1989–90	*York C*	3	—

HEBBERD, Trevor

Born Winchester 19.6.58. Ht 6 0
Wt 11 04
Midfield. From Apprentice.

Season	Club	Apps	Goals
1976–77	Southampton	12	2
1977–78		12	1
1978–79		22	2
1979–80		36	2
1980–81		11	—
1981–82		4	—
1981–82	*Bolton W*	6	—
1981–82	*Leicester C*	4	1
1981–82	Oxford U	15	2
1982–83		39	10
1983–84		46	11
1984–85		42	6
1985–86		41	3
1986–87		38	2
1987–88		39	3
1988–89	Derby Co	37	5
1989–90		23	4

HEDDLE, Ian

Born Dunfermline 2.3.63. Ht 5 10
Wt 11 00
Midfield. From Dunfermline Railway.

Season	Club	Apps	Goals
1983–84	Dunfermline Ath	1	—
1984–85		3	1
1985–86		25	3
1986–87		10	2
1986–87	St Johnstone	19	2
1987–88		36	9

Season	Club	League Appearances/Goals	
1988–89		36	2
1989–90		39	5

HEDMAN, Rudi

Born London 16.11.64. Ht 6 3 Wt 12 02
Defender. Local.

Season	Club	Apps	Goals
1983–84	Colchester U	4	—
1984–85		30	2
1985–86		39	3
1986–87		44	4
1987–88		42	—
1988–89		17	1
1988–89	Crystal Palace	5	—
1989–90		12	—
1989–90	*Leyton Orient*	5	—

HEDWORTH, Chris

Born Newcastle 5.1.64. Ht 6 1 Wt 10 11
Defender. From Apprentice.

Season	Club	Apps	Goals
1981–82	Newcastle U	—	—
1982–83		4	—
1983–84		—	—
1984–85		1	—
1985–86		4	—
1986–87	Barnsley	20	—
1987–88		5	—
1988–89	Halifax T	11	—
1989–90		27	—

HEEPS, Jimmy

Born Luton 16.5.71.
Goalkeeper. From Trainee.

Season	Club	Apps	Goals
1989–90	Swansea C	1	—

HEGARTY, Paul

Born Edinburgh 25.7.54. Ht 5 10
Wt 11 04
Defender. From Tynecastle BC. Scotland Under-21, 8 full caps.

Season	Club	Apps	Goals
1972–73	Hamilton A	36	7
1973–74		31	10
1974–75		12	5
1974–75	Dundee U	17	4
1975–76		33	8
1976–77		36	6
1977–78		36	4
1978–79		36	5
1979–80		27	—
1980–81		33	3
1981–82		36	2
1982–83		36	3
1983–84		36	4
1984–85		33	2
1985–86		36	5
1986–87		23	4
1987–88		41	1
1988–89		29	1
1989–90		5	—
1989–90	St Johnstone	14	1

HELLIWELL, Ian

Born Rotherham 7.12.62. Ht 6 3
Wt 13 12
Forward. From Matlock T.

Season	Club	Apps	Goals
1987–88	York C	32	8
1988–89		41	11
1989–90		46	14

HEMMING, Chris

Born Newcastle 13.4.66. Ht 5 10
Wt 12 10
Defender. From school.

Season	Club	Apps	Goals
1983–84	Stoke C	3	—
1984–85		16	1
1985–86		24	—
1986–87		22	—
1987–88		24	1
1988–89		4	—
1988–89	*Wigan Ath*	4	—
1989–90	Hereford U	35	2

HENDRIE, John

Born Lennoxtown 24.10.63. Ht 5 7
Wt 11 07
Forward. From Apprentice. Scotland Youth.

Season	Club	Apps	Goals
1981–82	Coventry C	6	—
1982–83		12	2
1983–84		3	—
1983–84	*Hereford U*	6	—
1984–85	Bradford C	46	9

Season	Club	League Appearances/Goals	
1985–86		42	10
1986–87		42	14
1987–88		43	13
1988–89	Newcastle U	34	4
1989–90	Leeds U	27	5

HENDRY, Colin

Born Keith 7.12.65. Ht 6 1 Wt 12 00
Defender. From Islavale. Scotland B.

Season	Club	Apps	Goals
1983–84	Dundee	4	—
1984–85		4	—
1985–86		20	—
1986–87		13	2
1986–87	Blackburn R	13	3
1987–88		44	12
1988–89		38	7
1989–90		7	—
1989–90	Manchester C	25	3

HENRY, Charlie

Born Acton 13.2.62. Ht 5 11 Wt 12 08
Forward. From Apprentice.

Season	Club	Apps	Goals
1980–81	Swindon T	32	—
1981–82		42	3
1982–83		19	—
1983–84		29	—
1984–85		16	—
1985–86		38	18
1986–87		10	1
1987–88		15	1
1986–87	*Torquay U*	6	1
1986–87	*Northampton T*	4	1
1988–89	Swindon T	22	3
1989–90	Aldershot	40	5

HENRY, Liburd

Born Dominica 29.8.67. Ht 5 11
Wt 11 00
Forward. From Colchester U, Rainham T, Millwall, Leytonstone/Ilford.

Season	Club	Apps	Goals
1987–88	Watford	—	—
1988–89		1	—
1988–89	*Halifax T*	5	—
1989–90	Watford	9	1

HENRY, Nick

Born Liverpool 21.2.69. Ht 5 6 Wt 9 08
Midfield. From Trainee.

Season	Club	Apps	Goals
1987–88	Oldham Ath	5	—
1988–89		18	—
1989–90		41	—

HENSHAW, Gary

Born Leeds 18.2.65. Ht 5 8 Wt 11 08
Midfield. From Apprentice.

Season	Club	Apps	Goals
1982–83	Grimsby T	—	—
1983–84		4	—
1984–85		7	1
1985–86		10	4
1986–87		29	4
1987–88	Bolton W	31	2
1988–89		21	1
1989–90		14	—
1989–90	*Rochdale*	9	1

HERITAGE, Peter

Born Bexhill 8.11.60.
Forward. From Hythe Town.

Season	Club	Apps	Goals
1989–90	Gillingham	42	9

HERRERA, Roberto

Born Torbay 12.6.70 Ht 5 7 Wt 10 06
Defender. From Trainee.

Season	Club	Apps	Goals
1987–88	QPR	—	—
1988–89		2	—
1989–90		1	—

HESELTINE, Wayne

Born Bradford 3.12.69. Ht 5 9
Wt 11 06
Defender. From Trainee.

Season	Club	Apps	Goals
1987–88	Manchester U	—	—
1988–89		—	—

Season	Club	League Appearances/Goals	
1989–90		—	—
1989–90	Oldham Ath	1	—

HESFORD, Iain

Born Zambia 4.3.60. Ht 6 2 Wt 14 10
Goalkeeper. From Apprentice. England Youth, Under-21.

Season	Club	League Appearances/Goals	
1977–78	Blackpool	14	—
1978–79		33	—
1979–80		30	—
1980–81		42	—
1981–82		39	—
1982–83		44	—
1983–84	Sheffield W	—	—
1984–85		—	—
1984–85	*Fulham*	3	—
1985–86	Sheffield W	—	—
1985–86	*Notts Co*	10	—
1986–87	Sunderland	38	—
1987–88		39	—
1988–89		20	—
1988–89	Hull C	22	—
1989–90		38	—

HETHERINGTON, Brent

Born Carlisle 6.12.61. Ht 5 7 Wt 11 10
Forward. From Penrith, Workington.

Season	Club	League Appearances/Goals	
1987–88	Carlisle U	37	10
1988–89		39	11
1989–90		12	2

HETZKE, Steve

Born Marlborough 3.6.55. Ht 6 2
Wt 14 00
Defender. From Apprentice.

Season	Club	League Appearances/Goals	
1971–72	Reading	4	—
1972–73		1	—
1973–74		22	1
1974–75		15	—
1975–76		17	1
1976–77		24	3
1977–78		16	—
1978–79		42	9
1979–80		43	2
1980–81		45	5
1981–82		32	2
1982–83	Blackpool	42	2
1983–84		45	7
1984–85		30	5
1985–86		23	4
1985–86	Sunderland	8	—
1986–87		23	—
1987–88	Chester C	14	—
1987–88	Colchester U	5	—
1988–89		24	2
1989–90		—	—

HEWITSON, Mark

Born Oxford 27.2.71. Ht 5 8 Wt 10 10
Midfield. From Trainee.

Season	Club	League Appearances/Goals	
1988–89	Oxford U	—	—
1989–90		—	—

HEWITT, Daren

Born Chichester 1.9.69 Ht 5 8 Wt 11 06
Forward. From Trainee.

Season	Club	League Appearances/Goals	
1988–89	Aldershot	2	—
1989–90		—	—

HEWITT, Jamie

Born Chesterfield 17.5.68. Ht 5 10
Wt 10 08
Defender. From school.

Season	Club	League Appearances/Goals	
1984–85	Chesterfield	—	—
1985–86		17	—
1986–87		42	2
1987–88		28	2
1988–89		40	1
1989–90		42	6

HEWITT, John

Born Aberdeen 9.2.63. Ht 5 8 Wt 10 08
Forward. From Middlefield Wasps. Scotland Schools, Youth, Under-21.

Season	Club	League Appearances/Goals	
1979–80	Aberdeen	4	—
1980–81		21	2
1981–82		25	11
1982–83		16	4
1983–84		32	12
1984–85		21	3
1985–86		23	6

Season	Club	League Appearances/Goals	
1986–87		34	11
1987–88		37	1
1988–89		27	3
1989–90	Celtic	12	—

HICKS, Martin

Born Stratford-on-Avon 27.2.57 Ht 6 3 Wt 13 06
Defender. From Stratford T.

Season	Club	League Appearances/Goals	
1976–77	Charlton Ath	—	—
1977–78		—	—
1977–78	Reading	19	1
1978–79		46	1
1979–80		1	1
1980–81		27	2
1981–82		44	3
1982–83		32	1
1983–84		46	1
1984–85		40	2
1985–86		34	2
1986–87		34	3
1987–88		44	1
1988–89		45	3
1989–90		44	2

HICKS, Stuart

Born Peterborough 30.5.67. Ht 6 1 Wt 12 06
Defender. From Peterborough U Apprentice, Wisbech.

Season	Club	League Appearances/Goals	
1987–88	Colchester U	7	—
1988–89		37	—
1989–90		20	—

HIGGINS, Dave

Born Liverpool 19.8.61 Ht 6 0 Wt 11 00
Defender. From Eagle.

Season	Club	League Appearances/Goals	
1983–84	Tranmere R	20	—
1984–85		8	—
From S. Liverpool, Caernarfon			
1987–88	Tranmere R	33	1
1988–89		43	1
1989–90		45	1

HIGGINS, Mark

Born Buxton 29.9.58. Ht 6 1 Wt 13 05
Defender. From Apprentice. England Schools Youth.

Season	Club	League Appearances/Goals	
1976–77	Everton	2	—
1977–78		26	1
1978–79		21	1
1979–80		19	—
1980–81		2	—
1981–82		29	3
1982–83		39	1
1983–84		14	—
Retired			
1985–86	Manchester U	6	—
1986–87		—	—
1986–87	Bury	22	—
1987–88		41	—
1988–89		5	—
1988–89	Stoke C	33	1
1989–90		6	—

HIGNETT, Craig

Born Whiston 12.1.70. Ht 5 10 Wt 11 00
Midfield.

Season	Club	League Appearances/Goals	
1987–88	Crewe Alex	—	—
1988–89		1	—
1989–90		35	8

HILAIRE, Vince

Born Forest Hill 10.10.59. Ht 5 6 Wt 10 07
Forward. From Apprentice. England Youth, Under-21, B.

Season	Club	League Appearances/Goals	
1976–77	Crystal Palace	3	—
1977–78		30	2
1978–79		31	6
1979–80		42	5
1980–81		31	4
1981–82		36	5
1982–83		42	5
1983–84		40	2
1984–85	Luton T	6	—
1984–85	Portsmouth	26	7

Season	Club	League Appearances/Goals	
1985–86		41	8
1986–87		41	8
1987–88		38	2
1988–89	Leeds U	42	6
1989–90		2	—
1989–90	*Stoke C*	5	1
1989–90	*Charlton Ath*	—	—

HILDERSLEY, Ron

Born Fife 6.4.65. Ht 5 4 Wt 9 2
Forward. From Apprentice. Scotland Schools.

Season	Club	Apps	Goals
1982–83	Manchester C	1	—
1983–84		—	—
1983–84	*Chester C*	9	—
1984–85	Chester C	9	—
1985–86	Rochdale	16	—
1986–87	Preston NE	33	2
1987–88		25	1
1988–89	Blackburn R	25	4
1989–90		5	—

HILDITCH, Mark

Born Royton 20.8.60. Ht 6 0 Wt 12 01
Forward. From Amateur.

Season	Club	Apps	Goals
1977–78	Rochdale	3	1
1978–79		27	3
1979–80		44	3
1980–81		44	12
1981–82		40	14
1982–83		39	7
1983–84	Tranmere R	39	8
1984–85		3	1
1985–86		7	3
1986–87	Wigan Ath	28	8
1987–88		29	8
1988–89		25	3
1989–90		21	7

HILEY, Scott

Born Plymouth 27.9.68. Ht 5 9 Wt 10 07
Midfield. From Trainee.

Season	Club	Apps	Goals
1986–87	Exeter C	—	—
1987–88		15	1
1988–89		37	5
1989–90		46	—

HILL, Andy

Born Maltby 20.1.65. Ht 5 10 Wt 12 00
Defender. From Apprentice. England Youth.

Season	Club	Apps	Goals
1982–83	Manchester U	—	—
1983–84		—	—
1984–85	Bury	43	3
1985–86		35	2
1986–87		42	1
1987–88		43	2
1988–89		43	—
1989–90		46	2

HILL, Colin

Born Hillingdon 12.11.63. Ht 5 11 Wt 12 02
Defender. From Apprentice. Northern Ireland 2 full caps.

Season	Club	Apps	Goals
1981–82	Arsenal	—	—
1982–83		7	—
1983–84		37	1
1984–85		2	—
1985–86		—	—
1985–86	*Brighton*	—	—
From Maritimo.			
1987–88	Colchester U	25	—
1988–89		44	—
1989–90	Sheffield U	43	—

HILL, David

Born Nottingham 6.6.66. Ht 5 10 Wt 11 03
Midfield. Local.

Season	Club	Apps	Goals
1983–84	Scunthorpe U	2	—
1984–85		29	2
1985–86		42	2
1986–87		41	3
1987–88		26	3

Season	Club	League Appearances/Goals	
1988–89	Ipswich T	36	—
1989–90		2	—

HILL, Jonathan

Born Wigan 20.8.70. Ht 5 10 Wt 11 10
Midfield. From Crewe Alex Trainee.

Season	Club	League Appearances/Goals	
1989–90	Rochdale	25	—

HILL, Keith

Born Bolton 17.5.69. Ht 6 0 Wt 11 03
Defender. From Apprentice.

Season	Club	League Appearances/Goals	
1986–87	Blackburn R	—	—
1987–88		1	—
1988–89		15	1
1989–90		25	—

HILL, Ricky

Born London 5.3.59. Ht 5 10 Wt 13 10
Midfield. From Apprentice.
England Youth, 3 full caps.

Season	Club	League Appearances/Goals	
1975–76	Luton T	2	1
1976–77		11	4
1977–78		40	5
1978–79		38	3
1979–80		40	6
1980–81		42	7
1981–82		38	5
1982–83		42	9
1983–84		26	2
1984–85		39	2
1985–86		38	3
1986–87		30	2
1987–88		17	2
1988–89		33	3

To Le Havre.

HILL, Richard

Born Hinckley 20.9.63. Ht 6 0 Wt 12 11
Forward.

Season	Club	League Appearances/Goals	
1981–82	Leicester C	—	—

From Grankulla, Nuneaton.

Season	Club	League Appearances/Goals	
1985–86	Northampton T	41	17
1986–87		45	29
1987–88	Watford	4	—
1987–88	Oxford U	24	3
1988–89		39	10
1989–90		—	—

HILLIER, David

Born Blackheath 19.12.69 Ht 5 10
Wt 11 06
Midfield. From Trainee.

Season	Club	League Appearances/Goals	
1987–88	Arsenal	—	—
1988–89		—	—
1989–90		—	—

HILLYARD, Ron

Born Rotherham 31.3.53. Ht 5 11
Wt 11 07
Goalkeeper. From Amateur.

Season	Club	League Appearances/Goals	
1969–70	York C	3	—
1970–71		34	—
1971–72		17	—
1971–72	*Hartlepool U*	23	—
1972–73	York C	4	—
1973–74		3	—
1973–74	*Bury*	—	—
1973–74	*Brighton*	—	—
1974–75	Gillingham	46	—
1975–76		44	—
1976–77		25	—
1977–78		44	—
1978–79		46	—
1979–80		46	—
1980–81		37	—
1981–82		44	—
1982–83		42	—
1983–84		8	—
1984–85		25	—
1985–86		46	—
1986–87		27	—
1987–88		18	—
1988–89		19	—
1989–90		42	—

HIMSWORTH, Gary

Born Appleton 19.12.69 Ht 5 7 Wt 9 08
Forward. From Trainee.

Season	Club	League Appearances/Goals	
1987–88	York C	31	2

Season	Club	League Appearances/Goals	
1988–89		32	2
1989–90		23	4

HINCHCLIFFE, Andy

Born Manchester 5.2.69 Ht 5 10
Wt 12 10
Defender. From Apprentice. England Youth, Under-21.

Season	Club	Apps	Goals
1986–87	Manchester C	—	—
1987–88		42	1
1988–89		39	5
1989–90		31	2

HINDMARCH, Rob

Born Stannington 27.4.61. Ht 6 1
Wt 13 04
Defender. From Apprentice. England Youth.

Season	Club	Apps	Goals
1977–78	Sunderland	2	—
1978–79		—	—
1979–80		21	—
1980–81		29	—
1981–82		36	2
1982–83		14	—
1983–84		13	—
1983–84	*Portsmouth*	2	—
1984–85	Derby Co	22	1
1985–86		39	6
1986–87		33	2
1987–88		19	—
1988–89		25	—
1989–90		26	—

HINDS, Peter

Born Barbados 8.6.62. Ht 6 2 Wt 12 11
Midfield. From Fujita.

Season	Club	Apps	Goals
1989–90	Dundee U	13	—

HINE, Mark

Born Middlesbrough 18.5.64. Ht 5 8
Wt 9 11
Midfield. Local.

Season	Club	Apps	Goals
1983–84	Grimsby T	—	—
1984–85		9	—
1985–86		13	1
1986–87	Darlington	43	2
1987–88		45	4
1988–89		40	2
1989–90		—	—
1989–90	Peterborough U	22	4

HINNIGAN, Joe

Born Liverpool 3.12.55. Ht 6 0 Wt 12 00
Defender. From South Liverpool.

Season	Club	Apps	Goals
1978–79	Wigan Ath	39	5
1979–80		27	5
1979–80	Sunderland	14	—
1980–81		16	4
1981–82		30	—
1982–83		3	—
1982–83	Preston NE	13	3
1983–84		39	5
1984–85	Gillingham	37	5
1985–86		39	2
1986–87		27	—
1987–88	Wrexham	29	1
1988–89	Chester C	39	2
1989–90		15	—

HIRONS, Paul

Born Bristol 6.3.71 Ht 5 11 Wt 11 00
Forward. From Bristol C trainee.

Season	Club	Apps	Goals
1988–89	Torquay U	5	—
1989–90		16	—

HIRST, David

Born Barnsley 7.12.67. Ht 5 11
Wt 13 01
Forward. From Apprentice. England Youth, Under-21.

Season	Club	Apps	Goals
1985–86	Barnsley	28	9
1986–87	Sheffield W	21	6
1987–88		24	3
1988–89		32	7
1989–90		38	14

HIRST, Lee

Born Sheffield 26.1.69. Ht 6 2 Wt 12 07
Defender.

Season	Club	League Appearances	Goals
1989–90	Scarborough	10	—

HITCHCOCK, Kevin

Born Custom House 5.10.62. Ht 6 1
Wt 12 02
Goalkeeper. From Barking.

Season	Club	League Appearances	Goals
1983–84	Nottingham F	—	—
1983–84	*Mansfield T*	14	—
1984–85	Mansfield T	43	—
1985–86		46	—
1986–87		46	—
1987–88		33	—
1987–88	Chelsea	8	—
1988–89		3	—
1989–90		—	—

HOBSON, Gordon

Born Sheffield 27.11.57. Ht 5 9 Wt 10 11
Forward. From Sheffield RGRS.

Season	Club	League Appearances	Goals
1977–78	Lincoln C	5	2
1978–79		33	6
1979–80		43	10
1980–81		44	21
1981–82		32	7
1982–83		41	14
1983–84		36	6
1984–85		38	7
1985–86	Grimsby T	41	15
1986–87		11	3
1986–87	Southampton	20	7
1987–88		13	1
1988–89		—	—
1988–89	Lincoln C	32	14
1989–90		29	8

HOCKADAY, David

Born Billingham 9.11.57. Ht 5 10
Wt 10 09
Defender. From Amateur.

Season	Club	League Appearances	Goals
1975–76	Blackpool	—	—
1976–77		5	—
1977–78		—	—
1978–79		18	4
1979–80		7	1
1980–81		36	4
1981–82		41	7
1982–83		40	8
1983–84	Swindon T	36	3
1984–85		22	1
1985–86		37	1
1986–87		40	1
1987–88		43	—
1988–89		44	—
1989–90		20	—

HODDLE, Carl

Born Harlow 8.3.67.
Midfield. From Bishop's Stortford.

Season	Club	League Appearances	Goals
1989–90	Leyton Orient	26	2

HODDLE, Glenn

Born Hayes 27.10.57. Ht 6 0 Wt 11 6
Midfield. From Apprentice.
England Youth, Under-21 B, 53 full caps.

Season	Club	League Appearances	Goals
1974–75	Tottenham H	—	—
1975–76		7	1
1976–77		39	4
1977–78		41	12
1978–79		35	7
1979–80		41	19
1980–81		38	12
1981–82		34	10
1982–83		24	1
1983–84		24	4
1984–85		28	8
1985–86		31	7
1986–87		35	3

To Monaco

HODGE, Martin

Born Southport 4.2.59. Ht 6 1 Wt 14 06
Goalkeeper. From Apprentice.

Season	Club	League Appearances	Goals
1976–77	Plymouth Arg	—	—
1977–78		5	—
1978–79		38	—
1979–80	Everton	23	—
1980–81		2	—
1981–82	*Preston NE*	28	—
1982–83	*Oldham Ath*	4	—
1982–83	*Gillingham*	4	—
1982–83	*Preston NE*	16	—
1983–84	Sheffield W	42	—

Season	Club	League Appearances/Goals	
1984–85		42	—
1985–86		42	—
1986–87		42	—
1987–88		29	—
1988–89	Leicester C	19	—
1989–90		46	—

HODGE, Steve

Born Nottingham 25.10.62. Ht 5 8
Wt 9 11
Midfield. From Apprentice.
England Under-21, B, 22 full caps.

Season	Club	League Appearances/Goals	
1980–81	Nottingham F	—	—
1981–82		1	—
1982–83		39	8
1983–84		39	10
1984–85		42	12
1985–86		2	—
1985–86	Aston Villa	36	8
1986–87		17	4
1986–87	Tottenham H	19	4
1987–88		26	3
1988–89	Nottingham F	34	7
1989–90		34	10

HODGES, David

Born Hereford 17.1.70 Ht 5 9 Wt 10 02
Midfield.

Season	Club	League Appearances/Goals	
1986–87	Mansfield T	3	—
1987–88		22	2
1988–89		39	4
1989–90		19	1

HODGES, Glyn

Born Streatham 30.4.63. Ht 6 0
Wt 12 03
Forward. From Apprentice. Wales Youth, Under-21, 13 full caps.

Season	Club	League Appearances/Goals	
1980–81	Wimbledon	30	5
1981–82		34	2
1982–83		37	9
1983–84		42	15
1984–85		22	3
1985–86		30	6
1986–87		37	9
1987–88	Newcastle U	7	—
1987–88	Watford	24	3
1988–89		27	5
1989–90		35	7

HODGES, Kevin

Born Bridport 12.6.60 Ht 5 8 Wt 10 00
Midfield. From Apprentice.

Season	Club	League Appearances/Goals	
1977–78	Plymouth Arg	—	—
1978–79		12	—
1979–80		44	5
1980–81		41	5
1981–82		46	11
1982–83		46	11
1983–84		43	4
1984–85		45	10
1985–86		46	16
1986–87		35	5
1987–88		37	6
1988–89		31	1
1989–90		44	4

HODKINSON, Andrew

Born Ashton 4.11.65. Ht 5 7 Wt 10 10
Midfield. From Bolton W. Apprentice.
England Schools.

Season	Club	League Appearances/Goals	
1983–84	Oldham Ath	4	1
1984–85		1	—
1985–86	Stockport Co	41	6
1986–87		38	6
1987–88		39	6
1988–89	Scunthorpe U	41	8
1989–90		21	—

HODSON, Simeon

Born Lincoln 5.3.66. Ht 5 10 Wt 11 06
Defender. From Apprentice.

Season	Club	League Appearances/Goals	
1983–84	Notts Co	13	—
1984–85		14	—
1984–85	Charlton Ath	5	—
1985–86		—	—
1985–86	Lincoln C	15	—
1986–87		41	—
1987–88	Newport Co	34	1
1987–88	WBA	7	—

Season	Club	League Appearances/Goals	
1988–89		9	—
1989–90		10	—

HOGG, Graeme

Born Aberdeen 17.6.64. Ht 6 1
Wt 13 01
Defender. From Apprentice. Scotland Under-21.

Season	Club	Apps	Goals
1982–83	Manchester U	—	—
1983–84		16	1
1984–85		29	—
1985–86		17	—
1986–87		11	—
1987–88		10	—
1987–88	*WBA*	7	—
1988–89	Portsmouth	41	1
1989–90		39	1

HOLDEN, Andy

Born Flint 14.9.62. Ht 6 1 Wt 13 10
Defender. From Rhyl. Wales Under-21, 1 full cap.

Season	Club	Apps	Goals
1983–84	Chester	44	7
1984–85		38	6
1985–86		10	2
1986–87		8	2
1986–87	Wigan Ath	11	1
1987–88		15	2
1988–89		23	1
1988–89	Oldham Ath	13	4
1989–90		6	—

HOLDEN, Rick

Born Skipton 9.9.64. Ht 5 11 Wt 12 07
Midfield.

Season	Club	Apps	Goals
1985–86	Burnley	1	—
1986–87	Halifax T	32	2
1987–88		35	10
1987–88	Watford	10	2
1988–89		32	6
1989–90	Oldham Ath	45	9

HOLDSWORTH, David

Born London 8.11.68. Ht 5 11 Wt 11 04
Defender. From Trainee. England Youth, Under-21.

Season	Club	Apps	Goals
1986–87	Watford	—	—
1987–88		—	—
1988–89		33	1
1989–90		44	3

HOLDSWORTH, Dean

Born London 8.11.68. Ht 5 11 Wt 11 13
Forward. From Trainee.

Season	Club	Apps	Goals
1986–87	Watford	2	—
1987–88	*Carlisle U*	4	1
1987–88	*Port Vale*	6	2
1988–89	Watford	10	2
1988–89	*Swansea C*	5	1
1988–89	*Brentford*	7	1
1989–90	Watford	4	1
1989–90	Brentford	39	24

HOLLOWAY, Ian

Born Kingswood 12.3.63. Ht 5 8
Wt 10 10
Midfield. From Apprentice.

Season	Club	Apps	Goals
1980–81	Bristol R	1	—
1981–82		1	—
1982–83		31	7
1983–84		36	1
1984–85		42	6
1985–86	Wimbledon	19	2
1985–86	*Brentford*	13	2
1986–87	Brentford	16	—
1986–87	*Torquay U*	5	—
1987–88		1	—
1987–88	Bristol R	43	5
1988–89		44	6
1989–90		46	8

HOLMES, Andy

Born Stoke 7.1.69. Ht 6 1 Wt 12 12
Defender. From Apprentice.

Season	Club	Apps	Goals
1986–87	Stoke C	—	—
1987–88		2	—
1988–89		—	—
1989–90		6	—

HOLMES, David

Born Derby 22.11.72.
Defender.

Season	Club	League Appearances/Goals	
1989–90	Scarborough	2	—

HOLMES, Matt

Born Luton 1.8.69 Ht 5 7 Wt 10 07
Forward. From Trainee.

Season	Club	Apps	Goals
1988–89	Bournemouth	4	1
1988–89	*Cardiff C*	1	—
1989–90	Bournemouth	22	2

HOLMES, Micky

Born Blackpool 9.9.65. Ht 5 8 Wt 10 12
Midfield.

Season	Club	Apps	Goals
1984–85	Bradford C	5	—
1985–86	Burnley	—	—
1985–86	Wolverhampton W	26	3
1986–87		37	8
1987–88		20	2
1988–89	Huddersfield T	7	—
1988–89	Cambridge U	11	—
1989–90	Rochdale	38	2

HOLMES, Paul

Born Wortley 18.2.68. Ht 5 10 Wt 11 00
Defender. From Apprentice.

Season	Club	Apps	Goals
1985–86	Doncaster R	5	1
1986–87		16	—
1987–88		26	—
1988–89	Torquay U	25	—
1989–90		44	2

HOLSGROVE, Paul

Born Wellington 26.8.69. Ht 6 1
Wt 12 00
Forward. From Trainee.

Season	Club	Apps	Goals
1986–87	Aldershot	—	—
1987–88		2	—
1988–89		1	—
1988–89	*Wimbledon*	—	—
1989–90	Aldershot	—	—
1989–90	*WBA*	—	—

HOLT, John

Born Dundee 21.11.56 Ht 5 9 Wt 11 10
Defender. 'S' Form. Scotland Youth.

Season	Club	Apps	Goals
1973–74	Dundee U	3	—
1974–75		—	—
1975–76		16	—
1976–77		8	—
1977–78		15	3
1978–79		27	3
1979–80		17	4
1980–81		24	—
1981–82		28	1
1982–83		26	4
1983–84		32	2
1984–85		25	—
1985–86		27	—
1986–87		18	—
1987–88		6	—
1987–88	Dunfermline Ath	35	1
1988–89		13	1
1988–89	Dundee	11	—
1989–90		2	—

HONE, Mark

Born Croydon 31.3.68. Ht 6 1 Wt 12 05
Defender.

Season	Club	Apps	Goals
1985–86	Crystal Palace	—	—
1986–87		—	—
1987–88		3	—
1988–89		1	—
1989–90		—	—

HONEYWOOD, Lee

Born Chelmsford 3.8.71. Ht 5 8
Wt 10 10
Defender. From Trainee.

Season	Club	Apps	Goals
1989–90	Ipswich T	—	—

HONOR, Chris

Born Bristol 5.6.68. Ht 5 9 Wt 10 09
Defender. From Apprentice.

Season	Club	Apps	Goals
1985–86	Bristol C	1	—
1986–87		2	—
1986–87	*Torquay U*	3	—
1987–88	Bristol C	17	—
1988–89		26	—

Season	Club	League Appearances/Goals	
1989–90		14	1
1989–90	*Hereford U*	3	—

HONOUR, Brian

Born Horden 16.2.64. Ht 5 7 Wt 12 05
Midfield. From Apprentice.

Season	Club	League Appearances/Goals	
1981–82	Darlington	1	—
1982–83		32	3
1983–84		41	1
From Peterlee			
1984–85	Hartlepool U	17	—
1985–86		46	8
1986–87		32	2
1987–88		44	—
1988–89		34	1
1989–90		9	—

HOOLE, David

Born Chesterfield 16.10.70
Defender. From Trainee.

Season	Club	League Appearances/Goals	
1988–89	Chesterfield	13	—
1989–90		1	—

HOOPER, Michael

Born Bristol 10.2.64. Ht 6 2 Wt 13 05
Goalkeeper.

Season	Club	League Appearances/Goals	
1983–84	Bristol C	—	—
1984–85		1	—
1984–85	*Wrexham*	20	—
1985–86	Wrexham	14	—
1985–86	Liverpool	—	—
1986–87		11	—
1987–88		2	—
1988–89		17	—
1989–90		—	—

HOPE, Darren

Born Stoke 3.4.71. Ht 5 6 Wt 10 05
Forward. From Trainee.

Season	Club	League Appearances/Goals	
1989–90	Stoke C	—	—
1989–90	Stockport Co	4	—

HOPKINS, Jeff

Born Swansea 14.4.64. Ht 6 0 Wt 12 12
Defender. From Apprentice.
Wales Youth, Under-21, 16 full caps.

Season	Club	League Appearances/Goals	
1980–81	Fulham	1	—
1981–82		35	—
1982–83		41	1
1983–84		33	—
1984–85		40	2
1985–86		23	—
1986–87		20	1
1987–88		26	—
1988–89	Crystal Palace	43	—
1989–90		27	2

HOPKINS, Robert

Born Birmingham 25.10.61. Ht 5 7
Wt 10 07
Midfield. From Apprentice.

Season	Club	League Appearances/Goals	
1979–80	Aston Villa	2	1
1980–81		—	—
1981–82		—	—
1982–83		1	—
1982–83	Birmingham C	11	2
1983–84		32	5
1984–85		39	9
1985–86		38	4
1986–87		3	1
1986–87	Manchester C	7	1
1986–87		25	4
1987–88		29	2
1988–89	WBA	29	5
1988–89	Birmingham C	9	—
1989–90		18	6

HORNE, Barry

Born St. Asaph 18.5.62. Ht 5 10
Wt 12 02
Midfield. From Rhyl. Wales 14 full caps.

Season	Club	League Appearances/Goals	
1984–85	Wrexham	44	6
1985–86		46	3
1986–87		46	8
1987–88	Portsmouth	39	3
1988–89		31	4

Season	Club	App	Gls
1988–89	Southampton	11	—
1989–90		29	4

HORNE, Brian

Born Billericay 5.10.67. Ht 5 11
Wt 13 13
Goalkeeper. From Apprentice. England Youth, Under-21.

Season	Club	App	Gls
1985–86	Millwall	—	—
1986–87		32	—
1987–88		43	—
1988–89		38	—
1989–90		22	—

HORNER, Philip

Born Leeds 10.11.66. Ht 6 1 Wt 12 07
Forward. From Lincoln C Schoolboy.

Season	Club	App	Gls
1984–85	Leicester C	—	—
1985–86		—	—
1985–86	*Rotherham U*	4	—
1986–87	Leicester C	3	—
1987–88		7	—
1988–89	Halifax T	38	3
1989–90		34	1

HORRIX, Dean (Deceased)

Born Taplow 21.11.61. Ht 5 11 Wt 11 10
Forward. From Apprentice.

Season	Club	App	Gls
1978–79	Millwall	—	—
1979–80		—	—
1980–81		13	4
1981–82		44	15
1982–83		15	—
1982–83	Gillingham	14	—
1983–84	Reading	43	8
1984–85		43	19
1985–86		41	6
1986–87		18	—
1986–87	*Cardiff C*	9	3
1987–88	Reading	13	2
1987–88	Millwall	2	1
1988–89		8	—
1989–90		1	—
1989–90	Bristol C	3	—

HOUCHEN, Keith

Born Middlesbrough 25.7.60. Ht 6 2
Wt 12 08
Forward. From Chesterfield Amateur.

Season	Club	App	Gls
1977–78	Hartlepool U	13	4
1978–79		39	12
1979–80		41	14
1980–81		45	17
1981–82		32	18
1981–82	Orient	14	1
1982–83		32	10
1983–84		30	9
1983–84	York C	7	1
1984–85		35	12
1985–86		25	6
1985–86	Scunthorpe U	9	3
1986–87	Coventry C	20	2
1987–88		21	3
1988–89		13	2
1988–89	Hibernian	7	2
1989–90		29	8

HOUGH, David

Born Crewe 20.2.66. Ht 5 11 Wt 11 10
Defender. From Apprentice. Wales Youth.

Season	Club	App	Gls
1983–84	Swansea C	2	—
1984–85		25	2
1985–86		31	3
1986–87		31	3
1987–88		20	—
1988–89		40	—
1989–90		32	1

HOUGHTON, Ray

Born Glasgow 9.1.62. Ht 5 8 Wt 11 04
Midfield. Amateur. Eire 34 full caps.

Season	Club	App	Gls
1979–80	West Ham U	—	—
1980–81		—	—
1981–82		1	—
1982–83	Fulham	42	5
1983–84		40	3
1984–85		42	8

Season Club League Appearances/Goals

Season	Club	Apps	Goals
1985–86	....	5	—
1985–86	Oxford U	35	4
1986–87	....	37	5
1987–88	....	11	1
1987–88	Liverpool	28	5
1988–89	....	38	7
1989–90	....	19	1

HOWARD, Mark

Born King's Lynn 21.10.64. Ht 5 8
Wt 10 08
Defender. From Norwich C.

Season	Club	Apps	Goals
1987–88	Stockport Co	2	—
1988–89	....	16	2
1988–89	*Cambridge U*	2	—
1989–90	Stockport Co	1	—

HOWARD, Matthew

Born Watford 5.12.70
Midfield. From Trainee.

Season	Club	Apps	Goals
1987–88	Brentford	1	—
1988–89	....	—	—
1989–90	....	—	—

HOWARD, Terence

Born Stepney 26.2.66. Ht 6 1 Wt 11 07
Defender. From Apprentice. England Youth.

Season	Club	Apps	Goals
1983–84	Chelsea	—	—
1984–85	....	4	—
1985–86	....	1	—
1985–86	*C Palace*	4	—
1986–87	Chelsea	1	—
1986–87	*Chester C*	2	—
1986–87	Orient	12	2
1987–88	....	41	2
1988–89	....	46	5
1989–90	....	45	7

HOWARTH, Neil

Born Farnworh 15.11.71.
Midfield. From Trainee.

Season	Club	Apps	Goals
1989–90	Burnley	1	—

HOWELLS, David

Born Guildford 15.12.67. Ht 5 11
Wt 11 01
Forward. From Trainee. England Youth.

Season	Club	Apps	Goals
1984–85	Tottenham H	—	—
1985–86	....	1	1
1986–87	....	1	—
1987–88	....	11	—
1988–89	....	27	3
1989–90	....	34	5

HOWELLS, Gareth

Born Guildford 13.6.70. Ht 6 1
Wt 12 08
Goalkeeper. From Trainee.

Season	Club	Apps	Goals
1988–89	Tottenham H	—	—
1989–90	....	—	—
1989–90	*Swindon T*	—	—
1989–90	*Leyton Orient*	—	—

HOWES, Jason

Born London 24.9.70 Ht 5 8 Wt 11 02
Forward.

Season	Club	Apps	Goals
1987–88	Fulham	—	—
1988–89	....	—	—
1989–90	....	—	—

HOWEY, Steve

Born Sunderland 26.10.71 Ht 6 1
Wt 10 05
Midfield. From Trainee.

Season	Club	Apps	Goals
1988–89	Newcastle U	1	—
1989–90	....	—	—

HOWLETT, Gary

Born Dublin 2.4.63. Ht 5 8 Wt 10 11
Midfield. From Home Farm. Eire Youth, 1 full cap.

Season	Club	Apps	Goals
1980–81	Coventry C	—	—
1981–82	....	—	—
1982–83	Brighton	9	1
1983–84	....	17	—

Season	Club	League Appearances/Goals	
1984–85		6	1
1984–85	Bournemouth	17	2
1985–86		20	2
1986–87		23	3
1987–88		—	—
1987–88	*Aldershot*	1	—
1987–88	*Chester C*	6	1
1987–88	York C	18	2
1988–89		23	4
1989–90		43	4

HOYLAND, Jamie

Born Sheffield 23.1.66. Ht 6 0 Wt 12 08
Midfield. From Apprentice. England Youth.

Season	Club	Apps	Goals
1983–84	Manchester C	1	—
1984–85		1	—
1985–86		—	—
1986–87	Bury	36	2
1987–88		44	8
1988–89		46	9
1989–90		46	16

HOYLE, Colin

Born Derby 15.1.72. Ht 5 11 Wt 12 03
Forward. From Trainee.

Season	Club	Apps	Goals
1989–90	Arsenal	—	—
1989–90	*Chesterfield*	3	—

HUCKER, Peter

Born London 28.10.59. Ht 6 2 Wt 12 12
Goalkeeper. From Apprentice. England Under-21.

Season	Club	Apps	Goals
1977–78	QPR	—	—
1977–78	*Cambridge U*	—	—
1978–79	QPR	—	—
1979–80		—	—
1980–81		1	—
1981–82		22	—
1982–83		42	—
1983–84		42	—
1984–85		42	—
1985–86		11	—
1986–87		—	—
1986–87	Oxford U	5	—
1987–88		27	—
1987–88	*WBA*	7	—
1988–89	Oxford U	26	—
1988–89	*Manchester U*	—	—
1989–90	Oxford U	8	—
1989–90	Millwall	—	—

HUGHES, Adrian

Born Billinge 19.12.70 Ht 6 2 Wt 12 12
Defender. From Everton schoolboy, Preston NE Trainee.

Season	Club	Apps	Goals
1987–88	Preston NE	1	—
1988–89		23	1
1989–90		35	1

HUGHES, Ceri

Born Pontypridd 26.2.71. Ht 5 9
Wt 11 06
Midfield. From Trainee.

Season	Club	Apps	Goals
1989–90	Luton T	1	—

HUGHES, Darren

Born Prescot 6.10.65. Ht 5 11 Wt 10 11
Defender. From Apprentice.

Season	Club	Apps	Goals
1983–84	Everton	1	—
1984–85		2	—
1985–86	Shrewsbury T	31	1
1986–87		6	—
1986–87	Brighton	26	2
1987–88		—	—
1987–88	Port Vale	43	1
1988–89		44	1
1989–90		38	1

HUGHES, John

Born Edinburgh 9.9.64. Ht 6 0 Wt 13 07
Forward. From Newtongrange Star

Season	Club	Apps	Goals
1988–89	Berwick R	27	10
1989–90		14	4
1989–90	Swansea C	24	4

HUGHES, Ken

Born Barmouth 9.1.66. Ht 6 0 Wt 11 06
Goalkeeper.

Season	Club	Apps	Goals
1985–86	Crystal Palace	—	—

Season	Club	League Appearances/Goals	
1986–87	Shrewsbury T	6	—
1987–88		2	—
1988–89		7	—
1989–90		—	—

HUGHES, Mark

Born Port Talbot 3.2.62. Ht 6 0
Wt 12 08
Defender. From Apprentice. Wales Youth.

Season	Club	League Appearances/Goals	
1979–80	Bristol R	1	—
1980–81		38	1
1981–82		22	2
1982–83		4	—
1982–83	*Torquay U*	9	1
1983–84	Bristol R	9	—
1984–85	Swansea C	12	—
1984–85	Bristol C	20	—
1985–86		2	—
1985–86	Tranmere R	32	—
1986–87		38	1
1987–88		20	—
1988–89		37	1
1989–90		45	4

HUGHES, Mark

Born Wrexham 1.11.63. Ht 5 9 Wt 11 12
Forward. From Apprentice.
Wales Youth, Under-21, 28 full caps.

Season	Club	League Appearances/Goals	
1980–81	Manchester U	—	—
1981–82		—	—
1982–83		—	—
1983–84		11	4
1984–85		38	16
1985–86		40	17
From Barcelona, *Bayern Munich*			
1988–89	Manchester U	38	14
1989–90		37	13

HUGHES, Michael

Born Larne 2.8.71 Ht 5 6 Wt 10 08
Forward. From Carrick R. Northern Ireland Under-23.

Season	Club	League Appearances/Goals	
1988–89	Manchester C	1	—
1989–90		—	—

HUGHES, Paul

Born Denton 19.12.68. Ht 5 9 Wt 11 06
Defender. From Trainee.

Season	Club	League Appearances/Goals	
1987–88	Bolton W	11	—
1988–89		—	—
1989–90		2	—

HUGHES, Philip

Born Manchester 19.11.64. Ht 5 11
Wt 13 08
Goalkeeper. From Manchester U. Apprentice. Northern Ireland Youth, 3 full caps.

Season	Club	League Appearances/Goals	
1982–83	Leeds U	—	—
1983–84		2	—
1984–85		4	—
1985–86	Bury	41	—
1986–87		32	—
1987–88		7	—
1987–88	Wigan Ath	31	—
1988–89		16	—
1989–90		33	—

HUGHES, Zac

Born Bentley 6.6.71 Ht 5 11 Wt 11 12
Defender. From Trainee.

Season	Club	League Appearances/Goals	
1987–88	Rochdale	2	—
1988–89		—	—
1989–90		—	—

HUGHTON, Chris

Born West Ham 11.12.58. Ht 5 7
Wt 11 05
Defender. From Amateur.
Eire Under-21, 50 full caps.

Season	Club	League Appearances/Goals	
1977–78	Tottenham H	—	—
1978–79		—	—
1979–80		39	1
1980–81		34	1
1981–82		37	2
1982–83		38	3
1983–84		34	3

Season	Club	League Appearances/Goals	
1984–85		31	1
1985–86		33	1
1986–87		9	—
1987–88		13	—
1988–89		21	—
1989–90		8	—

HULL, Alan

Born Rochford 4.9.62. Ht 5 9 Wt 11 00
Forward. From Southend U, Basildon Barking.

Season	Club	League Appearances/Goals	
1987–88	Leyton Orient	36	5
1988–89		17	5
1989–90		24	6

HULME, Kevin

Born Farnworth 2.12.67
Forward. From Radcliffe Borough.

Season	Club	League Appearances/Goals	
1988–89	Bury	5	—
1989–90		19	1
1989–90	*Chester C*	4	—

HUMES, Tony

Born Blyth 19.3.66. Ht 6 1 Wt 11 03
Defender. From Apprentice.

Season	Club	League Appearances/Goals	
1983–84	Ipswich T	—	—
1984–85		—	—
1985–86		—	—
1986–87		22	2
1987–88		27	—
1988–89		26	3
1989–90		24	3

HUMPHREY, John

Born Paddington 31.1.61. Ht 5 10
Wt 11 03
Defender. From Apprentice.

Season	Club	League Appearances/Goals	
1978–79	Wolverhampton W	—	—
1979–80		2	—
1980–81		12	—
1981–82		23	—
1982–83		42	3
1983–84		28	—
1984–85		42	—
1985–86	Charlton Ath	39	2
1986–87		39	—
1987–88		40	—
1988–89		38	1
1989–90		38	—

HUMPHRIES, Glenn

Born Hull 11.8.64. Ht 6 0 Wt 12 00
Defender. From Apprentice. England Youth

Season	Club	League Appearances/Goals	
1980–81	Doncaster R	1	—
1981–82		14	—
1982–83		40	5
1983–84		44	2
1984–85		27	—
1985–86		29	—
1986–87		17	1
1986–87	*Lincoln C*	9	—
1987–88		8	—
1987–88	Bristol C	24	—
1988–89		22	—
1989–90		37	—

HUNT, David

Born Leicester 17.4.59. Ht 5 11
Wt 13 09
Midfield. From Apprentice.

Season	Club	League Appearances/Goals	
1977–78	Derby Co	5	—
1977–78	Notts Co	12	—
1978–79		37	2
1979–80		38	4
1980–81		42	3
1981–82		30	3
1982–83		37	1
1983–84		39	2
1984–85		37	3
1985–86		34	8
1986–87		30	2
1987–88	Aston Villa	12	—
1988–89		1	—
1989–90	Mansfield T	22	—

HUNT, Paul

Born Swindon 8.10.71. Ht 5 5 Wt 10 02
Forward. From Trainee.

Season	Club	League Appearances/Goals	
1989–90	Swindon T	4	—

HUNT, Richard

Born Reading 5.1.71. Ht 6 0 Wt 12 10
Defender. From QPR Trainee.

Season	Club	Apps	Goals
1989–90	Aldershot	2	—

HUNTER, Geoff

Born Hull 27.10.59. Ht 5 10 Wt 10 10
Defender. From Apprentice.

Season	Club	Apps	Goals
1976–77	Manchester U	—	—
1977–78		—	—
1978–79		—	—
1979–80	Crewe Alex	41	4
1980–81		46	4
1981–82	Port Vale	41	3
1982–83		46	4
1983–84		42	1
1984–85		42	2
1985–86		45	5
1986–87		5	—
1987–88	Wrexham	39	4
1988–89		38	4
1989–90		21	3

HUNTER, Gordon

Born Wallyford 3.5.67. Ht 5 10
Wt 10 05
Midfield. From Musselburgh Windsor.
Scotland Youth, Under-21.

Season	Club	Apps	Goals
1983–84	Hibernian	1	—
1984–85		6	—
1985–86		25	—
1986–87		29	—
1987–88		35	—
1988–89		33	1
1989–90		34	—

HUNTER, Lee

Born Oldham 5.10.69 Ht 5 10 Wt 10 08
Defender. From Trainee.

Season	Club	Apps	Goals
1987–88	Colchester U	1	—
1988–89		8	—
1989–90		—	—

HUNTER, Paul

Born Kirkcaldy 30.8.68. Ht 6 0
Wt 12 09
Forward. From Leven Royal Colts.

Season	Club	Apps	Goals
1984–85	East Fife	5	1
1985–86		20	7
1986–87		38	8
1987–88		39	17
1988–89		33	9
1989–90		29	14
1989–90	Hull C	9	3

HURLOCK, Terry

Born Hackney 22.9.58. Ht 5 9 Wt 13 04
Midfield. From Leytonstone and Ilford.
England B.

Season	Club	Apps	Goals
1980–81	Brentford	42	4
1981–82		40	2
1982–83		39	3
1983–84		32	4
1984–85		40	3
1985–86		27	2
1985–86	Reading	16	—
1986–87		13	—
1986–87	Millwall	13	1
1987–88		28	4
1988–89		34	3
1989–90		29	—

HURST, Lee

Born Nuneaton 21.9.70. Ht 6 0
Wt 11 09
Midfield. From Trainee.

Season	Club	Apps	Goals
1989–90	Coventry C	—	—

HURST, Mark

Born Derby 18.8.70. Ht 5 8 Wt 10 02
Forward. From Trainee.

Season	Club	Apps	Goals
1988–89	Nottingham F	—	—

Season Club League Appearances/Goals

Season	Club	Apps	Goals
1989–90		—	—
1989–90	*Huddersfield T*	—	—

HUTCHINGS, Chris

Born Winchester 5.7.57. Ht 5 10
Wt 11 00
Defender. From Harrow Bor.

Season	Club	Apps	Goals
1980–81	Chelsea	12	1
1981–82		35	1
1982–83		36	—
1983–84		4	1
1983–84	Brighton	26	1
1984–85		42	1
1985–86		29	1
1986–87		36	—
1987–88		20	1
1987–88	Huddersfield T	23	—
1988–89		41	5
1989–90		46	5

HUTCHINSON, Thomas

Born Glasgow 15.5.71. Ht 5 11
Wt 11 00
Midfield. From Tullibody Hearts.

Season	Club	Apps	Goals
1989–90	St Mirren	1	—

HUTCHISON, Donald

Born Gateshead 9.5.71. Ht 6 2 Wt 11 04
Forward. From Trainee.

Season	Club	Apps	Goals
1989–90	Hartlepool U	13	2

HUTCHISON, Tommy

Born Cardenden 22.9.47. Ht 6 0
Wt 12 06
Midfield. From Dundonald Bluebell.
Scotland Under-23, 17 full caps.

Season	Club	Apps	Goals
1965–66	Alloa	16	1
1966–67		29	2
1967–68		23	1
1967–68	Blackpool	9	—
1968–69		32	2
1969–70		41	2
1970–71		38	1
1971–72		35	2
1972–73		10	3
1972–73	Coventry C	30	2
1973–74		41	3
1974–75		42	4
1975–76		42	1
1976–77		33	3
1977–78		40	3
1978–79		42	6
1979–80		40	1
1980–81		4	1
1981–82	Manchester C	24	3
1982–83		22	1

From Bulova, Hong Kong.

Season	Club	Apps	Goals
1983–84	Burnley	46	4
1984–85		46	—
1985–86	Swansea C	41	3
1986–87		41	1
1987–88		7	—
1988–89		44	3
1989–90		36	2

HYDE, Gary

Born Wolverhampton 28.12.69 Ht 6 0
Wt 9 08
Midfield. From Trainee.

Season	Club	Apps	Goals
1987–88	Darlington	2	—
1988–89		36	3
1989–90		—	—
1989–90	Leicester C	—	—

HYDE, Graham

Born Doncaster 10.11.70. Ht 5 7
Wt 11 07
Midfield. From Trainee.

Season	Club	Apps	Goals
1987–88	Sheffield W	—	—
1988–89		—	—
1989–90		—	—

HYSEN, Glenn

Born Gothenburg 30.10.59 Ht 6 1
Wt 12 08
Defender. From Fiorentina. Sweden full caps.

Season	Club	Apps	Goals
1989–90	Liverpool	35	1

INCE, Paul

Born Ilford 21.10.67. Ht 5 10 Wt 11 07
Midfield. From Trainee. England Youth, Under-21.

Season	Club	App	Goals
1985–86	West Ham U	—	—
1986–87		10	1
1987–88		28	3
1988–89		33	3
1989–90		1	—
1989–90	Manchester U	26	—

IORFA, Dominic

Born Lagos 1.10.68.
Forward. From Antwerp.

Season	Club	App	Goals
1989–90	QPR	1	—

IRONS, David

Born Glasgow 18.7.61. Ht 6 0 Wt 11 04
Midfield. From Kello Rovers.

Season	Club	App	Goals
1984–85	Ayr U	34	6
1985–86		37	6
1986–87		4	1
1986–87	Clydebank	23	1
1987–88		31	6
1987–88	Dunfermline Ath	11	1
1988–89		36	2
1989–90		23	2

IRONS, Kenny

Born Liverpool 4.11.70. Ht 5 9
Wt 11 00
Forward. From Trainee.

Season	Club	App	Goals
1989–90	Tranmere R	3	—

IRONSIDE, Ian

Born Sheffield 8.3.64. Ht 6 2 Wt 13 00
Goalkeeper. From Barnsley Apprentice, N. Ferriby U.

Season	Club	App	Goals
1987–88	Scarborough	6	—
1988–89		28	—
1989–90		14	—

IRVINE, Alan

Born Glasgow 12.7.58. Ht 5 9 Wt 11 03
Forward. From Glasgow BC.

Season	Club	App	Goals
1977–78	Queen's Park	4	—
1978–79		8	—
1979–80		38	5
1980–81		38	4
1981–82	Everton	25	3
1982–83		14	1
1983–84		21	—
1984–85	Crystal Palace	35	5
1985–86		41	3
1986–87		33	4
1987–88	Dundee U	16	2
1988–89		7	1
1989–90		1	—
1989–90	Blackburn R	25	1

IRVINE, Brian

Born Bellshill 24.5.65. Ht 6 2 Wt 13 0
Defender. From Victoria Park.

Season	Club	App	Goals
1983–84	Falkirk	3	—
1984–85		35	—
1985–86	Aberdeen	1	—
1986–87		20	1
1987–88		16	1
1988–89		27	2
1989–90		31	1

IRWIN, Dennis

Born Cork 31.70.65. Ht 5 8 Wt 11 00
Defender. From Apprentice. Eire Schools Youth, B, Under-21.

Season	Club	App	Goals
1983–84	Leeds U	12	—
1984–85		41	1
1985–86		19	—
1986–87	Oldham Ath	41	1
1987–88		43	—

Season	Club	League Appearances/Goals	
1988–89		41	2
1989–90		42	1

ISAAC, Robert

Born Hackney 30.11.65. Ht 5 11
Wt 13 06
Defender. From Apprentice. England Youth.

Season	Club	League Appearances/Goals	
1983–84	Chelsea	—	—
1984–85		1	—
1985–86		3	—
1986–87		5	—
1986–87	Brighton	11	—
1987–88		10	—
1988–89		9	—
1989–90		—	—

JACK, Ross

Born Inverness 21.3.59. Ht 5 11
Wt 12 00
Forward. From Apprentice.

Season	Club	League Appearances/Goals	
1976–77	Everton	—	—
1977–78		—	—
1978–79		1	1
1979–80		—	—
1979–80	*Cardiff C*	—	—
1979–80	Norwich C	—	—
1980–81		11	—
1981–82		35	10
1982–83		10	—
1983–84	Lincoln C	36	9
1984–85		24	7
1985–86	Dundee	6	—
1986–87		28	4
1987–88		4	—
1987–88	Dunfermline Ath	25	4
1988–89		36	18
1989–90		36	16

JACKETT, Kenny

Born Watford 5.1.62. Ht 5 11 Wt 12 00
Defender. From Apprentice.
Wales Youth, Under-21, 31 full caps.

Season	Club	League Appearances/Goals	
1979–80	Watford	2	—
1980–81		42	3
1981–82		18	2
1982–83		41	4
1983–84		31	1
1984–85		36	4
1985–86		41	4
1986–87		32	6
1987–88		33	2
1988–89		42	—
1989–90		17	—

JACKSON, Darren

Born Edinburgh 25.7.66. Ht 5 10
Wt 10 10
Forward. From Broxburn Am.

Season	Club	League Appearances/Goals	
1985–86	Meadowbank T	39	17
1986–87		9	5
1986–87	Newcastle U	23	3
1987–88		31	2

Season	Club	League Appearances/Goals	
1988–89		15	2
1988–89	Dundee U	1	—
1989–90		25	7

JACKSON, Darren

Born Bristol 24.9.71. Ht 6 1 Wt 12 08
Defender. From Trainee.

Season	Club	Apps	Goals
1989–90	Oxford U	1	—

JACKSON, Peter

Born Bradford 6.4.61. Ht 6 0 Wt 12 07
Defender. From Apprentice.

Season	Club	Apps	Goals
1978–79	Bradford C	9	1
1979–80		12	—
1980–81		45	1
1981–82		32	8
1982–83		41	3
1983–84		42	3
1984–85		45	8
1985–86		42	—
1986–87		10	—
1986–87	Newcastle U	31	1
1987–88		28	2
1988–89		1	—
1988–89	Bradford C	32	3
1989–90		26	2

JACOBS, Wayne

Born Sheffield 3.2.69. Ht 5 9 Wt 10 02
Defender. From Apprentice.

Season	Club	Apps	Goals
1986–87	Sheffield W	—	—
1987–88		6	—
1987–88	Hull C	6	—
1988–89		33	—
1989–90		46	3

JAKUB, Joe

Born Falkirk 7.12.56. Ht 5 6 Wt 9 06
Midfield. From Apprentice.

Season	Club	Apps	Goals
1973–74	Burnley	—	—
1974–75		—	—
1975–76		1	—
1976–77		5	—
1977–78		—	—
1978–79		13	—
1979–80		23	—
1980–81		—	—
1981–82	Bury	33	1
1982–83		46	2
1983–84		46	3
1984–85		46	11
1985–86		40	3
1986–87		44	6
1987–88		10	1
From AZ Alkmaar			
1988–89	Chester C	42	1
1989–90	Burnley	46	5

JAMES, David

Born Welwyn 1.8.70 Ht 6 4 Wt 14 13
Goalkeeper. From Trainee.

Season	Club	Apps	Goals
1988–89	Watford	—	—
1989–90		—	—

JAMES, Julian

Born Tring 22.3.70. Ht 5 10 Wt 11 11
Midfield. From Trainee. England Under-21.

Season	Club	Apps	Goals
1987–88	Luton T	3	—
1988–89		1	—
1989–90		20	1

JAMES, Robbie

Born Swansea 23.3.57. Ht 5 11 Wt 13 0
Forward. From Apprentice. Wales Under-21, 47 full caps.

Season	Club	Apps	Goals
1972–73	Swansea C	1	—
1973–74		29	2
1974–75		42	8
1975–76		45	8
1976–77		46	14
1977–78		42	16
1978–79		43	14
1979–80		29	6
1980–81		35	8
1981–82		42	14
1982–83		40	9
1983–84	Stoke C	40	6
1984–85		8	—
1984–85	QPR	20	2
1985–86		28	1

Season	Club	Apps	Goals
1986–87	....	39	1
1987–88	Leicester C..............	23	—
1987–88	Swansea C	19	3
1988–89	....	41	9
1989–90	....	30	4

JAMES, Tony

Born Sheffield 27.6.67 Ht 6 3 Wt 13 08
Defender. From Gainsborough T.

Season	Club	Apps	Goals
1988–89	Lincoln C................	28	—
1989–90	....	1	—
1989–90	Leicester C..............	31	2

JAMIESON, Willie

Born Barnsley 27.4.63. Ht 5 11
Wt 12 00
Defender. From Tynecastle BC.

Season	Club	Apps	Goals
1980–81	Hibernian	28	12
1981–82	....	12	5
1982–83	....	19	2
1983–84	....	33	4
1984–85	....	25	2
1985–86	Hamilton A.............	39	2
1986–87	....	15	—
1987–88	....	41	4
1988–89	....	34	1
1989–90	Dundee	14	—

JASPER, Dale

Born Croydon 14.1.64. Ht 6 0 Wt 12 00
Defender. From Amateur.

Season	Club	Apps	Goals
1981–82	Chelsea	—	—
1982–83	....	—	—
1983–84	....	3	—
1984–85	....	7	—
1985–86	....	—	—
1986–87	Brighton.................	35	2
1987–88	....	14	4
1988–89	Crewe Alex.............	39	1
1989–90	....	40	—

JEFFELS, Simon

Born Darton 18.1.66. Ht 6 1 Wt 11 08
Defender. From Apprentice.
England Youth.

Season Club League Appearances/Goals

Season	Club	Apps	Goals
1983–84	Barnsley	3	—
1984–85	....	18	—
1985–86	....	11	—
1986–87	....	3	—
1987–88	....	7	—
1987–88	*Preston NE*.............	1	—
1988–89	Carlisle U	29	—
1989–90	....	—	—

JEFFERS, John

Born Liverpool 5.10.68. Ht 5 10
Wt 11 10
Forward. From Trainee.

Season	Club	Apps	Goals
1986–87	Liverpool................	—	—
1987–88	....	—	—
1988–89	....	—	—
1988–89	Port Vale	15	—
1989–90	....	40	1

JEFFREY, Mike

Born Liverpool 11.8.71 Ht 5 9 Wt 10 06
Forward. From Trainee.

Season	Club	Apps	Goals
1988–89	Bolton W.................	9	—
1989–90	....	4	—

JEMSON, Nigel

Born Preston 10.8.69. Ht 5 10 Wt 11 10
Forward. From Trainee.

Season	Club	Apps	Goals
1985–86	Preston NE	1	—
1986–87	....	4	3
1987–88	....	27	5
1987–88	Nottingham F	—	—
1988–89	....	—	—
1988–89	*Bolton W*	5	—
1988–89	*Preston NE*.............	9	2
1989–90	Nottingham F	18	4

JENKINS, Grant

Born Dundee 11.4.58 Ht 5 11 Wt 11 1
Forward. From Jeanfield Swifts.

Season	Club	Apps	Goals
1980–81	Dunfermline Ath.......	11	2
1981–82	....	35	7
1982–83	....	22	3
1983–84	....	29	6
1984–85	....	33	9

Season	Club	Apps	Goals
1985–86		37	14
1986–87		40	6
1987–88		16	—
1987–88	St Johnstone	15	1
1988–89		33	9
1989–90		28	3

JENKINSON, Leigh

Born Thorne 9.7.69. Ht 6 0 Wt 12 02
Forward. From Trainee.

Season	Club	Apps	Goals
1987–88	Hull C	3	1
1988–89		11	—
1989–90		22	—

JEPSON, Ron

Born Stoke 12.5.63. Ht 6 1 Wt 13 02
Forward. From Nantwich.

Season	Club	Apps	Goals
1988–89	Port Vale	2	—
1989–90		5	—
1989–90	*Peterborough U*	18	5

JESS, Eoin

Born Aberdeen 13.12.70. Ht 5 7
Wt 10 10
Forward. From Rangers S Form. Scotland Under-21.

Season	Club	Apps	Goals
1987–88	Aberdeen	—	—
1988–89		2	—
1989–90		11	3

JEWELL, Paul

Born Liverpool 28.9.64. Ht 5 8 Wt 11 10
Forward. From Apprentice.

Season	Club	Apps	Goals
1982–83	Liverpool	—	—
1983–84		—	—
1984–85	Wigan Ath	26	9
1985–86		29	6
1986–87		39	9
1987–88		43	11
1988–89	Bradford C	39	4
1989–90		30	4

JOBLING, Kevin

Born Sunderland 1.1.68. Ht 5 9
Wt 10 11
Midfield. From Apprentice.

Season	Club	Apps	Goals
1985–86	Leicester C	—	—
1986–87		3	—
1987–88		6	—
1987–88	Grimsby T	15	1
1988–89		32	4
1989–90		33	1

JOBSON, Richard

Born Hull 9.5.63. Ht 6 1 Wt 13 05
Defender. From Burton Alb.

Season	Club	Apps	Goals
1982–83	Watford	13	1
1983–84		13	2
1984–85		2	1
1984–85	Hull C	8	—
1985–86		36	7
1986–87		40	5
1987–88		44	2
1988–89		46	1
1989–90		45	2

JOHNROSE, Lenny

Born Preston 29.11.69. Ht 5 11 Wt 12 00
Forward. From Trainee.

Season	Club	Apps	Goals
1987–88	Blackburn R	1	—
1988–89		—	—
1989–90		8	3

JOHNS, Nicky

Born Bristol 8.6.57. Ht 6 2 Wt 11 08
Goalkeeper. From Minehead.

Season	Club	Apps	Goals
1975–76	Millwall	—	—
1976–77		16	—
1977–78		34	—
From Tampa Bay R			
1978–79	*Sheffield U*	1	—
1978–79	Charlton Ath	10	—
1979–80		34	—
1980–81		37	—
1981–82		40	—
1982–83		42	—
1983–84		36	—
1984–85		30	—
1985–86		38	—
1986–87		16	—
1987–88		5	—

Season Club League Appearances/Goals

Season	Club	Apps	Goals
1987–88	QPR	7	—
1988–89		3	—
1989–90		—	—
1989–90	Maidstone U	13	—

JOHNSEN, Erland

Born Frederikstad (Norway) 5.4.67.
Ht 6 0 Wt 12 10
Defender. From Bayern Munich. Norway full caps.

Season	Club	Apps	Goals
1989–90	Chelsea	18	—

JOHNSON, Alan

Born Ince 19.2.71
Defender. From Trainee.

Season	Club	Apps	Goals
1988–89	Wigan Ath	8	1
1989–90		33	1

JOHNSON, David

Born Northampton 10.3.67.
Defender. From Irthlingborough D.

Season	Club	Apps	Goals
1989–90	Northampton T	7	—

JOHNSON, Gavin

Born Eye 10.10.70 Ht 6 0 Wt 10 07
Defender. From Trainee.

Season	Club	Apps	Goals
1988–89	Ipswich T	4	—
1989–90		6	—

JOHNSON, Marvin

Born Wembley 29.10.68. Ht 5 11
Wt 11 06
Defender. From Apprentice.

Season	Club	Apps	Goals
1986–87	Luton T	—	—
1987–88		9	—
1988–89		16	—
1989–90		12	—

JOHNSON, Nigel

Born Rotherham 23.6.64. Ht 6 2
Wt 13 04
Defender. From Apprentice.

Season	Club	Apps	Goals
1982–83	Rotherham U	11	—
1983–84		43	1
1983–84	*Nottingham F*	—	—
1984–85	Rotherham U	35	—
1985–86	Manchester C	4	—
1986–87		—	—
1987–88	Rotherham U	23	—
1988–89		26	2
1989–90		43	2

JOHNSON, Peter

Born Harrogate 5.10.58. Ht 5 9
Wt 11 06
Defender. From Apprentice.

Season	Club	Apps	Goals
1976–77	Middlesbrough	—	—
1977–78		4	—
1978–79		21	—
1979–80		18	—
1980–81	Newcastle U	16	—
1981–82		—	—
1982–83		—	—
1982–83	*Bristol C*	20	—
1982–83	Doncaster R	12	—
1983–84	Darlington	44	1
1984–85		45	1
1985–86	Crewe Alex	8	—
1985–86	Exeter C	5	—
1986–87	Southend U	44	2
1987–88		39	1
1988–89		43	—
1989–90	Gillingham	45	2

JOHNSON, Rob

Born Bedford 22.2.62. Ht 5 7 Wt 11 03
Midfield. From Apprentice.

Season	Club	Apps	Goals
1979–80	Luton T	—	—
1980–81		—	—
1981–82		—	—
1982–83		—	—
1983–84		2	—
1983–84	*Lincoln C*	4	—
1984–85	Luton T	—	—
1985–86		15	—
1986–87		34	—
1987–88		25	—

Season Club League Appearances/Goals

Season	Club	Apps	Goals
1988–89		21	—
1989–90	Leicester C	13	—

JOHNSON, Steve

Born Liverpool 23.6.57. Ht 6 0 Wt 12 09
Forward. From Altrincham.

Season	Club	Apps	Goals
1977–78	Bury	11	1
1978–79		8	1
1979–80		27	9
1980–81		43	18
1981–82		31	13
1982–83		34	10
1983–84	Rochdale	19	7
1984–85	Wigan Ath	21	7
1985–86		30	11
1984–85	Bristol C	8	3
1985–86		13	—
1985–86	*Rochdale*	6	1
1985–86	*Chester C*	10	6
1986–87	Scunthorpe U	40	16
1987–88		32	4
1988–89	Chester C	38	10
From Huskvarna.			
1989–90	Rochdale	24	4

JOHNSON, Tommy

Born Newcastle 15.1.71. Ht 5 10
Wt 11 02
Forward. From Trainee.

Season	Club	Apps	Goals
1988–89	Notts Co	10	4
1989–90		40	18

JOHNSTON, Craig

Born S. Africa 8.12.60. Ht 5 8 Wt 10 13
Midfield. From Lake McQuarrie, Sydney C and Apprentice. England Under-21.

Season	Club	Apps	Goals
1977–78	Middlesbrough	5	1
1978–79		2	—
1979–80		30	5
1980–81		27	10
1980–81	Liverpool	—	—
1981–82		18	6
1982–83		33	7
1983–84		29	2
1984–85		11	—
1985–86		41	7
1986–87		28	3
1987–88		30	5
1988–89		—	—
1989–90		—	—

JOHNSTON, Mo

Born Glasgow 30.4.63. Ht 5 9 Wt 10 06
Forward. From Milton Battlefield.
Scotland Under-21, 36 full caps.

Season	Club	Apps	Goals
1980–81	Partick T	—	—
1981–82		32	9
1982–83		39	22
1983–84		14	10
1983–84	Watford	29	20
1984–85		9	3
1984–85	Celtic	27	14
1985–86		32	15
1986–87		40	23
From Nantes			
1989–90	Rangers	36	15

JOHNSTON, Richard

Born Portadown 15.10.69. Ht 5 9
Wt 10 10
Forward. From Trainee.

Season	Club	Apps	Goals
1988–89	Tottenham H	—	—
1989–90		—	—
1989–90	*Dunfermline Ath*	—	—

JOHNSTON, Sammy

Born Glasgow 13.4.67. Ht 5 9 Wt 10 07
Midfield. From Bishopbriggs BC

Season	Club	Apps	Goals
1984–85	St Johnstone	3	—
1985–86		27	2
1986–87		39	6
1987–88		39	11
1988–89		30	3
1989–90		37	7

JONES, Alex

Born Blackburn 27.11.64. Ht 6 2
Wt 12 08
Defender. From Apprentice.

Season	Club	Apps	Goals
1982–83	Oldham Ath	2	—
1983–84		2	—

Season	Club	League Appearances/Goals	
1984–85	....	5	—
1984–85	*Stockport Co*	3	—
1985–86	Oldham Ath	—	—
1986–87	Preston NE	46	1
1987–88	....	22	2
1988–89	....	30	—
1989–90	....	3	—
1989–90	Carlisle U	36	4

JONES, Andy

Born Wrexham 9.1.63. Ht 5 11 Wt 13 06
Forward. From Rhyl. Wales 6 full caps.

Season	Club	League Appearances/Goals	
1985–86	Port Vale	41	12
1986–87	....	43	31
1987–88	....	6	6
1978–79	Charlton Ath	25	6
1988–89	....	9	4
1988–89	*Port Vale*	17	3
1989–90	Charlton Ath	25	5
1989–90	*Bristol C*	4	1

JONES, Barry

Born Liverpool 30.6.70. Ht 6 0
Wt 12 00
Defender. From Prescot T.

Season	Club	League Appearances/Goals	
1988–89	Liverpool	—	—
1989–90	....	—	—

JONES, David

Born Harrow 3.7.64
Forward.

Season	Club	League Appearances/Goals	
1987–88	Chelsea	—	—
1988–89	Bury	1	—
1988–89	Leyton Orient	2	—
1988–89	Burnley	4	—
1989–90	Ipswich T	—	—
1989–90	Doncaster R	27	12

JONES, David

Born Wrexham 6.5.71. Ht 5 9 Wt 11 04
Forward. From Trainee. Wales Schools.

Season	Club	League Appearances/Goals	
1989–90	Aston Villa..............	—	—

JONES, Gary

Born Huddersfield 6.4.69. Ht 5 11
Wt 11 06
Forward. From Huddersfield T,
Rossington Main.

Season	Club	League Appearances/Goals	
1988–89	Doncaster R	17	2
1989–90	....	3	—

JONES, Joey

Born Llandudno 4.3.55. Ht 5 10
Wt 11 09
Defender. From Amateur.
Wales Under-23, 72 full caps.

Season	Club	League Appearances/Goals	
1972–73	Wrexham	17	—
1973–74	....	41	—
1974–75	....	40	2
1975–76	Liverpool	13	—
1976–77	....	39	3
1977–78	....	20	—
1978–79	....	—	—
1979–80	Wrexham	30	2
1980–81	....	36	3
1981–82	....	37	1
1982–83	....	36	—
1983–84	....	7	—
1982–83	Chelsea	28	1
1983–84	....	34	1
1984–85	....	16	—
1985–86	Huddersfield T	38	1
1986–87	....	30	2
1987–88	Wrexham	35	—
1988–89	....	41	8
1989–90	....	24	1

JONES, Keith

Born Dulwich 14.10.64. Ht 5 8 Wt 11 03
Midfield. From Apprentice. England
Schools, Youth.

Season	Club	League Appearances/Goals	
1982–83	Chelsea	2	—
1983–84	....	—	—
1984–85	....	19	2
1985–86	....	14	2
1986–87	....	17	3
1987–88	....	—	—

Season	Club	League Appearances/Goals	
1987–88	Brentford	36	1
1988–89		40	3
1989–90		42	2

JONES, Linden

Born Tredegar 5.3.61. Ht 5 6 Wt 10 08
Defender. From Apprentice. Wales Under-21.

Season	Club	League Appearances/Goals	
1978–79	Cardiff C	14	—
1979–80		17	—
1980–81		29	1
1981–82		36	—
1982–83		43	—
1983–84		6	—
1983–84	Newport Co	32	—
1984–85		44	4
1985–86		31	1
1986–87		35	—
1987–88	Reading	28	3
1988–89		29	3
1989–90		39	—

JONES, Mark

Born Berinsfield 26.9.61. Ht 5 6
Wt 10 03
Midfield. From Apprentice.

Season	Club	League Appearances/Goals	
1979–80	Oxford U	2	—
1980–81		36	1
1981–82		21	3
1982–83		26	1
1983–84		20	2
1984–85		18	—
1985–86		6	—
1986–87		—	—
1986–87	Swindon T	40	9
1987–88		—	—
1988–89		—	—
1989–90		—	—

JONES, Mark

Born Walsall 4.1.68. Ht 5 8 Wt 10 01
Midfield. From Apprentice.

Season	Club	League Appearances/Goals	
1985–86	Walsall	—	—
1986–87		—	—
1987–88		8	—
1988–89		—	—
1988–89	*Exeter C*	5	—
1989–90	Hereford U	42	8

JONES, Mark

Born Warley 22.10.61. Ht 5 8 Wt 10 08
Defender. From Apprentice.

Season	Club	League Appearances/Goals	
1979–80	Aston Villa	—	—
1980–81		—	—
1981–82		2	—
1982–83		17	—
1983–84		5	—
1983–84	Brighton	6	—
1984–85		3	—
1984–85	Birmingham C	10	—
1985–86		19	—
1986–87		5	—
1986–87	Shrewsbury T	—	—
1987–88	Hereford U	28	—
1988–89		41	—
1989–90		41	1

JONES, Matthew

Born Chiswick 9.10.70. Ht 5 11
Wt 12 00
Midfield. From Trainee.

Season	Club	League Appearances/Goals	
1988–89	Southend U	1	—
1989–90		4	—

JONES, Murray

Born Bexley 7.10.64 Ht 6 4 Wt 14 00
Forward. From Carshalton.

Season	Club	League Appearances/Goals	
1989–90	Crystal Palace	—	—

JONES, Paul

Born Ellesmere Port 13.5.53 Ht 6 1
Wt 12 09
Defender. From Apprentice.

Season	Club	League Appearances/Goals	
1970–71	Bolton W	3	—
1971–72		38	1
1972–73		46	7
1973–74		38	—
1974–75		42	5
1975–76		41	6
1976–77		42	10
1977–78		21	4

Season	Club	League Appearances/Goals	
1978–79		32	1
1979–80		32	1
1980–81		35	—
1981–82		41	1
1982–83		33	1
1983–84	Huddersfield T	36	7
1984–85		23	1
1985–86		14	—
1985–86	Oldham Ath	18	1
From Galway.			
1988–89	Wigan Ath	—	—
1988–89	Rochdale	14	2
1989–90	Stockport Co	25	—

JONES, Paul

Born Walsall 6.9.65. Ht 6 1 Wt 11 04
Forward. From Apprentice.

Season	Club	Apps	Goals
1982–83	Walsall	2	—
1983–84		4	—
1984–85		22	—
1985–86		26	1
1986–87		27	3
1987–88		43	11
1988–89		16	—
1988–89	*Wrexham*	5	—
1989–90	Walsall	3	—
1989–90	Wolverhampton W	13	—

JONES, Philip

Born Liverpool 1.12.69. Ht 5 8 Wt 10 09
Midfield. From Trainee.

Season	Club	Apps	Goals
1987–88	Everton	1	—
1988–89		—	—
1989–90		—	—
1989–90	*Blackpool*	6	—

JONES, Richard

Born Pontypool 26.4.69 Ht 5 11
Wt 11 01
Defender.

Season	Club	Apps	Goals
1986–87	Newport Co	10	—
1987–88		31	1
1988–89	Hereford U	38	1
1989–90		19	3

JONES, Rob

Born Wrexham 5.11.71. Ht 5 11
Wt 11 00
Defender. From Schoolboy, Trainee.

Season	Club	Apps	Goals
1987–88	Crewe Alex	5	—
1988–89		19	1
1989–90		11	—

JONES, Robert

Born Liverpool 12.11.71.
Midfield. From Crewe Alex Schoolboy.

Season	Club	Apps	Goals
1989–90	Wrexham	1	—

JONES, Shane

Born Tredegar 8.11.72.
Midfield. From Trainee.

Season	Club	Apps	Goals
1989–90	Hereford U	15	—

JONES, Tommy

Born Aldershot 7.10.64 Ht 5 10
Wt 11 07
Midfield. From Chelsea apprentice, Farnborough, Weymouth.

Season	Club	Apps	Goals
1987–88	Aberdeen	28	3
1988–89		—	—
1988–89	Swindon T	40	6
1989–90		44	2

JONES, Vaughan

Born Tonyrefail 2.9.59. Ht 5 8 Wt 11 11
Defender. From Apprentice. Wales Under-21.

Season	Club	Apps	Goals
1976–77	Bristol R	1	—
1977–78		—	—
1978–79		22	1
1979–80		23	1
1980–81		21	1
1981–82		34	—
1982–83	Newport Co	43	—
1983–84		25	4
1984–85	Cardiff C	11	—

Season	Club	League Appearances/Goals	
1984–85	Bristol R	20	—
1985–86		32	—
1986–87		34	1
1987–88		46	3
1988–89		45	2
1989–90		46	2

JONES, Vinny

Born Watford 5.1.65. Ht 5 11 Wt 11 10
Midfield. From Wealdstone.

Season	Club	Apps	Goals
1986–87	Wimbledon	22	4
1987–88		24	2
1988–89		31	3
1989–90	Leeds U	45	5

JONSSON, Siggi

Born Akranes 27.9.66. Ht 5 11 Wt 12 06
Midfield. From I A Akranes. Iceland full caps.

Season	Club	Apps	Goals
1984–85	Sheffield W	3	—
1985–86		10	2
1985–86	*Barnsley*	5	—
1986–87	Sheffield W	13	—
1987–88		13	1
1988–89		28	1
1989–90	Arsenal	6	—

JORDAN, David

Born Gillingham 26.10.71. Ht 6 0
Wt 11 07
Forward. From Trainee.

Season	Club	Apps	Goals
1989–90	Gillingham	—	—

JORDAN, Joe

Born Carlisle 15.12.51. Ht 6 1 Wt 12 01
Forward. Scotland Under-23, 52 full caps.

Season	Club	Apps	Goals
1968–69	Morton	5	1
1969–70		5	1
1970–71		2	—
1970–71	Leeds U	—	—
1971–72		12	—
1972–73		26	9
1973–74		33	7
1974–75		29	4
1975–76		17	2
1976–77		32	10
1977–78		20	3
1977–78	Manchester U	14	3
1978–79		30	6
1979–80		32	13
1980–81		33	15
1981–82	AC Milan	22	2
1982–83		30	10
1983–84	Verona	12	1
1984–85	Southampton	34	12
1985–86		12	—
1986–87		2	—
1986–87	Bristol C	19	3
1987–88		28	4
1988–89		9	1
1989–90		1	—

JOSEPH, Francis

Born Kilburn 6.3.60. Ht 5 10 Wt 12 12
Forward. From Hillingdon Bor.

Season	Club	Apps	Goals
1980–81	Wimbledon	11	1
1981–82		40	13
1982–83	Brentford	43	24
1983–84		43	18
1984–85		3	—
1985–86		8	1
1986–87		13	1
1986–87	*Wimbledon*	5	1
1987–88	Reading	11	2
1987–88	*Bristol R*	3	—
1987–88	*Aldershot*	10	2
1988–89	Sheffield U	13	3
1988–89	Gillingham	15	1
1989–90		3	—
1989–90	Crewe Alex	16	2

JOSEPH, Roger

Born Paddington 24.12.65 Ht 5 11
Wt 11 10
Defender. From Juniors.

Season	Club	Apps	Goals
1984–85	Brentford	1	—
1985–86		28	1
1986–87		32	1
1987–88		43	—

Season	Club	League Appearances/Goals	
1988–89	Wimbledon	31	—
1989–90		19	—

JOYCE, Joe

Born Consett 18.3.61. Ht 5 9 Wt 10 05
Defender. From school.

Season	Club	League Appearances/Goals	
1979–80	Barnsley	8	—
1980–81		33	—
1981–82		20	—
1982–83		32	1
1983–84		40	1
1984–85		41	—
1985–86		40	—
1986–87		34	—
1987–88		38	2
1988–89		45	—
1989–90		—	—

JOYCE, Sean

Born Doncaster 15.2.67. Ht 5 8
Wt 10 05
Midfield.

Season	Club	League Appearances/Goals	
1985–86	Doncaster R	15	1
1986–87		14	—
1986–87	*Exeter C*	1	—
1987–88	Doncaster R	12	1
1988–89	Torquay U	30	3
1989–90		41	5

JOYCE, Warren

Born Oldham 20.1.65. Ht 5 8 Wt 11 5
Midfield. Local.

Season	Club	League Appearances/Goals	
1982–83	Bolton W	8	—
1983–84		45	3
1984–85		45	5
1985–86		31	4
1986–87		44	5
1987–88		11	—
1987–88	Preston NE	22	—
1988–89		40	9
1989–90		44	11

JUDGE, Alan

Born Kingsbury 14.5.60. Ht 5 11
Wt 11 06
Goalkeeper. From Amateur.

Season	Club	League Appearances/Goals	
1977–78	Luton T	—	—
1978–79		—	—
1979–80		1	—
1980–81		2	—
1981–82		4	—
1982–83		4	—
1982–83	*Reading*	33	—
1983–84	Reading	41	—
1984–85		3	—
1984–85	Oxford U	—	—
1985–86		19	—
1985–86	*Lincoln C*	2	—
1986–87	Oxford U	9	—
1987–88		9	—
1987–88	*Cardiff C*	8	—
1988–89	Oxford U	20	—
1989–90		17	—

JURYEFF, Ian

Born Gosport 24.11.62. Ht 5 11 Wt 12 0
Forward. From Apprentice.

Season	Club	League Appearances/Goals	
1980–81	Southampton	—	—
1981–82		—	—
1982–83		—	—
From Sweden			
1983–84	Southampton	2	—
1983–84	*Mansfield T*	12	5
1984–85	Southampton	—	—
1984–85	*Reading*	7	1
1984–85	Orient	19	7
1985–86		27	10
1986–87		13	2
1987–88		23	16
1988–89		29	9
1988–89	*Ipswich T*	2	—
1989–90	Halifax T	17	7
1989–90	Hereford U	25	3

KAMARA, Alan

Born Sheffield 15.7.58. Ht 5 9 Wt 10 12
Defender. From Kiveton Park.

Season	Club	Apps	Goals
1979–80	York C	10	—
1980–81	Darlington	45	—
1981–82		43	—
1982–83		46	1
From York RI, Retford, Burton Alb			
1987–88	Scarborough	29	—
1988–89		44	1
1989–90		45	1

KAMARA, Chris

Born Middlesbrough 25.12.57. Ht 6 1
Wt 12 00
Midfield. From Apprentice.

Season	Club	Apps	Goals
1975–76	Portsmouth	24	4
1976–77		39	3
1977–78	Swindon T	40	10
1978–79		28	2
1979–80		34	5
1980–81		45	4
1981–82	Portsmouth	11	—
1981–82	Brentford	31	5
1982–83		44	11
1983–84		38	6
1984–85		39	6
1985–86	Swindon T	20	1
1986–87		42	3
1987–88		25	2
1988–89	Stoke C	38	4
1989–90		22	1
1989–90	Leeds U	11	1

KANE, Paul

Born Edinburgh 20.6.65. Ht 5 8 Wt 9 09
Midfield. From Salvesen BC. Scotland Youth.

Season	Club	Apps	Goals
1982–83	Hibernian	—	—
1983–84		13	1
1984–85		34	8
1985–86		32	5
1986–87		37	1
1987–88		44	10
1988–89		35	5
1989–90		31	3

KASULE, Vic

Born Glasgow 28.5.65. Ht 5 10 Wt 10 03
Forward. From Motherwell M.

Season	Club	Apps	Goals
1982–83	Albion R	5	1
1983–84		31	3
1984–85		29	3
1985–86		36	6
1986–87		31	5
1986–87	Meadowbank T	7	1
1987–88		28	6
1987–88	Shrewsbury T	14	3
1988–89		21	1
1989–90		5	—
1989–90	Hamilton A	12	—

KAVANAGH, Jason

Born Birmingham 23.11.71 Ht 5 9
Wt 11 00
Midfield. From Birmingham C schoolboys. FA Schools.

Season	Club	Apps	Goals
1988–89	Derby Co	—	—
1989–90		—	—

KAY, John

Born Sunderland 29.1.64. Ht 5 10
Wt 11 06
Defender. From Apprentice.

Season	Club	Apps	Goals
1981–82	Arsenal	—	—
1982–83		7	—
1983–84		7	—
1984–85	Wimbledon	21	1
1984–85	*Middlesbrough*	8	—
1985–86	Wimbledon	26	1
1986–87		16	—
1987–88	Sunderland	46	—
1988–89		11	—
1989–90		32	—

KEARNEY, Mark

Born Ormskirk 12.6.62. Ht 5 10
Wt 11 00
Defender. From Marine.

Season	Club	App	Goals
1981–82	Everton	—	—
1982–83		—	—
1982–83	Mansfield T	11	1
1983–84		17	2
1984–85		38	4
1985–86		31	7
1986–87		43	10
1987–88		4	—
1988–89		45	2
1989–90		41	3

KEARNS, Ollie

Born Banbury 12.6.56. Ht 6 0 Wt 12 07
Forward. From Banbury U.

Season	Club	App	Goals
1976–77	Reading	5	2
1977–78		27	16
1978–79		27	11
1979–80		27	11
1980–81		—	—
1981–82	Oxford U	18	4
1982–83	Walsall	38	11
1983–84	Hereford U	41	10
1984–85		45	18
1985–86		33	13
1986–87		40	16
1987–88		11	1
1987–88	Wrexham	17	8
1988–89		17	4
1989–90		12	2

KEARTON, Jason

Born Ipswich (Australia) 9.7.69. Ht 6 1
Wt 11 10
Goalkeeper. From Brisbane Lions.

Season	Club	App	Goals
1988–89	Everton	—	—
1989–90		—	—

KEE, Paul

Born Belfast 8.11.69 Ht 6 3 Wt 12 05
Goalkeeper. From Ards. Northern Ireland 1 full cap.

Season	Club	App	Goals
1988–89	Oxford U	—	—
1989–90		21	—

KEELEY, John

Born Plaistow 27.7.61. Ht 6 1 Wt 14 02
Goalkeeper. From Apprentice.

Season	Club	App	Goals
1979–80	Southend U	4	—
1980–81		—	—
1981–82		27	—
1982–83		7	—
1983–84		16	—
From Chelmsford C			
1986–87	Brighton	20	—
1987–88		46	—
1988–89		37	—
1989–90		35	—

KEEN, Kevin

Born Amersham 25.2.67. Ht 5 6
Wt 10 03
Midfield. From Wycombe W and Apprentice. England Schools, Youth.

Season	Club	App	Goals
1983–84	West Ham U	—	—
1984–85		—	—
1985–86		—	—
1986–87		13	—
1987–88		23	1
1988–89		24	3
1989–90		44	10

KELLY, Alan

Born Preston 11.8.68. Ht 6 2 Wt 12 05
Goalkeeper. Eire Youth, Under-21, Under-23.

Season	Club	App	Goals
1985–86	Preston NE	13	—
1986–87		22	—
1987–88		19	—
1988–89		—	—
1989–90		42	—

KELLY, David

Born Birmingham 25.11.65. Ht 5 11
Wt 11 03
Forward. From Alvechurch. Eire B, Under-21, Under-23, 6 full caps.

Season	Club	League Appearances/Goals	
1983–84	Walsall	6	3
1984–85		32	7
1985–86		28	10
1986–87		42	23
1987–88		39	20
1988–89	West Ham U	25	6
1989–90		16	1
1989–90	Leicester C	10	7

KELLY, Gary

Born Fulwood 3.8.66. Ht 5 10 Wt 12 03
Goalkeeper. From Apprentice. Eire B, Under-21.

Season	Club	Apps	Goals
1984–85	Newcastle U	—	—
1985–86		—	—
1986–87		3	—
1987–88		37	—
1988–89		9	—
1988–89	*Blackpool*	5	—
1989–90	Newcastle U	4	—
1989–90	Bury	38	—

KELLY, Gavin

Born Beverley 29.9.68. Ht 6 0 Wt 12 13
Goalkeeper.

Season	Club	Apps	Goals
1987–88	Hull C	—	—
1988–89		3	—
1989–90		8	—
1989–90	*Bristol R*	—	—

KELLY, John

Born Bebbington 20.10.60. Ht 5 10
Wt 10 09
Forward. From Cammell Laird.

Season	Club	Apps	Goals
1979–80	Tranmere R	28	4
1980–81		29	5
1981–82		7	—
1981–82	Preston NE	30	5
1982–83		29	2
1983–84		34	13
1984–85		37	7
1985–86	Chester C	43	8
1986–87		42	9
1987–88	Swindon T	7	1
1987–88	Oldham Ath	10	—
1988–89		42	6
1989–90	Walsall	26	1
1989–90	*Huddersfield T*	10	—

KELLY, Mark

Born Blackpool 7.10.66. Ht 5 9
Wt 10 05
Midfield.

Season	Club	Apps	Goals
1985–86	Shrewsbury T	—	—
1986–87		—	—
1987–88	Cardiff C	36	1
1988–89		28	—
1989–90		41	1

KELLY, Mark

Born Sutton 27.11.69. Ht 5 8 Wt 9 10
Forward. England Youth, Eire, B, Under-21, Under-23, 3 full caps.

Season	Club	Apps	Goals
1986–87	Portsmouth	—	—
1987–88		3	—
1988–89		28	1
1989–90		13	—

KELLY, Norman

Born Belfast 10.10.70 Ht 5 8 Wt 11 00
Midfield. From Trainee. Northern Ireland Youth.

Season	Club	Apps	Goals
1987–88	Oldham	1	—
1988–89		1	—
1989–90		—	—
1989–90	*Wigan Ath*	4	—

KELLY, Paul

Born Bexley 12.10.69 Ht 5 7 Wt 10 13
Midfield. From Trainee. England Youth

Season	Club	Apps	Goals
1988–89	West Ham U	—	—
1989–90		1	—

KELLY, Robert

Born Birmingham 21.12.64. Ht 5 9
Wt 10 13
Midfield. From Apprentice.

Season	Club	Apps	Goals
1982–83	Leicester C	—	—
1983–84		1	—
1984–85		—	—

Season	Club	League Appearances/Goals	
1984–85	*Tranmere R*	5	2
1985–86	Leicester C	9	—
1986–87		14	1
1986–87	Wolverhampton W	14	2
1988–89		2	—
1989–90		—	—

KELLY, Tom

Born Bellshill 28.3.64. Ht 5 10 Wt 11 10
Defender. From Hibs.

Season	Club	Apps	Goals
1985–86	Hartlepool U	15	—
1986–87	Torquay U	38	—
1987–88		38	—
1988–89		44	—
1989–90	York C	35	2
1989–90	Exeter C	12	2

KELLY, Tony

Born Prescot 1.10.64. Ht 5 1 Wt 11 09
Midfield. From Liverpool Apprentice.

Season	Club	Apps	Goals
1983–84	Derby Co	—	—
1983–84	Wigan Ath	29	2
1984–85		40	4
1985–86		32	9
1985–86	Stoke C	1	—
1986–87		35	4
1987–88	WBA	26	1
1988–89		—	—
1988–89	*Chester C*	5	—
1988–89	*Colchester U*	13	2
1988–89	Shrewsbury T	20	5
1989–90		43	5

KELLY, Tony

Born Meridan 14.2.66.
Midfield. From St. Albans C.

Season	Club	Apps	Goals
1989–90	Stoke C	9	—

KENDALL, Mark

Born Blackwood 20.9.58. Ht 6 0
Wt 12 04
Goalkeeper. From Apprentice. Wales Schools, Under-21.

Season	Club	Apps	Goals
1976–77	Tottenham H	—	—
1977–78		—	—
1978–79		23	—
1979–80		2	—
1979–80	*Chesterfield*	9	—
1980–81	Tottenham H	4	—
1980–81	Newport Co	28	—
1981–82		46	—
1982–83		44	—
1983–84		43	—
1984–85		44	—
1985–86		46	—
1986–87		21	—
1986–87	Wolverhampton W	24	—
1987–88		46	—
1988–89		36	—
1989–90		41	—

KENNA, Jeff

Born Dublin 27.8.70. Ht 5 11 Wt 11 07
Defender. From Trainee.

Season	Club	Apps	Goals
1988–89	Southampton	—	—
1989–90		—	—

KENNEDY, Alan

Born Sunderland 31.8.54. Ht 5 9
Wt 10 07
Defender. From Apprentice. England Under-23, B, 2 full caps.

Season	Club	Apps	Goals
1973–74	Newcastle U	2	—
1974–75		18	—
1975–76		28	3
1976–77		42	1
1977–78		42	2
1978–79		26	3
1979–80	Liverpool	37	3
1980–81		37	1
1981–82		19	2
1982–83		34	3
1983–84		42	3
1984–85		42	2
1985–86		32	1
1986–87		8	—
1985–86	Sunderland	32	2
1986–87		22	—
1987–88	Hartlepool U	5	—

Season	Club	League Appearances/Goals	
1987–88	Wigan Ath	22	—
From Colne Dynamoes			
1989–90	Wrexham	7	—

KENNEDY, Andy

Born Stirling 8.10.64. Ht 6 1 Wt 11 10
Forward. From Sauchie Ath.

Season	Club	League Appearances/Goals	
1983–84	Rangers	13	3
1984–85		2	—
1984–85	Birmingham C	7	4
1985–86		32	6
1986–87		9	1
1986–87	*Sheffield U*	9	1
1987–88	Birmingham C	28	7
1988–89	Blackburn R	25	10
1989–90		34	13

KENNEDY, Mick

Born Salford 9.4.61. Ht 5 10 Wt 11 08
Midfield. From Apprentice. Eire Under-21, 2 caps.

Season	Club	League Appearances/Goals	
1978–79	Halifax T	30	—
1979–80		46	4
1980–81	Huddersfield T	42	2
1981–82		39	7
1982–83	Middlesbrough	38	5
1983–84		30	—
1984–85	Portsmouth	37	—
1985–86		39	2
1986–87		35	2
1987–88		18	—
1987–88	Bradford C	15	1
1988–89		30	1
1988–89	Leicester C	9	—
1989–90	Luton T	32	—

KENT, Kevin

Born Stoke 19.3.65. Ht 5 11 Wt 11 00
Forward. From Apprentice.

Season	Club	League Appearances/Goals	
1982–83	WBA	—	—
1983–84		2	—
1984–85	Newport Co	33	1
1985–86	Mansfield T	34	8
1986–87		46	6
1987–88		45	10
1988–89		39	5
1989–90		38	3

KENWORTHY, Tony

Born Leeds 30.10.58. Ht 5 10 Wt 11 04
Defender. From Apprentice. England Youth.

Season	Club	League Appearances/Goals	
1975–76	Sheffield U	6	—
1976–77		37	1
1977–78		20	1
1978–79		37	3
1979–80		41	3
1980–81		37	7
1981–82		45	15
1982–83		23	3
1983–84		8	1
1984–85		19	—
1985–86		13	—
1985–86	*Mansfield T*	13	—
1986–87	Mansfield T	36	—
1987–88		30	—
1988–89		20	—
1989–90		1	—

KEOWN, Martin

Born Oxford 24.7.66. Ht 6 1 Wt 13 04
Defender. From Apprentice. England Youth, Under-21.

Season	Club	League Appearances/Goals	
1983–84	Arsenal	—	—
1984–85		—	—
1984–85	*Brighton*	16	—
1985–86	Arsenal	22	—
1985–86	*Brighton*	7	1
1986–87	Aston Villa	36	—
1987–88		42	3
1988–89		34	—
1989–90	Everton	20	—

KERNAGHAN, Alan

Born Otley 25.4.67. Ht 6 2 Wt 13 00
Forward. From Apprentice.

Season	Club	League Appearances/Goals	
1984–85	Middlesbrough	8	1
1985–86		6	—
1986–87		13	—
1987–88		35	6

Season	Club	League Appearances/Goals	
1988–89		23	—
1989–90		37	4

KERR, Dylan

Born Valetta 14.1.67 Ht 5 11 Wt 12 05
Defender. From Arcadia Shepherds.

1988–89	Leeds U	3	—
1989–90		5	—

KERR, Michael

Born Greenock 6.4.71. Ht 5 9 Wt 9 10
Midfield. From Shamrock BC

1988–89	Dundee	—	—
1989–90		2	—

KERR, Paul

Born Portsmouth 9.6.64. Ht 5 8
Wt 11 03
Forward. From Apprentice.

1982–83	Aston Villa	—	—
1983–84		2	—
1984–85		10	—
1985–86		6	1
1986–87		6	2
1986–87	Middlesbrough	20	—
1987–88		44	5
1988–89		20	1
1989–90		17	1

KERSLAKE, David

Born London 19.6.66. Ht 5 8 Wt 11 00
Midfield. From Apprentice. England Schools, Youth, Under-21.

1983–84	QPR	—	—
1984–85		1	—
1985–86		14	1
1986–87		3	—
1987–88		18	5
1988–89		21	—
1989–90		1	—
1989–90	Swindon T	28	—

KEVAN, David

Born Wigtown 31.8.68. Ht 5 8 Wt 9 10
Midfield. From Apprentice.

Season	Club	League Appearances/Goals	
1985–86	Notts Co	3	—
1986–87		33	1
1987–88		32	—
1988–89		18	2
1989–90		3	—
1989–90	*Cardiff C*	7	—
1989–90	Stoke C	17	—

KIDD, Walter

Born Edinburgh 10.3.58. Ht 5 11
Wt 12 03
Defender. From Newtongrange Star.

1977–78	Hearts	23	—
1978–79		30	—
1979–80		34	2
1980–81		25	1
1981–82		30	—
1982–83		37	—
1983–84		31	1
1984–85		33	1
1985–86		28	—
1986–87		35	—
1987–88		18	—
1988–89		20	—
1989–90		17	1

KIELY, Dean

Born Manchester 10.10.70 Ht 6 1
Wt 11 08
Goalkeeper. From WBA schoolboy. FA Schools. England Youth.

1987–88	Coventry C	—	—
1988–89		—	—
1989–90		—	—
1989–90	*Ipswich T*	—	—
1989–90	*York C*	—	—

KILCLINE, Brian

Born Nottingham 7.5.62. Ht 6 2
Wt 12 00
Defender. From Apprentice. England Under-21.

1979–80	Notts Co	16	1
1980–81		42	1
1981–82		36	3
1982–83		40	3

Season Club League Appearances/Goals

Season	Club	Apps	Goals
1983–84		24	1
1984–85	Coventry C	26	2
1985–86		32	7
1986–87		29	3
1987–88		28	8
1988–89		33	4
1989–90		11	1

KIMBLE, Alan

Born Poole 6.8.66. Ht 5 9 Wt 11 07
Defender.

Season	Club	Apps	Goals
1984–85	Charlton Ath	6	—
1985–86		—	—
1985–86	*Exeter C*	1	—
1986–87	Cambridge U	35	—
1987–88		41	2
1988–89		45	6
1989–90		44	8

KIMBLE, Garry

Born Poole 6.8.66. Ht 5 8 Wt 11 00
Forward.

Season	Club	Apps	Goals
1984–85	Charlton Ath	9	1
1985–86		—	—
1985–86	*Exeter C*	1	—
1986–87	Cambridge U	29	2
1987–88		12	—
1987–88	Doncaster R	34	1
1988–89		31	—
1989–90	Fulham	3	—
1989–90	Maidstone U	—	—
1989–90	Gillingham	14	—

KING, Adam

Born Hillingdon 4.10.69 Ht 5 11
Wt 12 12
Forward. From Trainee. English Youth.

Season	Club	Apps	Goals
1988–89	West Ham U	—	—
1989–90		—	—
1989–90	Plymouth Arg	8	—

KING, Andy

Born Newbury 30.3.70 Ht 6 0 Wt 11 07
Forward.

Season	Club	Apps	Goals
1988–89	Reading	1	—
1989–90		—	—

KING, Phil

Born Bristol 28.12.67. Ht 5 8 Wt 11 09
Defender. From Apprentice.

Season	Club	Apps	Goals
1984–85	Exeter C	16	—
1985–86		11	—
1986–87	Torquay U	24	3
1986–87	Swindon T	21	—
1987–88		44	1
1988–89		37	2
1989–90		14	1
1989–90	Sheffield W	25	—

KINGSMORE, Kevin

Born Belfast 14.10.70 Ht 5 7 Wt 11 02
Forward. From Trainee.

Season	Club	Apps	Goals
1988–89	QPR	—	—
1989–90		—	—

KINNAIRD, Paul

Born Glasgow 11.11.66. Ht 5 8 Wt 10 10
Forward. From Apprentice.

Season	Club	Apps	Goals
1984–85	Norwich C	—	—
1985–86	Dundee U	—	—
1986–87		7	—
1987–88		11	—
1987–88	Motherwell	10	—
1988–89		24	—
1988–89	St Mirren	6	—
1989–90		25	—

KINSELLA, Mark

Born Dublin 12.8.72. Ht 5 9 Wt 11 00
Midfield. From Home Farm.

Season	Club	Apps	Goals
1989–90	Colchester U	6	—

KIRK, Steve

Born Kirkcaldy 3.1.63. Ht 5 11 Wt 11 04
Midfield. From Buckhaven Hibs.

Season	Club	Apps	Goals
1979–80	East Fife	25	2
1980–81	Stoke C	—	—
1981–82		12	—
1982–83	Partick T	—	—

Season	Club	League Appearances/Goals	
1982–83	East Fife	25	8
1983–84		33	5
1984–85		38	8
1985–86		39	14
1986–87	Motherwell	35	10
1987–88		38	4
1988–89		33	14
1989–90		34	8

KIRKWOOD, David

Born St Andrews 27.8.67 Ht 5 10
Wt 11 07
Midfield. From Leven Royal Colts. Scotland Under-21.

Season	Club	League Appearances/Goals	
1983–84	East Fife	14	2
1984–85		17	4
1985–86		34	2
1986–87		35	2
1987–88	Rangers	4	—
1988–89		2	—
1989–90	Hearts	19	—

KITE, Phil

Born Bristol 26.10.62. Ht 6 3 Wt 13 03
Goalkeeper. From Apprentice. England Youth.

Season	Club	League Appearances/Goals	
1980–81	Bristol R	4	—
1981–82		27	—
1982–83		46	—
1983–84		19	—
1983–84	*Tottenham H*	—	—
1984–85	Southampton	1	—
1985–86		3	—
1985–86	*Middlesbrough*	2	—
1986–87	Gillingham	17	—
1987–88		26	—
1988–89		27	—
1989–90	Bournemouth	7	—

KITSON, Paul

Born Co Durham 9.1.71. Ht 5 11
Wt 10 12
Forward. From Trainee.

Season	Club	League Appearances/Goals	
1988–89	Leicester C	—	—
1989–90		13	—

KIWOMYA, Chris

Born Huddersfield 2.12.69. Ht 5 9
Wt 10 07
Forward.

Season	Club	League Appearances/Goals	
1986–87	Ipswich T	—	—
1987–88		—	—
1988–89		26	2
1989–90		29	5

KNIGHT, Alan

Born Balham 3.6.61. Ht 6 0
Wt 13 00
Goalkeeper. From Apprentice. England Youth, Under-21.

Season	Club	League Appearances/Goals	
1977–78	Portsmouth	1	—
1978–79		—	—
1979–80		8	—
1980–81		1	—
1981–82		45	—
1982–83		46	—
1983–84		42	—
1984–85		42	—
1985–86		38	—
1986–87		42	—
1987–88		36	—
1988–89		32	—
1989–90		46	—

KNIGHT, Ian

Born Hartlepool 26.10.66. Ht 6 2
Wt 13 11
Defender. From Apprentice. England Under-21.

Season	Club	League Appearances/Goals	
1984–85	Barnsley	—	—
1985–86	Sheffield W	4	—
1986–87		15	—
1987–88		—	—
1988–89		2	—
1989–90		—	—

Season	Club	Apps	Goals
1989–90	*Scunthorpe U*	2	—
1989–90	Grimsby T	9	1

KNIGHT, Keith

Born Cheltenham 16.2.69
Forward. From Cheltenham T.

Season	Club	Apps	Goals
1988–89	Reading	29	7
1989–90		13	1

KNILL, Alan

Born Slough 8.10.64. Ht 6 4 Wt 11 10
Defender. From Apprentice. Wales Youth, 1 full cap.

Season	Club	Apps	Goals
1982–83	Southampton	—	—
1983–84		—	—
1984–85	Halifax T	44	1
1985–86		33	2
1986–87		41	3
1987–88	Swansea C	46	1
1988–89		43	2
1989–90	Bury	43	1

KNOWLES, Darren

Born Sheffield 8.10.70. Ht 5 6 Wt 10 01
Midfield. From Trainee.

Season	Club	Apps	Goals
1989–90	Sheffield U	—	—
1989–90	Stockport Co	9	—

KOZMA, Istvan

Born Paszto, Hungary 3.12.64. Ht 6 00 Wt 11 13
Midfield. From Ujpest Dozsa, Bordeaux. Hungary full caps.

Season	Club	Apps	Goals
1989–90	Dunfermline Ath	33	6

KRISTENSEN, Bjorn

Born Malling 10.10.63 Ht 6 1 Wt 12 05
Defender. From Aarhus. Denmark full caps.

Season	Club	Apps	Goals
1988–89	Newcastle U	5	—
1989–90		33	3

KRIVOKAPIC, Miodrag

Born Niksic 6.9.59 Ht 6 1 Wt 12 12
Defender. From Red Star Belgrade. Yugoslavia full caps.

Season	Club	Apps	Goals
1988–89	Dundee U	24	1
1989–90		26	—

KRUSZYNSKI, Detsi

Born Divschav 14.10.61 Ht 6 0 Wt 12 12
Midfield. From Homburg.

Season	Club	Apps	Goals
1988–89	Wimbledon	16	—
1989–90		27	2

KUHL, Martin

Born Frimley 10.1.65. Ht 5 11 Wt 11 13
Midfield. From Apprentice.

Season	Club	Apps	Goals
1982–83	Birmingham C	2	—
1983–84		22	1
1984–85		27	2
1985–86		37	1
1986–87		23	1
1986–87	Sheffield U	10	1
1987–88		28	3
1987–88	Watford	4	—
1988–89		—	—
1988–89	Portsmouth	32	1
1989–90		40	9

LAKE, Michael

Born Manchester 6.11.66. Ht 6 1
Wt 13 07
Midfield. From Macclesfield T.

1989–90	Sheffield U	4	—

LAKE, Paul

Born Manchester 28.10.68. Ht 6 0
Wt 12 02
Midfield. From Trainee. England Under-21.

1986–87	Manchester C	3	1
1987–88		33	3
1988–89		38	3
1989–90		31	—

LAMB, Alan

Born Gateshead 30.10.70. Ht 5 10
Wt 11 12
Forward.

1987–88	Nottingham F	—	—
1988–89		—	—
1988–89	*Hereford U*	10	2
1989–90	Nottingham F	—	—
1989–90	*Hartlepool U*	10	—

LAMBERT, Martin

Born Southampton 24.9.65. Ht 5 10
Wt 11 05
Forward. From Apprentice.

1983–84	Brighton	3	—
1984–85		—	—
1985–86	Torquay U	6	2
From Le Havre, Sedan.			
1989–90	Brighton	1	—

LAMBERT, Paul

Born Glasgow 7.8.69. Ht 5 8 Wt 9 08
Midfield. From Linwood Rangers BC.

1985–86	St Mirren	1	—
1986–87		36	2
1987–88		36	2
1988–89		16	2
1989–90		25	3

LAMONT, Lee

Born Leeds 16.5.71. Ht 5 11 Wt 11 10
Goalkeeper. From Trainee.

1989–90	Doncaster R	—	—
1989–90	Rochdale	—	—

LANE, Martin

Born Altrincham 12.4.61. Ht 5 9
Wt 11 04
Defender. From Amateur.

1979–80	Manchester U	—	—
1980–81		—	—
1981–82		—	—
1982–83	Chester	41	2
1983–84		38	—
1984–85		31	—
1985–86		44	1
1986–87		21	—
1986–87	Coventry C	1	—
1987–88		2	—
1988–89		—	—
1988–89	*Wrexham*	6	—
1988–89	Chester C	23	—
1989–90		36	—

LANGE, Tony

Born London 10.12.64. Ht 6 0 Wt 12 09
Goalkeeper. From Apprentice.

1982–83	Charlton Ath	—	—
1983–84		6	—
1984–85		2	—
1985–86		4	—
1985–86	*Aldershot*	7	—
1986–87	Aldershot	45	—
1987–88		35	—
1988–89		45	—
1989–90	Wolverhampton W	5	—

LANGLEY, Kevin

Born St. Helens 24.5.64. Ht 6 1
Wt 10 03
Midfield. From Apprentice.

Season	Club	Apps	Goals
1981–82	Wigan Ath	2	—
1982–83		28	2
1983–84		44	1
1984–85		43	1
1985–86		43	2
1986–87	Everton	16	2
1986–87	*Manchester C*	9	—
1987–88	Manchester C	—	—
1987–88	*Chester C*	9	—
1987–88	Birmingham C	7	—
1988–89		36	2
1989–90		33	—

LANGLEY, Richard

Born London 20.3.65. Ht 5 7 Wt 11 05
Defender. From Corinthian C.

Season	Club	Apps	Goals
1986–87	Fulham	1	—
1987–88		15	—
1988–89		19	—
1989–90		11	—

LAW, Brian

Born Merthyr 1.1.70. Ht 6 2 Wt 11 12
Defender. From Apprentice. Wales Under-21, 1 full cap.

Season	Club	Apps	Goals
1987–88	QPR	1	—
1988–89		6	—
1989–90		10	—

LAW, Nicky

Born London 8.9.61. Ht 6 0 Wt 13 05
Defender. From Apprentice.

Season	Club	Apps	Goals
1979–80	Arsenal	—	—
1980–81		—	—
1981–82	Barnsley	19	—
1982–83		28	—
1983–84		31	1
1984–85		35	—
1985–86		1	—
1985–86	Blackpool	39	1
1986–87		27	—
1986–87	Plymouth Arg	12	2
1987–88		26	3
1988–89	Notts Co	44	4
1989–90		3	—
1989–90	*Scarborough*	12	—

LAWFORD, Craig

Born Dewsbury 25.11.72.
Midfield. From Trainee.

Season	Club	Apps	Goals
1989–90	Bradford C	1	—

LAWRENCE, George

Born London 14.9.62. Ht 5 10 Wt 13 05
Forward. From Apprentice.

Season	Club	Apps	Goals
1980–81	Southampton	—	—
1981–82		4	—
1981–82	*Oxford U*	15	4
1982–83	Southampton	6	1
1982–83	Oxford U	22	9
1983–84		34	9
1984–85		7	3
1984–85	Southampton	11	1
1985–86		21	2
1986–87		36	8
1987–88	Millwall	17	4
1988–89		11	—
1989–90	Bournemouth	33	3

LAWS, Brian

Born Wallsend 14.10.61. Ht 5 9
Wt 11 00
Defender. From Apprentice.

Season	Club	Apps	Goals
1979–80	Burnley	1	—
1980–81		42	2
1981–82		44	6
1982–83		38	4
1983–84	Huddersfield T	31	—
1984–85		25	1
1984–85	Middlesbrough	11	1
1985–86		42	2
1986–87		26	8
1987–88		28	1
1988–89	Nottingham F	22	1
1989–90		38	3

LEABURN, Carl

Born Lewisham 30.3.69. Ht 6 3
Wt 11 03

Forward. From Apprentice. England Youth.

1986–87	Charlton Ath	3	1
1987–88		12	—
1988–89		32	2
1989–90		13	—
1989–90	*Northampton T*	9	—

LEADBITTER, Chris

Born Middlesbrough 17.10.67. Ht 5 9 Wt 10 07
Forward. From Apprentice.

1985–86	Grimsby T	—	—
1986–87	Hereford U	6	—
1987–88		30	1
1988–89	Cambridge U	31	6
1989–90		43	4

LEAKE, Gary

Born Hucknall 30.1.70 Ht 6 2 Wt 11 10
Goalkeeper. From Trainee.

1988–89	WBA	—	—
1988–89	*Chester C*	—	—
1989–90	Huddersfield T	—	—

LEANING, Andy

Born York 18.5.63. Ht 6 1 Wt 14 07
Goalkeeper. From Rowntree Mackintosh.

1984–85	York C	—	—
1985–86		30	—
1986–87		39	—
1987–88	Sheffield U	21	—
1988–89		—	—
1988–89	Bristol C	6	—
1989–90		19	—

LEE, Chris

Born Halifax 18.6.71. Ht 5 10 Wt 11 07
Midfield. From Trainee.

1989–90	Bradford C	—	—

LEE, Dave

Born Manchester 5.11.67. Ht 5 8 Wt 10 02
Midfield. From Blackburn schools.

1984–85	Bury	—	—
1985–86		1	—
1986–87		30	4
1987–88		40	3
1988–89		45	4
1989–90		45	8

LEE, David

Born Kingswood 26.11.69 Ht 6 3 Wt 13 12
Defender. From Trainee. England Youth, Under-21.

1988–89	Chelsea	20	4
1989–90		30	1

LEE, Jason

Born Newham 9.5.71.
Forward. From Trainee.

1989–90	Charlton Ath	1	—

LEE, Raymond

Born Bristol 19.9.70 Ht 5 8 Wt 11 12
Midfield. From Trainee.

1988–89	Arsenal	—	—
1989–90		—	—

LEE, Robert

Born West Ham 1.2.66. Ht 5 10 Wt 11 13
Forward. From Hornchurch. England Under-21.

1983–84	Charlton Ath	11	4
1984–85		39	10
1985–86		35	8
1986–87		33	3
1987–88		23	2
1988–89		31	5
1989–90		37	1

LEE, Sammy

Born Liverpool 7.2.59. Ht 5 7 Wt 10 01
Midfield. From Apprentice. England Youth, Under-21, 14 full caps.

Season	Club	League Appearances/Goals	
1976–77	Liverpool	—	—
1977–78		2	1
1978–79		2	—
1979–80		7	—
1980–81		37	4
1981–82		35	3
1982–83		40	3
1983–84		42	2
1984–85		17	—
1985–86		15	—
1986–87	QPR	30	—
From Osasuna			
1989–90	Southampton	2	—

LEE, Tony

Born Wirral 2.3.70. Ht 5 7 Wt 10 07
Forward. From Trainee.

Season	Club	League Appearances/Goals	
1988–89	Wrexham	—	—
1989–90		—	—

LEGG, Andy

Born Neath 28.7.66 Ht 5 8 Wt 10 07
Midfield. From Briton Ferry

Season	Club	League Appearances/Goals	
1988–89	Swansea C	6	—
1989–90		26	3

LEIGHTON, Jim

Born Johnstone 24.7.58. Ht 6 1
Wt 12 09
Goalkeeper. From Dalry Thistle. Scotland Under-21, 58 full caps.

Season	Club	League Appearances/Goals	
1978–79	Aberdeen	11	—
1979–80		1	—
1980–81		35	—
1981–82		36	—
1982–83		35	—
1983–84		36	—
1984–85		34	—
1985–86		26	—
1986–87		42	—
1987–88		44	—
1988–89	Manchester U	38	—
1989–90		35	—

LEISHMAN, Graham

Born Manchester 6.4.68 Ht 5 9
Wt 10 07
Forward. From Irlam T.

Season	Club	League Appearances/Goals	
1988–89	Mansfield T	12	1
1989–90		4	1

LEMON, Paul

Born Middlesbrough 3.6.66. Ht 5 10
Wt 11 06
Forward. From Apprentice.

Season	Club	League Appearances/Goals	
1984–85	Sunderland	11	—
1984–85	*Carlisle U*	2	—
1985–86	Sunderland	5	—
1986–87		32	5
1987–88		41	9
1988–89		18	1
1989–90		—	—
1989–90	*Walsall*	2	—
1989–90	*Reading*	3	—

LENNON, Neil

Born Lurgan 25.6.71. Ht 5 9
Wt 11 06
Defender. From Trainee. Northern Ireland Under-23.

Season	Club	League Appearances/Goals	
1987–88	Manchester C	1	—
1988–89		—	—
1989–90		—	—

LEONARD, Gary

Born Newcastle 28.11.65. Ht 5 9
Wt 10 12
Defender. From Apprentice.

Season	Club	League Appearances/Goals	
1983–84	WBA	—	—
1984–85		—	—
1985–86	Shrewsbury T	21	1
1986–87		31	—
1987–88		15	—
1987–88	*Hereford U*	11	1
1988–89	Bury	9	1

Season	Club	League Appearances/Goals	
1988–89	Stockport Co	11	1
1989–90		6	—

LEONARD, Mark

Born St Helens 27.9.62. Ht 5 11
Wt 11 10
Forward. From Witton Albion.

Season	Club	Apps	Goals
1981–82	Everton	—	—
1982–83		—	—
1982–83	*Tranmere R*	7	—
1983–84	Crewe Alex	38	10
1984–85		16	5
1984–85	Stockport Co	23	4
1985–86		44	20
1986–87		6	—
1986–87	Bradford C	24	3
1987–88		28	10
1988–89		44	7
1989–90		24	5

LEONARD, Mick

Born Carshalton 9.5.59. Ht 5 11
Wt 11 00
Goalkeeper. From Epsom & Ewell

Season	Club	Apps	Goals
1976–77	Halifax T	19	—
1977–78		20	—
1978–79		25	—
1979–80		5	—
1979–80	Notts Co	9	—
1980–81		4	—
1981–82		—	—
1982–83		6	—
1983–84		18	—
1984–85		31	—
1985–86		23	—
1986–87		41	—
1987–88		45	—
1988–89		27	—
1988–89	Chesterfield	16	—
1989–90		46	—

LE SAUX, Graeme

Born Jersey 17.10.68. Ht 6 0 Wt 12 00
Defender. England Under-21.

Season	Club	Apps	Goals
1987–88	Chelsea	—	—
1988–89		1	—
1989–90		7	1

LE TISSIER, Matthew

Born Guernsey 14.10.68. Ht 6 0
Wt 11 06
Forward. From Vale Recreation, Trainee. England Youth, B.

Season	Club	Apps	Goals
1986–87	Southampton	24	6
1987–88		19	—
1988–89		28	9
1989–90		35	20

LEVEIN, Craig

Born Dunfermline 22.10.64. Ht 6 0
Wt 11 04
Defender. From Lochore Welfare.
Scotland Youth, Under-21, 6 full caps.

Season	Club	Apps	Goals
1981–82	Cowdenbeath	15	—
1982–83		30	—
1983–84		15	—
1983–84	Hearts	22	—
1984–85		36	1
1985–86		33	2
1986–87		12	—
1987–88		21	—
1988–89		9	—
1989–90		35	—

LEVER, Mark

Born Beverley 29.3.70 Ht 6 3 Wt 12 08
Defender. From Trainee.

Season	Club	Apps	Goals
1987–88	Grimsby T	1	—
1988–89		37	2
1989–90		38	2

LEWINGTON, Ray

Born Lambeth 7.9.56. Ht 5 6 Wt 11 08
Midfield. From Apprentice.

Season	Club	Apps	Goals
1973–74	Chelsea	—	—
1974–75		—	—
1975–76		9	—
1976–77		42	2
1977–78		24	2

Season	Club	League Appearances/Goals	
1978–79		10	—
From Vancouver Whitecaps			
1979–80	*Wimbledon*	23	—
1979–80	Fulham	10	1
1980–81		20	—
1981–82		31	4
1982–83		42	10
1983–84		33	—
1984–85		38	5
1985–86	Sheffield U	36	—
1986–87	Fulham	25	—
1987–88		31	1
1988–89		—	—
1989–90		4	—

LEWIS, Allan

Born Pontypridd 31.5.71. Ht 6 2
Wt 13 00
Defender. From Trainee.

Season	Club	League Appearances/Goals	
1989–90	Cardiff C	11	—

LEWIS, Dudley

Born Swansea 17.11.62. Ht 5 11
Wt 10 10
Defender. From Apprentice. Wales Schools, Under-21, 1 full cap.

Season	Club	League Appearances/Goals	
1979–80	Swansea C	—	—
1980–81		12	—
1981–82		1	—
1982–83		23	1
1983–84		37	—
1984–85		43	1
1985–86		24	—
1986–87		32	—
1987–88		18	—
1988–89		40	—
1989–90	Huddersfield T	28	—

LEWIS, Mickey

Born Birmingham 15.2.65. Ht 5 6
Wt 10 10
Midfield. From school. England Youth.

Season	Club	League Appearances/Goals	
1981–82	WBA	4	—
1982–83		5	—
1983–84		14	—
1984–85		1	—
1984–85	Derby Co	22	—
1985–86		5	1
1986–87		—	—
1987–88		16	—
1988–89	Oxford U	36	—
1989–90		45	1

LEWORTHY, David

Born Portsmouth 22.10.62. Ht 5 9
Wt 12 00
Forward. From Apprentice.

Season	Club	League Appearances/Goals	
1980–81	Portsmouth	—	—
1981–82		1	—
From Fareham T			
1984–85	Tottenham H	6	3
1985–86		5	—
1985–86	Oxford U	7	4
1986–87		18	3
1987–88		—	—
1987–88	*Shrewsbury T*	6	3
1988–89	Oxford U	12	1
1989–90	Reading	28	7

LIGHTFOOT, Chris

Born Wimwick 1.4.70. Ht 6 1 Wt 12 00
Midfield. From Trainee.

Season	Club	League Appearances/Goals	
1987–88	Chester C	16	1
1988–89		36	7
1989–90		40	1

LILLIS, Jason

Born Chatham 1.10.69. Ht 5 11
Wt 11 10
Midfield. From Trainee.

Season	Club	League Appearances/Goals	
1987–88	Gillingham	7	—
1988–89		22	3
1989–90	Maidstone U	33	14

LILLIS, Mark

Born Manchester 17.1.60. Ht 6 0
Wt 13 06
Forward. Local.

Season	Club	League Appearances/Goals	
1978–79	Huddersfield T	12	—
1979–80		—	—
1980–81		34	7

Season	Club	League Appearances/Goals	
1981–82	....	42	5
1982–83	....	46	20
1983–84	....	37	11
1984–85	....	35	13
1985–86	Manchester C	39	11
1986–87	Derby Co.................	14	1
1987–88	....	1	—
1987–88	Aston Villa..............	29	4
1988–89	....	2	—
1989–90	....	—	—
1989–90	Scunthorpe U	29	13

LIM, Harvey

Born Halesworth 30.8.67. Ht 6 0
Wt 13 07
Goalkeeper. From Apprentice.

Season	Club	League Appearances/Goals	
1984–85	Norwich C	—	—
1985–86	....	—	—
1985–86	*Plymouth Arg*	—	—
1986–87	Norwich C	—	—
1987–88	....	—	—
From Sweden			
1989–90	Gillingham...............	4	—

LINEKER, Gary

Born Leicester 30.11.60. Ht 5 9
Wt 11 10
Forward. From Apprentice. England 58 full caps.

Season	Club	League Appearances/Goals	
1978–79	Leicester C...............	7	1
1979–80	....	19	3
1980–81	....	9	2
1981–82	....	39	17
1982–83	....	40	26
1983–84	....	39	22
1984–85	....	41	24
1985–86	Everton	41	30
From Barcelona			
1989–90	Tottenham H...........	38	24

LING, Martin

Born West Ham 15.7.66. Ht 5 7 Wt 9 12
Forward. From Apprentice.

Season	Club	League Appearances/Goals	
1983–84	Exeter C..................	29	—
1984–85	....	42	6
1985–86	....	45	8
1986–87	Swindon T	2	—
1986–87	Southend U.............	24	8
1987–88	....	42	7
1988–89	....	44	6
1989–90	....	25	10

LINIGHAN, Andy

Born Hartlepool 18.6.62. Ht 6 3
Wt 13 07
Defender. From Smiths BC. England B.

Season	Club	League Appearances/Goals	
1980–81	Hartlepool U	6	—
1981–82	....	17	—
1982–83	....	45	3
1983–84	....	42	1
1984–85	Leeds U	42	2
1985–86	....	24	1
1985–86	Oldham Ath	15	1
1986–87	....	40	3
1987–88	....	32	2
1987–88	Norwich C	12	2
1988–89	....	37	4
1989–90	....	37	2

LINIGHAN, David

Born Hartlepool 9.1.65. Ht 6 1 Wt 13 03
Defender. Local.

Season	Club	League Appearances/Goals	
1981–82	Hartlepool U	6	—
1982–83	....	6	1
1983–84	....	23	1
1984–85	....	17	2
1984–85	*Leeds* U..................	—	—
1985–86	Hartlepool U	39	1
1986–87	Derby Co.................	—	—
1986–87	Shrewsbury T...........	24	—
1987–88	....	41	1
1988–89	Ipswich T................	41	2
1989–90	....	41	—

LINTON, Des

Born Birmingham 5.9.71.
Defender. From Trainee.

Season	Club	League Appearances/Goals	
1989–90	Leicester C..............	2	—

LISTER, Steve

Born Doncaster 18.11.61. Ht 6 1
Wt 12 07

Midfield. From Apprentice.

Season	Club	Apps	Goals
1978–79	Doncaster R	9	—
1979–80		40	12
1980–81		39	3
1981–82		41	7
1982–83		41	4
1983–84		31	2
1984–85		36	2
1985–86	Scunthorpe U	37	2
1986–87		40	11
1987–88		39	6
1988–89		34	9
1989–90		6	1

LITCHFIELD, Peter

Born Manchester 27.7.56. Ht 6 1
Wt 13 07
Goalkeeper. From Manchester C and Droylsden.

Season	Club	Apps	Goals
1978–79	Preston NE	—	—
1979–80		—	—
1980–81		3	—
1981–82		18	—
1982–83		23	—
1983–84		45	—
1984–85		18	—
1985–86	Bradford C	42	—
1986–87		39	—
1987–88		2	—
1988–89		5	—
1988–89	*Oldham Ath*	3	—
1989–90	Scunthorpe U	17	—

LITTLEJOHN, Adrian

Born Wolverhampton 26.9.70. Ht 5 9
Wt 10 05
Forward. From WBA Trainee.

Season	Club	Apps	Goals
1989–90	Walsall	11	—

LIVETT, Simon

Born Newham 8.1.69. Ht 5 10 Wt 12 02
Forward. From Trainee.

Season	Club	Apps	Goals
1986–87	West Ham U	—	—
1987–88		—	—
1988–89		—	—
1989–90		—	—

LIVINGSTONE, Steve

Born Middlesbrough 8.9.69. Ht 6 1
Wt 12 07
Forward. From Trainee.

Season	Club	Apps	Goals
1986–87	Coventry C	3	—
1987–88		4	—
1988–89		1	—
1989–90		13	3

LLEWELLYN, Andy

Born Bristol 26.2.66. Ht 5 7 Wt 11 00
Defender. From Apprentice. England Youth.

Season	Club	Apps	Goals
1983–84	Bristol C	—	—
1984–85		22	—
1985–86		38	1
1986–87		31	—
1987–88		42	1
1988–89		16	1
1989–90		46	—

LLOYD, Philip

Born Hemsworth 26.12.64. Ht 5 11
Wt 11 11
Defender. From Apprentice.

Season	Club	Apps	Goals
1982–83	Middlesbrough	—	—
1983–84	Barnsley	—	—
1983–84	Darlington	14	—
1984–85		41	2
1985–86		29	—
1986–87		43	1
1987–88	Torquay U	46	2
1988–89		46	4
1989–90		46	1

LOCKE, Adam

Born Croydon 20.8.70 Ht 5 10 Wt 11 10
Midfield. From Trainee.

Season	Club	Apps	Goals
1988–89	Crystal Palace	—	—
1989–90		—	—

LOCKETT, Phil

Born Stockport 6.9.72.
Forward. From Oldham Ath Schoolboy and Rochdale Trainee.

Season	Club	Apps	Goals
1989–90	Rochdale	1	—

LOGAN, David

Born Middlesbrough 5.12.63. Ht 5 9 Wt 10 11
Defender. From Whitby.

Season	Club	Apps	Goals
1984–85	Mansfield T	17	—
1985–86		24	1
1986–87		26	—
1986–87	Northampton T	15	1
1987–88		26	—
1988–89	Halifax T	3	—
1988–89	Stockport Co	35	—
1989–90		25	4

LONGDEN, Paul

Born Wakefield 28.9.62. Ht 5 9 Wt 11 00
Defender. From Apprentice.

Season	Club	Apps	Goals
1981–82	Barnsley	4	—
1982–83		1	—
1983–84	Scunthorpe U	43	—
1984–85		14	—
1985–86		31	—
1986–87		42	—
1987–88		44	—
1988–89		41	—
1989–90		46	—

LONGHURST, David

Born Northampton 15.1.65. Ht 5 8 Wt 10 12
Forward. From Apprentice.

Season	Club	Apps	Goals
1982–83	Nottingham F	—	—
1983–84		—	—
1984–85		—	—
1985–86	Halifax T	44	14
1986–87		41	10
1987–88	Northampton T	35	7
1988–89		2	—
1988–89	Peterborough U	37	7
1989–90		21	—
1989–90	York C	4	2

LONGSTAFF, Jason

Born Leeds 8.2.71. Ht 5 10 Wt 12 03
Defender. From Trainee.

Season	Club	Apps	Goals
1989–90	Leeds U	—	—

LORAM, Mike

Born Brixham 13.8.67. Ht 6 0 Wt 12 00
Forward. From Brixham.

Season	Club	Apps	Goals
1984–85	Torquay U	14	2
1985–86		38	6
1985–86	*QPR*	—	—
1986–87	*Torquay U*	13	4
1987–88	Torquay U	45	8
1988–89		37	4
1989–90		42	12

LORMOR, Tony

Born Ashington 29.10.70 Ht 6 1 Wt 12 03
Forward. From Trainee.

Season	Club	Apps	Goals
1987–88	Newcastle U	5	2
1988–89		3	1
1988–89	*Norwich C*	—	—
1989–90	Newcastle U	—	—
1989–90	Lincoln C	21	8

LOUGHLAN, Anthony

Born Surrey 19.1.70 Ht 6 0 Wt 12 03
Midfield. From Leicester U

Season	Club	Apps	Goals
1989–90	Nottingham F	—	—

LOVE, Ian

Born Cardiff 1.3.58. Ht 5 11 Wt 11 04
Forward. From Barry T, Eastern.

Season	Club	Apps	Goals
1986–87	Swansea C	15	3
1987–88		12	6
1988–89		14	—

Season Club League Appearances/Goals

Season	Club	Apps	Goals
1988–89	Torquay U	9	—
1989–90	Cardiff C	2	—

LOVELL, Steve

Born Swansea 16.7.60. Ht 5 10 Wt 11 10
Forward. From Apprentice. Wales 6 full caps.

Season	Club	Apps	Goals
1977–78	Crystal Palace	—	—
1978–79		—	—
1979–80		—	—
1979–80	*Stockport Co*	12	—
1980–81	Crystal Palace	25	2
1981–82		30	1
1982–83		19	—
1982–83	Millwall	17	1
1983–84		46	7
1984–85		41	22
1985–86		42	14
1986–87		—	—
1986–87	*Swansea C*	2	1
1986–87	Gillingham	6	1
1987–88		46	25
1988–89		39	14
1989–90		41	16

LOWE, David

Born Liverpool 30.8.65. Ht 5 11
Wt 11 02
Forward. From Apprentice. England Youth, Under-21.

Season	Club	Apps	Goals
1982–83	Wigan Ath	28	6
1983–84		40	8
1984–85		29	5
1985–86		46	5
1986–87		45	16
1987–88	Ipswich T	41	17
1988–89		32	6
1989–90		34	13

LOWERY, Tony

Born Wallsend 6.7.61. Ht 5 9 Wt 10 06
Midfield. From Ashington.

Season	Club	Apps	Goals
1980–81	WBA	—	—
1981–82		1	—
1981–82	*Walsall*	6	1
1982–83		—	—
1982–83	Mansfield T	1	—
1983–84		45	6
1984–85		45	3
1985–86		40	5
1986–87		44	5
1987–88		44	—
1988–89		12	—
1989–90		14	—

LOWNDES, Steve

Born Cwmbran 17.6.60. Ht 5 10
Wt 10 06
Forward. From Amateur. Wales Under-21, 10 full caps.

Season	Club	Apps	Goals
1977–78	Newport Co	5	—
1978–79		43	8
1979–80		46	7
1980–81		40	9
1981–82		31	3
1982–83		43	12
1983–84	Millwall	20	3
1984–85		37	7
1985–86		39	6
1986–87	Barnsley	15	1
1987–88		44	9
1988–89		33	6
1989–90		24	4

LUCAS, Richard

Born Sheffield 22.9.70. Ht 5 10
Wt 11 04
Midfield. From Trainee.

Season	Club	Apps	Goals
1989–90	Sheffield U	—	—

LUCKETTI, Chris

Born Littleborough 28.9.71
Defender. From Trainee.

Season	Club	Apps	Goals
1988–89	Rochdale	1	—
1989–90		—	—

LUKE, Noel

Born Birmingham 28.12.64. Ht 5 10
Wt 12 05
Midfield. From school.

Season	Club	Apps	Goals
1981–82	WBA	—	—

Season	Club	Apps	Goals
1982–83		1	—
1983–84		8	1
1984–85	Mansfield T	36	6
1985–86		14	3
1986–87	Peterborough U	30	10
1987–88		43	7
1988–89		45	3
1989–90		43	5

LUKIC, John

Born Chesterfield 11.12.60. Ht 6 4
Wt 13 13
Goalkeeper. From Apprentice. England Youth, Under-21.

Season	Club	Apps	Goals
1978–79	Leeds U	—	—
1979–80		33	—
1980–81		42	—
1981–82		42	—
1982–83		29	—
1983–84	Arsenal	4	—
1984–85		27	—
1985–86		40	—
1986–87		36	—
1987–88		40	—
1988–89		38	—
1989–90		38	—

LUND, Gary

Born Grimsby 13.9.64 Ht 5 11 Wt 11 00
Forward. From school. England Youth. Under-21.

Season	Club	Apps	Goals
1983–84	Grimsby T	7	4
1984–85		24	12
1985–86		29	8
1986–87	Lincoln C	44	13
1987–88	Notts Co	40	20
1988–89		42	8
1989–90		40	9

LUNDON, Sean

Born Liverpool 7.3.69. Ht 5 10 Wt 10 10
Defender. From Apprentice.

Season	Club	Apps	Goals
1986–87	Chester C	12	—
1987–88		22	2
1988–89		6	—
1989–90		11	2

LUSCOMBE, Lee

Born Guernsey 16.7.71. Ht 6 0 Wt 11 10
Forward. From Trainee.

Season	Club	Apps	Goals
1988–89	Southampton	—	—
1989–90		—	—

LYNCH, Tommy

Born Limerick 10.10.64 Ht 6 0 Wt 12 06
Midfield. From Limerick.

Season	Club	Apps	Goals
1988–89	Sunderland	4	—
1989–90		—	—
1989–90	Shrewsbury T	22	—

LYNE, Neil

Born Leicester 4.4.70. Ht 6 1 Wt 12 04
Forward. From Leicester U

Season	Club	Apps	Goals
1989–90	Nottingham F	—	—
1989–90	*Walsall*	7	—

LYNEX, Steve

Born West Bromwich 23.1.58. Ht 5 9
Wt 11 05
Forward. From Apprentice.

Season	Club	Apps	Goals
1975–76	WBA	—	—
1976–77		—	—
From Shamrock R			
1978–79	Birmingham C	2	1
1979–80		30	8
1980–81		14	1
1980–81	Leicester C	12	5
1981–82		41	10
1982–83		38	9
1983–84		40	12
1984–85		42	13
1985–86		30	8
1986–87		10	—
1986–87	*Birmingham C*	10	2
1986–87	WBA	10	1
1987–88		19	2
1988–89	Cardiff C	36	—
1989–90		26	2

McADAM, Tom

Born Glasgow 9.4.54. Ht 6 0 Wt 12 9
Defender. From Glasgow Schools.

Season	Club	Apps	Goals
1971–72	Dumbarton	—	—
1972–73		17	9
1973–74		19	5
1974–75		33	11
1975–76		6	4
1975–76	Dundee U	26	12
1976–77		33	9
1977–78		2	—
1977–78	Celtic	33	8
1978–79		28	7
1979–80		34	8
1980–81		35	4
1981–82		34	5
1982–83		35	3
1983–84		28	1
1984–85		26	—
1985–86		5	—
1986–87	*Stockport Co*	5	1
1986–87	Hamilton A	3	—
1986–87	Motherwell	31	1
1987–88		34	1
1988–89		28	1
1989–90		6	—

McALLISTER, Brian

Born Glasgow 30.11.70 Ht 5 11
Wt 12 05
Defender. From Trainee.

Season	Club	Apps	Goals
1988–89	Wimbledon	—	—
1989–90		3	—

McALLISTER, Gary

Born Motherwell 25.12.64. Ht 6 1
Wt 10 11
Midfield. From Fir Park BC. Scotland B, Under-21, 3 full caps.

Season	Club	Apps	Goals
1981–82	Motherwell	1	—
1982–83		1	—
1983–84		21	—
1984–85		35	6
1985–86		1	—
1985–86	Leicester C	31	7
1986–87		39	10
1987–88		42	9
1988–89		46	11
1989–90		43	10

McALLISTER, Kevin

Born Falkirk 8.11.62. Ht 5 5 Wt 11 0
Forward.

Season	Club	Apps	Goals
1983–84	Falkirk	35	11
1984–85		29	7
1985–86	Chelsea	20	—
1986–87		8	—
1987–88		5	—
1987–88	*Falkirk*	6	3
1988–89	Chelsea	36	6
1989–90		24	1

McATEER, Andy

Born Preston 24.4.61. Ht 5 10 Wt 11 10
Defender. From Apprentice.

Season	Club	Apps	Goals
1978–79	Preston NE	—	—
1979–80		21	—
1980–81		20	—
1981–82		41	—
1982–83		44	5
1983–84		34	—
1984–85		33	2
1985–86		29	—
1986–87		16	1
1986–87	Blackpool	20	—
1987–88		21	—
1988–89	Preston NE	13	1
1989–90		—	—

McAVENNIE, Frank

Born Glasgow 22.11.59. Ht 5 9 Wt 11 0
Forward. From Johnstone Borough and Partick T trialist. Scotland Under-21, 5 full caps.

Season	Club	Apps	Goals
1981–82	St Mirren	31	13
1982–83		36	9
1983–84		34	12
1984–85		34	16
1985–86	West Ham U	41	26
1986–87		36	7
1987–88		8	—
1987–88	Celtic	32	15

Season	Club	League Appearances/Goals	
1988–89		23	12
1988–89	West Ham U	9	—
1989–90		5	—

McBRIDE, Joe

Born Glasgow 17.8.60. Ht 5 8 Wt 11 02
Forward. From Apprentice.
Scotland Schools, Youth. Under-21.

Season	Club	Apps	Goals
1978–79	Everton	—	—
1979–80		18	1
1980–81		31	7
1981–82		8	1
1982–83	Rotherham U	42	11
1983–84		3	1
1983–84	Oldham Ath	25	4
1984–85		11	1
1984–85	Hibernian	12	2
1985–86		14	1
1986–87		38	7
1987–88		13	1
1988–89		4	—
1988–89	Dundee	17	2
1989–90		18	1

McBRIDE, Martin

Born Bellshill 28.11.67. Ht 5 8 Wt 10 0
Forward. From Wishaw Juniors.

Season	Club	Apps	Goals
1984–85	Motherwell	—	—
1985–86		1	—
1986–87		2	—
1987–88		10	—
1988–89		16	1
1989–90		1	—

MacCABE, David

Born Port Glasgow 3.4.62. Ht 5 9
Wt 10 02
Forward. From Pollock Juniors.

Season	Club	Apps	Goals
1983–84	Airdrie	21	3
1984–85		37	21
1985–86		37	9
1986–87		36	13
1987–88		44	20
1988–89		5	—
1988–89	Motherwell	13	—
1989–90		1	—

McCAHILL, Stephen

Born Greenock 3.9.66 Ht 6 2 Wt 11 08
Defender. From Gleniffer Thistle.

Season	Club	Apps	Goals
1984–85	Dumbarton	26	—
1985–86		19	1
1986–87		39	2
1987–88		42	1
1988–89		21	—
1988–89	Celtic	5	—
1989–90		2	—

McCALL, Ian

Born Dumfries 13.9.64 Ht 5 10
Wt 11 07
Forward. From Motherwell Tech.

Season	Club	Apps	Goals
1983–84	Queen's Park	3	1
1984–85		28	—
1985–86		35	8
1986–87	Dunfermline Ath	43	8
1987–88		4	—
1987–88	Rangers	12	1
1988–89		5	1
1989–90		4	—
1989–90	Bradford C	12	1

McCALL, Steve

Born Carlisle 15.10.60. Ht 5 11
Wt 12 06
Midfield. From Apprentice.
England Youth, Under-21, B.

Season	Club	Apps	Goals
1978–79	Ipswich T	—	—
1979–80		10	—
1980–81		31	1
1981–82		42	1
1982–83		42	4
1983–84		42	1
1984–85		31	—
1985–86		33	—
1986–87		26	—
1987–88	Sheffield W	5	—
1988–89		2	—

Season	Club	League Appearances/Goals	
1989–90		3	—
1989–90	*Carlisle U*	6	—

McCALL, Stuart

Born Leeds 10.6.64. Ht 5 6 Wt 10 01
Midfield. From Apprentice. Scotland Under-21, 8 full caps.

Season	Club	Apps	Goals
1982–83	Bradford C	28	4
1983–84		46	5
1984–85		46	8
1985–86		38	4
1986–87		36	7
1987–88		44	9
1988–89	Everton	33	—
1989–90		37	3

McCARRICK, Mark

Born Liverpool 4.2.62. Ht 5 8 Wt 10 08
Defender. From Witton Albion.

Season	Club	Apps	Goals
1983–84	Birmingham C	15	—
1984–85	Lincoln C	30	—
1985–86		14	—
1985–86	Crewe Alex	11	—
From Koparit, Runcorn			
1987–88	Tranmere R	40	5
1988–89		42	3
1989–90		32	4

McCART, Chris

Born Motherwell 17.4.67. Ht 5 9
Wt 10 05
Midfield. From Fir Park BC.

Season	Club	Apps	Goals
1984–85	Motherwell	—	—
1985–86		13	—
1986–87		—	—
1987–88		1	—
1988–89		26	—
1989–90		34	1

McCARTHY, Mick

Born Barnsley 7.2.59. Ht 6 1 Wt 13 3
Defender. From Apprentice. Eire 47 full caps.

Season	Club	Apps	Goals
1977–78	Barnsley	46	1
1978–79		46	2
1979–80		44	1
1980–81		43	1
1981–82		42	1
1982–83		39	1
1983–84		12	—
1983–84	Manchester C	24	1
1984–85		39	—
1985–86		38	—
1986–87		39	1
1987–88	Celtic	22	—
1988–89		26	—
From Lyon.			
1989–90	Millwall	6	—

McCARTHY, Paul

Born Cork 4.8.71. Ht 6 0 Wt 13 06
Defender. From Apprentice

Season	Club	Apps	Goals
1989–90	Brighton	3	—

McCARTHY, Sean

Born Bridgend 12.9.67 Ht 6 0 Wt 12 05
Forward. From Bridgend.

Season	Club	Apps	Goals
1985–86	Swansea C	22	3
1986–87		44	14
1987–88		25	8
1988–89	Plymouth Arg	38	8
1989–90		32	11

McCATHIE, Norrie

Born Edinburgh 23.3.61. Ht 6 0
Wt 12 00
Midfield. From Edina Hibs.

Season	Club	Apps	Goals
1980–81	Cowdenbeath	11	—
1981–82	Dunfermline Ath	19	4
1982–83		24	3
1983–84		38	5
1984–85		37	8
1985–86		37	8
1986–87		44	6
1987–88		39	1
1988–89		20	1

Season	Club	League Appearances/Goals	
1988–89	*Ayr U*	2	—
1989–90	Dunfermline Ath	36	—

McCLAIR, Brian

Born Bellshill 8.12.63. Ht 5 9 Wt 12 00
Forward. From Apprentice. Scotland B, Under-21, 14 full caps.

Season	Club	Apps	Goals
1980–81	Aston Villa	—	—
1981–82	Motherwell	11	4
1982–83		28	11
1983–84	Celtic	35	23
1984–85		32	19
1985–86		34	22
1986–87		44	35
1987–88	Manchester U	40	24
1988–89		38	10
1989–90		37	5

McCLAREN, Steve

Born Fulford 3.5.61. Ht 5 7 Wt 9 04
Midfield. From Apprentice.

Season	Club	Apps	Goals
1978–79	Hull C	—	—
1979–80		1	—
1980–81		20	1
1981–82		37	4
1982–83		40	4
1983–84		40	3
1984–85		40	4
1985–86	Derby Co	23	—
1986–87		—	—
1986–87	*Lincoln C*	8	—
1987–88	Derby Co	2	—
1987–88	Bristol C	16	1
1988–89		45	1
1989–90		—	—
1989–90	Oxford U	22	—

McCLEAN, Christian

Born Colchester 17.10.63. Ht 6 4
Wt 14 00
Forward. From Colchester U, Clacton, Chelmsford C.

Season	Club	Apps	Goals
1987–88	Bristol R	6	—
1988–89		28	2
1989–90		15	4

McCLEAN, Wayne

Born Wordsley 8.1.71. Ht 6 1 Wt 12 03
Defender. From Trainee.

Season	Club	Apps	Goals
1989–90	Shrewsbury T	—	—

McCLELLAND, John

Born Belfast 7.12.55. Ht 6 2 Wt 13 02
Defender. From Portadown. Northern Ireland 53 full caps. Football League.

Season	Club	Apps	Goals
1973–74	Cardiff C	—	—
1974–75		4	1
From Bangor			
1978–79	Mansfield T	36	1
1979–80		43	1
1980–81		46	6
1981–82	Rangers	14	—
1982–83		35	2
1983–84		36	2
1984–85		11	—
1984–85	Watford	29	1
1985–86		31	1
1986–87		41	1
1987–88		40	—
1988–89		43	—
1989–90	Leeds U	3	—
1989–90	*Watford*	1	—

McCOIST, Ally

Born Bellshill 24.9.62. Ht 5 10 Wt 12 00
Forward. From Fir Park BC. Scotland Youth, Under-21, 26 full caps.

Season	Club	Apps	Goals
1978–79	St Johnstone	4	—
1979–80		15	—
1980–81		38	22
1981–82	Sunderland	28	2
1982–83		28	6
1983–84	Rangers	30	9
1984–85		25	12
1985–86		33	24
1986–87		44	33
1987–88		40	31

Season	Club	Apps	Goals
1988–89		19	9
1989–90		34	14

McCORD, Brian

Born Derby 24.8.68. Ht 5 10 Wt 11 06
Midfield. From Apprentice.

Season	Club	Apps	Goals
1987–88	Derby Co	1	—
1988–89		—	—
1989–90		4	—
1989–90	Barnsley	16	1

McCREERY, David

Born Belfast 16.9.57. Ht 5 6 Wt 9 07
Midfield. From Apprentice. Northern Ireland Schools. Youth Under-21, 67 full caps.

Season	Club	Apps	Goals
1974–75	Manchester U	2	—
1975–76		28	4
1976–77		25	2
1977–78		17	1
1978–79		15	—
1979–80	QPR	42	4
1980–81		15	—
From Tulsa R			
1982–83	Newcastle U	26	—
1983–84		40	—
1984–85		35	1
1985–86		41	—
1986–87		30	—
1987–88		35	1
1988–89		36	—
1989–90	Hearts	22	—

McDERMOTT, Brian

Born Slough 8.4.61. Ht 5 8 Wt 11 04
Forward. From Apprentice. England Youth.

Season	Club	Apps	Goals
1978–79	Arsenal	2	—
1979–80		1	—
1980–81		23	5
1981–82		13	1
1982–83		9	4
1982–83	*Fulham*	3	—
1983–84	Arsenal	13	2
1984–85	Oxford U	18	2
1985–86		4	—
1986–87		2	—
1986–87	Huddersfield T	4	1
1987–88	Cardiff C	45	7
1988–89		6	1
1988–89	Exeter C	19	1
1989–90		41	3

McDERMOTT, John

Born Middlesbrough 3.2.69. Ht 5 7
Wt 10 07
Defender.

Season	Club	Apps	Goals
1986–87	Grimsby T	13	—
1987–88		28	—
1988–89		38	1
1989–90		39	—

McDONALD, Alan

Born Belfast 12.10.63. Ht 6 2 Wt 12 07
Defender. From Apprentice.
Northern Ireland Youth, 25 full caps.

Season	Club	Apps	Goals
1981–82	QPR	—	—
1982–83		—	—
1982–83	*Charlton Ath*	9	—
1983–84	QPR	5	—
1984–85		16	1
1985–86		42	—
1986–87		39	4
1987–88		36	3
1988–89		30	—
1989–90		34	—

McDONALD, Gary

Born Sunderland 20.11.69. Ht 5 9
Wt 11 12
Forward. From Ipswich T. Trainee.

Season	Club	Apps	Goals
1989–90	Mansfield T	2	—

MACDONALD, Gary

Born Middlesbrough 26.3.62. Ht 6 0
Wt 12 01
Forward. From Apprentice.

Season	Club	Apps	Goals
1979–80	Middlesbrough	—	—
1980–81		7	—
1981–82		8	1
1982–83		9	1

Season	Club	League Appearances/Goals	
1983–84		29	3
1984–85	Carlisle U	9	—
1984–85	Darlington	33	4
1985–86		36	16
1986–87		10	3
1987–88		42	7
1988–89		41	5
1989–90	Stockport Co	1	—
1989–90	Hartlepool U	16	1

McDONALD, Ian

Born Barrow 10.5.53. Ht 5 7 Wt 10 05
Midfield. From Apprentice.

Season	Club	League Appearances/Goals	
1970–71	Barrow	12	—
1971–72		23	2
1972–73		—	—
1972–73	Workington	16	2
1973–74		26	2
1973–74	Liverpool	—	—
1974–75		—	—
1974–75	*Colchester U*	5	2
1975–76	Mansfield T	34	4
1976–77		22	—
1977–78		—	—
1977–78	York City	30	2
1978–79		43	6
1979–80		46	8
1980–81		46	11
1981–82		10	2
1981–82	Aldershot	31	3
1982–83		46	5
1983–84		46	11
1984–85		41	10
1985–86		46	2
1986–87		44	4
1987–88		43	8
1988–89		43	6
1989–90		—	—

MacDONALD, John

Born Glasgow 15.4.61. Ht 5 9 Wt 10 05
Forward. From Clydebank Strollers.
Scotland Schools, Youth, Under-21.

Season	Club	League Appearances/Goals	
1978–79	Rangers	2	—
1979–80		26	5
1980–81		30	11
1981–82		34	14
1982–83		30	10
1983–84		18	1
1984–85		18	3
1985–86		2	—
1986–87	Charlton Ath	2	—
1986–87	Barnsley	25	7
1987–88		33	7
1988–89		32	5
1989–90		4	1
1989–90	Scarborough	29	5

MACDONALD, Kevin

Born Inverness 22.12.60. Ht 6 1
Wt 12 01
Midfield. From Inverness Caley.

Season	Club	League Appearances/Goals	
1980–81	Leicester C	20	2
1981–82		25	1
1982–83		42	4
1983–84		38	1
1984–85		13	—
1984–85	Liverpool	13	—
1985–86		17	1
1986–87		6	—
1987–88		1	—
1987–88	*Leicester C*	3	—
1988–89	Liverpool	3	—
1988–89	*Rangers*	3	—
1989–90	Coventry C	22	—

McDONALD, Neil

Born Wallsend 2.11.65. Ht 5 11 Wt 11 4
Midfield. From Wallsend BC.
England Schools, Youth, Under-21.

Season	Club	League Appearances/Goals	
1982–83	Newcastle U	24	4
1983–84		12	—
1984–85		36	6
1985–86		28	4
1986–87		40	7
1987–88		40	3
1988–89	Everton	25	1
1989–90		31	1

McDONALD, Rob

Born Hull 22.1.59 Ht 6 2 Wt 13 00
Forward. From Apprentice.

Season	Club	League Appearances/Goals	
1976–77	Hull C	4	—

Season	Club	League Appearances	Goals
1977–78		1	—
1978–79		10	2
1979–80		10	—
From PSV Eindhoven			
1988–89	Newcastle U	10	1
1989–90		—	—

McDONOUGH, Darron

Born Antwerp 7.11.62. Ht 5 11
Wt 12 12
Defender. From Apprentice.

Season	Club	League Appearances	Goals
1979–80	Oldham Ath	—	—
1980–81		15	3
1981–82		36	1
1982–83		38	10
1983–84		38	—
1984–85		32	—
1985–86		20	—
1986–87		4	—
1986–87	Luton T	18	1
1987–88		27	4
1988–89		10	—
1989–90		15	—

McDONOUGH, Roy

Born Solihull 16.10.58. Ht 6 1 Wt 13 07
Forward. From Apprentice.

Season	Club	League Appearances	Goals
1976–77	Birmingham C	2	1
1977–78		—	—
1978–79		—	—
1978–79	Walsall	34	7
1979–80		42	7
1980–81		6	1
1980–81	Chelsea	—	—
1980–81	Colchester U	12	2
1981–82		40	14
1982–83		41	8
1983–84	Southend U	22	4
1983–84	Exeter C	16	—
1984–85		4	1
1984–85	Cambridge U	32	5
1985–86	Southend U	38	7
1986–87		33	4
1987–88		42	9

Season Club League Appearances/Goals

Season	Club	League Appearances	Goals
1988–89		40	5
1989–90		33	5

McDONNELL, Matthew

Born Keady 10.4.71. Ht 5 10 Wt 10 10
Forward. From Trainee.

Season	Club	League Appearances	Goals
1988–89	Oxford U	—	—
1989–90		—	—

McDOWALL, Kenny

Born Glasgow 29.7.63. Ht 5 10 Wt 10 03
Forward. From Drumchapel Amateurs.

Season	Club	League Appearances	Goals
1980–81	Partick T	—	—
1981–82		1	—
1982–83		24	5
1983–84		36	13
1984–85		6	1
1984–85	St Mirren	23	3
1985–86		12	1
1986–87		19	1
1987–88		27	3
1988–89		9	—
1989–90		23	3

McELHINNEY, Gerry

Born Londonderry 19.9.56 Ht 6 1
Wt 13 10
Defender. From Distillery. Northern Ireland 6 full caps.

Season	Club	League Appearances	Goals
1980–81	Bolton W	17	—
1981–82		19	1
1982–83		16	—
1982–83	*Rochdale*	20	1
1983–84	Bolton W	43	1
1984–85		14	—
1984–85	Plymouth Arg	21	—
1985–86		44	2
1986–87		20	—
1987–88		6	—
1988–89	Peterborough U	33	1
1989–90		34	—

McEWAN, Alexander

Born Glasgow 15.5.70. Ht 5 9 Wt 11 3
Defender. From Rangers S form.

Season	Club	League Appearances/Goals	
1989–90	St. Mirren	2	—

McEWAN, Stan

Born Cambusrethan 8.6.57. Ht 6 0 Wt 12 12
Defender. From Apprentice.

Season	Club	Apps	Goals
1974–75	Blackpool	1	—
1975–76		17	—
1976–77		11	—
1977–78		39	1
1978–79		46	5
1979–80		39	12
1980–81		36	1
1981–82		25	5
1982–83	Exeter C	37	6
1983–84		28	9
1983–84	Hull C	16	1
1984–85		37	11
1985–86		42	10
1986–87		17	3
1987–88		1	—
1987–88	Wigan Ath	23	4
1988–89		6	—
1989–90	Hartlepool U	14	2

McGARVEY, Frank

Born Glasgow 17.3.56. Ht 5 10 Wt 11 00
Forward. From Kilsyth Rangers. Scotland Under-21, 7 full caps.

Season	Club	Apps	Goals
1974–75	St Mirren	1	—
1975–76		25	5
1976–77		38	17
1977–78		35	17
1978–79		33	13
1979–80	Liverpool	—	—
1979–80	Celtic	12	2
1980–81		34	23
1981–82		26	10
1982–83		34	17
1983–84		30	10
1984–85		33	15
1985–86	St Mirren	35	6
1986–87		40	10
1987–88		25	2
1988–89		31	2
1989–90		3	—

McGARVEY, Scott

Born Glasgow 22.4.63. Ht 5 11 Wt 12 04
Forward. From Apprentice. Scotland Under-21.

Season	Club	Apps	Goals
1979–80	Manchester U	—	—
1980–81		2	—
1981–82		16	2
1982–83		7	1
1983–84		—	—
1983–84	*Wolverhampton W*	13	2
1984–85	Portsmouth	18	5
1985–86		5	1
1985–86	*Carlisle U*	10	3
1986–87	Carlisle U	25	8
1986–87	Grimsby T	11	1
1987–88		39	6
1988–89		—	—
1988–89	Bristol C	26	9
1989–90	Oldham Ath	4	1
1989–90	*Wigan Ath*	3	—

McGEACHIE, George

Born Skinflats 5.2.59. Ht 5 11 Wt 11 04
Defender. From Bo'ness United.

Season	Club	Apps	Goals
1977–78	Dundee	15	2
1978–79		5	—
1979–80		28	1
1980–81		30	2
1981–82		29	3
1982–83		22	—
1983–84		23	—
1984–85		35	1
1985–86		2	—
1986–87		28	—
1987–88		14	1
1988–89		6	—
1989–90		2	—

McGEE, Owen

Born Teeside 29.4.70 Ht 5 5 Wt 10 08
Defender. From Trainee.

Season	Club	League Appearances/Goals	
1988–89	Middlesbrough	—	—
1989–90		13	—

McGEE, Paul

Born Dublin 17.5.68 Ht 5 6 Wt 9 10
Forward. From Bohemians. Eire Under-21.

Season	Club	League Appearances/Goals	
1988–89	Colchester U	3	—
1988–89	Wimbledon	1	1
1989–90		13	—

McGHEE, Mark

Born Glasgow 25.5.57. Ht 5 10 Wt 12 00
Forward. From Apprentice. Scotland Under-21, 4 full caps.

Season	Club	League Appearances/Goals	
1974–75	Bristol C	—	—
1975–76	Morton	5	1
1976–77		39	20
1977–78		20	16
1977–78	Newcastle U	18	3
1978–79		10	2
1978–79	Aberdeen	11	4
1979–80		21	6
1980–81		36	13
1981–82		31	8
1982–83		32	16
1983–84		33	16
1984–85	SV Hamburg	26	6
1985–86		4	1
1985–86	Celtic	18	4
1986–87		17	1
1987–88		24	6
1988–89		29	16
1989–90	Newcastle U	46	19

McGILL, Daniel

Born Paisley 7.7.71. Ht 5 8 Wt 10 09
Midfield. From Gleniffer Th.

Season	Club	League Appearances/Goals	
1989–90	St Mirren	2	—

McGINLAY, John

Born Inverness 8.4.64 Ht 5 9 Wt 11 06
Forward. From Elgin C.

Season	Club	League Appearances/Goals	
1988–89	Shrewsbury T	16	5
1989–90		44	22

McGINLAY, Pat

Born Glasgow 30.5.67. Ht 5 10 Wt 10 10
Midfield. Scottish Junior.

Season	Club	League Appearances/Goals	
1985–86	Blackpool	—	—
1986–87		12	1
1987–88	Hibernian	—	—
1988–89		2	—
1989–90		28	3

McGINLEY, John

Born Rowlands Gill 11.6.59. Ht 6 2
Wt 13 08
Forward. From Gateshead.

Season	Club	League Appearances/Goals	
1981–82	Sunderland	3	—
From Charleroi and Nairn Co			
1984–85	Lincoln C	40	4
1985–86		29	7
1986–87		23	5
1986–87	Rotherham U	3	—
1986–87	*Hartlepool U*	2	—
1987–88	Lincoln C	*38*	*15*
1988–89		20	2
1989–90	Doncaster R	10	—

McGINNIS, Gary

Born Dundee 21.10.63. Ht 5 11
Wt 10 03
Defender. From Dundee BC. Scotland Schools, Youth, Under-21.

Season	Club	League Appearances/Goals	
1981–82	Dundee U	—	—
1982–83		—	—
1983–84		4	—
1984–85		10	—
1985–86		4	—
1986–87		20	—
1987–88		11	—
1988–89		11	—
1989–90		7	—
1989–90	St Johnstone	11	—

McGOLDRICK, Eddie

Born London 30.4.65. Ht 5 10 Wt 11 07
Midfield. From Nuneaton, Kettering T.

Season	Club	League Appearances/Goals	
1986–87	Northampton T	39	5
1987–88		46	2
1988–89		22	2
1988–89	Crystal Palace	21	—
1989–90		22	—

McGOWNE, Kevin

Born Kilmarnock 16.12.69. Ht 6 0
Wt 11 4
Defender. From Hurlford U.

Season	Club	League Appearances/Goals	
1989–90	St Mirren	2	—

McGRATH, Derek

Born Dublin 21.1.72. Ht 5 5 Wt 10 01
Midfield. From Apprentice.

Season	Club	League Appearances/Goals	
1989–90	Brighton	1	—

McGRATH, Lloyd

Born Birmingham 24.2.65. Ht 5 5
Wt 11 6
Midfield. From Apprentice. England Youth, Under-21.

Season	Club	League Appearances/Goals	
1982–83	Coventry C	—	—
1983–84		1	—
1984–85		23	—
1985–86		32	—
1986–87		30	3
1987–88		17	—
1988–89		8	—
1989–90		13	—

McGRATH, Paul

Born Greenford 4.12.59. Ht 6 0
Wt 13 09
Defender. From St Patrick's Ath. Eire 41 full caps. Football League.

Season	Club	League Appearances/Goals	
1981–82	Manchester U	—	—
1982–83		14	3
1983–84		9	1
1984–85		23	—
1985–86		40	3
1986–87		35	2
1987–88		22	2
1988–89		20	1
1989–90	Aston Villa	35	1

McGRORY, Shaun

Born Coventry 29.2.68. Ht 5 9 Wt 10 12
Defender.

Season	Club	League Appearances/Goals	
1986–87	Coventry C	—	—
1987–88	Burnley	16	1
1988–89		19	1
1989–90		11	—

McGUGAN, Paul

Born Glasgow 17.7.64. Ht 6 3 Wt 13 07
Defender. From Eastercraigs.

Season	Club	League Appearances/Goals	
1980–81	Celtic	—	—
1981–82		—	—
1982–83		—	—
1983–84		1	—
1984–85		3	—
1985–86		21	2
1986–87		22	—
1987–88		2	—
1987–88	Barnsley	29	1
1988–89		20	1
1989–90		—	—

McGUIRE, Doug

Born Bathgate 6.9.67 Ht 5 8 Wt 11 00
Midfield. From Celtic BC.

Season	Club	League Appearances/Goals	
1984–85	Celtic	—	—
1985–86		—	—
1986–87		1	—
1987–88		1	—
1987–88	*Sunderland*	1	—
1988–89	Celtic	—	—
1988–89	Coventry C	—	—
1989–90		4	—

McILHARGEY, Steve

Born Ferryhill 28.8.63. Ht 6 0 Wt 11 07
Goalkeeper. From Blantyre Celtic.

Season	Club	League Appearances/Goals	
1987–88	Walsall	—	—

Season	Club	League Appearances/Goals	
1988–89		—	—
1989–90	Blackpool	22	—

McILROY, Sammy

Born Belfast 2.8.54. Ht 5 10 Wt 11 08
Midfield. From Apprentice.
Northern Ireland 88 full caps.

Season	Club	Apps	Goals
1971–72	Manchester U	16	4
1972–73		10	—
1973–74		29	6
1974–75		42	7
1975–76		41	10
1976–77		40	2
1977–78		39	9
1978–79		40	5
1979–80		41	6
1980–81		32	5
1981–82		12	3
1981–82	Stoke C	18	3
1982–83		41	8
1983–84		40	1
1984–85		34	2
1985–86	Manchester C	12	1
1986–87		1	—
1986–87	Bury	15	2
1987–88		28	4
From Modling			
1988–89	Bury	45	2
1989–90		12	—
1989–90	Preston NE	20	—

McINALLY, Alan

Born Ayr 10.2.63. Ht 6 1 Wt 13 03
Forward. From Ayr U BC. Scotland 8 full caps.

Season	Club	Apps	Goals
1980–81	Ayr U	6	—
1981–82		17	9
1982–83		35	7
1983–84		35	16
1984–85	Celtic	11	1
1985–86		16	1
1986–87		38	15
1987–88	Aston Villa	25	4
1988–89		33	14

To Bayern Munich.

McINALLY, Jim

Born Glasgow 19.2.64. Ht 6 0 Wt 12 00
Midfield. From Celtic BC. Scottish Youth, Under-21. 3 full caps.

Season	Club	Apps	Goals
1982–83	Celtic	1	—
1983–84		—	—
1984–85	Nottingham F	24	—
1985–86		12	—
1985–86	Coventry C	5	—
1986–87	Dundee U	32	1
1987–88		36	2
1988–89		29	1
1989–90		35	3

McINERNEY, Ian

Born Liverpool 26.1.64 Ht 5 10
Wt 11 08
Forward. From Blue Star.

Season	Club	Apps	Goals
1988–89	Huddersfield T	10	1
1989–90	Stockport Co	40	8

McINTOSH, Martin

Born East Kilbride 19.3.71 Ht 6 2
Wt 12 00
Defender. From Tottenham H apprentice.

Season	Club	Apps	Goals
1988–89	St Mirren	2	—
1989–90		2	—

MACKAY, Gary

Born Edinburgh 23.1.64. Ht 5 9
Wt 10 05
Midfield. From Salvesan BC. Scotland Schools, Youth, 4 full caps.

Season	Club	Apps	Goals
1980–81	Hearts	12	—
1981–82		17	2
1982–83		34	6
1983–84		31	4
1984–85		17	2
1985–86		32	4
1986–87		37	7
1987–88		41	5

Season	Club	Apps	Goals
1988–89		29	2
1989–90		33	1

McKAY, Mark

Born Edinburgh 12.11.67.
Forward.

Season	Club	Apps	Goals
1989–90	Doncaster R	1	—

McKAY, Paul

Born Banbury 28.1.71.
Defender.

Season	Club	Apps	Goals
1989–90	Burnley	12	—

McKEARNEY, David

Born Crosby 20.6.68. Ht 5 10 Wt 11 02
Forward.

Season	Club	Apps	Goals
1987–88	Bolton W	—	—
1988–89		—	—
1989–90	Crewe Alex	17	1

McKELLAR, David

Born Ardrossan 22.5.56. Ht 6 0
Wt 12 03
Goalkeeper. From Apprentice.

Season	Club	Apps	Goals
1973–74	Ipswich T	—	—
1974–75		—	—
1975–76	*Colchester U*	—	—
1976–77	Ipswich T	—	—
1975–76	*Peterborough U*	—	—
From Ardrossan			
1977–78	Derby Co	—	—
1978–79		16	—
1979–80		25	—
1980–81		—	—
1980–81	Brentford	39	—
1981–82		45	—
1982–83		—	—
1983–84	Carlisle U	42	—
1984–85		40	—
1985–86	Hibernian	—	—
1985–86	*Manchester C*	—	—
1985–86	*Newcastle U*	10	—
1986–87	Hamilton A	36	—
1987–88		16	—
1987–88	Dunfermline Ath	6	—
1988–89		—	—
1988–89	*Hartlepool U*	5	—
1988–89	Carlisle U	34	—
1989–90		35	—
1989–90	Kilmarnock	5	—

McKENNA, Brian

Born Dublin 30.1.72. Ht 6 0 Wt 13 12
Goalkeeper. From Home Farm.

Season	Club	Apps	Goals
1989–90	Brighton	—	—

MACKENZIE, Steve

Born Romford 23.11.61. Ht 5 11
Wt 12 05
Midfield. From Apprentice. England Youth, Under-21, B.

Season	Club	Apps	Goals
1979–80	Crystal Palace	—	—
1979–80	Manchester C	19	2
1980–81		39	6
1981–82	WBA	37	5
1982–83		1	—
1983–84		19	4
1984–85		38	8
1985–86		31	4
1986–87		22	2
1987–88	Charlton Ath	32	2
1988–89		36	3
1989–90		17	1

McKEOWN, Gary

Born Oxford 19.10.70 Ht 5 10 Wt 11 07
Midfield. From Trainee. FA Schools, England Youth

Season	Club	Apps	Goals
1988–89	Arsenal	—	—
1989–90		—	—

McKERNON, Paul

Born Gloucester 23.2.68. Ht 5 8
Wt 10 02
Midfield. From Apprentice.

Season	Club	Apps	Goals
1984–85	Mansfield T	2	—
1985–86		11	—
1986–87		18	—
1987–88		14	—
1988–89		42	—

Season	Club	League Appearances/Goals	
1989–90		7	—
1989–90	Arsenal	—	—

McKILLOP, Alan

Born Perth 30.11.63. Ht 6 1 Wt 12 00
Defender. From Kinnoull Jun.

Season	Club	Apps	Goals
1984–85	Forfar Ath	1	—
1985–86		19	3
1986–87		27	—
1987–88	St Johnstone	38	5
1988–89		3	—
1989–90		5	—
1989–90	*Arbroath*	13	1

McKIMMIE, Stuart

Born Aberdeen 27.10.62. Ht 5 8
Wt 10 07
Defender. From Banks o'Dee. Scotland Under-21, 6 full caps.

Season	Club	Apps	Goals
1980–81	Dundee	17	—
1981–82		16	—
1982–83		31	—
1983–84		16	—
1983–84	Aberdeen	18	1
1984–85		34	3
1985–86		34	3
1986–87		37	—
1987–88		42	—
1988–89		35	—
1989–90		33	—

McKINLAY, Billy

Born Glasgow 22.4.69. Ht 5 9 Wt 9 13
Midfield. From Hamilton T. Scotland B, Under-21.

Season	Club	Apps	Goals
1986–87	Dundee U	3	—
1988–89		30	1
1989–90		13	—

McKINLAY, Tosh

Born Glasgow 3.12.64. Ht 5 7 Wt 10 03
Defender. From Celtic BC. Scotland Youth, Under-21.

Season	Club	Apps	Goals
1981–82	Dundee	—	—
1982–83		1	—
1983–84		36	3
1984–85		34	3
1985–86		22	—
1986–87		32	2
1987–88		19	—
1988–89		18	—
1988–89	Hearts	17	1
1989–90		29	1

McKINNON, Ray

Born Dundee 5.8.70 Ht 5 8 Wt 9 11
Defender. From S form.

Season	Club	Apps	Goals
1987–88	Dundee U	—	—
1988–89		1	—
1989–90		10	—

McKINNON, Rob

Born Glasgow 31.7.66. Ht 5 11 Wt 11 01
Defender. From Rutherglen Glencairn.

Season	Club	Apps	Goals
1984–85	Newcastle U	—	—
1985–86		1	—
1986–87	Hartlepool U	45	—
1987–88		42	2
1988–89		46	2
1989–90		46	1

McKINSTRY, Gary

Born Banbridge 7.1.72. Ht 5 9 Wt 10 08
Forward. From Portadown.

Season	Club	Apps	Goals
1989–90	Port Vale	—	—

McKNIGHT, Allen

Born Antrim 27.1.64 Ht 6 1 Wt 13 07
Goalkeeper. From Distillery. Northern Ireland Under-23, 10 full caps.

Season	Club	Apps	Goals
1986–87	Celtic	—	—
1986–87	*Albion R*	36	—
1987–88	Celtic	12	—
1988-89	West Ham U	23	—
1989–90		—	—

McLAREN, Alan

Born Edinburgh 4.1.71. Ht 5 11
Wt 11 06

Season	Club	League Appearances/Goals	

Defender. From Cavalry Bank. Scotland Under-21.

1987–88	Hearts	1	—
1988–89		12	1
1989–90		27	1

MacLAREN, Ross

Born Edinburgh 14.4.62. Ht 5 10
Wt 12 12
Midfield. From Glasgow Rangers.

1980–81	Shrewsbury T	4	—
1981–82		35	—
1982–83		40	5
1983–84		40	7
1984–85		42	6
1985–86	Derby Co	46	4
1986–87		42	—
1987–88		34	—
1988–89	Swindon T	37	4
1989–90		46	3

McLAUGHLIN, Joe

Born Greenock 2.6.60. Ht 6 1 Wt 12 00
Defender. From school. Scotland Under-21.

1977–78	Morton	—	—
1978–79		—	—
1979–80		30	2
1980–81		34	1
1981–82		36	—
1982–83		34	—
1983–84	Chelsea	41	—
1984–85		36	1
1985–86		40	1
1986–87		36	2
1987–88		36	1
1988–89		31	—
1989–90	Charlton Ath	31	—

McLEAN, Paul

Born Johnstone 25.7.64. Ht 5 10
Wt 12 00
Midfield. From Glenburn Am.

1983–84	Queen's Park	5	—
1984–85		1	—
1985–86		13	2
1986–87		19	—
1987–88		39	3
1988–89		39	2
1989–90	Motherwell	2	—

McLEARY, Alan

Born London 6.10.64. Ht 5 11
Wt 11 02
Defender. From Apprentice. England Youth, B, Under-21.

1981–82	Millwall	—	—
1982–83		3	1
1983–84		30	—
1984–85		21	—
1985–86		35	3
1986–87		42	—
1987–88		31	—
1988–89		38	1
1989–90		31	—

McLEISH, Alex

Born Glasgow 21.1.59. Ht 6 1 Wt 12 04
Defender. From Glasgow United.
Scotland Under-21, 72 full caps.

1977–78	Aberdeen	1	—
1978–79		19	1
1979–80		35	2
1980–81		32	3
1981–82		32	5
1982–83		34	2
1983–84		32	2
1984–85		30	1
1985–86		34	3
1986–87		40	3
1987–88		36	1
1988–89		34	—
1989–90		32	2

McLEOD, Andy

Born Glasgow 14.3.69 Ht 5 11 Wt 10 01
Forward. From Sunnybank 'A'.

Season	Club	League Appearances/Goals	
1988–89	Aberdeen	1	—
1989–90		—	—

McLEOD, Gordon

Born Edinburgh 2.10.67. Ht 5 8
Wt 10 04
Midfield. From Hutchison Vale BC.
Scotland Schools, Youth, Under-21.

Season	Club	Apps	Goals
1983–84	Dundee U	—	—
1984–85		3	—
1985–86		3	—
1986–87		8	—
1987–88		12	3
1988–89		3	—
1989–90	Dundee	27	—

MacLEOD, Joe

Born Edinburgh 30.12.67. Ht 5 7
Wt 9 11
Midfield. From Hutchison Vale BC.

Season	Club	Apps	Goals
1984–85	Dundee U	—	—
1985–86		—	—
1986–87	*Dumbarton*	5	—
1986–87	Dundee U	2	—
1987–88		10	1
1988–89		3	—
1989–90		2	—

MacLEOD, Murdo

Born Glasgow 24.9.58 Ht 5 8 Wt 12 00
Midfield. From Glasgow Amateurs.
Scotland Under-21, 17 full caps.

Season	Club	Apps	Goals
1974–75	Dumbarton	—	—
1975–76		7	—
1976–77		27	7
1977–78		39	1
1978–79		14	1
1978–79	Celtic	23	3
1979–80		36	7
1980–81		18	8
1981–82		36	10
1982–83		35	11
1983–84		34	7
1984–85		31	3
1985–86		30	3
1986–87		38	4

To Borussia Dortmund

McLOUGHLIN, Alan

Born Manchester 20.4.67. Ht 5 8
Wt 10 00
Midfield. From Local. Eire B, 3 full caps.

Season	Club	Apps	Goals
1984–85	Manchester U	—	—
1985–86		—	—
1986–87	Swindon T	9	—
1986–87	Torquay U	16	1
1987–88		8	3
1987–88	Swindon T	8	—
1988–89		26	3
1989–90		46	12

McLOUGHLIN, Paul

Born Bristol 23.12.63. Ht 5 10 Wt 10 07
Forward. From Bristol C and Gisborne C.

Season	Club	Apps	Goals
1984–85	Cardiff C	17	—
1985–86		32	4
From Gisborne C			
1987–88	Hereford U	29	1
1988–89		45	13
1989–90	Wolverhampton W	19	4

McLOUGHLIN, Stephen

Born Nottingham 21.11.69. Ht 5 10
Wt 10 09
Forward.

Season	Club	Apps	Goals
1987–88	Nottingham F	—	—
1988–89		—	—
1989–90		—	—

McMANAMAN, Steven

Born Liverpool 11.2.72. Ht 5 11
Wt 10 02
Forward. From School.

Season	Club	Apps	Goals
1989–90	Liverpool	—	—

McMAHON, Steve

Born Liverpool 20.8.61. Ht 5 9 Wt 11 08
Midfield. From Apprentice.
England Under-21, B, 16 full caps.

Season	Club	League Appearances/Goals	
1979–80	Everton	—	—
1980–81		34	5
1981–82		32	2
1982–83		34	4
1983–84	Aston Villa	37	5
1984–85		35	2
1985–86		3	—
1985–86	Liverpool	23	6
1986–87		37	5
1987–88		40	9
1988–89		29	3
1989–90		38	5

McMARTIN, Grant

Born Linlithgow 31.12.70. Ht 5 10
Wt 10 00
Forward. From Dunipace Jun.

1989–90	Dundee	4	—

McMILLAN, Andy

Born Bloemfontein 22.6.68. Ht 5 10
Wt 10 13
Defender.

1987–88	York C	22	—
1988–89		2	—
1989–90		25	—

McMINN, Ted

Born Castle Douglas 28.9.62. Ht 5 11
Wt 11 02
Forward. From Glenafton Athletic.

1982–83	Queen of the S	22	1
1983–84		32	3
1984–85		8	1
1984–85	Rangers	20	1
1985–86		28	2
1986–87		15	1
From Seville			
1987–88	Derby Co	7	1
1988–89		32	4
1989–90		15	—

McNAB, Neil

Born Greenock 4.6.57. Ht 5 7 Wt 11 00
Midfield. Scotland Schools. Under-21.

Season	Club	League Appearances/Goals	
1972–73	Morton	3	—
1973–74		11	—
1973–74	Tottenham H	1	—
1974–75		2	—
1975–76		15	—
1976–77		10	—
1977–78		42	3
1978–79		2	—
1978–79	Bolton W	23	3
1979–80		12	1
1979–80	Brighton	16	—
1980–81		33	1
1981–82		40	3
1982–83		14	—
1982–83	*Leeds U*	5	—
1982–83	*Portsmouth*	—	—
1983–84	Manchester C	33	1
1984–85		18	—
1985–86		37	4
1986–87		42	4
1987–88		37	2
1988–89		42	5
1989–90		12	—
1989–90	Tranmere R	22	1

McNAIR, Colin

Born Glasgow 20.3.69. Ht 5 11
Wt 12 00
Midfield. From Bishopbriggs BC.

1987–88	Falkirk	6	—
1988–89		33	4
1989–90		7	—
1989–90	Motherwell	2	—

McNALLY, Bernard

Born Shrewsbury 17.2.63. Ht 5 7
Wt 10 12
Midfield. From Apprentice. Northern Ireland 5 full caps.

1980–81	Shrewsbury T	1	—
1981–82		33	1
1982–83		25	1
1983–84		41	4
1984–85		42	2
1985–86		35	6
1986–87		40	5
1987–88		43	2

Season	Club	Apps	Goals
1988–89	4	22	2
1989–90	WBA	41	5

McNICHOL, Jim

Born Glasgow 9.6.58. Ht 6 0 Wt 12 10
Defender. From Ipswich T Apprentice.
Scotland Under-21.

Season	Club	Apps	Goals
1976–77	Luton T	2	—
1977–78		12	—
1978–79		1	—
1978–79	Brentford	32	4
1979–80		31	8
1980–81		14	—
1981–82		26	3
1982–83		32	3
1983–84		20	4
1984–85	Exeter C	42	5
1985–86		45	5
1986–87	Torquay U	42	3
1987–88		46	6
1988–89		36	4
1989–90	Exeter C	33	8

McPARLAND, Ian

Born Edinburgh 4.10.61. Ht 5 8
Wt 10 08
Forward. From Ormiston Primrose.

Season	Club	Apps	Goals
1980–81	Notts Co	2	—
1981–82		12	—
1982–83		11	1
1983–84		21	2
1984–85		20	—
1985–86		44	15
1986–87		45	24
1987–88		43	21
1988–89		23	6
1988–89	Hull C	11	1
1989–90		20	5

MacPHAIL, John

Born Dundee 7.12.55. Ht 6 0 Wt 12 03
Defender. From St. Columba's.

Season	Club	Apps	Goals
1975–76	Dundee	6	—
1976–77		25	—
1977–78		34	—
1978–79		3	—
1978–79	Sheffield U	15	1
1979–80		44	5
1980–81		39	—
1981–82		26	1
1982–83		11	—
1982–83	York C	12	2
1983–84		46	10
1984–85		42	5
1985–86		42	7
1986–87	Bristol C	26	1
1987–88	Sunderland	46	16
1988–89		45	4
1989–90		38	2

McPHERSON, Angus

Born Glasgow 11.10.68. Ht 5 11
Wt 10 04
Defender. From S Form.

Season	Club	Apps	Goals
1986–87	Rangers	—	—
1987–88		—	—
1988–89		—	—
1989–90		—	—
1989–90	*Exeter C*	11	1

McPHERSON, David

Born Paisley 28.1.64. Ht 6 3 Wt 11 11
Defender. From Gartcosh United.
Scotland Youth, B, Under-21, 7 full caps.

Season	Club	Apps	Goals
1980–81	Rangers	—	—
1981–82		—	—
1982–83		18	1
1983–84		36	2
1984–85		31	—
1985–86		34	5
1986–87		42	7
1987–88		44	4
1988–89	Hearts	32	4
1989–90		35	4

McPHERSON, Keith

Born Greenwich 11.9.63. Ht 5 11
Wt 10 11
Defender. From Apprentice.

Season	Club	Apps	Goals
1981–82	West Ham U	—	—
1982–83		—	—

Season	Club	League Appearances/Goals	
1983–84		—	—
1984–85		1	—
1985–86		—	—
1985–86	*Cambridge U*	11	1
1985–86	Northampton T	20	—
1986–87		46	5
1987–88		32	—
1988–89		41	2
1989–90		43	1

McPHILLIPS, Terry

Born Manchester 1.10.68. Ht 5 10
Wt 11 00
Forward. From Liverpool Trainee.

Season	Club	League Appearances/Goals	
1987–88	Halifax T	25	3
1988–89		41	22
1989–90		22	3
1989–90	*Northampton T*	1	—

McQUEEN, Tommy

Born Bellshill 1.4.63. Ht 5 11 Wt 11 00
Defender. From Gartcosh United.

Season	Club	League Appearances/Goals	
1981–82	Clyde	39	—
1982–83		35	—
1983–84		38	1
1984–85	Aberdeen	35	3
1985–86		17	1
1986–87		1	—
1986–87	West Ham U	9	—
1987–88		12	—
1988–89		2	—
1989–90		7	—

McQUILLAN, John

Born Stranraer 20.7.70. Ht 5 10
Wt 10 07
Defender. From Schools.

Season	Club	League Appearances/Goals	
1986–87	Stranraer	—	—
1987-88	Dundee	—	—
1988–89		—	—
1989–90		2	—

McQUILTER, Ron

Born Glasgow 24.12.70. Ht 6 2
Wt 12 01
Defender.

Season	Club	League Appearances/Goals	
1988–89	Bristol C	—	—
1989–90		—	—

McSKIMMING, Shaun

Born Stranraer 29.5.70. Ht 5 11
Wt 10 08
Defender. From Schools.

Season	Club	League Appearances/Goals	
1986–87	Stranraer	—	—
1987–88	Dundee	—	—
1988–89		—	—
1989–90		7	—

McSTAY, Paul

Born Hamilton 22.10.64. Ht 5 10
Wt 10 07
Midfield. From Celtic BC. Scotland Schools, Youth, Under-21, 48 full caps.

Season	Club	League Appearances/Goals	
1981–82	Celtic	10	1
1982–83		36	6
1983–84		34	3
1984–85		32	4
1985–86		34	8
1986–87		43	3
1987–88		44	5
1988–89		33	5
1989–90		35	3

McSTAY, Willie

Born Hamilton 26.11.61. Ht 5 11
Wt 11 02
Defender. From Celtic BC. Scotland Schools, Youth.

Season	Club	League Appearances/Goals	
1979–80	Celtic	—	—
1980–81		—	—
1981–82		—	—
1982–83		1	—
1983–84		19	1
1984–85		14	1
1985–86		18	—
1986–87		16	—
1986–87	Huddersfield T	1	—
1987–88		8	—
1987–88	Notts Co	9	—
1988–89		33	1
1989–90		3	—

Season	Club	Apps	Goals
1989–90	*Hartlepool U*	3	—
1989–90	*Partick T*	5	—

McVICAR, Don

Born Perth 6.11.62. Ht 5 9 Wt 11 06
Defender. From Blairgowrie Jun.

Season	Club	Apps	Goals
1981–82	St Johnstone	13	—
1982–83		26	—
1983–84		21	—
1984–85		26	1
1985–86	Tranmere R	7	—
1985–86	Montrose	12	—
1986–87	St Johnstone	23	2
1987–88		38	1
1988–89		28	3
1989–90		35	3

McWALTER, Mark

Born Arbroath 20.6.68. Ht 5 11
Wt 10 09
Forward. From Arbroath Lads Club.

Season	Club	Apps	Goals
1984–85	Arbroath	14	2
1985–86		37	14
1986–87		19	4
1987–88	St Mirren	4	—
1988–89		31	5
1989–90		22	—

McWHIRTER, Norman

Born Johnstone 4.9.69. Ht 5 9 Wt 9 06
Defender. From Linwood Rangers BC.

Season	Club	Apps	Goals
1986–87	St Mirren	5	—
1987–88		24	1
1988–89		4	—
1989–90		21	—

MABBUTT, Gary

Born Bristol 23.8.61. Ht 5 9 Wt 10 10
Defender . From Apprentice. England Youth, Under-21, B, 13 full caps.

Season	Club	Apps	Goals
1978–79	Bristol R	11	—
1979–80		33	—
1980–81		42	5
1981–82		45	5
1982–83	Tottenham H	38	10
1983–84		21	2
1984–85		25	2
1985–86		32	3
1986–87		37	1
1987–88		37	2
1988–89		38	1
1989–90		36	—

MACHIN, Scott

Born Leicester 29.9.70. Ht 6 0 Wt 12 00
Forward. From Trainee.

Season	Club	Apps	Goals
1988–89	Notts Co	—	—
1989–90		—	—

MADDEN, Craig

Born Manchester 25.9.58. Ht 5 7
Wt 11 08
Forward. From Northern Nomads.

Season	Club	Apps	Goals
1977–78	Bury	4	—
1978–79		13	1
1979–80		35	10
1980–81		30	10
1981–82		46	35
1982–83		43	20
1983–84		46	17
1984–85		46	22
1985–86		34	14
1985–86	WBA	9	2
1986–87		3	1
1986–87	Blackpool	19	5
1987–88		34	11
1988–89		27	4
1989–90		11	4

Season	Club	League Appearances/Goals	
1989–90	*Wrexham*	8	—
1989–90	York C	4	—

MADDEN, David

Born London 6.1.63. Ht 6 0 Wt 11 03
Defender. From Apprentice.

1980–81	Southampton	—	—
1981–82		—	—
1982–83		—	—
1982–83	*Bournemouth*	5	—
1983–84	Arsenal	2	—
1984–85	Charlton Ath	20	1
1985–86		—	—
1986–87		—	—
1987–88	Reading	9	1
1988–89	Crystal Palace	19	5
1989–90		8	—
1989–90	*Birmingham C*	5	1

MADDEN, Lawrie

Born London 28.9.55. Ht 6 0 Wt 13 07
Defender. From Arsenal Amateur.

1974–75	Mansfield T	7	—
1975–76		3	—
From Manchester Univ			
1977–78	Charlton Ath	4	—
1978–79		38	3
1979–80		36	1
1980–81		28	1
1981–82		7	2
1981–82	Millwall	10	—
1982–83		37	2
1983–84	Sheffield W	38	1
1984–85		19	—
1985–86		25	—
1986–87		35	1
1987–88		38	—
1988–89		27	—
1989–90		25	—

MADDISON, Neil

Born Darlington 2.10.69. Ht 5 9
Wt 11 08
Midfield. From Trainee.

1987–88	Southampton	—	—
1988–89		5	2
1989–90		2	—

MADDIX, Danny

Born Ashford 11.10.67. Ht 5 10
Wt 11 07
Defender. From Apprentice.

1985–86	Tottenham H	—	—
1986–87		—	—
1986–87	*Southend U*	2	—
1987–88	QPR	9	—
1988–89		33	2
1989–90		32	3

MAGILTON, John

Born Belfast 6.5.69 Ht 5 10 Wt 12 07
Midfield. From Apprentice. Northern Ireland Under-23.

1986–87	Liverpool	—	—
1987–88		—	—
1988–89		—	—
1989–90		—	—

MAGUIRE, Gavin

Born Hammersmith 24.11.67 Ht 5 10
Wt 11 08
Midfield. From Apprentice. Wales 5 full caps.

1985–86	QPR	—	—
1986–87		14	—
1987–88		18	—
1988–89		8	—
1988–89	Portsmouth	18	—
1989–90		29	—

MAGUIRE, Peter

Born Holmfirth 11.9.69. Ht 5 10
Wt 11 00
Forward. From Trainee.

1987–88	Leeds U	2	—
1988–89		—	—

1989–90		—	—
1989–90	Huddersfield T	3	—

MAHER, Gary

Born Corby 11.11.70. Ht 5 9 Wt 10 05
Midfield. From Blairgowrie Jun.

1987–88	St Johnstone	—	—
1988–89		3	—
1989–90		1	—

MAIL, David

Born Bristol 12.9.62. Ht 5 11 Wt 12 00
Defender. From Apprentice.

1980–81	Aston VIlla	—	—
1981–82	Blackburn R	—	—
1982–83		34	—
1983–84		11	1
1984–85		4	—
1985–86		18	1
1986–87		38	—
1987–88		36	—
1988–89		40	—
1989–90		25	2

MAIN, Alan

Born Elgin 5.12.67. Ht 5 11 Wt 12 03
Goalkeeper. From Elgin C. Scotland Under-21.

1986–87	Dundee U	2	—
1987–88		8	—
1988–89		—	—
1988–89	*Cowdenbeath*	3	—
1988–89	*East Stirling*	2	—
1989–90	Dundee U	27	—

MAIORANA, Giuliano

Born Cambridge 18.4.69 Ht 5 9
Wt 11 08
Forward. From Histon.

1988–89	Manchester U	6	—
1989–90		1	—

MAIR, Gordon

Born Bothwell 18.12.58 Ht 5 11
Wt 10 03
Midfield. From Apprentice. Scotland schools.

1976–77	Notts Co	5	—
1977–78		—	—
1978–79		4	1
1979–80		42	5
1980–81		4	—
1981–82		34	9
1982–83		25	4
1983–84		17	—
1984–85	Lincoln C	31	—
1985–86		26	3
1986–87	Motherwell	29	1
1987–88		21	1
1988–89		12	—
1989–90		9	—

MALKIN, Chris

Born Bebington 4.6.67. Ht 6 0 Wt 10 12
Forward. From Stork, Overpool.

1987–88	Tranmere R	5	—
1988–89		20	4
1989–90		40	18

MALONEY, Paul

Born St Helens 10.11.69. Ht 5 6 Wt 9 10
Midfield. From Trainee.

1988–89	Preston NE	—	—
1989–90		—	—

MALPAS, Maurice

Born Dunfermline 3.8.62. Ht 5 8
Wt 10 11
Defender. 'S' Form. Scotland Schools, Youth, Under-21, 37 full caps.

1979–80	Dundee U	—	—
1980–81		—	—
1981–82		19	—
1982–83		34	1
1983–84		34	2
1984–85		35	2
1985–86		36	2
1986–87		36	—
1987–88		44	—

Season	Club	League Appearances/Goals	
1988–89		36	1
1989–90		30	2

MANLEY, Roddy

Born Glasgow 23.7.65. Ht 5 11 Wt 11 4
Defender. From Knightswood Jun.

1984–85	Falkirk	11	—
1985–86		31	—
1986–87		39	—
1987–88		43	1
1988–89		35	1
1989–90	St Mirren	30	—

MANUEL, Billy

Born Hackney 28.6.69. Ht 5 5 Wt 10 00
Defender. From Apprentice.

1987–88	Tottenham H	—	—
1988–89		—	—
1988–89	Gillingham	17	1
1989–90		32	4

MARMON, Neale

Born Bournemouth 21.4.61.
Defender.

1978–79	Torquay U	4	—
From Hannover 96.			
1989–90	Colchester U	22	4

MARDON, Paul

Born Bristol 14.9.69. Ht 6 0 Wt 11 10
Defender. From Trainee.

1987–88	Bristol C	8	—
1988–89		20	—
1989–90		7	—

MARKER, Nick

Born Exeter 3.5.65. Ht 6 1 Wt 13 00
Defender. From Apprentice.

1981–82	Exeter C	14	1
1982–83		18	1
1983–84		31	—
1984–85		45	—
1985–86		40	—
1986–87		43	1

Season	Club	League Appearances/Goals	
1987–88		11	—
1987–88	Plymouth Arg	26	1
1988–89		43	6
1989–90		43	1

MARPLES, Chris

Born Chesterfield 3.8.64. Ht 5 11
Wt 11 12
Goalkeeper. From Sutton T and Goole

1984–85	Chesterfield	38	—
1985–86		32	—
1986–87		14	—
1986–87	Stockport Co	13	—
1987–88		44	—
1988–89	York C	45	—
1989–90		46	—

MARRIOTT, Andrew

Born Nottingham 11.10.70 Ht 6 0
Wt 12 07
Goalkeeper. From Trainee. FA Schools, England Youth.

1988–89	Arsenal	—	—
1989–90	Nottingham F	—	—
1989–90	*WBA*	3	—
1989–90	*Blackburn R*	2	—
1989–90	*Colchester U*	10	—

MARSDEN, Chris

Born Sheffield 3.1.69. Ht 5 11 Wt 10 12
Midfield. From Trainee.

1986–87	Sheffield U	—	—
1987–88		16	1
1988–89	Huddersfield T	14	1
1989–90		32	2

MARSH, Chris

Born Dudley 14.1.70. Ht 5 11 Wt 12 10
Midfield. From Trainee.

1987–88	Walsall	3	—

Season	Club	League Appearances/Goals	
1988–89		13	—
1989–90		9	—

MARSH, Ian

Born Swansea 27.10.69 Ht 5 8 Wt 11 00
Defender. From Trainee.

Season	Club	Apps	Goals
1987–88	Swansea C	1	—
1988–89		—	—
1989–90	Bradford C	—	—

MARSH, Mike

Born Liverpool 21.7.69 Ht 5 8 Wt 11 00
Forward. From Kirkby T.

Season	Club	Apps	Goals
1987–88	Liverpool	—	—
1988–89		1	—
1989–90		2	—

MARSHALL, Gary

Born Bristol 20.4.64. Ht 5 11 Wt 10 10
Forward. From Shepton Mallet.

Season	Club	Apps	Goals
1983–84	Bristol C	1	—
1984–85		5	2
1984–85	*Torquay U*	7	1
1985–86	Bristol C	19	2
1986–87		24	2
1987–88		19	1
1988–89	Carlisle U	21	2
1989–90	Scunthorpe U	34	3

MARSHALL, Gary

Born Glasgow 1.11.69. Ht 5 5 Wt 9 05
Midfield. From Trainee.

Season	Club	Apps	Goals
1987–88	Barnsley	—	—
1988–89		1	—
1989–90		2	—

MARSHALL, Ian

Born Oxford 20.3.66. Ht 6 1 Wt 12 12
Defender. From Apprentice.

Season	Club	Apps	Goals
1983–84	Everton	—	—
1984–85		—	—
1985–86		9	—
1986–87		2	1
1987–88		4	—
1987–88	Oldham Ath	10	—
1988–89		41	4
1989–90		25	3

MARSHALL, John

Born Surrey 18.8.64 Ht 5 10 Wt 12 01
Defender. From Apprentice.

Season	Club	Apps	Goals
1982–83	Fulham	—	—
1983–84		25	—
1984–85		32	1
1985–86		42	3
1986–87		29	4
1987–88		25	2
1988–89		41	7
1989–90		36	4

MARTIN, Alvin

Born Bootle 29.7.58. Ht 6 1 Wt 13 07
Defender. From Apprentice. England Youth, B, 17 full caps.

Season	Club	Apps	Goals
1976–77	West Ham U	—	—
1977–78		7	1
1978–79		22	1
1979–80		40	2
1980–81		41	1
1981–82		28	4
1982–83		38	3
1983–84		29	3
1984–85		40	1
1985–86		40	4
1986–87		16	2
1987–88		15	—
1988–89		27	1
1989–90		31	—

MARTIN, Brian

Born Bellshill 24.2.63. Ht 6 0 Wt 13 00
Defender. From Shotts Bon Accord.

Season	Club	Apps	Goals
1985–86	Falkirk	25	1
1986–87		34	1
1986–87	Hamilton A	7	—
1987–88		23	—
1987–88	St Mirren	12	1

Season	Club	League Appearances	Goals
1988–89		34	2
1989–90		35	2

MARTIN, David

Born East Ham 25.4.63. Ht 6 0
Wt 12 01
Defender. From Apprentice. England Youth.

Season	Club	League Appearances	Goals
1979–80	Millwall	3	—
1980–81		33	1
1981–82		38	1
1982–83		33	1
1983–84		31	3
1984–85		2	—
1984–85	Wimbledon	20	2
1985–86		15	1
1986–87	Southend U	32	2
1987–88		41	—
1988–89		37	1
1989–90		39	3

MARTIN, Dean

Born Halifax 9.9.67. Ht 5 10 Wt 10 02
Midfield. From Local.

Season	Club	League Appearances	Goals
1984–85	Halifax T	—	—
1985–86		—	—
1986–87		16	1
1987–88		40	3
1988–89		32	2
1989–90		37	—

MARTIN, Lee

Born Hyde 5.2.68. Ht 5 11 Wt 11 05
Defender. England Under-21.

Season	Club	League Appearances	Goals
1986–87	Manchester U	—	—
1987–88		1	—
1988–89		24	1
1989–90		32	—

MARTIN, Lee

Born Huddersfield 9.9.68. Ht 5 11
Wt 11 08
Goalkeeper. From Trainee.

Season	Club	League Appearances	Goals
1987–88	Huddersfield T	18	—
1988–89		—	—
1989–90		25	—

MARTINDALE, Dave

Born 9.4.64. Ht 5 11 Wt 11 10
Midfield. From Liverpool Apprentice, Southport, Caernarfon.

Season	Club	League Appearances	Goals
1987–88	Tranmere R	34	4
1988–89		32	1
1989–90		19	2

MARTYN, Nigel

Born St Austell 11.8.66. Ht 6 2 Wt 14 00
Goalkeeper. From St Blazey. England B, Under-21.

Season	Club	League Appearances	Goals
1987–88	Bristol R	39	—
1988–89		46	—
1989–90		16	—
1989–90	Crystal Palace	25	—

MARWOOD, Brian

Born Seaham Harbour 5.2.60. Ht 5 7
Wt 11 06
Midfield. From Apprentice. England 1 full cap.

Season	Club	League Appearances	Goals
1977–78	Hull C	—	—
1978–79		—	—
1979–80		6	—
1980–81		31	4
1981–82		42	12
1982–83		40	19
1983–84		39	16
1984–85	Sheffield W	41	7
1985–86		37	13
1986–87		32	5
1987–88		18	2
1987–88	Arsenal	4	1
1988–89		31	9
1989–90		17	6

MASEFIELD, Paul

Born Birmingham 21.10.70. Ht 5 11
Wt 12 08
Defender. From Trainee.

Season	Club	League Appearances/Goals	
1989–90	Birmingham C	—	—

MASKELL, Craig

Born Aldershot 10.4.68. Ht 5 10
Wt 11 04
Forward. From Apprentice.

1985–86	Southampton	2	1
1986–87		4	—
1986–87	*Swindon T*	—	—
1987–88	Southampton	—	—
1988–89	Huddersfield T	46	28
1989–90		41	15

MASKREY, Steve

Born Edinburgh 16.8.62. Ht 5 6
Wt 10 00
Forward. From Strathbrock Jun.

1984–85	East Stirling	37	12
1985–86		21	12
1985–86	Queen of the S	12	2
1986–87		31	2
1987–88	St Johnstone	33	5
1988–89		31	12
1989–90		29	11

MASON, Paul

Born Liverpool 3.9.63 Ht 5 8 Wt 11 09
Midfield. From Groningen.

1988–89	Aberdeen	28	4
1989–90		34	9

MASTERS, Paul

Born Southamptn 16.1.71. Ht 5 6
Wt 10 07
Midfield. From Trainee.

1988–89	Southampton	—	—
1989–90		—	—

MATHERS, Paul

Born Aberdeen 17.1.70. Ht 5 11
Wt 10 07
Goalkeeper. From Westfield Wasps.

Season	Club	League Appearances/Goals	
1989–90	Dundee	8	—

MATHIE, Alexander

Born Bathgate 22.12.68 Ht 5 10
Wt 10 07
Forward. From Celtic BC.

1987–88	Celtic	—	—
1988–89		1	—
1989–90		6	—

MATTHEW, Damian

Born Islington, London 23.9.70. Ht 5 11
Wt 10 10
Midfield. From Trainee. England Under-21.

1989–90	Chelsea	2	—

MATTHEWS, John

Born London 1.11.55. Ht 6 0 Wt 12 06
Midfield. From Apprentice.

1973–74	Arsenal	—	—
1974–75		20	—
1975–76		1	—
1976–77		17	2
1977–78		7	—
1978–79	Sheffield U	32	5
1979–80		32	5
1980–81		14	1
1981–82		25	3
1982–83	Mansfield T	40	3
1983–84		32	3
1984–85	Chesterfield	38	1
1985–86	Plymouth Arg	31	1
1986–87		39	2
1987–88		35	1
1988–89		30	—
1989–90	Torquay U	25	—

MATTHEWS, Mike

Born Hull 25.9.60. Ht 5 9 Wt 11 03
Midfield. From Apprentice.

1978–79	Wolverhampton W	—	—
1979–80		—	—
1980–81		1	—
1981–82		32	2

Season	Club	Apps	Goals
1982–83	....	40	5
1983–84	....	3	—
1983–84	Scunthorpe U	25	1
1984–85	....	22	3
1985–86	....	11	1
1986–87	Halifax T	39	4
1987–88	....	45	3
1988–89	....	15	1
1988–89	Scarborough	7	1
1988–89	Stockport Co	19	1
1989–90	....	16	2
1989–90	Scarborough	21	3

MATTHEWS, Neil

Born Grimsby 19.9.66. Ht 5 11 Wt 12 00
Forward.

Season	Club	Apps	Goals
1984–85	Grimsby T	4	1
1985–86	....	4	—
1985–86	*Scunthorpe U*	1	—
1986–87	Grimsby T	3	—
1986–87	*Halifax T*	9	2
1986–87	*Bolton W*	1	—
1987–88	Halifax T	32	10
1988–89	....	34	7
1989–90	....	39	12

MATTHEWS, Neil

Born Manchester 3.12.67. Ht 6 0
Wt 11 07
Defender. From Apprentice.

Season	Club	Apps	Goals
1985–86	Blackpool	1	—
1986–87	....	22	—
1987–88	....	27	—
1988–89	....	14	1
1989–90	....	12	—

MATTHEWSON, Trevor

Born Sheffield 12.2.63. Ht 6 1 Wt 12 05
Defender. From Apprentice.

Season	Club	Apps	Goals
1980–81	Sheffield W	1	—
1981–82	....	1	—
1982–83	....	1	—
1983–84	....	—	—
1983–84	Newport Co	32	—
1984–85	....	43	—
1985–86	Stockport Co	35	—
1986–87	....	45	—
1987–88	*Lincoln C*	*40*	*6*
1988–89	....	43	2
1989–90	Birmingham C	46	1

MAUCHLEN, Alister

Born Kilwinning 29.6.60. Ht 5 8
Wt 13 07
Midfield. From Irvine Meadow.

Season	Club	Apps	Goals
1978–79	Kilmarnock	20	—
1979–80	....	30	2
1980–81	....	31	3
1981–82	....	37	4
1982–83	....	2	1
1982–83	Motherwell..............	25	3
1983–84	....	20	—
1984–85	....	30	1
1985–86	....	1	—
1985–86	Leicester C..............	37	2
1986–87	....	30	1
1987–88	....	36	2
1988–89	....	38	3
1989–90	....	38	1

MAUGE, Ron

Born Islington 10.3.69 Ht 5 8 Wt 10 06
Defender. From Trainee.

Season	Club	Apps	Goals
1987–88	Charlton Ath	—	—
1988–89	Fulham....................	13	—
1989–90	....	37	2

MAXWELL, Alistair

Born Hamilton 29.6.60. Ht 5 7 Wt 10 05
Goalkeeper. From Fir Park BC.

Season	Club	Apps	Goals
1981–82	Motherwell..............	—	—
1982–83	....	—	—
1983–84	....	4	—
1984–85	....	15	—
1985–86	....	4	—
1986–87	....	21	—
1987–88	....	1	—
1987–88	*Clydebank*	1	—

Season	Club	Apps	Goals
1988–89	Motherwell	17	—
1989–90		36	—

MAY, Andy

Born Bury 26.2.64. Ht 5 8 Wt 11 01
Midfield. From Apprentice. England Under-21.

Season	Club	Apps	Goals
1980–81	Manchester C	1	—
1981–82		6	—
1982–83		8	—
1983–84		42	5
1984–85		39	3
1985–86		37	—
1986–87		17	—
1987–88	Huddersfield T	28	3
1987–88	*Bolton W*	10	2
1988–89	Huddersfield T	45	2
1989–90		41	—

MAY, David

Born Oldham 24.6.70 Ht 6 0 Wt 11 07
Defender. From Trainee.

Season	Club	Apps	Goals
1988–89	Blackburn R	1	—
1989–90		17	—

MAY, Edward

Born Edinburgh 30.8.67 Ht 5 7 Wt 10 03
Forward. From Hutchison Vale BC. Scotland Youth, Under-21.

Season	Club	Apps	Goals
1983–84	Dundee U	—	—
1984–85		—	—
1984–85	Hibernian	—	—
1985–86		19	1
1986–87		30	5
1987–88		35	2
1988–89		25	2
1989–90	Brentford	30	8

MAY, Larry

Born Sutton Coldfield 26.12.58. Ht 6 1
Wt 13 00
Defender. From Apprentice.

Season	Club	Apps	Goals
1976–77	Leicester C	1	—
1977–78		5	—
1978–79		36	4
1979–80		42	4
1980–81		34	—
1981–82		34	3
1982–83		35	1
1983–84	Barnsley	41	1
1984–85		23	1
1985–86		36	—
1986–87		22	1
1986–87	Sheffield W	13	—
1987–88		18	1
1988–89		—	—
1988–89	Brighton	24	3
1989–90		—	—

MEADE, Raphael

Born Islington 22.11.62. Ht 5 10
Wt 11 09
Forward. From Apprentice.

Season	Club	Apps	Goals
1980–81	Arsenal	—	—
1981–82		16	4
1982–83		4	2
1983–84		13	5
1984–85		8	3
From Sporting Lisbon			
1988–89	Dundee U	11	4
1988–89	Luton T	4	—
1989–90		—	—
1989–90	Ipswich T	1	—

MEASHAM, Ian

Born Barnsley 14.12.64. Ht 5 11
Wt 11 08
Defender. From Apprentice.

Season	Club	Apps	Goals
1982–83	Huddersfield T	—	—
1983–84		—	—
1984–85		17	—
1985–86		—	—
1985–86	*Lincoln C*	6	—
1985–86	*Rochdale*	12	—
1986–87	Cambridge U	46	—
1987–88		—	—
1988–89		—	—

Season	Club	League Appearances/Goals	
1988–89	Burnley	30	1
1989–90		35	—

MEGSON, Gary

Born Manchester 2.5.59. Ht 5 10
Wt 12 00
Midfield. From Apprentice.

Season	Club	Apps	Goals
1977–78	Plymouth Arg	24	2
1978–79		42	8
1979–80		12	—
1979–80	Everton	12	1
1980–81		10	1
1981–82	Sheffield W	40	5
1982–83		41	4
1983–84		42	4
1984–85	Nottingham F	—	—
1984–85	Newcastle U	20	1
1985–86		4	—
1985–86	Sheffield W	20	3
1986–87		35	6
1987–88		37	2
1988–89		18	1
1988–89	Manchester C	22	1
1989–90		19	—

MEGSON, Kevin

Born Halifax 1.7.71 Ht 5 11 Wt 11 00
Forward. From Trainee.

Season	Club	Apps	Goals
1989–90	Bradford C	23	—

MEHEW, David

Born Camberley 29.10.67. Ht 5 11
Wt 12 06
Forward.

Season	Club	Apps	Goals
1984–85	Leeds U	—	—
1985–86	Bristol R	4	—
1986–87		21	10
1987–88		18	8
1988–89		31	7
1989–90		46	18

MELON, Michael

Born Paisley 18.3.72.
Midfield. From Trainee.

Season	Club	Apps	Goals
1989–90	Bristol C	9	—

MELROSE, Jim

Born Glasgow 7.10.58. Ht 5 9 Wt 10 01
Forward. From Eastercraigs. Scottish Under-21, Scottish League.

Season	Club	Apps	Goals
1975–76	Partick T	2	—
1976–77		27	8
1977–78		25	4
1978–79		33	10
1979–80		35	9
1980–81	Leicester C	32	9
1981–82		35	11
1982–83		5	1
1982–83	Coventry C	24	8
1983–84	Celtic	29	7
1984–85		—	—
1984–85	*Wolverhampton W*	7	2
1984–85	Manchester C	24	7
1985–86		10	1
1985–86	Charlton Ath	11	5
1986–87		34	14
1987–88		3	—
1987–88	Leeds U	4	—
1987–88	Shrewsbury T	9	1
1988–89		21	2
1989–90		19	—

MELVILLE, Andy

Born Swansea 29.11.68. Ht 6 0 Wt 12 00
Defender. From school. Wales Under-21, 4 full caps.

Season	Club	Apps	Goals
1985–86	Swansea C	5	—
1986–87		42	3
1987–88		37	4
1988–89		45	10
1989–90		46	5

MENDONCA, Clive

Born Tullington 9.9.68. Ht 5 10
Wt 11 07
Forward. From Apprentice.

Season	Club	Apps	Goals
1986–87	Sheffield U	2	—
1987–88		11	4
1987–88	*Doncaster R*	2	—
1987–88	Rotherham U	8	2

Season	Club	Apps	Goals
1988–89		10	1
1989–90		32	14

MERCER, William

Born Liverpool 22.5.69. Ht 6 1 Wt 11 00
Goalkeeper. From Trainee.

Season	Club	Apps	Goals
1987–88	Liverpool	—	—
1988–89		—	—
1988–89	Rotherham U	—	—
1989–90		2	—

MERSON, Paul

Born London 20.3.68. Ht 5 10 Wt 11 08
Forward. From Apprentice. England Youth, Under-21.

Season	Club	Apps	Goals
1985–86	Arsenal	—	—
1986–87		7	3
1986–87	*Brentford*	7	—
1987–88	Arsenal	15	5
1988–89		37	10
1989–90		29	7

METGOD, Johnny

Born Amsterdam 27.2.58. Ht 6 4
Wt 13 6
Midfield. From DWS, Haarlem, AZ'67 and Real Madrid. Holland full caps.

Season	Club	Apps	Goals
1984–85	Nottingham F	40	6
1985–86		39	6
1986–87		37	3
1987–88	Tottenham H	12	—

To Feyenoord

METHVEN, Colin

Born India 10.12.55. Ht 6 2 Wt 12 06
Defender. From Leven Royals.

Season	Club	Apps	Goals
1974–75	East Fife	1	—
1975–76		26	1
1976–77		39	—
1977–78		39	2
1978–79		39	11
1979–80	Wigan Ath	35	2
1980–81		46	2
1981–82		46	9
1982–83		44	1
1983–84		39	—
1984–85		43	—
1985–86		43	7
1986–87	Blackpool	46	5
1987–88		40	2
1988–89		42	1
1989–90		45	3

MEYER, Adrian

Born Bristol 22.9.70. Ht 6 0 Wt 14 00
Defender. From Trainee.

Season	Club	Apps	Goals
1989–90	Scarborough	18	2

MICKLEWHITE, Gary

Born Southwark 21.3.61. Ht 5 7
Wt 10 04
Forward. From Apprentice.

Season	Club	Apps	Goals
1977–78	Manchester U	—	—
1978–79		—	—
1979–80	QPR	—	—
1980–81		1	—
1981–82		26	2
1982–83		34	6
1983–84		30	2
1984–85		15	1
1984–85	Derby Co	19	4
1985–86		46	11
1986–87		42	6
1987–88		16	1
1988–89		26	3
1989–90		18	2

MIDDLETON, Craig

Born Nuneaton 10.9.70. Ht 5 9
Wt 11 00
Forward. From Trainee.

Season	Club	Apps	Goals
1989–90	Coventry C	1	—

MIDDLETON, Lee

Born Nuneaton 10.9.70. Ht 5 9
Wt 11 09
Defender. From Trainee.

Season	Club	League Appearances/Goals	
1989–90	Coventry C	2	—

MIKLOSKO, Ludek

Born Ostrava 9.12.61.
Goalkeeper. From Banik Ostrava. Czechoslovakia full caps.

Season	Club	Apps	Goals
1989–90	West Ham U	18	—

MILLAR, Paul

Born Belfast 16.11.66. Ht 6 2 Wt 12 07
Forward. From Portadown. Nothern Ireland Under-23.

Season	Club	Apps	Goals
1988–89	Port Vale	—	—
1989–90		23	4

MILLAR, John

Born Lanark 8.12.66. Ht 5 10 Wt 10 00
Defender.

Season	Club	Apps	Goals
1984–85	Chelsea	—	—
1985–86		7	—
1986–87		4	—
1986–87	*Hamilton A*	10	—
1986–87	*Northampton T*	1	—
1987–88	Blackburn R	15	—
1988–89		38	—
1989–90		39	1

MILLEN, Keith

Born Croydon 26.9.66. Ht 6 2 Wt 12 04
Defender. From Juniors.

Season	Club	Apps	Goals
1984–85	Brentford	17	—
1985–86		32	2
1986–87		39	2
1987–88		40	3
1988–89		36	3
1989–90		32	—

MILLER, Alan

Born Preston 13.9.70.
Forward. From Bury Trainee.

Season	Club	Apps	Goals
1989–90	Torquay U	4	—

MILLER, Allan

Born Epping 29.3.70. Ht 6 2 Wt 13 08
Goalkeeper. From Trainee. FA Schools, England Under-21.

Season	Club	Apps	Goals
1987–88	Arsenal	—	—
1988–89		—	—
1988–89	*Plymouth Arg*	13	—
1989–90	Arsenal	—	—

MILLER, David

Born Burnley 8.1.64. Ht 5 11 Wt 11 12
Midfield. From Apprentice.

Season	Club	Apps	Goals
1981–82	Burnley	—	—
1982–83		1	—
1982–83	*Crewe Alex*	3	—
1983–84	Burnley	17	2
1984–85		14	1
1985–86	Tranmere R	29	1
1986–87	Preston NE	15	—
1987–88		28	2
1988–89		12	—
1988–89	*Burnley*	4	—
1989–90	Preston NE	3	—
1989–90	Carlisle U	42	3

MILLER, Ian

Born Perth 13.5.55. Ht 5 9 Wt 11 12
Forward.

Season	Club	Apps	Goals
1973–74	Bury	15	—
1974–75		—	—
1974–75	Nottingham F	—	—
1975–76	Doncaster R	43	9
1976–77		46	5
1977–78		35	—
1978–79	Swindon T	44	3
1979–80		40	2
1980–81		43	4
1981–82	Blackburn R	42	3
1982–83		32	4
1983–84		36	3
1984–85		38	4
1985–86		38	1
1986–87		28	—
1987–88		23	—

Season	Club	League Appearances/Goals	
1988–89		31	1
1989–90	Port Vale	21	1

MILLER, Joe

Born Glasgow 8.12.67. Ht 5 8 Wt 9 12
Forward. 'S' Form. Scotland Schools, Youth, Under-21.

Season	Club	Apps	Goals
1984–85	Aberdeen	1	—
1985–86		18	3
1986–87		27	6
1987–88		14	4
1987–88	Celtic	27	3
1988–89		22	8
1989–90		24	5

MILLER, Kevin

Born Falmouth 15.3.69 Ht 6 1 Wt 12 10
Goalkeeper. From Newquay.

Season	Club	Apps	Goals
1988–89	Exeter C	3	—
1989–90		28	—

MILLER, Paul

Born London 11.10.59. Ht 6 1 Wt 13 02
Defender. From Apprentice.

Season	Club	Apps	Goals
1977–78	Tottenham H	—	—
1978–79		7	—
1979–80		27	2
1980–81		25	2
1981–82		35	—
1982–83		23	1
1983–84		21	—
1984–85		39	—
1985–86		29	2
1986–87		2	—
1986–87	Charlton Ath	14	1
1987–88		23	1
1988–89		5	—
1988–89	Watford	20	—
1989–90	Bournemouth	31	—
1989–90	*Brentford*	3	—

MILLER, Paul

Born Bisley 31.1.68. Ht 6 0 Wt 11 00
Forward. From Trainee.

Season	Club	Apps	Goals
1987–88	Wimbledon	5	—
1987–88	*Newport Co*	6	2
1988–89	Wimbledon	18	5
1989–90		15	2
1989–90	*Bristol C*	3	—

MILLER, William

Born Edinburgh 1.11.69. Ht 5 8 Wt 10 6
Defender. From Edina Hibs BC.

Season	Club	Apps	Goals
1989–90	Hibernian	11	—

MILLER, Willie

Born Glasgow 2.5.55. Ht 5 10 Wt 11 08
Defender. From Eastercraigs. Scotland Youth, Under-21, Under-23, 65 full caps.

Season	Club	Apps	Goals
1971–72	Aberdeen	—	—
1972–73		—	—
1973–74		31	1
1974–75		34	1
1975–76		36	—
1976–77		36	—
1977–78		36	2
1978–79		34	—
1979–80		31	1
1980–81		33	2
1981–82		36	—
1982–83		36	2
1983–84		34	2
1984–85		34	3
1985–86		33	1
1986–87		36	2
1987–88		42	—
1988–89		21	1
1989–90		15	—

MILLIGAN, Mike

Born Manchester 20.2.67. Ht 5 8
Wt 11 00
Midfield. Eire B.

Season	Club	Apps	Goals
1984–85	Oldham Ath	—	—
1985–86		5	1
1986–87		38	2
1987–88		39	1

Season	Club	Apps	Goals
1988–89		39	6
1989–90		41	7

MILLIGAN, Steve

Born Hyde 13.6.73.
Midfield. From Ipswich T. Schoolboy and Rochdale Trainee.

Season	Club	Apps	Goals
1989–90	Rochdale	5	1

MILLS, Brian

Born Swynnerton 26.12.71. Ht 5 9 Wt 10 10
Forward. From Trainee.

Season	Club	Apps	Goals
1989–90	Port Vale	—	—

MILLS, Gary

Born Northampton 11.11.61. Ht 5 8 Wt 11 05
Forward. From Apprentice. England Schools, Youth, Under-21.

Season	Club	Apps	Goals
1978–79	Nottingham F	4	1
1979–80		13	1
1980–81		27	5
1981–82		14	1
From Seattle S			
1982–83	Derby Co	18	1
From Seattle S			
1983–84	Nottingham F	7	—
1984–85		26	4
1985–86		14	—
1986–87		32	—
1987–88	Notts Co	46	5
1988–89		29	3
1988–89	Leicester C	13	—
1989–90		29	4

MILLS, Simon

Born Sheffield 16.8.64. Ht 5 8 Wt 11 04
Midfield. From Apprentice. England Youth.

Season	Club	Apps	Goals
1982–83	Sheffield W	1	—
1983–84		2	—
1984–85		2	—
1985–86	York C	36	2
1986–87		45	1
1987–88		18	2
1987–88	Port Vale	19	5
1988–89		43	—
1989–90		45	1

MILNER, Andy

Born Kendal 10.2.67. Ht 5 11 Wt 11 07
Forward. From Netherfield.

Season	Club	Apps	Goals
1988–89	Manchester C	—	—
1989–90		—	—
1989–90	Rochdale	16	4

MILNE, Callum

Born Edinburgh 27.8.65. Ht 5 8 Wt 10 07
Defender. From Salvesen BC.

Season	Club	Apps	Goals
1983–84	Hibernian	—	—
1984–85		1	—
1985–86		7	—
1986–87		2	—
1987–88		3	—
1988–89		19	—
1989–90		3	—

MILNE, Ralph

Born Dundee 13.5.61. Ht 5 9 Wt 12 00
Forward. 'S' Form. Scotland Youth, Under-21.

Season	Club	Apps	Goals
1977–78	Dundee U	—	—
1978–79		—	—
1979–80		13	2
1980–81		21	7
1981–82		35	8
1982–83		34	16
1983–84		25	5
1984–85		19	4
1985–86		18	1
1986–87		14	1
1986–87	Charlton Ath	12	—
1987–88		10	—
1987–88	Bristol C	19	4
1988–89		11	2
1988–89	Manchester U	22	3

Season	Club	League Appearances/Goals	
1989–90	....	1	—
1989–90	*West Ham U*	—	—

MILTON, Simon

Born London 23.8.63. Ht 5 9 Wt 11 09
Midfield. From Bury St Edmunds.

Season	Club	Apps	Goals
1987–88	Ipswich T................	8	1
1987–88	*Exeter C*	2	3
1987–88	*Torquay U*	4	1
1988–89	Ipswich T................	35	10
1989–90	....	41	10

MILTON, Steve

Born Fulham 13.4.63.
Forward. From Apprentice.

Season	Club	Apps	Goals
1981–82	West Ham U	—	—
From Whyteleafe.			
1989–90	Fulham..................	34	9

MIMMS, Bobby

Born York 12.10.63. Ht 6 2 Wt 12 13
Goalkeeper. From Halifax T Apprentice.
England Under-21.

Season	Club	Apps	Goals
1981–82	Rotherham U	2	—
1982–83	....	13	—
1983–84	....	22	—
1984–85	....	46	—
1985–86	Everton	10	—
1985–86	*Notts Co*	2	—
1986–87	Everton	11	—
1986–87	*Sunderland*	4	—
1986–87	*Blackburn R*	6	—
1987–88	Everton	8	—
1987–88	*Manchester C*	3	—
1987–88	Tottenham H	13	—
1988–89	....	20	—
1989–90	....	4	—
1989–90	*Aberdeen*	6	—

MINETT, Jason

Born Peterborough 12.8.71. Ht 5 10
Wt 10 02
Midfield. From Trainee.

Season	Club	Apps	Goals
1989–90	Norwich C	—	—

MINTO, Scott

Born Cheshire 6.8.71 Ht 5 10 Wt 10 00
Defender. From Trainee.

Season	Club	Apps	Goals
1988–89	Charlton Ath	3	—
1989–90	....	23	2

MITCHELL, Brian

Born Stonehaven 16.7.63. Ht 6 1
Wt 13 1
Defender. From King St. Scotland
Schools.

Season	Club	Apps	Goals
1981–82	Aberdeen	1	—
1982–83	....	1	—
1983–84	....	9	—
1984–85	....	14	1
1985–86	....	23	—
1986–87	....	17	—
1986–87	Bradford C..............	16	—
1987–88	....	42	6
1988–89	....	45	1
1989–90	....	35	2

MITCHELL, David

Born Glasgow 13.6.62 Ht 6 1 Wt 12 07
Forward. Australia full caps.

Season	Club	Apps	Goals
1983–84	Rangers..................	12	2
1984–85	....	14	4
From Feyenoord			
1988–89	Chelsea	6	—
1989–90	....	—	—

MITCHELL, Graham

Born Glasgow 2.11.62. Ht 5 10 Wt 11 08
Midfield. From Auchengill BC.

Season	Club	Apps	Goals
1980–81	Hamilton A	4	—
1981–82	....	37	—
1982–83	....	32	1
1983–84	....	21	1
1984–85	....	30	—
1985–86	....	32	6
1986–87	....	23	1
1986–87	Hibernian	17	1
1987–88	....	41	1

Season	Club	League Appearances/Goals	
1988–89		20	—
1989–90		31	—

MITCHELL, Graham

Born Shipley 16.2.68. Ht 6 0 Wt 11 05
Defender. From Apprentice.

Season	Club	Apps	Goals
1986–87	Huddersfield T	17	—
1987–88		29	1
1988–89		34	—
1989–90		37	1

MOCKLER, Andrew

Born Stockton 18.11.70 Ht 5 11
Wt 11 13
Midfield. From Trainee.

Season	Club	Apps	Goals
1988–89	Arsenal	—	—
1989–90		—	—

MOHAN, Nicky

Born Middlesbrough 6.10.70. Ht 6 2
Wt 12 00
Defender. From Trainee.

Season	Club	Apps	Goals
1987–88	Middlesbrough	—	—
1988–89		6	—
1989–90		22	—

MOLBY, Jan

Born Kolding 4.7.63. Ht 6 1 Wt 14 7
Midfield. From Kolding, Ajax. Denmark full caps.

Season	Club	Apps	Goals
1984–85	Liverpool	22	1
1985–86		39	14
1986–87		34	7
1987–88		7	—
1988–89		13	—
1989–90		17	1

MONCUR, John

Born Stepney 22.9.66. Ht 5 7 Wt 9 10
Midfield. From Apprentice.

Season	Club	Apps	Goals
1984–85	Tottenham H	—	—
1985–86		—	—
1986–87		1	—
1986–87	*Cambridge U*	4	—
1986–87	*Doncaster R*	4	—
1987–88	Tottenham H	5	—
1988–89		1	—
1988–89	*Portsmouth*	7	—
1989–90	Tottenham H	5	1
1989–90	*Brentford*	5	1

MONEY, Campbell

Born Maybole 31.8.60. Ht 5 11 Wt 12 03
Goalkeeper. From Dailly Ams. Scotland Youth, B, Under-21.

Season	Club	Apps	Goals
1978–79	St Mirren	—	—
1979–80		—	—
1980–81		—	—
1981–82		1	—
1982–83		1	—
1983–84		6	—
1984–85		30	—
1985–86		33	—
1986–87		42	—
1987–88		41	—
1988–89		21	—
1989–90		28	—

MONEY, Richard

Born Lowestoft 13.10.55. Ht 5 11
Wt 11 07
Defender. From Lowestoft T. England B.

Season	Club	Apps	Goals
1973–74	Scunthorpe U	29	1
1974–75		43	—
1975–76		45	3
1976–77		38	—
1977–78		18	—
1977–78	Fulham	23	2
1978–79		42	1
1979–80		41	—
1979–80	Liverpool	—	—
1980–81		14	—
1981–82		—	—
1981–82	*Derby Co*	5	—
1981–82	Luton T	13	1
1982–83		31	—
1983–84	Portsmouth	16	—
1984–85		—	—
1985–86		1	—
1985–86	Scunthorpe U	25	—

Season	Club	League Appearances/Goals	
1986–87		42	—
1987–88		32	—
1988–89		6	—
1989–90		1	—

MONINGTON, Mark

Born Bilsthorpe 21.10.70 Ht 6 1
Wt 13 00
Midfield. From schoolboy.

Season	Club	League Appearances/Goals	
1988–89	Burnley	8	1
1989–90		13	—

MONKOU, Kenneth

Born Surinam 29.11.64 Ht 6 0 Wt 12 00
Defender. From Feyenoord.

Season	Club	League Appearances/Goals	
1988–89	Chelsea	2	—
1989–90		34	1

MOONEY, Brian

Born Dublin 2.2.66. Ht 5 10 Wt 11 02
Midfield. From Home Farm. Eire Youth, B, Under-23.

Season	Club	League Appearances/Goals	
1983–84	Liverpool	—	—
1984–85		—	—
1985–86		—	—
1985–86	*Wrexham*	9	2
1986–87	Liverpool	—	—
1987–88		—	—
1987–88	Preston NE	34	3
1988–89		40	6
1989–90		45	9

MOONEY, Tommy

Born Teeside North 11.8.71. Ht 5 10
Wt 12 05
Forward. From Trainee.

Season	Club	League Appearances/Goals	
1989–90	Aston Villa	—	—

MOORE, Allan

Born Glasgow 23.12.64. Ht 5 6 Wt 9 10
Forward. From Possil YM.

Season	Club	League Appearances/Goals	
1983–84	Dumbarton	4	—
1984–85		4	—
1985–86		33	4
1986–87		18	3
1986–87	Hearts	10	—
1987–88		7	1
1988–89		12	2
1989–90	St Johnstone	33	13

MOORE, Kevin

Born Grimsby 29.4.58. Ht 5 11 Wt 12 12
Defender. Local. England Schools.

Season	Club	League Appearances/Goals	
1976–77	Grimsby T	28	—
1977–78		42	—
1978–79		46	6
1979–80		41	4
1980–81		41	1
1981–82		36	4
1982–83		38	—
1983–84		41	1
1984–85		31	4
1985–86		31	2
1986–87		25	5
1986–87	Oldham Ath	13	1
1987–88	Southampton	35	3
1988–89		25	3
1989–90		21	1

MOORE, Martin

Born Middlesbrough 10.1.66.
Forward. From Stockton.

Season	Club	League Appearances/Goals	
1989–90	Peterborough U	7	—

MORAN, Kevin

Born Dublin 29.4.56. Ht 5 11 Wt 12 09
Defender. From Pegasus-Eire Gaelic Football. Eire 54 full caps.

Season	Club	League Appearances/Goals	
1977–78	Manchester U	—	—
1978–79		1	—
1979–80		9	1
1980–81		32	—
1981–82		30	7
1982–83		29	2
1983–84		38	7
1984–85		19	4
1985–86		19	—
1986–87		33	—

Season	Club	Apps	Goals
1987–88		21	—

From Sporting Gijon

Season	Club	Apps	Goals
1989–90	Blackburn R	19	2

MORAN, Paul

Born Enfield 22.5.68. Ht 5 10 Wt 11 00
Forward. From Trainee.

Season	Club	Apps	Goals
1984–85	Tottenham H	—	—
1985–86		—	—
1986–87		1	—
1987–88		13	1
1988–89		8	—
1988–89	*Portsmouth*	3	—
1989–90	Tottenham H	5	1
1989–90	*Leicester C*	10	1

MORAN, Steve

Born Croydon 10.1.61. Ht 5 8 Wt 11 03
Forward. From Amateur. England Under-21.

Season	Club	Apps	Goals
1979–80	Southampton	1	1
1980–81		31	18
1981–82		18	9
1982–83		36	10
1983–84		34	21
1984–85		32	11
1985–86		28	8
1986–87		—	—
1986–87	Leicester C	27	9
1987–88		16	5
1987–88	Reading	28	7
1988–89		34	4
1989–90		28	11

MORGAN, Darren

Born Camberwell 5.11.67. Ht 5 6
Wt 9 10
Defender. From Apprentice. Wales Youth.

Season	Club	Apps	Goals
1985–86	Millwall	—	—
1986–87		21	1
1987–88		4	—
1988–89		8	—
1989–90		2	1
1989–90	*Bradford C*	2	—

MORGAN, Jon

Born Cardiff 10.7.70 Ht 5 8 Wt 10 01
Midfield. From Trainee.

Season	Club	Apps	Goals
1988–89	Cardiff C	19	—
1989–90		32	3

MORGAN, Nicky

Born East Ham 30.10.59. Ht 5 10
Wt 13 10
Forward. From Apprentice.

Season	Club	Apps	Goals
1977–78	West Ham U	—	—
1978–79		2	—
1979–80		6	1
1980–81		6	1
1981–82		—	—
1982–83		7	1
1982–83	Portsmouth	6	1
1983–84		25	9
1984–85		30	8
1985–86		30	14
1986–87		4	—
1986–87	Stoke C	29	10
1987–88		28	5
1988–89		18	5
1989–90		13	1
1989–90	Bristol C	7	4

MORGAN, Simon

Born Birmingham 5.9.66. Ht 5 10
Wt 11 00
Defender. England Under-21.

Season	Club	Apps	Goals
1984–85	Leicester C	—	—
1985–86		30	—
1986–87		41	1
1987–88		40	—
1988–89		32	—
1989–90		17	2

MORGAN, Steve

Born Oldham 19.9.68. Ht 5 11 Wt 13 00
Defender. From Apprentice. England Youth.

Season	Club	League Appearances/Goals	
1985–86	Blackpool	5	—
1986–87		11	—
1987–88		46	6
1988–89		44	3
1989–90		38	1

MORGAN, Steve

Born Wrexham 28.12.70. Ht 5 9
Wt 11 05
Midfield. From Trainee.

Season	Club	Apps	Goals
1987–88	Oldham Ath	1	—
1988–89		1	—
1989–90		—	—
1989–90	*Wrexham*	7	1

MORGAN, Trevor

Born Forest Gate 30.9.56 Ht 6 2
Wt 13 04
Forward. From Leytonstone and Ilford.

Season	Club	Apps	Goals
1980–81	Bournemouth	42	10
1981–82		11	3
1981–82	Mansfield T	12	6
1981–82	Bournemouth	14	4
1982–83		45	16
1983–84		29	13
1983–84	Bristol C	15	5
1984–85		17	3
1984–85	Exeter C	26	9
1985–86		4	—
1985–86	Bristol R	36	16
1986–87		19	8
1986–87	Bristol C	19	8
1987–88	Bolton W	38	7
1988–89		39	10
1989–90		—	—
1989–90	Colchester U	32	12

MORLEY, Trevor

Born Nottingham 20.3.61. Ht 5 11
Wt 12 01
Forward. From Derby Co, Corby T, Nuneaton.

Season	Club	Apps	Goals
1985–86	Northampton T	43	13
1986–87		37	16
1987–88		27	10
1987–88	Manchester C	15	4
1988–89		40	12
1989–90		17	2
1989–90	West Ham U	19	10

MORRELL, Paul

Born Poole 23.3.61. Ht 5 11 Wt 13 05
Defender. From Poole, Bath & Weymouth.

Season	Club	Apps	Goals
1983–84	Bournemouth	22	2
1984–85		44	1
1985–86		38	1
1986–87		45	2
1987–88		42	—
1988–89		44	—
1989–90		21	—

MORRIS, Andy

Born Sheffield 17.11.67. Ht 6 5 Wt 15 07
Forward.

Season	Club	Apps	Goals
1984–85	Rotherham U	1	—
1985–86		—	—
1986–87		6	—
1987–88		—	—
1987–88	Chesterfield	10	—
1988–89		42	9
1989–90		43	4

MORRIS, Chris

Born Newquay 24.12.63. Ht 5 10
Wt 10 08
Defender. England Schools. Eire 26 full caps.

Season	Club	Apps	Goals
1982–83	Sheffield W	—	—
1983–84		13	1
1984–85		14	—
1985–86		30	—
1986–87		17	—
1987–88	Celtic	44	3
1988–89		33	3
1989–90		32	1

MORRIS, Colin

Born Blyth 22.8.53. Ht 5 7 Wt 10 05
Forward. From Apprentice.

Season	Club	Apps	Goals
1971–72	Burnley	—	—

Season	Club	Apps	Goals
1972–73		—	—
1973–74		—	—
1974–75		2	—
1975–76		8	—
1976–77		—	—
1976–77	Southend U	23	3
1977–78		46	11
1978–79		44	7
1979–80		20	4
1979–80	Blackpool	21	4
1980–81		44	12
1981–82		22	10
1981–82	Sheffield U	23	4
1982–83		41	14
1983–84		42	20
1984–85		32	8
1985–86		40	10
1986–87		34	8
1987–88		28	4
1988–89	Scarborough	23	3
1989–90		1	—

MORRIS, Mark

Born Morden 26.9.62. Ht 6 1 Wt 13 08
Defender. From Apprentice.

Season	Club	Apps	Goals
1980–81	Wimbledon	—	—
1981–82		33	1
1982–83		26	3
1983–84		39	3
1984–85		29	1
1985–86		20	1
1985–86	*Aldershot*	14	—
1986–87	Wimbledon	21	—
1987–88	Watford	39	1
1988–89		2	—
1989–90	Sheffield U	42	3

MORRIS, Mark

Born Chester 1.8.68. Ht 6 0 Wt 13 00
Goalkeeper.

Season	Club	Apps	Goals
1985–86	Wrexham	3	—
1986–87		—	—
1987–88		6	—
1988–89		3	—
1989–90		3	—

MORRIS, Ronnie

Born Birmingham 25.9.70. Ht 6 0
Wt 11 08
Forward. From Trainee. FA Schools.

Season	Club	Apps	Goals
1987–88	Birmingham C	1	—
1988–89		10	—
1989–90		—	—

MORRISON, Andy

Born Inverness 30.7.70 Ht 5 11
Wt 12 00
Midfield. From Trainee.

Season	Club	Apps	Goals
1987–88	Plymouth Arg	1	—
1988–89		2	—
1989–90		19	1

MORRISON, John

Born Kettering 27.7.70 Ht 5 6 Wt 10 04
Defender. From Trainee.

Season	Club	Apps	Goals
1988–89	Torquay U	18	—
1989–90		14	—

MORRISSEY, John

Born Liverpool 8.3.65. Ht 5 8 Wt 11 09
Midfield. From Apprentice. England
Youth.

Season	Club	Apps	Goals
1982–83	Everton	—	—
1983–84		—	—
1984–85		1	—
1985–86	Wolverhampton W	10	1
1985–86	Tranmere R	32	5
1986–87		38	7
1987–88		39	4
1988–89		42	4
1989–90		27	4

MORROW, Grant

Born Glasgow 4.10.70.
Forward. From Rowntree Mackintosh.

Season	Club	Apps	Goals
1989–90	Doncaster R	7	2

MORROW, Steve

Born Belfast 2.7.70. Ht 6 0 Wt 11 03
Defender. From Bangor, Arsenal Trainee. Northern Ireland Youth, Under-23, 1 full cap.

Season	Club	Apps	Goals
1987–88	Arsenal	—	—
1988–89		—	—
1989–90		—	—

MORTIMER, Paul

Born London 8.5.68. Ht 5 11 Wt 11 03
Midfield. From Fulham Apprentice. England Under-21.

Season	Club	Apps	Goals
1987–88	Charlton Ath	12	—
1988–89		33	5
1989–90		36	5

MORTENSEN, Henrik

Born Odder (Denmark) 12.2.68.
Ht 5 10 Wt 11 07
Forward. From Aarhus. Denmark full caps.

Season	Club	Apps	Goals
1989–90	Norwich C	15	—

MOULDEN, Paul

Born Farnworth 6.9.67. Ht 5 8 Wt 11 03
Forward. From Apprentice. England Youth.

Season	Club	Apps	Goals
1984–85	Manchester C	—	—
1985–86		2	—
1986–87		20	5
1987–88		6	—
1988–89		36	13
1989–90	Bournemouth	32	13
1989–90	Oldham Ath	8	—

MOUNTFIELD, Derek

Born Liverpool 2.11.62. Ht 6 1 Wt 12 07
Defender. From Apprentice. England B, Under-21.

Season	Club	Apps	Goals
1980–81	Tranmere R	5	—
1981–82		21	1

Season	Club	Apps	Goals
1982–83	Everton	1	—
1983–84		31	3
1984–85		37	10
1985–86		15	3
1986–87		13	3
1987–88		9	—
1988–89	Aston Villa	24	1
1989–90		32	4

MOVERLEY, Rob

Born Batley 16.1.69. Ht 6 3 Wt 12 00
Goalkeeper. From Trainee.

Season	Club	Apps	Goals
1987–88	Bradford C	—	—
1988–89		—	—
1988–89	Hartlepool U	23	—
1989–90		6	—

MOWBRAY, Tony

Born Saltburn 22.11.63. Ht 6 1 Wt 13 00
Defender. From Apprentice. England B.

Season	Club	Apps	Goals
1981–82	Middlesbrough	—	—
1982–83		26	—
1983–84		35	1
1984–85		40	2
1985–86		35	4
1986–87		46	7
1987–88		44	3
1988–89		37	3
1989–90		28	2

MOWER, Ken

Born Walsall 1.12.60 Ht 6 1 Wt 12 04
Defender. From Apprentice.

Season	Club	Apps	Goals
1978–79	Walsall	1	—
1979–80		44	1
1980–81		33	2
1981–82		34	—
1982–83		45	1
1983–84		44	1
1984–85		41	1
1985–86		43	1
1986–87		28	1

Season	Club	Apps	Goals
1987–88		26	—
1988–89		29	—
1989–90		30	—

MOYES, David

Born Blythswood 25.4.63. Ht 6 1
Wt 11 08
Defender. From Drumchapel A

Season	Club	Apps	Goals
1980–81	Celtic	—	—
1981–82		19	—
1982–83		5	—
1983–84		—	—
1983–84	Cambridge U	30	—
1984–85		40	1
1985–86		9	—
1985–86	Bristol C	27	2
1986–87		41	3
1987–88		15	1
1987–88	Shrewsbury T	17	2
1988–89		33	1
1989–90		46	8

MUDD, Paul

Born Hull 13.11.70
Defender. From Trainee.

Season	Club	Apps	Goals
1988–89	Hull C	1	—
1989–90		—	—

MUGGLETON, Carl

Born Leicester 13.9.68. Ht 6 1 Wt 11 13
Goalkeeper. From Apprentice. England Under-21.

Season	Club	Apps	Goals
1986–87	Leicester C	—	—
1987–88		—	—
1987–88	*Chesterfield*	17	—
1987–88	*Blackpool*	2	—
1988–89	Leicester C	3	—
1988–89	*Hartlepool U*	8	—
1989–90	Leicester C	—	—
1989–90	*Stockport Co*	4	—

MUIR, Ian

Born Coventry 5.5.63. Ht 5 8 Wt 11 00
Forward. From Apprentice. England Youth.

Season	Club	Apps	Goals
1980–81	QPR	2	2
1981–82		—	—
1982–83		—	—
1982–83	*Burnley*	2	1
1983–84	Birmingham C	1	—
1983–84	Brighton	2	—
1984–85		2	—
1984–85	*Swindon T*	2	—
1985–86	Tranmere R	32	14
1986–87		46	20
1987–88		43	27
1988–89		46	21
1989–90		46	23

MUIR, John

Born Sedgley 26.4.63.
Forward. From Dudley T.

Season	Club	Apps	Goals
1989–90	Doncaster R	16	4

MUMBY, Peter

Born Bradford 22.2.69. Ht 5 9
Wt 11 05
Forward. From Trainee.

Season	Club	Apps	Goals
1987–88	Leeds U	5	—
1988–89		1	—
1988–89	*Shamrock R*	—	—
1989–90	Burnley	25	4

MUNDEE, Denny

Born Swindon 10.10.68 Ht 5 10
Wt 11 00
Forward. From Apprentice.

Season	Club	Apps	Goals
1986–87	QPR	—	—
1986–87	Swindon T	—	—
1987–88	Bournemouth	—	—
1988–89		2	—
1989–90		10	—
1989–90	*Torquay U*	9	—

MUNGALL, Steve

Born Bellshill 22.5.58. Ht 5 8 Wt 11 05
Defender.

Season	Club	Apps	Goals
1976–77	Motherwell	3	—
1977–78		13	—
1978–79		4	—

Season	Club	League Appearances/Goals	
1979–80	Tranmere R	24	—
1980–81		38	3
1981–82		44	1
1982–83		31	1
1983–84		26	—
1984–85		23	—
1985–86		46	1
1986–87		46	—
1987–88		45	—
1988–89		42	1
1989–90		17	1

MUNRO, Stuart

Born Falkirk 15.9.62. Ht 5 8 Wt 10 05
Defender. From Bo'ness United. Scotland B.

Season	Club	Apps	Goals
1980–81	St Mirren	1	—
1981–82		—	—
1982–83	Alloa	39	5
1983–84		21	1
1983–84	Rangers	5	—
1984–85		13	—
1985–86		29	—
1986–87		43	—
1987–88		17	—
1988–89		22	2
1989–90		36	1

MURPHY, Aidan

Born Manchester 17.9.67. Ht 5 10
Wt 11 03
Midfield. From Apprentice. England Schools, Youth.

Season	Club	Apps	Goals
1984–85	Manchester U	—	—
1985–86		—	—
1986–87		—	—
1986–87	*Lincoln C*	2	—
1986–87	*Oldham Ath*	—	—
1987–88	Crewe Alex	20	2
1988–89		35	5
1989–90		35	3

MURRAY, Malcolm

Born Buckie 26.7.64. Ht 5 11 Wt 11 12
Defender. From Buckie Thistle.

Season	Club	Apps	Goals
1983–84	Hearts	1	—
1984–85		4	—
1985–86		—	—
1986–87		7	—
1987–88		7	—
1988–89		8	—
1988–89	Hull C	8	—
1989–90		3	—
1989–90	Mansfield T	28	—

MURRAY, Shaun

Born Newcastle 7.2.70. Ht 5 8 Wt 11 02
Forward. From Trainee. England Youth.

Season	Club	Apps	Goals
1987–88	Tottenham H	—	—
1988–89		—	—
1989–90	Portsmouth	—	—

MUSEMIC, Husref

Born Janja 4.7.61. Ht 6 2 Wt 12 04
Forward. From Red Star Belgrade.
Yugoslavia full caps.

Season	Club	Apps	Goals
1989–90	Hearts	6	3

MUSSELWHITE, Paul

Born Portsmouth 22.12.68 Ht 6 2
Wt 12 07
Goalkeeper.

Season	Club	Apps	Goals
1987–88	Portsmouth	—	—
1988–89	Scunthorpe U	41	—
1989–90		29	—

MUSTOE, Robbie

Born Oxford 28.8.68. Ht 5 10
Wt 10 08
Midfield.

Season	Club	Apps	Goals
1986–87	Oxford U	3	—
1987–88		17	—
1988–89		33	3
1989–90		38	7

MUTCH, Andy

Born Liverpool 28.12.63. Ht 5 10
Wt 11 00
Forward. From Southport. England B, Under-21.

Season	Club	League Appearances/Goals	
1985–86	Wolverhampton W	15	7
1986–87	....	41	12
1987–88	....	46	19
1988–89	....	45	21
1989–90	....	37	11

MUTTOCK, Jon

Born Oxford 23.12.71. Ht 6 2 Wt 13 00
Defender. From Trainee.

Season	Club	League Appearances/Goals	
1989–90	Oxford U	1	—

NARBETT, Jon

Born Birmingham 21.11.68. Ht 5 10
Wt 10 08
Midfield. From Apprentice.

Season	Club	League Appearances/Goals	
1986–87	Shrewsbury T...........	1	—
1987–88	....	25	3
1988–89	....	—	—
1988–89	Hereford U	36	7
1989–90	....	36	5

NAREY, David

Born Dundee 21.6.56. Ht 6 0 Wt 12 06
Defender. 'S' Form. Scotland Youth, Under-21, Under-23, 35 full caps.

Season	Club	League Appearances/Goals	
1973–74	Dundee U	12	—
1974–75	....	31	6
1975–76	....	33	—
1976–77	....	32	2
1977–78	....	35	—
1978–79	....	36	5
1979–80	....	35	1
1980–81	....	32	—
1981–82	....	34	1
1982–83	....	36	5
1983–84	....	34	1
1984–85	....	29	1
1985–86	....	35	—
1986–87	....	33	—
1987–88	....	39	—
1988–89	....	33	—
1989–90	....	31	—

NASSARI, Derek

Born Pendleton 20.10.71.
Midfield. From Trainee.

Season	Club	League Appearances/Goals	
1989–90	Chester C................	1	—

NAUGHTON, Willie

Born Catrine 20.3.62. Ht 6 0 Wt 12 08
Forward. From Apprentice.

Season	Club	League Appearances/Goals	
1979–80	Preston NE	3	—
1980–81	....	10	2
1981–82	....	33	3
1982–83	....	41	1
1983–84	....	42	3

Season	Club	League Appearances/Goals	
1984–85	....	33	1
1984–85	Walsall	13	—
1985–86	....	39	5
1986–87	....	23	1
1987–88	....	41	3
1988–89	....	35	7
1989–90	Shrewsbury T	43	3

NAYIM (Mohamed Ali Amar)

Born Morocco 5.11.66 Ht 5 8 Wt 11 04
Midfield. From Barcelona. Spain Under-21.

1988–89	Tottenham H	11	2
1989–90	....	19	—

NAYLOR, Dominic

Born Watford 12.8.62. Ht 5 9 Wt 11 07
Midfield. From Trainee.

1988–89	Watford	—	—
1989–90	....	—	—
1989–90	Halifax T	6	1

NAYLOR, Glenn

Born York 11.8.72. Ht 5 9 Wt 11.10
Forward. From Trainee.

1989–90	York C	1	—

NAYLOR, Stuart

Born Wetherby 6.12.62. Ht 6 4 Wt 12 02
Goalkeeper. From Yorkshire A. England Youth, B.

1980–81	Lincoln C	—	—
1981–82	....	3	—
1982–83	....	1	—
1982–83	*Peterborough U*	8	—
1983–84	Lincoln C	—	—
1983–84	*Crewe Alex*	38	—
1984–85	*Crewe Alex*	17	—
1984–85	Lincoln C	25	—
1985–86	....	20	—
1985–86	WBA	12	—
1986–87	....	42	—
1987–88	....	35	—
1988–89	....	44	—
1989–90	....	39	—

NAYLOR, Tony

Born Manchester 29.3.67. Ht 5 8
Wt 10 08
Forward. From Droylsden.

1989–90	Crewe Alex	2	—

NEAL, Phil

Born Irchester 20.2.51. Ht 5 11
Wt 12 02
Defender. From Apprentice.
England B, 50 full caps. Football League.

1968–69	Northampton T	21	4
1969–70	....	13	1
1970–71	....	17	2
1971–72	....	41	2
1972–73	....	38	9
1973–74	....	46	9
1974–75	....	10	2
1974–75	Liverpool	23	—
1975–76	....	42	6
1976–77	....	42	7
1977–78	....	42	4
1978–79	....	42	5
1979–80	....	42	1
1980–81	....	42	2
1981–82	....	42	2
1982–83	....	42	8
1983–84	....	41	1
1984–85	....	42	4
1985–86	....	13	1
1985–86	Bolton W	20	2
1986–87	....	28	1
1987–88	....	8	—
1988–89	....	8	—
1989–90	....	—	—

NEBBELING, Gavin

Born Johannesburg 15.5.63. Ht 6 0
Wt 12 10
Defender. From Arcadia Shepherds.

1981–82	Crystal Palace	1	—
1982–83	....	28	1
1983–84	....	16	—

Season	Club	League Appearances/Goals	
1984–85	....	16	—
1985–86	....	14	—
1985–86	*Northampton T*	11	—
1986–87	Crystal Palace	23	—
1987–88	....	39	6
1988–89	....	14	1
1989–90	Fulham	36	—

NEILL, Warren

Born Acton 21.11.62. Ht 5 9 Wt 11 05
Defender. From Apprentice. England Schools.

Season	Club	League Appearances/Goals	
1980–81	QPR	4	—
1981–82	....	11	—
1982–83	....	39	2
1983–84	....	41	1
1984–85	....	18	—
1985–86	....	16	—
1986–87	....	29	—
1987–88	....	23	—
1988–89	Portsmouth	43	—
1989–90	....	37	—

NELSON, Garry

Born Braintree 16.1.61. Ht 5 10
Wt 11 07
Forward. From Amateur.

Season	Club	League Appearances/Goals	
1979–80	Southend U	22	2
1980–81	....	22	3
1981–82	....	40	4
1982–83	....	45	8
1983–84	Swindon T	36	4
1984–85	....	43	3
1985–86	Plymouth Arg	42	13
1986–87	....	32	7
1987–88	Brighton	42	22
1988–89	....	46	15
1989–90	....	33	5

NEVILLE, Steve

Born Walthamstow 18.9.57. Ht 5 7
Wt 11 04
Forward. From Apprentice

Season	Club	League Appearances/Goals	
1975–76	Southampton	—	—
1976–77	....	—	—
1977–78	....	5	1
1978–79	....	—	—
1978–79	Exeter C	36	9
1979–80	....	43	8
1980–81	....	14	5
1980–81	Sheffield U	19	2
1981–82	....	30	4
1982–83	*Exeter C*	33	17
1983–84	Exeter C	43	9
1984–85	....	16	1
1984–85	Bristol C	28	8
1985–86	....	46	19
1986–87	....	20	8
1987–88	....	40	5
1988–89	Exeter C	38	14
1989–90	....	42	14

NEVIN, Pat

Born Glasgow 6.9.63. Ht 5 6 Wt 10 00
Forward. From Gartcosh U. Scotland, Youth, Under-21, B, 8 full caps.

Season	Club	League Appearances/Goals	
1981–82	Clyde	34	12
1982–83	....	39	5
1983–84	Chelsea	38	14
1984–85	....	41	4
1985–86	....	40	7
1986–87	....	37	5
1987–88	....	37	6
1988–89	Everton	25	2
1989–90	....	30	4

NEWBIGGING, Willie

Born Blairhall 7.9.68. Ht 5 10 Wt 13 00
Midfield. From Oakley U.

Season	Club	League Appearances/Goals	
1988–89	St Johnstone	1	—
1989–90	....	1	—

NEWELL, Mike

Born Liverpool 27.1.65. Ht 6 1 Wt 11 00
Forward. From Liverpool Amateur. England, B, Under-21.

Season	Club	League Appearances/Goals	
1983–84	Crewe Alex	3	—
1983–84	Wigan Ath	9	—
1984–85	....	39	9
1985–86	....	24	16
1985–86	Luton T	16	6
1986–87	....	42	12

Season	Club	League Appearances/Goals	
1987–88		5	—
1987–88	Leicester C	36	8
1988–89		45	13
1989–90	Everton	26	7

NEWELL, Paul

Born Greenwich 23.2.69. Ht 6 1
Wt 11 05
Goalkeeper. From Trainee.

1987–88	Southend U	13	—
1988–89		2	—
1989–90		—	—

NEWHOUSE, Aidan

Born Wallasey 23.5.72. Ht 6 2 Wt 13 05
Midfield. From Schoolboy, Trainee.

1987–88	Chester C	1	—
1988–89		25	2
1989–90		18	4
1989–90	Wimbledon	2	—

NEWMAN, Ricky

Born Guildford 5.8.70. Ht 5 9 Wt 10 07
Forward.

1987–88	Crystal Palace	—	—
1988–89		—	—
1989–90		—	—

NEWMAN, Rob

Born Bradford-on-Avon 13.12.63. Ht 6 0
Wt 13 00
Defender. From Apprentice.

1981–82	Bristol C	21	3
1982–83		43	3
1983–84		30	1
1984–85		34	3
1985–86		39	3
1986–87		45	6
1987–88		44	11
1988–89		46	6
1989–90		46	8

NEWSOME, Jon

Born Sheffield 6.9.70. Ht 6 2 Wt 13 11
Defender. From Trainee.

Season	Club	League Appearances/Goals	
1989–90	Sheffield W	6	—

NEWSON, Mark

Born Stepney 7.12.60. Ht 5 10 Wt 12 06
Defender. From Apprentice.

1979–80	Charlton Ath	—	—
From Maidstone U			
1985–86	Bournemouth	46	5
1986–87		46	7
1987–88		29	3
1988–89		40	7
1989–90		16	1
1989–90	Fulham	16	—

NEVILLE, Chris

Born Cambridge 22.10.70. Ht 6 0
Wt 11 10
Goalkeeper. From Trainee.

1989–90	Ipswich T	1	—

NGATA, Herry

Born New Zealand 24.8.71.
Midfield.

1989–90	Hull C	4	—

NICHOLAS, Charlie

Born Glasgow 30.12.61. Ht 5 10
Wt 11 00
Forward. From Celtic BC. Scotland Youth. Under-21, 20 full caps.

1980–81	Celtic	29	16
1981–82		10	3
1982–83		35	29
1983–84	Arsenal	41	11
1984–85		38	9
1985–86		41	10
1986–87		28	4
1987–88		3	—
1987–88	Aberdeen	16	3
1988–89		29	16
1989–90		33	11

NICHOLAS, Peter

Born Newport 10.11.59. Ht 5 8 Wt 11 08
Midfield. From Apprentice.

Wales Under-21, 65 full caps.

Season	Club	Apps	Goals
1976–77	Crystal Palace	—	—
1977–78		23	1
1978–79		37	3
1979–80		39	2
1980–81		28	1
1980–81	Arsenal	8	1
1981–82		31	—
1982–83		21	—
1983–84		—	—
1983–84	*Crystal Palace*	25	3
1984–85	Crystal Palace	22	4
1984–85	Luton T	19	—
1985–86		41	—
1986–87		42	1
1987–88	Aberdeen	39	3
1988–89	Chelsea	39	1
1989–90		29	—

NICHOLL, Jimmy

Born Canada 28.2.56. Ht 5 9 Wt 11 08
Defender. From Apprentice. Northern Ireland Under-21, 73 full caps.

Season	Club	Apps	Goals
1973–74	Manchester U	—	—
1974–75		1	—
1975–76		20	—
1976–77		30	—
1977–78		37	2
1978–79		21	—
1979–80		42	—
1980–81		36	1
1981–82		1	—
1981–82	Sunderland	3	—
From Toronto B.			
1982–83	Sunderland	29	—
From Toronto B.			
1983–84	Rangers	17	—
1984–85	WBA	27	—
1985–86		29	—
1986–87	Rangers	42	—
1987–88		22	—
1988–89		1	—
1989–90	Dunfermline Ath	17	—

NICOL, Paul

Born Scunthorpe 31.10.67 Ht 6 1
Wt 12 00
Defender.

Season	Club	Apps	Goals
1986–87	Scunthorpe U	9	—
1987–88		25	—
1988–89		23	1
1989–90		18	1

NICOL, Steve

Born Irvine 11.12.61. Ht 5 10 Wt 12 00
Midfield. From Ayr U. BC.
Scotland Under-21, 23 full caps.

Season	Club	Apps	Goals
1979–80	Ayr U	20	2
1980–81		39	2
1981–82		11	2
1981–82	Liverpool	—	—
1982–83		4	—
1983–84		23	5
1984–85		31	5
1985–86		34	4
1986–87		14	3
1987–88		40	6
1988–89		38	2
1989–90		23	6

NICHOLSON, Max

Born Leeds 3.10.71.
Forward. From Trainee.

Season	Club	Apps	Goals
1989–90	Doncaster R	2	—

NICHOLSON, Shane

Born Newark 3.6.70 Ht 5 10 Wt 11 00
Defender. From Trainee.

Season	Club	Apps	Goals
1986–87	Lincoln C	7	—
1987–88		*33*	*1*
1988–89		34	1
1989–90		23	—

NICOLSON, Keith

Born Perth 16.7.68. Ht 6 1 Wt 12 09
Defender. From East Craigie.

Season	Club	Apps	Goals
1988–89	St Johnstone	3	—
1989–90		1	—

NIELSEN, Kent

Born Frederiksberg 28.12.61. Ht 6 2
Wt 14 01

Defender. From Brondby (Denmark). Denmark full caps.

1989–90	Aston Villa	36	2

NISBET, Scott

Born Edinburgh 30.1.68. Ht 6 1 Wt 11 08
Defender. From Salvesen BC. Scotland Schools, Youth, Under-21.

1985–86	Rangers	5	—
1986–87		1	—
1986–87	*East Fife*	6	—
1987–88	Rangers	25	—
1988–89		7	1
1989–90		7	—

NILSSON, Roland

Born Helsingborg 27.11.63. Ht 6 0 Wt 11 06
Defender. From IFK Gothenburg. Sweden full caps.

1989–90	Sheffield W	20	—

NIXON, Eric

Born Manchester 4.10.62. Ht 6 2 Wt 14 03
Goalkeeper. From Curzon Ashton.

1983–84	Manchester C	—	—
1984–85		—	—
1985–86		28	—
1986–87		5	—
1986–87	*Wolverhampton W*	16	—
1986–87	*Bradford C*	3	—
1986–87	*Southampton*	4	—
1986–87	*Carlisle U*	16	—
1987–88	Manchester C	25	—
1987–88	*Tranmere R*	8	—
1988–89	Tranmere R	45	—
1989–90		46	—

NIXON, Paul

Born Seaham 23.9.63 Ht 5 10 Wt 11 03
Forward. From New Zealand.

1988–89	Bristol R	1	—
1989–90		27	5

NOBBS, Keith

Born Bishop Auckland 19.9.61. Ht 5 10 Wt 11 10
Defender. From Apprentice.

1979–80	Middlesbrough	—	—
1980–81		1	—
1981–82		—	—
1982–83	Halifax T	46	1
1983–84		41	—

From Bishop Auckland

1985–86	Hartlepool U	39	1
1986–87		40	—
1987–88		43	—
1988–89		18	—
1989–90		32	—

NOBLE, Daniel

Born Cardiff 2.9.70. Ht 5 11 Wt 12 09
Goalkeeper. From Trainee.

1989–90	Stoke C	1	—

NOGAN, Kurt

Born Cardiff 9.9.70. Ht 5 10 Wt 11 01
Forward. From Trainee. Wales Under-21.

1989–90	Luton T	10	2

NOGAN, Lee

Born Cardiff 21.5.69. Ht 5 10 Wt 11 00
Forward. From Apprentice.

1986–87	Oxford U	—	—
1986–87	*Brentford*	11	2
1987–88	Oxford U	3	—
1987–88	*Southend U*	6	1
1988–89	Oxford U	3	—
1989–90		4	—

NORMAN, John

Born Birkenhead 26.6.71. Ht 5 8 Wt 11 07
Defender/Midfield. From Trainee.

Season	Club	Apps	Goals
1989–90	Tranmere R	—	—

NORMAN, Tony

Born Mancot 24.2.58. Ht 6 2 Wt 13 10
Goalkeeper. From Amateur. Wales 5 full caps.

Season	Club	Apps	Goals
1976–77	Burnley	—	—
1977–78		—	—
1978–79		—	—
1979–80		—	—
1979–80	Hull C	17	—
1980–81		42	—
1981–82		36	—
1982–83		36	—
1983–84		46	—
1984–85		46	—
1985–86		42	—
1986–87		42	—
1987–88		44	—
1988–89		21	—
1988–89	Sunderland	24	—
1989–90		28	—

NORRIS, Russell

Born Chatham 1.2.71. Ht 5 9 Wt 10 12
Defender. From Trainee.

Season	Club	Apps	Goals
1989–90	Gillingham	5	—

NORRIS, Steve

Born Coventry 22.9.61 Ht 5 9 Wt 10 09
Forward. From Telford.

Season	Club	Apps	Goals
1988–89	Scarborough	31	9
1989–90		14	4
1989–90	*Notts Co*	1	—
1989–90	Carlisle U	24	3

NORTH, Marc

Born Ware 29.5.66. Ht 5 11 Wt 11 00
Forward. From Apprentice.

Season	Club	Apps	Goals
1983–84	Luton T	—	—
1984–85		—	—
1984–85	*Lincoln C*	4	—
1985–86	Luton T	13	3
1986–87		5	—
1986–87	*Scunthorpe U*	5	2
1986–87	*Birmingham C*	5	1
1987–88	Grimsby T	38	11
1988–89		29	6
1988–89	Leicester C	8	1
1989–90		24	6

NORTH, Stacey

Born Luton 25.11.64. Ht 6 2 Wt 12 08
Defender. From Apprentice. England Youth.

Season	Club	Apps	Goals
1982–83	Luton T	—	—
1983–84		1	—
1984–85		7	—
1985–86		2	—
1985–86	*Wolverhampton W*	3	—
1986–87	Luton T	14	—
1987–88		1	—
1987–88	WBA	18	—
1988–89		46	—
1989–90		34	—

NORTON, David

Born Cannock 3.3.65. Ht 5 7 Wt 11 03
Midfield. From Apprentice. England Youth.

Season	Club	Apps	Goals
1982–83	Aston Villa	—	—
1983–84		—	—
1984–85		2	—
1985–86		20	2
1986–87		20	—
1987–88		2	—
1988–89	Notts Co	8	—
1989–90		15	1

NOTEMAN, Kevin

Born Preston 15.10.69. Ht 5 10
Wt 10 09
Forward. From Trainee.

Season	Club	Apps	Goals
1987–88	Leeds U	1	—
1988–89		—	—
1989–90		—	—
1989–90	Doncaster R	30	3

NUGENT, Kevin

Born Edmonton 10.4.69. Ht 6 1
Wt 12 04

Forward. From Trainee.

Season	Club	App	Goals
1987–88	Leyton Orient	11	3
1988–89		3	—
1988–89	*Cork C*	—	—
1989–90	Leyton Orient	11	—

NUGENT, Stephen

Born Wigan 7.5.73.
Forward. From Trainee.

Season	Club	App	Goals
1989–90	Wigan Ath	1	—

OAKES, Keith

Born Bedworth 3.7.56. Ht 6 1 Wt 12 13
Defender. From Apprentice.

Season	Club	App	Goals
1972–73	Peterborough	4	—
1973–74		4	—
1974–75		12	—
1975–76		9	1
1976–77		23	1
1977–78		10	—
1978–79		—	—
1978–79	Newport Co	34	5
1979–80		45	11
1980–81		43	8
1981–82		45	1
1982–83		28	1
1983–84		37	1
1984–85	Gillingham	45	5
1985–86		40	2
1986–87		1	—
1986–87	Fulham	41	3
1987–88		35	—
1988–89	Peterborough U	41	5
1989–90		29	1

OAKES, Scott

Born Leicester 5.8.72.
Midfield. From Trainee.

Season	Club	App	Goals
1989–90	Leicester C	2	—

O'BOYLE, George

Born Belfast 14.12.67. Ht 5 7 Wt 10 2
Forward. From Linfield.

Season	Club	App	Goals
1989–90	Dunfermline Ath	28	3

O'BRIEN, Liam

Born Dublin 5.9.64. Ht 6 1 Wt 13 03
Midfield. From Shamrock R. Eire 8 full caps.

Season	Club	App	Goals
1986–87	Manchester U	11	—
1987–88		17	2
1988–89		3	—

Season	Club	League Appearances/Goals	
1988–89	Newcastle U	20	4
1989–90		19	2

O'BRIEN, Michael

Born Dublin 28.11.70. Ht 5 10 Wt 11 04
Midfield. From Trainee.

1988–89	Luton T	—	—
1988–89		—	—

O'CALLAGHAN, Kevin

Born London 19.10.61. Ht 5 8 Wt 11 07
Forward. From Apprentice. Eire Youth, Under-21, 20 full caps.

1978–79	Millwall	10	—
1979–80		10	3
1979–80	Ipswich T	4	—
1980–81		24	—
1981–82		19	1
1982–83		28	—
1983–84		25	2
1984–85		15	—
1984–85	Portsmouth	15	2
1985–86		39	11
1986–87		33	3
1987–88	Millwall	22	7
1988–89		34	5
1989–90		—	—

O'CONNELL, Brendan

Born London 12.11.66. Ht 5 10
Wt 10 09
Forward.

1984–85	Portsmouth	—	—
1985–86		—	—
1986–87	Exeter C	42	8
1987–88		39	11
1988–89	Burnley	43	13
1989–90		21	4
1989–90	*Huddersfield T*	11	1
1989–90	Barnsley	11	2

O'CONNELL, Iain

Born Rochford 9.10.70. Ht 6 1 Wt 12 07
Forward. From Trainee.

Season	Club	League Appearances/Goals	
1989–90	Southend U	4	—

O'CONNOR, Mark

Born Rochdale 10.3.63. Ht 5 7 Wt 10 02
Midfield. From Apprentice.

1980–81	QPR	—	—
1981–82		1	—
1982–83		2	—
1983–84		—	—
1983–84	*Exeter C*	38	1
1984–85	Bristol R	46	8
1985–86		34	2
1985–86	Bournemouth	9	1
1986–87		43	7
1987–88		37	2
1988–89		33	2
1989–90		6	—
1989–90	Gillingham	15	1

O'CONNOR, Paul

Born Co Durham 17.8.71. Ht 5 11
Wt 12 10
Goalkeeper. From Trainee.

1988–89	Leicester C	—	—
1989–90		—	—

O'DOHERTY, Ken

Born Dublin 30.3.63. Ht 6 0 Wt 12 00
Defender. From UCD.

1984–85	Crystal Palace	—	—
1985–86		13	—
1986–87		12	—
1987–88		17	—
1988–89	Huddersfield T	37	1
1989–90		18	—

O'DONNELL, Chris

Born Newcastle 26.5.68. Ht 5 11
Wt 12 13
Defender. From Apprentice.

1985–86	Ipswich T	—	—
1986–87		10	—
1987–88		2	—
1987–88	*Northampton T*	1	—

Season	Club	League Appearances/Goals	
1988–89	Ipswich T	2	—
1989–90	Leeds U	1	—

O'DRISCOLL, Sean

Born Wolverhampton 1.7.57. Ht 5 8 Wt 11 03
Midfield. From Alvechurch. Eire 3 full caps.

Season	Club	Apps	Goals
1979–80	Fulham	10	1
1980–81		42	2
1981–82		42	7
1982–83		42	3
1983–84		12	—
1983–84	*Bournemouth*	19	1
1984–85	Bournemouth	44	1
1985–86		46	5
1986–87		46	5
1987–88		39	4
1988–89		41	—
1989–90		39	—

OGDEN, Paul

Born Salford 19.10.69 Ht 5 10 Wt 11 02
Midfield. From Oldham Ath. Trainee.

Season	Club	Apps	Goals
1988–89	Hartlepool U	10	—
1989–90		2	—

OGHANI, George

Born Manchester 2.9.60. Ht 5 11 Wt 12 03
Forward. From Hyde.

Season	Club	Apps	Goals
1983–84	Bolton W	3	—
1984–85		41	16
1985–86		36	7
1986–87		19	4
1986–87	*Wrexham*	7	—
1987–88	Burnley	37	14
1988–89		37	7
1989–90	Stockport Co	8	2
1989–90	Hereford U	8	2
1989–90	Scarborough	14	4

OGLEY, Mark

Born Barnsley 10.3.67. Ht 5 10 Wt 11 07
Defender. From Apprentice.

Season	Club	League Appearances/Goals	
1984–85	Barnsley	—	—
1985–86		2	—
1986–87		17	—
1987–88		—	—
1987–88	*Aldershot*	8	—
1987–88	Carlisle U	3	—
1988–89		26	–
1989–90		4	1
1989–90	Aldershot	28	—

OGRIZOVIC, Steve

Born Mansfield 12.9.57. Ht 6 5 Wt 15 00
Goalkeeper. From ONRYC.

Season	Club	Apps	Goals
1977–78	Chesterfield	16	—
1977–78	Liverpool	2	—
1978–79		—	—
1979–80		1	—
1980–81		1	—
1981–82		—	—
1982–83	Shrewsbury T	42	—
1983–84		42	—
1984–85	Coventry C	42	—
1985–86		42	—
1986–87		42	1
1987–88		40	—
1988–89		38	—
1989–90		37	—

O'HANLON, Kelham

Born Saltburn 16.5.62. Ht 6 1 Wt 13 01
Goalkeeper. From Apprentice. Eire Under-21.

Season	Club	Apps	Goals
1980–81	Middlesbrough	—	—
1981–82		—	—
1982–83		19	—
1983–84		30	—
1984–85		38	—
1985–86	Rotherham U	46	—
1986–87		40	—
1987–88		40	—
1988–89		46	—
1989–90		43	—

O'HARA, Steve

Born Lanark 21.2.71. Ht 6 1 Wt 12 02
Defender. From Trainee.

Season	Club	League Appearances/Goals	
1989–90	Walsall	18	—

O'KEEFE, Eamon

Born Manchester 13.10.53. Ht 5 7
Wt 11 05
Forward. From Stalybridge C. Eire, 5 full caps.

Season	Club	Apps	Goals
1973–74	Plymouth Arg	—	—
From Hyde, Saudi Arabia, Mossley			
1979–80	Everton	4	—
1980–81		25	3
1981–82		11	3
1981–82	Wigan Ath	22	9
1982–83		36	16
1983–84	Port Vale	37	10
1984–85		22	7
1984–85	Blackpool	12	6
1985–86		22	17
1986–87		2	—
From Cork C			
1988–89	Chester C	14	4
1989–90		3	—

O'KEEFE, Vince

Born Birmingham 2.4.57. Ht 6 2
Wt 13 00
Goalkeeper. Local

Season	Club	Apps	Goals
1975–76	Birmingham C	—	—
1975–76	*Peterborough U*	—	—
1976–77	Walsall	—	—
From AP Leamington			
1978–79	Exeter C	33	—
1979–80		20	—
1979–80	Torquay U	16	—
1980–81		46	—
1981–82		46	—
1982–83	Blackburn R	9	—
1983–84		12	—
1983–84	*Bury*	2	—
1984–85	Blackburn R	5	—
1985–86		10	—
1986–87		25	—
1986–87	*Blackpool*	1	—
1987–88	Blackburn R	5	—
1988–89		2	—
1988–89	*Blackpool*	6	—
1989–90	Wrexham	43	—

O'KELLY, Richard

Born West Bromwich 8.1.57. Ht 5 10
Wt 11 08
Forward. From Alvechurch.

Season	Club	Apps	Goals
1979–80	Walsall	—	—
1980–81		38	7
1981–82		29	6
1982–83		35	7
1983–84		40	12
1984–85		34	16
1985–86		28	8
1986–87	Port Vale	12	3
1987–88		16	1
1987–88	Walsall	12	1
1988–89	Grimsby T	39	10
1989–90		—	—

OLDFIELD, David

Born Perth, Australia 30.5.68. Ht 6 0
Wt 12 02
Forward. From Apprentice. England Under-21.

Season	Club	Apps	Goals
1986–87	Luton T	—	—
1987–88		8	3
1988–89		21	1
1988–89	Manchester C	11	3
1989–90		15	3
1989–90	Leicester C	20	5

O'LEARY, David

Born London 2.5.58. Ht 6 1 Wt 13 02
Defender. From Apprentice.
Eire, 51 full caps.

Season	Club	Apps	Goals
1975–76	Arsenal	27	—
1976–77		33	2
1977–78		41	1
1978–79		37	2
1979–80		34	1
1980–81		24	1
1981–82		40	1
1982–83		36	1
1983–84		36	—
1984–85		36	—

Season	Club	League Appearances/Goals	
1985–86		35	—
1986–87		39	—
1987–88		23	—
1988–89		26	—
1989–90		34	—

OLIVER, Gavin

Born Felling 6.9.62. Ht 6 0 Wt 12 10
Defender. From Apprentice.

Season	Club	Apps	Goals
1980–81	Sheffield W	2	—
1981–82		—	—
1982–83		2	—
1982–83	*Tranmere R*	17	1
1983–84	Sheffield W	6	—
1984–85		10	—
1985–86		—	—
1985–86	*Brighton*	16	—
1985–86	Bradford C	27	1
1986–87		40	—
1987–88		43	—
1988–89		39	1
1989–90		22	—

OLIVER, Neil

Born Berwick 11.4.67. Ht 5 11 Wt 11 10
Defender. From Coldstream.

Season	Club	Apps	Goals
1985–86	Berwick R	5	—
1986–87		37	—
1987–88		12	—
1988–89		39	—
1989–90	Blackburn R	3	—

OLNEY, Ian

Born Luton 17.12.69 Ht 6 1 Wt 11 00
Forward. From Trainee. England Under-21.

Season	Club	Apps	Goals
1988–89	Aston Villa	15	2
1989–90		35	9

OLSEN, Jesper

Born Fakse 20.3.61. Ht 5 6 Wt 9 9
Forward. From Naestved and Ajax. Denmark full caps.

Season	Club	Apps	Goals
1984–85	Manchester U	36	5
1985–86		28	11
1986–87		28	3
1987–88		37	2
1988–89		10	—

To Bordeaux

OLSSON, Paul

Born Hull 24.12.65. Ht 5 8 Wt 10 11
Midfield. From Apprentice.

Season	Club	Apps	Goals
1983–84	Hull C	—	—
1984–85		—	—
1985–86		—	—
1986–87		—	—
1986–87	*Exeter C*	8	—
1987–88	Exeter C	35	2
1988–89	Scarborough	32	4
1989–90		16	1
1989–90	Hartlepool U	23	2

O'NEIL, John

Born Bellshill 6.7.71 Ht 5 7 Wt 10 02
Midfield. From Fir Park BC.

Season	Club	Apps	Goals
1988–89	Dundee U	1	—
1989–90		10	—

O'NEILL, Colin

Born Belfast 14.6.63 Ht 5 8 Wt 10 09
Midfield. From Portadown. Northern Ireland 2 full caps.

Season	Club	Apps	Goals
1988–89	Motherwell	19	2
1989–90		24	1

O'NEILL, Michael

Born Portadown 5.7.69. Ht 5 11 Wt 10 10
Forward. From Coleraine. Northern Ireland 12 full caps.

Season	Club	Apps	Goals
1987–88	Newcastle U	21	12
1988–89		27	3
1989–90	Dundee U	18	5

ONUORA, Iffy

Born Glasgow 28.7.67.
Forward.

Season Club League Appearances/Goals

Season	Club	App	Gls
1989–90	Huddersfield T	20	3

ORD, Richard

Born Easington 3.3.70 Ht 6 2 Wt 12 08
Defender. From Trainee.

Season	Club	App	Gls
1987–88	Sunderland	8	—
1988–89		34	1
1989–90		7	1
1989–90	*York C*	3	—

O'REGAN, Kieran

Born Cork 9.11.63. Ht 5 8 Wt 10 12
Midfield. From Tramore Ath.
Eire 4 full caps.

Season	Club	App	Gls
1982–83	Brighton	1	—
1983–84		31	1
1984–85		15	—
1985–86		15	1
1986–87		24	—
1987–88	Swindon T	26	1
1988–89	Huddersfield T	36	2
1989–90		37	3

O'REILLY, Gary

Born Isleworth 21.3.61. Ht 5 11
Wt 13 05
Defender. From Amateur. Eire Youth.

Season	Club	App	Gls
1979–80	Tottenham H	—	—
1980–81		2	—
1981–82		5	—
1982–83		26	—
1983–84		12	—
1984–85	Brighton	36	3
1985–86		35	—
1986–87		8	—
1986–87	Crystal Palace	13	—
1987–88		4	—
1988–89		32	2
1989–90		21	—

O'RIORDAN, Don

Born Dublin 14.5.57. Ht 6 0 Wt 11 12
Midfield. From Apprentice. Eire Under-21.

Season	Club	App	Gls
1975–76	Derby Co	—	—
1976–77		1	—
1977–78		5	1
1977–78	*Doncaster R*	2	—
From Tulsa			
1978–79	Preston NE	32	—
1979–80		18	—
1980–81		21	—
1981–82		46	4
1982–83		41	4
1983–84	Carlisle U	42	8
1984–85		42	10
1985–86	Middlesbrough	41	2
1986–87	Grimsby T	40	6
1987–88		46	8
1988–89	Notts Co	43	3
1989–90		17	—
1989–90	*Mansfield T*	6	—

ORLYGSSON, Thorvaldur

Born Odense 2.8.66. Ht 5 11 Wt 10 08
Midfield. From FC Akureyri. Iceland full caps.

Season	Club	App	Gls
1989–90	Nottingham F	12	1

ORMONDROYD, Ian

Born Bradford 22.9.64. Ht 6 4 Wt 13 07
Forward. From Thackley.

Season	Club	App	Gls
1985–86	Bradford C	12	3
1986–87		13	4
1986–87	*Oldham Ath*	10	1
1987–88	Bradford C	37	9
1988–89		25	4
1988–89	Aston Villa	12	1
1989–90		25	4

ORMSBY, Brendan

Born Birmingham 1.10.60. Ht 5 11
Wt 11 12
Defender. From Apprentice.
England Schools, Youth.

Season	Club	App	Gls
1978–79	Aston Villa	2	—
1979–80		23	—
1980–81		—	—
1981–82		12	—
1982–83		—	—
1983–84		34	2

Season Club League Appearances/Goals

Season	Club	Apps	Goals
1984–85		32	2
1985–86		14	—
1985–86	Leeds U	12	1
1986–87		33	4
1987–88		—	—
1988–89		1	—
1989–90		—	—
1989–90	*Shrewsbury T*	1	—

ORR, Neil

Born Airdrie 13.5.59. Ht 5 10 Wt 12 02
Defender. Scotland Under-21.

Season	Club	Apps	Goals
1975–76	Morton	4	—
1976–77		24	—
1977–78		39	—
1978–79		35	—
1979–80		35	1
1980–81		33	—
1981–82		16	—
1981–82	West Ham U	24	1
1982–83		14	—
1983–84		29	—
1984–85		20	—
1985–86		36	2
1986–87		22	1
1987–88		1	—
1987–88	Hibernian	38	1
1988–89		33	—
1989–90		29	1

OSBORN, Simon

Born New Addington 19.1.72. Ht 5 10
Wt 11 04
Midfield. From Apprentice.

Season	Club	Apps	Goals
1989–90	Crystal Palace	—	—

O'SHAUGHNESSY, Steve

Born Wrexham 13.10.67. Ht 6 2
Wt 13 00
Defender. Wales Youth.

Season	Club	Apps	Goals
1984–85	Leeds U	—	—
1985–86		—	—
1985–86	Bradford C	—	—
1986–87		—	—
1987–88		1	—
1988–89	Rochdale	41	6
1989–90		30	8

O'SHEA, Danny

Born Kennington 26.3.63. Ht 6 0
Wt 12 02
Defender. From Apprentice.

Season	Club	Apps	Goals
1980–81	Arsenal	—	—
1981–82		—	—
1982–83		6	—
1983–84		—	—
1983–84	*Charlton Ath*	9	—
1984–85	Exeter C	45	2
1985–86	Southend U	35	9
1986–87		41	2
1987–88		22	—
1988–89		20	1
1989–90	Cambridge U	26	—

O'SHEA, Tim

Born London 12.11.66. Ht 5 11 Wt 11 4
Defender. From Arsenal Schoolboy. Eire Youth.

Season	Club	Apps	Goals
1984–85	Tottenham H	—	—
1985–86		—	—
1986–87		2	—
1986–87	*Newport Co*	10	—
1987–88	Tottenham H	1	—
1988–89	Leyton Orient	9	1
1988–89	Gillingham	17	—
1989–90		36	2

OSBORNE, Steve

Born Middlesbrough 3.3.69 Ht 5 10
Wt 11 11
Forward. From South Bank.

Season	Club	Apps	Goals
1988–89	Peterborough U	9	1
1989–90		32	5

OSGOOD, Steve

Born Surrey 20.1.62 Ht 6 0 Wt 12 00
Goalkeeper. From Farnborough.

Season	Club	Apps	Goals
1988–89	Aldershot	1	—
1989–90		—	—

OSMAN, Russell

Born Repton 14.2.59. Ht 5 11 Wt 12 01
Defender. From Apprentice. England Under-21, B, 11 full caps.

Season	Club	Apps	Goals
1975–76	Ipswich	—	—
1976–77		—	—
1977–78		28	—
1978–79		39	2
1979–80		42	2
1980–81		42	1
1981–82		39	2
1982–83		38	4
1983–84		37	3
1984–85		29	3
1985–86	Leicester C	40	—
1986–87		31	3
1987–88		37	5
1988–89	Southampton	36	—
1989–90		35	5

O'SULLIVAN, Alan

Born Cork 26.8.71. Ht 5 5 Wt 10 01
Midfield.

Season	Club	Apps	Goals
1988–89	Luton T	—	—
1989–90		—	—

OVERSON, Vince

Born Kettering 15.5.62. Ht 6 0 Wt 13 00
Defender. From Apprentice.

Season	Club	Apps	Goals
1979–80	Burnley	22	—
1980–81		39	1
1981–82		36	4
1982–83		6	—
1983–84		38	—
1984–85		42	1
1985–86		28	—
1986–87	Birmingham C	34	1
1987–88		37	—
1988–89		41	—
1989–90		30	—

OWEN, Gareth

Born Chester 21.10.71.
Midfield. From Trainee.

Season	Club	Apps	Goals
1989–90	Wrexham	13	—

OWEN, Gordon

Born Barnsley 14.6.59. Ht 5 8 Wt 10 09
Forward. From Amateur.

Season	Club	Apps	Goals
1976–77	Sheffield W	1	—
1977–78		2	—
1978–79		22	3
1979–80		4	1
1979–80	*Rotherham U*	9	—
1980–81	Sheffield W	6	—
1981–82		6	—
1982–83		7	1
1982–83	*Doncaster R*	9	—
1982–83	*Chesterfield*	6	2
1983–84	Cardiff C	39	14
1984–85	Barnsley	36	14
1985–86		32	11
1986–87	Bristol C	35	5
1987–88		18	6
1987–88	*Hull C*	3	—
1987–88	Mansfield T	17	3
1988–89		41	5
1989–90	Blackpool	28	4

OWERS, Adrian

Born Banbury 26.2.65. Ht 5 8 Wt 10 02
Midfield. From Apprentice.

Season	Club	Apps	Goals
1982–83	Southend U	14	—
1983–84		1	—
1984–85		12	—
From Chelmsford C			
1987–88	Brighton	9	2
1988–89		24	2
1989–90		4	—

OWERS, Gary

Born Newcastle 3.10.68. Ht 5 10
Wt 11 10
Midfield. From Apprentice.

Season	Club	League Appearances/Goals	
1986–87	Sunderland	—	—
1987–88		37	4
1988–89		38	3
1989–90		43	9

OXBROW, Darren

Born Ipswich 1.9.69 Ht 6 1 Wt 12 06
Defender. From Trainee.

Season	Club	League Appearances/Goals	
1988–89	Ipswich T	—	—
1989–90	Maidstone U	24	—

PAATELAINEN, Mixu

Born Helsinki 3.2.67. Ht 6 0 Wt 13 11
Forward. From Valkeakosken Haka. Finland full caps.

Season	Club	League Appearances/Goals	
1987–88	Dundee U	19	9
1988–89		33	10
1989–90		31	7

PAGE, Don

Born Manchester 18.1.64 Ht 5 11
Wt 11 00
Forward. From Runcorn.

Season	Club	League Appearances/Goals	
1988–89	Wigan Ath	15	2
1989–90		25	—

PAINTER, Robert

Born Ince 26.1.71.
Midfield. From Trainee.

Season	Club	League Appearances/Goals	
1987–88	Chester C	2	—
1988–89		8	1
1989–90		32	4

PALIN, Leigh

Born Worcester 12.9.65. Ht 5 9
Wt 11 07
Midfield. From Apprentice. England Youth.

Season	Club	League Appearances/Goals	
1983–84	Aston Villa	—	—
1984–85		—	—
1984–85	*Shrewsbury T*	2	—
1985–86	Aston Villa	—	—
1985–86	Nottingham F	—	—
1986–87		—	—
1986–87	Bradford C	21	3
1987–88		20	3
1988–89		30	4
1989–90		—	—
1989–90	Stoke C	19	3
1989–90	Hull C	9	1

PALLISTER, Gary

Born Ramsgate 30.6.65. Ht 6 4
Wt 13 04
Defender. England B, 2 full caps

Season	Club	Apps	Goals
1984–85	Middlesbrough	—	—
1985–86		28	—
1985–86	*Darlington*	7	—
1986–87	Middlesbrough	44	1
1987–88		44	3
1988–89		37	1
1989–90		3	—
1989–90	Manchester U	35	3

PALMER, Carlton

Born West Bromwich 5.12.65. Ht 6 2
Wt 12 04
Defender. From Trainee. England B, Under-21.

Season	Club	Apps	Goals
1984–85	WBA	—	—
1985–86		20	—
1986–87		37	1
1987–88		38	3
1988–89		26	—
1988–89	Sheffield W	13	1
1989–90		34	—

PALMER, Charlie

Born Aylesbury 10.7.63. Ht 5 11
Wt 13 00
Defender. From Apprentice.

Season	Club	Apps	Goals
1981–82	Watford	—	—
1982–83		—	—
1983–84		10	1
1984–85	Derby Co	33	2
1985–86		18	—
1986–87		—	—
1986–87	Hull C	17	—
1987–88		35	—
1988–89		18	1
1988–89	Notts Co	11	—
1989–90		37	5

PALMER, Lee

Born Gillingham 19.9.70 Ht 6 0
Wt 12 04
Defender. From Trainee.

Season	Club	Apps	Goals
1987–88	Gillingham	1	—
1988–89		—	—
1989–90		39	3

PALMER, Roger

Born Manchester 30.1.59. Ht 5 10
Wt 11 00
Forward. From Apprentice.

Season	Club	Apps	Goals
1976–77	Manchester C	—	—
1977–78		5	3
1978–79		14	4
1979–80		7	1
1980–81		5	1
1980–81	Oldham Ath	21	6
1981–82		37	7
1982–83		42	15
1983–84		42	13
1984–85		36	9
1985–86		41	15
1986–87		42	16
1987–88		42	17
1988–89		46	15
1989–90		42	16

PALMER, Steve

Born Brighton 31.3.68 Ht 6 1 Wt 12 07
Midfield. From Cambridge University.

Season	Club	Apps	Goals
1989–90	Ipswich T	5	—

PAMPHLETT, Tony

Born Westminster 13.4.60. Ht 6 3
Wt 13 07
Defender. From Cray Wanderers and Dartford (1986)

Season	Club	Apps	Goals
1989–90	Maidstone U	7	—

PARDEW, Alan

Born Wimbledon 18.7.61. Ht 5 10
Wt 11 00
Midfield. From Yeovil.

Season	Club	Apps	Goals
1986–87	Crystal Palace	—	—
1987–88		20	—

Season	Club	Apps	Goals
1988–89		45	1
1989–90		36	6

PARIS, Alan

Born Slough 15.8.64. Ht 6 0 Wt 11 10
Defender. From Slough T.

Season	Club	Apps	Goals
1982–83	Watford	—	—
1983–84		—	—
1984–85		—	—
1985–86	Peterborough U	46	—
1986–87		45	—
1987–88		46	2
1988–89	Leicester C	37	1
1989–90		38	2

PARRISH, Sean

Born Wrexham 14.3.72.
Midfield. From Trainee.

Season	Club	Apps	Goals
1989–90	Shrewsbury T	2	—

PARKER, Garry

Born Oxford 7.9.65. Ht 5 10 Wt 12 06
Midfield. From Apprentice. England Youth, B, Under-21.

Season	Club	Apps	Goals
1982–83	Luton T	1	—
1983–84		13	2
1984–85		20	1
1985–86		8	—
1985–86	Hull C	12	—
1986–87		38	—
1987–88		34	8
1987–88	Nottingham F	2	—
1988–89		22	7
1989–90		37	6

PARKER, Paul

Born Essex 4.4.64. Ht 5 7 Wt 10 13
Defender. From Apprentice. England Youth, B, Under-21, 11 full caps.

Season	Club	Apps	Goals
1980–81	Fulham	1	—
1981–82		5	—
1982–83		16	—
1983–84		34	—
1984–85		36	—
1985–86		30	—
1986–87		31	2
1987–88	QPR	40	—
1988–89		36	—
1989–90		32	—

PARKES, Phil

Born Sedgeley 8.8.50. Ht 6 3 Wt 15 12
Goalkeeper. From Amateur. England Under-21, Under-23, B, 1 full cap.

Season	Club	Apps	Goals
1967–68	Walsall	—	—
1968–69		8	—
1969–70		44	—
1970–71	QPR	41	—
1971–72		42	—
1972–73		41	—
1973–74		42	—
1974–75		41	—
1975–76		42	—
1976–77		40	—
1977–78		31	—
1978–79		24	—
1978–79	West Ham U	18	—
1979–80		40	—
1980–81		42	—
1981–82		39	—
1982–83		42	—
1983–84		42	—
1984–85		10	—
1985–86		42	—
1986–87		33	—
1987–88		1	—
1988–89		13	—
1989–90		22	—

PARKIN, Brian

Born Birkenhead 12.10.65. Ht 6 1
Wt 12 0
Goalkeeper. Local.

Season	Club	Apps	Goals
1982–83	Oldham Ath	—	—
1983–84		5	—
1984–85		1	—
1984–85	*Crewe Alex*	12	—
1985–86	Crewe Alex	39	—
1986–87		44	—
1987–88		3	—
1987–88	*Crystal Palace*	—	—
1988–89	Crystal Palace	19	—

Season	Club	League Appearances/Goals	
1989–90		1	—
1989–90	Bristol R	30	—

PARKIN, Steve

Born Mansfield 7.11.65. Ht 5 6
Wt 11 00
Defender. From Apprentice. England Schools, Youth, Under-21.

Season	Club		
1982–83	Stoke C	2	—
1983–84		1	—
1984–85		13	1
1985–86		12	1
1986–87		38	—
1987–88		43	3
1988–89		4	—
1989–90	WBA	14	1

PARKIN, Tim

Born Penrith 31.12.57. Ht 6 2 Wt 13 02
Defender. From Apprentice.

Season	Club		
1976–77	Blackburn R	1	—
1977–78		—	—
1978–79		12	—
1979–80		—	—
From Malmo and Almondsbury Greenway			
1981–82	Bristol R	40	2
1982–83		41	3
1983–84		39	2
1984–85		43	3
1985–86		43	2
1986–87	Swindon T	32	2
1987–88		40	2
1988–89		32	1
1989–90		6	1
1989–90	Port Vale	12	1

PARKINSON, Gary

Born Middlesbrough 10.1.68. Ht 5 11
Wt 12 05
Defender. From Everton Amateur.

Season	Club		
1985–86	Middlesbrough	—	—
1986–87		46	—
1987–88		38	—
1988–89		36	2
1989–90		41	2

PARKINSON, Joe

Born Eccles 11.6.71
Midfield. From Trainee.

Season	Club		
1988–89	Wigan Ath	12	1
1989–90		33	2

PARKINSON, Philip

Born Chorley 1.12.67. Ht 6 0 Wt 11 06
Midfield. From Apprentice.

Season	Club		
1985–86	Southampton	—	—
1986–87		—	—
1987–88		—	—
1987–88	Bury	8	1
1988–89		39	—
1989–90		22	2

PARKS, Tony

Born Hackney 26.1.63. Ht 5 11
Wt 10 08
Goalkeeper. From Apprentice.

Season	Club		
1980–81	Tottenham H	—	—
1981–82		2	—
1982–83		1	—
1983–84		16	—
1984–85		—	—
1985–86		—	—
1986–87		2	—
1986–87	*Oxford U*	5	—
1987–88	Tottenham H	16	—
1987–88	*Gillingham*	2	—
1988–89	Brentford	33	—
1989–90		37	—

PARRIS, George

Born Ilford 11.9.64. Ht 5 9 Wt 13 00
Defender. From Apprentice. England Schools.

Season	Club		
1982–83	West Ham U	—	—
1983–84		—	—
1984–85		1	—
1985–86		26	1
1986–87		36	2

Season	Club	League Appearances/Goals	
1987–88		30	1
1988–89		27	1
1989–90		38	2

PARRISH, Sean

Born Wrexham 14.3.72.
Midfield.

Season	Club	Apps	Goals
1989–90	Shrewsbury T	2	—

PARROTT, Mark

Born Cheltenham 14.3.71. Ht 5 11
Wt 11 00
Forward. From Trainee. England schools, Youth.

Season	Club	Apps	Goals
1989–90	Aston Villa	—	—

PARSLEY, Neil

Born Liverpool 25.4.66 Ht 5 10
Wt 10 11
Defender. From Witton Alb.

Season	Club	Apps	Goals
1988–89	Leeds U	—	—
1989–90		—	—
1989–90	*Chester C*	6	—

PASCOE, Colin

Born Port Talbot 9.4.65. Ht 5 9
Wt 10 00
Forward. From Apprentice. Wales Youth, Under-21, 7 full caps.

Season	Club	Apps	Goals
1982–83	Swansea C	7	1
1983–84		32	2
1984–85		41	9
1985–86		19	3
1986–87		41	11
1987–88		34	13
1987–88	Sunderland	9	4
1988–89		39	10
1989–90		33	1

PASHLEY, Terry

Born Chesterfield 11.10.56. Ht 5 8
Wt 12 00
Defender. From Apprentice. England Schools.

Season	Club	League Appearances/Goals	
1973–74	Burnley	—	—
1974–75		—	—
1975–76		1	—
1976–77		11	—
1977–78		6	—
1978–79	Blackpool	35	—
1979–80		44	3
1980–81		30	—
1981–82		46	1
1982–83		46	3
1983–84	Bury	40	—
1984–85		29	1
1985–86		39	1
1986–87		38	1
1987–88		46	1
1988–89		25	1
1989–90		—	—

PASKIN, John

Born Capetown 1.2.62
Forward. From Seiko.

Season	Club	Apps	Goals
1988–89	WBA	25	5
1989–90	Wolverhampton W	17	2

PATERSON, Craig

Born South Queensferry 2.10.59. Ht 6 2
Wt 12 12
Defender. From Bonnyrigg Rose. Scotland Under-21.

Season	Club	Apps	Goals
1978–79	Hibernian	—	—
1979–80		30	—
1980–81		38	3
1981–82		36	1
1982–83	Rangers	20	—
1983–84		21	1
1984–85		22	2
1985–86		18	1
1986–87		2	—
1986–87	Motherwell	16	—
1987–88		44	2
1988–89		33	1
1989–90		33	3

PATES, Colin

Born Mitcham 10.8.61. Ht 5 11
Wt 11 00

Defender. From Apprentice. England Youth.

Season	Club	Apps	Goals
1979–80	Chelsea	16	—
1980–81		15	—
1981–82		42	1
1982–83		35	4
1983–84		42	—
1984–85		36	1
1985–86		35	1
1986–87		33	2
1987–88		17	—
1988–89		10	1
1988–89	Charlton Ath	21	—
1989–90		17	—
1989–90	Arsenal	2	—

PATTERSON, Darren

Born Belfast 15.10.69 Ht 6 2 Wt 11 10
Defender. From Trainee.

Season	Club	Apps	Goals
1988–89	WBA	—	—
1989–90	Wigan Ath	29	1

PATTERSON, Mark

Born Darwen 24.5.65. Ht 5 6 Wt 10 10
Forward. From Apprentice.

Season	Club	Apps	Goals
1983–84	Blackburn R	29	7
1984–85		9	—
1985–86		26	10
1986–87		24	1
1987–88		13	2
1988–89	Preston NE	42	15
1989–90		13	4
1989–90	Bury	20	4

PATTERSON, Mark

Born Leeds 13.9.68 Ht 5 10 Wt 11 05
Defender. From Trainee.

Season	Club	Apps	Goals
1986–87	Carlisle U	6	—
1987–88		16	—
1987–88	Derby Co	—	—
1988–89		1	—
1989–90		9	—

PATTISON, Martin

Born Bradford 21.7.71. Ht 6 0 Wt 11 07
Defender. From Trainee.

Season	Club	Apps	Goals
1989–90	Bradford C	—	—

PAYNE, Lee

Born Luton 12.12.66 Ht 5 10 Wt 11 05
Forward. From Barnet.

Season	Club	Apps	Goals
1988–89	Newcastle U	7	—
1988–89	Reading	15	3
1989–90		12	—

PAYNE, Mark

Born Cheltenham 3.8.60 Ht 5 9
Wt 11 09
Forward. From Cambuur.

Season	Club	Apps	Goals
1988–89	Stockport Co	22	1
1989–90		34	6

PAYNE, Russell

Born Wigan 8.7.70. Ht 5 10 Wt 11 08
Forward. From Skelmersdale U.

Season	Club	Apps	Goals
1989–90	Liverpool	—	—

PAYTON, Andy

Born Burnley 23.10.66. Ht 5 9 Wt 10 06
Midfield. From Apprentice.

Season	Club	Apps	Goals
1985–86	Hull C	—	—
1986–87		2	—
1987–88		22	2
1988–89		28	4
1989–90		39	17

PEACOCK, Darren

Born Bristol 3.2.68 Ht 6 2 Wt 12 06
Defender. From Apprentice.

Season	Club	Apps	Goals
1984–85	Newport Co	—	—
1985–86		18	—
1986–87		5	—
1987–88		5	-

Season	Club	League Appearances/Goals	
1988–89	Hereford U	8	—
1989–90		36	3

PEACOCK, Gavin

Born Kent 18.11.67. Ht 5 8 Wt 11 08
Midfield. England School, Youth.

Season	Club	Apps	Goals
1984–85	QPR	—	—
1985–86		—	—
1986–87		12	1
1987–88		5	—
1987–88	Gillingham	26	2
1988–89		44	9
1989–90	Bournemouth	41	4

PEAKE, Andy

Born Market Harborough 1.11.61.
Ht 5 10 Wt 12 00
Midfield. From Apprentice. England Youth, Under-21.

Season	Club	Apps	Goals
1978–79	Leicester C	18	2
1979–80		25	3
1980–81		24	1
1981–82		31	2
1982–83		4	—
1983–84		24	4
1984–85		21	1
1985–86	Grimsby T	36	4
1986–87		3	—
1986–87	Charlton Ath	29	—
1987–88		16	—
1988–89		31	1
1989–90		36	—

PEAKE, Trevor

Born Nuneaton 10.2.57. Ht 6 0 Wt 12 9
Defender. From Nuneaton Bor.

Season	Club	Apps	Goals
1979–80	Lincoln C	45	1
1980–81		43	1
1981–82		37	4
1982–83		46	1
1983–84	Coventry C	33	3
1984–85		35	1
1985–86		37	1
1986–87		39	—
1987–88		31	—

Season	Club	League Appearances/Goals	
1988–89		32	—
1989–90		33	—

PEARCE, Chris

Born Newport 7.8.61. Ht 6 0 Wt 11 04
Goalkeeper. From Wolverhampton W. Apprentice. Wales Schools, Youth.

Season	Club	Apps	Goals
1979–80	Blackburn R	—	—
1980–81	*Rochdale*	5	—
1981–82	*Barnsley*	—	—
1982–83	Rochdale	36	—
1983–84	Port Vale	7	—
1984–85		36	—
1985–86		5	—
1986–87	Wrexham	25	—
1987–88	Burnley	46	—
1988–89		39	—
1989–90		39	—

PEARCE, Graham

Born Hammersmith 8.7.59. Ht 5 9
Wt 11 00
Defender. From Barnet.

Season	Club	Apps	Goals
1981–82	Brighton	—	—
1982–83		14	—
1983–84		18	1
1984–85		24	—
1985–86		32	1
1986–87	Gillingham	33	—
1987–88		32	—
1988–89	Brentford	18	—
1989–90	Maidstone U	27	—

PEARCE, Stuart

Born London 24.4.62. Ht 5 10 Wt 12 08
Defender. From Wealdstone. England Under-21, 30 full caps.

Season	Club	Apps	Goals
1983–84	Coventry C	23	—
1984–85		28	4
1985–86	Nottingham F	30	1
1986–87		39	6
1987–88		34	5

Season	Club	League Appearances/Goals	
1988–89		36	6
1989–90		34	5

PEARCEY, Jason

Born Leamington Spa 2.7.71
Goalkeeper. From Trainee.

Season	Club	Apps	Goals
1988–89	Mansfield T	1	—
1989–90		5	—

PEARS, Steve

Born Brandon 22.1.62. Ht 6 0 Wt 12 11
Goalkeeper. From Apprentice.

Season	Club	Apps	Goals
1978–79	Manchester U	—	—
1979–80		—	—
1980–81		—	—
1981–82		—	—
1982–83		—	—
1983–84		—	—
1983–84	*Middlesbrough*	12	—
1984–85	Manchester U	4	—
1985–86	Middlesbrough	38	—
1986–87		46	—
1987–88		43	—
1988–89		26	—
1989–90		25	—

PEARSON, Andy

Born London 27.11.69 Ht 5 7 Wt 10 06
Defender. From Trainee. England Youth.

Season	Club	Apps	Goals
1988–89	West Ham U	—	—
1989–90		—	—

PEARSON, John

Born Sheffield 1.9.63. Ht 6 3 Wt 13 00
Forward. From Apprentice. England Youth.

Season	Club	Apps	Goals
1980–81	Sheffield W	15	4
1981–82		24	7
1982–83		30	7
1983–84		27	4
1984–85		9	2
1985–86	Charlton Ath	42	14
1986–87		19	1
1986–87	Leeds U	18	4
1987–88		28	6
1988–89		33	1
1989–90		7	—

PEARSON, Nigel

Born Nottingham 21.8.63. Ht 6 1
Wt 13 03
Defender. From Heanor T.

Season	Club	Apps	Goals
1981–82	Shrewsbury T	—	—
1982–83		39	1
1983–84		26	—
1984–85		—	—
1985–86		35	1
1986–87		42	3
1987–88		11	—
1987–88	Sheffield W	19	2
1988–89		37	2
1989–90		33	1

PEARSON, Rick

Born Maidstone 18.10.70 Ht 5 11
Wt 10 09
Defender. From Trainee.

Season	Club	Apps	Goals
1988–89	Gillingham	3	—
1989–90		6	—

PEER, Dean

Born Dudley 8.8.69. Ht 6 2 Wt 12 00
Midfield. From Trainee.

Season	Club	Apps	Goals
1986–87	Birmingham C	2	—
1987–88		—	—
1988–89		17	1
1989–90		27	3

PEJIC, Mel

Born Chesterton 27.4.59. Ht 5 9
Wt 10 08
Defender. Local.

Season	Club	Apps	Goals
1977–78	Stoke C	—	—
1978–79		—	—
1979–80		1	—
1980–81	Hereford U	13	—
1981–82		27	—
1982–83		45	1
1983–84		44	—
1984–85		46	1

Season	Club	League Appearances/Goals	
1985–86		45	1
1986–87		31	—
1987–88		44	1
1988–89		18	3
1989–90		38	5

PEMBERTON, John

Born Oldham 18.11.64. Ht 5 11
Wt 12 03
Defender. From Chadderton.

Season	Club	Apps	Goals
1984–85	Rochdale	1	—
1984–85	Crewe Alex	6	—
1985–86		41	—
1986–87		43	—
1987–88		31	1
1987–88	Crystal Palace	2	—
1988–89		42	1
1989–90		34	1

PEMBRIDGE, Mark

Born Methyr Tydfil 29.11.70. Ht 5 7
Wt 11 01
Defender. From Trainee.

Season	Club	Apps	Goals
1989–90	Luton T	—	—

PENDER, John

Born Luton 19.11.63. Ht 6 0 Wt 12 03
Defender. From Apprentice. Eire Youth, Under-21.

Season	Club	Apps	Goals
1981–82	Wolverhampton W	8	—
1982–83		39	1
1983–84		34	1
1984–85		36	1
1985–86	Charlton Ath	38	—
1986–87		1	—
1987–88		2	—
1987–88	Bristol C	28	2
1988–89		45	1
1989–90		10	—

PENNEY, David

Born Wakefield 17.8.64. Ht 5 8 Wt 10 7
Forward. From Pontefract.

Season	Club	Apps	Goals
1985–86	Derby Co	—	—
1986–87		1	—
1987–88		9	—
1988–89		9	–
1989–90	Oxford U	29	2

PENNEY, Steve

Born Ballymena 16.1.64. Ht 5 8
Wt 10 07
Midfield. From Ballymena U. Northern Ireland 17 full caps.

Season	Club	Apps	Goals
1983–84	Brighton	25	1
1984–85		26	4
1985–86		37	3
1986–87		27	3
1987–88		13	3
1988–89		10	1
1989–90		—	—

PENNOCK, Adrian

Born Ipswich 27.3.71. Ht 6 0 Wt 12 04
Defender. From Trainee.

Season	Club	Apps	Goals
1989–90	Norwich C	1	—

PENNYFATHER, Glenn

Born Billericay 11.2.63. Ht 5 8 Wt 11 08
Midfield. From Apprentice.

Season	Club	Apps	Goals
1980–81	Southend U	1	—
1981–82		33	4
1982–83		34	1
1983–84		33	4
1984–85		41	7
1985–86		41	7
1986–87		38	10
1987–88		17	3
1987–88	Crystal Palace	19	1
1988–89		15	—
1989–90		—	—
1989–90	Ipswich T	8	1

PENRICE, Gary

Born Bristol 23.3.64. Ht 5 8 Wt 10 06
Forward. From Bristol C. Apprentice.

Season	Club	Apps	Goals
1984–85	Bristol R	5	1
1985–86		39	5
1986–87		43	7
1987–88		46	18

Season	Club	League Appearances/Goals	
1988–89		43	20
1989–90		12	3
1989–90	Watford	29	13

PEPPER, Nigel

Born Rotherham 25.4.68. Ht 5 10
Wt 11 05
Midfield. From Apprentice.

Season	Club	Apps	Goals
1985–86	Rotherham U	7	—
1986–87		2	—
1987–88		15	—
1988–89		2	—
1989–90		19	1

PERKS, Steve

Born Bridgnorth 19.4.63. Ht 6 0
Wt 12 02
Goalkeeper. From Apprentice.

Season	Club	Apps	Goals
1980–81	Shrewsbury T	—	—
1981–82		—	—
1982–83		—	—
1983–84		—	—
1984–85		23	—
1985–86		42	—
1986–87		36	—
1987–88		42	—
1988–89		22	—
1989–90		46	—

PERRY, Jason

Born Newport 2.4.70. Ht 5 11 Wt 10 04
Defender. Wales Under-21.

Season	Club	Apps	Goals
1986–87	Cardiff C	1	—
1987–88		3	—
1988–89		—	—
1989–90		36	—

PERRYMAN, Steve

Born Ealing 21.12.51. Ht 5 8 Wt 10 07
Defender. From Apprentice. England Schools, Youth, Under-23, 1 full cap.

Season	Club	Apps	Goals
1968–69	Tottenham H	—	—
1969–70		23	1
1970–71		42	3
1971–72		39	1
1972–73		41	2
1973–74		39	1
1974–75		42	6
1975–76		40	6
1976–77		42	1
1977–78		42	1
1978–79		42	1
1979–80		40	1
1980–81		42	2
1981–82		42	1
1982–83		33	1
1983–84		41	1
1984–85		42	1
1985–86		23	1
1985–86	Oxford U	9	—
1986–87		8	—
1986–87	Brentford	24	—
1987–88		21	—
1988–89		5	—
1989–90		3	—

PETERS, Gary

Born Carshalton 3.8.54. Ht 5 11
Wt 11 12
Defender. From Aldershot Apprentice and Guildford C.

Season	Club	Apps	Goals
1975–76	Reading	30	2
1976–77		35	2
1977–78		46	2
1978–79		45	1
1979–80	Fulham	29	—
1980–81		34	2
1981–82		1	—
1982–83	Wimbledon	46	4
1983–84		37	3
1984–85	Aldershot	17	1
1984–85	Reading	18	—
1985–86		41	2
1986–87		25	1
1987–88		16	1
1988–89	Fulham	9	2
1989–90		2	—

PETERS, Rob

Born Kensington 18.5.71. Ht 5 8
Wt 11 02
Defender. From Trainee.

Season	Club	League Appearances/Goals	
1989–90	Brentford	2	—

PETTERSON, Andy

Born Freemantle 26.9.69. Ht 6 1
Wt 14 12
Goalkeeper.

Season	Club	Apps	Goals
1988–89	Luton T	—	—
1988–89	*Swindon T*	—	—
1989–90	Luton T	—	—
1989–90	*Swindon T*	—	—

PEYTON, Gerry

Born Birmingham 20.5.56. Ht 6 2
Wt 13 09
Goalkeeper. From Atherstone T. Eire 28 full caps.

Season	Club	Apps	Goals
1975–76	Burnley	20	—
1976–77		10	—
1976–77	Fulham	23	—
1977–78		42	—
1978–79		40	—
1979–80		31	—
1980–81		28	—
1981–82		44	—
1982–83		42	—
1983–84		27	—
1983–84	*Southend U*	10	—
1984–85	Fulham	32	—
1985–86		36	—
1986–87	Bournemouth	46	—
1987–88		42	—
1988–89		39	—
1989–90		39	—

PHELAN, Mike

Born Nelson 24.9.62. Ht 5 11 Wt 11 01
Defender. From Apprentice. England 1 full cap.

Season	Club	Apps	Goals
1980–81	Burnley	16	2
1981–82		23	1
1982–83		42	3
1983–84		44	2
1984–85		43	1
1985–86	Norwich C	42	3
1986–87		40	4
1987–88		37	—
1988–89		37	2
1989–90	Manchester U	38	1

PHELAN, Terry

Born Manchester 16.3.67. Ht 5 8
Wt 10 00
Defender. Eire Youth, B, Under-21, Under-23.

Season	Club	Apps	Goals
1984–85	Leeds U	—	—
1985–86		14	—
1986–87	Swansea C	45	—
1987–88	Wimbledon	30	—
1988–89		29	—
1989–90		34	—

PHILLIBEN, John

Born Stirling 14.3.64. Ht 5 10 Wt 11 00
Defender. From Gairdoch U. Scotland Youth.

Season	Club	Apps	Goals
1980–81	Stirling A	15	—
1981–82		37	1
1982–83		34	—
1983–84		23	—
1983–84	Doncaster R	12	—
1984–85		36	1
1985–86		22	—
1985–86	*Cambridge U*	6	—
1986–87	Doncaster R	1	—
1986–87	Motherwell	37	—
1987–88		35	2
1988–89		19	—
1989–90		24	—

PHILLIPS, David

Born Wegberg 29.7.63. Ht 5 10
Wt 11 02
Midfield. From Apprentice. Wales Under-21, 27 full caps.

Season	Club	Apps	Goals
1981–82	Plymouth Arg	8	1
1982–83		23	8
1983–84		42	6
1984–85	Manchester C	42	12
1985–86		39	1
1986–87	Coventry C	39	4
1987–88		35	2

Season	Club	League Appearances/Goals	
1988–89		26	2
1989–90	Norwich C	38	4

PHILLIPS, Gary

Born St. Albans 20.9.61. Ht 6 0 Wt 13 10
Goalkeeper. England Schools.

Season	Club		
1979–80	WBA	—	—
1980–81		—	—
From Barnet			
1984–85	Brentford	21	—
1985–86		43	—
1986–87		44	—
1987–88		35	—
1988–89		—	—
1988–89	Reading	24	—
1989–90		—	—
1989–90	*Hereford U*	6	—

PHILLIPS, Ian

Born Edinburgh 23.4.59. Ht 5 9 Wt 11 12
Defender. From Ipswich T Apprentice.

Season	Club		
1977–78	Mansfield T	18	—
1978–79		5	—
1979–80	Peterborough U	39	1
1980–81		41	—
1981–82		17	2
1982–83	Northampton T	42	1
1983–84		—	—
1983–84	Colchester U	43	5
1984–85		37	1
1985–86		37	2
1986–87		33	2
1987–88	Aldershot	32	—
1988–89		30	—
1989–90		44	2

PHILLIPS, Jimmy

Born Bolton 8.2.66. Ht 6 0 Wt 12 0
Defender. From Apprentice.

Season	Club		
1983–84	Bolton W	1	—
1984–85		40	1
1985–86		33	1
1986–87		34	—
1986–87	Rangers	6	—
1987–88		19	—
1988–89	Oxford U	45	5
1989–90		34	3
1989–90	Middlesbrough	12	—

PHILLIPS, Les

Born Lambeth 7.1.63. Ht 5 8 Wt 10 06
Midfield. From Apprentice.

Season	Club		
1980–81	Birmingham C	—	—
1981–82		11	1
1982–83		13	2
1983–84		20	—
1983–84	Oxford U	6	—
1984–85		3	—
1985–86		28	2
1986–87		35	—
1987–88		30	4
1988–89		26	2
1989–90		8	—

PHILLIPS, Stewart

Born Halifax 30.12.61. Ht 6 0 Wt 11 07
Forward. From Amateur.

Season	Club		
1977–78	Hereford U	1	—
1978–79		8	—
1979–80		11	2
1980–81		8	1
1981–82		43	12
1982–83		41	13
1983–84		46	17
1984–85		46	19
1985–86		20	5
1986–87		39	11
1987–88		30	3
1987–88	WBA	10	2
1988–89		5	2
1988–89	Swansea C	6	—
1989–90		14	1

PHILLIPS, Wayne

Born Bangor 15.12.70.
Defender. From Trainee.

Season	Club	League Appearances/Goals	
1989–90	Wrexham	5	—

PHILLISKIRK, Tony

Born Sunderland 10.2.65. Ht 6 1 Wt 12 02
Forward. From Amateur. England Schools.

Season	Club	Apps	Goals
1983–84	Sheffield U	21	8
1984–85		23	2
1985–86		4	—
1986–87		6	1
1986–87	*Rotherham U*	6	1
1987–88	Sheffield U	26	9
1988–89	Oldham Ath	10	1
1988–89	Preston NE	14	6
1989–90	Bolton W	45	18

PHILPOTT, Lee

Born Barnet 21.2.70
Midfield. From Trainee.

Season	Club	Apps	Goals
1987–88	Peterborough U	1	—
1988–89		3	—
1989–90	Cambridge U	42	5

PICKARD, Owen

Born Barnstaple 18.11.69 Ht 5 10 Wt 11 03
Forward. From Trainee.

Season	Club	Apps	Goals
1988–89	Plymouth Arg	2	—
1989–90		5	—

PICKERING, Ally

Born Manchester 22.6.67. Ht 5 9 Wt 10 08
Defender.

Season	Club	Apps	Goals
1989–90	Rotherham U	10	—

PICKERING, Nick

Born Newcastle 4.8.63. Ht 6 0 Wt 11 10
Midfield. From Apprentice. England Youth, Under-21, 1 full cap.

Season	Club	Apps	Goals
1981–82	Sunderland	37	3
1982–83		39	7
1983–84		42	1
1984–85		37	2
1985–86		24	5
1985–86	Coventry C	15	4
1986–87		36	5
1987–88		27	—
1988–89	Derby Co	8	—
1989–90		23	3

PIKE, Chris

Born Cardiff 19.10.61. Ht 6 2 Wt 13 07
Forward. From Barry T.

Season	Club	Apps	Goals
1984–85	Fulham	—	—
1985–86		26	4
1986–87		13	—
1986–87	*Cardiff C*	6	2
1987–88	Fulham	3	—
1988–89		—	—
1989–90	Cardiff C	41	18

PIKE, Geoff

Born Clapton 28.9.56. Ht 5 6 Wt 11 04
Midfield. From Apprentice.

Season	Club	Apps	Goals
1975–76	West Ham U	3	—
1976–77		20	6
1977–78		28	2
1978–79		14	2
1979–80		31	4
1980–81		42	6
1981–82		34	2
1982–83		40	6
1983–84		28	2
1984–85		30	2
1985–86		10	—
1986–87		11	—
1987–88	Notts Co	46	14
1988–89		36	3
1989–90		—	—
1989–90	Leyton Orient	14	—

PIKE, Martin

Born South Shields 21.10.64. Ht 5 11 Wt 11 07
Defender. From Apprentice.

Season	Club	Apps	Goals
1982–83	WBA	—	—
1983–84	Peterborough U	35	2
1984–85		45	4

Season | Club | League Appearances/Goals

Season | Club | League Appearances/Goals

Season	Club	Apps	Goals
1985–86		46	2
1986–87	Sheffield U	42	—
1987–88		39	—
1988–89		45	5
1989–90		3	—
1989–90	*Tranmere R*	2	—
1989–90	*Bolton W*	5	1
1989–90	Fulham	20	2

PILLING, Andy

Born Wigan 30.6.69. Ht 5 10 Wt 11 04
Midfield. From Trainee.

Season	Club	Apps	Goals
1985–86	Preston NE	1	—
1986–87		—	—
1987–88	Wigan Ath	20	3
1988–89		39	2
1989–90		26	6

PITCHER, Darren

Born London 12.10.69. Ht 5 9 Wt 12 02
Defender. From Trainee.

Season	Club	Apps	Goals
1987–88	Charlton Ath	—	—
1988–89		—	—
1988–89	*Galway*	—	—
1989–90	Charlton Ath	—	—

PITTMAN, Steve

Born North Carolina 18.7.67 Ht 5 10
Wt 11 07
Defender. From Broxburn J.

Season	Club	Apps	Goals
1986–87	East Fife	11	—
1987–88		32	2
1988–89		25	8
1988–89	Shrewsbury T	12	—
1989–90		20	2
1989–90	*Dunfermline Ath*	—	—

PLACE, Brendan

Born Ireland 13.12.65.
Defender. From Athlone T.

Season	Club	Apps	Goals
1989–90	Gillingham	4	—

PLACE, Mark

Born Mansfield 16.11.69 Ht 5 11
Wt 10 06
Defender. From Trainee.

Season	Club	Apps	Goals
1988–89	Mansfield T	14	—
1989–90		1	—

PLASKETT, Steve

Born Newcastle 24.4.71
Defender. From Trainee.

Season	Club	Apps	Goals
1988–89	Hartlepool U	12	—
1989–90		8	—

PLATNAUER, Nicky

Born Leicester 10.6.61. Ht 5 11
Wt 12 06
Defender. From Northampton T Amateur and Bedford T.

Season	Club	Apps	Goals
1982–83	Bristol R	24	7
1983–84	Coventry C	34	6
1984–85		10	—
1984–85	Birmingham C	11	1
1985–86		17	1
1985–86	*Reading*	7	—
1986–87	Cardiff C	38	3
1987–88		38	1
1988–89		39	2
1989–90	Notts Co	44	—

PLATT, David

Born Chadderton 10.6.66. Ht 5 10
Wt 11 12
Forward. From Chadderton. England B, Under-21, 11 full caps.

Season	Club	Apps	Goals
1984–85	Manchester U	—	—
1984–85	Crewe Alex	22	5
1985–86		43	8
1986–87		43	23
1987–88		26	19
1987–88	Aston Villa	11	5
1988–89		38	7
1989–90		37	19

PLUMMER, Calvin

Born Nottingham 14.2.63. Ht 5 8
Wt 11 03
Forward. From Apprentice.

Season	Club	Apps	Goals
1980–81	Nottingham F	—	—

Season	Club	League Appearances/Goals	
1981–82	....	9	2
1982–83	....	3	—
1982–83	Chesterfield.............	28	7
1983–84	Derby Co................	27	3
1983–84	Barnsley	2	1
1984–85	....	26	2
1985–86	....	23	3
1986–87	....	3	—
1986–87	Nottingham F	—	—
1987–88	....	8	2
1987–88	*Derry C*	—	—
1988–89	Nottingham F	—	—
1988–89	Plymouth Arg	23	1
1989–90	Chesterfield.............	44	8

POINTON, Neil

Born Church Warsop 28.11.64. Ht 5 10 Wt 11 00
Defender. From Apprentice.

Season	Club	Apps	Goals
1981–82	Scunthorpe U	5	—
1982–83	....	46	1
1983–84	....	45	1
1984–85	....	46	—
1985–86	....	17	—
1985–86	Everton	15	—
1986–87	....	12	1
1987–88	....	33	3
1988–89	....	23	—
1989–90	....	19	1

POLLARD, John

Born Chelmsford 17.11.71 Ht 5 10 Wt 12 07
Forward. From Trainee.

Season	Club	Apps	Goals
1988–89	Colchester U	2	1
1989–90	....	7	—

POLSTON, Andy

Born Walthamstow 26.7.70. Ht 5 10 Wt 11 00
Defender. From Trainee.

Season	Club	Apps	Goals
1988–89	Tottenham H...........	—	—
1989–90	....	1	—
1989–90	*Cambridge U*	3	—

POLSTON, John

Born London 10.6.68. Ht 5 11 Wt 11 03
Defender. From Apprentice. England Youth.

Season	Club	Apps	Goals
1985–86	Tottenham H...........	—	—
1986–87	....	6	—
1987–88	....	2	—
1988–89	....	3	—
1989–90	....	13	1

POOLE, Kevin

Born Bromsgrove 21.7.63. Ht 5 10 Wt 11 10
Goalkeeper. From Apprentice.

Season	Club	Apps	Goals
1981–82	Aston Villa.............	—	—
1982–83	....	—	—
1983–84	....	—	—
1984–85	....	7	—
1984–85	*Northampton T*	3	—
1985–86	Aston Villa.............	11	—
1986–87	....	10	—
1987–88	Middlesbrough.........	1	—
1988–89	....	12	—
1989–90	....	21	—

PORTER, Andy

Born Manchester 17.9.68. Ht 5 9 Wt 11 02
Midfield. From Trainee.

Season	Club	Apps	Goals
1986–87	Port Vale	1	—
1987–88	....	6	—
1988–89	....	14	1
1989–90	....	36	1

PORTER, Gary

Born Sunderland 6.3.66. Ht 5 6 Wt 10 01
Midfield. From Apprentice. England Youth, Under-21.

Season	Club	Apps	Goals
1983–84	Watford.................	2	—
1984–85	....	9	—
1985–86	....	8	1

Season	Club	League Appearances/Goals	
1986–87		26	4
1987–88		40	3
1988–89		42	10
1989–90		32	4

POTTS, Steven

Born Hartford (USA) 7.5.67. Ht 5 7 Wt 10 11
Defender. From Apprentice. England Youth.

1984–85	West Ham U	1	—
1985–86		1	—
1986–87		8	—
1987–88		8	—
1988–89		28	—
1989–90		32	—

POUTCH, Neil

Born Dublin 27.11.69. Ht 5 8 Wt 10 09
Defender. From Trainee. Eire Under-21

1987–88	Luton T	—	—
1988–89		—	—
1988–89		1	—
1989–90	*Leicester C*	—	—

POWELL, Chris

Born Lambeth 8.9.69. Ht 5 8 Wt 10 08
Defender.

1987–88	Crystal Palace	—	—
1988–89		3	—
1989–90		—	—
1989–90	*Aldershot*	11	—

POWELL, Cliff

Born Watford 21.2.68. Ht 6 0 Wt 12 00
Defender. From Apprentice.

1985–86	Watford	—	—
1986–87		—	—
1987–88		—	—
1987–88	*Hereford U*	7	—
1987–88	Sheffield U	6	—
1988–89		4	—
1988–89	Doncaster R	4	—
1989–90	Sheffield U	—	—
1989–90	*Cardiff C*	1	—

POWELL, Darryl

Born Lambeth 15.1.71 Ht 6 0 Wt 12 03
Forward. From Trainee.

1988–89	Portsmouth	3	—
1989–90		—	—

POWELL, Gary

Born Holylake 2.4.69. Ht 5 10 Wt 10 02
Forward. From Trainee.

1987–88	Everton	—	—
1988–89		—	—
1989–90		—	—

POWER, Lee

Born Lewisham 30.6.72. Ht 5 11 Wt 11 02
Forward. From Trainee.

1989–90	Norwich C	1	—

PRATLEY, Dick

Born Banbury 12.1.63. Ht 6 2 Wt 14 00
Defender. From Banbury U.

1983–84	Derby Co	2	—
1983–84	*Scunthorpe U*	10	—
1984–85	Derby Co	13	1
1985–86		7	—
1986–87		9	—
1987–88	Shrewsbury T	11	—
1988–89		28	—
1989–90		7	1

PREECE, Andy

Born Evesham 27.3.67
Midfield.

1988–89	Northampton T	1	—
From Worcester C.			
1989–90	Wrexham	7	1

PREECE, David

Born Bridgnorth 28.5.63. Ht 5 5 Wt 11 07

Midfield. From Apprentice. England B.

1980–81	Walsall	8	—
1981–82		8	—
1982–83		42	2
1983–84		41	3
1984–85		12	—
1984–85	Luton T	21	2
1985–86		41	2
1986–87		14	—
1987–88		13	—
1988–89		26	—
1989–90		32	1

PREECE, Roger

Born Much Wenlock 9.6.69. Ht 5 9
Wt 10 12
Midfield. From Coventry C Apprentice.

1986–87	Wrexham	7	2
1987–88		40	4
1988–89		31	5
1989–90		32	1

PRESSMAN, Kevin

Born Fareham 6.11.67. Ht 6 1 Wt 14 02
Goalkeeper. From Apprentice. England Schools, Youth, Under-21.

1985–86	Sheffield W	—	—
1986–87		—	—
1987–88		11	—
1988–89		9	—
1989–90		15	—

PRESTON, Allan

Born Edinburgh 16.8.68. Ht 5 10
Wt 10 01
Midfield. From Hutchison Vale BC.

1985–86	Dundee U	—	—
1986–87		—	—
1987–88		2	—
1988–89		9	1
1989–90		8	—

PRICE, Chris

Born Hereford 30.3.60. Ht 5 7 Wt 10 02
Defender. From Apprentice. England Youth.

1976–77	Hereford U	2	—
1977–78		13	—
1978–79		29	—
1979–80		42	—
1980–81		42	2
1981–82		41	10
1982–83		42	5
1983–84		37	1
1984–85		41	5
1985–86		41	4
1986–87	Blackburn R	40	1
1987–88		43	10
1988–89	Aston Villa	36	—
1989–90		34	1

PRICE, Gareth

Born Swindon 21.2.70 Ht 5 9 Wt 10 02
Defender. From Trainee.

1988–89	Mansfield T	—	—
1989–90	Bury	1	—

PRIDAY, Mark

Born Knighton 16.10.71.
Goalkeeper. From Trainee.

1989–90	Hereford U	3	—

PRIEST, Philip

Born Warley 9.9.66. Ht 5 7 Wt 10 10
Midfield. From school. England Schools, Youth.

1983–84	Chelsea	—	—
1984–85		—	—
1985–86		—	—
1986–87		—	—
1986–87	*Blackpool*	1	—
1986–87	*Brentford*	5	1
1987–88	Shrewsbury T	21	2

Season	Club	League Appearances/Goals	
1988–89		28	1
1989–90		11	—

PRIESTLEY, Jason

Born Leeds 25.10.70. Ht 5 11 Wt 12 02
Goalkeeper. From Trainee.

Season	Club	Apps	Goals
1989–90	Carlisle U	—	—
1989–90	*Hartlepool U*	16	—

PRINDIVILLE, Steve

Born Harlow 26.12.68 Ht 5 8 Wt 10 11
Defender. From Apprentice.

Season	Club	Apps	Goals
1986–87	Leicester C	—	—
1987–88		1	—
1988–89	Chesterfield	43	1
1989–90	Mansfield T	22	—

PRIOR, Spencer

Born Rochford 22.4.71 Ht 6 3 Wt 12 10
Defender. From Trainee.

Season	Club	Apps	Goals
1988–89	Southend U	14	1
1989–90		15	1

PRITCHARD, Howard

Born Cardiff 18.10.58. Ht 5 10 Wt 12 00
Forward. From Apprentice. Wales Youth, 1 full cap.

Season	Club	Apps	Goals
1976–77	Bristol C	—	—
1977–78		—	—
1978–79		1	—
1979–80		16	—
1980–81		21	2
1981–82	Swindon T	28	1
1982–83		37	10
1983–84	Bristol C	46	10
1984–85		39	6
1985–86		34	6
1986–87	Gillingham	46	12
1987–88		42	8
1988–89	Walsall	41	6
1989–90		4	1
1989–90	Maidstone U	24	4

PROCTOR, Mark

Born Middlesbrough 30.1.61. Ht 5 10 Wt 11 13
Midfield. From Apprentice. England Youth, Under-21.

Season	Club	Apps	Goals
1978–79	Middlesbrough	33	9
1979–80		38	2
1980–81		38	1
1981–82	Nottingham F	37	1
1982–83		27	4
1982–83	*Sunderland*	5	—
1983–84	Sunderland	41	2
1984–85		17	2
1985–86		19	7
1986–87		31	8
1987–88		4	—
1987–88	Sheffield W	35	2
1988–89		24	2
1988–89	Middlesbrough	10	—
1989–90		45	4

PROUDLOCK, Paul

Born Hartlepool 25.10.65 Ht 5 9 Wt 11 09
Forward. From Local.

Season	Club	Apps	Goals
1984–85	Hartlepool U	14	—
1985–86		1	—
1986–87	Middlesbrough	3	1
1987–88		1	—
1988–89		1	—
1988–89	Carlisle U	10	3
1989–90		40	6

PUCKETT, David

Born Southampton 29.10.60. Ht 5 7 Wt 10 4
Forward. From Apprentice.

Season	Club	Apps	Goals
1978–79	Southampton	—	—
1979–80		—	—
1980–81		7	—
1981–82		17	3
1982–83		25	3

Season	Club	League Appearances/Goals	
1983–84		18	3
1983–84	*Nottingham F*	—	—
1984–85	Southampton	13	1
1985–86		15	4
1986–87	Bournemouth	19	10
1987–88		12	4
1987–88	*Stoke C*	7	—
1988–89	Bournemouth	4	—
1988–89	*Swansea C*	8	3
1988–89	Aldershot	21	11
1989–90		46	18

PUGH, Daral

Born Crynant 5.6.61. Ht 5 8 Wt 10 03
Midfield. From Apprentice. Wales Under-21.

Season	Club	Apps	Goals
1978–79	Doncaster R	21	1
1979–80		40	5
1980–81		42	3
1981–82		45	6
1982–83		6	—
1982–83	Huddersfield T	27	2
1983–84		29	4
1984–85		28	1
1985–86	Rotherham U	37	2
1986–87		46	3
1987–88		29	1
1987–88	*Cambridge U*	6	1
1988–89	Torquay U	29	—
1989–90		3	—

PUGH, David

Born Liverpool 19.9.64.
Midfield. From Runcorn.

Season	Club	Apps	Goals
1989–90	Chester C	35	3

PULIS, Tony

Born Newport 16.1.58. Ht 5 10
Wt 11 08
Midfield. From Apprentice.

Season	Club	Apps	Goals
1975–76	Bristol R	4	—
1976–77		9	—
1977–78		23	—
1978–79		7	—
1979–80		34	3
1980–81		8	—
From Happy Valley, Hong Kong			
1982–83	Bristol R	17	—
1983–84		28	2
1984–85	Newport C	37	—
1985–86		40	—
1986–87	Bournemouth	35	—
1987–88		29	3
1988–89		10	—
1989–90	Gillingham	16	—

PULLAN, Chris

Born Durham 14.12.67. Ht 5 8 Wt 10 12
Midfield.

Season	Club	Apps	Goals
1986–87	Watford	1	—
1987–88		4	—
1988–89		1	—
1988–89	*Halifax T*	5	1
1989–90	Watford	4	—

PURDIE, Jon

Born Corby 22.2.67. Ht 5 9 Wt 11 12
Forward. From Apprentice. England Schools.

Season	Club	Apps	Goals
1984–85	Arsenal	—	—
1985–86	Wolverhampton W	42	6
1986–87		38	5
1987–88		9	1
1987–88	*Cambridge U*	7	2
1988–89	Oxford U	11	1
1988–89	Brentford	6	—
1989–90	Shrewsbury T	12	1

PURNELL, Philip

Born Bristol 16.9.64. Ht 5 6 Wt 9 08
Forward.

Season	Club	Apps	Goals
1985–86	Bristol R	11	2
1986–87		21	3
1987–88		41	8
1988–89		37	7
1989–90		22	2

PUTNEY, Trevor

Born Harold Hill 11.2.61. Ht 5 7
Wt 10 11

Season	Club	League Appearances/Goals	

Midfield. From Brentwood & W.

1980–81	Ipswich T	—	—
1981–82		—	—
1982–83		20	3
1983–84		35	2
1984–85		27	2
1985–86		21	1
1986–87	Norwich C	23	4
1987–88		26	1
1988–89		33	4
1989–90	Middlesbrough	25	—

PUTTNAM, David

Born Leicester 3.2.67
Midfield. From Leicester U.

1988–89	Leicester C	3	—
1989–90		4	—
1989–90	Lincoln C	23	1

QUAMINA, Mark

Born St Helier 25.11.69
Midfield. From Trainee.

1988–89	Wimbledon	1	—
1989–90		—	—

QUINN, Jimmy

Born Belfast 18.11.59. Ht 6 0 Wt 12 07
Forward. From Oswestry T. Northern Ireland 27 full caps.

1981–82	Swindon T	4	—
1982–83		13	3
1983–84		32	7
1984–85	Blackburn R	25	10
1985–86		31	4
1986–87		15	3
1986–87	Swindon T	22	9
1987–88		42	21
1988–89	Leicester C	31	6
1988–89	Bradford C	12	8
1989–90		23	6
1989–90	West Ham U	21	12

QUINN, Mick

Born Liverpool 2.5.62. Ht 5 10
Wt 13 04
Forward. From Derby Co Apprentice.

1979–80	Wigan Ath	4	1
1980–81		36	14
1981–82		29	4
1982–83	Stockport Co	39	24
1983–84		24	15
1983–84	Oldham Ath	14	5
1984–85		40	18
1985–86		26	11
1985–86	Portsmouth	11	6
1986–87		39	22
1987–88		32	8
1988–89		39	18
1989–90	Newcastle U	45	32

QUINN, Niall

Born Dublin 6.10.66. Ht 6 3 Wt 13 10
Forward. From Eire Youth, B, Under-21, Under-23, 18 full caps.

Season	Club	League Appearances/Goals	
1983–84	Arsenal	—	—
1984–85		—	—
1985–86		12	1
1986–87		35	8
1987–88		11	2
1988–89		3	1
1989–90		6	2
1989–90	Manchester C	9	4

QUOW, Trevor

Born Peterborough 28.9.60. Ht 5 8
Wt 11 07
Midfield. From Apprentice.

Season	Club	League Appearances/Goals	
1978–79	Peterborough U	8	—
1979–80		29	3
1980–81		44	4
1981–82		10	1
1982–83		18	1
1983–84		28	4
1984–85		36	1
1985–86		30	3
1986–87	Gillingham	19	1
1987–88		40	1
1988–89		20	1
1988–89	Northampton T	18	1
1989–90		30	1

RADFORD, Dean

Born London 14.11.70. Ht 5 11
Wt 11 05
Defender. From Trainee.

Season	Club	League Appearances/Goals	
1988–89	Southampton	—	—
1989–90		—	—

RADFORD, Mark

Born Leicester 20.12.68. Ht 6 1
Wt 11 08
Midfield. From Trainee.

Season	Club	League Appearances/Goals	
1987–88	Colchester U	14	—
1988–89		30	1
1989–90		20	4

RAE, Gordon

Born Edinburgh 3.5.58. Ht 6 0 Wt 13 05
Defender. From Whitehill Welfare.

Season	Club	League Appearances/Goals	
1977–78	Hibernian	2	1
1978–79		27	7
1979–80		33	4
1980–81		34	13
1981–82		29	11
1982–83		31	6
1983–84		16	—
1984–85		34	—
1985–86		32	2
1986–87		35	2
1987–88		40	—
1988–89		32	1
1989–90		2	—

RAFFELL, Steve

Born Blyth 27.4.70 Ht 5 11 Wt 11 02
Defender. From Trainee.

Season	Club	League Appearances/Goals	
1987–88	Doncaster R	14	—
1988–89		13	—
1989–90		27	—

RAFFERTY, Stuart

Born Port Glasgow 6.3.61. Ht 5 10
Wt 11 00
Midfield. From Port Glasgow. Scotland Youth.

Season	Club	Apps	Goals
1978–79	Motherwell	5	—
1979–80		7	2
1980–81		5	2
1981–82		13	5
1982–83		33	4
1983–84		26	4
1984–85	Dundee	36	4
1985–86		29	3
1986–87		36	4
1987–88		30	4
1988–89		32	1
1989–90	Dunfermline Ath	32	1

RAMAGE, Craig

Born Derby 30.3.70 Ht 5 9 Wt 11 08
Forward. From Trainee.

Season	Club	Apps	Goals
1988–89	Derby Co	—	—
1988–89	*Wigan Ath*	10	2
1989–90	Derby Co	12	1

RAMSEY, Paul

Born Londonderry 3.9.62. Ht 5 11
Wt 13 00
Defender. From Apprentice. Northern Ireland 14 full caps.

Season	Club	Apps	Goals
1970–80	Leicester C	—	—
1980–81		3	—
1981–82		10	—
1982–83		40	1
1983–84		33	1
1984–85		39	—
1985–86		13	1
1986–87		29	6
1987–88		42	1
1988–89		22	—
1989–90		35	3

RANDALL, Adrian

Born Amesbury 10.11.68. Ht 5 11
Wt 10 11
Forward. From Apprentice. England Youth.

Season	Club	Apps	Goals
1985–86	Bournemouth	2	—
1986–87		—	—
1987–88		1	—
1988–89		—	—
1988–89	Aldershot	37	2
1989–90		34	2

RANKINE, Mark

Born Doncaster 30.9.69 Ht 5 10
Wt 11 08
Midfield. From Trainee.

Season	Club	Apps	Goals
1987–88	Doncaster R	18	2
1988–89		46	11
1989–90		36	2

RANSON, Ray

Born St. Helens 12.6.60. Ht 5 9
Wt 11 12
Defender. From Apprentice. England Schools, Youth, Under-21.

Season	Club	Apps	Goals
1978–79	Manchester C	8	—
1979–80		40	—
1980–81		33	1
1981–82		36	—
1982–83		40	—
1983–84		26	—
1984–85		—	—
1984–85	Birmingham C	28	—
1985–86		37	—
1986–87		17	—
1987–88		38	—
1988–89		17	—
1988–89	Newcastle U	14	1
1989–90		33	—

RATCLIFFE, Kevin

Born Mancot 12.11.60. Ht 5 11
Wt 12 07
Defender. From Apprentice. Wales Schools, Youth, Under-21, 48 full caps.

Season	Club	Apps	Goals
1978–79	Everton	—	—
1979–80		2	—
1980–81		21	—
1981–82		25	—
1982–83		29	1
1983–84		38	—
1984–85		40	—
1985–86		39	1
1986–87		42	—
1987–88		24	—

Season	Club	League Appearances/Goals	
1988–89		30	—
1989–90		24	—

RATCLIFFE, Simon

Born Davyhulme 8.2.67. Ht 5 11
Wt 11 09
Defender. From Apprentice. England Schools, Youth.

Season	Club	Apps	Goals
1984–85	Manchester U	—	—
1985–86		—	—
1986–87		—	—
1987–88	Norwich C	9	—
1988–89		—	—
1988–89	Brentford	9	1
1989–90		35	2

RATHBONE, Mike

Born Birmingham 6.11.58. Ht 5 10
Wt 11 12
Defender. From Apprentice. England Youth.

Season	Club	Apps	Goals
1976–77	Birmingham C	16	—
1977–78		2	—
1978–79		2	—
1978–79	Blackburn R	15	—
1979–80		28	1
1980–81		27	—
1981–82		41	1
1982–83		42	—
1983–84		11	—
1984–85		42	—
1985–86		42	—
1986–87		25	—
1987–88	Preston NE	36	1
1988–89		34	2
1989–90		8	—

RAVEN, Paul

Born Salisbury 28.7.70
Defender. From Schoolboy.

Season	Club	Apps	Goals
1987–88	Doncaster R	17	3
1988–89		35	1

Season	Club	League Appearances/Goals	
1988–89	WBA	3	—
1989–90		7	—

RAYNOR, Paul

Born Nottingham 29.4.66. Ht 5 11
Wt 11 12
Forward. From Apprentice.

Season	Club	Apps	Goals
1983–84	Nottingham F	—	—
1984–85		3	—
1984–85	*Bristol R*	8	—
1985–86	Huddersfield T	30	5
1986–87		20	4
1986–87	Swansea C	12	1
1987–88		44	8
1988–89		26	5
1988–89	*Wrexham*	6	—
1989–90	Swansea C	40	6

RECK, Sean

Born Oxford 5.5.67. Ht 5 10 Wt 12 07
Midfield. From Apprentice.

Season	Club	Apps	Goals
1984–85	Oxford U	—	—
1985–86		—	—
1985–86	*Newport Co*	15	—
1985–86	*Reading*	1	—
1986–87	Oxford U	6	—
1987–88		2	—
1988–89		6	—
1989–90	Wrexham	32	1

REDDISH, Shane

Born Bolsover 5.5.71.
Midfield. From Mansfield T Trainee and Doncaster R Trainee.

Season	Club	Apps	Goals
1989–90	Doncaster R	1	—

REDFEARN, Neil

Born Dewsbury 20.6.65. Ht 5 10
Wt 12 09
Midfield. From Nottingham F Apprentice.

Season	Club	Apps	Goals
1982–83	Bolton W	10	—
1983–84		25	1
1983–84	*Lincoln C*	10	1
1984–85	Lincoln C	45	4
1985–86		45	8

Season	Club	League Appearances/Goals	
1986–87	Doncaster R	46	14
1987–88	Crystal Palace	42	8
1988–89		15	2
1988–89	Watford	12	2
1989–90		12	1
1989–90	Oldham Ath	17	2

REDFERN, David

Born Sheffield 8.11.62. Ht 6 2 Wt 13 12
Goalkeeper. From School.

Season	Club	Apps	Goals
1981–82	Sheffield W	—	—
1982–83		—	—
1983–84		—	—
1984–85		—	—
1984–85	*Doncaster R*	—	—
1984–85	*Rochdale*	19	—
1985–86	Rochdale	46	—
1986–87		22	—
1987–88		—	—
From Gainsborough T.			
1989–90	Stockport Co	11	—

REDFORD, Ian

Born Perth 5.4.60. Ht 5 11 Wt 11 10
Midfield. From Errol Rovers. Scotland Youth, Under-21.

Season	Club	Apps	Goals
1976–77	Dundee	1	—
1977–78		34	10
1978–79		37	15
1979–80		13	9
1979–80	Rangers	13	—
1980–81		35	9
1981–82		32	2
1982–83		34	3
1983–84		32	4
1984–85		26	5
1985–86	Dundee U	30	4
1986–87		37	8
1987–88		25	6
1988–89		9	2
1988–89	Ipswich T	24	2
1989–90		18	2

REDKNAPP, Jamie

Born Barton on Sea 25.6.73. Ht 5 11
Wt 11 08
Midfield. From Tottenham H Schoolboy, Bournemouth Trainee.

Season	Club	Apps	Goals
1989–90	Bournemouth	4	—

REDMOND, Steven

Born Liverpool 2.11.67. Ht 5 11
Wt 12 13
Defender. From Apprentice. England Youth, Under-21.

Season	Club	Apps	Goals
1984–85	Manchester C	—	—
1985–86		9	—
1986–87		30	2
1987–88		44	—
1988–89		46	1
1989–90		38	—

REECE, Andy

Born Shrewsbury 5.9.62. Ht 5 11
Wt 12 04
Midfield. From Walsall, Worcester C, Willenhall.

Season	Club	Apps	Goals
1987–88	Bristol R	40	1
1988–89		42	7
1989–90		43	2

REECE, Paul

Born Nottingham 16.7.68 Ht 5 11
Wt 12 07
Goalkeeper. From Kettering.

Season	Club	Apps	Goals
1988–89	Grimsby T	14	—
1989–90		15	—

REES, Jason

Born Pontypridd 22.12.69. Ht 5 5
Wt 9 08
Midfield. From Trainee. Wales Under-21.

Season	Club	Apps	Goals
1988–89	Luton T	—	—
1989–90		14	—

REES, Mark

Born Smethwick 13.10.61. Ht 5 10
Wt 11 10
Forward. From Apprentice. England Schools.

Season	Club	League Appearances/Goals	
1978–79	Walsall	10	—
1979–80		18	3
1980–81		25	6
1981–82		39	6
1982–83		18	3
1983–84		33	6
1984–85		27	9
1985–86		19	2
1986–87		13	—
1986–87	*Rochdale*	3	—
1987–88	Walsall	3	—
1988–89		25	1
1989–90		7	1

REES, Mel

Born Cardiff 25.1.67. Ht 6 3 Wt 13 05
Goalkeeper. From Plymouth Arg Schoolboy and Trainee. Wales Youth.

1984–85	Cardiff C	1	—
1985–86		9	—
1986–87		21	—
1987–88	Watford	3	—
1988–89		—	—
1989–90		—	—
1989–90	*Crewe Alex*	6	—
1989–90	*Southampton*	—	—
1989–90	*Leyton Orient*	9	—

REES, Tony

Born Merthyr Tydfil 1.8.64. Ht 5 9 Wt 11 08
Forward. From Apprentice. Wales Youth, Under-21, 1 full cap.

1982–83	Aston Villa	—	—
1983–84	Birmingham C	25	2
1984–85		9	2
1985–86		8	—
1985–86	*Peterborough U*	5	2
1985–86	*Shrewsbury T*	2	—
1986–87	Birmingham C	30	4
1987–88		23	4
1987–88	Barnsley	14	2
1988–89		17	1
1989–90	Grimsby T	35	13

REEVES, Alan

Born Birkenhead 19.11.67
Defender.

1988–89	Norwich C	—	—
1988–89	*Gillingham*	18	—
1989–90	Chester C	30	2

REEVES, David

Born Birkenhead 19.11.67. Ht 6 0 Wt 11 05
Forward. From Heswall.

1986–87	Sheffield W	—	—
1986–87	*Scunthorpe U*	4	2
1987–88	Sheffield W	—	—
1987–88	*Scunthorpe U*	6	4
1987–88	*Burnley*	16	8
1988–89	Sheffield W	17	2
1989–90	Bolton W	41	10

REGIS, Cyrille

Born French Guyana 9.2.58. Ht 6 0 Wt 13 5
Forward. From Moseley, Hayes. England Under-21, B, 5 full caps.

1977–78	WBA	34	10
1978–79		39	13
1979–80		26	8
1980–81		38	14
1981–82		37	17
1982–83		26	9
1983–84		30	10
1984–85		7	1
1984–85	Coventry C	31	5
1985–86		34	5
1986–87		40	12
1987–88		31	10
1988–89		34	7
1989–90		34	4

REHN, Stefan

Born Stockholm 22.9.66. Ht 5 10 Wt 10 10

Season	Club	League Appearances/Goals	

Midfield. From Djurgaarden. Sweden full caps.

1989–90	Everton	4	—

To IFK Gothenburg.

REID, Chris

Born Edinburgh 4.11.71. Ht 5 11 Wt 11 06
Goalkeeper. From Hutcheson Vale BC.

1989–90	Hibernian	2	—

REID, Mark

Born Kilwinning 15.9.61. Ht 5 8 Wt 11 5
Defender. From Celtic BC. Scotland Youth, Under-21.

1980–81	Celtic	22	—
1981–82		36	2
1982–83		26	1
1983–84		24	2
1984–85		16	—
1985–86	Charlton Ath	42	8
1986–87		42	—
1987–88		36	4
1988–89		36	1
1989–90		31	—

REID, Nicky

Born Ormston 30.10.60. Ht 5 10 Wt 12 00
Defender. From Apprentice. England Under-21.

1978–79	Manchester C	8	—
1979–80		23	—
1980–81		37	—
1981–82		36	—
1982–83		25	—
1983–84		19	2
1984–85		32	—
1985–86		30	—
1986–87		7	—
1987–88	Blackburn R	44	1
1988–89		37	1
1989–90		42	4

REID, Paul

Born Warley 19.1.68. Ht 5 8 Wt 10 08
Forward. From Apprentice.

1985–86	Leicester C	—	—
1986–87		6	—
1987–88		26	5
1988–89		45	6
1989–90		40	8

REID, Peter

Born Huyton 20.6.56. Ht 5 8 Wt 10 07
Midfield. From Apprentice. England Under-21, 13 full caps.

1974–75	Bolton W	27	—
1975–76		42	2
1976–77		42	5
1977–78		38	9
1978–79		14	—
1979–80		17	3
1980–81		18	2
1981–82		12	1
1982–83		15	1
1982–83	Everton	7	—
1983–84		35	2
1984–85		36	2
1985–86		15	1
1986–87		16	1
1987–88		32	1
1988–89		18	1
1988–89	QPR	14	1
1989–90		15	—
1989–90	Manchester C	18	1

REID, Shaun

Born Huyton 13.10.65. Ht 5 8 Wt 11 10
Midfield. Local.

1983–84	Rochdale	17	—
1984–85		21	1
1985–86		8	—
1985–86	*Preston NE*	3	—
1986–87	Rochdale	41	1
1987–88		28	—
1988–89		18	2

Season	Club	League Appearances/Goals	
1988–89	York C	24	2
1989–90		25	4

REID, Wesley

Born Lewisham 10.9.68. Ht 5 8
Wt 11 03
Midfield. From Trainee.

Season	Club	Apps	Goals
1986–87	Arsenal	—	—
1987–88	Millwall	—	—
1988–89		1	—
1989–90		5	—

REILLY, Mark

Born Bellshill 30.3.69. Ht 5 8 Wt 10 00
Defender. From Wishaw Jun.

Season	Club	Apps	Goals
1988–89	Motherwell	—	—
1989–90		4	—

RENNIE, David

Born Edinburgh 29.8.64. Ht 5 11
Wt 12 00
Defender. From Apprentice. Scotland Youth.

Season	Club	Apps	Goals
1982–83	Leicester C	—	—
1983–84		15	—
1984–85		3	1
1985–86		3	—
1985–86	Leeds U	16	2
1986–87		24	—
1987–88		28	2
1988–89		33	1
1989–90	Bristol C	45	4

RENNIE, Paul

Born Nantwich 26.10.71.
Defender. From Trainee.

Season	Club	Apps	Goals
1989–90	Crewe Alex	2	—

RESTARICK, Stephen

Born Barking 28.11.71.
Midfield. From Trainee.

Season	Club	Apps	Goals
1989–90	Colchester U	1	—

RHOADES-BROWN, Peter

Born Hampton 2.1.62. Ht 5 9 Wt 11 04
Forward. From Apprentice.

Season	Club	Apps	Goals
1979–80	Chelsea	4	—
1980–81		34	1
1981–82		27	1
1982–83		25	1
1983–84		6	1
1983–84	Oxford U	20	4
1984–85		31	4
1985–86		17	3
1986–87		6	—
1987–88		31	2
1988–89		7	—
1989–90		—	—

RHODES, Andy

Born Doncaster 23.8.64. Ht 6 1
Wt 13 06
Goalkeeper. From Apprentice.

Season	Club	Apps	Goals
1982–83	Barnsley	—	—
1983–84		31	—
1984–85		5	—
1985–86		—	—
1985–86	Doncaster R	30	—
1986–87		41	—
1987–88		35	—
1987–88	Oldham Ath	11	—
1988–89		27	—
1989–90		31	—

RICE, Brian

Born Glasgow 11.10.63. Ht 6 0
Wt 12 04
Midfield. From Whitburn Central.
Scotland Youth, Under-21.

Season	Club	Apps	Goals
1980–81	Hibernian	1	—
1981–82		1	—
1982–83		22	2
1983–84		25	5
1984–85		35	4
1985–86	Nottingham F	19	3
1986–87		3	1

Season	Club	League Appearances/Goals	
1987–88		30	2
1988–89		20	1
1988–89	*WBA*	3	—
1989–90	Nottingham F	18	2

RICHARDS, Carl

Born Jamaica 12.1.60. Ht 6 0 Wt 13 00
Forward. Dulwich H, Enfield.

Season	Club	Apps	Goals
1986–87	Bournemouth	43	11
1987–88		20	4
1988–89		8	—
1988–89	Birmingham C	19	2
1989–90	Peterborough U	20	5
1989–90	Blackpool	16	4

RICHARDS, Steve

Born Dundee 24.10.61. Ht 6 1 Wt 12 05
Defender. From Apprentice.

Season	Club	Apps	Goals
1979–80	Hull C	1	—
1980–81		25	1
1981–82		29	1
1982–83		3	—
From Gainsborough T.			
1984–85	York C	7	—
1985–86	Lincoln C	21	—
1985–86	Cambridge U	4	2
1986–87	Scarborough	—	—
1987–88		42	5
1988–89		42	1
1989–90		35	4

RICHARDSON, Barry

Born Willington Key 5.8.69. Ht 6 0
Wt 12 00
Goalkeeper. From Trainee.

Season	Club	Apps	Goals
1987–88	Sunderland	—	—
1988–89	Scunthorpe U	—	—
1989–90	Scarborough	24	—

RICHARDSON, Kevin

Born Newcastle 4.12.62. Ht 5 9
Wt 11 02
Midfield. From Apprentice.

Season	Club	Apps	Goals
1980–81	Everton	—	—
1981–82		18	2
1982–83		29	3
1983–84		28	4
1984–85		15	4
1985–86		18	3
1986–87		1	—
1986–87	Watford	39	2
1987–88	Arsenal	29	4
1988–89		34	1
1989–90		33	—

RICHARDSON, Lee

Born Halifax 12.3.69. Ht 5 11 Wt 11 00
Midfield.

Season	Club	Apps	Goals
1986–87	Halifax T	1	—
1987–88		30	1
1988–89		25	1
1988–89	Watford	9	—
1989–90		32	1

RICHARDSON, Nick

Born Halifax 11.4.67 Ht 6 0 Wt 12 07
Midfield. Local.

Season	Club	Apps	Goals
1988–89	Halifax T	7	—
1989–90		27	6

RICHARDSON, Neil

Born Sunderland 3.3.68. Ht 5 10
Wt 13 05
Defender.

Season	Club	Apps	Goals
1989–90	Rotherham U	2	—

RICHARDSON, Steve

Born Slough 11.2.62. Ht 5 5 Wt 10 03
Defender. From Apprentice.

Season	Club	Apps	Goals
1979–80	Southampton	—	—
1980–81		—	—
1981–82		—	—
1982–83	Reading	40	1
1983–84		34	—
1984–85		43	—
1985–86		32	—
1986–87		37	1
1987–88		27	—

Season	Club	League Appearances/Goals	
1988–89		39	—
1989–90		43	—

RIDEOUT, Paul

Born Bournemouth 14.8.64. Ht 5 11
Wt 12 01
Forward. From Apprentice. England Schools, Youth, Under-21.

Season	Club		
1980–81	Swindon T	16	4
1981–82		35	14
1982–83		44	20
1983–84	Aston Villa	25	5
1984–85		29	14
1985–86	Bari	28	6
1986–87		34	10
1987–88		37	7
1988–89	Southampton	24	6
1989–90		31	7

RILEY, David

Born Northampton 8.12.60. Ht 5 7
Wt 10 10
Forward. From Keyworth U.

Season	Club		
1983–84	Nottingham F	1	—
1984–85		10	2
1985–86		—	—
1986–87		1	—
1986–87	*Darlington*	6	2
1987–88	Nottingham F	—	—
1987–88	*Peterborough U*	12	2
1987–88	Port Vale	34	8
1988–89		40	3
1989–90		2	—
1989–90	Peterborough U	15	5

RIMMER, Neill

Born Liverpool 13.11.67. Ht 5 6
Wt 10 03
Midfield. From Apprentice. England Schools, Youth.

Season	Club		
1984–85	Everton	1	—
1985–86	Ipswich T	2	—
1986–87		1	—
1987–88		19	3

Season	Club	League Appearances/Goals	
1988–89	Wigan Ath	25	3
1989–90		38	1

RIMMER, Stuart

Born Southport 12.10.64. Ht 5 8
Wt 11 00
Forward. From Apprentice. England Youth.

Season	Club		
1981–82	Everton	2	—
1982–83		—	—
1983–84		1	—
1984–85		—	—
1984–85	Chester C	24	14
1985–86		18	16
1986–87		38	13
1987–88		34	24
1987–88	Watford	9	1
1988–89		1	—
1988–89	Notts Co	4	2
1988–89	Walsall	20	8
1989–90		41	10

RIPLEY, Stuart

Born Middlesbrough 20.11.67. Ht 5 11
Wt 12 05
Forward. From Apprentice. England Youth, Under-21.

Season	Club		
1984–85	Middlesbrough	1	—
1985–86		8	—
1985–86	*Bolton W*	5	1
1986–87	Middlesbrough	44	4
1987–88		43	8
1988–89		36	4
1989–90		39	1

RITCHIE, Andy

Born Manchester 28.11.60. Ht 5 10
Wt 11 11
Forward. From Apprentice. England Schools, Youth, Under-21.

Season	Club		
1977–78	Manchester U	4	—
1978–79		17	10
1979–80		8	3
1980–81		4	—
1980–81	Brighton	26	5
1981–82		39	13

Season	Club	League Appearances/Goals	
1982–83		24	5
1982–83	Leeds U	10	3
1983–84		38	7
1984–85		28	12
1985–86		29	11
1986–87		31	7
1987–88	Oldham Ath	36	19
1988–89		31	14
1989–90		38	15

RITCHIE, David

Born Newcastle 20.1.71. Ht 5 11
Wt 11 01
Forward. From Trainee.

Season	Club	League Appearances/Goals	
1989–90	Stoke C	—	—
1989–90	Stockport Co	1	—

RIX, Graham

Born Doncaster 23.10.57. Ht 5 9
Wt 11 0
Midfield. From Apprentice. England Under-21, 17 full caps.

Season	Club	League Appearances/Goals	
1974–75	Arsenal	—	—
1975–76		—	—
1976–77		7	1
1977–78		39	2
1978–79		39	3
1979–80		38	4
1980–81		35	5
1981–82		39	9
1982–83		36	6
1983–84		34	4
1984–85		18	2
1985–86		38	3
1986–87		18	2
1987–88		10	—
1987–88	*Brentford*	6	—

To Caen

ROAST, Jesse

Born Barking 16.3.64. Ht 6 1 Wt 12 07
Defender. From Walthamstow Avenue, Hornchurch, Dagenham, Brighton, Barking (1987)

Season	Club	League Appearances/Goals	
1989–90	Maidstone U	16	—

ROBERTS, Alan

Born Newcastle 8.12.64. Ht 5 9
Wt 10 00
Midfield. From Apprentice.

Season	Club	League Appearances/Goals	
1982–83	Middlesbrough	1	—
1983–84		7	1
1984–85		29	1
1985–86		1	—
1985–86	Darlington	38	5
1986–87		43	7
1987–88		38	7
1988–89	Sheffield U	29	2
1989–90		7	—
1989–90	Lincoln C	10	—

ROBERTS, Brian

Born Manchester 6.11.55. Ht 5 8
Wt 11 07
Defender. From Apprentice.

Season	Club	League Appearances/Goals	
1974–75	Coventry C	—	—
1974–75	*Hereford U*	5	—
1975–76	Coventry C	2	—
1976–77		12	—
1977–78		26	—
1978–79		17	—
1979–80		14	—
1980–81		42	—
1981–82		34	—
1982–83		38	1
1983–84		30	—
1983–84	Birmingham C	11	—
1984–85		41	—
1985–86		33	—
1986–87		24	—
1987–88		27	—
1988–89		41	—
1989–90		10	—

ROBERTS, Garreth

Born Hull 15.11.60. Ht 5 5 Wt 10 10
Midfield. From Apprentice. Wales Under-21.

Season	Club	League Appearances/Goals	
1978–79	Hull C	19	3
1979–80		44	2

Season	Club	League Appearances/Goals	
1980–81		20	3
1981–82		29	6
1982–83		44	6
1983–84		38	9
1984–85		29	3
1985–86		33	4
1986–87		35	5
1987–88		44	3
1988–89		35	3
1989–90		36	—

ROBERTS, Graham

Born Southampton 3.7.59. Ht 5 10
Wt 12 12
Defender. From Southampton, Sholing, Bournemouth, Portsmouth, Dorchester T and Weymouth. England B, 6 full caps.

Season	Club	Apps	Goals
1980–81	Tottenham H	24	—
1981–82		37	6
1982–83		24	2
1983–84		35	6
1984–85		40	7
1985–86		32	1
1986–87		17	1
1986–87	Rangers	18	2
1987–88		37	1
1988–89	Chelsea	46	15
1989–90		24	3

ROBERTS, Iwan

Born Bangor 26.6.68. Ht 6 3 Wt 12 06
Forward. Wales Youth, 1 full cap.

Season	Club	Apps	Goals
1985–86	Watford	4	—
1986–87		3	1
1987–88		25	2
1988–89		22	6
1989–90		9	—

ROBERTS, Jon

Born Llwynpia 30.12.68. Ht 6 0
Wt 12 05
Goalkeeper. From Trainee.

Season	Club	Apps	Goals
1987–88	Cardiff C	8	—
1988–89		1	—
1989–90		—	—

ROBERTS, Mark

Born Shrewsbury 20.7.71. Ht 5 8
Wt 10 10
Midfield. From Trainee.

Season	Club	Apps	Goals
1989–90	Shrewsbury T	—	—

ROBERTS, Paul

Born London 27.4.62. Ht 5 9 Wt 11 13
Defender. From Apprentice.

Season	Club	Apps	Goals
1978–79	Millwall	2	—
1979–80		27	—
1980–81		45	—
1981–82		41	—
1982–83		31	—
1983–84		—	—
1983–84	Brentford	34	—
1984–85		28	—
1985–86	Swindon T	27	—
1986–87	Southend U	38	—
1987–88	Aldershot	39	—
1988–89	Exeter C	3	—
1988–89	Southend U	23	—
1989–90		31	—

ROBERTS, Tony

Born Bangor 4.8.69. Ht 6 0
Goalkeeper. From Trainee.

Season	Club	Apps	Goals
1987–88	QPR	1	—
1988–89		—	—
1989–90		5	—

ROBERTSON, Alistair

Born Philipstown 9.9.52. Ht 5 9
Wt 12 04
Defender. From Apprentice. Scotland Schools, Youth.

Season	Club	Apps	Goals
1969–70	WBA	10	—
1970–71		4	—
1971–72		31	—
1972–73		36	1
1973–74		40	—
1974–75		21	1

Season	Club	League Appearances/Goals	
1975–76		42	1
1976–77		42	—
1977–78		42	1
1978–79		39	—
1979–80		38	1
1980–81		28	—
1981–82		33	1
1982–83		37	2
1983–84		6	—
1984–85		37	—
1985–86		20	—
1986–87	Wolverhampton W	31	—
1987–88		41	—
1988–89		30	—
1989–90		5	—

ROBERTSON, Alexander

Born Edinburgh 26.4.71 Ht 5 9
Wt 10 07
Midfield. From S Form.

Season	Club	Apps	Goals
1987–88	Rangers	—	—
1988–89		2	—
1989–90		1	—

ROBERTSON, Craig

Born Dunfermline 22.4.63. Ht 5 9
Wt 11 02
Midfield. From 'S' Form.

Season	Club	Apps	Goals
1979–80	Hearts	—	—
1980–81	Raith R	—	—
1981–82		11	—
1982–83		22	—
1983–84		38	3
1984–85		39	11
1985–86		25	2
1986–87		35	3
1987–88	Dunfermline Ath	42	13
1988–89		13	5
1988–89	Aberdeen	4	1
1989–90		22	2

ROBERTSON, David

Born Aberdeen 17.10.68. Ht 5 11
Wt 11 00
Defender. From Deeside BC. Scotland Under-21.

Season	Club	Apps	Goals
1986–87	Aberdeen	34	—
1987–88		23	—
1988–89		23	—
1989–90		20	1

ROBERTSON, Ian

Born Inverness 14.10.66. Ht 5 9
Wt 10 10
Midfield. 'S' Form. Scotland Youth.

Season	Club	Apps	Goals
1983–84	Aberdeen	—	—
1984–85		—	—
1985–86		4	—
1986–87		4	—
1987–88		—	—
1988–89		7	—
1989–90		5	—

ROBERTSON, Graeme

Born Dumfries 4.6.62. Ht 5 7 Wt 11 00
Defender. From Lochar Th.

Season	Club	Apps	Goals
1978–79	Queen of South	1	—
1979–80		4	1
1980–81		14	2
1981–82		26	1
1982–83		14	1
1983–84		34	8
1984–85		39	3
1985–86		39	1
1986–87		43	—
1987–88	Dunfermline Ath	17	—
1988–89		29	1
1989–90		17	2

ROBERTSON, Jimmy

Born Gateshead 24.11.69 Ht 5 7
Wt 10 08
Defender. From Trainee.

Season	Club	Apps	Goals
1987–88	Carlisle U	5	—
1988–89		7	—
1989–90		1	—

ROBERTSON, John

Born Edinburgh 2.10.64. Ht 5 7
Wt 11 06

Forward. From Edina Hibs. Scotland B, Under-21.

1980–81	Hearts	—	—
1981–82		1	—
1982–83		23	19
1983–84		35	15
1984–85		33	8
1985–86		35	20
1986–87		37	16
1987–88		39	26
1987–88	Newcastle U	—	—
1988–89		12	—
1988–89	Hearts	15	4
1989–90		32	17

ROBERTSON, Paul

Born Stockport 5.2.72. Ht 5 7 Wt 11 06
Defender. From York C Trainee.

1989–90	Stockport Co	9	—

ROBINS, Mark

Born Ashton-under-Lyme. 22.12.69.
Ht 5 7 Wt 10 01
Forward. From Apprentice. England Under-21.

1986–87	Manchester U	—	—
1987–88		—	—
1988–89		10	—
1989–90		17	7

ROBINSON, Colin

Born Birmingham 15.5.60. Ht 5 10
Wt 10 12
Forward. From Mile Oak Rovers.

1982–83	Shrewsbury T	12	3
1983–84		30	4
1984–85		42	14
1985–86		42	10
1986–87		41	9
1987–88		27	1
1987–88	Birmingham C	4	1
1988–89		33	5
1989–90	Hereford U	29	4

ROBINSON, David

Born Cleveland 14.1.65. Ht 6 0
Wt 12 03
Defender.

1983–84	Hartlepool U	7	—
1984–85		38	—
1985–86		21	1
1986–87	Halifax T	10	—
1987–88		32	—
1988–89		30	1
1989–90	Peterborough U	45	4

ROBINSON, David

Born Newcastle 27.11.69 Ht 6 0
Wt 13 02
Forward. From Trainee.

1988–89	Newcastle U	1	—
1989–90		1	—

ROBINSON, John

Born Bulawayo, Rhodesia 29.8.71.
Ht 5 10 Wt 11 02
Midfield. From Apprentice.

1989–90	Brighton	5	—

ROBINSON, Les

Born Mansfield 1.3.67. Ht 5 8 Wt 11 1
From Local.

1984–85	Mansfield T	6	—
1985–86		7	—
1986–87		2	—
1986–87	Stockport Co	30	1
1987–88		37	2
1987–88	Doncaster R	7	1
1988–89		43	3
1989–90		32	8
1989–90	Oxford U	1	—

ROBINSON, Liam

Born Bradford 29.12.65. Ht 5 7
Wt 11 05
Forward. From Nottingham F schoolboy.

Season	Club	League Appearances/Goals	
1983–84	Huddersfield T	5	1
1984–85		15	1
1985–86		1	—
1985–86	*Tranmere R*	4	3
1986–87	Bury	33	13
1987–88		43	19
1988–89		43	20
1989–90		45	17

ROBINSON, Mark

Born Manchester 21.11.68. Ht 5 9
Wt 11 08
Midfield. From Trainee.

Season	Club	Apps	Goals
1985–86	WBA	1	—
1986–87		1	—
1987–88	Barnsley	3	—
1988–89		18	2
1989–90		24	—

ROBINSON, Martin

Born Ilford 17.7.57. Ht 5 8 Wt 11 11
Forward. From Apprentice.

Season	Club	Apps	Goals
1975–76	Tottenham H	2	1
1976–77		—	—
1977–78		4	1
1977–78	Charlton Ath	16	7
1978–79		35	15
1979–80		33	7
1980–81		40	10
1981–82		39	5
1982–83		32	4
1982–83	*Reading*	6	2
1983–84	Charlton Ath	27	8
1984–85		6	2
1984–85	Gillingham	33	10
1985–86		33	10
1986–87		30	4
1987–88	Southend U	37	8
1988–89		19	6
1989–90	Cambridge U	16	1

ROBINSON, Michael

Born Leicester 12.7.58. Ht 6 0 Wt 13 04
Forward. From Apprentice. Eire, 23 full caps.

Season	Club	Apps	Goals
1975–76	Preston NE	2	—
1976–77		—	—
1977–78		10	2
1978–79		36	13
1979–80	Manchester C	30	8
1980–81	Brighton	42	19
1981–82		35	11
1982–83		36	7
1983–84	Liverpool	24	6
1984–85		6	—
1984–85	QPR	11	1
1985–86		26	5
1986–87		11	—

To Osasuna

ROBINSON, Paul

Born Notingham 21.2.71. Ht 6 4
Wt 14 07
Forward. From Notts Co & Bury Trainee.

Season	Club	Apps	Goals
1989–90	Scarborough	20	3

ROBINSON, Philip

Born Stafford 6.1.67. Ht 5 9 Wt 10 10
Defender. From Apprentice.

Season	Club	Apps	Goals
1984–85	Aston Villa	—	—
1985–86		—	—
1986–87		3	1
1987–88	Wolverhampton W	41	5
1988–89		30	3
1989–90	Notts Co	46	2

ROBINSON, Ronnie

Born Sunderland 22.10.66. Ht 5 9
Wt 11 05
Defender.

Season	Club	Apps	Goals
1984–85	Ipswich T	—	—
From Vaux Breweries			
1985–86	Leeds U	16	—
1986–87		11	—
1986–87	Doncaster R	12	—
1987–88		37	1
1988–89		29	4

Season	Club	League Appearances/Goals	
1988–89	WBA	1	—
1989–90	Rotherham U	43	1

ROBSON, Bryan

Born Chester-le-Street 11.1.57. Ht 5 10
Wt 11 11
Midfield. From Apprentice. England Schools, Youth, Under-21, B, 87 full caps.

1974–75	WBA	3	2
1975–76		16	1
1976–77		23	8
1977–78		35	3
1978–79		41	7
1979–80		34	8
1980–81		40	10
1981–82		5	—
1981–82	Manchester U	32	5
1982–83		33	10
1983–84		33	12
1984–85		33	9
1985–86		21	7
1986–87		30	7
1987–88		36	11
1988–89		34	4
1989–90		20	2

ROBSON, Gary

Born Durham 6.7.65. Ht 5 7 Wt 10 12
Midfield. From Apprentice.

1982–83	WBA	2	—
1983–84		7	—
1984–85		11	—
1985–86		14	—
1986–87		5	1
1987–88		31	1
1988–89		38	8
1989–90		25	5

ROBSON, Mark

Born Newham 22.5.69. Ht 5 7 Wt 10 05
Forward. From Trainee.

1986–87	Exeter C	26	7
1987–88	Tottenham H	—	—
1987–88	*Reading*	7	—
1988–89	Tottenham H	5	—
1989–90		3	—
1989–90	*Watford*	1	—
1989–90	*Plymouth Arg*	7	—

ROBSON, Mark

Born Newcastle 25.4.71. Ht 5 10
Wt 11 00
Midfield. From Trainee.

1989–90	Hartlepool U	—	—

ROBSON, Stewart

Born Billericay 6.11.64. Ht 5 11
Wt 12 04
Midfield. From Apprentice. England Youth, Under-21.

1981–82	Arsenal	20	2
1982–83		31	2
1983–84		28	6
1984–85		40	2
1985–86		27	4
1986–87		5	—
1986–87	West Ham U	18	1
1987–88		37	2
1988–89		6	—
1989–90		7	1

ROCASTLE, David

Born Lewisham 2.5.67. Ht 5 9 Wt 11 12
Forward. From Apprentice. England Under-21, 11 full caps.

1984–85	Arsenal	—	—
1985–86		16	1
1986–87		36	2
1987–88		40	7
1988–89		38	6
1989–90		33	2

ROCHE, David

Born Newcastle 13.12.70 Ht 5 11
Wt 12 01
Defender. From Trainee.

Season	Club	League Appearances/Goals	
1988–89	Newcastle U	2	—
1989–90		—	—

ROCHE, Paddy

Born Dublin 4.1.51. Ht 6 1 Wt 11 09
Goalkeeper. From Shelbourne. Eire, 8 full caps.

Season	Club	Apps	Goals
1973–74	Manchester U	—	—
1974–75		2	—
1975–76		4	—
1976–77		2	—
1977–78		19	—
1978–79		14	—
1979–80		—	—
1980–81		2	—
1981–82		3	—
1982–83	Brentford	46	—
1983–84		25	—
1984–85	Halifax T	43	—
1985–86		46	—
1986–87		24	—
1987–88		46	—
1988–89		25	—
1989–90		—	—
1989–90	Chester C	—	—

RODGER, Graham

Born Glasgow 1.4.67. Ht 6 2 Wt 11 11
Defender. From Apprentice. England Under-21.

Season	Club	Apps	Goals
1983–84	Wolverhampton W	1	—
1984–85	Coventry C	—	—
1985–86		10	—
1986–87		6	—
1987–88		12	1
1988–89		8	1
1989–90	Luton T	2	—

RODGERSON, Ian

Born Hereford 9.4.66. Ht 5 10 Wt 10 07
Midfield. From Pegasus Juniors.

Season	Club	Apps	Goals
1984–85	Hereford U	—	—
1985–86		19	2
1986–87		44	1
1987–88		37	3
1988–89	Cardiff C	40	—
1989–90		45	4

ROEDER, Glenn

Born Woodford 13.12.55. Ht 6 0
Wt 12 13
Defender. From Apprentice. England B.

Season	Club	Apps	Goals
1974–75	Orient	6	—
1975–76		25	2
1976–77		42	2
1977–78		42	—
1978–79	QPR	27	4
1979–80		40	9
1980–81		39	2
1981–82		41	2
1982–83		9	—
1983–84		1	—
1983–84	*Notts Co*	4	—
1983–84	Newcastle U	23	—
1984–85		36	—
1985–86		42	6
1986–87		37	1
1987–88		37	1
1988–89		18	—
1989–90	Watford	45	1

ROGAN, Anton

Born Belfast 25.3.66. Ht 5 11 Wt 12 06
Defender. From Distillery. Northern Ireland, 12 full caps.

Season	Club	Apps	Goals
1986–87	Celtic	10	1
1987–88		33	1
1988–89		34	1
1989–90		18	—

ROGERS, Darren

Born Birmingham 9.4.71 Ht 5 10
Wt 11 02
Defender. From Trainee.

Season	Club	Apps	Goals
1988–89	WBA	—	—
1989–90		—	—

ROGERS, Lee

Born Bristol 8.4.67. Ht 5 11 Wt 12 08
Defender. From Apprentice.

Season Club League Appearances/Goals

Season	Club	Apps	Goals
1984–85	Bristol C	6	—
1985–86		21	—
1986–87		3	—
1986–87	*Hereford U*	13	—
1987–88	Bristol C	—	—
1987–88	*York C*	7	—
1988–89	Exeter C	45	—
1989–90		16	—

ROGERS, Lee

Born Doncaster 21.10.66. Ht 5 10
Wt 12 00
Defender. From Doncaster R.

Season	Club	Apps	Goals
1986–87	Chesterfield	36	—
1987–88		43	—
1988–89		24	—
1989–90		32	—

ROGERSON, Lee

Born Darwen 21.3.67.
Midfield. From Clitheroe.

Season	Club	Apps	Goals
1989–90	Wigan Ath	3	—

ROLPH, Andy

Born Birmingham 28.10.69 Ht 5 6
Wt 10 00
Forward. From Birmingham C Trainee.

Season	Club	Apps	Goals
1988–89	Chesterfield	12	1
1989–90		9	—

ROLPH, Darren

Born Romford 19.11.68. Ht 5 8
Wt 11 04
Defender.

Season	Club	Apps	Goals
1987–88	Barnsley	2	—
1988–89		—	—
1989–90		—	—

ROOKE, Rodney

Born Orsett 7.4.70. Ht 5 5 Wt 10 03
Defender. From Trainee.

Season	Club	Apps	Goals
1988–89	Colchester U	—	—
1989–90		4	—

ROONEY, Simon

Born Manchester 10.7.70. Ht 5 11
Wt 11 08
Midfield. From Trainee.

Season	Club	Apps	Goals
1987–88	Blackpool	8	—
1988–89		1	—
1989–90		—	—

ROSARIO, Robert

Born Hammersmith 4.3.66. Ht 6 3
Wt 12 01
Forward. From Hillingdon Bor. England Youth.

Season	Club	Apps	Goals
1983–84	Norwich C	8	1
1984–85		4	1
1985–86		8	2
1985–86	*Wolverhampton W*	2	1
1986–87	Norwich C	25	3
1987–88		14	2
1988–89		27	4
1989–90		31	5

ROSE, Kevin

Born Evesham 23.11.60. Ht 6 1
Wt 13 03
Goalkeeper. From Ledbury T.

Season	Club	Apps	Goals
1979–80	Lincoln C	—	—
1980–81		—	—
From Ledbury T			
1982–83	Hereford U	15	—
1983–84		46	—
1984–85		46	—
1985–86		46	—
1986–87		46	—
1987–88		46	—
1988–89		23	—
1989–90	Bolton W	6	—
1989–90	*Halifax T*	—	—
1989–90	*Carlisle U*	11	—

ROSENIOR, Leroy

Born London 24.3.64. Ht 6 1 Wt 11 10
Forward. From school. England Schools.

Season	Club	Apps	Goals
1982–83	Fulham	1	—
1983–84		23	8
1984–85		30	8
1985–86	QPR	18	3
1986–87		20	4
1987–88	Fulham	34	20
1987–88	West Ham U	9	5
1988–89		28	7
1989–90		5	2

ROSENTHAL, Ronny

Born Haifa 11.10.63.
Forward. From Maccabi Haifa, FC Brugge, Standard Liege. Israel full caps.

Season	Club	Apps	Goals
1989–90	*Luton T*	—	—
1989–90	*Liverpool*	8	7

ROSS, David

Born Durham 21.11.69. Ht 6 1 Wt 10 03
Forward.

Season	Club	Apps	Goals
1987–88	Barnsley	—	—
1988–89		—	—
1989–90		—	—

ROSS, Mike

Born Southampton 2.9.71. Ht 5 6 Wt 9 13
Forward.

Season	Club	Apps	Goals
1988–89	Portsmouth	1	—
1989–90		—	—

ROSTRON, Wilf

Born Sunderland 29.9.56. Ht 5 6 Wt 11 01
From Apprentice. England Schools.

Season	Club	Apps	Goals
1973–74	Arsenal	—	—
1974–75		6	2
1975–76		5	—
1976–77		6	—
1977–78	Sunderland	34	6
1978–79		34	11
1979–80		8	—
1979–80	Watford	31	3
1980–81		27	1
1981–82		27	2
1982–83		42	3
1983–84		39	4
1984–85		38	3
1985–86		30	5
1986–87		39	1
1987–88		37	—
1988–89		7	—
1988–89	Sheffield W	7	—
1989–90	Sheffield U	26	3

ROUGVIE, Doug

Born Ballingry 24.5.56. Ht 6 2 Wt 14 00
Defender. Scotland 1 full cap.

Season	Club	Apps	Goals
1976–77	Aberdeen	6	1
1977–78		1	—
1978–79		20	—
1979–80		25	2
1980–81		28	3
1981–82		28	6
1982–83		35	3
1983–84		35	4
1984–85	Chelsea	27	1
1985–86		34	2
1986–87		13	—
1987–88	Brighton	35	2
1988–89	Shrewsbury T	21	3
1988–89	Fulham	18	1
1989–90	Dunfermline Ath	28	—

ROWBOTHAM, Darren

Born Cardiff 22.10.66. Ht 5 10 Wt 11 05
Midfield. From Trainee.

Season	Club	Apps	Goals
1984–85	Plymouth Arg	7	—
1985–86		14	1
1986–87		16	1
1987–88		9	—
1987–88	Exeter C	23	2
1988–89		45	20
1989–90		32	21

ROWBOTHAM, Jason

Born Cardiff 3.1.69.
Defender. From Trainee.

Season	Club	Apps	Goals
1987–88	Plymouth Arg	4	—

Season	Club	League Appearances/Goals	
1988–89		5	—
1989–90		—	—

ROWE, Ben

Born Hull 1.10.70. Ht 5 7 Wt 10 07
Midfield. From Bristol C.

Season	Club	League Appearances/Goals	
1989–90	Exeter C	10	2

ROWE, Paul

Born Wadebridge 1.8.71. Ht 5 10
Wt 10 12
Forward. From Trainee.

Season	Club	League Appearances/Goals	
1989–90	Plymouth Arg	—	—

ROWELL, Gary

Born Seaham 6.6.57. Ht 5 10 Wt 11 03
Forward. From Apprentice. England Under-21.

Season	Club	League Appearances/Goals	
1974–75	Sunderland	—	—
1975–76		4	1
1976–77		32	5
1977–78		39	18
1978–79		32	21
1979–80		17	—
1980–81		31	10
1981–82		30	9
1982–83		35	16
1983–84		34	8
1984–85	Norwich C	6	1
1985–86	Middlesbrough	27	10
1986–87	Brighton	10	—
1987–88		2	—
1987–88	Dundee	1	—
1987–88	Carlisle U	7	—
1988–89	Burnley	18	1
1989–90		1	—

RUDDOCK, Neil

Born London 9.5.68. Ht 6 2 Wt 12 6
Defender. From Apprentice. England Youth, Under-21.

Season	Club	League Appearances/Goals	
1985–86	Millwall	—	—
1985–86	Tottenham H	—	—
1986–87		4	—
1987–88		5	—
1988–89	Millwall	2	1
1988–89	Southampton	13	3
1989–90		29	3

RUMBLE, Paul

Born Hemel Hempstead 14.3.69.
Ht 5 11 Wt 11 05
Defender. From Trainee.

Season	Club	League Appearances/Goals	
1986–87	Watford	—	—
1987–88		—	—
1988–89		—	—
1988–89	*Scunthorpe U*	8	1
1989–90	Maidstone U	23	2

RUSH, Ian

Born St. Asaph 20.10.61. Ht 6 0
Wt 12 06
Forward. From Apprentice. Wales Schools, Under-21, 44 full caps.

Season	Club	League Appearances/Goals	
1978–79	Chester	1	—
1979–80		33	14
1979–80	Liverpool	—	—
1980–81		7	—
1981–82		32	17
1982–83		34	24
1983–84		41	32
1984–85		28	14
1985–86		40	22
1986–87		42	30
1987–88	Juventus	29	7
1988–89	Liverpool	24	7
1989–90		36	18

RUSSELL, Billy

Born Glasgow 14.9.59. Ht 5 10
Wt 11 03
Defender. From Apprentice. Scotland Youth.

Season	Club	League Appearances/Goals	
1977–78	Everton	—	—
From Glasgow Celtic			
1979–80	Doncaster R	42	—
1980–81		46	1
1981–82		37	3
1982–83		40	5
1983–84		41	6
1984–85		38	—

Season	Club	League Appearances/Goals	
1985–86	Scunthorpe U	42	—
1986–87		41	3
1987–88		34	4
1988–89	Rotherham U	44	2
1989–90		29	—

RUSSELL, Bobby

Born Glasgow 11.2.57. Ht 5 8 Wt 10 03
Midfield. From Shettleston. Scotland Under-21.

Season	Club	League Appearances/Goals	
1976–77	Rangers	—	—
1977–78		33	3
1978–79		36	4
1979–80		23	7
1980–81		28	6
1981–82		32	6
1982–83		21	4
1983–84		31	4
1984–85		18	—
1985–86		27	—
1986–87		1	—
1987–88	Motherwell	32	3
1988–89		31	5
1989–90		33	3

RUSSELL, Kevin

Born Portsmouth 6.12.66. Ht 5 8
Wt 10 10
Forward. From Brighton Apprentice. England Youth.

Season	Club	League Appearances/Goals	
1984–85	Portsmouth	—	—
1985–86		1	—
1986–87		3	1
1987–88	Wrexham	38	21
1988–89		46	22
1989–90	Leicester C	10	—

RUSSELL, Lee

Born Southampton 3.9.69 Ht 5 11
Wt 11 04
Defender. From Trainee.

Season	Club	League Appearances/Goals	
1988–89	Portsmouth	2	—
1989–90		3	—

RUSSELL, Martin

Born Dublin 27.4.67. Ht 5 11 Wt 11 00
Midfield. From Apprentice. Eire Youth, Under-21, Under-23.

Season	Club	League Appearances/Goals	
1984–85	Manchester U	—	—
1985–86		—	—
1986–87		—	—
1986–87	*Birmingham C*	5	—
1986–87	*Norwich C*	—	—
1986–87	Leicester C	5	—
1987–88		5	—
1988–89		10	—
1988–89	Scarborough	20	2
1989–90		31	7
1989–90	Middlesbrough	—	—

RUTHERFORD, Mark

Born Birmingham 25.3.72. Ht 5 11
Wt 11 00
Forward. From Trainee.

Season	Club	League Appearances/Goals	
1989–90	Birmingham C	2	—

RUTHERFORD, Michael

Born Greenwich 6.6.72.
Forward. From Trainee.

Season	Club	League Appearances/Goals	
1989–90	QPR	2	—

RYAN, John

Born Ashton 18.2.62. Ht 5 10 Wt 11 07
Defender. From Apprentice. England Under-21.

Season	Club	League Appearances/Goals	
1979–80	Oldham Ath	—	—
1980–81		—	—
1981–82		37	—
1982–83		40	8
1983–84	Newcastle U	22	1
1984–85		6	—
1984–85	Sheffield W	8	1
1985–86	Oldham Ath	22	—
1986–87		1	—
1987–88		—	—
1987–88	Mansfield T	32	1

Season	Club	Apps	Goals
1988–89	....	30	—
1989–90	Chesterfield.............	43	4

RYAN, Laurie

Born Watford 15.10.63. Ht 5 9 Wt 10 12
Forward. From Dunstable.

Season	Club	Apps	Goals
1987–88	Cambridge U...........	2	—
1988–89	....	39	12
1989–90	....	10	1

RYAN, Vaughan

Born Westminster 2.9.68. Ht 5 8
Wt 10 12
Midfield.

Season	Club	Apps	Goals
1986–87	Wimbledon	1	—
1987–88	....	22	1
1988–89	....	5	—
1988–89	*Sheffield U*	3	—
1989–90	Wimbledon	31	—

SADDINGTON, Nigel

Born Sunderland 9.12.65. Ht 6 1
Wt 12 02
Defender.

Season	Club	Apps	Goals
1984–85	Doncaster R	6	—
1985–86	....	—	—
1985–86	Sunderland..............	—	—
1986–87	....	3	—
1987–88	....	—	—
1987–88	Carlisle U	13	1
1988–89	....	40	5
1989–90	....	44	10

SAGE, Mel

Born Gillingham 24.3.64. Ht 5 8
Wt 10 04
Defender. From Apprentice.

Season	Club	Apps	Goals
1981–82	Gillingham..............	1	—
1982–83	....	9	—
1983–84	....	40	2
1984–85	....	36	1
1985–86	....	46	2
1986–87	Derby Co................	26	2
1987–88	....	13	—
1988–89	....	16	1
1989–90	....	34	—

SALAKO, John

Born Nigeria, 11.2.69. Ht 5 10 Wt 11 00
Forward. From Trainee.

Season	Club	Apps	Goals
1986–87	Crystal Palace	4	—
1987–88	....	31	—
1988–89	....	28	—
1989–90	....	17	2
1989–90	*Swansea C*..............	13	3

SALATHIEL, Neil

Born Wrexham 19.11.62. Ht 5 7
Wt 10 00
Defender. From Sheffield W Amateur.
Wales Schools, Youth.

Season	Club	Apps	Goals
1980–81	Wrexham................	4	—
1981–82	Crewe Alex.	44	—
1982–83	....	21	—

From Arcadia Shepherds

Season	Club	League Appearances/Goals	
1983–84	Wrexham	29	—
1984–85		36	—
1985–86		42	1
1986–87		45	2
1987–88		24	—
1988–89		35	—
1989–90		29	—

SALE, Mark

Born Burton-on-Trent 27.2.72.
Defender. From Trainee.

Season	Club	Apps	Goals
1989–90	Stoke C	2	—

SALMAN, Danis

Born Cyprus 12.3.60. Ht 5 10 Wt 11 13
Defender. From Apprentice. England Youth.

Season	Club	Apps	Goals
1975–76	Brentford	6	—
1976–77		18	1
1977–78		37	—
1978–79		40	1
1979–80		41	3
1980–81		38	—
1981–82		40	—
1982–83		1	—
1983–84		21	—
1984–85		43	3
1985–86		40	—
1986–87	Millwall	31	2
1987–88		36	1
1988–89		19	1
1989–90		7	—
1989–90	Plymouth Arg	11	—

SALMON, Mike

Born Leyland 14.7.64. Ht 6 2 Wt 12 12
Goalkeeper. Local.

Season	Club	Apps	Goals
1981–82	Blackburn R	1	—
1982–83		—	—
1982–83	*Chester C*	16	—
1983–84	Stockport Co	46	—
1984–85		46	—
1985–86		26	—
1986–87	Bolton W	26	—
1986–87	*Wrexham*	17	—
1987–88	Wrexham	40	—
1988–89		43	—
1989–90	Charlton Ath	—	—

SALTON, Darren

Born Edinburgh 16.3.72. Ht 6 1
Wt 13 08
Forward. From Trainee.

Season	Club	Apps	Goals
1988–89	Luton T	—	—
1989–90		—	—

SAMWAYS, Mark

Born Doncaster 11.11.68. Ht 6 0
Wt 11 12
Goalkeeper. From Trainee.

Season	Club	Apps	Goals
1987–88	Doncaster R	11	—
1988–89		12	—
1989–90		46	—

SAMWAYS, Vinny

Born Bethnal Green 27.10.68. Ht 5 8
Wt 9 00
Midfield. From Apprentice. England Youth, Under-21.

Season	Club	Apps	Goals
1985–86	Tottenham H	—	—
1986–87		2	—
1987–88		26	—
1988–89		19	3
1989–90		23	3

SANCHEZ, Lawrie

Born Lambeth 22.10.59. Ht 5 11
Wt 12 00
Midfield. From Thatcham. Northern Ireland 3 caps.

Season	Club	Apps	Goals
1977–78	Reading	8	1
1978–79		39	4
1979–80		46	5
1980–81		37	2
1981–82		35	3
1982–83		37	1
1983–84		45	10
1984–85		15	2
1984–85	Wimbledon	20	5
1985–86		42	9
1986–87		29	—

Season	Club	League Appearances/Goals	
1987–88		38	4
1988–89		36	5
1989–90		18	1

SANDEMAN, Bradley

Born Northampton 24.2.70 Ht 5 10
Wt 10 08
Midfield. From Trainee.

Season	Club	Apps	Goals
1987–88	Northampton T	2	—
1988–89		22	2
1989–90		29	1

SANDFORD, Lee

Born Basingstoke 22.4.68. Ht 6 01
Wt 12 00
Defender. From Apprentice. England Youth.

Season	Club	Apps	Goals
1985–86	Portsmouth	7	—
1986–87		—	—
1987–88		21	1
1988–89		31	—
1989–90		13	—
1989–90	Stoke C	23	2

SANDISON, James

Born Edinburgh 22.6.65. Ht 6 0
Wt 11 02
Midfield. From Edinburgh Emmet.

Season	Club	Apps	Goals
1983–84	Hearts	—	—
1984–85		3	—
1985–86		3	—
1986–87		13	—
1987–88		2	—
1988–89		14	—
1989–90		12	2

SANSOM, Kenny

Born Camberwell 26.9.58. Ht 5 7
Wt 10 04
Defender. From Apprentice. England Schools, Youth, Under-21, B, 86 full caps. Football League.

Season	Club	Apps	Goals
1974–75	Crystal Palace	1	—
1975–76		6	—
1976–77		46	—
1977–78		41	2
1978–79		42	—
1979–80		36	1
1980–81	Arsenal	42	3
1981–82		42	—
1982–83		40	—
1983–84		40	1
1984–85		39	1
1985–86		42	—
1986–87		35	—
1987–88		34	1
1988–89		—	—
1988–89	Newcastle U	20	—
1989–90	QPR	36	—

SANSOME, Paul

Born N. Addington 6.10.61. Ht 5 11
Wt 12 00
Goalkeeper. From Crystal Palace Apprentice.

Season	Club	Apps	Goals
1979–80	Millwall	—	—
1980–81		—	—
1981–82		8	—
1982–83		24	—
1983–84		31	—
1984–85		46	—
1985–86		36	—
1986–87		10	—
1987–88		1	—
1987–88	Southend U	6	—
1988–89		44	—
1989–90		46	—

SAUNDERS, Carl

Born Marston Green 26.11.64. Ht 5 8
Wt 11 02
Forward. Local.

Season	Club	Apps	Goals
1982–83	Stoke C	1	—
1983–84		—	—
1984–85		23	2
1985–86		37	2
1986–87		31	13
1987–88		17	3
1988–89		33	2

Season	Club	League Appearances/Goals	
1989–90		22	1
1989–90	Bristol R	20	5

SAUNDERS, Dean

Born Swansea 21.6.64. Ht 5 8 Wt 10 06
Forward. From Apprentice. Wales 19 full caps.

Season	Club		
1982–83	Swansea C	—	—
1983–84		19	3
1984–85		30	9
1984–85	*Cardiff C*	4	—
1985–86	Brighton	42	15
1986–87		30	6
1986–87	Oxford U	12	6
1987–88		37	12
1988–89		10	4
1988–89	Derby Co	30	14
1989–90		38	11

SAUNDERS, Steve

Born Warrington 21.9.64. Ht 5 7 Wt 10 06
Forward. From Apprentice.

Season	Club		
1982–83	Bolton W	—	—
1983–84		3	—
1984–85		—	—
1985–86	Crewe Alex	22	1
1986–87	Preston NE	—	—
1987–88	Grimsby T	35	3
1988–89		41	10
1989–90	Scarborough	32	1

SAUNDERS, Wes

Born Sunderland 23.2.63. Ht 6 0 Wt 11 11
Defender. From school.

Season	Club		
1981–82	Newcastle U	29	—
1982–83		13	—
1983–84		16	—
1984–85		21	—
1984–85	*Bradford C*	4	—
1985–86	Carlisle U	35	3
1986–87		37	3
1987–88		25	5
1987–88	Dundee	11	—
1988–89		30	1
1989–90		9	1

SAVAGE, Bob

Born Liverpool 8.1.60. Ht 5 7 Wt 11 1
Midfield. From Apprentice.

Season	Club		
1977–78	Liverpool	—	—
1978–79		—	—
1979–80		—	—
1980–81		—	—
1981–82		—	—
1982–83		—	—
1982–83	*Wrexham*	27	10
1983–84	Stoke C	7	—
1983–84	Bournemouth	23	5
1984–85		43	9
1985–86		—	—
1986–87		16	4
1986–87	Bradford C	8	—
1987–88		3	—
1987–88	Bolton W	39	5
1988–89		38	6
1989–90		10	—

SAVILLE, Andrew

Born Hull 12.12.64. Ht 6 0 Wt 12 06
Forward. From local.

Season	Club		
1983–84	Hull C	1	—
1984–85		4	1
1985–86		9	1
1986–87		35	9
1987–88		31	6
1988–89		20	1
1988–89	Walsall	12	4
1989–90		26	1
1989–90	Barnsley	15	3

SAYER, Andy

Born Brent 6.6.66 Ht 5 9 Wt 10 12
Forward. From Apprentice.

Season	Club		
1983–84	Wimbledon	2	—
1984–85		20	8
1985–86		7	—
1986–87		20	7
1987–88		9	—
1987–88	*Cambridge U*	5	—

Season	Club	Apps	Goals
1988–89	Fulham	28	10
1989–90		25	5
1989–90	Leyton Orient	10	1

SCALES, John

Born Harrogate 4.7.66. Ht 6 2 Wt 12 07
Defender.

Season	Club	Apps	Goals
1984–85	Leeds U	—	—
1985–86	Bristol R	29	1
1986–87		43	1
1987–88	Wimbledon	25	1
1988–89		38	5
1989–90		28	2

SCHOFIELD, Jon

Born Barnsley 16.5.65 Ht 5 11 Wt 11 03
Midfield. From Gainsborough T.

Season	Club	Apps	Goals
1988–89	Lincoln C	29	2
1989–90		29	2

SCOPE, David

Born Newcastle 10.5.67.
Forward. From Blyth Spartans.

Season	Club	Apps	Goals
1989–90	Northampton T	7	—

SCOTT, Colin

Born Glasgow 19.5.70. Ht 6 1 Wt 12 04
Goalkeeper. From Dalry Thistle.

Season	Club	Apps	Goals
1987–88	Rangers	—	—
1988–89		—	—
1989–90		—	—
1989–90	*Brentford*	6	—

SCOTT, Ian

Born Luton 25.11.68. Ht 5 10 Wt 11 05
Midfield. From Apprentice.

Season	Club	Apps	Goals
1986–87	Luton T	—	—
1987–88		—	—

Season Club League Appearances/Goals

Season	Club	Apps	Goals
1988–89		—	—
1989–90		—	—

SCOTT, Ian

Born Radcliffe 20.9.67. Ht 5 9 Wt 11 04
Forward. From Apprentice. England Schools.

Season	Club	Apps	Goals
1985–86	Manchester C	—	—
1986–87		—	—
1987–88		23	3
1988–89		1	—
1989–90	Stoke C	19	1

SCOTT, Keith

Born London 10.6.67. Ht 6 3 Wt 12 00
Forward. From Leicester U.

Season	Club	Apps	Goals
1989–90	Lincoln C	10	2

SCOTT, Kevin

Born Easington 17.12.66. Ht 6 2
Wt 11 06
Defender.

Season	Club	Apps	Goals
1984–85	Newcastle U	—	—
1985–86		—	—
1986–87		3	1
1987–88		4	1
1988–89		29	—
1989–90		42	3

SCOTT, Martin

Born Sheffield 7.1.68. Ht 5 8 Wt 10 10
Midfield. From Apprentice.

Season	Club	Apps	Goals
1984–85	Rotherham U	3	—
1985–86		—	—
1986–87		12	—
1987–88		19	—
1987–88	*Nottingham F*	—	—
1988–89	Rotherham U	19	1
1989–90		28	1

SCOTT, Morrys

Born Swansea 17.12.70. Ht 6 3 Wt 12 06
Forward. From Swansea C Trainee and Cardiff C Trainee.

Season	Club	League Appearances/Goals	
1989–90	Cardiff C	9	—

SCOTT, Peter

Born London 1.10.63. Ht 5 9 Wt 11 12
Midfield. From Apprentice.

Season	Club	Apps	Goals
1981–82	Fulham	1	—
1982–83		—	—
1983–84		32	4
1984–85		19	1
1985–86		32	5
1986–87		30	6
1987–88		23	2
1988–89		37	3
1989–90		41	3

SCOTT, Robert

Born Broxburn 13.1.64 Ht 5 10
Wt 11 07
Forward. From Whitburn J.

Season	Club	Apps	Goals
1988–89	Colchester U	12	5
1989–90		25	3

SCULLY, Pat

Born Dublin 23.6.70. Ht 6 1 Wt 12 07
Defender. Eire Schools, B, Under-21, Under-23, 1 full cap.

Season	Club	Apps	Goals
1987–88	Arsenal	—	—
1988–89		—	—
1989–90		—	—
1989–90	*Preston NE*	13	1

SEAGRAVES, Mark

Born Bootle 22.10.66. Ht 6 1 Wt 12 10
Defender. From England Schools, Youth.

Season	Club	Apps	Goals
1983–84	Liverpool	—	—
1984–85		—	—
1985–86		—	—
1986–87		—	—
1986–87	*Norwich C*	3	—
1987–88	Liverpool	—	—
1987–88	Manchester C	17	—
1988–89		23	—
1989–90		2	—

SEALEY, Les

Born Bethnal Green 29.9.57. Ht 6 1
Wt 13 06
Goalkeeper. From Apprentice.

Season	Club	Apps	Goals
1975–76	Coventry C	—	—
1976–77		11	—
1977–78		2	—
1978–79		36	—
1979–80		20	—
1980–81		35	—
1981–82		15	—
1982–83		39	—
1983–84	Luton T	42	—
1984–85		26	—
1984–85	*Plymouth Arg*	6	—
1985–86	Luton T	35	—
1986–87		41	—
1987–88		31	—
1988–89		32	—
1989–90		—	—
1989–90	*Manchester U*	2	—

SEALY, Tony

Born London 7.5.59 Ht 5 8 Wt 11 08
Forward. From Apprentice.

Season	Club	Apps	Goals
1977–78	Southampton	2	—
1978–79		5	—
1978–79	Crystal Palace	5	—
1979–80		—	—
1979–80	*Port Vale*	17	6
1980–81	Crystal Palace	19	5
1980–81	QPR	8	2
1981–82		7	—
1981–82	*Port Vale*	6	4
1982–83	QPR	40	16
1983–84		8	—
1983–84	*Fulham*	5	1
1984–85	QPR	—	—
1984–85	Fulham	13	6
1985–86		7	3
1985–86	Leicester C	21	6
1986–87		18	1
1986–87	*Bournemouth*	13	2

From Braga

Season	Club	League Appearances/Goals	
1988–89	Brentford	12	4
1989–90	Swindon T	—	—
1989–90	Bristol R	19	3

SEAMAN, David

Born Rotherham 19.9.63. Ht 6 3 Wt 13 00
Goalkeeper. From Apprentice. England B, Under-21, 3 full caps.

Season	Club	League Appearances/Goals	
1981–82	Leeds U	—	—
1982–83	Peterborough U	38	—
1983–84		45	—
1984–85		8	—
1984–85	Birmingham C	33	—
1985–86		42	—
1986–87	QPR	41	—
1987–88		32	—
1988–89		35	—
1989–90		33	—

SEDGLEY, Steve

Born Enfield 26.5.68. Ht 6 1 Wt 12 06
Midfield. From Apprentice. England Under-21.

Season	Club	League Appearances/Goals	
1986–87	Coventry C	26	—
1987–88		27	2
1988–89		31	1
1989–90	Tottenham H	32	—

SEGERS, Hans

Born Eindhoven 30.10.61. Ht 5 11 Wt 12 12
Goalkeeper. From PSV Eindhoven.

Season	Club	League Appearances/Goals	
1984–85	Nottingham F	28	—
1985–86		11	—
1986–87		14	—
1986–87	*Stoke C*	1	—
1987–88	Nottingham F	5	—
1987–88	*Sheffield U*	10	—
1987–88	*Dunfermline Ath*	4	—
1988–89	Nottingham F	—	—
1988–89	Wimbledon	33	—
1989–90		38	—

SELLARS, Scott

Born Sheffield 27.11.65 Ht 5 7 Wt 9 10
Midfield. From Apprentice. England Under-21.

Season	Club	League Appearances/Goals	
1982–83	Leeds U	1	—
1983–84		19	3
1984–85		39	7
1985–86		17	2
1986–87	Blackburn R	32	4
1987–88		42	7
1988–89		46	2
1989–90		43	14

SENDALL, Richard

Born Stamford 10.7.67. Ht 5 10 Wt 11 06
Forward. From Watford Apprentice.

Season	Club	League Appearances/Goals	
1985–86	Blackpool	8	—
1986–87		3	—
1987–88		—	—
1988–89	Carlisle U	29	6
1989–90		19	4
1989–90	*Cardiff C*	4	—

SENIOR, Steve

Born Sheffield 15.5.63. Ht 5 8 Wt 12 07
Defender. From Apprentice.

Season	Club	League Appearances/Goals	
1980–81	York C	3	—
1981–82		17	1
1982–83		10	1
1983–84		39	1
1984–85		28	—
1984–85	*Darlington*	5	—
1985–86	York C	34	3
1986–87		37	—
1987–88	Northampton T	4	—
1987–88	Wigan Ath	22	1
1988–89		44	2
1989–90		43	—

SENIOR, Karl

Born Northwich 3.9.72.
Midfield. From School.

Season	Club	Apps	Goals
1989–90	Chester C	1	—

SENIOR, Trevor

Born Dorchester 28.11.61. Ht 6 1
Wt 13 07
Forward. From Dorchester T.

Season	Club	Apps	Goals
1981–82	Portsmouth	9	2
1982–83		2	—
1982–83	*Aldershot*	10	7
1983–84	Reading	45	36
1984–85		31	22
1985–86		46	27
1986–87		42	17
1987–88	Watford	24	1
1987–88	Middlesbrough	6	2
1988–89		4	—
1988–89	Reading	37	16
1989–90		35	14

SERMANNI, Peter

Born Glasgow 9.9.71. Ht 5 9 Wt 11 02
Midfield. From Celtic BC.

Season	Club	Apps	Goals
1989–90	Liverpool	—	—

SERTORI, Mark

Born Manchester 1.9.67. Ht 6 3
Wt 13 04
Forward.

Season	Club	Apps	Goals
1986–87	Stockport Co	3	—
1987–88		1	—
1987–88	Lincoln C	*28*	*6*
1988–89		26	4
1989–90		24	5
1989–90	Wrexham	18	2

SHAKESPEARE, Craig

Born Birmingham 26.10.63. Ht 5 10
Wt 12 05
Midfield. From Apprentice.

Season	Club	Apps	Goals
1981–82	Walsall	—	—
1982–83		31	4
1983–84		46	6
1984–85		41	9
1985–86		32	4
1986–87		44	11
1987–88		45	8
1988–89		45	3
1989–90	Sheffield W	17	—
1989–90	WBA	18	1

SHANLEY, Kevin

Born Ireland 8.9.70. Ht 5 11 Wt 11 11
Defender. From Trainee.

Season	Club	Apps	Goals
1989–90	Luton T	—	—

SHANNON, Rab

Born Bellshill 20.4.66. Ht 5 11 Wt 11 08
Defender. From St Columba's BC.
Scotland Youth, Under-21.

Season	Club	Apps	Goals
1982–83	Dundee	—	—
1983–84		6	—
1984–85		3	—
1985–86		33	—
1986–87		39	5
1987–88		41	—
1988–89		29	1
1989–90		36	1

SHARP, Graeme

Born Glasgow 16.10.60. Ht 6 1
Wt 11 09
Forward. From Eastercraigs. Scotland
Under-21, 12 full caps.

Season	Club	Apps	Goals
1978–79	Dumbarton	6	1
1979–80		34	16
1979–80	Everton	2	—
1980–81		4	—
1981–82		29	15
1982–83		41	15
1983–84		28	7
1984–85		36	21
1985–86		37	19
1986–87		27	5
1987–88		32	13
1988–89		26	7
1989–90		33	6

SHARP, Kevin

Born Stapleford 1.11.70. Ht 5 11
Wt 10 13

Defender. From Trainee.

1988–89	Nottingham F	—	—
1989–90		—	—

SHARP, Raymond

Born Stirling 16.11.69. Ht 5 6 Wt 9 04
Defender. From Gairdoch U.

1986–87	Dunfermline Ath	—	—
1987–88		—	—
1988–89	*Stenhousemuir*	5	—
1988–89	Dunfermline Ath	9	—
1989–90		27	—

SHARPE, Lee

Born Halesowen 25.7.71 Ht 5 11
Wt 11 04
Midfield. From Trainee. England Under-21.

1987–88	Torquay U	14	3
1988–89	Manchester U	22	—
1989–90		18	1

SHAW, Adrian

Born Easington 13.4.66. Ht 5 9
Wt 11 03
Forward. From Apprentice.

1983–84	Nottingham F	—	—
1984–85	Halifax T	21	1
1985–86		34	—
1986–87		21	—
1987–88		24	—
1988–89	York C	5	—
1988–89	Chesterfield	25	1
1989–90		24	2

SHAW, Gary

Born Birmingham 21.1.61. Ht 5 10
Wt 11 13
Forward. From Apprentice. England Under-21.

1978–79	Aston Villa	3	—
1979–80		28	9
1980–81		40	18
1981–82		26	9
1982–83		39	17
1983–84		12	5
1984–85		—	—
1985–86		12	1
1986–87		1	—
1987–88		4	—
1987–88	*Blackpool*	6	—

From Klagenfurt.

1989–90	Walsall	9	3

SHAW, George

Born Glasgow 10.2.69. Ht 5 7 Wt 9 02
Forward. From Ayresome N.

1987–88	St Mirren	2	—
1988–89		10	1
1989–90		23	2

SHAW, Graham

Born Stoke 7.6.67. Ht 5 8 Wt 10 05
Forward. From Apprentice.

1985–86	Stoke C	20	5
1986–87		18	2
1987–88		33	6
1988–89		28	5
1989–90	Preston NE	31	5

SHAW, Richard

Born Brentford 11.9.68. Ht 5 9 Wt 11 08
Defender. From Apprentice.

1986–87	Crystal Palace	—	—
1987–88		3	—
1988–89		14	—
1989–90		21	—
1989–90	Hull C	4	—

SHEARER, Alan

Born Newcastle 13.8.70. Ht 5 11
Wt 11 03
Forward. From Trainee. England Youth.

1987–88	Southampton	5	3
1988–89		10	—
1989–90		26	3

SHEARER, Duncan

Born Fort William 28.8.62. Ht 5 10
Wt 10 09

Forward. From Inverness Clach.

Season	Club	App	Goals
1983–84	Chelsea	—	—
1984–85		—	—
1985–86		2	1
1985–86	Huddersfield T	8	7
1986–87		42	21
1987–88		33	10
1988–89	Swindon T	36	14
1989–90		42	20

SHEARER, Peter

Born Birmingham 4.2.67 Ht 6 0
Wt 11 06
Forward. From Apprentice.

Season	Club	App	Goals
1984–85	Birmingham C	4	—
1985–86		—	—
1986–87	Rochdale	1	—
From Cheltenham T			
1988–89	Bournemouth	4	1
1989–90		34	4

SHEEDY, Kevin

Born Builth Wells 21.10.59. Ht 5 9
Wt 10 11
Midfield. From Apprentice.
Eire Youth, Under-21, 32 full caps.

Season	Club	App	Goals
1975–76	Hereford U	1	—
1976–77		16	1
1977–78		34	3
1978–79	Liverpool	—	—
1979–80		—	—
1980–81		1	—
1981–82		2	—
1982–83	Everton	40	11
1983–84		28	4
1984–85		29	11
1985–86		31	5
1986–87		28	13
1987–88		17	1
1988–89		26	8
1989–90		37	9

SHEFFIELD, Jon

Born Bedworth 1.2.69. Ht 5 11 Wt 11 07
Goalkeeper.

Season	Club	App	Goals
1986–87	Norwich C	—	—
1987–88		—	—
1988–89		1	—
1989–90		—	—
1989–90	*Aldershot*	11	—
1989–90	*Ipswich T*	—	—

SHELTON, Gary

Born Nottingham 21.3.58. Ht 5 7
Wt 10 12
Midfield. From Apprentice.
England Under-21.

Season	Club	App	Goals
1975–76	Walsall	2	—
1976–77		10	—
1977–78		12	—
1977–78	Aston Villa	—	—
1978–79		19	7
1979–80		4	—
1979–80	*Notts Co*	8	—
1980–81	Aston Villa	—	—
1981–82		1	—
1981–82	Sheffield W	9	1
1982–83		40	4
1983–84		40	5
1984–85		41	4
1985–86		31	1
1986–87		37	3
1987–88	Oxford U	32	—
1988–89		33	1
1989–90	Bristol C	43	9

SHELTON, Richard

Born Sheffield 8.6.68. Ht 5 8 Wt 10 11
Midfield. From Trainee.

Season	Club	App	Goals
1987–88	Huddersfield T	—	—
1988–89		—	—
1989–90		—	—

SHEPHERD, Glen

Born Dudley 4.1.71. Ht 5 9 Wt 10 00
Midfield. From Trainee.

Season Club League Appearances/Goals

Season	Club	Apps	Goals
1988–89	Port Vale	—	—
1989–90		—	—

SHEPHERD, Tony

Born Glasgow 16.11.66. Ht 5 9 Wt 10 07
Midfield. From Celtic BC. Scotland Schools, Youth.

Season	Club	Apps	Goals
1983–84	Celtic	—	—
1984–85		—	—
1985–86		1	—
1986–87		21	2
1987–88		6	1
1988–89		—	—
1988–89	*Bristol C*	3	—
1989–90	Carlisle U	31	2

SHEPSTONE, Paul

Born Coventry 8.11.70.
Midfield. FA Schools.

Season	Club	Apps	Goals
1987–88	Coventry C	—	—
1988–89		—	—
1989–90	Blackburn R	—	—
1989–90	Birmingham C	—	—

SHERIDAN, John

Born Manchester 1.10.64. Ht 5 9 Wt 10 08
Midfield. Local. Eire Youth, Under-21, Under-23, 9 full caps.

Season	Club	Apps	Goals
1981–82	Leeds U	—	—
1982–83		27	2
1983–84		11	1
1984–85		42	6
1985–86		32	4
1986–87		40	15
1987–88		38	12
1988–89		40	7
1989–90	Nottingham F	—	—
1989–90	Sheffield W	27	2

SHERINGHAM, Teddy

Born Highams Park 2.4.66. Ht 6 0 Wt 12 05
Forward. From Apprentice. England Youth.

Season	Club	Apps	Goals
1983–84	Millwall	7	1
1984–85		—	—
1984–85	*Aldershot*	5	—
1985–86	Millwall	18	4
1986–87		42	13
1987–88		43	22
1988–89		33	11
1989–90		31	9

SHERWOOD, Steve

Born Selby 10.12.53. Ht 6 4 Wt 14 07
Goalkeeper. From Apprentice.

Season	Club	Apps	Goals
1970–71	Chelsea	—	—
1971–72		1	—
1972–73		3	—
1973–74		—	—
1973–74	*Brighton*	—	—
1973–74	*Millwall*	1	—
1973–74	*Brentford*	16	—
1974–75	Chelsea	—	—
1974–75	*Brentford*	46	—
1975–76	Chelsea	12	—
1976–77		—	—
1976–77	Watford	8	—
1977–78		16	—
1978–79		16	—
1979–80		4	—
1980–81		22	—
1981–82		41	—
1982–83		42	—
1983–84		40	1
1984–85		9	—
1985–86		2	—
1986–87		11	—
1987–88	Grimsby T	46	—
1988–89		32	—
1989–90		31	—

SHERWOOD, Tim

Born St Albans 6.2.69. Ht 6 1 Wt 11 04
Midfield. From Trainee. England Under-21.

Season	Club	Apps	Goals
1986–87	Watford	—	—
1987–88		13	—

 Season Club League Appearances/Goals

Season	Club	Apps	Goals
1988–89		19	2
1989–90	Norwich C	27	3

SHILTON, Peter

Born Leicester 18.9.49. Ht 6 0 Wt 14 00
Goalkeeper. From Apprentice. England Schools, Youth, Under-23, 125 full caps. Football League.

Season	Club	Apps	Goals
1965–66	Leicester C	1	—
1966–67		4	—
1967–68		35	1
1968–69		42	—
1969–70		39	—
1970–71		40	—
1971–72		37	—
1972–73		41	—
1973–74		42	—
1974–75		5	—
1974–75	Stoke C	25	—
1975–76		42	—
1976–77		40	—
1977–78		3	—
1977–78	Nottingham F	37	—
1978–79		42	—
1979–80		42	—
1980–81		40	—
1981–82		41	—
1982–83	Southampton	39	—
1983–84		42	—
1984–85		41	—
1985–86		37	—
1986–87		29	—
1987–88	Derby Co	40	—
1988–89		38	—
1989–90		35	—

SHIRTLIFF, Peter

Born Barnsley 6.4.61. Ht 5 11 Wt 12 2
Defender. From Apprentice.

Season	Club	Apps	Goals
1978–79	Sheffield W	26	1
1979–80		3	—
1980–81		28	—
1981–82		31	2
1982–83		8	—
1983–84		36	1
1984–85		35	—
1985–86		21	—
1986–87	Charlton Ath	33	3
1987–88		36	2
1988–89		34	2
1989–90	Sheffield W	33	2

SHORT, Chris

Born Munster 9.5.70 Ht 5 10 Wt 12 02
Defender.

Season	Club	Apps	Goals
1988–89	Scarborough	2	—
1989–90		41	1

SHORT, Craig

Born Bridlington 25.6.68. Ht 6 0
Wt 11 04
Defender. From Pickering T. England Schools.

Season	Club	Apps	Goals
1987–88	Scarborough	21	2
1988–89		42	5
1989–90	Notts Co	44	2

SHORTE, Grenville

Born Leeds 14.10.70. Ht 6 1 Wt 12 08
Defender. From Trainee.

Season	Club	Apps	Goals
1989–90	Leeds U	—	—

SHOTTON, Malcolm

Born Newcastle 16.2.57. Ht 6 3
Wt 13 12
Defender. From Apprentice.

Season	Club	Apps	Goals
1974–75	Leicester C	—	—
1975–76		—	—
From Nuneaton Bor			
1980–81	Oxford U	38	5
1981–82		40	4
1982–83		46	1
1983–84		43	1
1984–85		42	1
1985–86		42	—
1986–87		11	—
1987–88		1	—
1987–88	Portsmouth	10	—
1987–88	Huddersfield T	14	—
1988–89		2	1
1988–89	Barnsley	37	5

Season	Club	League Appearances/Goals	
1989–90	....	29	1
1989–90	Hull C....................	16	2

SHUTT, Carl

Born Sheffield 10.10.61. Ht 5 10
Wt 11 13
Forward. From Spalding U.

Season	Club	Apps	Goals
1984–85	Sheffield W	—	—
1985–86	....	19	9
1986–87	....	20	7
1987–88	....	1	—
1987–88	Bristol C..................	22	9
1988–89	....	24	1
1988–89	Leeds U	3	4
1989–90	....	20	2

SIDDALL, Barry

Born Ellesmere Port 12.9.54. Ht 6 1
Wt 14 02
Goalkeeper. From Apprentice.
England Youth.

Season	Club	Apps	Goals
1971–72	Bolton W................	—	—
1972–73	....	4	—
1973–74	....	42	—
1974–75	....	42	—
1975–76	....	42	—
1976–77	....	7	—
1976–77	Sunderland..............	34	—
1977–78	....	42	—
1978–79	....	41	—
1979–80	....	12	—
1980–81	....	15	—
1980–81	*Darlington*	8	—
1981–82	Sunderland..............	23	—
1982–83	Port Vale................	33	—
1983–84	....	39	—
1983–84	*Blackpool*	7	—
1984–85	Port Vale................	9	—
1984–85	Stoke C	15	—
1985–86	....	5	—
1985–86	*Tranmere R*	12	—
1985–86	*Manchester C*	6	—
1986–87	Blackpool	37	—
1987–88	....	38	—
1988–89	....	35	—
1989–90	Stockport Co	21	—
1989–90	Hartlepool U	11	—

SIMPSON, Fitzroy

Born Trowbridge 26.2.70 Ht 5 8
Wt 10 07
Midfield. From Trainee.

Season	Club	Apps	Goals
1988–89	Swindon T	7	—
1989–90	....	30	2

SIMPSON, Neil

Born London 15.11.61. Ht 5 10
Wt 11 06
Midfield. From Middlefield Wasps.
Scotland Youth, Under-21, 4 full caps.

Season	Club	Apps	Goals
1978–79	Aberdeen	—	—
1979–80	....	—	—
1980–81	....	16	2
1981–82	....	29	4
1982–83	....	33	5
1983–84	....	24	2
1984–85	....	33	4
1985–86	....	22	1
1986–87	....	9	—
1987–88	....	15	1
1988–89	....	16	—
1989–90	....	9	—

SIMPSON, Paul

Born Carlisle 26.7.66. Ht 5 7 Wt 11 04
Forward. From Apprentice. England
Youth, Under-21.

Season	Club	Apps	Goals
1983–84	Manchester C	—	—
1984–85	....	10	6
1985–86	....	37	8
1986–87	....	32	3
1987–88	....	38	1
1988–89	....	1	—
1988–89	Oxford U................	25	8
1989–90	....	42	9

SIMS, Steve

Born Lincoln 2.7.57. Ht 6 1 Wt 14 04
Defender. From Apprentice. England
Youth, Under-21 B.

Season	Club	League Appearances/Goals	
1974–75	Leicester C	—	—
1975–76		10	—
1976–77		32	1
1977–78		29	2
1978–79		8	—
1978–79	Watford	14	1
1979–80		34	2
1980–81		37	1
1981–82		17	—
1982–83		28	—
1983–84		22	—
1984–85		—	—
1984–85	Notts Co	34	2
1985–86		41	—
1986–87		10	3
1986–87	Watford	19	1
1987–88	Aston Villa	29	—
1988–89		12	—
1989–90		—	—

SINCLAIR, Chris

Born Sheffield 11.11.70. Ht 5 9
Wt 10 05
Midfield. From Sauchie Ath.

Season	Club	Apps	Goals
1989–90	Dunfermline Ath	1	—

SINCLAIR, Jade

Born Saltburn 6.11.71.
Midfield. From Trainee.

Season	Club	Apps	Goals
1989–90	Hartlepool U	4	—

SINCLAIR, Ron

Born Stirling 19.11.64. Ht 5 9 Wt 11 13
Goalkeeper. From Apprentice. Scotland Schools, Youth.

Season	Club	Apps	Goals
1982–83	Nottingham F	—	—
1983–84		—	—
1983–84	*Wrexham*	11	—
1984–85	Nottingham F	—	—
1984–85	*Derby Co*	—	—
1985–86	Nottingham F	—	—
1985–86	*Sheffield U*	—	—
1985–86	*Leeds U*	—	—
1986–87	Leeds U	8	—
1986–87	*Halifax T*	4	—
1987–88	Leeds U	—	—
1988–89		—	—
1988–89	*Halifax T*	10	—
1989–90	Leeds U	—	—
1989–90	Bristol C	27	—

SINCLAIR, Trevor

Born Dulwich 2.3.73.
Midfield. From Trainee.

Season	Club	Apps	Goals
1989–90	Blackpool	9	—

SINGLETON, Martin

Born Banbury 2.8.63. Ht 5 10 Wt 11 00
Midfield. From Apprentice. England Youth.

Season	Club	Apps	Goals
1980–81	Coventry C	—	—
1981–82		3	1
1982–83		5	—
1983–84		13	—
1984–85		2	—
1984–85	Bradford C	17	—
1985–86		36	2
1986–87		18	1
1986–87	WBA	7	—
1987–88		12	1
1987–88	Northampton T	29	3
1988–89		11	1
1989–90		10	—

SINNOTT, Lee

Born Pelsall 12.7.65. Ht 6 1 Wt 12 07
Defender. From Apprentice. England Youth, Under-21.

Season	Club	Apps	Goals
1981–82	Walsall	4	—
1982–83		32	2
1983–84		4	—
1983–84	Watford	20	—
1984–85		30	—
1985–86		18	2
1986–87		10	—
1987–88	Bradford C	42	1
1988–89		42	2
1989–90		45	2

SINTON, Andy

Born Newcastle. 19.3.66. Ht 5 8
Wt 10 10

Season	Club	League Appearances/Goals	

Midfield. From Apprentice. England Schools, B.

1982–83	Cambridge U	13	5
1983–84		34	6
1984–85		26	2
1985–86		20	—
1985–86	Brentford	26	3
1986–87		46	5
1987–88		46	11
1988–89		31	9
1988–89	QPR	10	3
1989–90		38	6

SITTON, John

Born Hackney 21.10.59. Ht 5 11 Wt 12 04
Defender. From Apprentice.

1978–79	Chelsea	12	—
1979–80		1	—
1979–80	Millwall	13	1
1980–81		32	—
1981–82		—	—
1981–82	Gillingham	30	2
1982–83		30	—
1983–84		42	3
1984–85		5	—
1985–86	Orient	39	—
1986–87		13	—
1987–88		20	1
1988–89		37	4
1989–90		37	2

SKINNER, Justin

Born London 30.1.69. Ht 6 0 Wt 11 03
Midfield. From Apprentice.

1986–87	Fulham	3	—
1987–88		32	6
1988–89		38	8
1989–90		30	4

SKIPPER, Peter

Born Hull 11.4.58. Ht 6 0 Wt 13 08
Defender. Local.

1978–79	Hull C	17	2
1979–80		6	—
1979–80	*Scunthorpe U*	1	—
1980–81	Darlington	46	2
1981–82		45	2
1982–83	Hull C	46	4
1983–84		46	1
1984–85		46	5
1985–86		40	1
1986–87		41	4
1987–88		43	2
1988–89		3	—
1988–89	Oldham Ath	27	1
1989–90	Walsall	40	1

SLACK, Trevor

Born Peterborough 26.9.62. Ht 6 1 Wt 13 00
Defender. From Apprentice.

1980–81	Peterborough U	35	4
1981–82		7	2
1982–83		40	1
1983–84		39	3
1984–85		41	3
1985–86		40	5
1986–87	Rotherham U	15	1
1987–88	Grimsby T	21	—
1987–88	Northampton T	13	1
1988–89	Chesterfield	21	—
1989–90		2	—

SLATER, Stuart

Born Sudbury 27.3.69. Ht 5 9 Wt 10 04
Forward. From Apprentice. England Under-21.

1986–87	West Ham U	—	—
1987–88		2	—
1988–89		18	1
1989–90		40	7

SLATTER, Neil

Born Cardiff 30.5.64. Ht 5 11 Wt 10 09
Defender. From Apprentice.
Wales Youth, Under-21, 22 full caps.

1980–81	Bristol R	4	—
1981–82		28	1
1982–83		36	—
1983–84		43	1

Season	Club	League Appearances/Goals	
1984–85		37	2
1985–86	Oxford U	22	2
1986–87		18	1
1987–88		16	3
1988–89		25	—
1989–90		10	—
1989–90	*Bournemouth*	6	—

SLAVEN, Bernie

Born Paisley 13.11.60. Ht 5 11 Wt 12 00
Forward. Eire 4 full caps.

Season	Club	League Appearances/Goals	
1981–82	Morton	31	1
1982–83		9	—
1983–84	Airdrie	2	—
1983–84	Queen of the South	2	—
1983–84	Albion R	3	—
1984–85		39	27
1985–86	Middlesbrough	32	8
1986–87		46	17
1987–88		44	21
1988–89		37	15
1989–90		46	21

SLEEUWENHOEK, Kris

Born Oldham 2.10.71 Ht 5 7 Wt 10 00
Forward. From Wolverhampton W schoolboys.

Season	Club	League Appearances/Goals	
1988–89	Derby Co	—	—
1989–90		—	—

SLINGSBY, Lee

Born Doncaster 27.11.70. Ht 5 7 Wt 11 04
Midfield. From Doncaster R. Trainee.

Season	Club	League Appearances/Goals	
1989–90	Scarborough	1	—

SMALL, Colin

Born Stockport 9.11.70.
Midfield. From Manchester C. Trainee.

Season	Club	League Appearances/Goals	
1989–90	Rochdale	7	1

SMALLER, Paul

Born Scunthorpe 18.9.70
Forward. From Trainee.

Season	Club	League Appearances/Goals	
1988–89	Grimsby T	1	—
1989–90		1	—

SMALLEY, Mark

Born Newark 2.1.65. Ht 5 11 Wt 11 06
Defender. From Apprentice. England Youth.

Season	Club	League Appearances/Goals	
1982–83	Nottingham F	1	—
1983–84		1	—
1984–85		1	—
1985–86		—	—
1985–86	*Birmingham C*	7	—
1986–87	Orient	22	1
1986–87	Nottingham F	—	—
1986–87	*Bristol R*	10	—
1987–88	Leyton Orient	35	3
1988–89		4	—
1989–90		3	—
1989–90	Mansfield T	28	1

SMALLEY, Paul

Born Nottingham 17.11.66. Ht 5 11 Wt 11 0
Defender. From Apprentice. England Youth.

Season	Club	League Appearances/Goals	
1984–85	Notts Co	—	—
1985–86		26	—
1986–87		46	—
1987–88		46	—
1988–89		—	—
1988–89	Scunthorpe U	39	1
1989–90		44	—

SMART, Gary

Born Totnes 29.4.64 Ht 5 9 Wt 11 03
Defender. From Wokingham.

Season	Club	League Appearances/Goals	
1988–89	Oxford U	17	—
1989–90		40	—

SMART, Jason

Born Rochdale 15.2.69. Ht 6 0 Wt 12 10
Defender. From Trainee.

Season	Club	League Appearances/Goals	
1985–86	Rochdale	1	—
1986–87		38	1
1987–88		36	3

Season	Club	League Appearances/Goals	
1988–89		42	—
1989–90	Crewe Alex	41	2

SMILLIE, Neil

Born Barnsley 19.7.58. Ht 5 6 Wt 10 07
Forward. From Apprentice.

Season	Club		
1975–76	Crystal Palace	—	—
1976–77		1	—
1976–77	*Brentford*	3	—
1977–78	Crystal Palace	1	—
1978–79		8	1
1979–80		8	1
1980–81		24	2
1981–82		41	3
1982–83	Brighton	25	—
1983–84		26	2
1984–85		24	—
1985–86	Watford	16	3
1986–87		—	—
1986–87	Reading	16	—
1987–88		23	—
1988–89	Brentford	28	2
1989–90		43	5

SMITH, Alan

Born Birmingham 21.11.62. Ht 6 3
Wt 12 08
Forward. From Alvechurch. England B, 4 full caps. Football League.

Season	Club		
1982–83	Leicester C	39	13
1983–84		40	15
1984–85		39	12
1985–86		40	19
1986–87		33	14
1986–87	*Leicester C*	9	3
1987–88	Arsenal	39	11
1988–89		36	23
1989–90		38	10

SMITH, Brian

Born Sheffield 27.10.66. Ht 5 10
Wt 11 06
Defender. Local.

Season	Club		
1984–85	Sheffield U	6	—
1985–86		8	—
1986–87		12	—
1986–87	*Scunthorpe U*	6	1
1987–88	Sheffield U	23	—
1988–89		35	—
1989–90		—	—

SMITH, Colin

Born Ruddington 3.11.58. Ht 6 0
Wt 12 10
Defender. Local.

Season	Club		
1981–82	Nottingham F	—	—
1982–83	Norwich C	4	—
From Sea Bee, Hong Kong			
1983–84	Cardiff C	34	2
1984–85		16	1
1984–85	Aldershot	17	—
1985–86		34	1
1986–87		27	—
1987–88		42	1
1988–89		45	2
1989–90		25	—

SMITH, David

Born Sidcup 25.6.61. Ht 6 0 Wt 11 00
Forward. From Welling U.

Season	Club		
1986–87	Gillingham	27	1
1987–88		35	7
1988–89		42	2
1989–90	Bristol C	45	4

SMITH, David

Born Gloucester 29.3.68. Ht 5 8
Wt 10 02
Midfield. England Under-21.

Season	Club		
1986–87	Coventry C	—	—
1987–88		16	4
1988–89		35	3
1989–90		37	6

SMITH, David

Born Liverpool 26.12.70. Ht 5 9
Wt 11 12
Midfield. From Trainee.

Season	Club	Apps	Goals
1989–90	Norwich C	1	—

SMITH, Dean

Born West Bromwich 19.3.71 Ht 6 1 Wt 12 00
Defender. From Trainee.

Season	Club	Apps	Goals
1988–89	Walsall	15	—
1989–90		7	—

SMITH, Shaun

Born Leeds 9.4.71
Midfield. From Trainee.

Season	Club	Apps	Goals
1988–89	Halifax T	1	—
1989–90		6	—

SMITH, Gary

Born Lichfield 30.12.68.
Midfield.

Season	Club	Apps	Goals
1987–88		—	—
1988–89	Walsall	—	—
1989–90	Gillingham	1	—

SMITH, Henry

Born Lanark 10.3.56. Ht 6 2 Wt 12 00
Goalkeeper. From school. Scotland Under-21.

Season	Club	Apps	Goals
1978–79	Leeds U	—	—
1979–80		—	—
1980–81		—	—
1981–82	Hearts	33	—
1982–83		39	—
1983–84		36	—
1984–85		36	—
1985–86		36	—
1986–87		43	—
1987–88		44	—
1988–89		36	—
1989–90		36	—

SMITH, Jim

Born Elderslie 14.5.61. Ht 6 1 Wt 11 04
Defender. From Greenock Juniors.

Season	Club	Apps	Goals
1980–81	Dundee	—	—
1981–82		17	1
1982–83		36	1
1983–84		34	—
1984–85		23	1
1985–86		32	—
1986–87		39	—
1987–88		40	2
1988–89		7	—
1989–90		4	—

SMITH, Jim

Born Johnstone 22.11.69 Ht 5 9 Wt 10 02
Midfield. From Trainee.

Season	Club	Apps	Goals
1987–88	Torquay U	1	—
1988–89		34	4
1989–90		10	1

SMITH, John

Born Liverpool 23.7.70. Ht 5 7 Wt 10 12
Midfield.

Season	Club	Apps	Goals
1987–88	Tranmere R	—	—
1988–89		2	—

SMITH, Malcolm

Born Maidstone 3.8.70 Ht 5 7 Wt 11 04
Midfield. From Trainee.

Season	Club	Apps	Goals
1987–88	Gillingham	2	—
1988–89		—	—

SMITH, Mark

Born Sheffield 21.3.60. Ht 6 0 Wt 11 11
Defender. From Apprentice. England Under-21.

Season	Club	Apps	Goals
1977–78	Sheffield W	2	—
1978–79		21	—
1979–80		44	9
1980–81		41	1
1981–82		41	—
1982–83		41	2
1983–84		27	2
1984–85		36	2
1985–86		13	—
1986–87		16	—
1987–88	Plymouth Arg	41	6
1988–89		35	—

Season	Club	League Appearances/Goals	
1989–90		6	—
1989–90	Barnsley	25	3

SMITH, Mark

Born Sheffield 19.12.61. Ht 5 9 Wt 12 0
Forward.

Season	Club	Apps	Goals
1979–80	Sheffield U	—	—
1980–81		—	—
1981–82		—	—
From Worksop, Gainsborough T.			
1985–86	Scunthorpe U	1	—
From Kettering			
1988–89	Rochdale	27	7
1988–89	Huddersfield T	20	2
1989–90		44	7

SMITH, Mark

Born Bell Hill 16.12.64. Ht 5 9 Wt 10 01
Forward. From St Mirren BC.

Season	Club	Apps	Goals
1983–84	Queen's Park	15	2
1984–85		36	2
1985–86		31	3
1986–87	Celtic	6	1
1987–88	Dunfermline Ath	30	5
1988–89		23	1
1989–90		—	—
1989–90	*Stoke C*	2	—
1989–90	Nottingham F	—	—

SMITH, Michael

Born Hull 19.12.68. Ht 5 8 Wt 12 03
Forward.

Season	Club	Apps	Goals
1987–88	Hull C	—	—
1988–89		12	1
1989–90		1	—

SMITH, Mick

Born Sunderland 28.10.58. Ht 6 0
Wt 11 09
Defender. Lambton St BC.

Season	Club	Apps	Goals
1977–78	Lincoln C	5	—
1978–79		20	—
1979–80		—	—
1979–80	Wimbledon	20	—
1980–81		45	2
1981–82		39	2
1982–83		24	4
1983–84		24	3
1984–85		23	—
1984–85	*Aldershot*	7	—
1985–86	Wimbledon	24	3
1986–87		6	—
1987–88		—	—
From Seaham Red Star.			
1989–90	Hartlepool U	35	5

SMITH, Mike

Born Bangor 30.4.69. Ht 5 10 Wt 10 9
Midfield. From Livingston Colts.

Season	Club	Apps	Goals
1986–87	St Johnstone	2	—
1987–88		17	2
1988–89		12	—
1989–90		2	—
1989–90	*Cowdenbeath*	11	—

SMITH, Neil

Born Warley 10.2.70. Ht 5 11 Wt 12 00
Midfield. From Trainee.

Season	Club	Apps	Goals
1988–89	Shrewsbury T	1	—
From Reddich			
1989–90	Lincoln C	4	—

SMITH, Nick

Born Berkley 28.1.69. Ht 5 8
Wt 10 00
Midfield.

Season	Club	Apps	Goals
1986–87	Southend U	1	—
1987–88		34	5
1988–89		11	—
1989–90		14	1

SMITH, Nigel

Born Leeds 21.12.69.
Midfield. From Leeds U.

Season	Club	Apps	Goals
1989–90	Burnley	11	—

SMITH, Paul

Born Currie 2.11.62 Ht 5 11 Wt 11 04
Forward. From Edinburgh BC.

Season	Club	League Appearances/Goals	
1980–81	Dundee	—	—
1981–82		—	—
1982–83	Dundee U	—	—
1982–83	Raith R	16	2
1983–84		38	8
1984–85		38	19
1985–86		35	21
1986–87	Motherwell	44	9
1987–88		30	4
1988–89		4	—
1988–89	Dunfermline Ath	35	5
1989–90		33	4

SMITH, Paul

Born Rotherham 9.11.64. Ht 5 10
Wt 10 09
Forward. From Apprentice.

Season	Club	League Appearances/Goals	
1982–83	Sheffield U	7	—
1983–84		3	—
1984–85		8	1
1985–86		18	—
1985–86	*Stockport Co*	7	5
1986–87	Port Vale	42	7
1987–88		2	—
1987–88	Lincoln C	*33*	*8*
1988–89		28	10
1989–90		33	5

SMITH, Paul

Born London 5.10.67. Ht 5 8 Wt 9 09
Forward. From Apprentice.

Season	Club	League Appearances/Goals	
1985–86	Arsenal	—	—
1986–87		—	—
1987–88	Brentford	17	1
1988–89	Bristol R	16	1
1988–89	Torquay U	11	1
1989–90		33	6

SMITH, Paul

Born Lenham 18.9.71.
Forward. From Trainee.

Season	Club	League Appearances/Goals	
1989–90	Southend U	10	1

SMITH, Richard

Born Leicester 3.10.70.
Defender. From Trainee.

Season	Club	League Appearances/Goals	
1988–89	Leicester C	—	—
1989–90		4	—
1989–90	*Cambridge U*	4	—

SMYTH, John

Born Dundalk 28.4.70. Ht 5 10 Wt 11 00
Defender. From Dundalk.

Season	Club	League Appearances/Goals	
1987–88	Liverpool	—	—
1988–89		—	—
1989–90		—	—

SNEDDON, Alan

Born Baillieston 12.3.58. Ht 5 11
Wt 12 03
Defender. From Larkhall Thistle. Scotland Under-21.

Season	Club	League Appearances/Goals	
1977–78	Celtic	15	—
1978–79		4	—
1979–80		32	1
1980–81		15	—
1980–81	Hibernian	14	—
1981–82		36	—
1982–83		36	—
1983–84		35	1
1984–85		36	2
1985–86		31	2
1986–87		26	—
1987–88		32	—
1988–89		26	—
1989–90		29	2

SNELDERS, Theo

Born Westervoort 7.12.63 Ht 6 2
Wt 14 02
Goalkeeper. From Twente. Holland full caps.

Season	Club	League Appearances/Goals	
1988–89	Aberdeen	36	—
1989–90		23	—

SNODIN, Glynn

Born Rotherham 14.2.60. Ht 5 6
Wt 9 05
Midfield. From Apprentice.

Season	Club	League Appearances/Goals	
1976–77	Doncaster R	4	—
1977–78		22	2

Season	Club	League Appearances/Goals	
1978–79		34	3
1979–80		41	1
1980–81		44	3
1981–82		40	7
1982–83		38	14
1983–84		43	13
1984–85		43	18
1985–86	Sheffield W	28	1
1986–87		31	—
1987–88	Leeds U	35	7
1988–89		35	3
1989–90		4	—

SNODIN, Ian

Born Rotherham 15.8.63. Ht 5 7
Wt 8 11
Midfield. From Apprentice. England Youth, Under-21.

Season	Club	Apps	Goals
1979–80	Doncaster R	9	1
1980–81		32	2
1981–82		33	2
1982–83		34	3
1983–84		39	9
1984–85		41	8
1985–86	Leeds U	37	5
1986–87		14	1
1986–87	Everton	16	—
1987–88		31	2
1988–89		23	—
1989–90		25	—

SNOOK, Eddie

Born Washington 18.10.68. Ht 5 7
Wt 10 01
Midfield. From Apprentice.

Season	Club	Apps	Goals
1986–87	Notts Co	—	—
1987–88		—	—
1988–89		—	—
1989–90		—	—

SNOW, Simon

Born Sheffield 3.4.66.
Forward. From Sutton T.

Season	Club	Apps	Goals
1989–90	Preston NE	1	—

SOLOMAN, Jason

Born Welwyn 6.10.70. Ht 6 1 Wt 11 09
Defender. From Trainee.

Season	Club	Apps	Goals
1988–89	Watford	—	—
1989–90		—	—

SORBIE, Stuart

Born Glasgow 7.9.63. Ht 5 9 Wt 10 05
Forward. From Milngavie Wanderers.

Season	Club	Apps	Goals
1983–84	Alloa	2	1
1984–85		36	5
1985–86		32	11
1986–87		38	14
1987–88		39	12
1988–89	St Johnstone	35	7
1989–90		3	—
1989–90	Raith R	14	1
1989–90	*Alloa*	10	2

SORRELL, Tony

Born London 17.10.66. Ht 5 10
Wt 12 04
Midfield. From Barking and Bishop's Stortford (1988).

Season	Club	Apps	Goals
1989–90	Maidstone U	28	3

SOUNESS, Graeme

Born Edinburgh 6.5.53. Ht 5 11
Wt 12 13
Midfield. From Apprentice.
Scotland Schools, Under-23, 54 full caps.

Season	Club	Apps	Goals
1970–71	Tottenham H	—	—
1971–72		—	—
1972–73		—	—
1972–73	Middlesbrough	11	—
1973–74		35	7
1974–75		38	7
1975–76		35	3
1976–77		38	2
1977–78		19	3
1977–78	Liverpool	15	2
1978–79		41	8
1979–80		41	1

Season	Club	League Appearances/Goals	
1980–81		37	6
1981–82		35	5
1982–83		41	9
1983–84		37	7
1984–85	Sampdoria	28	5
1985–86		28	3
1986–87	Rangers	25	1
1987–88		18	2
1988–89		6	—
1989–90		1	—

SOUTHALL, Neville

Born Llandudno 16.9.58. Ht 6 1
Wt 12 02
Goalkeeper. From Winsford.
Wales Under-21, 44 full caps.

Season	Club	League Appearances/Goals	
1980–81	Bury	39	—
1981–82	Everton	26	—
1982–83		17	—
1982–83	*Port Vale*	9	—
1983–84	Everton	35	—
1984–85		42	—
1985–86		32	—
1986–87		31	—
1987–88		32	—
1988–89		38	—
1989–90		38	—

SOUTHGATE, Gareth

Born Watford 3.9.70. Ht 5 10 Wt 11 12
Defender. From Trainee.

Season	Club	League Appearances/Goals	
1988–89	Crystal Palace	—	—
1989–90		—	—

SPACKMAN, Nigel

Born Romsey 2.12.60. Ht 6 1 Wt 13 02
Midfield. From Andover.

Season	Club	League Appearances/Goals	
1980–81	Bournemouth	44	3
1981–82		35	3
1982–83		40	4
1983–84	Chelsea	40	3
1984–85		42	1
1985–86		39	7
1986–87		20	1
1986–87	Liverpool	12	—
1987–88		27	—
1988–89		12	—
1988–89	QPR	16	1
1989–90		13	—
1989–90	Rangers	21	1

SPARHAM, Sean

Born Bexley 4.12.68. Ht 5 7 Wt 10 10
Defender.

Season	Club	League Appearances/Goals	
1986–87	Millwall	—	—
1987–88		—	—
1988–89		12	—
1989–90		9	—
1989–90	*Brentford*	5	1

SPEARING, Tony

Born Romford 7.10.64. Ht 5 9 Wt 10 12
Defender. From Apprentice. England Youth.

Season	Club	League Appearances/Goals	
1982–83	Norwich C	—	—
1983–84		4	—
1984–85		—	—
1984–85	*Stoke C*	9	—
1984–85	*Oxford U*	5	—
1985–86	Norwich C	8	—
1986–87		39	—
1987–88		18	—
1988–89	Leicester C	36	—
1989–90		20	1

SPEED, Gary

Born Hawarden 8.9.69 Ht 5 9 Wt 10 06
Midfield. From Trainee. Wales Under-21, 1 full cap.

Season	Club	League Appearances/Goals	
1988–89	Leeds U	1	—
1989–90		25	3

SPEEDIE, David

Born Glenrothes 20.2.60. Ht 5 7
Wt 11 00
Forward. From Amateur. Scotland Under-21, 10 full caps.

Season	Club	League Appearances/Goals	
1978–79	Barnsley	10	—
1979–80		13	—
1980–81	Darlington	44	4
1981–82		44	17

Season	Club	League Appearances/Goals	
1982–83	Chelsea	34	7
1983–84		37	13
1984–85		35	10
1985–86		34	14
1986–87		22	3
1987–88	Coventry C	36	6
1988–89		36	14
1989–90		32	8

SPEIRS, Gardner

Born Airdrie 14.4.63. Ht 5 8 Wt 10 00
Forward. From St Mirren BC. Scotland Youth.

Season	Club	Apps	Goals
1979–80	St Mirren	—	—
1980–81		2	—
1981–82		3	—
1982–83		1	—
1983–84		10	—
1984–85		17	6
1985–86		31	7
1986–87		26	2
1987–88		—	—
1988–89	Kilmarnock	5	—
1988–89	Dunfermline Ath	4	—
1989–90	Hartlepool U	1	—

SPINK, Nigel

Born Chelmsford 8.8.58. Ht 6 1
Wt 14 10
Goalkeeper. From Chelmsford C. England, 1 full cap.

Season	Club	Apps	Goals
1976–77	Aston Villa	—	—
1977–78		—	—
1978–79		—	—
1979–80		1	—
1980–81		—	—
1981–82		—	—
1982–83		22	—
1983–84		28	—
1984–85		19	—
1985–86		31	—
1986–87		32	—
1987–88		44	—

Season	Club	League Appearances/Goals	
1988–89		34	—
1989–90		38	—

SPINK, Dean

Born Birmingham 22.1.67.
Forward. From Halesowen.

Season	Club	Apps	Goals
1989–90	Aston Villa	—	—
1989–90	*Scarborough*	3	2
1989–90	*Bury*	6	1
1989–90	Shrewsbury T	13	5

SPOONER, Steve

Born London 25.1.61. Ht 5 10 Wt 12 00
Midfield. From Apprentice.

Season	Club	Apps	Goals
1978–79	Derby Co	1	—
1979–80		1	—
1980–81		2	—
1981–82		4	—
1981–82	Halifax T	29	2
1982–83		43	11
1983–84	Chesterfield	20	3
1984–85		41	6
1985–86		32	5
1986–87	Hereford U	42	11
1987–88		42	8
1988–89	York C	31	5
1989–90		41	6

SPROSON, Phil

Born Trent Vale 13.10.59. Ht 6 0
Wt 12 00
Defender. From Amateur.

Season	Club	Apps	Goals
1977–78	Port Vale	2	—
1978–79		23	—
1979–80		39	3
1980–81		44	1
1981–82		42	6
1982–83		42	4
1983–84		38	2
1984–85		44	3
1985–86		44	4
1986–87		44	5
1987–88		44	3

Season	Club	League Appearances	Goals
1988–89	....	20	2
1989–90	Birmingham C	12	—

STAFFORD, Clive

Born Ipswich 4.4.63 Ht 6 1 Wt 12 02
Defender. From Diss T.

Season	Club	League Appearances	Goals
1988–89	Colchester U	16	—
1989–90	....	17	—
1989–90	*Exeter C*	2	—

STAINROD, Simon

Born Sheffield 1.2.59. Ht 5 10 Wt 12 9
Forward. From Apprentice. England Youth.

Season	Club	League Appearances	Goals
1975–76	Sheffield U	7	2
1976–77	....	21	3
1977–78	....	25	6
1978–79	....	14	3
1978–79	Oldham Ath	14	5
1979–80	....	37	11
1980–81	....	18	5
1980–81	QPR	15	4
1981–82	....	39	17
1982–83	....	31	9
1983–84	....	41	13
1984–85	....	19	5
1984–85	Sheffield W	9	1
1985–86	....	6	1
1985–86	Aston Villa..............	30	10
1986–87	....	29	6
1987–88	....	4	—
1987–88	Stoke C	12	2
1988–89	....	16	4

To Strasbourg

STANCLIFFE, Paul

Born Sheffield 5.5.58. Ht 6 2 Wt 13 03
Defender. From Apprentice.

Season	Club	League Appearances	Goals
1975–76	Rotherham U	42	2
1976–77	....	46	—
1977–78	....	32	3
1978–79	....	33	—
1979–80	....	33	1
1980–81	....	44	—
1981–82	....	42	2
1982–83	....	13	—
1983–84	Sheffield U	43	1
1984–85	....	33	1
1985–86	....	40	1
1986–87	....	36	2
1987–88	....	41	3
1988–89	....	42	3
1989–90	....	40	1

STANISLAUS, Roger

Born Hammersmith 2.11.68. Ht 5 9
Wt 12 11
Defender. From Trainee.

Season	Club	League Appearances	Goals
1986–87	Arsenal	—	—
1987–88	Brentford................	37	2
1988–89	....	43	1
1989–90	....	31	1

STANNARD, Jim

Born London 6.10.62. Ht 6 0 Wt 13 02
Goalkeeper. Local.

Season	Club	League Appearances	Goals
1980–81	Fulham....................	17	—
1981–82	....	2	—
1982–83	....	—	—
1983–84	....	15	—
1984–85	....	7	—
1984–85	*Charlton Ath*	1	—
1984–85	*Southend U*	17	—
1985–86	Southend U	46	—
1986–87	....	46	—
1987–88	Fulham....................	46	—
1988–89	....	45	—
1989–90	....	44	1

STANT, Phil

Born Bolton 13.10.62. Ht 6 1 Wt 12 07
Forward. From Camberley.

Season	Club	League Appearances	Goals
1982–83	Reading..................	4	2
From Army			
1986–87	Hereford U	9	1
1987–88	....	39	9
1988–89	....	41	28
1989–90	Notts Co	22	6

STAPLETON, Frank

Born Dublin 10.7.56. Ht 6 0 Wt 13 01
Forward. From Apprentice.

Season	Club	League Appearances/Goals	

Season Club League Appearances/Goals

Eire Youth, 70 full caps.

1973–74	Arsenal	—	—
1974–75		1	—
1975–76		25	4
1976–77		40	13
1977–78		39	13
1978–79		41	17
1979–80		39	14
1980–81		40	14
1981–82	Manchester U	41	13
1982–83		41	14
1983–84		42	13
1984–85		24	6
1985–86		41	7
1986–87		34	7
1987–88	Ajax	4	—
1987–88	Derby Co	10	1

From Le Havre

1989–90	Blackburn R	43	3

STARBUCK, Philip

Born Nottingham 24.11.68. Ht 5 10
Wt 10 13
Forward. From Apprentice.

1986–87	Nottingham F	5	2
1987–88		10	—
1987–88	*Birmingham C*	3	—
1988–89	Nottingham F	7	—
1989–90		2	—
1989–90	*Hereford U*	6	—

STARK, Billy

Born Glasgow 1.12.56. Ht 6 1 Wt 11 04
Midfield. From Anniesland W. Scotland Under-21.

1975–76	St Mirren	21	6
1976–77		35	11
1977–78		33	7
1978–79		32	9
1979–80		36	8
1980–81		34	5
1981–82		33	10
1982–83		31	4
1983–84	Aberdeen	14	6
1984–85		32	15
1985–86		30	8
1986–87		35	12
1987–88	Celtic	37	8
1988–89		25	9
1989–90		2	—

STATHAM, Brian

Born Zimbabwe 21.5.69. Ht 5 11
Wt 11 00
Defender. From Apprentice. England Under-21.

1987–88	Tottenham H	18	—
1988–89		6	—
1989–90		—	—

STATHAM, Derek

Born Wolverhampton 24.3.59. Ht 5 5
Wt 11 10
Defender. From Apprentice.
England Youth, Under-21, B, 3 full caps.

1976–77	WBA	16	1
1977–78		40	—
1978–79		39	1
1979–80		16	—
1980–81		31	—
1981–82		35	—
1982–83		32	2
1983–84		16	—
1984–85		30	4
1985–86		37	—
1986–87		6	—
1987–88		1	—
1987–88	Southampton	38	—
1988–89		26	2
1989–90	Stoke C	19	—

STAUNTON, Steve

Born Drogheda 19.1.69. Ht 5 11
Wt 11 02
Defender. From Dundalk. Eire Under-21, 18 full caps.

1986–87	Liverpool	—	—
1987–88		—	—
1987–88	*Bradford C*	8	—

Season	Club	League Appearances/Goals	
1988–89	Liverpool	21	—
1989–90		20	—

STEBBING, Gary

Born Croydon 11.8.65. Ht 5 9 Wt 11 06
Defender. From Apprentice. England Youth.

Season	Club	Apps	Goals
1982–83	Crystal Palace	—	—
1983–84		31	2
1984–85		24	1
1985–86		3	—
1985–86	*Southend U*	5	—
1986–87	Crystal Palace	23	—
1987–88		21	—
From KV Ostend.			
1989–90	Maidstone U	6	—

STEEL, Jim

Born Dumfries 4.12.59. Ht 6 3 Wt 14 00
Forward. From Apprentice.

Season	Club	Apps	Goals
1978–79	Oldham Ath	7	4
1979–80		33	10
1980–81		24	3
1981–82		37	7
1982–83		7	—
1982–83	*Wigan Ath*	2	2
1982–83	*Wrexham*	9	6
1982–83	Port Vale	13	3
1983–84		15	3
1983–84	Wrexham	21	—
1984–85		45	14
1985–86		43	14
1986–87		37	17
1987–88		18	6
1987–88	Tranmere R	29	7
1988–89		44	7
1989–90		36	5

STEELE, Tim

Born Coventry 1.2.67. Ht 5 9 Wt 10 10
Forward. From Apprentice.

Season	Club	Apps	Goals
1985–86	Shrewsbury T	2	—
1986–87		11	1
1987–88		33	3
1988–89		15	1
1988–89	Wolverhampton W	11	1
1989–90		15	1

STEIN, Brian

Born S. Africa 19.10.57. Ht 5 10
Wt 11 08
Forward. From Edgware T.
England Under-21, 1 full cap.

Season	Club	Apps	Goals
1977–78	Luton T	24	3
1978–79		34	10
1979–80		42	8
1980–81		42	18
1981–82		42	21
1982–83		21	15
1983–84		42	9
1984–85		42	9
1985–86		33	14
1986–87		38	12
1987–88		28	9
To Caen			

STEIN, Mark

Born S. Africa 28.1.66. Ht 5 5 Wt 11 04
Forward. England Youth.

Season	Club	Apps	Goals
1983–84	Luton T	1	—
1984–85		1	—
1985–86		6	—
1985–86	*Aldershot*	2	1
1986–87	Luton T	21	8
1987–88		25	11
1988–89	QPR	31	4
1989–90		2	—
1989–90	Oxford U	41	9

STEMP, Wayne

Born Epsom 9.9.70. Ht 5 11 Wt 11 02
Defender. From Trainee.

Season	Club	Apps	Goals
1988–89	Brighton	—	—
1989–90		2	—

STEPHENSON, Geoff

Born Tynemouth 28.4.70 Ht 5 7
Wt 11 00
Defender. From Trainee.

Season	Club	Apps	Goals
1987–88	Grimsby T	—	—

Season	Club	League Appearances/Goals	
1988–89		14	—
1989–90		7	—

STEPHENSON, Paul

Born Wallsend 2.1.68. Ht 5 10 Wt 10 9
Forward. From Apprentice. England Youth.

Season	Club	League Appearances/Goals	
1985–86	Newcastle U	22	1
1986–87		24	—
1987–88		7	—
1988–89		8	—
1989–90	Millwall	12	1
1989–90		23	2

STERLAND, Mel

Born Sheffield 1.10.61. Ht 6 0 Wt 13 05
Defender. From Apprentice.
England Under-21, B, 1 full cap. Football League.

Season	Club	League Appearances/Goals	
1978–79	Sheffield W	2	1
1979–80		2	—
1980–81		22	2
1981–82		27	—
1982–83		35	—
1983–84		39	8
1984–85		24	2
1985–86		38	8
1986–87		30	2
1987–88		38	8
1988–89		22	6
1988–89	Rangers	9	3
1989–90	Leeds U	42	5

STERLING, Worrell

Born Bethnal Green 8.6.65. Ht 5 7
Wt 10 11
Midfield. From Apprentice.

Season	Club	League Appearances/Goals	
1982–83	Watford	3	—
1983–84		10	1
1984–85		15	4
1985–86		24	3
1986–87		18	4
1987–88		21	2
1988–89		3	—
1988–89	Peterborough U	12	3
1989–90		46	5

STEVEN, Trevor

Born Berwick 21.9.63. Ht 5 8 Wt 10 09
Midfield. From Apprentice. England Under-21, 29 full caps.

Season	Club	League Appearances/Goals	
1980–81	Burnley	1	—
1981–82		36	3
1982–83		39	8
1983–84	Everton	27	1
1984–85		40	12
1985–86		41	9
1986–87		41	14
1987–88		36	6
1988–89		29	6
1989–90	Rangers	34	3

STEVENS, David

Born Plumstead 19.10.70. Ht 5 11
Wt 11 00
Midfield. From Trainee.

Season	Club	League Appearances/Goals	
1988–89	Crystal Palace	—	—
1989–90		—	—

STEVENS, Gary

Born Barrow 27.3.63. Ht 5 11 Wt 10 11
Defender. From Apprentice. England 41 full caps.

Season	Club	League Appearances/Goals	
1980–81	Everton	—	—
1981–82		19	1
1982–83		28	—
1983–84		27	1
1984–85		37	3
1985–86		41	1
1986–87		25	2
1987–88		31	—
1988–89	Rangers	35	1
1989–90		35	1

STEVENS, Gary

Born Birmingham 30.8.54. Ht 6 2
Wt 11 01
Defender. From Evesham.

Season	Club	League Appearances/Goals	
1978–79	Cardiff C	34	13

Season	Club	League Appearances/Goals	
1979–80		38	11
1980–81		40	7
1981–82		38	13
1982–83		—	—
1982–83	Shrewsbury T	35	4
1983–84		38	1
1984–85		39	20
1985–86		38	4
1986–87	Brentford	32	10
1986–87	Hereford U	10	—
1987–88		45	7
1988–89		33	3
1989–90		6	—

STEVENS, Gary

Born Hillingdon 30.3.62. Ht 6 0
Wt 12 00
Defender. From Apprentice.
England Under-21, 7 full caps.

Season	Club	Apps	Goals
1979–80	Brighton	26	1
1980–81		34	1
1981–82		32	—
1982–83		41	—
1983–84	Tottenham H	40	4
1984–85		28	—
1985–86		29	2
1986–87		20	—
1987–88		18	—
1988–89		5	—
1989–90		7	—
1989–90	Portsmouth	21	1

STEVENS, Ian

Born Malta 21.10.66. Ht 5 9 Wt 12 00
Forward. From Trainee.

Season	Club	Apps	Goals
1984–85	Preston NE	4	1
1985–86		7	1
1986–87	Stockport Co	2	—
From Lancaster C			
1986–87	Bolton W	8	2
1987–88		9	—
1988–89		21	5
1989–90		4	—

STEVENS, Keith

Born Merton 21.6.64. Ht 6 0 Wt 12 12
Defender. From Apprentice.

Season	Club	League Appearances/Goals	
1980–81	Millwall	1	—
1981–82		7	—
1982–83		26	—
1983–84		17	—
1984–85		41	—
1985–86		33	1
1986–87		35	1
1987–88		35	1
1988–89		23	—
1989–90		28	—

STEVENSON, Andy

Born Scunthorpe 29.9.67. Ht 6 0
Wt 12 03
Midfield. From school.

Season	Club	Apps	Goals
1985–86	Scunthorpe U	2	—
1986–87		7	—
1987–88		8	—
1988–89		26	—
1989–90		24	1

STEWART, Billy

Born Liverpool 1.1.65. Ht 5 11
Wt 11 07
Goalkeeper. From Apprentice.

Season	Club	Apps	Goals
1982–83	Liverpool	—	—
1983–84		—	—
1984–85	Wigan Ath	6	—
1985–86		8	—
1986–87	Chester C	29	—
1987–88		27	—
1988–89		46	—
1989–90		46	—

STEWART, Ian

Born Belfast 10.9.61. Ht 5 7 Wt 10 9
Forward. From juniors. Northern Ireland Schools Youth, 31 full caps.

Season	Club	Apps	Goals
1980–81	QPR	1	—
1981–82		3	—
1982–83		19	—
1982–83	*Millwall*	11	3
1983–84	QPR	31	2
1984–85		13	—
1985–86	Newcastle U	28	2
1986–87		14	1

Season	Club	Apps	Goals
1987–88	Portsmouth	1	—
1987–88	*Brentford*	7	—
1988–89	Portsmouth	—	—
1988–89	Aldershot	22	—
1989–90		43	—

STEWART, Mark

Born Bury 26.7.67. Ht 6 0 Wt 12 00
Forward.

Season	Club	Apps	Goals
1988–89	Oldham Ath	—	—
1989–90		—	—

STEWART, Paul

Born Manchester 7.10.64. Ht 5 11
Wt 11 03
Forward. From Apprentice.
England Youth, B.

Season	Club	Apps	Goals
1981–82	Blackpool	14	3
1982–83		38	7
1983–84		44	10
1984–85		31	7
1985–86		42	8
1986–87		32	21
1986–87	Manchester C	11	2
1987–88		40	24
1988–89	Tottenham H	30	12
1989–90		28	8

STEWART, Ray

Born Perth 7.9.59. Ht 5 11 Wt 11 13
Defender. From Errol Rovers.
Scotland Schools, Under-21, 10 full caps.

Season	Club	Apps	Goals
1975–76	Dundee U	—	—
1976–77		1	—
1977–78		6	1
1978–79		34	4
1979–80		3	—
1979–80	West Ham U	38	10
1980–81		41	5
1981–82		42	10
1982–83		39	8
1983–84		42	7
1984–85		37	6
1985–86		39	6
1986–87		23	4
1987–88		33	4
1988–89		6	2
1989–90		—	—

STICKROTH, Thomas

Born Stuttgart 13.4.65.
Midfield. From Bayer Uerdingen.

Season	Club	Apps	Goals
1989–90	St Mirren	7	—

STILES, John

Born Manchester 6.5.64. Ht 5 9
Wt 11 08
Midfield. From Vancouver W.

Season	Club	Apps	Goals
1984–85	Leeds U	1	—
1985–86		12	1
1986–87		29	—
1987–88		13	1
1988–89		10	—
1989–90	Doncaster R	42	2

STIMSON, Mark

Born Plaistow 27.12.67. Ht 5 11
Wt 11 00
Defender. From Trainee.

Season	Club	Apps	Goals
1984–85	Tottenham H	—	—
1985–86		—	—
1986–87		1	—
1987–88		—	—
1987–88	*Leyton Orient*	10	—
1988–89	Tottenham H	1	—
1988–89	*Gillingham*	18	—
1989–90	Newcastle U	37	1

STOCKWELL, Mike

Born Chelmsford 14.2.65. Ht 5 6
Wt 10 2
Midfield. From Apprentice.

Season	Club	Apps	Goals
1982–83	Ipswich T	—	—
1983–84		—	—
1984–85		—	—
1985–86		8	—
1986–87		21	1
1987–88		43	1

Season	Club	League Appearances/Goals	
1988–89	....	23	2
1989–90	....	34	3

STOKES, Wayne

Born Birmingham 16.2.65. Ht 6 1
Wt 13 00
Defender. From Coventry C Apprentice.

Season	Club	League Appearances/Goals	
1982–83	Gillingham..............	2	—
1983–84	....	1	—
From Finland			
1986–87	Stockport Co	18	1
1987–88	Hartlepool U............	24	—
1988–89	....	37	1
1989–90	....	1	—

STOKLE, David

Born Hartlepool 1.12.69 Ht 6 3
Wt 13 00
Defender. From Trainee.

Season	Club	League Appearances/Goals	
1986–87	Hartlepool U............	5	—
1987–88	....	3	—
1988–89	....	—	—
1989–90	....	1	—

STONE, Steven

Born Gateshead 20.8.71. Ht 5 9
Wt 11 03
Midfield. From Trainee.

Season	Club	League Appearances/Goals	
1988–89	Nottingham F	—	—
1989–90	....	—	—

STONEHOUSE, Kevin

Born Bishop Auckland 20.9.59. Ht 5 11
Wt 11 01
Forward. From Shildon.

Season	Club	League Appearances/Goals	
1979–80	Blackburn R............	7	2
1980–81	....	26	10
1981–82	....	37	11
1982–83	....	15	4
1982–83	Huddersfield T..........	5	—
1983–84	....	17	4
1983–84	Blackpool	13	5
1984–85	....	26	11
1985–86	....	16	3
1986–87	....	—	—
1987–88	Darlington	43	13
1988–89	....	29	7
1988–89	*Carlisle U*................	3	—
1989–90	Rochdale	14	2

STORER, Stuart

Born Harborough 16.1.67. Ht 5 11
Wt 11 08
Forward. Local.

Season	Club	League Appearances/Goals	
1983–84	Mansfield T	1	—
1984–85	Birmingham C	—	—
1985–86	....	2	—
1986–87	....	6	—
1986–87	Everton	—	—
1987–88	....	—	—
1987–88	*Wigan Ath*...............	12	—
1987–88	Bolton W..................	15	1
1988–89	....	23	2
1989–90	....	38	4

STOUTT, Stephen

Born Halifax 5.4.64. Ht 5 8 Wt 11 06
Defender. Local.

Season	Club	League Appearances/Goals	
1983–84	Huddersfield T.........	3	—
1984–85	....	3	—
1984–85	Wolverhampton W	—	—
1985–86	....	28	—
1986–87	....	44	4
1987–88	....	22	1
1988–89	Grimsby T	2	1
1989–90	....	1	—
1989–90	Lincoln C.................	21	—

STOWELL, Mike

Born Preston 19.4.65. Ht 6 2 Wt 11 10
Goalkeeper. From Leyland Motors.

Season	Club	League Appearances/Goals	
1984–85	Preston NE	—	—
1985–86	....	—	—
1985–86	Everton	—	—
1986–87	....	—	—
1987–88	*Chester C*................	14	—
1987–88	*York C*....................	6	—
1987–88	*Manchester C*...........	14	—
1988–89	Everton	—	—
1988–89	*Port Vale*	7	—
1988–89	*Wolverhampton W*	7	—

Season	Club	League Appearances/Goals	
1989–90	Everton	—	—
1989–90	*Preston NE*	2	—

STRACHAN, Gordon

Born Edinburgh 9.2.57. Ht 5 6 Wt 10 06
Midfield. Scotland Youth, Under-21, 43 full caps.

Season	Club	League Appearances/Goals	
1974–75	Dundee	1	—
1975–76		23	6
1976–77		36	7
1977–78	Aberdeen	12	2
1978–79		31	5
1979–80		33	10
1980–81		20	6
1981–82		30	7
1982–83		32	12
1983–84		25	13
1984–85	Manchester U	41	15
1985–86		28	5
1986–87		34	4
1987–88		36	8
1988–89		21	1
1988–89	Leeds U	11	3
1989–90		46	16

STREETE, Floyd

Born W. Indies 5.5.59. Ht 5 11 Wt 14 00
Defender. From Rivet Sports.

Season	Club	League Appearances/Goals	
1976–77	Cambridge U	3	1
1977–78		21	3
1978–79		13	1
1979–80		21	1
1980–81		22	4
1981–82		31	5
1982–83		14	4
From Utrecht and SC Cumbuur.			
1984–85	Derby Co	30	—
1985–86		5	—
1985–86	Wolverhampton W	25	1
1986–87		35	—
1987–88		44	—
1988–89		38	5
1989–90		17	—

STRINGFELLOW, Ian

Born Nottingham 8.5.69. Ht 5 9
Wt 10 03
Forward. From Apprentice.

Season	Club	League Appearances/Goals	
1985–86	Mansfield T	3	—
1986–87		22	4
1987–88		30	8
1988–89		8	1
1989–90		19	3

STRODDER, Gary

Born Leeds 1.4.65. Ht 6 1 Wt 12 06
Defender. From Apprentice.

Season	Club	League Appearances/Goals	
1982–83	Lincoln C	8	—
1983–84		22	1
1984–85		26	2
1985–86		43	1
1986–87		33	2
1986–87	West Ham U	12	—
1987–88		30	1
1988–89		7	—
1989–90		16	1

STUART, Graham

Born Tooting, London 24.10.70. Ht 5 8
Wt 11 06
Forward. From Trainee. England Under-21.

Season	Club	League Appearances/Goals	
1989–90	Chelsea	2	1

STUART, Mark

Born Hammersmith 15.12.66. Ht 5 10
Wt 11 03
Forward. From QPR Schoolboy.

Season	Club	League Appearances/Goals	
1984–85	Charlton Ath	6	1
1985–86		30	12
1986–87		36	9
1987–88		31	6
1988–89		4	—
1988–89	Plymouth Arg	32	5
1989–90		25	6
1989–90	*Ipswich T*	5	2

STURRIDGE, Simon

Born Birmingham 9.12.69 Ht 5 5
Wt 10 07
Forward. From Trainee.

Season	Club	Apps	Goals
1988–89	Birmingham C	21	3
1989–90		31	10

SUCKLING, Perry

Born Leyton 12.10.65. Ht 6 1 Wt 11 02
Goalkeeper. From Apprentice.
England Youth, Under-21.

Season	Club	Apps	Goals
1982–83	Coventry C	3	—
1983–84		24	—
1984–85		—	—
1985–86		—	—
1986–87	Manchester C	37	—
1987–88		2	—
1987–88	Crystal Palace	17	—
1988–89		27	—
1989–90		12	—
1989–90	*West Ham U*	6	—

SULLEY, Chris

Born Camberwell 3.12.59. Ht 5 8
Wt 10 00
Defender. From Apprentice.

Season	Club	Apps	Goals
1978–79	Chelsea	—	—
1979–80		—	—
1980–81		—	—
1980–81	Bournemouth	8	—
1981–82		46	—
1982–83		46	1
1983–84		46	2
1984–85		23	—
1985–86		37	—
1986–87	Dundee U	7	—
1986–87	Blackburn R	13	—
1987–88		34	—
1988–89		19	—
1989–90		36	—

SULLIVAN, Neil

Born Sutton 24.2.70 Ht 6 0 Wt 12 01
Goalkeeper. From Trainee.

Season	Club	Apps	Goals
1988–89	Wimbledon	—	—
1989–90		—	—

SUMMERBEE, Nicky

Born Altrincham 26.8.71. Ht 5 11
Wt 11 08
Forward. From Trainee.

Season	Club	Apps	Goals
1989–90	Swindon T	1	—

SUMMERFIELD, Kevin

Born Walsall 7.1.59. Ht 5 11 Wt 11 00
Midfield. From Apprentice.

Season	Club	Apps	Goals
1976–77	WBA	—	—
1977–78		—	—
1978–79		2	1
1979–80		3	1
1980–81		—	—
1981–82		4	2
1982–83	Birmingham C	5	1
1982–83	Walsall	21	9
1983–84		33	8
1984–85	Cardiff C	10	1
1984–85	Plymouth Arg	17	2
1985–86		26	7
1986–87		28	9
1987–88		37	5
1988–89		20	2
1989–90		10	1
1989–90	*Exeter C*	4	—

SUMNER, Justin

Born Harrogate 19.10.70.
Midfield. From Leeds U. Trainee.

Season	Club	Apps	Goals
1989–90	Doncaster R	2	—

SUSSEX, Andy

Born Enfield 23.11.64. Ht 6 0 Wt 11 06
Forward. From Apprentice.

Season	Club	Apps	Goals
1981–82	Orient	8	1
1982–83		24	2
1983–84		29	6
1984–85		19	2
1985–86		36	4
1986–87		20	1
1987–88		8	1
1988–89	Crewe Alex	25	4
1989–90		33	9

SUTCH, Daryl

Born Lowestoft 11.9.71. Ht 6 0
Wt 12 00

Season	Club	League Appearances/Goals	

Midfield. From Trainee.

1989–90	Norwich C	—	—

SUTTON, Steve

Born Hartington 16.4.61. Ht 6 1 Wt 13 07
Goalkeeper. From Apprentice.

1980–81	Nottingham F	1	—
1980–81	*Mansfield T*	8	—
1981–82	Nottingham F	1	—
1982–83		17	—
1983–84		6	—
1984–85		14	—
1984–85	*Derby Co*	14	—
1985–86	Nottingham F	31	—
1986–87		28	—
1987–88		35	—
1988–89		36	—
1989–90		30	—

SWAILES, Chris

Born Gateshead 19.10.70. Ht 6 1 Wt 12 11
Defender. From Trainee.

1989–90	Ipswich T	—	—

SWAIN, Kenny

Born Birkenhead 28.1.52. Ht 5 9 Wt 11 07
Defender. From Wycombe W.

1973–74	Chelsea	7	1
1974–75		—	—
1975–76		25	4
1976–77		36	13
1977–78		36	4
1978–79		15	4
1978–79	Aston Villa	24	2
1979–80		41	—
1980–81		42	—
1981–82		39	—
1982–83		2	—
1982–83	Nottingham F	32	1
1983–84		41	1
1984–85		39	—
1985–86	Portsmouth	39	—
1986–87		42	—
1987–88		32	—
1988–89	Crewe Alex	41	—
1989–90		43	1

SWAN, Peter

Born Leeds 29,9.66. Ht 6 0 Wt 12 00
Forward. Local.

1984–85	Leeds U	—	—
1985–86		16	3
1986–87		7	—
1987–88		25	8
1988–89		1	—
1988–89	Hull C	11	1
1989–90		31	11

SWANN, Gary

Born York 11.4.62. Ht 5 9 Wt 11 12
Midfield. From Apprentice.

1980–81	Hull C	20	2
1981–82		20	—
1982–83		25	—
1983–84		41	2
1984–85		32	3
1985–86		39	2
1986–87		9	—
1986–87	Preston NE	30	5
1987–88		46	12
1988–89		18	2
1989–90		46	8

SWEENEY, Paul

Born Glasgow 10.1.65 Ht 5 8 Wt 11 05
Midfield. From St Kentigerns Acad.

1981–82	Raith R	—	—
1982–83		2	—
1983–84		29	1
1984–85		32	—
1985–86		37	3
1986–87		38	—
1987–88		39	2
1988–89		28	2

1988–89	Newcastle U	8	—
1989–90		19	—

SYMONS, Kit

Born Basingstoke 8.3.71 Ht 6 1
Wt 10 10
Defender. From Trainee.

1988–89	Portsmouth	2	—
1989–90		1	—

TAGGART, Gerry

Born Belfast 18.10.70
Defender. From Trainee. Northern Ireland Under-23, 2 full caps.

1988–89	Manchester C	11	1
1989–90		1	—
1989–90	Barnsley	21	2

TAIT, Mick

Born Wallsend 30.9.56. Ht 5 11
Wt 12 05
Midfield. From Apprentice.

1974–75	Oxford U	4	—
1975–76		37	12
1976–77		23	11
1976–77	Carlisle U	13	3
1977–78		43	10
1978–79		46	7
1979–80		4	—
1979–80	Hull C	33	3
1980–81	Portsmouth	38	8
1981–82		35	9
1982–83		44	6
1983–84		36	3
1984–85		33	1
1985–86		26	2
1986–87		28	1
1987–88		—	—
1987–88	Reading	35	2
1988–89		36	4
1989–90		28	3

TAIT, Paul

Born Sutton Coldfield 31.1.71.
Midfield. From Trainee.

1987–88	Birmingham C	1	—
1988–89		10	—
1989–90		14	2

TALBOT, Brian

Born Ipswich 21.7.53. Ht 5 10 Wt 12 00
Midfield. From Apprentice.
England Under-21, B, 6 full caps.

1972–73	Ipswich T	—	—
1973–74		15	3

Season	Club	League Appearances/Goals	
1974–75		40	8
1975–76		19	2
1976–77		42	5
1977–78		40	4
1978–79		21	3
1978–79	Arsenal	20	—
1979–80		42	1
1980–81		40	7
1981–82		42	7
1982–83		42	9
1983–84		27	6
1984–85		41	10
1985–86	Watford	41	7
1986–87		7	1
1986–87	Stoke C	32	3
1987–88		22	2
1987–88	WBA	15	2
1988–89		39	2
1989–90		20	1

TANKARD, Allen

Born Fleet 21.5.69. Ht 5 10 Wt 11 07
Defender. From Trainee. England Youth.

Season	Club	Apps	Goals
1985–86	Southampton	3	—
1986–87		2	—
1987–88		—	—
1988–89	Wigan Ath	33	1
1989–90		45	1

TANNER, Nick

Born Bristol 24.5.65. Ht 6 2 Wt 13 07
Defender. From Mangotsfield.

Season	Club	Apps	Goals
1984–85	Bristol R	—	—
1985–86		37	2
1986–87		44	1
1987–88		26	—
1988–89	Liverpool	—	—
1989–90		4	—
1989–90	*Norwich C*	6	—

TARRY, Matt

Born Northampton 14.10.70.
Defender. From Trainee.

Season	Club	Apps	Goals
1989–90	Northampton T	—	—

TAYLOR, Alex

Born Baillieston 13.6.62 Ht 5 7
Wt 10 11
Midfield. From Blantyre St. J.

Season	Club	Apps	Goals
1982–83	Dundee U	3	—
1983–84		9	1
1984–85		21	5
1985–86		—	—
1986–87	Hamilton A	25	1
1987–88		41	4
1988–89	Walsall	13	3
1989–90		32	3

TAYLOR, Bob

Born Horden 3.2.67. Ht 5 10 Wt 11 09
Forward. From Horden CW.

Season	Club	Apps	Goals
1985–86	Leeds U	2	—
1986–87		2	—
1987–88		32	9
1988–89		6	—
1988–89	Bristol C	12	8
1989–90		37	27

TAYLOR, Colin

Born Liverpool 25.12.71. Ht 6 0
Wt 12 07
Forward. From Trainee.

Season	Club	Apps	Goals
1989–90	Wolverhampton W	—	—

TAYLOR, Craig

Born Leeds 10.12.70. Ht 5 11 Wt 11 00
Defender. From Trainee.

Season	Club	Apps	Goals
1989–90	Bradford C	—	—

TAYLOR, John

Born Norwich 24.10.64 Ht 6 2 Wt 11 12
Forward. Local.

Season	Club	Apps	Goals
1982–83	Colchester U	—	—
1983–84		—	—
1984–85		—	—

From Sudbury

Season Club League Appearances/Goals

Season	Club	Apps	Goals
1988–89	Cambridge U	40	12
1989–90		45	15

TAYLOR, Kevin

Born Wakefield 22.1.61. Ht 5 9
Wt 11 01
Midfield. From Apprentice.

Season	Club	Apps	Goals
1978–79	Sheffield W	5	—
1979–80		21	6
1980–81		30	5
1981–82		35	7
1982–83		29	3
1983–84		5	—
1984–85	Derby Co	22	2
1984–85	Crystal Palace	13	—
1985–86		31	6
1986–87		41	8
1987–88		2	—
1987–88	Scunthorpe U	35	5
1988–89		41	8
1989–90		39	8

TAYLOR, Les

Born North Shields 4.12.56. Ht 5 8
Wt 11 07
Midfield. From Apprentice.

Season	Club	Apps	Goals
1974–75	Oxford U	5	—
1975–76		35	—
1976–77		32	2
1977–78		46	6
1978–79		46	1
1979–80		36	6
1980–81		19	—
1980–81	Watford	24	1
1981–82		42	4
1982–83		39	5
1983–84		27	—
1984–85		39	3
1985–86		1	—
1986–87		—	—
1986–87	Reading	31	1
1987–88		30	2
1988–89		14	—

Season	Club	Apps	Goals
1988–89	Colchester U	16	—
1989–90		36	1

TAYLOR, Mark

Born Hartlepool 20.11.64. Ht 5 7
Wt 10 00
Midfield. Local.

Season	Club	Apps	Goals
1982–83	Hartlepool U	—	—
1983–84		6	—
1984–85		36	4
1985–86		5	—
1985–86	*Crewe Alex*	3	—
1986–87	Blackpool	40	14
1987–88		41	21
1988–89		9	3
1989–90		—	—

TAYLOR, Mark

Born Walsall 22.2.66. Ht 5 8 Wt 11 08
Midfield. Local.

Season	Club	Apps	Goals
1984–85	Walsall	4	—
1985–86		18	2
1986–87		17	—
1987–88		40	1
1988–89		34	1
1989–90	Sheffield W	9	—

TAYLOR, Martin

Born Tamworth 9.12.66. Ht 5 11
Wt 12 04
Goalkeeper. From Mile Oak R.

Season	Club	Apps	Goals
1986–87	Derby Co	—	—
1987–88		—	—
1987–88	*Carlisle U*	10	—
1987–88	*Scunthorpe U*	8	—
1988–89	Derby Co	—	—
1989–90		3	—

TAYLOR, Robert

Born Norwich 30.4.71. Ht 6 0 Wt 11 07
Forward. From Trainee.

Season	Club	League Appearances/Goals	
1989–90	Norwich C	—	—

TAYLOR, Robbie

Born Plymouth 3.12.67.
Forward. From Apprentice.

1986–87	Portsmouth	—	—
1986–87	Newport Co	10	3
1987–88		34	4
1988–89		—	—
1989–90	Torquay U	18	1

TAYLOR, Robin

Born Rinteln 14.1.71.
Midfield. From Leicester C.

1989–90	Wigan Ath	1	—

TAYLOR, Scott

Born Portsmouth 23.11.70
Midfield. From Trainee.

1988–89	Reading	3	—
1989–90		29	2

TAYLOR, Shaun

Born Plymouth 26.3.63. Ht 6 1 Wt 13 00
Defender. From Bideford.

1986–87	Exeter C	23	—
1987–88		41	1
1988–89		46	6
1989–90		45	5

TAYLOR, Steve

Born Royton 18.10.55. Ht 5 10 Wt 10 09
Forward. From Apprentice.

1974–75	Bolton W	5	—
1975–76		3	—
1975–76	*Port Vale*	4	2
1976–77	Bolton W	31	16
1977–78		1	—
1977–78	Oldham Ath	32	20
1978–79		15	5
1978–79	Luton T	20	1
1979–80	Mansfield T	37	7
1980–81	Burnley	38	16
1981–82		22	9
1982–83		26	12
1983–84	Wigan Ath	30	7
1983–84	Stockport Co	12	6
1984–85		14	2
1984–85	Rochdale	30	12
1985–86		45	25
1986–87		9	5
1986–87	Preston NE	5	2
1987–88		—	—
1987–88	Burnley	42	6
1988–89		3	—
1988–89	Rochdale	17	4
1989–90		—	—

TAYLOR, Steve

Born Holbrook 10.1.70. Ht 5 8
Wt 10 04
Midfield. From Trainee.

1988–89	Derby Co	—	—
1989–90		—	—

TEALE, Shaun

Born Southport 10.3.64 Ht 6 0 Wt 13 07
Defender. From Southport, Northwich Vics, Weymouth.

1988–89	Bournemouth	20	—
1989–90		34	—

TELFER, Paul

Born Edinburgh 21.10.71. Ht 5 9
Wt 10 02
Midfield. From Trainee.

1988–89	Luton T	—	—
1989–90		—	—

TERRY, Steve

Born Clapton 14.6.62. Ht 6 1 Wt 13 05
Defender. From Apprentice.

1979–80	Watford	2	—
1980–81		5	—
1981–82		26	2
1982–83		7	1
1983–84		17	1
1984–85		38	4
1985–86		41	4
1986–87		18	2

Season	Club	League Appearances	Goals
1987–88		6	—
1988–89	Hull C	33	1
1989–90		29	3
1989–90	Northampton T	17	2

TESTER, Paul

Born Stroud 10.3.59. Ht 5 8 Wt 10 12
Forward. From Cheltenham T.

Season	Club	League Appearances	Goals
1983–84	Shrewsbury T	8	—
1984–85		23	5
1984–85	*Hereford U*	4	—
1985–86	Shrewsbury T	9	1
1986–87		29	5
1987–88		29	1
1988–89	Hereford U	44	6
1989–90		26	5

THACKERAY, Andy

Born Huddersfield 13.2.68. Ht 5 9
Wt 11 00
Midfield.

Season	Club	League Appearances	Goals
1985–86	Manchester C	—	—
1986–87	Huddersfield T	2	—
1986–87	Newport Co	11	3
1987–88		43	1
1988–89	Wrexham	35	2
1989–90		34	7

THEODOSIOU, Andy

Born Stoke Newington 30.10.70. Ht 6 0
Wt 12 10
Defender. From Tottenham H Trainee.

Season	Club	League Appearances	Goals
1989–90	Norwich C	—	—

THOMAS, Andy

Born Oxford 16.12.62. Ht 6 0 Wt 10 10
Forward. From Apprentice.

Season	Club	League Appearances	Goals
1980–81	Oxford U	9	1
1981–82		39	14
1982–83		24	7
1982–83	*Fulham*	4	2
1982–83	*Derby Co*	1	—
1983–84	Oxford U	23	7
1984–85		4	1
1985–86		17	2
1986–87		—	—
1986–87	Newcastle U	27	6
1987–88		4	—
1988–89	Bradford C	23	5
1989–90	Plymouth Arg	36	12

THOMAS, Dean

Born Bedworth 19.12.61 Ht 5 9
Wt 11 08
Defender. From Nuneaton Borough.

Season	Club	League Appearances	Goals
1981–82	Wimbledon	18	—
1982–83		24	5
1983–84		15	3
From Fortuna Dusseldorf			
1988–89	Northampton T	43	9
1989–90		31	2
1989–90	Notts Co	10	1

THOMAS, Geoff

Born Manchester 5.8.64. Ht 5 10
Wt 12 04
Midfield. Local.

Season	Club	League Appearances	Goals
1981–82	Rochdale	—	—
1982–83		1	—
1983–84		10	1
1983–84	Crewe Alex	8	1
1984–85		40	4
1985–86		37	6
1986–87		40	9
1987–88	Crystal Palace	41	6
1988–89		22	5
1989–90		35	1

THOMAS, Glen

Born Hackney 6.10.67. Ht 6 1 Wt 12 02
Defender. From Apprentice.

Season	Club	League Appearances	Goals
1985–86	Fulham	—	—
1986–87		1	—
1987–88		27	—
1988–89		40	1
1989–90		17	1

THOMAS, Gwyn

Born Swansea 26.9.57. Ht 5 8 Wt 11 00
Midfield. From Apprentice. Wales Under-21.

Season	Club	League Appearances/Goals	
1974–75	Leeds U	1	—
1975–76		—	—
1976–77		7	1
1977–78		3	1
1978–79		2	—
1979–80		3	—
1980–81		2	—
1981–82		15	—
1982–83		39	1
1983–84		17	—
1983–84	Barnsley	13	—
1984–85		40	1
1985–86		39	5
1986–87		40	5
1987–88		42	4
1988–89		24	2
1989–90		3	—
1989–90	Hull C	11	—

THOMAS, John

Born Wednesbury 5.8.58. Ht 5 8
Wt 11 03
Forward.

Season	Club	League Appearances/Goals	
1978–79	Everton	—	—
1978–79	*Tranmere R*	11	2
1979–80	Everton	—	—
1979–80	*Halifax T*	5	—
1980–81	Bolton W	17	5
1981–82		5	1
1982–83	Chester	44	20
1983–84	Lincoln C	37	15
1984–85		30	5
1985–86	Preston NE	40	17
1986–87		38	21
1987–88	Bolton W	44	22
1988–89		29	9
1989–90	WBA	18	1
1989–90	Preston NE	11	3

THOMAS, Lee

Born Tredegar 1.11.70. Ht 5 7 Wt 11 02
Defender. From Newport Co Trainee.

Season	Club	League Appearances/Goals	
1989–90	Hereford U	1	—

THOMAS, Martin

Born Caerphilly 28.11.59. Ht 6 1
Wt 13 00
Goalkeeper. From Apprentice. Wales Under-21, 1 full cap.

Season	Club	League Appearances/Goals	
1976–77	Bristol R	1	—
1977–78		37	—
1978–79		42	—
1979–80		38	—
1980–81		25	—
1981–82		19	—
1982–83	*Cardiff C*	15	—
1982–83	*Tottenham H*	—	—
1982–83	*Southend U*	6	—
1982–83	*Newcastle U*	3	—
1983–84	Newcastle U	23	—
1984–85		18	—
1984–85	*Middlesbrough*	4	—
1985–86	Newcastle U	32	—
1986–87		39	—
1987–88		3	—
1988–89		—	—
1988–89	Birmingham C	36	—
1989–90		42	—

THOMAS, Michael

Born Lambeth 24.8.67. Ht 5 10
Wt 12 02
Midfield. From Apprentice. England Schools, Youth, B, Under-21, 2 full caps.

Season	Club	League Appearances/Goals	
1985–86	Arsenal	—	—
1986–87		12	—
1986–87	*Portsmouth*	3	—
1987–88	Arsenal	37	9
1988–89		37	7
1989–90		36	5

THOMAS, Mickey

Born Mochdre 7.7.54. Ht 5 6 Wt 10 07
Midfield. From Amateur. Wales Under-23, 51 full caps.

Season	Club	League Appearances/Goals	
1971–72	Wrexham	20	3
1972–73		26	—
1973–74		19	4
1974–75		31	5
1975–76		30	2
1976–77		45	6
1977–78		43	7
1978–79		16	6
1978–79	Manchester U	25	1

Season	Club	Apps	Goals
1979–80		35	8
1980–81		30	2
1981–82	Everton	10	—
1981–82	Brighton	20	—
1982–83	Stoke C	41	11
1983–84		16	3
1983–84	Chelsea	17	4
1984–85		27	5
1985–86		—	—
1985–86	WBA	20	—
1985–86	*Derby Co*	9	—
From Wichita W			
1988–89	Shrewsbury T	40	1
1989–90	Leeds U	3	—
1989–90	*Stoke C*	5	—

THOMAS, Mitchell

Born Luton 2.10.64 Ht 6 0 Wt 12 00
Defender. From Apprentice. England Youth, Under-21.

Season	Club	Apps	Goals
1982–83	Luton T	4	—
1983–84		26	—
1984–85		36	—
1985–86		41	1
1986–87	Tottenham H	39	4
1987–88		36	—
1988–89		25	1
1989–90		26	1

THOMAS, Rod

Born London 10.10.70. Ht 5 6 Wt 10 03
Forward. From Trainee. England Youth, Under-21.

Season	Club	Apps	Goals
1987–88	Watford	4	—
1988–89		18	2
1989–90		32	6

THOMAS, Tony

Born Liverpool 12.7.71 Ht 5 11
Wt 12 05
Defender. From Trainee.

Season	Club	Apps	Goals
1988–89	Tranmere R	9	2
1989–90		42	2

THOMPSON, Andy

Born Carnock 9.11.67. Ht 5 4 Wt 10 06
Midfield. From Apprentice.

Season	Club	Apps	Goals
1985–86	WBA	15	1
1986–87		9	—
1986–87	Wolverhampton W	29	8
1987–88		42	2
1988–89		46	6
1989–90		33	4

THOMPSON, Chris

Born Walsall 24.1.60. Ht 5 11 Wt 12 04
Forward. From Apprentice. England Youth.

Season	Club	Apps	Goals
1977–78	Bolton W	—	—
1978–79		—	—
1979–80		15	1
1980–81		6	1
1981–82		36	12
1982–83		16	4
1982–83	*Lincoln C*	6	—
1983–84	Blackburn R	33	8
1984–85		35	15
1985–86		17	1
1986–87	Wigan Ath	43	9
1987–88		31	5
1988–89	Blackpool	36	8
1989–90		3	—
1989–90	Cardiff C	2	—

THOMPSON, David

Born Ashington 20.11.68. Ht 6 3
Wt 12 07
Defender. From Trainee.

Season	Club	Apps	Goals
1986–87	Millwall	—	—
1987–88		—	—
1988–89		15	1
1989–90		27	2

THOMPSON, David

Born Manchester 27.5.62. Ht 5 11
Wt 12 10
Forward. Local.

Season	Club	League Appearances/Goals	
1981–82	Rochdale	2	—
1982–83		46	5
1983–84		40	4
1984–85		40	2
1985–86		27	2
1985–86	*Manchester U*	—	—
1986–87	Notts Co	46	7
1987–88		9	1
1987–88	Wigan Ath	27	2
1988–89		42	7
1989–90		39	5

THOMPSON, Garry

Born Birmingham 7.10.59. Ht 6 1 Wt 14 00
Forward. From Apprentice. England Under-21.

Season	Club	Apps	Goals
1977–78	Coventry C	6	2
1978–79		20	8
1979–80		17	6
1980–81		35	8
1981–82		36	10
1982–83		20	4
1982–83	WBA	12	7
1983–84		37	13
1984–85		42	19
1985–86	Sheffield W	36	7
1986–87	Aston Villa	31	6
1987–88		24	11
1988–89		5	—
1988–89	Watford	21	7
1989–90		13	1
1989–90	Crystal Palace	9	2

THOMPSON, Gary

Born Glasgow 11.6.56. Ht 5 6 Wt 11 06
Midfield. From Benburb.

Season	Club	Apps	Goals
1976–77	Morton	1	—
1977–78		—	—
1978–79	Falkirk	17	6
1979–80		20	7
1980–81		19	2
1981–82		22	3
1982–83		21	1
1983–84	Alloa	31	1
1984–85		33	4
1985–86		21	2
1985–86	Dunfermline Ath	8	2
1986–87		41	—
1987–88		5	—
1987–88	St Johnstone	29	1
1988–89		30	—
1989–90		7	—
1989–90	Forfar Ath	14	—

THOMPSON, Keith

Born Birmingham 24.4.65. Ht 5 9 Wt 11 2
Forward. From Apprentice. England Youth.

Season	Club	Apps	Goals
1982–83	Coventry C	5	—
1983–84		6	—
1983–84	*Wimbledon*	3	—
1984–85	Coventry C	1	—
1984–85	*Northampton T*	10	1
1985–86	Coventry C	—	—
From Oviedo			
1988–89	Coventry C	9	1
1989–90		1	—

THOMPSON, Les

Born Cleethorpes 23.9.68. Ht 5 10 Wt 11 00
Forward.

Season	Club	Apps	Goals
1986–87	Hull C	—	—
1987–88		7	2
1988–89		7	—
1988–89	*Scarborough*	3	1
1989–90	Hull C	1	—

THOMPSON, Neil

Born Beverley 2.10.63. Ht 6 0 Wt 13 07
Defender. From Nottingham F Apprentice.

Season	Club	Apps	Goals
1981–82	Hull C	23	—
1982–83		8	—
To Scarborough			
1987–88	Scarborough	41	6

Season	Club	Apps	Goals
1988–89		46	9
1989–90	Ipswich T	45	3

THOMPSON, Nigel

Born Leeds 1.3.67. Ht 5 7 Wt 10 07
Defender. From Apprentice.

Season	Club	Apps	Goals
1983–84	Leeds U	1	—
1984–85		—	—
1985–86		1	—
1986–87		5	—
1987–88		—	—
1987–88	*Rochdale*	5	—
1987–88	Chesterfield	4	—
1988–89		6	—
1989–90		10	1

THOMPSON, Simon

Born Sheffield 27.2.70 Ht 5 9 Wt 10 06
Forward. From Trainee.

Season	Club	Apps	Goals
1988–89	Rotherham U	1	—
1989–90		11	—

THOMPSON, Steve

Born Oldham 2.11.64. Ht 5 11 Wt 11 12
Midfield. From Apprentice.

Season	Club	Apps	Goals
1982–83	Bolton W	3	—
1983–84		40	3
1984–85		34	4
1985–86		35	8
1986–87		44	7
1987–88		44	7
1988–89		43	9
1989–90		45	6

THOMPSON, Steve

Born Sheffield 28.7.55. Ht 6 1 Wt 13 10
Defender. From Boston U.

Season	Club	Apps	Goals
1979–80	Lincoln C	—	—
1980–81		31	2
1981–82		30	2
1982–83		36	2
1983–84		16	1
1984–85		41	1
1985–86	Charlton Ath	38	—
1986–87		34	—

Season Club League Appearances/Goals

Season	Club	Apps	Goals
1987–88		23	—
1988–89	Leicester C	—	—
1988–89	Sheffield U	20	1
1989–90	Lincoln C	27	—

THOMPSON, Steven

Born Manchester 17.2.72.
Defender. From Trainee.

Season	Club	Apps	Goals
1989–90	Gillingham	2	—

THOMPSTONE, Ian

Born 17.1.71. Ht 6 0 Wt 11 03
Midfield. From Trainee.

Season	Club	Apps	Goals
1987–88	Manchester C	1	1
1988–89		—	—

THOMSON, Billy

Born Linwood 10.2.58. Ht 6 2 Wt 12 03
Goalkeeper. From Glasgow United.
Scotland Under-21, 7 full caps.

Season	Club	Apps	Goals
1975–76	Partick T	—	—
1976–77		—	—
1977–78		—	—
1978–79	St Mirren	34	—
1979–80		36	—
1980–81		36	—
1981–82		35	—
1982–83		35	—
1983–84		30	—
1984–85	Dundee U	11	—
1985–86		28	—
1986–87		42	—
1987–88		36	—
1988–89		36	—
1989–90		7	—

THOMSON, Ken

Born Dunfermline 9.11.51. Ht 5 10
Wt 10 12
Defender. From Dunfermline U.

Season	Club	Apps	Goals
1970–71	Dunfermline Ath	3	1
1971–72		15	1
1972–73		35	—
1973–74		30	—
1974–75		34	—

Season	Club	League Appearances/Goals	
1975–76		26	—
1976–77		38	2
1977–78	Alloa	39	1
1978–79		39	1
1979–80		39	—
1980–81		39	—
1981–82		16	—
1982–83	Alloa	39	1
1983–84		30	—
1984–85		39	—
1985–86		36	—
1986–87		39	—
1987–88		3	—
1987–88	St Johnstone	36	1
1988–89		34	—
1989–90		24	—

THOMSON, Scott

Born Edinburgh 8.11.66. Ht 6 0
Wt 11 04
Goalkeeper. From Hutcheson Vale BC.

Season	Club	Apps	Goals
1984–85	Dundee U	—	—
1985–86		—	—
1986–87		—	—
1987–88		—	—
1988–89		1	—
1989–90		2	—

THORN, Andy

Born Carshalton 12.11.66. Ht 6 0
Wt 11 05
Defender. From Apprentice. England Under-21.

Season	Club	Apps	Goals
1984–85	Wimbledon	10	—
1985–86		28	—
1986–87		34	2
1987–88		35	—
1988–89	Newcastle U	26	1
1989–90		10	1
1989–90	Crystal Palace	17	1

THORNBER, Stephen

Born Dewsbury 11.10.65. Ht 5 10
Wt 11 02
Forward. Local.

Season	Club	Apps	Goals
1983–84	Halifax T	4	1
1984–85		31	3
1985–86		18	—
1986–87		16	—
1987–88		35	—
1988–89	Swansea C	31	—
1989–90		34	1

THORPE, Adrian

Born Chesterfield 20.11.63. Ht 5 7
Wt 11 06
Forward. From Heanor T.

Season	Club	Apps	Goals
1984–85	Bradford C	—	—
1985–86		10	1
1986–87		5	—
1986–87	*Tranmere R*	5	3
1987–88	Bradford C	2	—
1987–88	Notts Co	23	5
1988–89		36	4
1989–90	Walsall	27	1
1989–90	Northampton T	13	3

THORPE, Andy

Born Stockport 15.9.60. Ht 5 11
Wt 12 02
Defender. From Amateur.

Season	Club	Apps	Goals
1977–78	Stockport Co	4	—
1978–79		38	—
1979–80		36	1
1980–81		38	1
1981–82		46	—
1982–83		46	—
1983–84		45	1
1984–85		31	—
1985–86		30	—
1986–87	Tranmere R	39	—
1987–88		14	—
1987–88	Stockport Co	20	—
1988–89		41	—
1989–90		40	—

THORSTVEDT, Erik

Born Stavanger 28.10.62 Ht 6 0
Wt 12 01
Goalkeeper. From IFK Gothenburg. Norway full caps.

Season	Club	League Appearances/Goals	
1988–89	Tottenham H	18	—
1989–90		34	—

TIERNEY, Grant

Born Falkirk 11.10.61. Ht 6 0 Wt 11 06
Defender. From Bainsford F.

1978–79	Hearts	—	—
1979–80		—	—
1980–81	Cowdenbeath	32	1
1981–82		32	2
1982–83		32	2
1983–84		35	1
1984–85		25	3
1984–85	Meadowbank Th	8	—
1985–86		35	4
1986–87		36	4
1987–88		36	2
1988–89		18	—
1988–89	Dunfermline Ath	18	1
1989–90		33	2

TIGHE, Aaron

Born Banbury 11.7.69. Ht 5 9 Wt 10 09
Midfield. From Apprentice. Eire Under 21.

1986–87	Luton T	—	—
1987–88		—	—
1988–89		—	—
1989–90	*Leicester C*	—	—

TILER, Carl

Born Sheffield 11.2.70. Ht 6 2 Wt 13 00
Defender. From Trainee. England Under-21.

1987–88	Barnsley	1	—
1988–89		4	—
1989–90		21	1

TILLSON, Andy

Born Huntingdon 30.6.66 Ht 6 2
Wt 12 07
Defender. From Kettering.

Season	Club	League Appearances/Goals	
1988–89	Grimsby T	45	2
1989–90		42	3

TILSON, Steve

Born Essex 27.7.66 Ht 5 11 Wt 11 10
Forward. From Burnham.

1988–89	Southend U	16	2
1989–90		16	—

TINKLER, John

Born Trimdon 24.8.68. Ht 5 8 Wt 11 07
Midfield.

1986–87	Hartlepool U	2	—
1987–88		20	—
1988–89		38	3
1989–90		45	2

TINNION, Brian

Born Stanley 23.2.68. Ht 5 11 Wt 11 05
Defender. From Apprentice.

1985–86	Newcastle U	—	—
1986–87		3	—
1987–88		16	1
1988–89		13	1
1988–89	Bradford C	14	1
1989–90		37	5

TITTERTON, David

Born Hatton 25.9.71.
Midfield. From Trainee.

1989–90	Coventry C	1	—

TODD, Mark

Born Belfast 4.12.67. Ht 5 7 Wt 10 00
Midfield. From Trainee. Northern Ireland Under-23.

1985–86	Manchester U	—	—
1986–87		—	—
1987–88	Sheffield U	12	—

Season	Club	Apps	Goals
1988–89		39	4
1989–90		16	1

TOMLINSON, Neil

Born Birmingham 14.10.69 Ht 5 11 Wt 12 00
Forward. From Shrewsbury T.

Season	Club	Apps	Goals
1988–89	Swindon T	—	—
1989–90		—	—

TOMLINSON, Paul

Born Brierley Hill 22.2.64. Ht 6 2 Wt 13 12
Goalkeeper. From Middlewood R.

Season	Club	Apps	Goals
1983–84	Sheffield U	30	—
1984–85		2	—
1985–86		—	—
1986–87		5	—
1986–87	*Birmingham C*	11	—
1987–88	Bradford C	42	—
1988–89		38	—
1989–90		41	—

TORPEY, Stephen

Born Islington 8.12.70 Ht 6 2 Wt 12 11
Forward. From Trainee.

Season	Club	Apps	Goals
1988–89	Millwall	—	—
1989–90		7	—

TORFASON, Gudmundor

Born Westann Isles 13.12.61. Ht 6 1 Wt 13 02
Forward. From RSC Genk. Iceland full caps.

Season	Club	Apps	Goals
1989–90	St Mirren	29	12

TORTOLANO, Joe

Born Stirling 6.4.66. Ht 5 8 Wt 11 02
Forward. From Apprentice. Scotland Under-21.

Season	Club	Apps	Goals
1983–84	WBA	—	—
1984–85		—	—
1985–86	Hibernian	20	3
1986–87		33	—

Season Club League Appearances/Goals

Season	Club	Apps	Goals
1987–88		21	4
1988–89		25	—
1989–90		7	—

TOSHACK, Cameron

Born Cardiff 7.3.70 Ht 6 2 Wt 12 00
Forward. From Trainee.

Season	Club	Apps	Goals
1988–89	Swansea C	—	—
1989–90	Bristol C	—	—

TOWNSEND, Andy

Born Maidstone 23.7.63. Ht 5 11 Wt 12 13
Midfield. From Welling and Weymouth. Eire 17 full caps.

Season	Club	Apps	Goals
1984–85	Southampton	5	—
1985–86		27	1
1986–87		14	1
1987–88		37	3
1988–89	Norwich C	36	5
1989–90		35	3

TRACEY, Simon

Born Woolwich 9.12.67. Ht 6 0 Wt 12 00
Goalkeeper. From Apprentice.

Season	Club	Apps	Goals
1985–86	Wimbledon	—	—
1986–87		—	—
1987–88		—	—
1988–89		1	—
1988–89	Sheffield U	7	—
1989–90		46	—

TREACY, Darren

Born Lambeth 6.9.70 Ht 5 10 Wt 12 09
Forward. From Trainee.

Season	Club	Apps	Goals
1988–89	Millwall	3	—
1989–90		4	—

TREANOR, Mark

Born Glasgow 1.4.63. Ht 6 0 Wt 11 00
Defender. From Eastercraigs.

Season	Club	Apps	Goals
1979–80	Clydebank	1	—
1980–81		16	—

Season	Club	League Appearances/Goals	
1981–82		35	—
1982–83		36	3
1983–84		18	1
1984–85		38	1
1985–86		32	—
1986–87		33	—
1987–88		37	3
1988–89		27	5
1988–89	St Johnstone	3	—
1989–90		30	4

TREVITT, Simon

Born Dewsbury 20.12.67. Ht 5 11 Wt 11 02
Defender. From Apprentice.

Season	Club	Apps	Goals
1986–87	Huddersfield T	11	—
1987–88		37	1
1988–89		39	—
1989–90		7	—

TREWICK, John

Born Bedlington 3.6.57. Ht 5 10 Wt 10 13
Midfield. From Apprentice. England Schools, Youth.

Season	Club	Apps	Goals
1974–75	WBA	3	—
1975–76		11	1
1976–77		7	1
1977–78		18	3
1978–79		21	3
1979–80		21	2
1980–81		15	1
1980–81	Newcastle U	21	1
1981–82		40	6
1982–83		1	—
1983–84		16	1
1983–84	*Oxford U*	3	—
1984–85	Oxford U	42	—
1985–86		35	3
1986–87		31	1
1987–88		3	—
1987–88	Birmingham C	26	—
1988–89		11	—
1989–90	Hartlepool U	8	—

TRICK, Des

Born Swansea 7.11.69 Ht 5 11 Wt 12 00
Defender. From Trainee.

Season	Club	Apps	Goals
1988–89	Swansea C	—	—
1989–90		14	—

TROLLOPE, Paul

Born Swindon 3.6.72. Ht 6 0 Wt 12 02
Midfield. From Trainee.

Season	Club	Apps	Goals
1989–90	Swindon T	—	—

TROTTER, Michael

Born Hartlepool 27.10.69. Ht 6 3 Wt 12 02
Defender. From Trainee.

Season	Club	Apps	Goals
1987–88	Middlesbrough	—	—
1988–89		—	—
1988–89	*Doncaster R*	3	—
1989–90	Middlesbrough	—	—

TRUSSON, Mike

Born Northolt 26.5.59. Ht 6 0 Wt 12 04
Forward. From Apprentice.

Season	Club	Apps	Goals
1976–77	Plymouth Arg	4	—
1977–78		15	2
1978–79		27	5
1978–79	*Stoke C*	—	—
1979–80	Plymouth Arg	27	8
1980–81	Sheffield U	39	8
1981–82		44	11
1982–83		32	9
1983–84		11	3
1983–84	Rotherham U	25	2
1984–85		45	7
1985–86		37	6
1986–87		17	4
1987–88	Brighton	15	2
1988–89		22	—

Season	Club	League Appearances/Goals	
1989–90		—	—
1989–90	Gillingham	25	2

TUCKER, Gordon

Born Manchester 5.1.68. Ht 5 11 Wt 11 12
Defender. From Derby County.

Season	Club	Apps	Goals
1987–88	Huddersfield T	23	—
1988–89		12	—
1989–90	Scunthorpe U	15	1

TUNKS, Roy

Born W. Germany 21.1.51. Ht 6 1 Wt 13 11
Goalkeeper. From Apprentice.

Season	Club	Apps	Goals
1967–68	Rotherham U	—	—
1968–69		1	—
1968–69	*York C*	4	—
1969–70	Rotherham U	—	—
1970–71		11	—
1971–72		42	—
1972–73		37	—
1973–74		23	—
1973–74	*Ipswich T*	—	—
1974–75	Rotherham U	24	—
1974–75	*Newcastle U*	—	—
1974–75	Preston NE	27	—
1975–76		43	—
1976–77		38	—
1977–78		46	—
1978–79		42	—
1979–80		42	—
1980–81		39	—
1981–82	Wigan Ath	31	—
1982–83		46	—
1983–84		42	—
1984–85		40	—
1985–86		38	—
1986–87		38	—
1987–88		10	—
1988–89	Hartlepool U	5	—
1988–89	Preston NE	23	—
1989–90		2	—

TUPLING, Steve

Born Wensleydale 11.7.64. Ht 6 0 Wt 11 03
Midfield. From Apprentice.

Season	Club	Apps	Goals
1982–83	Middlesbrough	—	—
1983–84		—	—
1984–85	*Carlisle U*	1	—
1984–85	Darlington	39	4
1985–86		40	4
1986–87		32	—
1987–88	Newport Co	33	2
1988–89	Cardiff C	4	—
1988–89	*Torquay U*	3	—
1988–89	*Exeter C*	9	1
1989–90	Cardiff C	1	—
1989–90	Hartlepool U	26	1

TURNBULL, Lee

Born Teesside 27.9.67. Ht 6 0 Wt 11 09
Midfield. Local.

Season	Club	Apps	Goals
1985–86	Middlesbrough	2	—
1986–87		14	4
1987–88		—	—
1987–88	Aston Villa	—	—
1987–88	Doncaster R	30	1
1988–89		32	4
1989–90		42	10

TURNER, Chris

Born Sheffield 15.9.58. Ht 5 11 Wt 11 12
Goalkeeper. From Apprentice. England Youth.

Season	Club	Apps	Goals
1976–77	Sheffield W	45	—
1977–78		23	—
1978–79		23	—
1978–79	*Lincoln C*	5	—
1979–80	Sunderland	30	—
1980–81		27	—
1981–82		19	—
1982–83		35	—
1983–84		42	—
1984–85		42	—
1985–86	Manchester U	17	—
1986–87		23	—
1987–88		24	—
1988–89		—	—
1988–89	Sheffield W	29	—

Season	Club	League Appearances/Goals	
1989–90	....	23	—
1989–90	*Leeds U*	2	—

TURNER, Phil

Born Sheffield 12.2.62. Ht 5 8 Wt 10 07
Midfield. From Apprentice.

Season	Club	League Appearances/Goals	
1979–80	Lincoln C	14	1
1980–81	....	38	4
1981–82	....	28	1
1982–83	....	40	3
1983–84	....	42	3
1984–85	....	36	3
1985–86	....	43	4
1986–87	Grimsby T	34	3
1987–88	....	28	5
1987–88	Leicester C	8	—
1988–89	....	16	2
1988–89	Notts Co	16	2
1989–90	....	44	6

TURNER, Robert

Born Durham 18.9.66. Ht 6 3 Wt 14 00
Forward. From Apprentice.

Season	Club	League Appearances/Goals	
1984–85	Huddersfield T	1	—
1985–86	Cardiff C	34	7
1986–87	....	5	1
1986–87	*Hartlepool U*	7	1
1986–87	Bristol R	17	1
1987–88	....	9	1
1987–88	Wimbledon	4	—
1988–89	....	6	—
1988–89	Bristol C	19	6
1989–90	....	33	6

TUTILL, Steve

Born Derwent 1.10.69. Ht 6 0 Wt 11 10
Defender. From Trainee.

Season	Club	League Appearances/Goals	
1987–88	York C	21	—
1988–89	....	22	1
1989–90	....	42	—

TWENTYMAN, Geoff

Born Liverpool 10.3.59. Ht 6 1 Wt 13 02
Defender. From Southport, Maghull, Formby and Chorley.

Season	Club	League Appearances/Goals	
1983–84	Preston NE	28	2
1984–85	....	44	2
1985–86	....	26	—
1986–87	Bristol R	43	—
1987–88	....	38	1
1988–89	....	46	1
1989–90	....	46	3

TYNAN, Tommy

Born Liverpool 17.11.55. Ht 5 10
Wt 11 11
Forward. From Apprentice.

Season	Club	League Appearances/Goals	
1972–73	Liverpool	—	—
1973–74	....	—	—
1974–75	....	—	—
1975–76	....	—	—
1975–76	*Swansea C*	6	2
1976–77	Liverpool	—	—
1976–77	Sheffield W	39	14
1977–78	....	44	16
1978–79	....	8	1
1978–79	Lincoln C	9	1
1978–79	Newport Co	20	7
1979–80	....	34	8
1980–81	....	45	13
1981–82	....	38	13
1982–83	....	46	25
1983–84	Plymouth Arg	35	12
1984–85	....	45	31
1985–86	Rotherham U	30	13
1985–86	*Plymouth Arg*	9	9
1986–87	Rotherham U	2	—
1986–87	Plymouth Arg	40	18
1987–88	....	43	16
1988–89	....	46	24
1989–90	....	44	15

ULLATHORNE, Robert

Born Wakefield 11.10.71. Ht 5 8
Wt 10 00
Defender. From Trainee.

Season	Club	Apps	Goals
1989–90	Norwich C	—	—

UNDERHILL, Phil

Born Bristol 26.10.69. Ht 5 6 Wt 9 09
Midfield. From Trainee.

Season	Club	Apps	Goals
1987–88	Southampton	—	—
1988–89		—	—
1988–89	Torquay U	—	—
1989–90		—	—

UZZELL, John

Born Plymouth 31.3.59. Ht 5 10
Wt 11 03
Defender. From Apprentice.

Season	Club	Apps	Goals
1976–77	Plymouth Arg	—	—
1977–78		44	1
1978–79		21	—
1979–80		1	—
1980–81		16	—
1981–82		35	2
1982–83		42	1
1983–84		42	—
1984–85		29	1
1985–86		8	—
1986–87		21	—
1987–88		10	1
1988–89		33	—
1989–90	Torquay U	36	2

VALENTINE, Peter

Born Huddersfield 16.6.63. Ht 5 11
Wt 12 00
Defender. From Apprentice.

Season	Club	Apps	Goals
1980–81	Huddersfield T	—	—
1981–82		14	1
1982–83		5	—
1983–84	Bolton W	42	1
1984–85		26	—
1985–86	Bury	46	3
1986–87		46	2
1987–88		42	2
1988–89		30	1
1989–90		38	—

VAN DEN HAUWE, Pat

Born Dendermonde 16.12.60. Ht 6 0
Wt 10 08
Defender. From Apprentice. Wales 13 full caps.

Season	Club	Apps	Goals
1978–79	Birmingham C	8	—
1979–80		1	—
1980–81		4	—
1981–82		31	—
1982–83		31	1
1983–84		42	—
1984–85		6	—
1984–85	Everton	31	—
1985–86		40	1
1986–87		11	1
1987–88		28	—
1988–89		25	—
1989–90		—	—
1989–90	Tottenham H	31	—

VAN DER ARK, Willem

Born Groningen 13.11.63. Ht 6 5
Wt 13 06
Forward. From Willem II

Season	Club	League Appearances/Goals	
1988–89	Aberdeen	8	2
1989–90		26	7

VAN DER HOORN, Freddy

Born Den Bosch 12.10.63. Ht 6 0 Wt 12 06
Defender. From BVV Den Bosch.

Season	Club		
1989–90	Dundee U	31	2

VARADI, Imre

Born Paddington 8.7.59. Ht 5 8 Wt 12 09
Forward. From Letchworth G.C.

Season	Club		
1977–78	Sheffield U	—	—
1978–79		10	4
1978–79	Everton	—	—
1979–80		4	—
1980–81		22	6
1981–82	Newcastle U	42	18
1982–83		39	21
1983–84	Sheffield W	38	17
1984–85		38	16
1985–86	WBA	32	9
1986–87		—	—
1986–87	Manchester C	30	9
1987–88		32	17
1988–89		3	—
1988–89	Sheffield W	20	3
1989–90		2	—
1989–90	Leeds U	13	2

VAUGHAN, John

Born Isleworth 26.6.64. Ht 5 10 Wt 13 01
Goalkeeper. From Apprentice.

Season	Club		
1981–82	West Ham U	—	—
1982–83		—	—
1983–84		—	—
1984–85		—	—
1984–85	*Charlton Ath*	6	—
1985–86		—	—
1985–86	*Bristol R*	6	—
1985–86	*Wrexham*	4	—
1985–86	*Bristol C*	2	—
1986–87	Fulham	44	—
1987–88		—	—
1987–88	*Bristol C*	3	—
1988–89	Cambridge U	29	—
1989–90		46	—

VAUGHAN, Nigel

Born Caerleon 20.5.59. Ht 5 5 Wt 8 10
Midfield. From Apprentice. Wales Under-21, 10 full caps.

Season	Club		
1976–77	Newport Co	1	—
1977–78		11	—
1978–79		27	4
1979–80		46	12
1980–81		45	1
1981–82		44	3
1982–83		43	7
1983–84		7	5
1983–84	Cardiff C	36	8
1984–85		38	16
1985–86		43	12
1986–87		32	6
1986–87	*Reading*	5	1
1987–88	Wolverhampton W	36	6
1988–89		32	4
1989–90		25	—

VENISON, Barry

Born Consett 16.8.64. Ht 5 9 Wt 11 09
Defender. From Apprentice. England Youth, Under-21.

Season	Club		
1981–82	Sunderland	20	1
1982–83		37	—
1983–84		41	—
1984–85		39	1
1985–86		36	—
1986–87	Liverpool	33	—
1987–88		18	—
1988–89		15	—
1989–90		25	—

VENUS, Mark

Born Hartlepool 6.4.67. Ht 6 0 Wt 11 08
Defender.

Season	Club		
1984–85	Hartlepool U	4	—
1985–86	Leicester C	1	—
1986–87		39	—

Season	Club	Apps	Goals
1987–88		21	1
1987–88	Wolverhampton W	4	—
1988–89		35	—
1989–90		44	2

VERTANNES, Des

Born Hounslow 25.4.72.
Midfield. From Chelsea and Fulham Trainee.

Season	Club	Apps	Goals
1989–90	Fulham	2	—

VEYSEY, Ken

Born Hackney 8.6.67. Ht 5 11 Wt 11 08
Goalkeeper.

Season	Club	Apps	Goals
1987–88	Torquay U	—	—
1988–89		25	—
1989–90		46	—

VICKERS, Steve

Born Bishop Auckland 13.10.67. Ht 6 2
Wt 12 00
Defender. From Spennymoor U.

Season	Club	Apps	Goals
1985–86	Tranmere R	3	—
1986–87		36	2
1987–88		46	1
1988–89		46	3
1989–90		42	3

VINNICOMBE, Chris

Born Exeter 20.10.70 Ht 5 9 Wt 10 04
Midfield.

Season	Club	Apps	Goals
1988–89	Exeter C	25	—
1989–90		14	1
1989–90	Rangers	7	—

VIVEASH, Adrian

Born Swindon 30.9.69 Ht 6 1 Wt 11 12
Forward. From Trainee.

Season	Club	Apps	Goals
1988–89	Swindon T	—	—
1989–90		—	—

WADDLE, Chris

Born Hepworth 14.12.60. Ht 6 0
Wt 11 05
Forward. From Tow Law T. England Under-21, 59 full caps. Football League.

Season	Club	Apps	Goals
1980–81	Newcastle U	13	1
1981–82		42	7
1982–83		37	7
1983–84		42	18
1984–85		36	13
1985–86	Tottenham H	39	11
1986–87		39	6
1987–88		22	2
1988–89		38	14

To Marseille

WADE, Bryan

Born Bath 25.6.63. Ht 5 8 Wt 11 05
Forward. From Trowbridge T.

Season	Club	Apps	Goals
1985–86	Swindon T	34	10
1986–87		23	9
1987–88		3	—
1988–89	Swansea C	25	4
1989–90		11	1

WADDOCK, Gary

Born Alperton 17.3.62. Ht 5 10
Wt 11 12
Midfield. From Apprentice. Eire B, Under-21, Under-23, 20 full caps.

Season	Club	Apps	Goals
1979–80	QPR	16	1
1980–81		33	3
1981–82		35	—
1982–83		33	—
1983–84		36	3
1984–85		31	1
1985–86		15	—
1986–87		4	—
1987–88		—	—
From Charleroi			
1989–90	Millwall	18	—

WAITES, Paul

Born Hull 24.1.71. Ht 5 10 Wt 12 08
Defender. From Trainee.

Season	Club	Apps	Goals
1989–90	Hull C	1	—

WAITT, Mick

Born Newcastle 25.6.60. Ht 6 4
Wt 12 00
Forward. From Keyworth U and Arnold Kingswell.

Season	Club	Apps	Goals
1984–85	Notts Co	13	1
1985–86		37	14
1986–87		32	12
1987–88	Lincoln C	*15*	*8*
1988–89		—	—
1989–90		8	1

WALKER, Alan

Born Mossley 17.12.59. Ht 6 2 Wt 12 04
Defender. From Stockport Co and Telford U.

Season	Club	Apps	Goals
1983–84	Lincoln C	33	2
1984–85		42	2
1985–86	Millwall	26	3
1986–87		40	1
1987–88		26	4
1987–88	Gillingham	7	—
1988–89		22	1
1989–90		38	1

WALKER, Andy

Born Glasgow 6.4.65. Ht 5 8 Wt 10 07
Forward. From Baillieston Juniors. Scotland, Under-21, 1 full cap.

Season	Club	Apps	Goals
1984–85	Motherwell	11	3
1985–86		22	4
1986–87		43	10
1987–88	Celtic	42	16
1988–89		22	8
1989–90		32	6

WALKER, Clive

Born Oxford 26.5.57. Ht 5 7 Wt 11 09
Forward. From Apprentice. England Schools.

Season	Club	Apps	Goals
1974–75	Chelsea	—	—
1975–76		—	—
1976–77		1	—
1977–78		23	7
1978–79		30	4
1979–80		36	13
1980–81		37	11
1981–82		36	16
1982–83		29	6
1983–84		6	3
1984–85	Sunderland	38	10
1985–86		12	—
1985–86	QPR	5	1
1986–87		16	—
1987–88		—	—
1987–88	Fulham	26	8
1988–89		38	8
1989–90		45	13

WALKER, Des

Born Hackney 26.11.65. Ht 5 10
Wt 11 05
Defender. From Apprentice. England Under-21, 25 full caps

Season	Club	Apps	Goals
1983–84	Nottingham F	4	—
1984–85		3	—
1985–86		39	—
1986–87		41	—
1987–88		35	—
1988–89		34	—
1989–90		38	—

WALKER, Keith

Born Edinburgh 17.4.66. Ht 6 0
Wt 11 09
Midfield. From ICI Juveniles

Season	Club	Apps	Goals
1984–85	Stirling Albion	38	6
1985–86		32	5
1986–87		21	6
1987–88	St Mirren	19	3
1988–89		14	1
1989–90		10	2
1989–90	Swansea C	13	—

WALKER, Nicky

Born Aberdeen 29.9.62. Ht 6 2
Wt 11 12
Goalkeeper. From Elgin C. Scotland Youth.

Season	Club	League Appearances/Goals	
1980–81	Leicester C	—	—
1981–82		6	—
1982–83	Motherwell	16	—
1983–84		15	—
1983–84	Rangers	8	—
1984–85		14	—
1985–86		34	—
1986–87		2	—
1987–88		5	—
1987–88	*Dunfermline Ath*	1	—
1988–89	Rangers	12	—
1989–90		—	—

WALKER, Ray

Born North Shields 28.9.63. Ht 5 10
Wt 11 12
Midfield. From Apprentice. England Youth.

Season	Club	Apps	Goals
1981–82	Aston Villa	—	—
1982–83		1	—
1983–84		8	—
1984–85		7	—
1984–85	*Port Vale*	15	1
1985–86	Aston Villa	7	—
1986–87	Port Vale	45	4
1987–88		42	6
1988–89		43	5
1989–90		40	—

WALLACE, Danny

Born London 21.1.64. Ht 5 4 Wt 10 04
Forward. From Apprentice. England Youth, Under-21, 1 full cap.

Season	Club	Apps	Goals
1980–81	Southampton	2	—
1981–82		7	—
1982–83		35	12
1983–84		41	11
1984–85		35	7
1985–86		35	8
1986–87		31	8
1987–88		33	11
1988–89		31	5
1989–90		5	2
1989–90	Manchester U	26	3

WALLACE, Ray

Born Lewisham 2.10.69. Ht 5 6
Wt 10 02
Defender. From Trainee, England Under-21.

Season	Club	Apps	Goals
1987–88	Southampton	—	—
1988–89		26	—
1989–90		9	—

WALLACE, Rodney

Born Lewisham 2.10.69. Ht 5 7
Wt 10 01
Forward. From Trainee. England B, Under-21

Season	Club	Apps	Goals
1987–88	Southampton	15	1
1988–89		38	12
1989–90		38	18

WALLER, David

Born Urmston 20.12.63. Ht 5 10
Wt 12 10
Forward. Local.

Season	Club	Apps	Goals
1981–82	Crewe Alex	1	—
1982–83		37	17
1983–84		42	10
1984–85		44	15
1985–86		44	13
1986–87	Shrewsbury T	11	3
1986–87	Chesterfield	—	—
1987–88		40	19
1988–89		36	18
1989–90		43	16

WALLING, Dean

Born Leeds 17.4.69. Ht 6 0 Wt 10 08
Forward.

Season	Club	Apps	Goals
1986–87	Leeds U	—	—
1987–88	Rochdale	12	2

Season	Club	League Appearances/Goals	
1988–89		34	3
1989–90		19	3

WALLINGTON, Mark

Born Sleaford 17.9.52. Ht 6 1 Wt 14 11
Goalkeeper. England Youth, Under-23.

Season	Club	Apps	Goals
1971–72	Walsall	11	—
1971–72	Leicester C	5	—
1972–73		1	—
1973–74		—	—
1974–75		30	—
1975–76		42	—
1976–77		42	—
1977–78		42	—
1978–79		42	—
1979–80		42	—
1980–81		42	—
1981–82		36	—
1982–83		42	—
1983–84		35	—
1984–85		11	—
1985–86	Derby Co	33	—
1986–87		34	—
1987–88		—	—
1988–89	Lincoln C	38	—
1989–90		26	—

WALSH, Colin

Born Hamilton 22.7.62. Ht 5 10
Wt 12 02
Midfield. From Apprentice. Scotland Youth, Under-21.

Season	Club	Apps	Goals
1979–80	Nottingham F	—	—
1980–81		16	4
1981–82		15	3
1982–83		37	5
1983–84		38	13
1984–85		13	1
1985–86		20	6
1986–87		—	—
1986–87	Charlton Ath	33	6
1987–88		11	3
1988–89		5	—
1988–89	*Peterborough U*	5	1
1989–90	Charlton Ath	27	2

WALSH, Derek

Born Hamilton 24.10.67. Ht 5 7
Wt 10 01
Midfield. From Apprentice.

Season	Club	Apps	Goals
1984–85	Everton	1	—
1985–86		—	—
1986–87		—	—
1987–88	Hamilton A.	2	—
1988–89	Carlisle U	35	3
1989–90		28	3

WALSH, Gary

Born Wigan 21.3.68. Ht 6 1 Wt 13 01
Goalkeeper. England Under-21.

Season	Club	Apps	Goals
1984–85	Manchester U	—	—
1985–86		—	—
1986–87		14	—
1987–88		16	—
1988–89		—	—
1988–89	*Airdrie*	3	—
1989–90	Manchester U	—	—

WALSH, Mario

Born Paddington 19.1.66. Ht 6 1
Wt 12 04
Forward. From Apprentice.

Season	Club	Apps	Goals
1983–84	Portsmouth	—	—
1984–85		—	—
1984–85	Torquay U	21	5
1985–86		41	7
1986–87		38	6
1987–88	Colchester U	11	2
1988–89		27	10
1989–90	Southend U	11	2

WALSH, Mick

Born Manchester 20.5.56. Ht 6 0
Wt 13 00
Defender. Eire 5 full caps.

Season	Club	Apps	Goals
1974–75	Bolton W	5	—
1975–76		9	—
1976–77		8	—

Season	Club	League Appearances/Goals	
1977–78		41	1
1978–79		42	1
1979–80		42	1
1980–81		30	1
1981–82	Everton	18	—
1982–83		2	—
1982–83	*Norwich C*	5	—
1982–83	*Burnley*	3	—
From Ft Lauderdale			
1983–84	Manchester C	4	—
1983–84	Blackpool	20	1
1984–85		35	1
1985–86		25	1
1986–87		34	2
1987–88		30	—
1988–89		9	—
1989–90	Bury	—	—

WALSH, Paul

Born Plumstead 1.10.62. Ht 5 7
Wt 10 08
Forward. From Apprentice. England Youth, Under-21, 3 full caps.

Season	Club	Apps	Goals
1979–80	Charlton Ath	9	—
1980–81		40	11
1981–82		38	13
1982–83	Luton T	41	13
1983–84		39	11
1984–85	Liverpool	26	8
1985–86		20	11
1986–87		23	6
1987–88		8	—
1987–88	Tottenham H	11	1
1988–89		33	6
1989–90		26	2

WALSH, Steve

Born Fulwood 3.11.64. Ht 6 3 Wt 13 08
Defender. Local.

Season	Club	Apps	Goals
1982–83	Wigan Ath	31	—
1983–84		42	1
1984–85		40	2
1985–86		13	1
1986–87	Leicester C	21	—
1987–88		32	7
1988–89		30	2
1989–90		34	3

WALTER, David

Born Barnstaple 3.9.64 Ht 6 3 Wt 13 03
Goalkeeper. From Bideford T.

Season	Club	Apps	Goals
1988–89	Exeter C	26	—
1989–90		18	—
1989–90	*Plymouth Arg*	—	—

WALTERS, Mark

Born Birmingham 12.1.61. Ht 5 9
Wt 10 12
Forward. From Apprentice. England Youth, Under-21.

Season	Club	Apps	Goals
1981–82	Aston Villa	1	—
1982–83		22	1
1983–84		37	8
1984–85		36	10
1985–86		40	10
1986–87		21	3
1987–88		24	7
1987–88	Rangers	18	7
1988–89		31	8
1989–90		27	5

WALTERS, Steve

Born Plymouth 9.1.72 Ht 5 10
Wt 11 08
Forward. From Schoolboy, Trainee. FA Schools.

Season	Club	Apps	Goals
1987–88	Crewe Alex	1	—
1988–89		22	1
1989–90		30	1

WALTON, Mark

Born Merthyr 1.6.69. Ht 6 2 Wt 13 13
Goalkeeper. From Swansea C.

Season	Club	Apps	Goals
1986–87	Luton T	—	—
1987–88		—	—
1987–88	Colchester U	17	—

Season	Club	League Appearances/Goals	
1988–89		23	—
1989–90	Norwich C	1	—

WALWYN, Keith

Born W Indies 17.2.56. Ht 6 1 Wt 13 04
Forward. From Winterton.

Season	Club	League Appearances/Goals	
1979–80	Chesterfield	—	—
1980–81		3	2
1981–82	York C	44	23
1982–83		41	21
1983–84		45	25
1984–85		27	9
1985–86		46	22
1986–87		42	19
1987–88	Blackpool	39	13
1988–89		30	3
1989–90	Carlisle U	40	11

WARBURTON, Ray

Born Rotherham 7.10.67. Ht 6 0
Wt 12 00
Defender. From Apprentice.

Season	Club	League Appearances/Goals	
1984–85	Rotherham U	1	—
1985–86		—	—
1986–87		3	—
1987–88		—	—
1988–89		—	—
1989–90	York C	43	2

WARD, Ashley

Born Manchester 24.11.70. Ht 6 1
Wt 11 07
Forward. From Trainee.

Season	Club	League Appearances/Goals	
1989–90	Manchester C	1	—

WARD, Gavin

Born Sutton Coldfield 30.6.70 Ht 6 2
Wt 12 12
Goalkeeper. From Aston Villa Trainee.

Season	Club	League Appearances/Goals	
1988–89	Shrewsbury T	—	—
1989–90	WBA	—	—
1989–90	Cardiff C	2	—

WARD, Kenny

Born Blairhall 16.8.63. Ht 5 8 Wt 9 07
Forward. From Oakley U.

Season	Club	League Appearances/Goals	
1983–84	Cowdenbeath	31	5
1984–85		36	16
1985–86		16	8
1985–86	Forfar Ath	16	1
1986–87		33	4
1987–88		37	7
1988–89		35	12
1989–90		2	—
1989–90	St Johnstone	18	4

WARD, Mark

Born Prescot 10.10.62. Ht 5 6 Wt 10 12
Midfield. From Everton Apprentice and Northwich Vic.

Season	Club	League Appearances/Goals	
1983–84	Oldham Ath	42	6
1984–85		42	6
1985–86	West Ham U	42	3
1986–87		37	1
1987–88		37	1
1988–89		30	2
1989–90		19	5
1989–90	Manchester C	19	3

WARD, Mitchum

Born Sheffield 18.6.71. Ht 5 8 Wt 10 07
Defender. From Trainee

Season	Club	League Appearances/Goals	
1989–90	Sheffield U	—	—

WARD, Paul

Born Sedgefield 15.9.63. Ht 5 11
Wt 12 05
Midfield. From Apprentice.

Season	Club	League Appearances/Goals	
1981–82	Chelsea	—	—
1982–83	Middlesbrough	15	—
1983–84		28	1
1984–85		30	—
1985–86		3	—
1985–86	Darlington	35	2
1986–87		44	1

Season Club League Appearances/Goals

Season	Club	Apps	Goals
1987–88	....	45	6
1988–89	Leyton Orient	28	1
1989–90	....	3	—
1989–90	Scunthorpe U	25	4

WARD, Peter

Born Durham 15.10.64. Ht 6 0 Wt 11 10
Forward. From Chester-le-Street.

Season	Club	Apps	Goals
1986–87	Huddersfield T	7	—
1987–88	....	26	2
1988–89	....	4	—
1989–90	Rochdale	40	5

WARD, Tony

Born Warrington 4.4.70 Ht 5 7 Wt 10 08
Midfield. From Trainee.

Season	Club	Apps	Goals
1988–89	Everton	—	—
1988–89	*Doncaster R*	4	—
1989–90	Wigan Ath	11	2

WARDLE, Ian

Born Doncaster 27.3.70 Ht 5 9 Wt 11 00
Goalkeeper. From School.

Season	Club	Apps	Goals
1988–89	Barnsley	—	—
1989–90	....	9	—

WARE, Paul

Born Congleton 7.11.70. Ht 5 8
Wt 11 02
Midfield. From Trainee.

Season	Club	Apps	Goals
1987–88	Stoke C	1	—
1988–89	....	11	1
1989–90	....	16	—

WARHURST, Paul

Born Stockport 26.9.69. Ht 6 1 Wt 14 00
Defender. From Trainee.

Season	Club	Apps	Goals
1987–88	Manchester C	—	—
1988–89	Oldham Ath	4	—
1989–90	....	30	1

WARK, John

Born Glasgow 4.8.57. Ht 5 11 Wt 12 12
Midfield. From Apprentice. Scotland Under-21, 29 full caps.

Season	Club	Apps	Goals
1974–75	Ipswich T	3	—
1975–76	....	3	—
1976–77	....	33	10
1977–78	....	18	5
1978–79	....	42	6
1979–80	....	41	12
1980–81	....	40	18
1981–82	....	42	18
1982–83	....	42	20
1983–84	....	32	5
1983–84	Liverpool	9	2
1984–85	....	40	18
1985–86	....	9	3
1986–87	....	11	5
1987–88	....	1	—
1987–88	Ipswich T	7	—
1988–89	....	41	13
1989–90	....	41	10

WARNER, John

Born Paddington 20.11.61 Ht 5 10
Wt 12 03
Forward. From Burnham Ramblers.

Season	Club	Apps	Goals
1988–89	Colchester U	15	3
1989–90	....	2	—

WARREN, Lee

Born Manchester 28.2.69. Ht 6 0
Wt 11 10
Midfield. From Trainee.

Season	Club	Apps	Goals
1987–88	Leeds U	—	—
1987–88	Rochdale	31	1
1988–89	Hull C	28	—
1989–90	....	10	—

WASSALL, Darren

Born Edgbaston 27.6.68. Ht 5 11
Wt 11 09
Defender.

Season Club League Appearances/Goals

Season	Club	Apps	Goals
1987–88	Nottingham F	3	—
1987–88	*Hereford U*	5	—
1988–89	Nottingham F	—	—
1988–89	*Bury*	7	1
1989–90	Nottingham F	3	—

WASSELL, Kim

Born Wolverhampton 9.6.57. Ht 5 8
Wt 11 08
Forward. From WBA Apprentice.

Season	Club	Apps	Goals
1977–78	Northampton T	7	—
1978–79		13	—
1979–80	Aldershot	—	—
Frim Finland.			
1983–84	Hull C	1	—
1984–85	Swansea C	2	—
1985–86	Wolverhampton W	2	—
From Finland.			
1989–90	Shrewsbury T	2	—

WATERS, Graham

Born St Austell 5.11.71. Ht 5 8
Wt 11 02
Midfield. From Trainee

Season	Club	Apps	Goals
1989–90	Oxford U	—	—

WATKINS, Dale

Born Peterborough 4.11.71.
Forward. From Sheffield U, Grimsby T and Peterborough U Trainee.

Season	Club	Apps	Goals
1989–90	Peterborough U	1	—

WATSON, Alex

Born Liverpool 5.4.68. Ht 5 11 Wt 11 09
Defender. From Apprentice. England Youth.

Season	Club	Apps	Goals
1984–85	Liverpool	—	—
1985–86		—	—
1986–87		—	—
1987–88		2	—
1988–89		2	—
1989–90		—	—

WATSON, Andy

Born Huddersfield 1.4.67. Ht 5 9
Wt 11 02
Defender. From Harrogate T

Season	Club	Apps	Goals
1988–89	Halifax T	45	5
1989–90		38	10

WATSON, Dave

Born Liverpool 20.11.61. Ht 6 0
Wt 11 12
Defender. From Amateur. England Under-21, 12 full caps.

Season	Club	Apps	Goals
1979–80	Liverpool	—	—
1980–81		—	—
1980–81	Norwich C	18	3
1981–82		38	3
1982–83		35	1
1983–84		40	1
1984–85		39	—
1985–86		42	3
1986–87	Everton	35	4
1987–88		37	4
1988–89		32	3
1989–90		29	1

WATSON, Gordon

Born Kent 20.3.71. Ht 6 0 Wt 12 00
Forward. From Trainee.

Season	Club	Apps	Goals
1988–89	Charlton Ath	—	—
1989–90		9	—

WATSON, Graham

Born St Andrews 16.8.63. Ht 5 8
Wt 10 10
Defender. From Deeside BC.

Season	Club	Apps	Goals
1986–87	Aberdeen	—	—
1987–88		—	—

Season	Club	Apps	Goals
1988–89		—	—
1989–90		4	1

WATSON, Gregg

Born Glasgow 21.9.70. Ht 5 9 Wt 10 09
Midfield. From Aberdeen Lads. Scotland Youth.

Season	Club	Apps	Goals
1987–88	Aberdeen	—	—
1988–89		4	—
1989–90		4	—

WATSON, John

Born Edinburgh 13.2.59. Ht 6 0 Wt 12 06
Forward. From Hong Kong R.

Season	Club	Apps	Goals
1983–84	Dunfermline Ath	21	3
1984–85		37	15
1985–86		37	24
1986–87		40	13
1987–88		25	3
1988–89		35	14
1989–90	Fulham	14	—
1989–90	Airdrie	11	1

WATSON, Tommy

Born Liverpool 29.9.69 Ht 5 8 Wt 10 10
Midfield. From Trainee.

Season	Club	Apps	Goals
1987–88	Grimsby T	19	—
1988–89		21	4
1989–90		16	1

WATT, Michael

Born Aberdeen 27.11.70. Ht 6 1 Wt 11 10
Goalkeeper. From Cove R.

Season	Club	Apps	Goals
1989–90	Aberdeen	7	—

WAUGH, Keith

Born Sunderland 27.10.56. Ht 6 1 Wt 13 00
Goalkeeper. From Apprentice.

Season Club League Appearances/Goals

Season	Club	Apps	Goals
1974–75	Sunderland	—	—
1975–76		—	—
1976–77	Peterborough U	32	—
1977–78		26	—
1978–79		46	—
1979–80		46	—
1980–81		45	—
1981–82	Sheffield U	45	—
1982–83		28	—
1983–84		16	—
1984–85		10	—
1984–85	*Bristol C*	3	—
1984–85	*Cambridge U*	4	—
1985–86	Bristol C	44	—
1986–87		46	—
1987–88		40	—
1988–89		37	—
1989–90	Coventry C	1	—

WDOWCZYK, Dariusz

Born Warsaw 21.9.62.
Defender. From Legia Warsaw, Poland full caps.

Season	Club	Apps	Goals
1989–90	Celtic	23	1

WEATHERHEAD, Shaun

Born Halifax 3.9.70. Ht 5 11 Wt 12 03
Defender. From Trainee.

Season	Club	Apps	Goals
1989–90	Huddersfield T	—	—

WEBB, Alan

Born Wellington 1.1.63. Ht 5 10 Wt 12 00
Defender. From Apprentice.

Season	Club	Apps	Goals
1979–80	WBA	—	—
1980–81		—	—
1981–82		6	—
1982–83		13	—
1983–84		5	—
1983–84	*Lincoln C*	11	—
1984–85	Port Vale	46	—
1985–86		39	1
1986–87		21	1
1987–88		26	—

Season	Club	League Appearances/Goals	
1988–89		37	—
1989–90		14	—

WEBB, Jamie

Born Portsmouth 7.12.69. Ht 5 8
Wt 10 06
Midfield. From Trainee.

Season	Club	Apps	Goals
1987–88	Southampton	—	—
1988–89		—	—
1989–90		—	—

WEBB, Neil

Born Reading 30.7.63. Ht 6 0 Wt 13 03
Midfield. From Apprentice. England Youth, B, Under-21, 20 full caps. Football League.

Season	Club	Apps	Goals
1979–80	Reading	5	—
1980–81		27	7
1981–82		40	15
1982–83	Portsmouth	42	8
1983–84		40	10
1984–85		41	16
1985–86	Nottingham F	38	14
1986–87		32	14
1987–88		40	13
1988–89		36	6
1989–90	Manchester U	11	2

WEBSTER, Simon

Born Earl Shilton 20.1.64. Ht 6 0
Wt 11 07
Defender. From Apprentice.

Season	Club	Apps	Goals
1981–82	Tottenham H	—	—
1982–83		2	—
1983–84		1	—
1983–84	*Exeter C*	26	—
1984–85	Tottenham H	—	—
1984–85	*Norwich C*	—	—
1984–85	Huddersfield T	16	1
1985–86		41	2
1986–87		39	1
1987–88		22	—
1987–88	Sheffield U	5	1

Season	Club	League Appearances/Goals	
1988–89		12	2
1989–90		20	—

WEGERLE, Roy

Born South Africa 19.3.64. Ht 5 11
Wt 11 00
Forward. From Tampa Bay R.

Season	Club	Apps	Goals
1986–87	Chelsea	12	2
1987–88		11	1
1987–88	*Swindon T*	7	1
1988–89	Luton T	30	8
1989–90		15	2
1989–90	QPR	19	6

WEIR, Billy

Born Baillieston 11.4.68. Ht 5 5 Wt 9 12
Forward. From Baillieston Juniors.

Season	Club	Apps	Goals
1989–90	Shrewsbury T	9	—

WEIR, Michael

Born Edinburgh 16.1.66. Ht 5 4 Wt 9 02
Midfield. From Portobello Thistle.

Season	Club	Apps	Goals
1982–83	Hibernian	—	—
1983–84		—	—
1984–85		12	—
1985–86		7	—
1986–87		24	4
1987–88		5	1
1987–88	Luton T	8	—
1987–88	Hibernian	13	2
1988–89		7	—
1989–90		18	3

WEIR, Peter

Born Johnstone 18.1.58. Ht 6 0
Wt 11 09
Forward. From Neilston Juniors. Scotland, 6 full caps.

Season	Club	Apps	Goals
1978–79	St Mirren	6	—
1979–80		26	2
1980–81		28	2
1981–82	Aberdeen	25	2
1982–83		31	6
1983–84		27	5
1984–85		16	3

Season	Club	League Appearances/Goals	
1985–86		22	5
1986–87		34	2
1987–88		5	—
1987–88	Leicester C	18	2
1988–89		10	—
1988–89	St Mirren	16	6
1989–90		12	—

WELCH, Keith

Born Bolton 3.10.68. Ht 6 0 Wt 12 0
Goalkeeper. From Trainee.

Season	Club	League Appearances/Goals	
1986–87	Bolton W	—	—
1986–87	Rochdale	24	—
1987–88		46	—
1988–89		46	—
1989–90		46	—

WELSH, Brian

Born Edinburgh 23.2.69 Ht 6 2
Wt 12 01
Defender. From Tynecastle BC.

Season	Club	League Appearances/Goals	
1986–87	Dundee U	1	—
1987–88		1	1
1988–89		1	—
1989–90		5	—

WELSH, Steve

Born Glasgow 19.4.68.
Defender. From Army.

Season	Club	League Appearances/Goals	
1989–90	Cambridge U	—	—

WEST, Colin

Born Middlesbrough 19.9.67. Ht 5 7
Wt 11 00
Forward. From Apprentice.

Season	Club	League Appearances/Goals	
1985–86	Chelsea	—	—
1986–87		7	1
1986–87	*Partick T*	24	10
1987–88	Chelsea	9	3
1988–89		—	—
1988–89	*Swansea C*	14	3
1989–90	Chelsea	—	—

WEST, Colin

Born Wallsend 13.11.62. Ht 6 0
Wt 13 11
Forward. From Apprentice.

Season	Club	League Appearances/Goals	
1980–81	Sunderland	—	—
1981–82		18	6
1982–83		23	3
1983–84		38	9
1984–85		23	3
1984–85	Watford	12	7
1985–86		33	13
1986–87	Rangers	9	2
1987–88		1	—
1987–88	Sheffield W	25	7
1988–89		20	1
1988–89	WBA	17	8
1989–90		21	4

WEST, Gary

Born Scunthorpe 25.8.64. Ht 6 2
Wt 13 02
Defender. From Apprentice. England Youth.

Season	Club	League Appearances/Goals	
1982–83	Sheffield U	26	1
1983–84		24	—
1984–85		25	—
1985–86	Lincoln C	38	2
1986–87		45	2
1987–88	Gillingham	42	2
1988–89		10	1
1988–89	Port Vale	14	1
1989–90		3	—

WESTLEY, Shane

Born Canterbury 16.6.65. Ht 6 2
Wt 13 08
Defender. From Apprentice.

Season	Club	League Appearances/Goals	
1983–84	Charlton Ath	8	—
1984–85		—	—
1984–85	Southend U	12	—
1985–86		36	5
1986–87		32	—
1986–87	*Norwich C*	—	—

Season	Club	League Appearances/Goals	
1987–88	Southend U	36	5
1988–89		28	—
1989–90	Wolverhampton W	37	—

WESTON, Ian

Born Bristol 6.5.68. Ht 5 10 Wt 11 10
Midfield.

Season	Club	Apps	Goals
1986–87	Bristol R	11	—
1987–88		5	—
1988–89	Torquay U	37	2
1989–90		25	—
1989–90	*Shamrock R*	—	—

WESTWATER, Ian

Born Loughborough 8.11.63. Ht 6 0
Wt 13 00
Goalkeeper. From Salvesen BC.

Season	Club	Apps	Goals
1980–81	Hearts	2	—
1981–82		—	—
1982–83		—	—
1983–84		—	—
1984–85		—	—
1984–85	Dunfermline Ath	8	—
1985–86		38	—
1986–87		42	—
1987–88		28	—
1988–89		39	—
1989–90		36	—

WETHERALL, David

Born Sheffield 14.3.71. Ht 6 3 Wt 12 00
Defender. From School.

Season	Club	Apps	Goals
1989–90	Sheffield W	—	—

WHARTON, Ken

Born Newcastle 28.11.60 Ht 5 8 Wt 8 10
Midfield. From Grainger Park BC.

Season	Club	Apps	Goals
1978–79	Newcastle U	2	—
1979–80		1	—
1980–81		36	—
1981–82		33	5
1982–83		41	5
1983–84		41	4
1984–85		35	6
1985–86		15	2
1986–87		37	2
1987–88		31	2
1988–89		18	—
1989–90	Middlesbrough	—	—
1989–90	Carlisle U	1	—
1989–90	Bradford C	5	—
1989–90	WBA	—	—

WHEELER, Paul

Born Caerphilly 3.1.65. Ht 5 9 Wt 11 00
Forward. From Apprentice.

Season	Club	Apps	Goals
1982–83	Bristol R	—	—
1983–84		—	—
From Aberaman			
1985–86	Cardiff C	21	2
1986–87		37	7
1987–88		16	—
1988–89		27	1
1989–90		—	—
1989–90	Hull C	5	—
1989–90	Hereford U	21	8

WHELAN, Ronnie

Born Dublin 25.9.61. Ht 5 9 Wt 10 13
Midfield. From Home Farm. Eire Under-21, 39 full caps.

Season	Club	Apps	Goals
1979–80	Liverpool	—	—
1980–81		1	1
1981–82		32	10
1982–83		28	2
1983–84		23	4
1984–85		37	7
1985–86		39	10
1986–87		39	3
1987–88		28	1
1988–89		37	4
1989–90		34	1

WHELLANS, Robbie

Born Harrogate 10.12.69. Ht 5 6
Wt 10 07
Forward. From Trainee.

Season	Club	Apps	Goals
1987–88	Bradford C	—	—
1987–88	*Hartlepool U*	11	1

Season	Club	League Appearances/Goals	
1988–89	Bradford C	—	—
1989–90	Rochdale	11	1

WHISTON, Peter

Born Widnes 4.1.68. Ht 6 0 Wt 11 06
Forward.

Season	Club		
1987–88	Plymouth Arg	—	—
1988–89		2	—
1989–90		8	—
1989–90	*Torquay U*	8	1

WHITBREAD, Adrian

Born Epping 22.10.71.
Defender. From Trainee

Season	Club		
1989–90	Leyton Orient	8	—

WHITE, David

Born Manchester 30.10.67. Ht 6 1
Wt 12 09
Forward. England Youth, Under-21.

Season	Club		
1985–86	Manchester C	—	—
1986–87		24	1
1987–88		44	13
1988–89		45	6
1989–90		37	8

WHITE, Devon

Born Nottingham 2.3.64. Ht 6 3
Wt 14 00
Forward. From Arnold T.

Season	Club		
1984–85	Lincoln C	7	1
1985–86		22	3
1986–87		—	—
From Boston U			
1987–88	Bristol R	39	15
1988–89		40	5
1989–90		43	12

WHITE, Steve

Born Chipping Sodbury 2.1.59. Ht 5 10
Wt 11 04
Forward. From Mangotsfield U.

Season	Club		
1977–78	Bristol R	8	4
1978–79		27	10
1979–80		15	6
1979–80	Luton T	9	—
1980–81		21	7
1981–82		42	18
1982–83	Charlton Ath	29	12
1982–83	*Lincoln C*	3	—
1982–83	*Luton T*	4	—
1983–84	Bristol R	43	9
1984–85		18	3
1985–86		40	12
1986–87	Swindon T	35	15
1987–88		25	11
1988–89		43	13
1989–90		43	18

WHITE, Winston

Born Leicester 26.10.58. Ht 5 10
Wt 10 12
Midfield. From Apprentice.

Season	Club		
1976–77	Leicester C	4	—
1977–78		6	1
1978–79		2	—
1978–79	Hereford U	15	3
1979–80		34	2
1980–81		43	5
1981–82		46	8
1982–83		37	3
1983–84	Chesterfield	1	—
1983–84	Port Vale	1	—
1983–84	Stockport Co	4	—
1983–84	Bury	29	1
1984–85		46	4
1985–86		43	5
1986–87		7	1
1986–87	*Rochdale*	4	—
1986–87	Colchester U	14	1
1987–88		41	7
1988–89		10	—
1988–89	Burnley	35	5
1989–90		40	7

WHITEHEAD, Clive

Born Birmingham 24.11.55. Ht 5 10
Wt 12 03
Defender. From Northfield J.

Season	Club		
1973–74	Bristol C	12	2
1974–75		14	—

Season	Club	League Appearances/Goals	
1975–76		22	4
1976–77		41	—
1977–78		33	2
1978–79		30	2
1979–80		40	—
1980–81		31	—
1981–82		6	—
1981–82	WBA	8	1
1982–83		36	1
1983–84		34	1
1984–85		32	—
1985–86		24	—
1985–86	*Wolverhampton W*	2	—
1986–87	WBA	34	3
1987–88	Portsmouth	33	2
1988–89		32	—
1989–90	Exeter C	38	5

WHITEHEAD, Philip

Born Halifax 17.12.69 Ht 6 3 Wt 13 07
Goalkeeper. From Trainee.

Season	Club	League Appearances/Goals	
1986–87	Halifax T	12	—
1987–88		—	—
1988–89		11	—
1989–90		19	—
1989–90	Barnsley	—	—

WHITEHOUSE, Dane

Born Sheffield 14.10.70 Ht 5 8 Wt 10 12
Midfield. From Trainee.

Season	Club	League Appearances/Goals	
1988–89	Sheffield U	5	—
1989–90		12	1

WHITEHOUSE, Phil

Born Wolverhampton 23.3.71.
Defender. From Trainee

Season	Club	League Appearances/Goals	
1989–90	WBA	—	—
1989–90	Walsall	9	—

WHITEHURST, Billy

Born Thurnscoe 10.6.59. Ht 6 0
Wt 14 09
Forward. From Mexborough.

Season	Club	League Appearances/Goals	
1980–81	Hull C	26	1
1981–82		36	6
1982–83		36	3
1983–84		37	10
1984–85		40	20
1985–86		18	7
1985–86	Newcastle U	20	7
1986–87		8	—
1986–87	Oxford U	20	2
1987–88		20	2
1987–88	Reading	15	6
1988–89		2	2
1988–89	Sunderland	17	3
1988–89	Hull C	21	5
1989–90		15	—
1989–90	Sheffield U	14	2

WHITESIDE, Norman

Born Belfast 7.5.65. Ht 6 0 Wt 12 11
Forward. From Apprentice. Northern Ireland Schools, Youth, 38 full caps.

Season	Club	League Appearances/Goals	
1981–82	Manchester U	2	1
1982–83		39	8
1983–84		37	10
1984–85		27	9
1985–86		37	4
1986–87		31	8
1987–88		27	7
1988–89		6	—
1989–90	Everton	27	9

WHITLOCK, Mark

Born Portsmouth 14.3.61. Ht 6 0
Wt 12 02
Defender. From Apprentice.

Season	Club	League Appearances/Goals	
1978–79	Southampton	—	—
1979–80		—	—
1980–81		—	—
1981–82		9	1
1982–83	*Grimsby T*	8	—
1982–83	*Aldershot*	14	—
1983–84	Southampton	16	—
1984–85		22	—
1985–86		14	—
1986–87	Bournemouth	45	1
1987–88		41	—
1988–89		13	—

Season	Club	Apps	Goals
1988–89	Reading	17	—
1989–90		10	—

WHITLOW, Mike

Born Northwich 13.1.68 Ht 5 11
Wt 12 01
Midfield. From Witton Alb.

Season	Club	Apps	Goals
1988–89	Leeds U	20	1
1989–90		29	1

WHITTAKER, Brian

Born Glasgow 23.9.56. Ht 6 0 Wt 11 09
Defender. From Sighthill Amateurs.

Season	Club	Apps	Goals
1974–75	Partick T	1	—
1975–76		1	—
1976–77		36	1
1977–78		35	—
1978–79		36	—
1979–80		35	1
1980–81		34	1
1981–82		28	—
1982–83		35	1
1983–84	Celtic	10	2
1984–85	Hearts	28	1
1985–86		25	—
1986–87		37	—
1987–88		42	—
1988–89		24	—
1989–90		6	—

WHITTINGHAM, Guy

Born Evesham 10.11.64. Ht 5 10
Wt 11 12
Forward. From Yeovil and Army.

Season	Club	Apps	Goals
1989–90	Portsmouth	42	23

WHITTON, Steve

Born East Ham 4.12.60. Ht 6 0
Wt 12 07
Forward. From Apprentice.

Season	Club	Apps	Goals
1978–79	Coventry C	—	—
1979–80		7	—
1980–81		1	—
1981–82		28	9
1982–83		38	12
1983–84	West Ham U	22	5
1984–85		17	1
1985–86		—	—
1985–86	*Birmingham C*	8	2
1986–87	Birmingham C	39	9
1987–88		33	14
1988–89		23	5
1988–89	Sheffield W	12	3
1989–90		19	1

WHITWORTH, Neil

Born Ince 12.4.72.
Defender. From Trainee

Season	Club	Apps	Goals
1989–90	Wigan Ath	2	—

WHYTE, David

Born Greenwich 20.4.71. Ht 5 9
Wt 10 06
Forward.

Season	Club	Apps	Goals
1988–89	Crystal Palace	—	—
1989–90		—	—

WHYTE, Chris

Born London 2.9.61. Ht 6 1 Wt 11 10
Defender. From Amateur. England
Under-21.

Season	Club	Apps	Goals
1979–80	Arsenal	—	—
1980–81		—	—
1981–82		32	2
1982–83		36	3
1983–84		15	2
1984–85		—	—
1984–85	*Crystal Palace*	13	—
1985–86	Arsenal	7	1
From Los Angeles R			
1988–89	WBA	40	3
1989–90		44	4

WHYTE, Derek

Born Glasgow 31.8.68. Ht 5 11 Wt 11 05
Defender. From Celtic BC. Scotland
Schools, Youth, B, Under-21, 3 full caps.

Season	Club	Apps	Goals
1985–86	Celtic	11	—
1986–87		42	—
1987–88		41	3

Season	Club	League Appearances/Goals	
1988–89		22	—
1989–90		35	1

WIGLEY, Steve

Born Ashton 15.10.61. Ht 5 9 Wt 10 05
Forward. From Curzon Ashton.

Season	Club	League Appearances/Goals	
1980–81	Nottingham F	—	—
1981–82		—	—
1982–83		4	—
1983–84		35	1
1984–85		35	1
1985–86		8	—
1985–86	Sheffield U	10	1
1986–87		18	—
1986–87	Birmingham C	11	1
1987–88		43	2
1988–89		33	1
1988–89	Portsmouh	11	—
1989–90		45	4

WIGNALL, Steve

Born Liverpool 17.9.54. Ht 5 11
Wt 11 11
Defender. From Liverpool Amateur.

Season	Club	League Appearances/Goals	
1971–72	Doncaster R	—	—
1972–73		23	—
1973–74		38	—
1974–75		35	1
1975–76		23	—
1976–77		11	—
1976–77	*Nottingham F*	—	—
1977–78	Doncaster R	—	—
1977–78	Colchester U	34	2
1978–79		42	4
1979–80		40	3
1980–81		42	1
1981–82		43	—
1982–83		44	4
1983–84		36	8
1984–85	Brentford	36	—
1985–86		28	2
1986–87		3	—
1986–87	Aldershot	40	1
1987–88		37	1

Season	Club	League Appearances/Goals	
1988–89		32	1
1989–90		38	1

WILCOX, Jason

Born Bolton 15.7.71.
Forward. From Trainee

Season	Club	League Appearances/Goals	
1989–90	Blackburn R	1	—

WILCOX, Russell

Born Hemsworth 25.3.64. Ht 6 0
Wt 11 10
Defender. From Apprentice.

Season	Club	League Appearances/Goals	
1980–81	Doncaster R	1	—
From Cambridge U, Frickley Ath.			
1986–87	Northampton T	35	1
1987–88		46	4
1988–89		11	1
1989–90		46	3

WILDER, Chris

Born Wortley 23.9.67 Ht 5 11 Wt 10 10
Defender. From Apprentice.

Season	Club	League Appearances/Goals	
1985–86	Southampton	—	—
1986–87	Sheffield U	11	—
1987–88		25	—
1988–89		29	1
1989–90		8	—
1989–90	*Walsall*	4	—

WILKINS, Dean

Born Hillingdon 12.7.62. Ht 5 8
Wt 11 08
Midfield. From Apprentice.

Season	Club	League Appearances/Goals	
1980–81	QPR	2	—
1981–82		1	—
1982–83		3	—
1983–84	Brighton	2	—
1983–84	*Orient*	10	—
From PEC Zwolle			
1987–88	Brighton	44	2

Season	Club	Apps	Goals
1988–89		43	1
1989–90		46	6

WILKINS, Ray

Born Hillingdon 14.9.56. Ht 5 8 Wt 11 02
Midfield. From Apprentice. England Under-21, Under-23, 84 full caps. Football League.

Season	Club	Apps	Goals
1973–74	Chelsea	6	—
1974–75		21	2
1975–76		42	11
1976–77		42	7
1977–78		33	7
1978–79		35	3
1979–80	Manchester U	37	2
1980–81		13	—
1981–82		42	1
1982–83		26	1
1983–84		42	3
1984–85	AC Milan	28	—
1985–86		29	2
1986–87		16	—
From Paris St Germain			
1987–88	Rangers	24	1
1988–89		31	1
1989–90		15	—
1989–90	QPR	23	1

WILKINS, Richard

Born London 28.5.65. Ht 6 0 Wt 12 00
Midfield. From Haverhill R.

Season	Club	Apps	Goals
1986–87	Colchester U	23	2
1987–88		46	9
1988–89		40	7
1989–90		43	4

WILKINSON, Paul

Born Louth 30.10.64. Ht 6 0 Wt 11 09
Forward. From Apprentice. England Under-21.

Season	Club	Apps	Goals
1982–83	Grimsby T	4	1
1983–84		37	12
1984–85		30	14
1984–85	Everton	5	2
1985–86		4	1
1986–87		22	4
1986–87	Nottingham F	8	—
1988–89	Watford	45	19
1989–90		43	15

WILKINSON, Steve

Born Lincoln 1.9.68. Ht 6 0 Wt 10 12
Forward. From Apprentice.

Season	Club	Apps	Goals
1986–87	Leicester C	1	–
1987–88		5	1
1988–89		1	—
1988–89	*Rochdale*	—	—
1988–89	*Crewe Alex*	5	2
1989–90	Leicester C	2	—
1989–90	Mansfield T	37	15

WILLIAMS, Adrian

Born Reading 16.8.71
Defender. From Trainee.

Season	Club	Apps	Goals
1988–89	Reading	8	—
1989–90		16	2

WILLIAMS, Andy

Born Birmingham 29.7.62. Ht 6 2 Wt 12 00
Midfield. From Dudley and Solihull B.

Season	Club	Apps	Goals
1985–86	Coventry C	8	—
1986–87		1	—
1986–87	Rotherham U	36	4
1987–88		36	6
1988–89		15	3
1988–89	Leeds U	18	1
1989–90		16	2

WILLIAMS, Bill

Born Rochdale 7.10.60. Ht 5 10 Wt 12 11
Defender. Local.

Season	Club	Apps	Goals
1981–82	Rochdale	6	—
1982–83		37	—
1983–84		27	2
1984–85		25	—
1985–86	Stockport Co	22	—
1986–87		30	—
1987–88		45	1

Season	Club	League Appearances/Goals	
1988–89	....	7	—
1988–89	Manchester C	1	—
1988–89	Stockport Co	28	2
1989–90	....	37	—

WILLIAMS, Brett

Born Dudley 19.3.68. Ht 5 10 Wt 11 12
Defender. From Apprentice.

Season	Club	League Appearances/Goals	
1985–86	Nottingham F	11	—
1986–87	....	3	—
1986–87	*Stockport Co*	2	—
1987–88	Nottingham F	4	—
1987–88	*Northampton T*	4	—
1988–89	Nottingham F	2	—
1989–90	....	1	—
1989–90	*Hereford U*	14	—

WILLIAMS Brian

Born Salford 5.11.55. Ht 5 9 Wt 12 01
Defender. From Apprentice

Season	Club	League Appearances/Goals	
1971–72	Bury	1	—
1972–73	....	10	1
1973–74	....	35	9
1974–75	....	35	1
1975–76	....	46	5
1976–77	....	32	3
1977–78	QPR	19	—
1978–79	Swindon T	25	2
1979–80	....	43	3
1980–81	....	31	3
1981–82	Bristol R.................	37	4
1982–83	....	43	2
1983–84	....	46	10
1984–85	....	46	4
1985–86	Bristol C.................	36	1
1986–87	....	41	2
1987–88	Shrewsbury T...........	42	—
1988–89	....	23	1
1989–90	....	—	—

WILLIAMS, Darren

Born Birmingham 15.12.68. Ht 5 10
Wt 10 05
Midfield. From Trainee.

Season	Club	League Appearances/Goals	
1986–87	Leicester C..............	—	—
1987–88	....	—	—
1988–89	....	6	1
1989–90	....	4	1
1989–90	*Lincoln C*	9	—

WILLIAMS, David

Born Cardiff 11.3.55. Ht 5 10 Wt 11 08
Midfield. From Clifton Ath. Wales Under-23, Under-21, 5 full caps.

Season	Club	League Appearances/Goals	
1975–76	Bristol R.................	41	2
1976–77	....	39	10
1977–78	....	33	8
1978–79	....	42	10
1979–80	....	40	4
1980–81	....	25	3
1981–82	....	46	11
1982–83	....	25	9
1983–84	....	24	3
1984–85	....	37	6
1985–86	Norwich C	39	8
1986–87	....	12	3
1987–88	....	9	—
1988–89	....	—	—
1989–90	....	—	—

WILLIAMS, David

Born Liverpool 18.9.68. Ht 6 0 Wt 12 00
Goalkeeper. From Trainee.

Season	Club	League Appearances/Goals	
1987–88	Oldham Ath	—	—
1987–88	Burnley	—	—
1988–89	....	7	—
1989–90	....	7	—

WILLIAMS, Dean

Born Lichfield 5.1.72. Ht 6 0 Wt 11 07
Goalkeeper, From Trainee.

Season	Club	League Appearances/Goals	
1989–90	Birmingham C	3	—

WILLIAMS, Gareth

Born Isle of Wight 12.3.67 Ht 5 10
Wt 11 08
Forward. From Gosport Borough.

Season	Club	League Appearances/Goals	
1987–88	Aston Villa..............	1	—

Season	Club	League Appearances/Goals	
1988–89		1	—
1989–90		10	—

WILLIAMS, Gary

Born Bristol 8.6.63. Ht 5 8 Wt 10 11
Midfield. From Apprentice.

Season	Club	Apps	Goals
1980–81	Bristol C	1	—
1981–82		33	1
1982–83		36	—
1983–84		30	—
1984–85	Portsmouth	—	—
1984–85	Swansea C	6	—
1984–85	Bristol R	—	—
1985–86	Oldham Ath	9	1
1986–87		32	9
1987–88		9	1
1988–89		6	1
1989–90		3	—

WILLIAMS, Gary

Born Wolverhampton 17.6.60. Ht 5 9
Wt 11 12
Defender. From Apprentice.

Season	Club	Apps	Goals
1978–79	Aston Villa	23	—
1979–80		2	—
1979–80	*Walsall*	9	—
1980–81	Aston Villa	22	—
1981–82		28	—
1982–83		36	—
1983–84		40	—
1984–85		38	—
1985–86		25	—
1986–87		26	—
1987–88	Leeds U	31	3
1988–89		8	—
1989–90		—	—
1989–90	Watford	18	—

WILLIAMS, Geraint

Born Treorchy 5.1.62. Ht 5 7 Wt 10 6
Midfield. From Apprentice. Wales Youth, Under-21, 11 full caps.

Season	Club	Apps	Goals
1979–80	Bristol R	—	—
1980–81		28	1
1981–82		16	—
1982–83		35	3
1983–84		34	4
1984–85		28	—
1984–85	Derby Co	12	—
1985–86		40	4
1986–87		40	1
1987–88		40	1
1988–89		37	1
1989–90		38	—

WILLIAMS, Jeremy

Born Didcot 24.3.60. Ht 5 11 Wt 11 10
Midfield. From Apprentice.

Season	Club	Apps	Goals
1976–77	Reading	5	—
1977–78		13	2
1978–79		1	—
1979–80		15	2
1980–81		27	3
1981–82		45	—
1982–83		41	2
1983–84		38	—
1984–85		38	1
1985–86		31	4
1986–87		34	2
1987–88		21	1
1988–89	Gillingham	13	—
1989–90	Aldershot	28	1

WILLIAMS, John

Born Liverpool 3.10.60. Ht 6 1
Wt 13 12
Defender. From Amateur.

Season	Club	Apps	Goals
1978–79	Tranmere R	1	—
1979–80		3	—
1980–81		27	2
1981–82		44	6
1982–83		35	—
1983–84		20	1
1984–85		43	4
1985–86	Port Vale	36	2
1986–87		14	—
1986–87	Bournemouth	26	3
1987–88		38	2

Season	Club	League Appearances/Goals	
1988–89		37	2
1989–90		16	2

WILLIAMS, Mike

Born Mancot 6.2.65. Ht 5 10 Wt 11 00
Midfield. From Apprentice. Wales Youth.

1981–82	Chester	2	—
1982–83		12	2
1983–84		20	2
1984–85	Wrexham	27	—
1985–86		27	—
1986–87		42	1
1987–88		42	2
1988–89		27	—
1989–90		13	—

WILLIAMS, Neil

Born Waltham Abbey 23.10.64. Ht 5 11 Wt 11 04
Midfield. From Apprentice. England Youth.

1982–83	Watford	—	—
1983–84		—	—
1984–85	Hull C	17	3
1985–86		19	3
1986–87		30	2
1987–88		25	2
1988–89	Preston NE	41	2
1989–90		41	3

WILLIAMS, Paul

Born London 16.8.65. Ht 5 7 Wt 10 03
Forward. From Woodford T. England B, Under-21.

1986–87	Charlton Ath	—	—
1987–88		12	—
1987–88	*Brentford*	7	3
1988–89	Charlton Ath	32	13
1989–90		38	10

WILLIAMS, Paul

Born Sheffield 8.9.63 Ht 6 3 Wt 14 06
Forward. From Distillery, Leeds U, Grenaker R, Nuneaton.

1986–87	Preston NE	1	—
1987–88	Newport Co	26	3
1987–88	Sheffield U	6	—
1988–89		2	—
1989–90	Hartlepool U	8	—

WILLIAMS, Paul

Born Burton 26.3.71. Ht 5 11 Wt 12 00
Midfield. From Trainee.

1989–90	Derby Co	10	1
1989–90	*Lincoln C*	3	—

WILLIAMS, Paul

Born Leicester 11.9.69. Ht 5 7 Wt 10 00
Forward. From Trainee

1988–89	Leicester C	—	—
1989–90	Stockport Co	7	—

WILLIAMS, Paul

Born Liverpool 25.9.70.
Midfield. From Trainee.

1988–89	Sunderland	1	—
1989–90		1	—

WILLIAMS, Steve

Born London 12.7.58. Ht 5 9 Wt 11 04
Midfield. From Apprentice. England Under-21, B, 6 full caps.

1974–75	Southampton	—	—
1975–76		1	—
1976–77		33	—
1977–78		39	5
1978–79		39	—
1979–80		32	2
1980–81		33	4
1981–82		21	—
1982–83		39	3
1983–84		27	3
1984–85		14	1
1984–85	Arsenal	15	1
1985–86		17	—
1986–87		34	2
1987–88		29	1

Season	Club	League Appearances/Goals	
1988–89	Luton T	10	—
1989–90		14	1

WILLIAMS, Steven

Born Mansfield 18.7.70 Ht 5 11
Wt 10 06
Midfield. From Trainee.

Season	Club	Apps	Goals
1986–87	Mansfield T	4	—
1987–88		4	—
1988–89		3	—
1989–90	Chesterfield	11	1

WILLIAMS, Tommy

Born West Lothian 18.12.57. Ht 5 9
Wt 11 06
Defender. From Apprentice.

Season	Club	Apps	Goals
1976–77	Leicester C	—	—
1977–78		32	3
1978–79		35	2
1979–80		40	1
1980–81		42	4
1981–82		31	—
1982–83		4	—
1983–84		22	—
1984–85		27	—
1985–86		8	—
1986–87	Birmingham C	29	—
1987–88		33	1
1988–89	Grimsby T	19	—
1989–90		1	—

WILLIAMS, Wayne

Born Delford 17.11.63. Ht 5 11
Wt 11 09
Defender. From Apprentice.

Season	Club	Apps	Goals
1981–82	Shrewsbury T	—	—
1982–83		42	4
1983–84		40	—
1984–85		28	—
1985–86		30	1
1986–87		40	—
1987–88		31	2
1988–89		10	—
1988–89	Northampton T	26	1
1989–90		15	—

WILLIAMSON, Andy

Born Kirkcaldy 4.9.69. Ht 6 0 Wt 11 00
Midfield. From Glenrothes Strollers.

Season	Club	Apps	Goals
1987–88	Dunfermline Ath	2	—
1988–89		6	—
1989–90		1	—

WILLIAMSON, Bobby

Born Glasgow 13.8.61. Ht 5 10 Wt 11 00
Forward. From Auchengill BC.

Season	Club	Apps	Goals
1980–81	Clydebank	2	—
1981–82		12	1
1982–83		39	23
1983–84		17	4
1983–84	Rangers	17	6
1984–85		1	—
1985–86		23	6
1986–87	WBA	31	8
1987–88		22	3
1988–89	Rotherham U	42	27
1989–90		42	19

WILLIS, Roger

Born Sheffield 17.6.67 Ht 6 1 Wt 11 06
Forward.

Season	Club	Apps	Goals
1989–90	Grimsby T	9	—

WILMOT, Rhys

Born Newport 21.2.62. Ht 6 1 Wt 12 00
Goalkeeper. From Apprentice. Wales Youth, Under-21.

Season	Club	Apps	Goals
1979–80	Arsenal	—	—
1980–81		—	—
1981–82		—	—
1982–83		—	—
1982–83	*Hereford U*	9	—
1983–84	Arsenal	—	—
1984–85	*Orient*	46	—
1985–86	Arsenal	2	—
1986–87		6	—
1987–88		—	—
1988–89		—	—

Season	Club	League Appearances/Goals	
1988–89	*Swansea C*	16	—
1988–89	*Plymouth Arg*	17	—
1989–90	Plymouth Arg	46	—

WILLMOTT, Ian

Born Bristol 10.7.68 Ht 5 10 Wt 12 07
Defender. From Weston-super-Mare.

Season	Club	League Appearances/Goals	
1988–89	Bristol R	—	—
1989–90		17	—

WILSON, Clive

Born Manchester 13.11.61. Ht 5 7
Wt 10 00
Midfield Local.

Season	Club	League Appearances/Goals	
1979–80	Manchester C	—	—
1980–81		—	—
1981–82		4	—
1982–83		—	—
1982–83	*Chester*	21	2
1983–84	Manchester C	11	—
1984–85		27	4
1985–86		25	5
1986–87		31	—
1986–87	Chelsea	—	—
1986–87	*Manchester C*	11	—
1987–88	Chelsea	31	2
1988–89		32	3
1989–90		18	—

WILSON, Danny

Born Wigan 1.1.60. Ht 5 6 Wt 11 00
Midfield. From Wigan Ath. Northern Ireland 18 full caps.

Season	Club	League Appearances/Goals	
1977–78	Bury	12	1
1978–79		46	7
1979–80		32	—
1980–81	Chesterfield	33	3
1981–82		43	3
1982–83		24	7
1982–83	Nottingham F	10	1
1983–84	*Scunthorpe U*	6	3
1983–84	Brighton	26	10
1984–85		38	5
1985–86		33	11
1986–87		38	7
1987–88	Luton T	38	8
1988–89		37	9
1989–90		35	7

WILSON, Darren

Born Manchester 30.9.71.
Defender.

Season	Club	League Appearances/Goals	
1989–90	Manchester C	—	—
1989–90		—	—

WILSON, David

Born Burnley 20.3.69. Ht 5 9 Wt 10 10
Midfield. From Apprentice.

Season	Club	League Appearances/Goals	
1986–87	Manchester U	—	—
1987–88		—	—
1988–89		4	—
1989–90		—	—

WILSON, Kevin

Born Banbury 18.4.61. Ht 5 8 Wt 11 06
Forward. From Banbury U. Northern Ireland 16 full caps.

Season	Club	League Appearances/Goals	
1979–80	Derby Co	4	—
1980–81		27	7
1981–82		24	9
1982–83		22	4
1983–84		32	2
1984–85		13	8
1984–85	Ipswich T	17	7
1985–86		39	7
1986–87		42	20
1987–88	Chelsea	25	5
1988–89		46	13
1989–90		37	14

WILSON, Paul

Born Bradford 2.8.68 Ht 5 10 Wt 13 00
Defender. From Trainee.

Season	Club	League Appearances/Goals	
1985–86	Huddersfield T	7	—
1986–87		8	—
1987–88	Norwich C	—	—
1987–88	Northampton T	15	1

Season	Club	League Appearances/Goals	
1988–89		39	1
1989–90		27	—

WILSON, Phil

Born Hemsworth 16.10.60. Ht 5 6 Wt 11 13
Midfield. From Apprentice.

Season	Club	Apps	Goals
1978–79	Bolton W	—	—
1979–80		17	1
1980–81		22	3
1981–82	Huddersfield T	34	2
1982–83		45	6
1983–84		41	3
1984–85		40	3
1985–86		35	1
1986–87		38	1
1987–88	York C	36	1
1988–89		10	1
From Macclesfield			
1989–90	Scarborough	24	1

WILSON, Phil

Born Teeside 5.2.72.
Midfield. From Trainee.

Season	Club	Apps	Goals
1989–90	Hartlepool U	1	—

WILSON, Robert

Born Kensington 5.6.61. Ht 5 10 Wt 12 00
Midfield. From Apprentice. Eire Under-21.

Season	Club	Apps	Goals
1979–80	Fulham	2	—
1980–81		35	4
1981–82		43	5
1982–83		40	11
1983–84		16	3
1984–85		39	11
1985–86	Millwall	28	12
1986–87	Luton T	21	1
1987–88		3	—
1987–88	Fulham	20	3
1988–89		27	1
1989–90	Huddersfield T	28	6

WILSON, Terry

Born Broxburn 8.2.69. Ht 6 0 Wt 10 10
Midfield. From Apprentice. Scotland Under-21.

Season	Club	Apps	Goals
1986–87	Nottingham F	—	—
1987–88		36	5
1988–89		27	1
1989–90		21	—

WILSON, Tommy

Born Paisley 2.8.61. Ht 5 8 Wt 9 07
Defender. From School. Scotland Under-21.

Season	Club	Apps	Goals
1979–80	Queens Park	1	—
1980–81		1	—
1981–82		30	—
1982–83	St Mirren	36	—
1983–84		1	—
1984–85		35	—
1985–86		27	—
1986–87		25	1
1987–88		35	—
1988–89		31	—
1989–90		9	—
1989–90	Dunfermline Ath	15	—

WIMBLETON, Paul

Born Havant 13.11.64. Ht 5 8 Wt 10 12
Midfield. From Apprentice. England Schools, Youth.

Season	Club	Apps	Goals
1981–82	Portsmouth	8	—
1982–83		—	—
1983–84		2	—
1984–85		—	—
1985–86		—	—
1986–87	Cardiff C	46	8
1987–88		37	9
1988–89		36	—

Season	Club	League Appearances/Goals	
1989–90	Bristol C	16	2
1989–90	Shrewsbury T	16	—

WINNIE, David

Born Glasgow 26.10.66. Ht 5 1 Wt 10 07
Defender. S Form. Scotland Schools, Youth, Under-21.

Season	Club	Apps	Goals
1983–84	St Mirren	8	—
1984–85		30	3
1985–86		20	1
1986–87		14	—
1987–88		26	2
1988–89		30	—
1989–90		17	—

WINSTANLEY, Mark

Born St. Helens 22.1.68. Ht 6 1
Wt 12 04
Defender. From Trainee.

Season	Club	Apps	Goals
1984–85	Bolton W	—	—
1985–86		3	—
1986–87		13	—
1987–88		8	1
1988–89		44	—
1989–90		43	1

WINTER, Julian

Born Huddersfield 6.9.65. Ht 6 0
Wt 11 10
Midfield. Local.

Season	Club	Apps	Goals
1983–84	Huddersfield T	—	—
1984–85		16	2
1985–86		4	—
1986–87		31	1
1987–88		7	—
1988–89		35	2
1988–89	*Scunthorpe U*	4	—
1989–90	Sheffield U	—	—

WINTERBURN, Nigel

Born Nuneaton 11.12.63. Ht 5 10
Wt 10 09
Defender. Local. England Youth, B, Under-21, 1 full cap.

Season	Club	Apps	Goals
1981–82	Birmingham C	—	—
1982–83		—	—
1983–84	Oxford U	—	—
1983–84	Wimbledon	43	1
1984–85		41	4
1985–86		39	1
1986–87		42	2
1987–88	Arsenal	17	—
1988–89		38	3
1989–90		36	—

WISE, Dennis

Born Kensington 15.12.66. Ht 5 6
Wt 9 05
Forward. From Southampton Apprentice. England B, Under-21.

Season	Club	Apps	Goals
1984–85	Wimbledon	1	—
1985–86		4	—
1986–87		28	4
1987–88		30	10
1988–89		37	5
1989–90		35	8

WISHART, Fraser

Born Johnstone 1.3.65. Ht 5 8 Wt 10 00
Defender. From Pollok.

Season	Club	Apps	Goals
1983–84	Motherwell	6	—
1984–85		—	—
1985–86		26	—
1986–87		44	3
1987–88		43	1
1988–89		35	1
1989–90	St Mirren	20	—

WITHE, Chris

Born Liverpool 25.9.62. Ht 5 10
Wt 11 02
Defender. From Apprentice.

Season	Club	Apps	Goals
1980–81	Newcastle U	2	—
1981–82		—	—
1982–83		—	—
1983–84	Bradford C	45	1
1984–85		45	—
1985–86		33	—
1986–87		18	1
1987–88		2	—
1987–88	Notts Co	35	2

Season	Club	League Appearances/Goals	
1988–89		45	1
1989–90	Bury	31	1

WITHE, Peter

Born Liverpool 30.8.51. Ht 6 1 Wt 12 00
Forward. From Skelmersdale. England. 11 full caps.

Season	Club	League Appearances/Goals	
1970–71	Southport	2	—
1971–72		1	—
1971–72	Barrow	1	—
From Port Elizabeth C and Arcadia Shepherds			
1973–74	Wolverhampton W	3	1
1974–75		14	2
From Portland T			
1975–76	Birmingham C	32	9
1976–77		3	—
1976–77	Nottingham F	34	16
1977–78		40	12
1978–79		1	—
1978–79	Newcastle U	39	14
1979–80		37	11
1980–81	Aston Villa	36	20
1981–82		35	10
1982–83		35	16
1983–84		36	16
1984–85		40	12
1985–86	Sheffield U	30	11
1986–87		35	5
1987–88		9	2
1987–88	*Birmingham C*	8	2
1988–89	Huddersfield T	26	—
1989–90		12	1

WOAN, Ian

Born Wirrall 14.12.67 Ht 5 10 Wt 11 09.
Midfield. From Runcorn.

Season	Club	League Appearances/Goals	
1989–90	Nottingham F	—	—

WOOD, Darren

Born Derby 22.10.68. Ht 6 1 Wt 12 08
Defender. From Trainee.

Season	Club	League Appearances/Goals	
1986–87	Chesterfield	10	1
1987–88		35	1
1988–89		22	1
1989–90	Reading	32	2

WOOD, Darren

Born Scarborough 9.6.64. Ht 5 10
Wt 11 00
Defender. From Apprentice. England Schools.

Season	Club	League Appearances/Goals	
1981–82	Middlesbrough	11	1
1982–83		42	3
1983–84		42	2
1984–85		6	—
1984–85	Chelsea	19	1
1985–86		28	—
1986–87		41	—
1987–88		34	1
1988–89		22	1
1988–89	Sheffield W	8	—
1989–90		3	—

WOOD, George

Born Douglas 26.9.52. Ht 6 3 Wt 14 00
Goalkeeper. From East Stirling. Scotland 4 full caps.

Season	Club	League Appearances/Goals	
1970–71	East Stirling	23	1
1971–72		21	—
1971–72	Blackpool	4	—
1972–73		20	—
1973–74		12	—
1974–75		4	—
1975–76		35	—
1976–77		42	—
1977–78	Everton	42	—
1978–79		42	—
1979–80		19	—
1980–81	Arsenal	11	—
1981–82		26	—
1982–83		23	—
1983–84	Crystal Palace	42	—
1984–85		42	—
1985–86		39	—
1986–87		42	—
1987–88		27	—
1987–88	Cardiff C	13	—
1988–89		45	—

Season	Club	Apps	Goals
1989–90		9	—
1989–90	*Blackpool*	15	—

WOOD, Paul

Born Middlesbrough 1.11.64. Ht 5 9
Wt 10 04
Forward. From Apprentice.

Season	Club	Apps	Goals
1982–83	Portsmouth	—	—
1983–84		8	1
1984–85		6	1
1985–86		25	4
1986–87		8	—
1987–88		—	—
1987–88	Brighton	31	4
1988–89		35	1
1989–90		26	3
1989–90	Sheffield U	17	3

WOOD, Steve

Born Bracknell 2.2.63. Ht 6 1 Wt 12 02
Defender. From Apprentice.

Season	Club	Apps	Goals
1979–80	Reading	2	—
1980–81		6	—
1981–82		32	—
1982–83		18	—
1983–84		37	3
1984–85		46	1
1985–86		46	4
1986–87		32	1
1987–88	Millwall	22	—
1988–89		35	—
1989–90		21	—

WOOD, Trevor

Born Jersey 3.11.68 Ht 5 11 Wt 13 00
Goalkeeper. From Apprentice.

Season	Club	Apps	Goals
1986–87	Brighton	—	—
1987–88		—	—
1988–89	Port Vale	2	—
1989–90		3	—

WOODMAN, Andy

Born Denmark Hill 11.8.71. Ht 6 1
Wt 12 04
Goalkeeper. From Apprentice.

Season	Club	Apps	Goals
1989–90	Crystal Palace	—	—

WOODS, Chris

Born Boston 14.11.59. Ht 6 2 Wt 12 08
Goalkeeper. From Apprentice. England B,Under-21, 16 full caps.

Season	Club	Apps	Goals
1976–77	Nottingham F	—	—
1977–78		—	—
1978–79		—	—
1979–80	QPR	41	—
1980–81		22	—
1980–81	*Norwich C*	10	—
1981–82	Norwich C	42	—
1982–83		42	—
1983–84		42	—
1984–85		38	—
1985–86		42	—
1986–87	Rangers	42	—
1987–88		39	—
1988–89		24	—
1989–90		32	—

WOODS, Neil

Born York 30.7.66. Ht 6 1 Wt 12 12
Forward. From Apprentice.

Season	Club	Apps	Goals
1982–83	Doncaster R	4	—
1983–84		7	1
1984–85		6	2
1985–86		30	7
1986–87		18	6
1986–87	Rangers	3	—
1987–88	Ipswich T	19	4
1988–89		1	—
1989–90		7	1
1989–90	Bradford C	14	2

WOODS, Ray

Born Birkenhead 7.6.65 Ht 5 11
Wt 10 00
Forward. From Apprentice.

Season	Club	Apps	Goals
1982–83	Tranmere R	1	—
1983–84		6	2

From Colne D.

Season	Club	League Appearances/Goals	
1988–89	Wigan Ath	8	—
1989–90		—	—

WOODTHORPE, Colin

Born Ellesmere Pt 13.1.69. Ht 5 11
Wt 11 08
Defender. From Apprentice.

Season	Club	Apps	Goals
1986–87	Chester C	30	2
1987–88		35	—
1988–89		44	3
1989–90		46	1

WORSLEY, Graeme

Born Liverpool 4.1.69 Ht 5 10 Wt 11 02
Defender. From Bootle.

Season	Club	Apps	Goals
1988–89	Shrewsbury T	6	—
1989–90		15	—

WORTHINGTON, Gary

Born Cleethorpes 10.11.66. Ht 5 10
Wt 10 05
Forward. From Apprentice. England Youth.

Season	Club	Apps	Goals
1984–85	Manchester U	—	—
1985–86		—	—
1986–87	Huddersfield T	—	—
1987–88	Darlington	9	3
1988–89		31	12
1989–90	Wrexham	42	12

WORTHINGTON, Nigel

Born Ballymena 4.11.61. Ht 5 11
Wt 12 05
Defender. From Ballymena U. Northern Ireland Youth, 28 full caps.

Season	Club	Apps	Goals
1981–82	Notts Co	2	—
1982–83		41	3
1983–84		24	1
1983–84	Sheffield W	14	1
1984–85		38	1
1985–86		15	—
1986–87		35	—
1987–88		38	—
1988–89		28	—
1989–90		32	2

WRATTEN, Paul

Born Middlesbrough 29.11.70 Ht 5 7
Wt 9 13
Midfield. From Trainee. England Youth.

Season	Club	Apps	Goals
1988–89	Manchester U	—	—
1989–90		—	—

WRENCH, Mark

Born Warrington 27.9.69 Ht 5 10
Wt 11 00
Defender. From Trainee.

Season	Club	Apps	Goals
1988–89	Wrexham	4	—
1989–90		2	—

WRIGHT, Alan

Born Ashton-under-Lyme 28.9.71.
Midfield. From Schoolboy, Trainee.

Season	Club	Apps	Goals
1987–88	Blackpool	1	—
1988–89		16	—
1989–90		24	—

WRIGHT, Darren

Born West Bromwich 14.3.68. Ht 5 10
Wt 11 04
Defender. From Apprentice.

Season	Club	Apps	Goals
1984–85	Wolverhampton W	—	—
1985–86		1	—
1986–87	Wrexham	14	—
1987–88		35	—
1988–89		37	3
1989–90		24	1

WRIGHT, George

Born South Africa 22.12.69. Ht 5 7
Wt 10 02
Defender. From Hutcheson Vale BC.

Season	Club	Apps	Goals
1987–88	Hearts	—	—

Season	Club	Apps	Goals
1988–89		—	—
1989–90		1	—

WRIGHT, Ian

Born Woolwich 3.11.63. Ht 5 11
Wt 11 06
Forward. From Greenwich Bor. England B.

Season	Club	Apps	Goals
1985–86	Crystal Palace	32	9
1986–87		38	8
1987–88		41	20
1988–89		42	24
1989–90		26	8

WRIGHT, Ian

Born Lichfield 10.3.72.
Defender. From Trainee.

Season	Club	Apps	Goals
1989–90	Stoke C	1	—

WRIGHT, Keith

Born Edinburgh 17.5.65. Ht 5 11
Wt 11 00
Forward. From Melbourne T.

Season	Club	Apps	Goals
1983–84	Raith R	37	5
1984–85		38	22
1985–86		39	21
1986–87		17	13
1986–87	Dundee	20	10
1987–88		42	15
1988–89		35	8
1989–90		34	11

WRIGHT, Mark

Born Dorchester 1.8.63. Ht 6 3
Wt 12 01
Defender. From Amateur. England Under-21, 30 full caps.

Season	Club	Apps	Goals
1980–81	Oxford U	—	—
1981–82		10	—
1981–82	Southampton	3	—
1982–83		39	2
1983–84		29	1
1984–85		36	—
1985–86		33	3
1986–87		30	1
1987–88		—	—
1987–88	Derby Co	38	3
1988–89		33	1
1989–90		36	6

WRIGHT, Mark

Born Manchester 29.1.70 Ht 5 11
Wt 10 12
Defender. From Trainee.

Season	Club	Apps	Goals
1988–89	Everton	—	—
1989–90		1	—

WRIGHT, Paul

Born East Kilbride 17.8.67. Ht 5 8
Wt 10 08
Forward. S Form. Scotland Youth, Under-21.

Season	Club	Apps	Goals
1983–84	Aberdeen	1	—
1984–85		—	—
1985–86		10	2
1986–87		25	4
1987–88		9	4
1988–89		23	6
1989–90	QPR	15	5
1989–90	Hibernian	3	1

WRIGHT, Stephen

Born Bellshill 27.8.71. Ht 5 10 Wt 10 10
Defender. From Aberdeen Lads.

Season	Club	Apps	Goals
1987–88	Aberdeen	—	—
1988–89		—	—
1989–90		1	—

WRIGHT, Tommy

Born Belfast 29.8.63. Ht 6 1 Wt 13 05
Goalkeeper. From Linfield. Northern Ireland 4 full caps.

Season	Club	Apps	Goals
1987–88	Newcastle U	—	—
1988–89		9	—
1989–90		14	—

WRIGHT, Tommy

Born Dunfermline 10.1.66. Ht 5 7
Wt 9 10
Forward. From Apprentice. Scotland Under-21.

Season	Club	Apps	Goals
1982–83	Leeds U	4	1
1983–84		25	8
1984–85		42	14
1985–86		10	1
1986–87		—	—
1986–87	Oldham Ath	28	7
1987–88		41	9
1988–89		43	7
1989–90	Leicester C	41	3

WRIGHTSON, Jeff

Born Newcastle 18.5.68. Ht 5 11
Wt 11 00
Defender. From Apprentice.

Season	Club	Apps	Goals
1986–87	Newcastle U	4	—
1987–88	Preston NE	25	—
1988–89		38	—
1989–90		26	—

WYNNE, Darren

Born St. Asaph 12.10.70 Ht 5 9
Wt 11 05
Midfield. From Trainee.

Season	Club	Apps	Goals
1988–89	Chester C	6	—
1989–90		6	—

YALLOP, Frank

Born Watford 4.4.64. Ht 5 11 Wt 11 04
Defender. From Apprentice. England Youth.

Season	Club	Apps	Goals
1981–82	Ipswich T	—	—
1982–83		—	—
1983–84		6	—
1984–85		10	—
1985–86		34	—
1986–87		31	—
1987–88		41	2
1988–89		40	2
1989–90		31	—

YATES, Dean

Born Leicester 26.10.67. Ht 6 1
Wt 10 04
Defender. From Apprentice. England Under-21.

Season	Club	Apps	Goals
1984–85	Notts Co	8	—
1985–86		44	4
1986–87		42	9
1987–88		46	2
1988–89		41	6
1989–90		45	6

YATES, Mark

Born Birmingham 24.1.70. Ht 5 11
Wt 11 09
Midfield. From Trainee.

Season	Club	Apps	Goals
1987–88	Birmingham C	3	—
1988–89		20	3
1989–90		20	2

YATES, Steve

Born Bristol 29.1.70. Ht 5 11 Wt 11 00
Defender. From Trainee.

Season	Club	Apps	Goals
1986–87	Bristol R	2	—
1987–88		—	—

Season	Club	League Appearances/Goals	
1988–89		35	—
1989–90		42	—

YORKE, Dwight

Born Tobago 3.12.71. Ht 5 10 Wt 11 12
Forward. From St Clair's Coaching School, Tobago.

Season	Club	Apps	Goals
1989–90	Aston Villa	2	—

YOUDS, Edward

Born Liverpool 3.5.70 Ht 6 0 Wt 10 00
Defender. From Trainee.

Season	Club	Apps	Goals
1988–89	Everton	—	—
1989–90		—	—
1989–90	*Cardiff C*	1	—
1989–90	*Wrexham*	20	2

YOUNG, Eric

Born Singapore 25.3.60. Ht 6 3
Wt 12 06
Defender. From Slough Town. Wales 1 full cap.

Season	Club	Apps	Goals
1982–83	Brighton	—	—
1983–84		30	4
1984–85		35	3
1985–86		32	2
1986–87		29	1
1987–88	Wimbledon	29	3
1988–89		35	1
1989–90		35	5

YOUNG, Richard

Born Nottingham 31.12.68 Ht 6 3
Wt 13 07
Forward. From Apprentice.

Season	Club	Apps	Goals
1986–87	Notts Co	35	5
1987–88	Southend U	7	—
1988–89		2	—
1988–89	*Wimbledon*	—	—
1988–89	Exeter C	14	4
1989–90		28	6

ZONDERVAN, Romeo

Born Surinam 4.3.59. Ht 5 11 Wt 10 10
Midfield. From Den Haag and Twente. Holland Schools, Under-21, full caps.

Season	Club	Apps	Goals
1981–82	WBA	14	—
1982–83		41	2
1983–84		29	3
1983–84	Ipswich T	8	2
1984–85		41	1
1985–86		28	2
1986–87		39	1
1987–88		29	4
1988–89		37	3
1989–90		30	—